Ancient Greek Scholarship

AMERICAN PHILOLOGICAL ASSOCIATION
CLASSICAL RESOURCES SERIES

Series Editor
JUSTINA GREGORY

A Casebook on Roman Family Law
BRUCE W. FRIER AND THOMAS A. J. MCGINN

When Dead Tongues Speak
Teaching Beginning Greek and Latin
JOHN GRUBER-MILLER

Ancient Greek Scholarship
A Guide to Finding, Reading, and Understanding Scholia,
Commentaries, Lexica, and Grammatical Treatises,
from Their Beginnings to the Byzantine Period
ELEANOR DICKEY

Ancient Greek Scholarship

*A Guide to Finding, Reading,
and Understanding Scholia, Commentaries,
Lexica, and Grammatical Treatises,
from Their Beginnings to the Byzantine Period*

ELEANOR DICKEY

OXFORD
UNIVERSITY PRESS

2007

OXFORD
UNIVERSITY PRESS

Oxford University Press, Inc., publishes works that further
Oxford University's objective of excellence
in research, scholarship, and education.

Oxford   New York
Auckland   Cape Town   Dar es Salaam   Hong Kong   Karachi
Kuala Lumpur   Madrid   Melbourne   Mexico City   Nairobi
New Delhi   Shanghai   Taipei   Toronto

With offices in
Argentina   Austria   Brazil   Chile   Czech Republic   France   Greece
Guatemala   Hungary   Italy   Japan   Poland   Portugal   Singapore
South Korea   Switzerland   Thailand   Turkey   Ukraine   Vietnam

Published by Oxford University Press, Inc.
198 Madison Avenue, New York, New York 10016

www.oup.com

Oxford is a registered trademark of Oxford University Press

Library of Congress Cataloging-in-Publication Data
Dickey, Eleanor.
Ancient Greek scholarship : a guide to finding, reading, and understanding scholia,
commentaries, lexica, and grammatical treatises, from their beginnings to the Byzantine
period / Eleanor Dickey.
p. cm. — (American Philological Association classical resources series ; no. 7)
Includes bibliographical references.
ISBN 978-0-19-531292-8; 978-0-19-531293-5 (pbk.)
1. Greek philology—History.   2. Scholia.   3. Greek literature—Criticism, Textual.
4. Transmission of texts.   5. Greece—Civilization.   I. Title.   II. Classical resources
series; no. 7
PA53.D53 2006
480.9—dc22   2006008424

Printed in the United States of America
on acid-free paper

Dedicated to my mother, BARBARA DICKEY,
who put up with a great deal while this book was being written.

Preface

IN RECENT YEARS A GROWING INTEREST IN ANCIENT SCHOLARSHIP has brought sources that used to be considered obscure into the mainstream of modern classical scholarship. This development is welcome, not only because the extant remains of ancient scholarship shed valuable light on ancient literature, but also because ancient scholarship is a fascinating subject in its own right, and its study can teach us a great deal about our own profession. But the increase in interest has brought with it some problems of access. It is more and more the case that Classicists, both graduate students and professors, need to consult ancient works of scholarship that they find difficult to use because of a lack of familiarity with the resources of the genre and with the peculiarities of scholarly Greek. This book is intended to remedy that problem and make ancient scholarship accessible to all Classicists.

Some types of ancient scholarship, of course, are already widely available: many treatises on rhetorical theory and literary criticism, such as Aristotle's *Rhetoric* and *Poetics* and ps.-Longinus' *On the Sublime*, are well supplied with good editions, translations, commentaries, and abundant modern discussions. The same applies to biographies of writers by mainstream authors such as Plutarch and Diogenes Laertius, and to the numerous commentaries on and interpretations of the Bible and other works of Judeo-Christian religious literature. This book therefore omits all these categories of material and concentrates on those that are currently most difficult to find and use: scholia, secular commentaries, lexica, grammatical treatises, and a few closely related works such as the *Suda*. Metrical treatises and notes have generally been omitted because metrical studies form a separate, specialized field with its own conventions and a large body of terminology that it would not have been practical to include here; the most useful metrical works are nevertheless discussed to give an introduction to that subject. For convenience the term "scholarship" will be used in this book as a cover term for the particular genres included in the book, in other words to refer to any type of work concentrating on the words, rather than the ideas, of ancient pagan authors: textual criticism, interpretation, literary criticism of specific passages, grammar, syntax, lexicography, etc. No implication that biblical, rhetorical, or other studies are inherently "unscholarly" is intended by this usage.

This book has two aims: to explain what ancient scholarship exists, where to find it, and when and how to use it; and to help readers acquire the facility in scholarly Greek necessary to use that material. Traditionally, the first of these goals has been addressed by a teacher or other mentor when a student begins to work on this subject, making the field difficult to enter for those without the good fortune to have a mentor with this knowledge. The second aim is traditionally met by the students' sitting down with a text and dictionary and teaching themselves, a method that requires considerable proficiency in Greek. This traditional method is certainly effective for those with the right combination of luck and ability, and virtually all the current experts on ancient scholarship have used it. Even for such people, however, it is not exactly efficient, and as interest in the subject grows the amount of wasted energy and frustration caused by hundreds of people rediscovering the same facts laboriously and independently becomes less and less tolerable. It is therefore my hope that this book will make access to ancient scholarship easier and more enjoyable for all, as well as possible for some for whom the field might otherwise have remained inaccessible.

The first three chapters of this work are directed toward the first aim. They are not a history of ancient scholarship in its entirety, but merely an explanation of those portions of it that happen to survive. In Chapter 2 are discussed, author by author, ancient literary works on which scholarship survives intact or as scholia; this chapter includes virtually any type of commentary, scholia, or author-specific lexicon, whether text-critical, literary, rhetorical, metrical, philosophical, etc., though types of material for which good guidance is available elsewhere (such as the philosophical commentaries on Plato and Aristotle) are treated in less detail than the obscurer material. Chapter 3 discusses lexica, grammatical treatises, and a few related works. In this chapter are treated, scholar by scholar, the works of those ancient scholars who now have an autonomous existence as authors: those whose works still survive or whose fragments are normally consulted in a collected edition. Many important ancient scholars do not currently have such an autonomous existence, as the fragments of their writings must be consulted in the various works in which they are preserved; information on using these authors is provided in footnotes to Chapter 1, which offers a general overview of ancient scholarship.

The authors treated in Chapters 2 and 3 are discussed not in chronological order, but in the order most likely to be helpful to the novice. Thus texts belonging to similar genres are kept together, as texts of similar genres tend to have similar problems, and within each genre the authors with the greatest and most typical amount of surviving ancient scholarship are treated first. Thus in Chapter 2 scholarship on Euripides, Sophocles, and Aeschylus is discussed in that order because much of what is known about scholarship on Aeschylus is extrapolated from more plentiful information on Euripides and, to a lesser extent, Sophocles. Similarly in Chapter 3 the voluminous and indubitably authentic works of Apollonius Dyscolus are discussed before Dionysius Thrax, whose treatise is enmeshed in complex questions of authenticity that make it atypical, and also before Trypho, of whose writings very little survives. A similar policy has been adopted in giving lists of modern references: generally speaking, when several secondary sources are listed without differentiation, the reader is advised to consult them in the order listed.

Readers of these chapters are advised to pay particular attention to the discussion of the relative merits of different editions, for one of the worst mistakes a novice in the use of ancient scholarship can make is the use of the wrong edition. Good editions of classical literature abound, so that when working on a standard literary author such as Plato or Euripides one often has a choice of four or five perfectly good texts with only minimal differences between them. Really bad editions of such authors—that is, editions that present a text substantially different from that found in a good edition—are rare. This situation, one of the most precious fruits of modern classical scholarship, has the drawback of lulling us into a false sense of security about published texts: in dealing with ancient scholarship, one must be far more cautious, for really bad editions abound.

This problem is not simply due to the fact that ancient scholarship has received less attention from editors than works of literature and that in consequence many latest editions are very old. More fundamentally, it stems from the different nature of the textual tradition of secondary sources, which were freely altered, abridged, or enlarged even by scribes who would copy the words of a classical literary work much more faithfully. As a result it is normal for scholarly works to appear in radically different form from one manuscript to the next, putting a tremendous responsibility upon editors to analyze the tradition correctly and choose the best variants. The differences between one modern edition and another can be huge, and therefore it is worth making a considerable effort to obtain the best text. Moreover, good texts do not exist for many works, and therefore when using the flawed editions of those works it is important to be aware of their drawbacks and to pay scrupulous attention to the apparatus criticus and introduction.

In selecting editions and explanatory works for inclusion I hope I have not failed to meet the needs of those who have access to excellent libraries and who can benefit from the knowledge that a rare edition is slightly better than a common one or that the very best study of a particular question is in an utterly unknown periodical. I have however also tried to remember the difficulties confronting those at institutions where library budgets prohibit the purchase of many new texts and periodicals or where older material is not available, and therefore I have tried whenever feasible to give not only a first choice of text, but also a readily available alternative, and to alert readers to the drawbacks of certain widely available but flawed editions.

For those without access to a good library, the most convenient way to access the Greek texts of many authors is electronically via the *Thesaurus Linguae Graecae*.[1] Though this resource is an invaluable one, it offers only the bare text without whatever apparatus criticus, notes, translation, or introduction may be available in the printed edition; not even an explanation of the use of brackets or other

1. Available at http://www.tlg.uci.edu and on disk.

symbols appears in the electronic version. The editions used as the basis for the *TLG* are usually well chosen, however, and in many cases it is better to consult the best edition via this medium than a printed version of any other edition. But when the *TLG* edition is a poor one, the combination of that fact with the absence of all the material that could allow one to mitigate the poor quality of the edition can be catastrophic: for example if one were to consult Timaeus' lexicon to Plato via the *TLG*, one would be presented with a perfectly good-looking text and have no way of knowing that a large part of the material in it is not from Timaeus' lexicon at all, nor would there be any way of identifying the genuine material even if one were aware of the problem.

In listing editions I have indicated (with the sign "=*TLG*") whenever one that is mentioned is also to be found on the *TLG*; such an indication does not necessarily imply that the complete text of the printed version is available electronically, and for many texts that is not the case. As new works are still being added to the database, some that are not so indicated may yet appear. In some cases, however, the reason no reference to the *TLG* is given is that the edition used there is not one of the ones that is worth mentioning.

The references given to discussions of ancient scholarship are necessarily highly selective, and many excellent works have been omitted, especially in the case of topics like the scholia to Homer or to Aristophanes on which a great deal has been written. Most topics are covered by most of the standard reference works (*OCD*, *NP*, *RE*, etc.), so I have mentioned such reference works only when they are unusually helpful; they are however often a good source of further information even when not expressly mentioned. When possible, I have tried to mention which works will provide further bibliography, but in many cases the best source of further references is simply *L'Année philologique*.[2] I have tried whenever practical to mention at least some scholarship in English, but in most cases those who confine themselves to works in English will find themselves cut off from the most accurate, most interesting, or most up-to-date literature, so I have listed many works in other languages as well.

Chapters 4 to 6 are dedicated to the second aim of this book, an introduction to scholarly Greek. The basic facts are laid out in Chapter 4, but in order to absorb them effectively most readers will need practice reading scholarly texts; the purpose of Chapter 5 is to provide such practice.

Users of this book are encouraged to read Chapters 1 and 4 in their entirety, for familiarity with the main points laid out there is assumed in later chapters. They should also read the sections of Chapters 2 and 3 that relate to the particular type of ancient scholarship in which they are interested, and turn to the rele-

2. Also available online at http://www.annee-philologique.com/aph. Users of the electronic version should be aware that since entries are written in a variety of languages, text searches need to be done with multiple keywords; for example entries pertaining to scholia can be found under the keywords *scholia, scholion, scholium, scholie, scholien, scholies, scoli, scolie, scolies,* and *scolii.*

vant sections of Chapter 5 for practice in reading that material. Users are encouraged to translate the pertinent passages in section 5.1, making use of the glossary and commentary and checking their results with the key in 5.2. This practice will often be sufficient; for those who wish to practice their skills further, and for teachers who wish to assign exercises in this book for homework, additional exercises without key are provided in 5.3.

The material included here is all Greek, both in the sense of being itself written in Greek and in the sense of being scholarship on Greek texts and on the Greek language. Of course, some scholarship on Greek texts is in Latin, either because it was originally written in that language or because a Greek original was translated into Latin before being lost. This material is discussed in Chapter 2 where relevant, but it would have been impractical to include Latin in Chapters 4–6. It is to be hoped that someone who finds this book useful will one day produce its Latin equivalent.

When I first embarked on this project, many people told me that it was impossible; I thought only that it would be tremendous fun and would give me an excuse to learn things I would never otherwise be able to enjoy. As it turned out, the project was just as much fun as I had hoped, but it also proved to be as impossible as those who are older and wiser had warned me it would be. One reason it is impossible to write a book like this in a way that will generally give satisfaction to the intended audience is that scholia (and to a lesser extent other types of ancient scholarship) are used for very different purposes by different groups such as historians, students of literature, linguists, philosophers, and archaeologists. It is by now painfully obvious to me that a book of this nature must therefore have several very different types of reader with different needs and little sympathy for each other, and I have decided to deal with this issue by providing all (or as much as possible) of the information that each group is likely to need, on the grounds that such a course will make the book as useful as it can be—though, alas, it is unlikely to earn me the goodwill of any particular group. Thus on certain topics some readers may feel insulted by the provision of very basic information while others are irritated by encountering apparently obscure details in which they have no interest. I beg each group of readers to remember the existence of the others before condemning me too harshly for not catering exclusively to their own interests.

The other reason that writing this book was an impossible task is that no-one could be an expert in all the areas it covers, and I, alas, am not an expert in any of them. Basic proficiency in dealing with ancient scholarship is not too hard to acquire (and of course it is my hope that with the publication of this book it will become much easier), but expertise is quite another matter; after working diligently on the subject for five years I am still clearly not an expert. I have, however, learned a huge amount: much of it about the need for humility, and much of it about the goodness of the people who actually are experts. I am greatly touched by the way that the scholars who have the necessary knowledge have been happy to give me hours or even days of their valuable time, in order that the finished product might be good enough to benefit readers as it was intended to do. That world-famous Classicists were willing to painstakingly scrutinize details so that future students would be able to learn from this book effectively is, to me, deeply touching. We have a wonderful profession: I cannot imagine experts in many other fields being so willing to give their time and energy, without any reward at all, in the cause of making their own expertise easier to obtain. And it is a glorious thing that a Classicist who embarks on a valuable but impossible task with youthful folly and enthusiasm is supported and aided by her older and wiser colleagues rather than being left to waste years of her life and produce a book that will do no-one any good.

Thus my gratitude to those who have helped with this book is immense, but their sheer number makes it impossible for me to express even a fraction of the debt I owe to each individually. Martin West, Ineke Sluiter, Leofranc Holford-Strevens, David Sider, and Philomen Probert nobly read the entire work, including Chapters 5 and 6, and made many suggestions that resulted in substantial improvements, as well as saving me from a number of horrifying errors. Each of them deserves not only my eternal gratitude, but also that of anyone who relies on this book to provide accurate information. Robert Parker, Nicholas Horsfall, David Blank, and Robin Schlunk read almost all the book and provided invaluable comments. Robert Kaster, Nigel Wilson, Christian Habicht, Jim Zetzel, Leonardo Tarán, René Nünlist, Alan Cameron, Gregory Nagy, and Frederick Laurizten read substantial portions and provided extremely useful advice. Alexander Verlinsky, Heinrich von Staden, Friedemann Buddensiek, Andrew Dyck, Helmut van Thiel, Richard Sorabji, Valerio Casadio, Michael Haslam, John Lundon, Patrick Finglass, and Christian Brockmann offered valuable advice and information on particular sections. Philomen Probert and my heroic research assistant Nina Papathanasopoulou both tested out all the exercises in Chapter 5 and made tremendous improvements to them. The students in my Homer seminar at the University of Ottawa gave me the original idea, and those in my Greek 6260 class at Columbia University, on whom this book was tested, had sharp eyes and penetrating questions that resulted in numerous improvements. Joel Lidov, acting on behalf of the American Philological Association, guided this project from its outset, offering not only thoughtful advice but also extraordinary patience and encouragement in the face of my doubts and delays, while Justina Gregory, who oversaw the project in its latter stages, provided an excellent combination of sympathy and prodding. Julian Ward did a wonderful job on the copyediting, and Robert Kaster generously oversaw the publication process. I am deeply grateful to all these people for their help, especially to those who found mistakes that might not otherwise have been caught, and they are not responsible for the errors that remain.

Columbia University librarians Andrew Carriker and Karen Green, Center for Hellenic Studies librarians Jill Robbins and Temple Wright, and Jacqueline Dean at the Bodleian Library all made unusual efforts to locate the obscure materials on which so much of this project is based; they were also unusually kind and patient. I am also grateful to Columbia University for several research grants, to the Classics Department of Yale University for offering me access to their wonderful libraries, and to the Center for Hellenic Studies for providing ideal working conditions in which to complete the majority of this project.

Contents

Ancient Greek Scholarship

1

Introduction to Ancient Scholarship

For almost four thousand years, the peoples living around the Mediterranean have been attempting to improve their ability to understand ancient texts by systematic study of their language, context, and textual tradition. The Greeks seem to have come to this practice relatively late in comparison with Near Eastern civilizations such as that of the Babylonians, who produced dictionaries of Sumerian in the second millennium BC. The earliest traces of Greek scholarship can be found in the fifth century BC, when philosophers and rhetors began thinking and writing about language in a way that led towards systematic linguistic scholarship and when attempts to explain Homer to schoolchildren resulted in the earliest ancestors of some of our scholia. In the fourth century Plato and Aristotle continued to think systematically about language, while the establishment of an official text of the Athenian tragedies showed a new concern for textual authenticity and the creation of texts like that preserved on the Derveni papyrus showed the development of exegesis. The Stoic philosophers also made important observations about the Greek language that laid much of the foundation for the later grammatical tradition.[1]

The real beginning of Greek scholarship in our sense of the term, however, occurred with the foundation of the library and Museum at Alexandria in the early third century BC, and for centuries the librarians and other scholars there were the most important Greek scholars. By the first century BC noted grammarians, lexicographers, and textual critics could be found in many parts of the Greco-Roman world, and scholarship was a flourishing and highly respected profession. These ancient scholars brought to their work a host of advantages that their modern counterparts lack: native-speaker fluency in ancient Greek, access to vast numbers

---

1. Exactly how much is a disputed matter: since both the ideas of the early Stoics and those of the early grammarians must be reconstructed from later writings, it is possible to make widely differing assessments of the extent to which the latter were dependent on the former. For the beginnings of Greek linguistic thought and the links between the Alexandrians and these earlier thinkers, see Pfeiffer (1968), Matthews (1994), Ildefonse (1997), Siebenborn (1976), Frede (1977, 1978), Richardson (1994), Sluiter (1990, 1997a), Swiggers (1997), Swiggers and Wouters (1990), Belardi (1985), Pinborg (1975), Ax (1986, 1991), Blank (1994), Hovdhaugen (1982), Diels (1910), and Koller (1958).

of papyrus texts hundreds of years older and usually far less corrupt than our medieval manuscripts, knowledge of much of the ancient literature that is now lost, and contact with an explanatory oral tradition going back to the time of the classical writers themselves.[2]

Scholarship was very important in intellectual and literary circles from the Alexandrian period onwards. Hellenistic and Roman poetry is heavily influenced by research into earlier poetry; indeed some of it can only be understood in the light of ancient interpretations of those earlier works. Thus we find the word στῆτα "woman" (Theocritus, *Syrinx* 14) derived perhaps humorously from Homer's διαστήτην ἐρίσαντε (*Iliad* 1. 6, "they stood apart, having quarreled"), which in antiquity was sometimes read διὰ στήτην ἐρίσαντε "having quarreled over a woman." Educated Greeks and Romans did not read Homer (or other poets) in a vacuum; they studied the Homeric poems at schools in which obscure words and complex passages were authoritatively explained, and they discussed criticism and interpretation. It was thus inevitable that Vergil and Apollonius Rhodius, in composing their own epics, relied not only on the text of Homer itself, but on the traditional scholarly explanations and interpretations of his poems.[3]

It is very unfortunate, not only for our understanding of Homer and other early texts but also for our comprehension of the *Argonautica, Aeneid*, and other Hellenistic and Roman literature, that most ancient scholarly works have been lost. Ancient scholarship is thus now of three types: works that survive (intact or in epitomes), those that now exist only in quotations, papyrus fragments, and marginalia, and those that are altogether lost. Optimistic attempts are periodically made to reconstruct works of the second type and to discuss the content of some in the third category, and many modern scholars have a tendency to refer to lost works as if they still existed, which can blur the distinction. Such blurring is risky, however, as many of the modern reconstructions and hypotheses rest on very dubious foundations. The present work, since it is intended for those who wish to read works of ancient scholarship, is directly concerned only with works that are still extant or of which a substantial body of fragments remains, and the lost material is considered only to the extent that an appreciation of it is necessary in order to understand the remains we possess.

The earliest scholarship, that from the Alexandrian period, is often considered to be the most valuable to us, because of the extraordinary intellectual abilities of Aristarchus and his fellow librarians and the unique body of resources to which they had access.[4] None of their work, however, survives in its original form; we

---

2. See e.g. Henrichs (1971–3: 99–100) and Wackernagel (1914*b*).

3. See e.g. Schmit-Neuerburg (1999) and Rengakos (1993).

4. For further information on the Alexandrian scholars see, in addition to the specific works cited below, Pfeiffer (1968), Fraser (1972), M. L. West (2001: esp. chs. 2–3), Rengakos (1993), F. Montanari (1994), Ax (1991), Turner (1962), Susemihl (1891–2), Laum (1928), *RE, NP,* and *OCD.*

have only fragments gathered from the works of later scholars, some (but by no means all) of whom are important primarily for preserving Alexandrian material.

The library at Alexandria was founded c.285 BC, and its first head was Zenodotus of Ephesus (c.325–c.270 BC).[5] Zenodotus worked primarily on establishing texts of Homer and the lyric poets, and our knowledge of his work comes chiefly through notes in later commentaries indicating Zenodotus' preferred readings.[6] The second librarian was Apollonius Rhodius (c.295–c.215 BC), who is now more famous for his poetry than for his scholarship, though a few fragments of the latter survive as well.[7] The same can be said of Apollonius' teacher[8] Callimachus (c.305–c.240 BC), who compiled the Πίνακες, a 120-book catalog of authors and their works.[9] Eratosthenes of Cyrene (c.280–c.194 BC), the third librarian, was also a scholar, though he is now more famous for scientific works.[10]

The fourth librarian, Aristophanes of Byzantium (c.257–c.180 BC), marks the beginning of the developed period of Alexandrian scholarship, when its greatest achievements were produced (see 3.2.4). In addition to editing many poetic texts and dividing lyric poetry into separate lines of verse, Aristophanes wrote important lexicographical works, fragments of which are still extant, and invented the accent marks still in use today. He also wrote introductions to many plays, some of which are the ancestors of extant hypotheses. Aristarchus of Samothrace (c.216–c.145 BC), the sixth[11] librarian, was the greatest of all ancient scholars.[12] He produced not only texts but also hypomnemata—self-standing commentaries—on a wide range of poetic and prose works and made many crucial contributions, especially to Homeric scholarship. His editorial and critical judgements were widely quoted by later commentators whose work still survives, and a fragment of his commentary on Herodotus is preserved on papyrus (see 2.2.6).

Shortly before the death of Aristarchus the scholars fled Alexandria to escape persecution by Ptolemy VIII, whose succession to the throne was preceded by a contest in which Aristarchus had supported the rival candidate; this move ultimately resulted in the dispersal of Alexandrian learning throughout the ancient

---

5. Zendotus' reputed teacher Philitas, born c.340 BC, was also important for early Alexandrian scholarship and compiled a glossary of obscure words that became a standard reference work—though he is better known for his poetry. For the remaining fragments of Philitas' scholarship see Kuchenmüller (1928).

6. On Zenodotus see Duentzer (1848), Nickau (1977), F. Montanari (1998), and M. L. West (2001: ch. 2).

7. On Apollonius see Rengakos (1994).

8. According to ancient sources, though this formulation of their relationship is now sometimes questioned.

9. On Callimachus see Blum (1977, 1991).

10. On Eratosthenes see Geus (2002).

11. Between Aristophanes and Aristarchus was an obscure Apollonius ὁ εἰδογράφος "classifier of forms").

12. On Aristarchus see Matthaios (1999), Schironi (2004), Lührs (1992), Apthorp (1980), Ludwich (1884–5), Lehrs (1882), and Erbse (1959).

world and its enormous influence on the Romans. Aristarchus' pupils established themselves in a variety of cities; one, Dionysius Thrax (*c*.170–*c*. 90 BC), founded a school in Rhodes and produced grammatical treatises, one of which may still be extant (see 3.1.3). Another disciple of Aristarchus, Apollodorus of Athens[13] (*c*. 180–*c*.110 BC), moved to Pergamum,[14] where a school rivaling[15] that at Alexandria had grown up under the leadership of the Stoic scholar Crates of Mallos[16] (second century BC). Crates made important contributions to grammatical analysis, while Apollodorus produced, among other writings, an authoritative work of chronology and a commentary on Homer's catalog of ships.

In the late second century Hipparchus of Nicaea produced an astronomical commentary on Aratus that has the distinction of being the only Hellenistic commentary to survive intact to this day (see 2.3.1). This feat of survival is still more impressive considering that the commentary is not a chance papyrus find but was preserved via the manuscript tradition; it survived at least in part because Hipparchus' work had independent value as an astronomical treatise. From Hipparchus one can learn much about the genre of the Hellenistic commentary, but because of its heavily scientific orientation his work is not typical of ancient commentaries on literary works.

In the first century BC scholarship entered a new phase. The Alexandrians had established good texts to the important works of classical literature and produced excellent commentaries on them, so there was little original work remaining to be done in those areas. Some scholars of the Roman period branched out into composing grammatical treatises and producing commentaries on postclassical or nonliterary authors, particularly the difficult and erudite poetry of Hellenistic scholars such as Apollonius and Callimachus and the scientific works of mathematicians and physicians. Others sacrificed their originality and continued to work on classical authors, producing syntheses or reworkings of earlier commentaries. These scholars' lack of originality, a frequent ground for nineteenth- and twentieth-century disdain, at the same time incurs gratitude insofar as we owe to it virtually all our knowledge of the Alexandrians' work: such fragments of Alexandrian scholarship as survive today normally come via composite commentaries of the Roman period.

13. For the fragments of Apollodorus see Jacoby (1929: 1022–1128), Theodoridis (1972), and Mette (1978: 20–3).

14. On the Pergamene scholars and their library see F. Montanari (1993*b*) and Nagy (1998).

15. Because of statements in Varro and Gellius, this rivalry is often thought to have taken the form of a controversy between "Analogists" (Aristarchus and his followers, who believed in principles of regularity in language) and "Anomalists" (Crates and his followers, who believed in irregularity). Some scholars (e.g. Fehling 1956–7; Pinborg 1975; Blank 1982: 1–4, 1994) doubt the reality of this controversy, but others (e.g. Ax 1991; Siebenborn 1976: 2–13; Colson 1919) support its existence. See also Schenkeveld (1994: 281–91).

16. On Crates see Broggiato (2002), Mette (1952), Janko (1995), and Ax (1991).

The establishment of Alexandrian scholarship in Rome was at least partly the work of Tyrannio(n) the elder (*c*.100–*c*.25 BC), a pupil of Dionysius Thrax who produced a variety of scholarly works that survive only in fragments (see 3.1.9). Rome then became the main place of work for a number of Greek scholars.[17] Trypho(n) (second half of the first century BC) produced glossaries and grammatical treatises, some of which may survive in excerpts (see 3.1.8). Philoxenus (first century BC) produced an etymological treatise, and Diocles (first century BC to first century AD) wrote a commentary on the works of his teacher Tyrannio(n); fragments of both are still extant (see 3.1.10 and 3.1.9). The second-oldest extant commentary, dating to the first century BC, is that of Apollonius of Citium on Hippocrates (see 2.2.1); this work owes its survival to factors similar to those that preserved Hipparchus' commentary on Aratus.

The greatest producer of composite commentaries, and probably the most prolific of all ancient scholars, was the Alexandrian Didymus Chalcenterus ("brazenguts"), who lived in the second half of the first century BC and the beginning of the first century AD.[18] Didymus is said to have written 3,500 or 4,000 books and was nicknamed βιβλιολάθας because he allegedly could not remember what he had written. He put together the writings of Aristarchus and other scholars in order to compile hundreds of composite commentaries on Homer, Demosthenes, and other literary works, as well as producing lexica and monographs; the remains of his commentaries are our primary source of knowledge of the Alexandrians' critical work. Most of the commentaries survive only in extracts preserved in later works, but part of the commentary on Demosthenes has been found on papyrus.[19] Another important commentator of this period is Theon, whose works now survive only in fragments.[20]

---

17. In addition to the ones mentioned here, there were a number of other Greek scholars working at Rome; these are less well known today because less of their work suvives. Two particularly notable scholars, both from the Augustan age, are Aristonicus (who wrote Homeric commentaries and a work on Aristarchus' signs) and Seleucus (who also wrote on Aristarchus' signs, as well as on many other topics). For Aristonicus see 2.1.1.1 below, Friedlaender (1853) and Carnuth (1869); for Seleucus see M. L. West (2001: esp. 47–8 with n. 7).

18. This Didymus is (probably) to be distinguished from a number of other scholars named Didymus, including Didymus minor / Δίδυμος ὁ νεώτερος, a Greek grammarian in Alexandria in the 1st cent. AD; Didymus Claudius, a Greek grammarian in Rome in the early 1st cent. AD; Didymus son of Heraclides, a Greek grammarian in Rome in the mid-1st cent. AD; and Didymus the Blind, a theologian in Alexandria in the 4th cent. AD. See *NP* iii: 553–4, *RE* v.i: 472–4, and Fraser (1972: ii. 686).

19. For the fragments of Didymus see Moritz Schmidt (1854), Ludwich (1884–5: i. 175–631), Miller (1868: 399–406 =*TLG*), and Pearson and Stephens (1983 =*TLG*); for discussion see C. Gibson (2002), F. Montanari (1992: esp. 262–4), Van der Valk (1963–4: i. 536–53), and works cited in Pearson and Stephens (1983).

20. Although he worked in Alexandria, this Theon is not to be confused with Theon of Alexandria, an important mathematical writer of the 4th cent. AD, nor with Theon of Samos, Theon of Smyrna, and numerous other Theons. The surviving fragments of his work have been collected by Guhl (1969).

From the first century AD we have Heraclitus' allegorical exegesis of Homer
(see 2.1.1.3), and that century was also a source of several lexica of which we have
surviving epitomes: the Homer lexicon of Apollonius Sophista (see 2.1.1.3) and
the Hippocratic lexicon of Erotian (see 2.2.1), both of which preserve elements
of much earlier scholarship. These early lexica, and probably their immediate
predecessors as well, were arranged in a simple form of alphabetical order, in which
only the first or first two or three letters of each word were taken into account in
determining their order; this type of alphabetization is characteristic of much
ancient scholarship and was not completely replaced by full alphabetical order
until the Byzantine period.[21]

In addition, it is in this century that we find the first evidence of an interesting
development in post-Alexandrian scholarship: the proliferation of popularizing
commentaries and summaries of literary works, usually with an emphasis on
mythology.[22] The Alexandrian commentaries and their direct descendants were
deeply scholarly and written for a sophisticated audience; they contained discussion of textual problems, alternative interpretations, critical judgements, and factual background, including detailed historical information and excerpts from
related literary works. Their commentaries were never the only type of commentary in existence, for elementary aids to school readings existed even before the
Alexandrian period. In the Roman period, however, the scholarly commentaries
faced considerable competition from a different type of work aimed at a less sophisticated adult audience.

Some of these works were prose summaries of famous poetry, often focusing
on mythological details; these included a set of summaries of individual books of
the *Iliad* and *Odyssey* (see 2.1.1.3) and a collection of summaries of the plays of
Euripides known today as the "Tales from Euripides" (see 2.1.3). Such works may
have been intended to be read instead of rather than along with the original poems
or plays. Other examples of the popularizing tendency, such as the Φ commentary on Aratus (see 2.3.1) and the Mythographus Homericus (see 2.1.1.3), were
still commentaries tied to the original work but contained in place of textual or
historical information extensive prose paraphrases aimed at helping readers grasp
the basic sense of the unfamiliar Greek, and/or increased discussion of the mythological background, sometimes with an eye-catching set of illustrations. Some
scholarly information might be retained from the older commentaries, but most
was simply excised to make room for the new material. The scholarly commentaries themselves did not usually disappear at this period, however; rather the two
types of commentary existed side by side.

The popularizing works appear to have continued and even increased in popularity in the second century and later, but at the same time the second century
saw much high-quality scholarly activity; it is also the first period from which a

21. For more information on ancient alphabetization, see Daly (1967).
22. On the use of such material in the Roman period see Rossum-Steenbeek (1998)
and Cameron (2004).

substantial amount of scholarly material has survived until the present day. It is probably not coincidental that this century was the period of the Second Sophistic, a movement that involved widespread revival of interest in the language of the classical writers. Second-century authors like Lucian learned to produce literary works in nearly flawless imitations of fifth-century Attic, and even in other classical dialects. The perfection of these imitations is especially impressive considering that non-literary Greek (as seen for example in documentary papyri) had undergone considerable evolution in the intervening five or six centuries, becoming a language markedly different from that of Plato or Herodotus.

Some of the most important results of the second-century developments seem to have come in the areas least covered by the Alexandrians, such as grammar.[23] Apollonius Dyscolus, probably the greatest of the grammarians, was active in the mid-second century AD; of his many works analyzing the structure of Greek, four still survive and are crucial to our understanding of ancient grammar (see 3.1.1). Apollonius' son Herodian produced important treatises on topics such as accentuation, of which portions are still extant (see 3.1.2). Hephaestion's treatise on metre, the main source of our knowledge of ancient metrical theory (see 3.3.2), is also from this period.

The second century was also a good era for lexica. Many of these were Atticist lexica that provided lists of words acceptable in Atticizing writing, though often they included material from authors such as Homer or Herodotus who would not today be considered Attic. There was considerable debate among the Atticists as to which authors should be admitted to their canon, and we can see the results of that debate both in the work of broad-based lexicographers such as the "Antiatticist," who took pains to justify by citation of Attic authors the use of words that were intelligible to second-century Greeks, and in the lexica of strict Atticists such as Phrynichus, who rejected such words in favor of obscurer alternatives gleaned from Old Comedy. Not all second-century lexica simply focused on the Attic dialect, however; we also have Galen's glossary of Hippocratic words (see 2.2.1), Pollux' *Onomasticon* (see 3.2.7), Harpocration's lexicon of terms used by the Attic orators (see 3.2.5), and remains of Herennius Philo's collection of synonyms and homonyms (see 3.2.6). Diogenianus' lexicon of rare words, which is lost but formed the basis of Hesychius' work (see 3.2.1), also dates to the second century.

Many commentaries were also produced in the second century, and a number of these are still extant. Galen (c.129–c.216) is responsible for thirteen surviving commentaries on Hippocrates that are crucial for our understanding of the nature of ancient scholarship (see 2.2.1), as well as some extant work on Plato (see 2.2.2). The earliest surviving commentaries on Aristotle likewise date to the second century, and the most important of the Aristotle commentators, Alexander of Aphrodisias, comes from the second and third centuries (see 2.2.3). Writers of

---

23. For more information on ancient grammatical theories, see Steinthal (1890–1), Pinborg (1975), Siebenborn (1976), Ax (1986), Sluiter (1990), Matthews (1994), Swiggers and Wouters (1996), Ildefonse (1997), and the works cited in section 3.1.

the third century too produced numerous commentaries and exegetical works on ancient literature, a substantial amount of which survives: from Porphyry alone we have works on Homer, Plato, Aristotle, and Ptolemy.

Towards the end of the Roman period commentaries were sometimes written on works of the earlier Roman period, such as those of Lucian (see 2.3). The remaining fragments of such commentaries can be of considerable value today, in part because their authors had access to older scholarship, and when treating an archaizing author a commentator often needs to discuss matters that significantly predate the author himself. Even historical details about fifth-century Athens can be gleaned from the remains of these commentaries.

Many late antique commentaries have survived more or less intact, but these all concern philosophical, mathematical, or medical writers.[24] Most plentiful are commentaries on Aristotle, Plato, Hippocrates, Galen, Ptolemy, and Euclid, but Archimedes and Apollonius of Perga are also represented. These works are usually concerned with the subject-matter rather than the text of the commented author and so preserve little scholarship in our sense of the term, but they are often very interesting as expositions of late antique thought in these disciplines. The best-preserved commentators are Simplicius, who wrote on Aristotle, Euclid, and Epictetus, and Proclus, who wrote a phenomenal number of works on authors as diverse as Hesiod, Plato, and Ptolemy. It is clear that commentaries to literary works were also composed during this period, in some cases by the same scholars as the surviving commentaries, but succeeding generations preserved only the philosophical and mathematical ones.

We also have some scholarship of other types surviving from the late antique period, but most of it is highly derivative. Since the scholars of the Roman period had done for lexica and grammars what the Alexandrians did for texts and commentaries, late antique scholars had few opportunities for constructive originality. Many of their works are now valued primarily for their preservation of earlier scholarship; Hesychius' lexicon of obscure words (fifth or sixth century) and the lexica of Orus, Orion, and Cyrillus (all fifth century) belong to this group, as does the geographical lexicon of Stephanus of Byzantium (sixth century).

Others were elementary, aimed at drilling the basic grammar of classical Greek into children who spoke a language as many centuries removed from Pericles as we are from Chaucer. Schoolbooks had of course existed for many centuries, but those from the Hellenistic and Roman periods, designed for an audience whose native language was not dramatically different from that of the classical period, were not usually preserved (though they are sometimes found on papyri). By contrast the *Canones* of Theodosius (fourth–fifth century) is a set of rules for declension and conjugation that has survived to the present day via the manuscript tradition.

---

24. For further information on late antique scholarship see N. Wilson (1983*a*: 28–60), Kaster (1988), Reynolds and Wilson (1991), and Robins (1993).

The next major development in the history of commentary, the transformation of commentaries on literary works into scholia,[25] was a momentous one.[26] In one sense this transition was chiefly one of format, for ancient commentaries (hypomnemata) were separate books, while medieval scholia took the form of marginalia around the text on which they commented.[27] This change is usually thought to

25. The word "scholia" now has different meanings when used by different groups of scholars. In recent works on Greek literary texts it means "commentary or notes written in the margins of a text," as opposed to "hypomnema," which refers to an ancient self-standing commentary, and to "gloss," which generally refers to a short definition found between the lines of a literary text (often the distinction is that a marginal comment is a scholion and an interlinear one is a gloss, though sometimes marginal notes consisting of short definitions are also called glosses, and the term can also be used for an entry in a lexicon). Since this usage of these terms is now the most common one, it is also followed in this book. Scholars working on philosophical and scientific texts, however, have a tendency to use "scholia" (and sometimes even "glosses") for a commentary consisting of short notes on specific passages rather than a continuous exegesis, regardless of whether that commentary is found in the margins of a manuscript or as its only text; sometimes they even use "scholia" for a continuous commentary.

The original meaning of σχόλια is "notes," regardless of location (see Lundon 1997), but while the ancients referred to their self-standing commentaries as ὑπομνήματα, the Byzantines called commentaries σχόλια, irrespective of location or character. This usage is continued into modern Greek, where σχόλια is still the regular word for "commentary." Nineteenth-century scholars working on authors for whose works self-standing late antique commentaries are preserved intact as well as being the source of most marginalia (i.e. philosophical, mathematical, and medical texts) tended to keep the Byzantine usage of σχόλια or to temper it with the ancient usage by restricting the word to commentaries consisting of discrete notes. Since for such texts marginal and self-standing commentaries have similar content and origins, the location of the commentary in the manuscripts is not of much importance, so scholars working on them had no need to develop a terminology that identified commentaries by location. But 19th-cent. scholars studying authors for whose works ancient scholarship is preserved (at least via the manuscript tradition) only in marginalia came quite naturally to use σχόλια only for marginalia. When papyrus fragments of ancient self-standing commentaries on those authors turned up, the major differences between the content of those fragments and that of the marginalia necessitated a distinction in terminology and led to the resurrection of the ancient term "hypomnema" for the self-standing commentaries, as well as a more deliberate restriction of the term "scholia" to marginalia. In the last half-century or so research on the conversion of the hypomnemata into marginalia has solidified this terminology among students of literary texts, but it has spread only gradually to other areas; for example scholars working on medical texts now use "scholia" only for marginalia, but those working on Aristotle still use "scholia" for commentaries.

26. For more information on this transition see N. Wilson (1967, 1971, 1984), McNamee (1995, 1998), Zuntz (1975; 1965: 272–5), H. Maehler (1994, 2000), Andorlini (2000), and Irigoin (1994: 67–82); n.b. also Zetzel (1975).

27. For more information on the hypomnema and scholia formats and ancient commentary in general, see in addition to the works already cited Slater (1989a), Rutherford

be connected to the shift in book production that occurred in the late antique period: most ancient books were written on papyrus rolls in short parallel columns with little space between them and virtually no room for marginalia, while most medieval ones were written on parchment codices (i.e. manuscripts shaped like a modern book), often with wide margins around each page. At some point a few hypomnemata were copied into the margins of codices, and then both they and the uncopied hypomnemata were lost, leaving only the marginalia extant.

But the relationship between hypomnemata and scholia is more complex, and the differences between them more significant, than this formulation suggests. Hypomnemata were unified works by a single author; even composite commentaries like those of Didymus presented a fairly seamless appearance and smoothly integrated pieces of information from various sources. Though written on separate rolls, they were not intended to be read independently of the text but were connected to it by lemmata, short quotations indicating the word or passage under discussion. When a hypomnema was intended to accompany a particular edition,[28] like the texts and commentaries of Aristarchus, the two could be linked by marginal signs in the text pointing to notes in the commentary. At the same time marginal and interlinear annotation on papyrus texts is by no means unknown; we have numerous annotated papyri of literary texts from many genres.[29] But such annotation normally consists of brief notes rather than the complex discussions found in hypomnemata and in medieval scholia, and it is clear that our scholia are descended from ancient hypomnemata rather than from ancient marginalia.

Medieval scholia are not simply transcripts, or even abbreviated transcripts, of ancient hypomnemata, nor are many of them readers' casual notes; they are dense and systematic collections of extracts from different sources. They make no claim to be the work of an individual, and little or no attempt to reconcile the contents or integrate the syntax of the different extracts, which often involve multiple entries on the same passage (frequently separated simply by ἄλλως[30]). The authors of (some of) the hypomnemata used may be given in a general note on the sources of the scholia, and the sources of individual notes are often explicitly stated at their beginnings. The original lemmata may be retained (and in such cases provide a valuable independent witness to the text, since they sometimes escape corruptions undergone by the main text), but often they are lost, made redundant by the note's proximity to the text it explains.

(1905), Sluiter (2000), Pasquali (1934), Bühler (1977), C. Gibson (2002), N. Wilson (1983*b*), Meijering (1987), Tosi (1988: 59–86), Lamberz (1987), Arrighetti (1977), and numerous articles in Geerlings and Schulze (2002), Goulet-Cazé (2000), and Most (1999).

28. The texts produced by ancient scholars, which clearly differed from those of other scholars to some extent, are now usually called their "editions." They did not, however, have all the characteristics of a modern "critical edition."

29. For further information on annotated papyri see McNamee (1977, 1992, forthcoming) and Van Thiel (1992).

30. See Ch. 4.1.5 for the use of ἄλλως.

Scholia often represent severe abridgements, and sometimes mutilations, of hypomnemata, but at the same time the initial selection of material appears to have been excellent. Most of the papyrus commentary we possess is fairly elementary, and only a small percentage preserves Alexandrian scholarship, but the scholia are often based on Alexandrian material, suggesting that their first compilers made an effort to find the most scholarly commentaries to copy into their margins. Such commentaries were not, unfortunately, those of the Alexandrians themselves, which seem to have disappeared before the end of the Roman period, but rather the composite commentaries of Didymus and his contemporaries. Material from these scholarly works was often mixed with that from more popularizing works of the Roman period, and frequently with later material as well, but it is still true that much more Alexandrian material can be recovered from scholia than from papyri.

The precise date and manner in which this crucial change from separate commentary to scholia took place are disputed, with suggested dates ranging from the fourth to the tenth century.[31] Clearly the change was complete by the time of our earliest manuscripts with scholia, which date to the ninth and tenth century, but some independent hypomnemata could have survived until that date (indeed we know that ninth-century authors like Photius had access to large quantities of ancient scholarship that disappeared not long afterwards), so our earliest manuscripts could contain scholia copied directly from hypomnemata. Alternatively one can point to the early parchment codices of the late antique period (a number of which contain substantial marginal annotation, though this annotation often fails to show the composite characteristics of medieval scholia), and to late antique legal and Biblical commentaries in the medieval scholia format, and argue that hypomnemata began to be converted into scholia in the fifth century. In the latter case the process was probably a gradual one, for it is clear that information continued to be copied out of self-standing texts into the margins of other texts throughout much of the Byzantine period.

In a sense the act that is most significant for us is not the copying of the hypomnemata as scholia, but the subsequent loss of the hypomnemata themselves—something that did not necessarily happen as soon as the scholia were copied. By no means all ancient commentaries disappeared; those on philosophical, medical, and mathematical works often survived intact or nearly intact, as did those on Christian texts. Scholia on such works are usually considered valueless and are rarely published, because they are mostly drawn from commentaries that still survive; by contrast the scholia on poetic texts, since they come from lost commentaries, are highly prized.

---

31. e.g. White (1914: p. lxiv) opts for the 4th or 5th cent., McNamee (e.g. 1998: 285) the 5th cent., N. Wilson (e.g. 1983a: 34–6) and Dover (1993: 96–7) the late antique period, H. Maehler (e.g. 1994) the 9th cent., and Zuntz (e.g. 1975: 109) the 9th or 10th cent. Erbse (1969–88: ii. 547) believes that the scholia to other texts may have been compiled in the 5th or 6th cent., but that those to the *Iliad* come from the 9th cent.

An interesting exception to all these principles consists of the "D scholia" to Homer, which were not originally hypomnemata but which appear as a self-standing commentary, without the text of Homer, in several medieval manuscripts of varying dates (as well as in the margins of many manuscripts containing the text of Homer). These scholia must at some point have been copied from different sources into a self-standing commentary, showing that the flow of information between different formats could go in both directions.

An apparent (though perhaps illusory) period of scholarly inactivity after the late antique period was ended by a revival in Byzantium in the ninth century.[32] Many scholars of this period are not respected by Classicists, but they had access to lost works of earlier scholarship and thus can be of considerable significance now; in addition, the study of the evolution of Byzantine scholarship is an interesting field in its own right. Early Byzantine scholars include George Choeroboscus (eighth–ninth century), who wrote a number of didactic works containing information from lost works of the early grammarians; some of these survive, including a long commentary on Theodosius as well as (probably) the *Epimerismi Homerici*. His contemporary Michael Syncellus has left us a basic textbook on syntax, and Photius (c.810–c.893) contributed the massive *Bibliotheca*, a compendium of information on earlier literary works, in addition to a lexicon. The *Etymologicum genuinum*, a ninth-century etymological lexicon, and the *Suda*, a tenth-century literary encyclopedia, both survive intact (and enormous) and preserve many valuable fragments of earlier scholarship.

The earliest surviving manuscripts of many literary texts date to the early Byzantine period, and these manuscripts often contain scholia. But the scholia as they appear in our manuscripts are not always what they were when they first became marginalia. In order to survive, scholia had to be recopied with each successive copying of the main text, and this did not always happen; in many cases the sheer quantity of marginalia defeated copyists, leading to the omission of large amounts of material. It is common for scholia on small bodies of text (such as the speeches of Aeschines) to be much richer than the scholia on longer works (such as the dialogues of Plato), and it is also usual for scholia to be much more plentiful at the beginning of a long work than in subsequent sections. Sometimes correction for these omissions was made by Byzantine readers who, having originally copied a text with few or no scholia, then found a different source with scholia and copied those; such hybrid manuscripts can be important for the preservation of scholia but are highly problematic for those who use scholia to determine manuscript stemmata (see O. L. Smith 1981: 53).

Moreover, even when they were copied, the scholia suffered many kinds of corruption. They were frequently abbreviated, displaced, miscopied, or inappropriately run together. Their text was treated much more casually by copy-

---

32. For further information on Byzantine scholarship see N. Wilson (1983a), Hunger (1978: ii. 3–83), Reynolds and Wilson (1991), and Robins (1993).

ists than the main text, so that some scribes felt free to rephrase the notations as they saw fit (see H. Fränkel 1964: 99). As a result, the scholia to a single author often appear in radically different form in different manuscripts, and frequently the divergences are so great that no reconstruction of the original is possible.

The situation is further complicated by the fact that some Byzantine scholars composed their own notes on ancient literature, sometimes based on the older scholia and sometimes on their own researches, and these notes have been transmitted in the margins of manuscripts as well. The Byzantine scholia are known as *scholia recentiora* and receive on the whole less attention than the older scholia (known as *scholia vetera* or "old scholia"), but they cannot be ignored entirely. In the first place one has to identify them in order to tell which scholia are old and which are not, since scholia from different sources are frequently mixed together in the same manuscript. In addition, since the writers had access to manuscripts now lost, they often used old scholia that we do not possess and that we can only recover from a study of the Byzantine notes. Moreover Byzantine scholars occasionally had good ideas of their own—and of course the *scholia recentiora* are crucial for the study of Byzantine scholarship.

The earliest significant body of Byzantine scholia comes from Arethas of Caesarea (*c*.850–*c*.944), whose recasting of older scholia preserves much ancient material. John Tzetzes (*c*.1110–*c*.1180) produced numerous surviving commentaries on classical authors, many of which contain important information on the work of earlier scholars. Eustathius' (*c*.1115–*c*.1195) immense commentaries on Homer are now considered probably the most important of all surviving Byzantine commentaries and contain much ancient material. Maximus Planudes (*c*.1255–*c*.1305), Manuel Moschopulus (*c*.1265–after 1305), Thomas Magister (active 1301–46), and Demetrius Triclinius (*c*.1280–1340) also produced significant commentaries on a number of authors. The latest of these, Triclinius, is often called the first modern scholar; he went far beyond the resources handed down to him to develop his own metrical analyses and write original commentaries. While these qualities make his work interesting and important in the history of classical scholarship, they also mean that it is often less reliable than that of his predecessors as a source of ancient material. Fortunately Triclinius' ideas evolved over a considerable period, and we have manuscripts of his work at widely differing dates. In many cases his initial work on a text involved the faithful repetition of ancient scholia, and only later did he depart from them significantly. When both versions are preserved, scholars tend to use the earlier ("proto-Triclinian") work for reconstruction of ancient commentary, and the later ("Triclinian") for evaluation of his own theory.

The Byzantine period produced other types of scholarship as well, some of it original, some of it preserving valuable ancient material, and some of it falling into neither category. Important works of this period include those of Gregory of Corinth (eleventh–twelfth century), who discussed Greek dialectology, and several lexica, of which the most significant are the *Etymologicum magnum* (twelfth century), *Etymologicum Gudianum* (eleventh century), and lexicon of Zonaras (thirteenth century). Maximus Planudes (*c*.1255–*c*.1305) is responsible for a wide variety of extant works, including collections of texts and some important theoretical discussions of grammar, and John Glykys (fourteenth century) has left us a work on correct syntax.

After this period old material known to scholars was rarely lost, and therefore authors later than the 14th century are not used as sources of ancient scholarship. In modern times the surviving self-standing works of ancient and Byzantine scholarship, such as the grammars, have been edited and published like other surviving ancient texts, though on the whole they have received less editorial attention and so present more challenges for readers, and more opportunities for future editors, than do works of classical literature. Scholia are more problematic; at first they were either ignored or published together with the texts they accompanied (either at the bottom of the page or as an appendix), but now they are usually collected and published in separate volumes. Such collections often include not only manuscript scholia but also papyrus fragments with commentaries or marginal scholia to the works concerned.

The body of surviving scholia is enormous; often the scholia on a literary work fill more volumes than the work itself. Much of this material is late, and it is not always easy to distinguish the ancient elements in the mixture. Modern editors often deal with this problem by marking individual scholia with signs to indicate their origins or by editing only a portion of the surviving scholia, such as the old scholia, the metrical scholia, the scholia from certain manuscripts, or the marginal scholia (as opposed to interlinear glosses). Often this pre-selection is helpful, but often it causes much inconvenience, since it means that there may be no complete text of the scholia on a given author when one is trying to follow up a reference consisting only of the location of the lemma in the original work.

In either case the reader is presented with editorial decisions that may or may not be trustworthy. In the case of certain authors the division of scholia is easy, because those from different sources appear in different manuscripts or are marked with different signs in a single manuscript. In other cases the matter is much more complex, and sometimes editors are relying simply on the assumption that any comments on certain topics must come from certain sources. As the value of a scholion depends largely on its source, it is important to understand the editor's judgements in this respect and their level of reliability. For this reason it is important to choose editions carefully and to read the preface to one's chosen edition in order to find out what sort of evidence underlies these editorial decisions; the present work is intended to help with the choice of editions but can be no substitute for a careful perusal of prefaces.

The value of ancient scholarship as a whole is immense, but the usefulness of individual works varies widely. Some offer large quantities of generally reliable, accurate information on subjects like the language or the world of classical Athens. Others contain very little such information but are nevertheless important for the light they shed on classical scholarship in their writers' times or on the textual history of a literary work. Still others seem to offer valuable information about antiquity but are unreliable and mingle a bit of real knowledge with a deluge of guesswork. Though it is normally the case that factual information about the classical period is more to be trusted from a Hellenistic source than from a Byzantine one, date alone is not an adequate guage of reliability. Just as some modern scholars are much more trustworthy than others, there was considerable synchronic variation in the reliability of ancient scholars; this variation is particularly apparent in the Roman period, from which we have both very trustworthy works such as those of Galen and Harpocration and others of much more dubious character. The nature of a source is therefore at least as important to know as its date. This is the reason for the great emphasis, in modern studies of scholia and other composite works of ancient scholarship, on identifying and separating material from different sources.

2

Scholia, Commentaries, and Lexica
on Specific Literary Works

2.1 ARCHAIC AND CLASSICAL POETRY

This category includes the most famous and most often cited scholia. By far the most important are the Homer scholia, but those on Pindar and the Attic dramatists are also significant.

2.1.1 Homer

Ancient scholarship on Homer was extensive and of high quality, for the best scholars of antiquity devoted much of their time and energy to the Homeric poems. Work on Homer that could be described as scholarship goes back at least to the classical period and probably to the sixth century BC, and editing the text of Homer was one of the main tasks of the first Alexandrian scholars. Zenodotus, Aristophanes of Byzantium, and Aristarchus probably all produced editions of the *Iliad* and *Odyssey*, and Aristarchus wrote extensive commentaries, while Zenodotus and Aristophanes compiled glossaries of primarily Homeric words. In addition, the early and persistent use of Homer as a school text meant that there was a tradition of school exegesis that reached back as far as the classical period. Though none of the very early work on Homer survives in its original form, a surprising amount is preserved in various later compilations, so we often know, for example, the readings of several different Alexandrian scholars for a particular passage, and even some of the arguments behind these readings (although the arguments preserved in later sources cannot always be assumed to be those of the editor himself).

Two principal sources for the ancient scholarship on Homer survive: the scholia and Eustathius' commentaries, both of which are gigantic works filling many volumes in modern editions. There are also some smaller works, some of which are more valuable than others.

2.1.1.1 Scholia

Most of the old scholia to the *Iliad* fall into three groups: A, bT, and D. The A scholia come from the margins of the most famous *Iliad* manuscript, Venetus A (tenth century), where they were entered systematically by a single scribe. (A scholia are also found in other manuscripts, including those whose scholia fall primarily into one of the other categories, for they contain material that was widespread long before the writing of Venetus A. They are, however, defined by their occurrence in that manuscript: a scholion found elsewhere is considered to be an A scholion if it duplicates material from Venetus A.[1]) The origins of the A scholia are clearer than is the case with most scholia, for at the end of almost every book the scribe added a subscription indicating their source: παράκειται τὰ 'Αριστονίκου Σημεῖα καὶ τὰ Διδύμου Περὶ τῆς 'Αρισταρχείου διορθώσεως, τινὰ δὲ καὶ ἐκ τῆς 'Ιλιακῆς προσῳδίας 'Ηρωδιανοῦ καὶ ἐκ τοῦ Νικάνορος Περὶ στιγμῆς "Written beside [the text] are Aristonicus' 'Signs' and Didymus' 'On the Aristarchean edition', and also some extracts from Herodian's 'Iliadic prosody' and from Nicanor's 'On punctuation'." The principal basis of the A scholia is therefore the four works cited in this subscription (all of which are now lost except insofar as they are preserved in the scholia), but it is unlikely that the scribe who wrote it was actually copying from the works themselves. Rather his source, or more likely his source's source, was a compilation of these four works (and some other material) probably made around the fourth century AD and known today as the "Viermännerkommentar" or VMK.

All four elements of the VMK represent Alexandrian scholarship to a significant extent. Aristonicus' treatise on signs, composed in the Augustan period, was a compilation of excerpts from one of Aristarchus' commentaries and from other works, focusing on critical signs. Didymus' work, probably also from the Augustan period but later than that of Aristonicus (which Didymus probably used), was a compilation based primarily on Aristarchus' commentaries, though his focus was on textual variants. Herodian's treatise on Homeric accentuation, from the late second century AD, also drew heavily on Aristarchus' commentaries, and Nicanor's work on punctuation, from the first half of the second century AD, was based on earlier works including those of the Alexandrians. The A scholia are thus a major source of information about the opinions of Aristarchus and, to a lesser extent, other Alexandrian scholars; they contain more than a thousand explicit references to Aristarchus. They are of crucial importance for our knowledge of the text of Homer, the goals and methods of Alexandrian scholarship, and ancient systems of accentuation, punctuation, etc.

The A scholia also contain material that probably does not derive from VMK. This information is more interpretive in nature and is related to material found in the bT scholia; A scholia of this type are also called exegetical scholia and as such are grouped with the bT scholia.

The bT scholia are so called because they are found in manuscript T (eleventh century) and in the descendants of the lost manuscript b (6th century). They contain some Alexandrian material (much of it attributable to Didymus) but seem to

---

1. Except that identification as a D scholion takes precedence over identification as an A scholion, so material found in the main D-scholia manuscripts is considered to be D-scholia material even if it also occurs in A. Thus the different groups of scholia are grouped hierarchically in the order D, A, bT, other, and material is assigned to the first of these groups in which it is found. It is not accidental that this hierarchy matches the chronological order of creation of the earliest elements of each group.

come more immediately from a commentary of the late antique period (known as "c"), of which b produced a popular and T a more scholarly version. These scholia are also known as the exegetical scholia, because they are concerned primarily with exegesis rather than textual criticism. They include extensive extracts from theὉμηρικὰ ζητήματα of Porphyry and the Ὁμηρικὰ προβλήματα of Heraclitus (see 2.1.1.3). Until recently the bT scholia were thought to be much less valuable than the A scholia (whose worth has been recognized since the eighteenth century), because of the limited extent to which they can aid in establishing the text of the Homeric poems. In the past few decades, however, an increasing interest in ancient literary criticism has brought these scholia into new prominence, and they are currently at the center of modern work on ancient Homeric scholarship.

The D scholia are unfortunately named after Didymus, with whom they are now known to have no connection; they are also known as "scholia minora" or "scholia vulgata." They are the largest group of Homeric scholia, and our earliest manuscript evidence for them is older than that for the other types of scholia, for the chief witnesses to the D scholia are manuscripts Z and Q, which date to the ninth and eleventh centuries respectively. D scholia are also found in a wide range of other manuscripts, including A and T, where they can be identified by their resemblance to notes found in Z, Q, or other manuscripts not part of the A or bT traditions. Many D scholia are very short and appear as interlinear glosses in A (and other manuscripts), but others are more substantial and take their place in the margins of A.

The D scholia have diverse origins and form a heterogeneous group, but there is no doubt that much of the material in them is very old, for there are remarkable similarities between the D scholia and Homeric scholarship found on papyri; in fact such similarities are much more frequent with the D scholia than with A or bT scholia. One major component of the D scholia is lexicographical, consisting of short definitions or explanations of difficult words. Many of these definitions can also be found in papyrus glossaries and/or as marginalia or interlinear glosses in papyrus texts of Homer, for they come from an ancient vulgate tradition of interpretation. The basis of this tradition goes back to the schoolrooms of the classical period, so that it predates the Alexandrians and represents the oldest surviving stratum of Homeric scholarship. Other components of the D scholia include mythological explanations, plot summaries, and prose paraphrases; these too are paralleled in the papyri and must be ancient, though they probably do not go back as far as the lexicographical element.

The D scholia have the distinction of existing in a number of medieval manuscripts as a self-standing commentary, without the text of Homer; they have thus reversed the path usually taken by scholia, since a self-standing work has been created out of notes from different sources, rather than a self-standing commentary being broken down into separate notes. Partly as a result of their unusual manuscript position, and partly because of their inherent usefulness for those who need help to read Homer, they were the first Homeric scholia to be published in printed form (in 1517) and remained pre-eminent until superseded by the A scholia. Subsequently they have been much neglected—until a few years ago the 1517 edition was the standard text—and it is only very recently that modern scholars have begun to pay them serious attention. Now, however, it is recognized that D-scholia lemmata sometimes preserve variant readings of the text that are not otherwise attested, that their definitions can provide important evidence for the meaning of Homeric words, and that they contain crucial information about the history and evolution of ancient scholarship, the ancient education system, and the way Homer was read and understood in antiquity.

The scholia to the *Odyssey* are much fewer and less well preserved than those to the *Iliad*. This distinction goes back to antiquity, when the *Iliad* was considered the superior work and so was read and copied much more often than the *Odyssey*. Nevertheless it is clear that the Alexandrians produced texts and commentaries on both poems, and that ancient scholars discussed the interpretation of the *Odyssey* as well as that of the *Iliad*. Thus equivalents of all three groups of *Iliad* scholia can be found for the *Odyssey* scholia: there are Alexandrian text-critical scholia, exegetical scholia of the bT type, and D scholia. However, because there is no equivalent of Venetus A among the *Odyssey* manuscripts the different types are not so easily separable by manuscript source.

Byzantine annotations to texts of the *Iliad* and *Odyssey* also exist, but these are generally ignored and remain largely unpublished. The best-known group of Byzantine scholia is the "h-scholia" to the *Iliad*, because these were once thought to be ancient, though they are now dated to the eleventh century.[2]

In addition to the uses of the Homer scholia already mentioned, they are important for the understanding of post-Homeric literature. Much of this literature, both Greek and Latin, was based to some extent on the Homeric poems, but not on the Homeric poems as we read them: rather on the Homer of the scholiasts. Authors such as Apollonius Rhodius and Vergil drew on and alluded to Homer based on the readings and interpretations current in their own time, and therefore the scholia provide us with information crucial for understanding their poems.

Most of the A and bT scholia to the *Iliad* are best consulted in the superb edition of Erbse (1969–88 =*TLG*). This edition is highly selective and tries to represent an early stage of the A and bT traditions, a feature that makes the most famous scholia readily available and easy to consult but also results in the omission of many scholia from different traditions, some of which are important. The omitted material includes all the D scholia, the bT scholia derived from Porphyry and Heraclitus, and some other material that cannot be easily assigned to any of the three main groups of scholia, not to mention all the Byzantine scholia. The seven volumes of Erbse's edition thus represent only a small fraction of all the preserved scholia, and since many scholia appearing in codex A are omitted from the edition because they belong to the D family, while others appearing in manuscripts of the b family are ignored because they come from Porphyry or Heraclitus, the

---

2. Erbse (1960: 208) dates them to the 12th cent., but evidence of their use in the *Etymologicum magnum* shows that they must be earlier; see Alpers (1981: 93 n. 36).

edition is not even a complete collection of the scholia appearing in the manuscripts included.

Of the scholia omitted from Erbse the most important are the D scholia, which can be found in Van Thiel's edition (2000*b*). The Porphyry and Heraclitus scholia are best consulted in editions of the works from which they came (see 2.1.1.3). Even together, however, these editions do not cover all the *Iliad* scholia, nor do they allow one to work out the full extent of the material in an individual manuscript; even the contents of A, the most famous, cannot all be found in recently published editions alone. For such purposes one must resort to the older editions of *Iliad* scholia, which cover the most important manuscripts individually: W. Dindorf (1875–8) for A and B, Maass (1887–8) for T, Nicole (1891 =*TLG*) for the Geneva manuscript,[3] and Lascaris (1517) and De Marco (1946) for the two branches of the D scholia. A complete facsimile of A has been published by De Vries (1901) and is useful for understanding the printed versions of the A and D scholia.

The situation regarding editions of the *Odyssey* scholia is both less complex and less satisfactory. The standard edition for most scholia is that of W. Dindorf (1855 =*TLG*), which is decidedly inadequate (and note that the D scholia are marked "V" in this edition). The first 309 lines of the first book only have received a better edition by Ludwich (1888–90 =*TLG*). The D scholia to the *Odyssey* are being edited by Conrad (forthcoming) and are otherwise to be found only in Asulanus' edition (1528).

It is possible to collect from the scholia the fragments of each of their sources, so that these can be studied as a group. Such collections have been made for the lost works of a number of ancient scholars, and these are sometimes convenient, but they are usually based on superseded texts and so should not be used in isolation. Collections include those of Duentzer (1848) on Zenodotus, Slater (1986) and Nauck (1848) on Aristophanes of Byzantium, Friedlaender (1853 =*TLG*, 1850) and Carnuth (1869 =*TLG*, 1875) on Aristonicus and Nicanor, Moritz Schmidt (1854) and Ludwich (1884–5: i. 175–631) on Didymus, Lentz (1867–70 = *GG* iii) on Herodian, and Schrader (1880–2, 1890) on Porphyry.

There is a vast corpus of papyrus Homerica (commentaries, glossaries, anthologies, explanations, paraphrases, summaries) and annotated papyrus texts of Homer, and each year it is augmented by new discoveries. This material is not normally included in editions of the manuscript scholia and so is difficult to find; it is however often important. A few papyrus commentaries are incorporated into Erbse's edition, and the annotated texts are listed and in most cases reprinted by McNamee (1992) and Van Thiel (1992). For guides to the rest of this material see M. L.

---

3. This manuscript contains bT and h scholia, including many (probably late) scholia omitted by both Erbse and Van Thiel, as well as some independent old material esp. on book 21. It is especially interesting for the later history of Homer scholarship because it was owned by Manuel Moschopulus and by H. Stephanus (Henri Estienne).

West (2001: 130–6), Lundon (1999), F. Montanari (1984, 1988*b*), Henrichs (1971–3), and Raffaelli (1984);[4] further publications in Spooner (2002).

The literature on the Homer scholia is enormous. Important studies include those of Erbse (1960), Van der Valk (1963–4), Martin Schmidt (1976), F. Montanari (1979), Henrichs (1971–3), and van Thiel (2000*a*), and general introductions include Nagy (1997), Gudeman (1921: 630–45), and the preface to Erbse (1969–88); Lamberton and Keaney (1992) offer a look at ancient readings of Homer as illustrated in the scholia and a variety of other sources. Works on some of the themes of modern interest in these scholia include: on the connection between the Homer scholia and later literature, Schmit-Neuerburg (1999), Schlunk (1974), and Rengakos (1993, 1994); on literary criticism, Richardson (1980), Meijering (1987), and many recent articles, e.g. Nünlist (2003); on the work of particular ancient scholars, Lührs (1992), Matthaios (1999), Erbse (1959), Lehrs (1882), and Ludwich (1884–5) on Aristarchus, Nickau (1977) on Zenodotus, Blank (1983*a*) on Nicanor, Dyck (1987) and Latte (1924) on the glossographers, and Ludwich (1912–14) on Demo.[5] In addition, most works on the textual history of the Homeric poems devote considerable attention to evaluating the ancient Homeric scholarship preserved in the scholia; recent examples of such works include Apthorp (1980), M. L. West (2001), and Nagy (2004).

2.1.1.2 Eustathius

Eustathius, archbishop of Thessalonica (not to be confused with several other Eustathii), wrote a number of commentaries on ancient authors in the twelfth century AD. The most important of these is his massive work on Homer, but we also possess a commentary on Dionysius Periegeta and the introduction to a commentary on Pindar, as well as historical and religious works dealing with Eustathius' own times. He is also sometimes credited with writing an epitome of Athenaeus' *Deipnosophistae*, but this attribution is now frequently rejected.

Eustathius based his commentaries on an impressive range of ancient sources, many of which are now lost to us in their original form. He consulted different manuscripts of the texts with which he worked and recorded variant readings, thus preserving for us the readings of manuscripts that have since disappeared. He also made extensive use of scholia, lexica, and other scholarly works, some of which no longer exist. In addition, he used works of ancient literature other than the ones upon which he commented and thus sometimes preserves fragments of those texts and variants otherwise lost.

The longest and most important of Eustathius' works is his commentary on the *Iliad*. This was written for students and educated general readers, rather than

4. General lists of Homeric papyri, such as those in Pack (1965) or the *Homer and the Papyri* website (www.chs.harvard.edu/homer_papyri), may also be helpful.

5. Though greatly neglected at present, Demo is worthy of further study, for numerous fragments of her work are preserved, and she offers a rare example of a female scholar (of the late antique/early Byzantine period).

for scholars, and is designed to be read with or without the text of the *Iliad*. The author provided it with a marginal index, which appears to be an invention of his own. The main source is the Homeric scholia (both those we possess and others), but many other works are also used (see the introduction to Van der Valk's edition for details). The commentary on the *Odyssey* is similar but much shorter and less important.

Eustathius' commentaries have reached us in excellent condition. For the *Iliad* commentary we possess, in addition to numerous copies, the author's own autograph manuscript. The identity of this manuscript (Codex Laurentianus Plut. LIX 2 and 3) was discovered fairly recently, and in consequence the only edition of the text to be based on it (that of Van der Valk, 1971–87 =*TLG*) is by far the best.[6] For the *Odyssey* commentary there is no equivalent of Van der Valk's edition, and one must use Stallbaum's text (1825–6 =*TLG*). Stallbaum also produced a text of the *Iliad* commentary (1827–30), but as he did not use the autograph manuscript at all, Van der Valk's text is always superior. There are separate indices both to Van der Valk's text (Keizer 1995) and to Stallbaum's (Devarius 1828).

Modern scholarship on Eustathius is fairly extensive. Accessible introductions in English include Browning (1992: 141–4) and N. Wilson (1983a: 196–204). The introduction to Van der Valk's edition of the *Iliad* commentary (beginning in volume one and continuing in volume two) is excellent, thorough, and written in highly comprehensible Latin. More wide-ranging discussions, covering the non-scholarly aspects of Eustathius' life and works, can be found in Browning (1962–3: 186–93), Kazhdan (1984: 115–95), and Wirth (1980).

References to Eustathius normally follow marginal numbers like references to a classical text.[7] On the rare occasions when references are given using the Homeric book and line numbers, patience is needed to pursue them; Eustathius' discussions do not always proceed in strict linear order, but Van der Valk inserts Homeric line numbers into the text whenever Eustathius moves from one line to another.

2.1.1.3 Other Sources of Ancient Scholarship on Homer

A number of ancient works on Homer have survived as separate entities to some extent, and there are also some Byzantine works that preserve ancient scholarship. Though these have traditionally received much less attention than the scholia, interest has grown in the past few decades, and a number have recently received good new editions that make them much easier to consult.

The primary Homeric lexicon of the late antique period was that compiled by Apollonius Sophista[8] in the first century AD, with sources including Apion, the

---

6. Readers interested in diacritics should, however, note that this edition does not re-produce Eustathius' own accent and breathing marks but regularizes these signs to fit modern conventions; Eustathius' own system is explained in the introduction, pp. xxvi–xxx.

7. Unfortunately, these numbers are omitted from the *TLG* version of the text, which instead gives references by page and line of Van der Valk's edition.

8. Also known as Apollonius son of Archibios, but to be distinguished from all the other Apollonii involved with ancient scholarship.

ancestors of the D scholia, and, indirectly, Aristarchus' commentaries. Apollonius' lexicon is for us one of the most important works of Greek lexicography, for it is a key source of information on ancient understandings of Homer's vocabulary and how Homer was read in antiquity. In addition, the lexicon preserves many fragments of earlier work, including but not limited to that of Aristarchus; for example the obscure Homerist Heliodorus[9] is known primarily from Apollonius. An epitome of Apollonius' work has come down to us in a single manuscript, and we also have several papyrus fragments of fuller versions, ranging in date from the first to the fifth century AD; these differ among themselves to some extent, showing that numerous alterations to the lexicon were made in the late antique period. Apollonius' lexicon was a source for Hesychius and the etymologica, which can also provide some further information on its original state. The work is in approximate alphabetical order; that is, most of the entries are grouped together by their first two or three letters, but the other letters of the words are not usually taken into account in determining their arrangement.

The text of the epitome can be found in Bekker (1833a =*TLG*), and the longest papyrus in Henrichs and Müller (1976).[10] Dyck (1993b) provides an edition of the fragments of Heliodorus, including those from sources other than Apollonius. Useful studies of the lexicon include those of Haslam (1994), Erbse (1960: 407–32), and Schenck (1974). F. Montanari (1996b) offers a good introduction with further bibliography.

Apion,[11] who lived in the late first century BC and first century AD, compiled an etymologizing Homeric lexicon entitled Γλῶσσαι Ὁμηρικαί, and a work of that title with Apion's name attached has survived, but the surviving work is probably not the one Apion wrote. Apion's own work was one of the principal sources of Apollonius Sophista, who quotes from it extensively, showing that this lexicon was different from the one we possess. The surviving lexicon is evidently a poorly made collection of excerpts from a longer work, and is alphabetized by the first letters of the words. The fragments of Apion's own lexicon (including those from sources

---

9. This Heliodorus is probably the same person as the Herodorus mentioned by Eustathius, who misattributed a version of the "Viermännerkommentar" to Apion and Herodorus. It is unclear whether this Heliodorus the Homerist can be identified with the metrician Heliodorus mentioned in the scholia to Aristophanes, but he is certainly to be distinguished from several other writers of the same name, including the author of the novel *Aethiopica*; the grammarian whose name is attached to Choeroboscus' commentary on Dionysius Thrax; a Neoplatonist philosopher who was the son of Hermeias and brother of Ammonius; Heliodorus Periegeta the antiquarian; and Heliodorus Arabius the sophist.

10. For editions of and bibliography on the other six fragments see Henrichs and Müller (1976: 29 n. 5) and Haslam (1994: 107–8). There is also an unpublished dissertation with a re-edition of letters α–δ of the epitome (Steinicke 1957).

11. This Apion is the same as the one against whom Josephus' *Contra Apionem* is directed, and produced other works in addition to the lexicon; fragments of these works can be found in Jacoby (1958: 122–44). See Dillery (2003).

other than Apollonius) have been collected and discussed by Neitzel (1977 =*TLG*), with an addendum by Theodoridis (1989); the other lexicon has been published and discussed by Ludwich (1917–18 =*TLG*). Neitzel and Ludwich provide the principal studies of these works, but other useful discussions include those of Haslam (1994: 26–9, 35–43), Van der Valk (1963–4: esp. i. 294–302), and Bossi (1998); see F. Montanari (1996*a*) for further bibliography.

The Mythographus Homericus is a somewhat amorphous entity. This term is used to refer to the author of a lost work, probably composed in the first century AD, that related the full versions of myths alluded to in the Homeric poems. The work could be called a mythological commentary, for it was arranged in the order in which the allusions occurred in the poems. It tended to give only one particular version of each myth, attributed to a specific source; a number of the attributions can be shown to be genuine, and it seems that the compiler was using important and now lost scholarly commentaries, probably Alexandrian. Although most of this compiler's work is lost in its original form, a number of papyrus fragments (dated from the first/second to the fifth century AD) have survived, and much material from the commentary was incorporated into the D scholia, where it can often be identified; although clearly related, the papyrus and D-scholia versions of the same entries are not identical. The papyri have all been collected and in some cases re-edited by Rossum-Steenbeek (1998: 278–309), who also provides a good study and further bibliography; other useful discussions include those of F. Montanari (1995) and Haslam (1990).

Another type of material found both in the papyri and in medieval manuscripts is Homeric hypotheses, or summaries of small sections (usually individual books) of the poems. These hypotheses, like those to dramatic texts, are found without the poetic text in the papyri but are prefixed to it in manuscripts. A discussion of the phenomenon and collection of the papyrus evidence can be found in Rossum-Steenbeek (1998), and the medieval versions are published in editions of the D scholia.

The Ὁμηρικὰ προβλήματα (*Quaestiones Homericae* or *Allegoriae Homericae*) attributed to Heraclitus offers allegorical interpretations and defenses of Homer's treatments of the gods. The Heraclitus in question is not Heraclitus of Ephesus, the pre-Socratic philosopher, nor can he be identified with any of the other known Heracliti; he seems to have written in the first century AD. His sources included Apollodorus and Crates of Mallos, and there is some debate about whether his work can be considered particularly Stoic in orientation. Heraclitus' work survives, largely intact, in a number of manuscripts; much of it is also to be found in the bT scholia, for which it was a major source (though Erbse's edition omits the scholia based on Heraclitus). The work is best consulted in the edition of Russell and Konstan (2005), which includes an English translation and excellent introduction; another good option is Buffière's edition (1962 =*TLG*), which offers a French translation and another good introduction. Discussions include those of Long (1992: 45–8) and Bernard (1990, with further bibliography).

A substantial essay entitled Περὶ τοῦ βίου καὶ τῆς ποιήσεως τοῦ Ὁμήρου (*De Homero*) is attributed to Plutarch but probably dates to the second or third century AD. The first part contains a short biography of Homer, and the second part discusses interpretation. The best text is that of Kindstrand (1990), but Keaney and Lamberton (1996) offer a usable text of the second part with (unreliable) English translation. The definitive study is that of Hillgruber (1994–9), and both editions offer discussion and further bibliography.

The third-century (AD) Neoplatonic philosopher Porphyry[12] has left us two works on Homer. One is an extended allegory on *Odyssey* 13.102–12, the cave of the nymphs; this piece is crucial for understanding the Neoplatonic interpretation of Homer. For discussion of its various editions see Alt (1998: 466).

Porphyry also composed a treatise entitled Ὁμηρικὰ ζητήματα (*Quaestiones Homericae*), which is believed to be based in part on Aristotle's six-book Ἀπορήματα Ὁμηρικά (now lost except for a few fragments). Porphyry's work is exegetical in nature and consists not of a linear commentary but of a series of essays that use discussion of specific passages to make larger points about Homeric interpretation. Only the first book survives in its original form, in a single fourteenth-century manuscript. Almost all the material in this manuscript is also found, in a very similar form, in the bT scholia to Homer, showing that one of the major sources of these scholia was Porphyry's work, which was probably systematically cut up and rearranged as scholia at a relatively late date. The later book(s) of Porphyry's work, though lost in their original form, are therefore probably all or almost all preserved in the bT scholia (though the scholia from this source are systematically omitted from Erbse's edition).

The standard text of the preserved first book is that of Sodano (1970 =*TLG*), where the self-standing and scholia versions of Porphyry's words are given in parallel columns. For the rest of the work one must rely on Schrader (1880–2 =*TLG*, 1890 =*TLG*), who used inferior manuscripts, made poor editorial judgements, and arranged the material in the order in which it appears in the scholia, rather than in Porphyry's order. (This order is probably unavoidable for the later books, since we have little chance of reconstructing the overall themes and arrangement of Porphyry's essays from the rearranged fragments, but Schrader follows it for the first book as well.) Schlunk (1993) provides an English translation of Sodano's text, and there are good discussions in Sodano's introduction and in Erbse (1960: 17–77).

The *Epimerismi Homerici* is a commentary consisting of grammatical explanations and definitions of Homeric words; the ἐπιμερισμός format was an instructional

---

12. Also referred to by his Latin name *Porphyrius*, but not to be confused with Porfyrius, or Publilius Optatianus Porfyrius, a Latin poet of the 4th cent. AD, nor with the Pomponius Porphyrio who commented on Horace. He is also to be distinguished from the Byzantine Porphyry associated with the Περὶ προσῳδίας commentary on a supplement to [ps.-] Dionysius Thrax.

method of the Byzantine school tradition (rather like sentence-parsing in English several generations ago), so most of the explanations in the *Epimerismi Homerici* are elementary. The work was based on a wide range of sources, including Herodian, Apion, the D scholia, and several lost works of ancient scholarship. Though anonymously transmitted, the *Epimerismi* are likely to have been composed by Choeroboscus in the ninth century. They are useful not only for what they tell us about the Byzantine reading of Homer, but also because they preserve ancient scholarship that is lost in its original form.

The *Epimerismi* were originally arranged in the order in which the words treated appeared in the poems, but at a later stage the entries pertaining to the first three books of the *Iliad* were reorganized in approximate alphabetical order. We have several manuscripts of this later version, known as the "alphabetical epimerismi," as well as a few texts of the entries for the first book of the *Iliad* in their original order, known as the "scholia-epimerismi." Thus entries for the first book of the *Iliad* are preserved in both versions (though each version contains some entries that do not appear in the other), those for books 2 and 3 are preserved only in the alphabetical version, and those after *Iliad* 3 are lost altogether. Additional material that originally belonged to the *Epimerismi* can be found in the *Etymologicum Gudianum*, which can be used to reconstruct the archetype. The standard edition of the *Epimerismi* is that of Dyck (1983–95 =*TLG*), who gives in the first volume all the entries pertaining to the first book of the *Iliad* (regardless of which manuscript tradition they are found in) and in the second volume the alphabetical epimerismi (with the exception of those presented in the first volume); this work also provides a comprehensive discussion and further bibliography.

A number of ancient works on Homer with subject-matter outside the limits of this book, including numerous biographies, survive and often contain information that is still useful for scholarly purposes. This material has been collected in the fifth volume of Allen's edition of Homer (1912 =*TLG*), where it is conveniently accessible with a reasonable text, and in M. L. West (2003), which offers a better text and English translation. There are also other usable versions; for example the Περὶ Ὁμήρου (*Vita Homeri*) of Proclus (a Neoplatonic philosopher of the fifth century AD) has been edited with French translation and extensive discussion by Severyns (1963). For a guide to editions of this material, and of the remains of other ancient scholarship on Homer that is too insignificant to be discussed here, see the list of abbreviations and editions in Erbse (1969–88); Graziosi (2002) provides a discussion of the biographical tradition.

2.1.2 Aristophanes

The scholia to Aristophanes are among the most important sets of scholia, in part because they provide historical background without which many of the jokes and allusions in the comedies would be incomprehensible. They are relatively well preserved, and most of them can be found in a sound and reliable modern edition, making them easier to use than many scholia.

Most Aristophanes scholia fall into one of four groups: the old scholia, Tzetzes' scholia, Thomas Magister's scholia, and Demetrius Triclinius' scholia. Scholarly attention tends to focus on the old scholia, which are the most useful in terms of the information they provide on Aristophanes, but the later annotations preserve some old material and are interesting in their own right because of the perspective they offer on Byzantine scholarship.

The old scholia to Aristophanes are derived from a variety of sources going back to the beginning of Alexandrian scholarship. Callimachus, Eratosthenes, and Lycophron (a contemporary of Zenodotus) all worked on Aristophanes to some extent, and the first continuous commentary on his plays was produced by Euphronius, the teacher of Aristophanes of Byzantium. Aristophanes of Byzantium himself produced an edition of the plays, providing an introduction to each (the extant verse hypotheses of the plays are thought to be distant descendants of these introductions) and may also have written a commentary; Callistratus and Aristarchus probably wrote commentaries on the plays, and Timachidas of Rhodes wrote one on the *Frogs*.

The work of these and other scholars was combined into a single commentary by Didymus in the late first century BC or early first century AD, and sometime in the first two centuries AD Symmachus compiled another commentary, using Didymus as his main source but also consulting other works. At a later date Symmachus' commentary or one of its descendants, along with some other material, was copied into the generous margins of a book of the plays of Aristophanes and formed the archetype of our extant scholia.

Perhaps the most important of the additional sources of our scholia is the metrical commentary on Aristophanes written by Heliodorus[13] around AD 100. This commentary is often studied apart from the other scholia, for it is crucial for our understanding of ancient metrical theory but of limited use in understanding Aristophanes. Heliodorus' work has been preserved to varying extents for the different plays; one can reconstruct from the scholia nearly all of it for the *Peace*, as well as substantial sections of it for the *Acharnians* and *Knights* and some fragments for the *Clouds* and *Wasps*, but little else.

In addition to the direct tradition of the scholia, which is well attested in several manuscripts, there is an indirect tradition via the *Suda*, whose writer had access to the same body of material when it was more complete and therefore often preserves scholia that did not survive in the direct tradition. There are also a number

---

13. It is unclear whether this Heliodorus can be identified with the Homeric commentator preserved by Apollonius Sophista (on whom see 2.1.1.3 above), but he is clearly not to be identified with many other writers of the same name, including the author of the novel *Aethiopica*; the grammarian whose name is attached to Choeroboscus' commentary on Dionysius Thrax; a Neoplatonist philosopher who was the son of Hermeias and brother of Ammonius; Heliodorus Periegeta the antiquarian; and Heliodorus Arabius the sophist.

of papyri and ancient parchment fragments with commentaries or scholia on Aristophanes; on the whole, those of the fourth century and later seem to reflect a body of material very similar to the ancestor of our scholia (though in some places more complete), while the earlier ones, which are much rarer, apparently belong to different traditions.

Byzantine scholarship, at least in its later centuries, focused primarily on the triad of plays made up of the *Plutus, Clouds,* and *Frogs,* but *scholia recentiora* on other plays also exist. Tzetzes and Triclinius each produced several editions of the plays with commentary, making their scholia somewhat complex; whether Thomas Magister also made two editions of Aristophanes is debated.[14] From Tzetzes' edition (the original scope of which is unknown) we have long commentaries on the triad, a shorter set of notes on the *Birds,* and a preface to the *Knights.* His notes make use of old scholia that are no longer extant, as well as manuscripts with better texts of the plays than we now possess, but also contain a considerable amount of guesswork. Thomas's commentaries, which are less extensive, are confined to the *Plutus, Clouds,* and *Frogs.* Triclinius' notes, which are often based on Thomas's as well as on old scholia, cover the *Plutus, Clouds, Frogs, Knights, Acharnians, Wasps, Birds,* and *Peace;* he is probably responsible for nearly all the metrical scholia not traceable to Heliodorus. Eustathius also wrote a commentary on Aristophanes, which is lost apart from fragments in later scholia, and additional contributions to our corpus of *scholia recentiora* were made by Moschopulus and Maximus Planudes.

The best edition of the scholia is a multivolume work edited first by W. J. W. Koster and later by D. Holwerda (1960– =*TLG*[15]), which includes both old and Byzantine scholia, usually in separate volumes. The volumes containing the *Thesmophoriazusae* and *Ecclesiazusae* have not yet appeared, so for those plays the standard text of the scholia is still that of Dübner (1842 =*TLG*).[16] While the Koster–Holwerda edition is unquestionably the best in terms of completeness and quality of the text presented, a number of older ones are still useful for specific purposes. Rutherford's edition (1896) of the scholia in the Ravenna manuscript provides translations and commentary in English. White's edition of the Heliodorus fragments (1912: 384–421) extracts all the Heliodorus fragments from the scholia, groups them together, and provides an excellent introduction (in English) with explanation of Heliodorus' Greek. Jorsal *et al.* (1970) collect the Byzantine metrical scholia to the *Frogs.* White's edition of the *Birds* scholia (1914) has much

14. See Koster (1964) and O. L. Smith (1976*b*).

15. For the Aristophanes scholia the *TLG* uses the new edition for only a few plays, and Dübner for the rest.

16. This text must be treated with caution, particularly because it includes some material from the *Suda* that is not actually found in manuscripts of Aristophanes, and makes this material seem to be scholia. One result of this problem is that modern literature sometimes contains references to "Aristophanes scholia" that cannot be found in the Koster–Holwerda edition, only in Dübner and in the *Suda.*

more detailed indices than the new edition, and Koster (1927) provides an important supplement for *Plutus* and *Clouds*.

Papyri with Aristophanes commentaries or scholia are not uncommon, and are conveniently collected with German translation and excellent discussion by Trojahn (2002). In addition, most of those relating to extant plays are included in the Koster–Holwerda edition, and those relating to lost plays can be found in Austin (1973).

Discussions of the Aristophanes scholia are numerous, lengthy, and extremely varied in character and conclusions. The best overview in English is still White's exceptionally lucid introduction to his edition of the *Birds* scholia (1914), which covers the entire history of the creation and transmission of the scholia and includes detailed information on Didymus and Symmachus; this work is, however, out of date in places and is concerned almost exclusively with the old scholia. Dunbar's introduction (1995: 31–49) is briefer but up to date and covers all types of scholarship. Rutherford (1905) offers a detailed and highly informative examination of the nature and contents of the old scholia, but many of his views are no longer accepted, and the author's evident grumpiness can make the book difficult to read. Additional discussions of textual history can be found in Koster (1985), Hangard (1983, 1985), and the prefaces to the individual volumes of the Koster–Holwerda edition (particularly volumes i.i a, i.iii.i, and ii.i). Montana (1996) discusses the information the old scholia provide on the Ἀθηναίων πολιτεία.

The papyrus scholia and commentaries are particularly interesting for the question of the dating of the transition from self-standing commentary to marginal scholia, as the marginal commentaries in Aristophanes papyri of the fourth century and later tend to resemble the medieval scholia more than is the case with other authors. Discussions of this and other issues relating to the papyri can be found in Trojahn (2002), Zuntz (1975), H. Maehler (1994: 124–6), Luppe (1978, 1982), and McNamee (1977: 175–96, 356; forthcoming). The best sources for discussion of Heliodorus are White (1912: 384–95) and Holwerda (1964, 1967). For the *scholia recentiora* one can consult N. Wilson (1962), O. L. Smith (1976b), Koster (1964), Koster and Holwerda (1954), Holzinger (1930), and the prefaces to volumes i.iii.ii, iii.iv b, and iv.i of the Koster–Holwerda edition. For examples of the way scholars use the Aristophanes scholia for historical information on the plays and on Athenian history and culture, see Carawan (1990), Lavelle (1989), Sutton (1980), Bicknell (1975), and Holwerda (1958).

2.1.3 Euripides

The scholia to Euripides are of great importance but difficult to use with confidence because of the lack of a reliable edition. Of the nineteen surviving plays of Euripides, only nine have preserved scholia: a large amount of annotation exists for the "Byzantine triad" of *Orestes*, *Hecuba*, and *Phoenissae*, and less extensive but still substantial notes survive on the *Medea*, *Hippolytus*, *Alcestis*, *Andromache*, *Rhesus*, and *Troades*. For most plays the scholia are easily divisible into old and Byzantine scholia, though in the case of *Rhesus* and *Troades* the two types are more difficult to separate.

The old scholia go back to the work of Aristophanes of Byzantium, who established the Alexandrian text and colometry of Euripides' plays, wrote introductions to them, and passed on a number of additional pieces of scholarly information (probably via notes or lectures rather than a complete commentary). Aristophanes' textual resources included the official Athenian copy of the tragedies, established less than a century after Euripides' death and purloined by the library at Alexandria, and he also had detailed historical information going back to Euripides' own time, since he provided information on the original productions of the plays. Other Alexandrians subsequently wrote commentaries on the plays, and these were combined into a composite commentary by Didymus around the end of the first century BC. The scholia have a note stating that they were taken from the commentaries of Didymus and Dionysius, but we have no idea who Dionysius was or when he flourished. However, there do not seem to have been significant additions to the old scholia after the mid-third century AD.

The old scholia are very important for establishing the text of the plays, not only because their evidence for textual transmission makes it possible to sort out the intricate manuscript tradition of the plays, but also because their lemmata and commentary often preserve correct readings that have been lost from the text itself in all branches of the tradition. They also contain much valuable information from the Alexandrian commentators, on the productions, the staging, the poet's sources, textual variants, etc.; this is mixed with lexicographical and mythological information dating to the early Roman period, and with paraphrases from school editions.

A number of late papyri contain commentaries on Euripides or marginal scholia; these agree closely with those found in the manuscripts.

Most of the plays, including a number for which there are no surviving scholia, are accompanied by hypotheses. There are three types of hypotheses: one group descends from the introductions written by Aristophanes of Byzantium (though the degree to which the surviving versions resemble his originals is a matter of dispute), a second set was composed by Byzantine scholars using earlier material, and a third group descends from plot summaries originally intended as substitutes for the plays rather than introductions to them. None of the sets is extant for all the plays; for some plays only one type of hypothesis is preserved, but for others multiple surviving hypotheses allow direct comparison between the different groups. The ancestor of the third group of hypotheses was a complete set of epitomes of Euripides' plays, arranged in alphabetical order. This work, now known as the "Tales from Euripides," circulated widely in the Roman period, quite independently of the tragedies themselves, and we have substantial fragments of it on a number of papyri from the first to third centuries AD, including the epitomes of many lost plays. The "Tales from Euripides" are often attributed to Aristotle's pupil Dicaearchus of Messene, though many scholars consider the attribution spurious, or suspect that only some material from Dicaearchus' epitomes survived as part of a collection compiled in the first century BC or AD.

The Byzantine scholia, which are most numerous for the Byzantine triad but also found with other plays, consist of a well-preserved commentary by Moschopulus (based in part on the work of his teacher Planudes), a partially preserved commentary by Thomas Magister, and two sets of work by Thomas's pupil Demetrius Triclinius: some early ("proto-Triclinian") commentary and a substantial and largely original later commentary. There are also some anonymous Byzantine scholia. At present the Byzantine work is used primarily to establish the history of the text in the Byzantine period, but these commentaries are also important for understanding the history of Byzantine scholarship, particularly in the field of meter. The non-metrical Byzantine scholia are generally ignored, but that may be a mistake, for it has been shown that some Byzantine commentators had access to ancient material now lost to us (see Barrett 1965).

The best text of the old scholia is that of Schwartz (1887–91 =*TLG*), but this is based on a small number of manuscripts and omits scholia found elsewhere, as well as recording inadequately the different variations in the scholia that are included. The result is that some ancient material on Euripides remains unpublished and hence unused; moreover Schwartz's text could be corrected to give us a better understanding of the published portion of the ancient material. Corrections and additions are scattered through the literature of the past century; the largest contribution is that of Daitz (1979 =*TLG*), who provides a complete edition of the scholia in one of the manuscripts not consulted by Schwartz.

Schwartz did not include the Byzantine scholia, and as a result the only reasonably complete edition of those scholia remains that of W. Dindorf (1863*b*), who published them together with the old scholia. Dindorf's edition is most inadequate, particularly in the case of Triclinius, for whose final commentary Dindorf did not make any use of the still-extant autograph manuscript (T). In recent years, however, reliance on Dindorf has been reduced by the appearance of several partial editions of the Byzantine scholia: one of Demetrius Triclinius' metrical scholia (De Faveri 2002, based on the autograph), one of a group of anonymous metrical scholia, descended from the proto-Triclinian commentary, that were entirely omitted by Dindorf (O. L. Smith 1977), and one of anonymous Byzantine exegetical scholia to the *Phoenissae* (Schartau 1981).

The hypotheses to extant plays are traditionally printed with the texts of the tragedies and can be found in almost any edition; the best is that of Diggle (1981–94), which includes the papyrus material. The papyrus hypotheses to both lost and extant plays have been collected and in some cases re-edited by Rossum-Steenbeek (1998) and can also be consulted in their original editions; the most important are *P.Oxy.* xxvii. 2455 and *PSI* xii.ii. 1286. New fragments continue to be published.

Discussions of ancient and medieval scholarship on Euripides are numerous and fall into several categories. For general information see Barrett (1964: 45–57, 78–81), Zuntz (1965: 249–75), Page (1934), Gudeman (1921: 662–72), and Wilamowitz (1889: 120–219), and for the papyrus commentaries and marginalia see H. Maehler (1994: 109–14), McNamee (1977: 168–75; forthcoming), and Luppe (2002). An extraordinary amount of work has been done on the hypotheses (particularly the "Tales from Euripides") and their history and influence, and the flow of publications continues unabated as new papyrus fragments appear. Of particular note are Zuntz (1955: 129–52), Barrett (1965), Rusten (1982), and especially Rossum-Steenbeek (1998, with further bibliography); for more references see also Van Looy (1991–2), but much work has appeared subsequent to both bibliographies, perhaps most notably Luppe (1996, 2002).

A great deal has also been written on the textual tradition of the scholia (especially in the Byzantine period) and on the history and authorship of various Byzantine commentaries; the definitive work on this subject is now that of Günther (1995, with references to earlier works). Delcourt (1933) presents the ancient biographies of Euripides. There is also a substantial body of articles that use the old scholia and hypotheses to provide insights into the text of Euripides, the history of the plays and of the myths involved, the methods and knowledge of the Alexandrians, etc.; because of the poorly edited state of the old scholia, new discoveries, including discoveries of fragments of other ancient works, are not uncommon. For examples of such work see Holwerda (1976), Luppe (1992), Poltera (1997), and Theodoridis (1996).

2.1.4 Sophocles

The scholia to Sophocles contain much ancient and valuable information. They are divided into old and Byzantine scholia, but the separation is not always straightforward.

The old scholia, which fill a substantial volume, are based on a composite commentary by Didymus (drawing on Alexandrian sources), along with material from the Roman-period scholars Pius, Sal(l)ustius, Herodian, Diogenianus, and others. For reasons that are not quite clear, the *Oedipus at Colonus* has the most useful and informative old scholia. The most important manuscript of Sophocles, the tenth-century L, has only old scholia and is our primary source for the ancient material. However, some other manuscripts also contain old scholia, which they sometimes report more fully than does L, and the *Suda* and the *Etymologicum genuinum* contain remnants of more old scholia in a fuller form than that found in L.

There is also a large mass of Byzantine scholia, attached primarily to the "Byzantine triad" (the texts usually read in the later Byzantine period) of *Ajax*, *Electra*, and *Oedipus Rex*. The Byzantine scholia derive from commentaries by Moschopulus, Thomas Magister, Triclinius, and sometimes Planudes or other scholars; these writers had access to old scholia, including some that have since disappeared, and certain of the Byzantine commentaries incorporated a considerable amount of ancient material. As the contributions from different sources are marked in a number of manuscripts, it is possible to separate the different Byzantine commentaries with reasonable confidence. Identifying the old material in them when it is not also in L is trickier, but for that reason the Byzantine scholia continue to hold out hopes of new discoveries of ancient material.

The Byzantine scholia are now used primarily for reconstructing the textual tradition of Sophocles and for understanding Byzantine scholarship. The old scholia are frequently used for historical, textual, lexical, and interpretive information.

Papyri have provided fewer contributions of commentary on Sophocles than on other important authors, but a few papyri of Sophocles do contain marginal scholia. Those in the Ἰχνευταί papyrus (second century AD) attribute certain variant readings to Theon, but it is unclear which Theon is meant.

The hypotheses to Sophocles' plays show many similarities to those of Euripides. As in the case of Euripides, multiple hypotheses to individual plays have been preserved via the manuscript tradition, and it is clear that several different types of hypothesis existed already in antiquity, with the oldest being based on the introductions written by Aristophanes of Byzantium. Papyri of non-Aristophanic hypotheses without the plays themselves exist, indicating a phenomenon like that of the "Tales from Euripides," but because these papyri are fewer and differ in some important respects from the "Tales from Euripides" papyri, the nature and purpose of these hypotheses is less well understood than that of their Euripidean equivalents.

The old scholia to the *Ajax* have been well edited by Christodoulou (1977 =*TLG*), the old scholia to the *Oedipus at Colonus* by De Marco (1952 =*TLG*), and the Byzantine scholia to the *Oedipus Rex* by Longo (1971 =*TLG*). For the rest of the scholia no good editions exist. The old scholia to all the plays (edited from L with insufficient attention to other manuscripts) can be consulted in Papageorgius's text (1888 =*TLG*) or failing that in Elmsley's (1825), and some of the Byzantine material is given by W. Dindorf (1852*b*), though some remains unpublished. There is a detailed discussion of these and earlier editions in Turyn (1949: 96–102), and Scattolin (2003) provides a text of some additional scholia to the *Electra*. The papyrus marginalia can be found in Carden (1974) and McNamee (1977: 162–7; forthcoming). The hypotheses to extant plays are published in most editions of Sophocles; those found on papyrus, including ones to lost plays, have been collected and in some cases re-edited by Rossum-Steenbeek (1998).

Discussions of the sources and textual history of the scholia include Havekoss (1961), Dawe (1973), De Marco (1936, 1937), Bollack (1990: i. 157–61), and Gudeman (1921: 656–62), most with further bibliography. For examples of the use of the scholia see Meijering (1985), Kopff (1976), Turyn (1944, 1949, 1952, 1958), Piérart (1993), O. L. Smith (1982*c*, 1992), Van der Valk (1984), and Aubreton (1949). On the hypotheses see Rossum-Steenbeek (1998, with further bibliography) and Gelzer (1976).

2.1.5 Aeschylus

The scholia to Aeschylus are less rewarding than most and at the same time pose many serious difficulties. The scholia are of crucial importance in attempts to understand the highly problematic Aeschylean textual tradition[17] and in consequence

---

17. In fact the scholia are now less useful for these purposes than they once were, not only because much of the tradition has finally been understood but also because it is now clear that Aeschylean scholia were sometimes copied from sources other than those used for the main text of a manuscript and hence are difficult to use in establishing stemmata for the text (cf. O. L. Smith 1981).

have been the subject of vast amounts of scholarly attention, but there is still no complete text of the scholia to Aeschylus, and some of the partial editions that do exist are less than fully reliable.

Six different types of Aeschylean scholia can be distinguished. Most highly regarded are the old scholia, which contain material from the Hellenistic and Roman periods, including some that is almost certainly Alexandrian; it is sometimes argued that these scholia derive from a commentary by Didymus, but this theory remains unproven.[18] All the scholia found in the oldest and most important Aeschylus manuscript, the tenth-century M,[19] are old; as scholia to the *Choephori* and *Supplices* are found only in M, all the scholia on those plays are old.

Next in order of age are the A or Φ scholia,[20] which derive from a commentary ascribed (probably falsely) to John Tzetzes. As their author (like a number of other Byzantine scholiasts) had access to a version of the old scholia, some scholia are, strictly speaking, both old and Φ; nevertheless some writers use the term "old" only for the scholia found in M. The Φ scholia are much longer and more numerous than the other classes of scholia but exist only for the "Byzantine triad" (*Prometheus*, *Persae*, and *Septem*, the plays normally read in the later Byzantine period). The Φ scholia are sometimes nearly valueless, but at other times they provide ancient material omitted or abridged in M; it is clear that their author was using a manuscript with ancient scholia very similar to those in M but without some of M's errors and omissions.

Also confined to the "Byzantine triad" are the Thoman or B scholia[21] composed by Thomas Magister at the end of the thirteenth century. The Triclinian scholia produced by Demetrius Triclinius in the early fourteenth century, as well as the proto-Triclinian scholia representing an earlier version of his commentary, exist both for the triad and for the *Agamemnon* and *Eumenides*. The proto-Triclinian scholia are based on a better text of the old scholia than that now surviving in M, so they are useful for reconstructing the old material, particularly for the sections of the *Agamemnon* missing from M. The Triclinian scholia represent more origi-

18. See Gudeman (1921: 654); Wartelle (1971: 185–95, 344); Dawe (1975: 642–3).

19. This is actually the same manuscript as the one called "L" when dealing with Sophocles (and Apollonius Rhodius); its full name is "Laurentianus Mediceus 32.9."

20. The designation "A" goes back to Butler and is much more commonly used than "Φ," which originated with Wilamowitz; Φ is nevertheless preferable because it avoids confusion with manuscript A (with which these scholia have no special connection, though Φ scholia do appear in that manuscript). The designation Φ is therefore gaining popularity and is used e.g. in the most recent Teubner text of Aeschylus.

21. The B scholia have no more connection to manuscript B than the A/Φ scholia have to manuscript A (in fact less, since manuscript B tends to have Φ scholia), but in this case there is no accepted alternative designation. The classification of Aeschylus scholia into the various types is also less than straightforward, and many individual scholia have been reclassified as they were better understood, with the result that scholars of previous generations do not always mean exactly the same thing as more recent writers when they discuss B (or A) scholia.

nal work by Triclinius and so are useful primarily for understanding Byzantine scholarship; they are exceptionally well preserved, because we have Triclinius' autograph manuscript (T).[22] In addition, there are a few later (post-Triclinian) scholia and some "minority" scholia that cannot be assigned with confidence to any of the above classes.

For scholia on the *Agamemnon*, *Choephori*, *Eumenides*, and *Supplices*, the best text is unquestionably that of O. L. Smith (1976a =TLG), which includes all extant scholia on those plays. Old, proto-Triclinian, and Triclinian scholia are given in separate sections, making it easy to tell the type of material in the scholion one is reading but less than straightforward to follow up a reference. If Smith's text is unavailable, the next best choice for the *Oresteia* is Thomson's edition (1966: i. 211–77), though this is not complete; in addition, one may safely use Wecklein (1885) for the scholia from M, and Van Heusde's edition (1864) is fairly reliable.

For the *Septem* the best text is O. L. Smith's (1982a =TLG); although not absolutely complete with respect to late scholia, this edition contains anything anyone is reasonably likely to want. Material is presented simply in order of line numbers, not classified by type of scholion as in Smith's other volume, so references are easy to follow but one has to judge the antiquity of each scholion for oneself based on the manuscripts in which it occurs (given in full at the end of each entry). Such judgements are not always easy to make, but the following simplified rules will work most of the time: everything in M and I^1 is old; scholia in B, C, N, Nc, P, Pd, V, Y, and Yb are normally Φ scholia; scholia in F, Fb, Fc, K, Lc, Lh, Ra, Rb, or θ (the symbol for the agreement of all these manuscripts) are Thoman; scholia occurring only in F are proto-Triclinian; scholia in T are Triclinian; and post-Triclinian material occurs in manuscripts A^2 and Ξa.

In the absence of Smith's text one could attempt to use Morocho Gayo's (1989) edition, which has the advantage of being even more comprehensive (except for the interlinear scholia and glosses, which are all omitted) but the disadvantage of containing many errors. Otherwise one must use different publications for the different manuscripts: Wecklein (1885) for M, O. L. Smith (1975: 240–6) for the proto-Triclinian material, W. Dindorf (1863a, 1864) for the Triclinian scholia, and W. Dindorf (1851a) for the Φ scholia.

For the *Prometheus* and the *Persae* no comprehensive editions of scholia exist. Herington (1972 =TLG) provides an excellent text of M, Φ, and minority scholia to the former play, while Smyth (1921 =TLG) records all the Triclinian scholia to the *Prometheus* (important supplements in O. L. Smith 1974). For the *Persae*

---

22. When using editions of this manuscript (which is sometimes necessary), one should observe that Triclinius marked the marginal scholia to indicate their origins: Triclinius' own work is preceded by a cross (+) and sometimes the word ἡμέτερα or ἡμέτερον, while older material (including the B scholia) is indicated by a capital letter and sometimes the word παλαιόν or παλαιά. Interlinear glosses are not so marked, but it is clear that some of these are old and some are Triclinian—though not always clear which are which.

Massa Positano (1963 =*TLG*) has edited the Triclinian scholia, and the scholia from M can be found in Wecklein (1885); the Φ scholia have been edited by Zabrowski (1984), in the absence of which text either Dähnhardt (1894 =*TLG*) or W. Dindorf (1851*a* =*TLG*) can be used, though neither is very accurate. In using both Dindorf and Wecklein one should beware of variant readings labelled "sch. rec." (and listed in the *TLG Canon* as "scholia recentiora"); in many cases these are not alternative manuscript readings at all, but corrections to the scholia made by a sixteenth-century editor (see O. L. Smith 1982*b*; Zabrowski 1987).

Discussions of the Aeschylus scholia are numerous and sometimes confusing. The most useful are probably Herington's introduction (1972: 3–51, in English with bibliography) and the prefaces to O. L. Smith's two volumes (1976*a*, 1982*a*, both in highly readable Latin and the former with a good bibliography). Also useful are Spoerri (1980), O. L. Smith (1967, 1975 (with good bibliography), 1979, 1980), Thomson (1966: i. 63–4; 1967), Turyn (1943), Smyth (1921), and Gudeman (1921: 652–6). The papyri are discussed by McNamee (1977: 160–2; forthcoming).

Most of the plays are accompanied by hypotheses, which are printed with the text in standard editions. See also Rossum-Steenbeek (1998: 35–6, 233–6).

2.1.6 Pindar

The voluminous scholia to Pindar offer abundant ancient material unmixed with later additions and are useful for a number of different purposes. Because of the extent to which these purposes diverge, discussions and even editions of Pindar scholia often cover only one type of material. The main divisions are between metrical and non-metrical and between old and Byzantine scholia.

There is a large body of old metrical scholia, compiled probably in the fifth century AD and based on a metrical analysis of the *Odes* written in the second century AD. This analysis incorporated a commentary by Didymus that transmitted the work of Alexandrian scholars and was based on the text and metrical divisions established by Aristophanes of Byzantium; its medieval transmission was in part separate from that of the text of the *Odes* and their non-metrical scholia. Scholars now generally agree that Aristophanes' colometry and the Alexandrian metrical analysis do not go back to Pindar himself and that in consequence the metrical scholia are of little use for understanding Pindar's own metrical intentions. They are, however, very important for our understanding of ancient metrical theory, since their detailed, line-by-line analysis (with continuous texts often resembling a treatise rather than traditional scholia) offers one of the few surviving examples of the practical application of the theories preserved in Hephaestion's manual.

Several Byzantine works on Pindaric meters are also preserved, including an influential verse treatise by Isaac Tzetzes, brother of the more famous John Tzetzes, and a substantial set of scholia by Demetrius Triclinius. Both of these contain ancient material and so are important for reconstructions of the original text of our metrical scholia, as well as for an understanding of the revival of metrical study in the Byzantine period. Tzetzes' work is, however, based much more on ancient sources than is Triclinius' largely original analysis.

The old metrical scholia are best consulted in the editions of Tessier (1989) or Irigoin (1958); if necessary they can also be found in Drachmann's text of all the old Pindar scholia (1903–27 =*TLG*). An edition of Tzetzes' work is given by Drachmann (1925), and that of Triclinius is split between Abel (1891 =*TLG*), who edits the scholia to the *Olympian Odes* and *Pythians* 1 and 2, and Irigoin (1958), who provides the scholia to *Pythians* 2–12. Günther (1998) has edited a third Byzantine treatise. Discussions, however, are more unified: Budelmann (1999) offers a brief introduction to all the metrical scholia, and Irigoin (1958) provides an excellent detailed study of the corpus.

The exegetical scholia to Pindar are more numerous than the metrical scholia and have an equally impressive pedigree, since they preserve the remains of commentaries by Aristarchus and several of his successors, incorporated into a comprehensive work by Didymus and then epitomized in the second century AD. Like the old metrical scholia, they are virtually free of late interpolations, so that almost any piece of information found in them can be assumed to come from the Alexandrians (though not necessarily without abridgement and alteration). These scholia attempt to explain the difficulties of the *Odes* and offer an interpretation of the poet's meaning. In doing so they invoke historical, biographical, and mythological data, some of which appear to derive from accurate transmission of information going back to Pindar's own time, though parts seem to be simply Alexandrian conjecture based on the poems themselves. The proportions in which these two types of material occur, and therefore the extent to which one can rely on information provided by the scholia but not otherwise verifiable, are the subject of debate (see Lefkowitz 1975*a*; P. Wilson 1980). It is, however, clear that the interpretations found in the scholia were widely accepted in antiquity, for they are reflected in later poetry influenced by Pindar, such as that of Theocritus, Callimachus, and Horace (see Lefkowitz 1985: 280–2). The best edition of these scholia is that of Drachmann (1903–27 =*TLG*); their sources and transmission are discussed by Deas (1931), Gudeman (1921: 647–52), Irigoin (1952), and Grandolini (1984).[23]

Two substantial fragments of ancient commentaries on Pindar are preserved on papyrus,[24] and there are also some fragments of the text with marginalia.[25]

23. Pindar's *Odes* have two sets of line numbers, an ancient one (based on the work of Aristophanes of Byzantium) that divides the poems into very short lines and a modern one (based on the rediscovery of the underlying metrical structure by Boeckh in the early 19th cent.) yielding longer lines. Though modern scholarship on Pindar uses the newer line numbers, many editions of the scholia, including Drachmann's, use the older line numbers. Conversion is possible by reference to the text, since most editions include both sets of line numbers.

24. *P.Berol.* 13419, from the 3rd cent. AD or later (published by Wilamowitz 1918: 749–50) and *P.Oxy.* xxxi. 2536, from the 2nd cent. AD.

25. *P.Oxy.* v. 841 (2nd cent. AD), *P.Rain.* i. 23 (6th cent. AD).

These fragments, unlike those on many other authors, seem to be related to the extant manuscript scholia. For details see H. Maehler (1994: 114–20), McNamee (1977: 271–302; forthcoming), and the editions of the papyri concerned.

Eustathius of Thessalonica, author of the famous twelfth-century commentary on Homer, also wrote a commentary on Pindar. Only the introduction now remains, but it is useful for quotations from odes that have since disappeared. Though the work survives only in a single manuscript, the text is generally good. The definitive edition is that of A. Kambylis (1991a =TLG); when this is not available the best alternative is the edition appended to Drachmann (1903–27). The main studies are by Kambylis (1991b and introduction to Kambylis 1991a). A few minor Byzantine works on Pindar also exist, some containing older metrical material; some can be found in Drachmann (1903–27: vol. iii) and others in Abel (1891).

The scholia to Pindar are frequently cited by modern scholars, most often in discussions of Pindaric interpretation, for which they remain crucial, but also for historical and mythological information that can be used for other purposes; they are of course also very useful for work on ancient metrical theory and on the evolution of scholia. Their value for establishing the text of Pindar is high, as they sometimes preserve the correct reading for passages that have been corrupted in all extant manuscripts of the text. For examples of how the scholia are used see Barrett (1973), Hubbard (1987), Lambin (1986), Lefkowitz (1975b), and works cited in the sources already mentioned. Arrighetti et al. (1991) provide a concordance to the scholia.

2.1.7 Hesiod

The scholia to Hesiod are voluminous, useful, and of impressive antiquity. Ancient scholarship on Hesiod began early, for lost interpretive works appear to date at least as early as Aristotle, and the first critical text was produced by Zenodotus. Zenodotus, Apollonius Rhodius, Aristophanes of Byzantium, Aristarchus, Crates, Aristonicus, and Didymus all left textual or interpretive comments on Hesiod that are still preserved under their names, though they did not all write full commentaries on the poems.

The oldest portion of our surviving scholia comprises the remains of a composite commentary of uncertain authorship (Choeroboscus and Dionysius of Corinth have both been suggested, but the author could be completely unknown). This commentary was a compilation of earlier writings, including both grammatical and critical notes from Alexandrian and other scholars and paraphrases from school texts; an important source seems to be the commentaries of Seleucus (first century AD). In general, the material seems mostly to come from before AD 100.

In addition to the direct transmission of this commentary as scholia attached to the text of Hesiod, there is an indirect transmission via several etymological works, particularly the *Etymologicum genuinum*. The authors of these etymologica quoted extensively from the scholia to Hesiod, and the scholia to which they had access were better preserved than those in the manuscripts we possess, as well as being unmixed with any later commentaries.

In the fifth century AD the Neoplatonist Proclus wrote a philosophical commentary on the *Works and Days*. Proclus made extensive use of the earlier composite commentary, of which he had a fuller version than that now preserved in the scholia, and he also drew heavily on a commentary by Plutarch on the *Works and Days*. Plutarch's commentary is now lost in its original form, but Proclus' survives largely intact in the scholia and preserves significant portions of Plutarch's work. In our manuscript scholia to the *Works and Days* Proclus' commentary has been mixed with the scholia derived from the earlier composite commentary, but a few manuscripts mark the notes from Proclus' commentary with special symbols, so they are relatively easy to separate.

There is also a substantial amount of Byzantine commentary on Hesiod. For the *Theogony* the major Byzantine sources are a continuous allegorical commentary by Ioannes Diaconus Galenus (date unknown) and a similar commentary known as the *Anonymous Exegesis*; there are also reworkings of the old scholia by Triclinius. For the *Works and Days* we have extensive Byzantine scholia that reproduce, largely intact, the text of lectures by John Tzetzes (twelfth century) and commentaries by Moschopulus (c.1300) and Triclinius (c.1318). There are also two self-standing numerological commentaries, as well as some scholia by Planudes. A small body of scholia to the *Scutum* is ascribed to Ioannes Diaconus Pediasimus (fourteenth century). The Byzantine commentaries on the *Theogony* sometimes preserve readings lost from the main tradition of the text and so can be useful for textual criticism, and Tzetzes seems to have had access to a version of the old scholia fuller than has otherwise survived, but in general the Byzantine commentaries are little used by modern scholars.

There is no unified text of the Hesiod scholia, nor are all of them available in satisfactory editions. The standard text of the old *Theogony* scholia is that of Di Gregorio (1975 =*TLG*), which is excellent and includes Byzantine versions and passages from the etymologica (the former clearly marked, and the latter in a "parallels" section at the bottom of the page). Flach's edition of the *Theogony* scholia (1876 =*TLG*) can and should be avoided for the old scholia, but for the self-standing Byzantine commentaries one must choose between Flach and Gaisford (1823). The old scholia on the *Works and Days*, including those from Proclus, are best consulted in Pertusi's edition (1955 =*TLG*), where Proclus' notes are marked with an asterisk and the apparatus and parallels are printed separately at the end of the book. For the remains of Plutarch's commentary (including a few from sources other than Proclus) one can also use Sandbach's edition of Plutarch fragments (1967), in which they appear as fragments 25–112 and so are provided with an English translation (Sandbach 1969). Tzetzes' prolegomena and life of Hesiod are given by Colonna (1953), but for the rest of the Byzantine scholia on the *Works and Days* one must resort to Gaisford (1823 =*TLG*). However, Gaisford omits one of the numerological commentaries, which is given by H. Schultz (1910: 34–40), as well as Planudes' scholia, which remain unpublished. The scholia to the *Scutum* were last edited by Ranke (1840: 19–65) but can also be found, in a radically different form, in Gaisford (1823 =*TLG*).

Much has been written on the Hesiod scholia. Excellent overviews can be found in M. L. West (1978: 63–75, with bibliography, p. 91) and Rzach (1912). The history of the commentaries and the manuscript tradition have been explained by H. Schultz (1910, 1913a), Pertusi (1955, with references to earlier literature), Di Gregorio (1975, with more references), and Faraggiana di Sarzana (1978, 1981, 1987), and the connection with the etymologica is examined by M. L. West (1974: 162–3). Among the articles that use the scholia for interpreting Hesiod or for historical information are those of Rechenauer (1993), Follet (1992), Van der Valk (1984: 41–3), Pritchett (1976), Meritt (1974), and Sicking (1970).

2.1.8 Other Early Poetry

Most other poetry from the classical and archaic periods survives not via a direct manuscript tradition, but on papyrus or as fragments gathered from quotations by later authors. There are therefore no manuscript scholia to such poems. At the same time their study often involves the study of manuscript scholia, since the scholia on better-preserved authors are a major source of fragments of lost poetry. When poems are preserved on papyrus, we sometimes have commentary or marginalia from the papyrus as well; in fact some poetic fragments themselves derive from papyrus commentaries on the author concerned. The hypotheses to some dramatic texts, particularly those of Menander, are also preserved on papyrus.

Many papyrus scholia to fragmentary authors can be consulted only in the original publications of the papyri concerned, which in general tend to provide the fullest publication and most comprehensive discussion of papyrus marginalia and commentaries. The most legible and important material is often reprinted with the poetic fragments in collections such as that of Davies (1991), but the ancient scholarship printed in such editions usually represents only a selection of what is available. For hypotheses, however, Rossum-Steenbeek (1998) provides a comprehensive collection. The new collection *Commentaria et Lexica Graeca in Papyris reperta*, to be published by K. G. Saur, may eventually provide a comprehensive set of texts of papyrus commentaries with up-to-date discussion, but little has appeared so far.

A thorough overview of such papyrus material cannot be undertaken in a book of this type, so only a few examples will be given here; a more comprehensive discussion is provided by McNamee (1977, forthcoming). Some of the most extensive remains are those pertaining to the poetry of Alcman, on which we have a large body of marginal scholia (coming especially from *P.Louvre* E 3320) and two substantial pieces of commentary (*P.Oxy.* xxiv. 2389, 2390), as well as numerous smaller commentary and lexicon fragments. Discussions include those of Most (1987), Cataudella (1972), M. L. West (1965a), and Gudeman (1921: 646–7); see also *CPF* iii #1.

Large fragments of papyrus scholarship on other authors include *P.Oxy.* xxix. 2506 and xxxii. 2637, both long commentaries on lyric poetry from the second century AD. The spectacular Derveni papyrus from the fourth century BC contains

extensive exegesis of Orphic poems.[26] There are also individual commentaries on
Bacchylides (*P.Oxy.* xxiii. 2367, 2368), Simonides (*P.Oxy.* xxv. 2434), Hipponax
(*P.Oxy.* xviii. 2176), Anacreon (*P.Oxy.* liv. 3722), Eupolis (Tojahn 2002), Anti-
machus (Wyss 1936), and other authors (e.g. in *P.Oxy.* xxxvii). For ancient scholarship on Alcaeus see Porro (1994), for that on comedies see Austin (1973), and
for hypotheses to Menander and other dramatists see Rossum-Steenbeek (1998).

2.2 CLASSICAL PROSE

The ancient scholarship on prose authors is less well known than that on poetry,
though it is much more plentiful and in some ways richer. Ancient commentaries
on a number of prose authors survive intact or in substantial fragments, offering
vital information on the nature and history of ancient scholarship as well as on
the texts concerned and providing a framework within which the poetic scholia
can be understood. While the scholia to prose authors are in general less exciting
than the scholia to Homer or the dramatists, they often contain valuable information, and several large corpora of such scholia remain unpublished and largely
unexplored, offering excellent prospects for future work.

2.2.1 Hippocrates and Galen

Probably the most interesting ancient scholarship on prose authors is that on the
two most famous physicians of antiquity, Hippocrates (fifth century BC) and Galen
(second century AD). Scholarship on these two writers cannot be fully separated,
for many of Galen's works are commentaries on Hippocrates, so that commentary on Galen is often also commentary on Hippocrates. The medical works attributed to Hippocrates (most of which were probably not written by Hippocrates
himself, though many must have been composed within a century of his death)
attracted a huge body of commentary. The commentators' primary interest was in
medical knowledge, and their works were often important medical treatises in their
own right, but some, particularly Galen, also paid attention to the sort of textual
and historical questions found in ancient scholarship on literary works. Many
of the commentaries, including some of impressive antiquity, still exist as self-
standing works (sometimes as many as four different ancient commentaries on a
single work of Hippocrates survive), so they are an important source for our understanding of ancient scholarly techniques.

Interpretation of the Hippocratic corpus began very early and continued
throughout antiquity; for few other writers do we have evidence of such an un-
broken tradition of scholarship. The earliest commentaries on Hippocrates were
probably produced by the physician Herophilus, who worked at Alexandria in the
early third century BC, and glossaries of Hippocratic words first appeared at the
end of that century. Though these early works are lost, we have a fair amount of
information about them from discussions in extant commentaries and glossaries.

26. See Betegh (2004), Janko (2002), Laks and Most (1997), and *CPF* iii. 565–85.

The earliest surviving commentary, that of Apollonius of Citium to Hippocrates' *On joints* (a treatise on reducing dislocations), dates to the first century BC. It is thus the second-oldest commentary to have survived via the manuscript tradition, surpassed only by Hipparchus' commentary on Aratus (from the second century BC); it is, however, a simplified retelling rather than a commentary in the strict sense of the word and is concerned with medical rather than scholarly questions. The work is accompanied in one manuscript by a set of illustrations thought to descend directly from ones designed by Apollonius himself.

The second surviving commentator, Galen, was by far the most important of the commentators on Hippocrates, as well as being a famous physician, intellectual, and medical writer in his own right. Thirteen of Galen's commentaries on Hippocrates survive, as well as some commentaries falsely attributed to Galen. Not all are intact, but some commentaries and portions of commentaries that do not survive in Greek are preserved in Arabic translations, or occasionally in Latin or Hebrew. Though primarily concerned with medical questions, Galen's work is of particular interest to students of ancient scholarship because of his occasional discussions of the authenticity of specific works and passages, textual corruption, and proposed emendations. Galen brings linguistic, historical, and medical arguments to bear on such questions; sometimes he summarizes the views of earlier scholars on a given point, thereby providing us with most of our information about their methods and opinions and revealing much about ancient editorial theory and practice that we cannot learn from the scholia's abbreviated and mutilated fragments of similar debates over the text of literary works. In discussion of textual variants Galen even distinguishes between older and newer manuscripts. The extended quotations in the lemmata to the commentaries also provide a crucial source for the text of Hippocrates.

In addition to the commentaries, Galen has left us a number of other writings devoted to discussion of Hippocrates' work and general questions of interpretation. These include *De captionibus*, a discussion of linguistic ambiguity and interpretation that offers intriguing insights into second-century views of a number of linguistic and textual issues, including the role of accentuation.

Late antique and Byzantine writers produced numerous commentaries on both Hippocrates and Galen; many of these works survive at least partially, but they are less respected and less exciting than Galen's commentaries, and not all have been edited. Most were not written for publication but are students' transcripts of the "author's" lectures. The most important late commentators are Palladius (sixth century), from whom we have works on Hippocrates' *On fractures* and book 6 of his *Epidemics*, as well as on Galen's *De sectis*; Stephanus of Athens[27] (sixth–seventh century AD), to whom are attributed extant commentaries on Hippocrates' *Aphorisms*, *Prognostic*, and *On fractures* (this last actually belongs to an unknown earlier commentator) and one on Galen's *Therapeutics*; and John of Alexandria,

---

27. Also known as Stephanus of Alexandria and as Stephanus the Philosopher, and probably the same person as the Stephanus who commented on Aristotle.

of whose commentaries on Hippocrates' *Epidemics* book 6 and *On the nature of the child* only fragments survive in Greek (though more exists in Latin). There are also fragmentary and Byzantine commentaries on both Hippocrates and Galen by a variety of authors.[28] Some commentaries now survive only in Latin or Arabic translation, and some were originally written in those languages.

Several papyrus commentaries on Hippocrates and Galen survive, and there are also papyrus texts with marginalia.

Almost as important and ancient as the Hippocratic commentaries are the Hippocratic glossaries. Compilation of these glossaries, which were the first author-specific lexica, probably began with Bacchius of Tanagra, who worked in Alexandria in the late third century BC. Though Bacchius' work is no longer extant, it was a major source for the earliest surviving glossary, that of Erotian (first century AD). Erotian's work was originally a large lexicon of obscure words found in thirty-seven Hippocratic treatises, arranged in the order of their occurrence in the texts; now we have an abridged version, rearranged in partial alphabetical order, and a collection of fragments. The material in Erotian's glossary overlaps to some extent with that found in literary glossaries and scholia on several poetic works, suggesting that his sources included scholarship on literary texts. The preface, in which Erotian discusses earlier Hippocratic glossography, is particularly valuable.

We also have a Hippocratic glossary by Galen, based heavily on earlier glossaries; unlike Galen's commentaries it is largely scholarly rather than scientific in orientation, and the preface contains much useful information on the work of earlier scholars. Galen's glossary has the distinction of being the earliest surviving Greek work to employ complete alphabetical order (i.e. words are not merely grouped together by their first letters, or by their first two or three letters, but fully alphabetized as in a modern dictionary), though it is thought that this feature may be due not to Galen but to one of his predecessors.

In addition to the commentaries and glossaries, there is a large body of scholia to the works of Hippocrates and Galen, though very few of these have been studied or published: Dietz's *Scholia in Hippocratem et Galenum* (1834) and most other editions of "scholia" to medical writers are actually editions of self-standing commentaries, not of marginal scholia.[29] Although a few selections from the scholia have been published piecemeal, the bulk of unpublished, unexplored material remains a promising field for further research.

Editions of the ancient scholarship on Hippocrates and Galen are too numerous to be fully listed here, but a fairly comprehensive listing for the commentaries and such scholia as are published can be found in Ihm (2002). Key editions include the *Corpus Medicorum Graecorum*, known as *CMG* (which often includes translations), Dietz (1834 =*TLG*), Kühn (1821–33 =*TLG*), Dickson (1998), Irmer

---

28. Ihm (2002) lists 271 known commentaries on medical writers; most of these are now lost, but many survive at least in fragments.

29. On the different use of the term "scholia" by scholars working on scientific texts, see Ch. 1 n. 25 above.

(1977 =*TLG*), and *CPF* iii (#3, 4). Ihm is also the best source for bibliography on the various commentators; particularly useful as an introduction is the overview of ancient scholarship on Hippocrates up to and including Galen by W. D. Smith (1979). Good discussions of Galen include those of Bröcker (1885), Manetti and Roselli (1994), Hankinson (1994), Hanson (1998), and Von Staden (2002); Galen's statements on his own commentaries are collected by Moraux (1985: 150–2). Garzya and Jouanna (1999) and Geerlings and Schulze (2002) provide useful collections of articles. On the papyri see *CPF* iii (#3, 4) and Andorlini (2000). The glossaries are not covered by Ihm, but Nachmanson (1918 =*TLG*) gives a text of Erotian, and Galen's glossary is in Kühn (1821–33: vol. xix =*TLG*). Useful studies of the glossaries (with further references) include Giuliani (1997), Salazar (1997), Von Staden (1992; 1989: 484–500), Wellmann (1931), and several pieces in Garzya and Jouanna (1999). Ihm also omits those works of Galen that are not commentaries; most of these are to be found in *CMG* or Kühn (1821–33), but Ebbesen (1981 =TLG) gives a text of *De captionibus* and Edlow (1977) a text and translation. Durling (1993) is a useful aid for reading any of Galen's works.

2.2.2 Plato

The corpus of ancient Platonic scholarship is extensive: two separate sets of scholia, a lexicon of Platonic words, a large number of Neoplatonic commentaries, and some shorter Neoplatonic and Middle Platonic writings. Most of this work, however, is philosophical in nature, and there is little that deals with the text or language; in particular it is striking that we have no certain remains of Alexandrian or other Hellenistic scholarship among the surviving scholia and commentaries on Plato.[30]

The scholia are divided into two groups, the *scholia vetera* and the *scholia Arethae*. The latter are so called because they were added to manuscript B, in which they first appear, by Archbishop Arethas (of Caesarea in Cappadocia) in his own hand (*c*.900 AD). The *scholia Arethae* are primarily exegetical and seem to be derived from lost Neoplatonic commentaries.

The *scholia vetera* also have a large exegetical component derived from Neoplatonic commentaries (though apparently not the same commentaries), but they also preserve some earlier material. This consists of lexicographical notes that because of their similarity to Hesychius' entries probably come from the second-century lexicon of Diogenianus, Hesychius' source; notes on Atticisms that probably derive from second-century lexica by Aelius Dionysius and Pausanias; and notes on proverbs that appear to come directly from the collection of Lucillus Tarrhaeus (first century AD and thus the earliest significant source for the scholia). The scholia have no transmitted lemmata (those now found with the scholia are modern additions) and so are of little use for establishing the text of Plato, and

---

30. Whether there was even an Alexandrian edition of Plato is a matter of dispute; see e.g. Tarán (1976) and Solmsen (1981). The anonymous commentary on the *Theaetetus* could, however, belong to the late 1st cent. BC; see Sedley (1996: 84).

their exegetical components are less interesting than they would be if we did not have so many intact Neoplatonic commentaries. The lexical material, however, is valuable, and the scholia are useful for their preservation of quotations from lost works of literature and for information on Greek religion and culture, the history of Greek literature, biography, and mythology. The standard text, for both sets of scholia, is that of Greene (1938 =*TLG*); Hermann (1853) is a poor second choice, but Naddei (1976) is usable for the *Gorgias* scholia and provides an Italian translation and commentary for that dialog. Discussions can be found in Greene (1937), Cohn (1884), Beutler (1938), Erbse (1950: 48–57), Gudeman (1921: 687–92), Dodds (1959), and N. Wilson (1983*a*: 121–3); cf. also Chroust (1965) and Solmsen (1981). Kougeas (1985) discusses Arethas, and McNamee (1977: 148–53; forthcoming) provides information on papyri with marginalia.

In addition to the scholia, we have a lexicon to Plato attributed to Timaeus the Sophist, which survives in a single manuscript. Nothing is known about Timaeus, who probably wrote sometime between the first and fourth centuries AD, and the work has clearly suffered significant additions and subtractions at later periods, leading to the inclusion of many non-Platonic words and to non-Platonic definitions of words that do occur in Plato. The lexicon is nevertheless important as the sole surviving witness to a genre: two other Platonic lexica, by Boethus and Clement, are known only from insubstantial fragments. Timaeus seems to have used earlier commentaries on Plato that are now lost, and his lexicon also appears to be one of the sources of our extant scholia. There is no consensus on the best text of Timaeus; the most easily accessible is that of Hermann (1853), but this is based largely on the work of Ruhnken (1789), and Ruhnken's original, which is equipped with a detailed commentary, is preferred by true connoisseurs. F. Dübner's text, printed in Baiter *et al.* (1839 =*TLG*), is important because it represents a new study of the manuscript, but this work is difficult to use effectively because it combines glosses from Timaeus' lexicon with material from other sources, so it is rarely cited. Discussion of the lexicon, and of the fragments of other Platonic lexica, can be found in Dyck (1985), Bonelli (1997), Von Fritz (1936), Roselli (1996), Theodoridis (1982–: ii, pp. xlvii–l), and Dörrie and Baltes (1987–: iii. 229–35), as well as in many of the discussions of the scholia listed above.

Timaeus' was not the only Platonic glossary circulating in antiquity, and while it is the only one to survive in substantial bulk, there is also a short work entitled Περὶ τῶν ἀπορουμένων παρὰ Πλάτωνι λέξεων. This glossary bears the name of Didymus, but the attribution is considered false. A text can be found in Miller (1868: 399–406) or reprinted in Latte and Erbse (1965: 245–52).

The Neoplatonic commentaries represent the bulk of ancient scholarship on Plato. Many of their authors were famous philosophers in their own right, and the commentaries are important for the study of Neoplatonism, so most of them can easily be found in good editions and even translations. There is also a large body of secondary literature on the commentaries and their authors. Precisely because of their originality and philosophical nature, however, the commentaries are now considered to be of little use for the study of Plato's own writings, and in consequence only the briefest summary of this body of work can be given here. For more information, including further editions of the texts, secondary literature, and other Platonist writings, see the bibliographies of Göransson (1995), R. Jackson et al. (1998), and other works mentioned below; Coulter (1976), Tarrant (2000), and Dörrie and Baltes (1987–) are also useful.

Many of the surviving Neoplatonic commentaries were composed by Proclus Diadochus, head of the Neoplatonist school at Athens in the fifth century AD and a prolific scholar. Proclus' surviving works include lengthy commentaries on the *Republic*, *Parmenides*, *Timaeus*, and *Alcibiades I*, excerpts from a commentary on the *Cratylus*, and numerous other works having to do with Plato but less easily categorized as Platonic scholarship. Texts can be found in Kroll (1899–1901 =*TLG*), Cousin (1864 =*TLG*), Diehl (1903–6 =*TLG*), Segonds (1985–6), Pasquali (1908 =*TLG*), and Romano (1989); translations in Festugière (1970, 1966–8), Morrow and Dillon (1987), O'Neill (1965), Segonds (1985–6), and Romano (1989); further information in Pépin and Saffrey (1987). A thirteenth-century Latin version of the *Parmenides* commentary by William of Moerbeke preserves some sections that are now lost in Greek; see Klibansky and Labowsky (1953).

Another major source of Neoplatonic commentaries is Olympiodorus, a member of the Neoplatonist school at Alexandria in the sixth century AD. His surviving commentaries, which are based on lost commentaries by Ammonius, were not composed for publication but are transcripts of his lectures on Plato's dialogs. We have Olympiodorus' commentaries on the *Gorgias*, *Phaedo*, and *Alcibiades I*. All three have been edited by Westerink (1956, 1970, 1976, all =*TLG*); earlier editions by Norvin (1913, 1936) are less good but still usable. The commentaries to the *Gorgias* and *Phaedo* have been translated into English, in both cases with good introductions (Westerink 1976; R. Jackson et al. 1998).

Other Neoplatonic works have also survived. These include a commentary on the *Phaedrus* by the fifth-century Hermeias of Alexandria (edited by Couvreur 1901 =*TLG*) that largely reproduces the views of Hermeias' teacher Syrianus, and anonymous prolegomena to Platonic philosophy derived from sixth-century lecture notes from the Neoplatonist school at Alexandria (edited by Westerink 1962 =*TLG*; Westerink et al. 1990). Damascius (early sixth century) left commentaries on the *Philebus*, *Phaedo*, and *Parmenides* (Westerink 1959 =*TLG*, 1977 =*TLG*; Westerink and Combès 1997–2003), though these used to be attributed to Olympiodorus.

Earlier works have fared less well, but there are a few survivals from the early centuries of the empire. The best-preserved author of this group is Plutarch, from whose numerous works on Plato two survive: the Πλατωνικὰ ζητήματα ("Platonic questions") and a treatise on the generation of the soul in the *Timaeus* (*Moralia* 999c–1011e and 1012b–1032f). In addition, a short prologue by the second-century philosopher Albinus, discussing the genre of the philosophical dialog, is preserved intact (see Nüsser 1991; Le Corre 1956), as is a work by an otherwise unknown Alcinous entitled Διδασκαλικός or *Handbook of Platonism* (see Whittaker 1990; Dillon 1993; Invernizzi 1976). Until very recently it was believed that Alcinous was the same person as Albinus, but now that identity is often rejected, though a second-century date for Alcinous is still likely. From Galen (second century AD) we have a treatise *On the doctrines of Plato and Hippocrates* and fragments of a commentary on the *Timaeus* (see *CMG* v.iv.i.ii and Larrain 1992). Porphyry, an important Neoplatonist who was head of the school at Rome in the third century AD, has left us fragments of commentaries on several dialogs (A. Smith 1993; Sodano 1964 =*TLG*) and perhaps a surviving (but not intact) work on the *Parmenides*, though this anonymous commentary is sometimes dated to earlier or later periods (see Bechtle 1999; P. Hadot 1968 =*TLG*). The remains of commentaries on the dialogs by the third-century Platonist Iamblichus fill a substantial volume of fragments (Dillon 1973).

Several papyri with commentaries on the Platonic dialogs survive; the most important of these is a long piece of commentary on the *Theaetetus* (*BKT* ii, *CPF* iii #9) that is normally dated to the second century AD but might be as early as the late first century BC. A number of others, all from the second century AD and later, are also interesting (*CPF* iii #5–13).

2.2.3 Aristotle

The amount of surviving ancient commentary on Aristotle is vast, more than double that on any other ancient writer. Much of this material consists of self-standing exegetical commentaries that are works of philosophy in their own right, like the Neoplatonic commentaries to Plato. There is also an enormous mass of scholia, most of which consist of extracts from the self-standing commentaries, usually from ones that are still extant but occasionally from ones that have been lost as independent works.

The commentaries that survive more or less intact are generally known and easily available, except for some of the less interesting Byzantine works. They are both numerous and lengthy, but in some cases heavily derivative from each other (as well as from lost commentaries). The earliest of these commentators, Aspasius of Athens, was an Aristotelian of the second century AD; the prolific and original Alexander of Aphrodisias (second–third century) and the paraphraser Themistius (fourth century) were also Aristotelians. Most commentators, however, were Neoplatonists, whose commentaries can be divided into two types: the works of Porphyry (third century), Dexippus (fourth century), Syrianus (fifth century), and Simplicius (sixth century) were written for publication like the commentaries of the Aristotelians, and the same is true of Ammonius' (fifth–sixth century) commentary on the *De interpretatione*; but Ammonius' other commentaries, and those of his followers Ioannes Philoponus, Olympiodorus, Asclepius of Tralles, Elias, David (all sixth century), and Stephanus (sixth–seventh century) are transcripts of lectures (sometimes Ammonius' lectures rather than those of the philosophers whose names they bear) rather than written commentaries. There is much overlap in content among the works of this latter group. After the Neoplatonists, there is a hiatus of several centuries followed by numerous later Byzantine commentaries. In addition, there are anonymous commentaries of each type (Aristotelian,

Neoplatonist, and Byzantine), and the fragments of numerous lost commentaries can be extracted from the surviving material.

Most of the commentaries have been edited as part of the *Commentaria in Aristotelem graeca* (known as *CAG*); this massive 23-volume set includes texts of almost all ancient commentaries of which substantial portions survive, as well as the most important of the Byzantine commentaries. Some additional commentaries have been edited later outside this corpus (e.g. Tarán 1978 =*TLG*; Westerink 1967), and there are also some post-*CAG* collections of fragments (e.g. Larsen 1972); some other commentaries can be found only in Brandis (1836), and some still remain unpublished. Much of the *CAG* corpus is currently being translated into English in the "Ancient Commentators on Aristotle" series, many volumes of which are already available.[31] Modern scholarship on the commentaries forms a field in itself and cannot be summarized here, but an overview and introduction to both the ancient commentaries and modern work on them is provided by Sorabji (1990, with further bibliography), who also gives a survey of the contents of *CAG* and references to supplementary editions.

As Aristotle was one of the most widely read Greek authors in the medieval period, there are more than a thousand extant manuscripts of his works, many of which contain scholia. Because of the sheer bulk of these scholia, they have never been systematically studied, and most remain unpublished. The scholia consist primarily of extracts from the extant commentaries, usually transmitted in poorer condition than in the self-standing versions of those commentaries, and this duplication is one of the reasons for the lack of attention to the scholia. But there is also some Byzantine material, largely unexplored and perhaps interesting for the history of Byzantine thought, as well as a few old manuscripts whose scholia contain fragments of lost Neoplatonic or Aristotelian commentaries; a number of collections of newly discovered fragments have been published in the past several decades on the basis of these scholia. The scholia can also give us hints as to how Aristotle was read and understood at different periods.

There are several texts that purport to be editions of scholia to Aristotle. The main one, the *Scholia in Aristotelem* of Brandis (1836), is not primarily an edition of scholia but rather of extracts from the commentaries, among which a few actual scholia are scattered; it is therefore superseded by *CAG* except for a few passages.[32] The same applies to Waitz's edition (1844) of some "scholia" to the *Organon*, which mixes marginal scholia with extracts from separate commentaries. There are some true editions of scholia, but only of very small selections of the whole; these include De Falco (1926), Bülow-Jacobsen and Ebbesen (1982), Tarán (1978: pp. xxv–xli), Ebbesen (1981), and Moraux (1979: 51–7, etc.). A glossary attributed to Alexander of Aphrodisias has been published by Kapetanaki

---

31. For a list see abbreviations at the beginning of the Annotated Bibliography, under ACA. The technical glossaries at the back of these volumes will also be of use.

32. For the different use of the word "scholia" by scholars working on Aristotle and certain other authors, see Ch. 1 n. 25 above.

and Sharples (2000). For further discussion of the Aristotle scholia see Wartelle (1963: pp. x–xi), Moraux (1967: 29–37; 1979: 7–8), Ebbesen (1981), Saffrey (1969), and Rashed (1995, 1997), the last three with further references.

There is a first-century (AD) papyrus fragment of a commentary on the *Topica*; see *CPF* iii #2.

Ancient scholarship on Aristotle is not confined to the Greek language. Some commentaries or parts thereof are lost in Greek but preserved in Arabic translation; these are included in *CAG* with the Greek commentaries. The Roman philosopher Boethius, a contemporary of the Greek Neoplatonists, wrote Latin commentaries using Greek sources now lost, and valuable witnesses to the text of the extant Greek commentaries come from literal Latin translations made in the later Middle Ages. Though these works are beyond the scope of this book, they are important for anyone seriously interested in Aristotelian scholarship.

2.2.4 Demosthenes

The ancient scholarship on Demosthenes offers a particularly fruitful field for study, since we possess not only two sets of manuscript scholia (one of them very large) and a small lexicon, but also numerous substantial papyrus fragments with commentaries or other works on Demosthenes, one of them expressly attributed to Didymus himself.

The majority of the scholia come from manuscripts of Demosthenes' orations, as is usual for scholia, but a second group has been found without the text in a tenth-century manuscript from Patmos. Both sets of scholia are important for establishing the text of Demosthenes, but the Patmos ones are particularly useful in this regard because they were separately transmitted from an early date. The scholia to Demosthenes are also helpful in terms of the historical details they transmit and the evidence they give for the practical application of ancient rhetorical theory. Unfortunately, they rarely identify the sources of their information, and so although it is known that many important figures worked on Demosthenes, it is not always clear what these scholars contributed to our extant scholia.

The primary basis of the scholia is a detailed commentary by Didymus (Augustan age), which in turn drew on earlier scholarly works, including a lexicon of Demosthenic words and a commentary from the second century BC. Didymus' work was primarily historical, biographical, and lexicographical in nature, but rhetorical and stylistic commentary on Demothenes was also practiced from an early period, beginning with Peripatetics who wrote soon after Demosthenes' own time. In the early Roman period this type of material was merged with Didymus' commentary, and as time went on the elements of rhetorical exegesis and elementary grammatical explanation seem to have increased at the expense of the historical material, which forms a relatively small part of the manuscript scholia.

A short, elementary lexicon to Demosthenes also survives via the manuscript tradition; the entries are arranged not in alphabetical order but in order of their appearance in the text. The lexicon's editor believes it could have served as a basic

Greek textbook and that it has little connection with the Demosthenic lexica preserved on papyrus.

As well as historical data and fragments of lost literary works quoted by the commentators, the papyrus commentaries offer a valuable glimpse into the evolution of ancient Demosthenic scholarship. By far the most important is the Didymus papyrus, which is much longer than most surviving fragments of papyrus commentaries: fifteen columns, covering *Philippics* 9, 10, 11, and 13. Didymus is explicitly named as the author of the commentary, and the papyrus dates to the early second century AD, so it is relatively close in time to Didymus himself—though the work appears nevertheless to have undergone some abbreviation and alteration in the interval, and it may even be a set of excerpts from Didymus' commentary. The other papyri (from the first to fourth centuries AD) comprise smaller, but still significant, pieces of anonymous commentary, hypotheses, and lexica.[33] One, from the third century, contains several entries that are virtually identical to ones in the manuscript scholia, showing a surprisingly high level of continuity through the late antique and early medieval periods.

There is now a good text of the main group of manuscript scholia, that of Dilts (1983–6 =*TLG*); W. Dindorf (1851*b*) is a poor second choice. Unfortunately, however, Dilts (like Dindorf) includes neither the Patmos scholia nor the papyri. The text of the Patmos scholia is given only by Sakkelion (1877), and the manuscript lexicon by Kazazis (1986). The Didymus papyrus is well edited by Pearson and Stephens (1983), though the original edition (*BKT* i) is also usable; both editions also include the fragments (gathered from Harpocration) of the rest of Didymus' work on Demosthenes. A translation and commentary of the papyrus and the other Didymus fragments is provided by C. Gibson (2002: 77–156). The major studies of ancient scholarship on Demosthenes and the history of the scholia are those of C. Gibson (2002) and Lossau (1964), but for the textual tradition of the primary group of manuscript scholia one should consult Dilts (1984, 1985, and works cited therein), and for the Patmos scholia Kontos (1877), Riemann (1877), and Luschnat (1958). Much has been written on the Didymus papyrus and its contributions to our historical and literary knowledge; see the bibliographies in Pearson and Stephens (1983) and also Arrighetti (1987) and Savorelli (1992). For other work on ancient Demosthenic scholarship see the bibliogra-

---

33. They are: a hypothesis and beginning of a commentary on Κατὰ Μειδίου (*Or.* 21) from c.100 (see C. Gibson 2002: 201–9; Blass 1892; Kenyon 1892: 215–19), part of some sort of work on Κατὰ 'Ανδροτίωνος (*Or.* 22) from c.50–150 and nicknamed "Anonymus Argentinensis" (see C. Gibson 2002: 175–89; Wilcken 1907), part of a commentary on Περὶ τῆς εἰρήνης (*Or.* 5) from the 2nd cent. (see C. Gibson 2002: 172–4; H. Maehler 1992, 1994: 122–4), part of a commentary on Κατὰ 'Αριστοκράτους (*Or.* 23) from the late 2nd cent. (see Hubbell 1957), part of a commentary on Περὶ τῆς παραπρεσβείας (*Or.* 19) from the 3rd cent. (*P.Rain.* i. 25), part of a lexicon to *Or.* 23 from the 4th cent. (see C. Gibson 2002: 157–71; Blass 1882; *BKT* i: 78–82), and part of a lexicon to *Or.* 21 from the 4th or 5th cent. (see C. Gibson 2002: 190–9).

phies of C. Gibson (2002), Lossau (1964), Dilts (1983–6), and Gudeman (1921: 697–703), and for examples of the use of the scholia by modern scholars see Harris (1986) and M. Hansen (1993).

2.2.5 Aeschines

The scholia to Aeschines are among the most useful and enjoyable of scholia to prose writers. It is thought that this high quality is due at least in part to the short length of the preserved works of Aeschines, which did not tempt later copyists to shorten the speeches or commentary by epitomizing. The scholia clearly derive from a commentary by an ancient scholar, probably Didymus, who had access to a considerable amount of information now lost to us. They are particularly useful for explanations of the orator's allusions to contemporary events, but they also provide quotations from lost works of literature and valuable information on language and Athenian history.

The best edition of these scholia is that of Dilts (1992), who provides a generally reliable text and apparatus (though it is not free of typographical errors and has some other flaws: see MacDowell 1993 and Hillgruber 1996 for some corrections) as well as a supplementary apparatus with a generous selection of references to parallel passages. Readers should note that the numbers in bold type at the start of each scholion are not references to the paragraphs of the text of Aeschines, as one might expect, but a numbering system for the scholia themselves; cross-references to the text are in the margins. This edition omits some late scholia included in earlier texts.

In the absence of Dilts, the second best text is F. Schultz's 1865 (=*TLG*) edition of the speeches of Aeschines, which includes the scholia (or rather those of which Schultz was aware); a few more are added, and some important corrections made, in a later article (F. Schultz 1868). Even with this supplement, Schultz's edition is less complete than Dilts's, and it is based on an inadequate understanding of the manuscript tradition. Even fewer scholia, less reliably edited, are found in W. Dindorf (1852*a*).

Little has been written on the interpretation of the scholia, particularly in the twentieth century. Dilts's introduction deals only with textual issues, so the most useful work is probably that of Gudeman (1921: 694–7); other good sources include articles by A. Schaefer (1866) and F. Schultz (1866) and a dissertation by Freyer (1882). Further references can be found in Dilts's bibliography (1992: pp. xvi–xvii).

2.2.6 Herodotus

Ancient scholars displayed considerable interest in Herodotus, both because of the importance of his work and because his Ionic dialect had become a rarity. Many ancient works relating to Herodotus survive intact, including a number that are scholarly in nature: two glossaries, a fragment of a commentary by Aristarchus, a small body of scholia, and a work of dialectology by Moschopulus.

The two glossaries are essentially different versions of the same work, one arranged in the order of the words' appearance in Herodotus' text and one in alphabetical order. They are often referred to together as the Λέξεις, with the two versions designated by A and B, but sometimes the title Λέξεις Ἡροδότου is reserved for the non-alphabetical version, while the alphabetical one is called the Λεξικὸν τῶν Ἡροδοτείων λέξεων. The non-alphabetical version is older; its date is unknown, but it was clearly written to accompany an unaccented version of the text (i.e. before c.900 AD). It seems to be based (at least in part) on a commentary, for it sometimes offers definitions intended to clarify the interpretation, in a specific context, of common words easily confused with homonyms. The alphabetical version of the Λέξεις appears in several manuscripts and differs from one to another; it seems to consist primarily of rearrangements of the older version into alphabetical order but also contains some additions (including words that do not occur in the text of Herodotus as we have it), subtractions, and other modifications. The glossaries are best edited by Rosén (1962: 222–31), where the two versions are merged; essentially the same text can be found in Asheri et al. 1977–98), while Stein's text (1871: 441–82 =TLG) helpfully separates the alphabetical and non-alphabetical versions. Rosén also prints extracts from the glossaries at the bottom of the relevant pages of his Herodotus edition (1987–97).

The commentary fragment, preserved on papyrus, is important because it carries a specific attribution to Aristarchus. It seems, however, to be an abridgement or set of extracts rather than a full version of the original commentary, and it is considerably later than Aristarchus himself, probably from the third century AD. The fragment is also rather short, with only one legible column, containing the end of the commentary on book 1. It is published in Paap (1948) and as P.Amh. ii. 12.

The scholia to Herodotus are few and mostly late, but they contain some remnants of early work. They have never been completely published; the best and most extensive edition is that of Rosén (1987–97), but most of the scholia can also be found in the editions of Asheri et al. (1977–98, with facing Italian translation) and Stein (1871: 431–40). They have never been properly studied.

Moschopulus' Περὶ Ἰάδος is a description of the Ionic dialect with special reference to Herodotus. It is of interest primarily for the history of the text of Herodotus and for the insight it offers into Byzantine views of dialectology; there is an edition in Rosén (1987–97: i, pp. lxviii–lxxxviii). Gregory of Corinth's work on the Ionic dialect also contains numerous references to Herodotus. Other ancient works bearing on Herodotus but less scholarly in nature include Plutarch's De Herodoti malignitate (Moralia 854e–874c) and Lucian's De Syria dea, a highly amusing parody.

At present, ancient scholarship on Herodotus is used chiefly in investigations of the possibility that Herodotus' dialect, as it appears in our manuscripts, comes more from ancient editors than from Herodotus' own pen. In general, however, modern scholars pay little attention to the ancient scholarship on Herodotus, which in consequence is ripe for serious study. Information can be found in Rosén (1962: 218–35) and Jacoby (1913), and an example of the way the scholia can be used is given by Corcella (1996). Rosén (1987–97: ii. 456–67) provides an index of words treated in the surviving ancient scholarship to Herodotus.

2.2.7 Thucydides

The Thucydides scholia, though substantial and based in part on ancient sources, are generally neglected. Half a century ago Luschnat (1954: 14) pointed out that they were underestimated and the time was ripe for a re-evaluation, but that re-evaluation is still awaited, and they are rarely mentioned in modern work on Thucydides. The one usable text, that of Hude (1927 =*TLG*), is largely sound but unreliable for the scholia from certain sources (see Powell 1936); it does, however, contain all the manuscript scholia and the two papyrus fragments of ancient commentary on Thucydides (from the second and third centuries AD), which have little in common with the manuscript scholia. The definitive study of the Thucydides scholia is that of Luschnat (1954, with further bibliography); see also Maurer (1995: 58–85), Dover (1955), Kleinlogel (1964, 1965), Luschnat (1958), Luzzatto (1993, 1999), and Tosi (1980–2).

2.2.8 Isocrates

Ancient scholars appear to have devoted considerable efforts to the elucidation of Isocrates, but almost all their work has perished. We now have only a biography of Isocrates, hypotheses to some of the speeches, and a very small body of scholia, derived in part from a commentary by Didymus. This material is in desperate need of a good edition to replace W. Dindorf (1852*a* =*TLG*), and of some serious study; for what is known so far, see Gudeman (1921: 693–4).

2.2.9 Xenophon

There is very little surviving ancient scholarship on Xenophon. His works were popular in antiquity, and some of the scraps of surviving commentary appear to be of considerable antiquity, so it is assumed that ancient commentaries on his writings once existed but have been lost. A few fragments of scholia survive but are generally considered to be of little value; not all of these have been published. The largest publication, containing only scholia to the *Anabasis*, is that of L. Dindorf (1855 =*TLG*), but since that publication a better manuscript has been discovered (see Piccolomini 1895). Some scholia from that manuscript (pertaining to the *Anabasis*, but completely different from Dindorf's) have been edited by Lundström (1913), who indicates the presence of further, unpublished scholia. For an overview see Gudeman (1921: 692–3).

2.3 HELLENISTIC LITERATURE

Ancient scholarship on Hellenistic literature is more important and more extensive than is generally believed. The best-preserved portions of such scholarship are scientific in orientation: numerous commentaries on Hellenistic mathematical works survive, and we even have an intact commentary, dating to the second century BC, on an astronomical work. In addition, several of the Alexandrian scholars wrote poetry, and the scholia to those poems contain some important material.

2.3.1 Aratus

Ancient scholarship on Aratus Soleus offers us a unique prize: a complete, self-standing ancient commentary that survived intact through the medieval manuscript tradition without being converted into scholia. At first glance such a survival seems particularly astonishing in the case of Aratus, who lived in the third century BC and produced an astronomical poem entitled *Phaenomena*, because he is largely ignored today. In antiquity and the middle ages, however, the *Phaenomena* achieved great popularity: it was translated repeatedly into Latin, imitated and followed by poets and astronomers both Greek and Latin, and was the subject of a vast amount of commentary.[34] This prolonged and intense interest contributed to the survival not only of the intact commentary, but also of a large corpus of ancient scholia and introductory material.

The oldest extant scholarship on Aratus is the self-standing commentary, entitled Ἱππάρχου τῶν Ἀράτου καὶ Εὐδόξου Φαινομένων ἐξηγήσεως βιβλία τρία and written by Hipparchus of Nicaea in the later second century BC. The commentary is concerned principally with correcting Aratus' astronomy—Hipparchus was a noted astronomer in his own right, and the commentary survives in part because of its intrinsic astronomical value—but also discusses textual issues to some extent. Hipparchus' textual comments give us an insight into the early period of transmission, before a canonical text of Aratus had been established (cf. Martin 1956: 33). He also serves as one of our major sources of information on Eudoxus of Cnidus, on whose lost astronomical writings Aratus (himself more a poet than an astronomer) is said to have based the *Phaenomena*; Hipparchus compares Aratus' work to Eudoxus' own writings and quotes the latter at length.[35]

The standard text of this commentary is that of Manitius (1894 =*TLG*), which is equipped not only with indices and notes, but also with a facing German translation (highly useful in view of the mathematical Greek).[36] Discussions of Hipparchus can be found in Hübner (1998), Kidd (1997: 18–21), Bowen and Goldstein (1991), Nadal and Brunet (1984, 1989), Martin (1956: 22–9; 1998: i, pp. lxxxvi–xcvii, 124–31), and Maass (1892: 61–117), as well as in Manitius (1894: 282–306) and elsewhere. For information on Germanicus Caesar's use of Hipparchus' commentary in his translation of the *Phaenomena*, see Gain (1976: 14–16) and Le Bœuffle (1975: pp. xix–xx).

Hipparchus also preserves substantial remnants of an even earlier commentary by Attalus of Rhodes (earlier second century BC). This work was also heavily astronomical in content, but it differed from Hipparchus' in that Attalus tended to jus-

34. For possible explanations of this popularity, see Lewis (1992).

35. For further information on Eudoxus and Hipparchus' value in understanding his work, see Lasserre (1966), Maass (1892: 279–304), and Kidd (1997: 14–18). Martin (1998: i. pp. lxxxvi–xcvii, cf. also 124–31) argues that Hipparchus has exaggerated the extent of Aratus' dependency on Eudoxus.

36. For help with the Greek, there is also Mugler's dictionary of geometrical terminology (1958–9).

tify Aratus' astronomy rather than to correct it; Hipparchus thus quotes Attalus in order to disagree with him. The fragments of Attalus have been collected from Hipparchus' text by Maass (1898: 1–24), and discussions of his work can be found in Martin (1956: 22–8), Kidd (1997: 18), and Maass (1898: pp. xi–xv).

As time went on work on Aratus grew to include research into the myths about the stars included in the *Phaenomena*, as well as textual criticism and astronomy. The definitive edition of the *Phaenomena* was produced in the first century BC[37] and included an introduction with a life of Aratus, extensive commentary, and a corrected text of the *Phaenomena* (Martin 1956: 196–204). The remains of this commentary form the core of our preserved scholia, though not all of it survives and many scholia have other sources (see below).

Plutarch (first to second centuries AD) wrote an explanation of Aratus entitled Αἰτίαι τῶν Ἀράτου Διοσημιῶν; this work is now lost, but fragments of it have been preserved in the scholia to Aratus. The best text of these fragments is that of the scholia (see below), but they have also been collected as fragments 13–20 of Plutarch's *Moralia* and hence provided with an English translation (Sandbach 1969: 88–97; text also at Sandbach 1967: 17–21).

The grammarian Achilles (third century AD) wrote a work entitled Περὶ τοῦ παντός ("On the universe") that was probably not intended to be a commentary on Aratus. A collection of extracts from this work, however, was pressed into service as an introduction to the *Phaenomena*. The original is lost, but the extracts survive; a text of them may be found in Maass (1898: 25–75) and discussion in Martin (1956: 131–2) and Maass (1892: 7–59; 1898: pp. xvi–xviii, espousing views no longer accepted).

In the seventh century the Byzantine engineer Leontius wrote a manual on the construction of globes used for understanding Aratus; for his works see Maass (1898: p. lxxi, 559–70). Much later Maximus Planudes (*c.*1290) and Demetrius Triclinius (early fourteenth century) wrote their own comments on Aratus; see Martin (1956: 196, 290–1, 295–9; 1974: pp. xxix–xxxiii; Kidd 1997: 55–7).

Several anonymous commentaries also survive. The work known as "Anonymus I" is a general astronomical introduction, not especially relevant to Aratus, which was composed sometime after the first century AD and later incorporated into the explanatory material on Aratus; scholars have traditionally displayed little interest in it. For the text see Maass (1898: 87–98), for brief discussion Martin (1956: 130–2) and Maass (1898: pp. xix–xx). "Anonymus III" is essentially a short Latin epitome of Aratus, a description of the constellations following Aratus' order, and is usually ignored like "Anonymus I." A text of it and some discussion can be found in Maass (1898: pp. xlv–xlvi, 307–12).

---

37. Martin attributes this commentary to the grammarian Theon, but Cameron has argued (1995: 197–8) that the Theon mentioned in the Aratus scholia is in fact Theon of Alexandria, the 4th-cent. mathematician; if so, neither Theon is likely to be the author of the commentary.

Of much greater importance is the work known as "Anonymus II." This extensive body of explanatory material goes back to the second edition of the *Phaenomena*, known as Φ (for which see Martin 1956: 35–126; 1998: i, pp. cxxvi–cxxx),
and is witness to an intriguing development in the history of the text. In the second or third century AD, when the old scholarly edition had been widely accepted
for centuries, another editor decided to create a new and more popular version of
the poem. To do so he took the earlier edition's text and removed most of the
commentary (which was often difficult and technical), keeping only the biography of Aratus and extracts from the preface and commentary. He then replaced
the omitted notes with a new and more attractive body of explanatory material.
This new material was drawn from a range of sources, including extracts from
commentaries and works on Aratus and from other astronomical and mythological works that had not been intended as commentaries; in addition, an appealing
series of illustrations was provided. Most of the new material came from a work
known as the *Catasterismi* of Eratosthenes, which appears to be the late epitome
of a lost astronomical treatise probably written by the third-century BC scholar
and mathematician Eratosthenes as an elementary and literary astronomy manual
designed to complete and explain Aratus. The editor of Φ apparently took extracts
from this original work and rearranged them in the order of Aratus' poem to en-
hance the appeal of his new edition.[38]

The Φ edition proved wildly popular and soon replaced the scholarly edition
entirely in the West; in the Byzantine world both editions existed side by side,
resulting in extensive cross-fertilization of the explanatory material. As a result,
while some surviving manuscripts (most notably M) contain scholia largely derived from the earlier edition and others (notably S and Q) contain substantial
amounts of explanatory material from the Φ edition, manuscripts of the earlier
edition generally show at least some influence from Φ. Much of the Φ commentary has, however, been lost in Greek; the "Anonymus II" consists primarily of a
Latin translation of the Φ edition made in the seventh or eighth century and known
as the *Aratus Latinus*.[39] Portions of the work's introductions and biographies sur-

38. See Martin (1956: esp. 58–62, 95–103). The *Catasterismi* epitome exists independently; the best text of it is that of Olivieri (1897) with additions by Rehm (1899),
and there is an English translation by Condos (1970) and an annotated Spanish one by
Del Canto Nieto (1993). Martin (1956: 63–126) has shown that Hyginus' *De astronomia*
(for which see Viré (1992) for the text and Le Bœuffle (1983: pp. ix–xviii) for discussion
of sources) is based on the lost original of this work, and Robert (1878) has produced an
edition that attempts to come as close as possible to (his pre-Martin understanding of)
the original, by printing in parallel columns the epitome and relevant sections of Hyginus,
the scholia to Aratus, and the scholia to Germanicus. For general information on Eratosthenes see Geus (2002).

39. For further information on the *Aratus Latinus* see Le Bourdellès (1985), Martin
(1956: 42–51), and Kidd (1997: 52–5); for the text of "Anonymus II," see Maass (1898:
99–306, cf. also pp. xxi–xliv). For a new and important manuscript fragment of this text
(in Greek), see Moraux (1981) and Erren (1994: 200–3).

vive in Greek as well, and these are given in parallel columns with the Latin in Maass's edition.

The *Aratus Latinus* is not the only Latin witness to Φ. The *Phaenomena* were translated into Latin repeatedly before the creation of Φ, and the most successful of these translations was that created in the early first century AD and attributed to Germanicus Caesar. In the third century the Φ commentary was translated into Latin and attached to Germanicus' translation to become the so-called scholia to Germanicus, which are still extant.[40]

There are thus two separate bodies of explanatory material that one might wish to recover when editing scholia to Aratus, that of the early scholarly edition and that of Φ; each contains not only scholia but also other material such as introductions and biographies of Aratus. The two cannot be fully separated, for the Φ edition incorporated some of the earlier edition's material and some of the commentary of that earlier edition survives only as part of Φ. As the earlier commentary contains information now valued much more highly than that of the Φ commentary, editions of the scholia focus on the older material. The definitive edition, that of Martin (1974 =*TLG*), not only gives scholia from Greek manuscripts (both texts of Aratus and manuscripts of Aeschylus' *Prometheus Vinctus*, which include some old Aratus scholia as part of the Aeschylus "A" scholia; see Martin 1974: pp. xxv–xxviii), but also quotes lengthy portions of the *Aratus Latinus* and the scholia to Germanicus where these are thought to reflect material from the earlier edition. Martin also includes scholia that preserve later interpolations from Plutarch, Sporus (a writer of unknown date who probably produced a lost commentary on Aratus; see Martin 1956: 205–9), and Apollinarius (an astronomer, probably of the first or second century AD; see Kidd 1997: 48). He does not, however, include the purely medieval scholia (some of which can be found in Dell'Era 1974) or the *Catasterismi* fragments. In the absence of Martin one can consult the scholia from two of the manuscripts in Maass's edition (1898: 334–555).

A number of papyri also contain scholia or commentary on Aratus. The most important of these is a fragment from the third or fourth century AD with a popular commentary on Aratus that bears little relationship to our scholia.[41] Other papyrus scholia are not included in Martin's edition and are generally of little interest; for overviews of them see Kidd (1997: 49–52), Martin (1956: 213–18; 1998: i, pp. clxxvi–clxxviii), and McNamee (1977: 212–13; forthcoming).

Discussions of the scholia to Aratus can be found in Martin's preface (1974) and scattered through his earlier work (1956), in both cases with a focus on textual history (for a good overview of which see Martin 1998: i, pp. cxxvi–clxxviii).

---

40. Part of the scholia to Germanicus have been edited by Dell'Era (1979*a* and *b*); for the rest, and in the absence of Dell'Era for all these scholia, one can consult Breysig (1867: 55–258). Discussion of these scholia can be found in Dell'Era (esp. 1979*b*, with bibliography), Martin (1956: 38–41), Bartalucci (1984), and Robert (1878: 201–20).

41. For a recent edition of this piece with discussion, see M. Maehler (1980); Martin (1974: 560–2) merely reprints an uncorrected version of Maass's text (1898: 556–8).

A brief discussion in English is given by Kidd (1997: 43–8, see also 49–68 on textual history), and further information can be found in Luck (1976) and Maass (1898: pp. xlix–lxix). For further bibliography see Martin (1998: i, pp. clxxix–clxxxv), Kidd (1997), and especially Erren (1994). Since all the extant Latin translations of Aratus used scholia and commentaries to some extent, editions and discussions of those translations often treat such material as well; see Lausdei (1981) and Soubiran (1972: 93) on Cicero's version, Le Bœuffle (1975: pp. xix–xx) and Santini (1981) on Germanicus' version, and Soubiran (1981: 53–7) and Robert (1878: 26–9) on Avienus' version (fourth century AD).

2.3.2 Euclid

Euclid (fourth–third century BC) was probably the most important mathematician of antiquity. His *Elements* is a technical work that requires considerable explanation, so it is unsurprising that much commentary on it survives. We have not only a substantial body of scholia, but also an intact commentary by Proclus (fifth century AD) and part of a commentary by Pappus (fourth century AD), as well as a variety of other works.

Proclus' commentary, a four-book work that covers only the first book of the *Elements*, is of considerable interest. It is based on a number of earlier works, including Eudemus of Rhodes' lost *History of geometry* (c.330 BC), lost works of Porphyry (third century AD), and commentaries on Euclid from the Roman period. The commentary is oriented toward the curriculum of the Neoplatonist school and has philosophical and historical as well as mathematical value; as a result it has been translated into several modern languages. It is frequently cited by modern scholars in discussions of philosophy, mathematics, Euclid, and its lost sources. The standard text of the commentary is that of Friedlein (1873 =TLG), and translations are provided by Morrow (1992), Ver Eecke (1948), Schönberger and Steck (1945), and Cardini (1978). For examples of recent use of the commentary see Zhmud (2002), Cleary (2000), Netz (1999*b*), Eide (1995), and Glasner (1992).

Pappus' commentary originally dealt with the entire *Elements*, but the two surviving books cover book 10 only. The original Greek version is lost in its entirety, and the two books that survive exist only in an Arabic translation. Pappus' commentary, which is less respected than Proclus' but not without value, includes a philosophical introduction to book 10 as well as detailed mathematical discussion. There is a good edition with full English translation in Junge and Thomson (1930).

Heron of Alexandria (first century AD) wrote a commentary on books 1 through 9 of the *Elements*. The work itself is lost, but extensive fragments are preserved in Proclus' commentary and in a tenth-century commentary by Anaritius (Al-Nayrizi), which was originally written in Arabic and translated into Latin. (For editions and translations see Mansfeld 1998: 26 n. 90). Anaritius' commentary also preserves fragments of a commentary by Simplicius (sixth century) on book 1 of the *Elements*.

Theon of Alexandria (fourth century) produced revised editions of the *Elements* and (probably) the *Optica*. Traces of his work on the *Elements* are preserved in scholia and commentaries, and an introduction to the *Optica* attributed to him survives intact. See Heiberg (1882) and Heiberg and Menge (1883–1916: vol. vii).

Marinus of Neapolis (fifth–sixth century), a pupil of Proclus, has left an introduction (often referred to as a commentary) to the *Data*. See Heiberg and Menge (1883–1916: vol. vi =*TLG*) and Michaux (1947). Later commentaries also exist.

The scholia to Euclid are extensive but less interesting than the commentaries. For the *Elements*, the scholia's oldest sources seem to be Proclus' commentary (for book 1) and Pappus' commentary (for books 2 through 13). There are also some scholia to the *Data*, *Optica*, and *Phaenomena*. The standard edition is that of Heiberg and Menge (1883–1916: vols. v–viii =*TLG*), but some additional scholia are provided by Heiberg (1903: 328–52). The key study is that of Heiberg (1888).

For discussion of the commentaries and scholia, with further bibliography, see Mansfeld (1998) and Knorr (1989). Mugler's dictionaries of technical terminology (1958–9, 1964) are useful for reading these texts.

2.3.3 Archimedes

The Syracusan mathematician Archimedes (third century BC) was almost as important as Euclid, but we have considerably less commentary on his works. What we have, however, is quite valuable: intact commentaries on three of Archimedes' works by Eutocius of Ascalon (fifth–sixth century). The three commentaries are on *De sphaera et cylindro*, *De planorum aequilibriis*, and *De dimensione circuli*. They are important mathematical works in their own right and significant for our understanding of Greek mathematics and its history. Later commentaries also exist.

In addition to the commentaries, there are some scholia to Archimedes. These are not considered important or of significant antiquity, but they are interesting because they contain mathematical diagrams.[42] Only a selection (those that appear to go back to the archetype of the Greek manuscripts) has been published.

Heiberg (1915 =*TLG*) provides a good text of Eutocius' commentaries and the scholia from the archetype and equips the commentaries (but not the scholia) with a facing Latin translation. Mugler (1972) offers another good edition of the commentaries, with French translation; he omits the scholia but includes a few odd scraps of other ancient comments on Archimedes. There is also an English translation of some of Eutocius' commentaries by Netz (2004–), and another French translation by Ver Eecke (1960). For examples of recent work on Eutocius see Cameron (1990), Netz (1999–2000), Knorr (1989), and Mansfeld (1998, with further references). Mugler's dictionaries of technical terminology (1958–9, 1964) are useful for reading these texts.

---

42. The scholia and commentaries on other mathematicians often contain diagrams too, but in many modern editions it is difficult to ascertain the extent to which the diagrams published with the text come from the manuscripts or are the editors' creations; see Netz (1999a). Some of the scholia to Archimedes consist only of diagrams, which have been published from the manuscripts.

2.3.4 Apollonius of Perga

The mathematician Apollonius of Perga produced his *Conica* around 200 BC; half of this work has survived in Greek, accompanied by a commentary by Eutocius of Ascalon (fifth–sixth century). Though not as famous as Eutocius' commentary on Archimedes, this work has some philosophical and mathematical value. It has been edited and provided with a Latin translation by Heiberg (1891–3 =*TLG*), and there is a good introduction with further bibliography in Mansfeld (1998); see also Knorr (1989) and Decorps-Foulquier (1998).

2.3.5 Apollonius Rhodius

Apollonius Rhodius lived in the third century BC and was one of the librarians at Alexandria, rather than one of the classical poets they so diligently edited, so it is perhaps surprising to find that there is a large body of scholia on Apollonius' *Argonautica*, including much ancient material and going back at least to the first century BC. While not as useful to us as the scholia on Aristophanes or Euripides, the Apollonius scholia contain much information that is still valuable, particularly when they shed light on how Apollonius used Homer, on how ancient authors who imitated Apollonius understood his text, and on the details of Greek mythology; they are of course also of use for establishing the text of the *Argonautica*.

A few papyri with marginal or interlinear scholia to Apollonius' works survive,[43] though these are too fragmentary to be of much use; there is also one fragment of a self-standing commentary.[44] The vast majority of our evidence for ancient scholarship on the *Argonautica*, however, is derived from medieval sources. The scholia to Apollonius state (at the end of book 4) that they are derived from the commentaries of Theon (first century BC), Lucillus Tarrhaeus (mid-first century AD), and Sophocles (second century AD). The last of these commentaries was also used (perhaps indirectly) by Stephanus of Byzantium, and the scholia themselves, in a state of preservation better than that of the present day, were used extensively by the compilers of the *Etymologicum genuinum* and more sparingly by Eustathius and John Tzetzes. The transmission is thus double, "direct" in manuscripts of Apollonius and "indirect" in the other sources, and quotations from the *Etymologicum* and other indirect sources are considered to be (and in editions printed as) part of the corpus of scholia to Apollonius. The direct transmission of the scholia has several distinct branches, L, P, and A (this last being closely related to, but not directly descended from, L); these are reproduced to varying degrees in different publications.

The best edition of Apollonius scholia, that of Wendel (1935 =*TLG*), is not really satisfactory. Wendel attempts to print all important scholia, but he frequently does not note major variations in order and wording among the different witnesses; a perusal of the explanation of the principles used in his apparatus (1935: pp. xxv–

---

43. *P.Köln* 12 + *P.Mil. Vogl.* 6, from the early 1st cent. AD (for combined publication see Henrichs 1970); also *P.Oxy.* xxxiv. 2693 and 2694, both 2nd cent. AD.

44. *P.Berol.* 13413, from 1st or 2nd cent. AD, pub. in Wifstrand (1932).

xxvi) is both enlightening and alarming. In many cases, moreover, material from the indirect transmission is given only in the apparatus, so that sometimes when one is trying to follow up a reference to an Apollonius scholion one has to look in the apparatus rather than in the main text. The P tradition, still more unfortunately, is given rather short shrift, so that material found only in P is sometimes omitted entirely from Wendel's text; if one needs to find this material, the only real option is to use G. Schaefer's (1813) text of the P scholia. Wendel's text is, however, the only unified text of the *Argonautica* scholia; if it is unavailable, one must use Schaefer for the P scholia and Keil (1854) for the L scholia. (The A scholia can be found only in Wendel and in very early editions of Apollonius, but they rarely show significant differences from the L scholia.)

Discussion of the Apollonius scholia is fairly extensive. Wendel provides, in addition to the introduction to his edition of the scholia (1935), a separate monograph on the textual history of the scholia (1932) and some later discussion (1942); his work is based on that of Deicke (1901 and unpublished). Wendel's discussions are not always easy to follow, and many of his views are no longer generally accepted, so that anyone interested in textual history should consult H. Fränkel (1964: 92–110; 1968), who provides many corrections to Wendel's text as well as to his analyses, and Herter (1955). The papyri are discussed by H. Maehler (1994: 105–9), H. Fränkel (1964: 92–3), McNamee (1977: 204–6; forthcoming), and their editors; their more legible portions are reproduced in Wendel (1935) at the appropriate line numbers.

Perhaps the most fruitful area of scholarship involving the Apollonius scholia is that of how they were used by other ancient writers who imitated Apollonius (such as Valerius Flaccus). There is no doubt that some ancient writers were familiar with the ancestors of our *Argonautica* scholia, and the interpretations contained in such commentaries seem to have influenced their creative activity to some extent. On this point see Nelis (2001), Scaffai (1997, with good discussion of earlier work), Bessone (1991), H. Fränkel (1964: 94–8), and Herter (1955: 243).

2.3.6 Theocritus

The scholia to Theocritus are useful and relatively unproblematic. Of ancient scholarship on Theocritus we possess introductory material, hypotheses to the individual poems, and marginal and interlinear scholia; some of the scholia are Byzantine, but many are ancient.

The old scholia, which fill a volume much thicker than that of Theocritus' own work, derive from a massive composite commentary assembled from at least two earlier works. One was a scholarly commentary dating to the Augustan period, composed primarily by Theon but also incorporating the work of Asclepiades of Myrlea (first century BC); in addition to many of the scholia, the surviving prolegomena and hypotheses have their bases in this commentary. The second major source of the composite commentary appears to be a work independently composed by Munatius of Tralles in the second century AD and containing a number of gross errors. It is thought that Munatius, who clearly had little interest in achieving high standards of scholarship, produced primarily paraphrases of the poems and identifications of the people mentioned in them. These two commentaries were later combined, along with the work of the second-century commentators Theaetetus and Amarantus; it is likely but not certain that the compilation was done by Theaetetus in the second century. From the fourth to sixth centuries a revival of Theocritan studies resulted in some further alterations to the commentaries, but since no scholars later than the second century are named in the old scholia it is likely that no significant additions were made at that period.

The scholia as they have come down to us represent a severely abridged version of the original commentaries, which were used by a number of early scholars in their fuller forms. There is thus a significant indirect tradition for the Theocritus scholia, involving Eustathius, Hesychius, various etymological works, and especially the scholia to Vergil.

The Byzantine scholia are easily separable from the old scholia and are generally considered to have no value except for the study of Byzantine scholarship itself, since they are based entirely on extant sources. They consist primarily of the work of Moschopulus and Planudes, with fragments of an earlier commentary by Tzetzes and notes by Triclinius.

Separate in origin from both these groups is the body of scholia on the *Technopaegnia*, a group of poems whose lines form shapes on the page. This group includes Theocritus' *Syrinx*, as well as a number of works by other poets, and was ultimately incorporated into the *Greek Anthology*. The scholia go back to the late antique period and are of particular interest for the history of this unusual poetic genre.

In addition to the manuscript scholia, we have a papyrus fragment from the first or second century AD containing a small piece of a commentary on Theocritus[45] and substantial marginal scholia on papyrus texts of the poems from the late second century and from c.500 AD (Hunt and Johnson 1930; Meliadò 2004). None of these remains shows close agreement with the manuscript scholia, and the commentaries from which they derive were clearly far less good than that of Theon.

The scholia are useful particularly for the interpretation of Theocritus, but also for establishing the text. They can also aid in the interpretation of other ancient poetry, for later poets, particularly Vergil, made use of Theocritus and understood his poems in the light of ancient commentaries. Ancient scholars' discussions of Theocritus' literary Doric dialect are also important for our understanding of the history of Greek dialectology.

The standard edition of the old scholia is that of Wendel (1914 =*TLG*), which includes material derived from the indirect tradition and the *Technopaegnia* scholia but omits the papyri and the Byzantine scholia. The latter can be found in earlier editions of the Theocritus scholia, preferably that of Ahrens (1859), in which they are marked with "*Rec*"; the papyri must be consulted in their original editions. The definitive discussion of the scholia is also by Wendel (1920, with further

---

45. *P.Berol.* 7506, pub. in *BKT* v.i, p. 56.

references), but Gow (1952: i, pp. lxxx–lxxxiv) offers a briefer explanation that is more cautious than Wendel's on some points, and H. Maehler (1994: 97–105), McNamee (1977: 217–28; forthcoming), and Meliadò (2004) discuss the papyri. For examples of use of the scholia in modern work on Theocritus, see Gow (1952: ii, *passim*), Payne (2001), and S. Jackson (1999).

2.3.7 Lycophron

The *Alexandra* of Lycophron (third or second century BC) is an abstruse poem on Trojan War themes. Though not popular in modern times, it attracted considerable attention at earlier periods and was the subject of commentaries by Theon and Tzetzes, among others.

A considerable body of scholia to the *Alexandra* (in fact much larger than the poem itself) survives and is divided into two groups: old scholia and Tzetzes' scholia. Tzetzes drew heavily on the old scholia and is in consequence an important witness to the ancient tradition, but some old material is also preserved separately. It is uncertain whether the Tzetzes in question was John or Isaac.

The standard edition of the scholia to Lycophron is that of Scheer (1908 =*TLG*); this text combines the two types of scholia, and most of those presented are Tzetzes', but where Tzetzes and the old scholia diverge, Scheer prints the text in two columns, with the old scholia on the left and Tzetzes' on the right. Gualandri provides indices to Scheer's edition (1962, 1965). Leone has published two studies of the manuscript tradition in preparation for a new edition (1991, 1992–3).

The principal discussion of the scholia is that of Scheer (1908). They are rich in mythographical information and also useful as evidence in the debate as to whether the author of the *Alexandra* can be identified with the Lycophron who was a tragedian of the third century BC or whether the poem was composed by another Lycophron in the second century BC; on this point see Ceccarelli and Steinrück (1995) and S. West (1984), both with further references.

2.3.8 Nicander

Nicander, a poet of the third or second century BC, produced two surviving works: the *Theriaca*, a didactic poem explaining remedies for the bites of snakes and other poisonous animals, and the *Alexipharmaca*, a similar explanation of remedies for poisons. Though these works are now somewhat neglected, and the information they contain is generally regarded as false, they were popular in antiquity and attracted the attention of many ancient commentators, including Theon and Plutarch.

There is a large body of surviving scholia for each poem; in both cases the mass of scholia is considerably larger than the poem itself. The scholia cover a wide variety of topics; while much of this material is late, some of it preserves valuable ancient commentary. The scholia are used particularly for the information they provide on the history of the poems and Nicander's other writings. There are also full-length prose paraphrases to both poems, attributed to one Eutecnius and dating perhaps to the fourth century AD. An interesting piece of papyrus commentary,

P.Oxy. xix. 2221 from the first century AD, shows no overlap with either scholia or paraphrases.

The standard edition of the *Theriaca* scholia is that of Crugnola (1971 =*TLG*), and the *Alexipharmaca* scholia have been edited by Geymonat (1974 =*TLG*). The editions of both in O. Schneider's edition of Nicander (1856) are also acceptable. The paraphrases can be found in Geymonat (1976) and Bussemaker (1849). A short overview is given by Gow and Scholfield (1953: 16), and examples of the use of the scholia are provided by Gallavotti (1988), Geymonat (1970), and Cazzaniga (1976).

2.3.9 Callimachus

The scholia to Callimachus appear to have originally resembled those for Apollonius Rhodius and Theocritus, but their state of preservation is much worse. Few scholia are found in the manuscripts, and little ancient scholarship can be extracted from them, though a respectable quantity has been recovered on papyri (both as marginalia and as separate commentaries). We also have a number of Roman-period papyri with *diegeses*, or summaries of the content of Callimachean poems; as in the case of the hypotheses to dramatic texts and to Homer, groups of these summaries circulated on papyrus without the poetic texts, but related summaries are found with the text in medieval manuscripts.

The main edition is that of Pfeiffer (1949–53 =*TLG*), but see also *P.Oxy.* xx. 2258, F. Montanari (1976), Henrichs (1969), Parsons (1977), Cameron (1995), and especially Rossum-Steenbeek (1998). Examples of recent use of the Callimachus scholia include Ambühl (1995), Krevans (1986), and McNamee (1982). For further references see Lehnus (2000).

2.3.10 *Batrachomyomachia*

The scholia to the *Batrachomyomachia* are mostly Byzantine and have attracted little attention in recent years. Many are short glosses, but there are also lengthier notations and a prose paraphrase of the poem. They make up a substantial body of work, much of which derives from the work of Moschopulus (*c.*1300) and other scholars of the same period. Such ancient material as is preserved comes primarily from extant sources such as lexica. The scholia are useful primarily for establishing the text of the poem. The standard edition and definitive study is that of Ludwich (1896: 117–35 and 198–318); Gudeman (1921: 645–6) provides an overview and Keaney (1979) offers some corrections to the attribution of individual notes.

2.4 LITERATURE OF THE ROMAN PERIOD

Most scholarship on authors of the Roman period (except Galen, for whose works see 2.2.1) is less significant than that on earlier writers. Some of it, however, is important, and in certain cases such scholarship can be shown to use lost sources that considerably predate the author under discussion; thus material going back to the classical period can sometimes be found in scholarship on writers of the second century AD. The number of Roman-period authors on whose works commentary survives is so great that only those with the most significant scholarship can be discussed here.

2.4.1 Ptolemy

Claudius Ptolemy of Alexandria, the great mathematician and astronomer, lived in the second century AD. His most famous composition is the *Almagest*, or Μαθηματικὴ σύνταξις, but he also wrote many other works. A great deal of scholarship on Ptolemy survives; not only are there numerous extant commentaries, but even commentaries on the commentaries. Much of this material is unpublished, and some that is published lacks modern editions. Only a minimal overview can be given here.

Pappus (fourth century) is responsible for the earliest surviving commentary on the *Almagest*. His work seems to have originally covered at least books 1 to 6 of the *Almagest*, but only the portion on books 5 and 6 is still extant. The standard edition is that of Rome (1931–43: vol. i =*TLG*).

Theon's commentary on the *Almagest* (fourth century) is only slightly later than Pappus' and much better preserved, though not complete. It originally covered books 1 through 13, but the section on book 11 is lost. Of the section on book 5 only a small fragment survived via the direct manuscript tradition, but most of the remainder has been preserved as scholia to the *Almagest*. The commentary on book 3 provides a rare glimpse of ancient scholarship produced by a woman, for it was based on a text edited by Theon's daughter Hypatia, who was made famous in the nineteenth century by Charles Kingsley's novel *Hypatia*. (Hypatia was an important Neoplatonist teacher until lynched by Christian monks; she also wrote her own commentaries, which unfortunately do not survive. See Dzielska 1995 and, on her editing, Cameron 1990 and Knorr 1989: 753–804.) Rome (1931–43: vols. ii–iii =*TLG*) provides a good edition of the commentary on the first four books of the *Almagest*, but there is no modern edition of the rest of the commentary. The portions that survived in the direct transmission can be found in Grynaeus and Camerarius (1538), and the scholia containing the remains of commentary on book 5 are unpublished but discussed in Tihon (1987).

An anonymous Neoplatonist of the late antique period has left us an introduction and partial commentary on book 1 of the *Almagest*. This commentary is based on earlier sources, including both Pappus and Theon. Only portions of it have been published, by Mogenet (1956) and Hultsch (1878).

In addition to his *Almagest* commentary, Theon composed two works on Ptolemy's Πρόχειροι κανόνες ("Handy Tables"). Both are self-standing treatises rather than commentaries in the strict sense of the word. The "Great Commentary" originally comprised five books, of which the first four are still extant, and the "Little Commentary," which has survived intact, is in one book. Marinus of Neapolis (fifth–sixth century) composed a commentary on Theon's Little Commentary; this secondary commentary is lost in its original form, but some of it is preserved as scholia to the Little Commentary. The Great Commentary and Little

Commentary have been edited and translated by Tihon (1978 =*TLG*, 1991 =*TLG*, 1999) and Mogenet and Tihon (1985 =*TLG*). The scholia deriving from Marinus' commentary are mostly unpublished, but there is a discussion of them by Tihon (1976), who also discusses the scholia to the Great Commentary (Mogenet and Tihon 1981).

We also have a fragment of an elementary commentary on the "Handy Tables" from the early third century. This has been edited and translated by Jones (1990).

Ptolemy's Ἀποτελεσματικά or Τετράβιβλος concerned astrology and so attracted particular attention from commentators. An introduction and explanation is attributed to Porphyry (third century) and edited by Boer and Weinstock (1940 =*TLG*). A long anonymous commentary of somewhat later date has no modern edition (text in Wolf 1559). There is also a paraphrase/commentary attributed (probably incorrectly) to Proclus, of which there is no modern edition (text in Allatius 1635). For more information on these commentaries see Gundel and Gundel (1966: 213–16).

Porphyry (third century) has left us a commentary on the *Harmonica*, of which there is a good edition by Düring (1932 =*TLG*), updated by Alexanderson (1969). Many later commentaries on Ptolemy's works also exist in a variety of languages.

For discussion of the commentaries to Ptolemy see especially the introductions to the editions, and Knorr (1989), and Mansfeld (1998, with further bibliography); for examples of their recent use see Cameron (1990), Jones (1999), and Gersh (1992).

There is also a large body of scholia to Ptolemy's works, though it has never been properly studied or edited. As a result it is still possible to make major discoveries by working on the scholia: the remains of Theon's commentary on *Almagest* 5 were found there only recently. See for example Mogenet (1975), Tihon (1973, 1987), Antoniou (1997), and Mansfeld (2000).

2.4.2 Nicomachus

There are four extant commentaries to the *Introductio arithmetica* of the mathematician Nicomachus of Gerasa (*c*.100 AD), as well as a prologue and a body of scholia. The earliest commentary is that of Iamblichus from the third century, while the next two are both based on lectures of the Neoplatonist Ammonius in the sixth century: Asclepius of Tralles reports the lectures directly, while Philoponus' commentary is more removed and may be based on Asclepius' work rather than personal memory of the lectures. Philoponus' commentary survives in two versions, of which the second has sometimes been ascribed to Isaac Argyros. Then there is an anonymous Byzantine commentary ("recensio IV") that is sometimes confused with Asclepius' commentary in manuscript catalogs; though this work was for a while attributed to Arsenius Olbiodorus, its authorship is unknown. The prologue is also anonymous, and the scholia are Byzantine.

Iamblichus' commentary has been edited by Pistelli (1894 =*TLG*), Asclepius' by Tarán (1969), and the first version of Philoponus' by Hoche (1864–7). The second version of Philoponus' commentary is published only in the form of collections of variants from the first version: the divergences from Philoponus' first book are given by Hoche (1864–7: ii, pp. ii–xiv), and those from Philoponus' second (and final) book by Delatte (1939: 129–87). The anonymous commentary is unpublished, as are the scholia, but the prologue has been edited by Tannery (1893–5: ii. 73–7). Giardina (1999) has reproduced Hoche's text of Philoponus, with an Italian translation. For further information see D'Ooge (1926), the introduction to Tarán (1969), and Mansfeld (1998).

2.4.3 Lucian

Since Lucian lived in the second century AD, well after the great age of Hellenistic scholarship, one might reasonably expect that the scholia to his works would have little to offer. But the scholiasts to Lucian drew on lost works of ancient scholarship that go back long before his time, so their products are useful even for historical information on classical Athens. There is of course also a significant Byzantine component, including much amusing castigation of the author by Christian readers.

The scholia are divided into five classes, of which class I represents the oldest commentary (dated, in its final form, to anywhere from the fifth to the ninth century), class II represents the commentary of Arethas (ninth–tenth century, but using earlier material), and classes III–V represent a combination of the two. The most important ancient sources of the scholia seem to be lexica and lost paroemiographical works.

The standard text of the scholia is that of Rabe (1906 =*TLG*), which does not include all the scholia that appear in the manuscripts. The main studies are those of Helm (1908) and Winter (1908). J. Schneider (1994: 196–9) offers a good summary of previous research with further references, and Lowe (1998), Skov (1975), and Baldwin (1980–1, with further references) provide examples of the way the scholia can be used.

2.4.4 Aelius Aristides

A large body of ancient and Byzantine scholarship on Aelius Aristides (a rhetorician of the second century AD) remains; it comprises a substantial set of scholia as well as prolegomena and hypotheses to some speeches. Much of this material goes back to the fourth-century rhetorician Sopater, who made use of earlier sources, but Sopater's work has been considerably tampered with by subsequent scholiasts and is not always easy to distinguish. There is also a body of scholia by Arethas (ninth–tenth century, but based on Sopater).

The ancient scholarship on Aristides is useful not only for the information it provides about the author and his works, but also for historical information going as far back as classical Athens. However, use of the scholia is hindered by the lack of a reliable edition.

The standard and only complete text of the scholia is that of W. Dindorf (1829 =*TLG*), which simply prints the eighteenth-century collation of Reiske and is completely untrustworthy. For orations 1–3 a better choice is Frommel's edition

(1826), but this work has its own flaws and is rarely cited because of its obscurity. A new edition of the whole is urgently needed. There is, however, a good study by Lenz (1934); see also Pernot (1981: 260–5). The prolegomena have been well edited and thoroughly studied by Lenz (1959); see also Behr (1968: 142–7). Examples of the uses of the scholia are provided by Piccirilli (1983), Thompson (1985), and Stichel (1988).

2.4.5 Oppian

Oppian, a poet of the second century AD, has left us a little-noticed poem about fish entitled *Halieutica*; a *Cynegetica* is also attributed to him but now considered spurious. Scholarly material is preserved for both poems and includes extensive scholia as well as full-length prose paraphrases attributed to one Eutecnius, who may have lived in the fourth century AD.

The paraphrase of the *Halieutica*, of which only the second half survives, is preserved in a very early manuscript (*c*.500 AD) and so is important for the establishment of the text of the poem itself, which is not found in manuscripts earlier than the twelfth century and is seriously corrupt. The standard text of this paraphrase is that of Papathomopoulos (1976), but Gualandri's edition (1968) is also usable; there are studies by Fajen (1979) and Gualandri (1968). The paraphrase of the *Cynegetica* is generally ignored but can be found in Bussemaker (1849).

The scholia, which seem to be at least primarily Byzantine, have an interesting history, in that some of them were transmitted independently of the text from the sixteenth century. The *Cynegetica* scholia consist largely of glosses and are rarely mentioned; a text can be found in Bussemaker (1849 =*TLG*). The *Halieutica* scholia are substantial (much larger than the poem itself) and fall into three groups, A, B, and C, of which only A has been published, and that only partially and inadequately (by Bussemaker 1849 (=*TLG*) and Vári 1909). The A scholia appear to derive primarily from the work of Tzetzes. There are a number of studies of their textual history; see Fajen (1969: 32–3) and Leverenz (1999, with further references). For an example of the use of the scholia see Dyck (1982*a*).

2.4.6 Other Authors

Scholia or commentaries to a number of other authors exist but are rarely mentioned, usually because of their poor quality or their inaccessibility. Some of these are:

A set of Byzantine scholia to the *De materia medica* of Dioscorides Pedanius (first century AD) is published in the apparatus of Wellmann (1906–14) and discussed by Riddle (1984) and N. Wilson (1971: 557–8).

A few scholia to the geometrical works of Hero of Alexandria (first century AD) have been published by Heiberg (1914: 222–32).

A Neoplatonist commentary on the *Encheiridion* of the Stoic Epictetus (first–second century), composed by Simplicius (6th century), has been edited and discussed by I. Hadot (1996) and translated by Brittain and Brennan (2002).

Some Byzantine scholia to Plutarch have been edited and discussed by Manfredini (1975, 1979).

Dionysius Periegeta (second century) produced a didactic poem with a description of the world. There is an extant commentary by Eustathius, far longer than the poem itself and important for its preservation of portions of Strabo and of Stephanus of Byzantium that do not survive elsewhere; also a substantial body of scholia and a detailed prose paraphrase. All this material can be found in Bernhardy's edition (1828), which is essentially reproduced in Müller (1861 =TLG) and of which a critique, corrections, and partial re-edition are provided by Ludwich (1884–5: ii. 553–97 =TLG); see also Sakellaridou-Sotiroudi (1993).

A small body of scholia to Pausanias has been published by Spiro (1894 =TLG; 1903: iii. 218–22). These scholia are Byzantine (but drawing on earlier material) and useful primarily for studies of the history of the text of Pausanias and of classical scholarship in the Byzantine period. They have been studied by Reitzenstein (1894), Wilamowitz (1894), and Diller (1956: 87, 96).

The scholia to Marcus Aurelius' *Meditations* are of little value except for establishing the history of the text. They consist primarily of Byzantine glosses and have never been fully published. A few are printed by Schenkl (1913: 160–1), and Dalfen (1978) offers a detailed discussion.

A few scholia to the works of Maximus of Tyre (a philosopher of the second century) are printed at the bottom of relevant pages of Hobein's edition (1910).

There is a small set of tenth-century scholia to the *Anaplus Bospori* of Dionysius of Byzantium, a minor geographer from the second century. They can be found in Güngerich (1927 =TLG).

The works of Hermogenes, a rhetorician who lived in the second and third centuries, attracted commentary from the third century onward. Two long commentaries by the fifth-century Aristotelian commentator Syrianus are preserved intact and have been edited by Rabe (1892–3). An enormous body of scholia is also preserved, including much material from the fourth and fifth centuries AD; it can be found in Walz (1832–6: vols. iv–vii).

A few scholia to the *Progymnasmata* of Aelius Theon,[46] a rhetorician of unknown date, are published by Walz (1832–6: i. 257–62 =TLG); they appear to be taken from the scholia to Aphthonius.

Later authors are beyond the scope of this study, but scholia and commentaries on their works are not uncommon. Gregory of Nazianzus, Oribasius, Diophantus, and Aphthonius, for example, are the subject of extensive surviving commentary. For further information on Byzantine commentary on these (and earlier) authors see Hunger (1978: ii. 55–77).

---

46. Listed in reference works under Theon, not Aelius.

3

Other Scholarly Works

WHILE THE PRODUCTION OF TEXTS AND COMMENTARIES on literary works was probably the primary goal of ancient scholarship, other lines of work were pursued as well, particularly in the later Hellenistic and Roman periods. Among these other scholarly genres were the grammatical treatise, in which scholars analysed the classical Greek language and tried to codify the underlying principles of correct usage, and the lexicon, in which unusual words were collected, classified, and explained. (Two other popular genres, mythography and paroemiography, have been excluded from this book but were clearly related to the scholarly genres discussed here.) Modern interest currently focuses on the grammatical writings much more than on lexica, and thus it is much easier to find reliable texts, commentaries, and translations of grammatical works than of lexica; precisely for this reason, however, the latter offer greater opportunities for future work.

This section includes only authors whose works still survive and ones whose fragments are normally consulted in a collected edition; that is, those who currently have an independent existence as authors. Many other ancient scholars have left traces in scholia or later authors, but the issues involved in finding and reading those traces have less to do with the original scholar than with the works in which the fragments are preserved, so they are not treated here. (For further information on using them, see the footnotes in Chapter 1.) A useful source of additional information on the authors in this chapter, and on many grammarians not covered here, is the *Lessico dei grammatici greci antichi* (*LGGA*), available at http://www.aristarchus.unige.it/lgga. This site provides very detailed information but currently includes only a few authors; it is hoped that eventually it will become a major resource for the study of ancient grammarians.

3.1 GRAMMATICAL TREATISES

Our understanding of the evolution of Greek grammar is complicated by the loss of most of the early works on the subject and by controversy over the authenticity of the earliest surviving treatise. Fortunately, much remains from the writings of two crucial figures from the second century AD, Apollonius Dyscolus and Herodian.

3.1.1 Apollonius Dyscolus

The works of Apollonius Dyscolus[1] are the most important and influential of surviving grammatical treatises. In antiquity and the Byzantine world Apollonius was
considered the greatest grammarian, and it is no coincidence that far more remains of his work than of any other Greek grammarian before the Byzantine period. Apollonius, who lived in Alexandria in the mid-second century AD and was
the father of the grammarian Herodian, wrote numerous treatises, of which four
survive: the *Syntax* (a major work in four books) and shorter treatises on pronouns,
adverbs, and conjunctions. Considerable portions of his other writings can be
extracted from Priscian, who translated much of Apollonius' work into Latin (and
through whom Apollonius exerted a powerful influence on the entire Western
grammatical tradition), and from scholia and commentaries, especially the "scholia"
to Dionysius Thrax.[2]

Apollonius may have invented syntax as a grammatical discipline; even if he
did not, his works are the earliest surviving discussions of the topic and represent
an important and original contribution that laid the foundations for future discussion. His analyses are theoretical rather than didactic and are concerned with
discovering the underlying rules that govern the regularities of language; his goal
is the construction of a theoretical framework that accounts for all the observed
facts about the aspects of the Greek language he considers. Although his works
are primarily important for their portrayal of Apollonius' own ideas, they are also
useful as sources of information on the lost writings of earlier scholars, since they
include numerous references to Zenodotus, Aristarchus, and others. Apollonius
seems to have been particularly indebted to Trypho, though (perhaps because the
latter was a scholarly "grandchild" of Aristarchus) Aristarchus' direct and indirect
influence is also considerable.

There are two editions with a good claim to be the standard text of the *Syntax*:
that of Uhlig (*Grammatici Graeci* (*GG*) ii.ii =*TLG*) and Lallot's text (1997), which
is based on Uhlig's and scrupulously notes all deviations from it. Bekker's version
(1817) is seriously out of date. There is an English translation of the *Syntax* (Householder 1981), but the French version (Lallot 1997) is much better; one can also
find Spanish (Bécares Botas 1987) and German (Buttmann 1877) versions, and
Uhlig gives a running Latin paraphrase in his edition.

The minor works are more problematic, since they survive in only one manuscript, and since damage to that manuscript makes the text very difficult to establish in a number of places. The standard edition of these works is currently that
of R. Schneider (*GG* ii.i (=*TLG*), with extensive commentary in *GG* i.ii = ii.i.ii),

---

1. This Apollonius is sometimes known as Apollonius Alexandrinus but is to be distinguished from the numerous other Apollonii involved with ancient scholarship, many
of whom are also associated with Alexandria.

2. When these "scholia" agree with Priscian, both are usually assumed to be derived
from Apollonius even if his name is not explicitly mentioned.

but it is possible that Dalimier's edition (2001) will supersede Schneider's for the *Conjunctions*, of which any text is something of a creative reconstruction. Brandenburg (2005) has produced a new edition of the *Pronouns* (differing little from that of Schneider) that will probably win adherents, and Maas (1911*b*) gives a text (based on Schneider) of *Pronouns* 3.1–49.7. Part of the text preserved with the *Adverbs* (201.1–210.5) appears to belong not to that work but to the lost portion of the fourth book of the *Syntax*, and in consequence is reprinted in Lallot (1997). All the minor works have also been edited by Bekker (1813; 1814–21: vol. ii), though that edition is now a last resort. Translations are sparse: Dalimier gives a French translation of the *Conjunctions* (2001) and Brandenburg a German one of the *Pronouns* (2005), while Lallot (1997) and Householder (1981) both include translations of the portion of *Adverbs* thought to belong to the *Syntax* (a complete translation of the *Adverbs* is in preparation by Sylvain Broquet). There are also Schneider's Latin summaries (*GG* ii.i).

Numerous fragments of Apollonius' lost works survive (many of them in Latin, since Priscian is one of the chief sources). The most important of the lost works are Περὶ ὀνομάτων and Περὶ ῥημάτων; others include Περὶ ὀρθογραφίας, Περὶ διαλέκτων, Περὶ στοιχείων, and Περὶ προσῳδιῶν. They are usually best consulted in R. Schneider's edition of Apollonius' fragments (*GG* ii.iii), though when the source text of a fragment has received a good new edition since 1910, it is prudent to consult that version as well.

References to Apollonius' works are usually given by work, page, and line number of the *Grammatici Graeci* texts; these numbers are reproduced in the margins by Lallot and Dalimier (but not Householder). Older works, including some (but not all) cross-references within the *Grammatici Graeci* edition, use Bekker's numeration, which Uhlig, Schneider, and Householder print in their margins but which does not appear in Lallot's or Dalimier's editions. LSJ uses Bekker's numeration for the *Syntax* but Schneider's pagination for the other works. Occasionally one also finds references by book and paragraph numbers, which remain constant in all editions but do not allow for sufficient precision when dealing with an author as difficult as Apollonius.

Apollonius' style is notoriously opaque and elliptical, and his terminology is idiosyncratic; indeed since antiquity one of the explanations offered for his nickname δύσκολος "troublesome" has been a reference to the sufferings he inflicted on his readers. As a result, there are a number of special aids to understanding Apollonius' writings. Uhlig and Schneider provide glossaries/indices (*GG* ii.ii: 507–29; *GG* ii.iii: 162–283) with Latin translations of much of Apollonius' terminology, and Dalimier (2001: 437–75) offers a similar tool for the words appearing in *Conjunctions*. Bednarski (1994) has even produced a book-length study of Apollonius' grammatical terminology. Schneider also provides a detailed discussion of the peculiarities of Apollonius' grammar and syntax (*GG* ii.iii: 141–61). Both Uhlig (*GG* ii.ii: 530–7) and Lallot (1997: i. 88–95) give detailed tables of contents of the *Syntax*, Dalimier (2001: 61–2) does the same for the *Conjunctions*, and Schneider provides such help for all the minor works (*GG* ii.i: 259–64).

Modern scholarship on Apollonius, which is abundant, tends to focus on the *Syntax*. The importance of Apollonius' work, combined with its difficulty, offers fertile ground for debate about the meanings of his theories; other topics investigated include Apollonius' originality, his debt to the Stoics and other predecessors, the interpretation of his terminology, the textual tradition, and the extent to which Apollonius can be claimed to have anticipated modern syntactic theories. An excellent introduction to Apollonius, with commentary on earlier work, is offered by Blank (1993), while extensive discussions are provided by Lallot (1997), Dalimier (2001), Blank (1982), Ildefonse (1997), Thierfelder (1935), Egger (1854), and Lange (1852). Treatments of specific points include those of Kemp (1991: 316–30), Lallot (1985, 1994a, 1994b), Blank (1994), Van Ophuijsen (1993a), and Sluiter (1990); for further bibliography see the recent major studies and Schmidhauser (forthcoming).

3.1.2 Herodian

Aelius Herodianus[3] (second century AD), son of Apollonius Dyscolus, is responsible for most of our knowledge of ancient accentuation. His main work, the Περὶ καθολικῆς προσῳδίας, is said originally to have given the rules for attaching accents and breathings to perhaps as many as 60,000 Greek words, with explanations based on their terminations, number of syllables, gender, and other qualities; it now survives in fragments and epitomes and is one of the major extant grammatical works despite being considerably reduced in size. The only one of Herodian's works to survive intact is the Περὶ μονήρους λέξεως, a treatise on anomalous words. Two smaller works that predate the Περὶ καθολικῆς προσῳδίας, the Περὶ Ἰλιακῆς προσῳδίας and the Περὶ Ὀδυσσειακῆς προσῳδίας, focus on Homeric accentuation and are preserved in fragments gathered from the Homeric scholia. Other grammatical works of which substantial fragments survive include the Περὶ παθῶν (on modifications of words), Περὶ ὀρθογραφίας (on spelling), and Περὶ κλίσεως ὀνομάτων (on the declension of nouns).

Herodian's rules were meant to apply to classical and Homeric words, i.e. to a state of the language six centuries and more before his own time. It is clear that he possessed some knowledge of this earlier state of the language and the ways in which its accentuation system differed from that of the language he spoke, for his pronouncements can sometimes be proven right by modern techniques of comparative philology. Yet it is uncertain what his ultimate source was: we know that Alexandrian scholars from Aristophanes of Byzantium (c.257–c.180 BC) onward worked on accentuation, and Herodian certainly built on a tradition going back to these scholars, but even they were too distanced from classical and Homeric Greek to possess any native-speaker knowledge of those dialects. Many modern scholars believe that the Alexandrians drew on a living tradition of accentuation going back to the classical period and perhaps beyond, but there is some debate as to the form and extent of that tradition.

---

3. Not to be confused with the historian Herodian (2nd–3rd cent. AD).

Working with Herodian is difficult because of the dubious state of the text. The only collected edition of his works is that of Lentz (*GG* iii.i–ii = Lentz 1867– 70 =*TLG*), but this edition often presents a somewhat fanciful attempt at a reconstruction of Herodian's work, rather than laying out the surviving evidence; Lentz's text can never be assumed to be Herodian's without further examination. Fortunately Dyck (1993*a*) provides a detailed, work-by-work explanation of the problems and available aids; this piece should always be consulted when using Lentz (or any other work on Herodian). References to Herodian are usually given by volume, page, and line number of Lentz.

In many cases use of Lentz's edition can be avoided by going back to his sources, and this is usually advisable where practical. The main sources for the Καθολικὴ προσῳδία are two epitomes, one misattributed to Arcadius and the other by Joannes Philoponus of Alexandria; although there are no real critical editions of the epitomes, the first of them can be consulted in Moritz Schmidt (1860 =*TLG*), or failing that in E. Barker (1820), and the second in W. Dindorf (1825). We now also have portions of two other epitomes, both unknown to Lentz: a palimpsest containing portions of books 5–7 (Hunger 1967) and a fourth-century papyrus fragment containing part of book 5 (*P.Ant.* ii. 67; see Wouters 1979: 216–24).

For the remains of the Περὶ Ἰλιακῆς προσῳδίας, which is entirely fragmentary, Lentz (*GG* iii.ii: 22–128) reprints Lehrs's edition (1848: 191–336), a text not without its own problems. Our source for this treatise is the scholia to the *Iliad*, which specifically acknowledge their overall use of Herodian; individual scholia do not usually specify a source, but it is normally assumed that scholia pertaining to accentuation are derived from Herodian's Περὶ Ἰλιακῆς προσῳδίας. Since Erbse's edition of the *Iliad* scholia (1969–88) is much better than the texts at Lehrs's disposal, Lentz can profitably be circumvented by direct consultation of the scholia.[4]

The Περὶ Ὀδυσσειακῆς προσῳδίας likewise survives only in fragments gathered from the scholia, but because the *Odyssey* scholia are less extensive than those to the *Iliad*, less remains of this treatise. The absence of a good edition of the *Odyssey* scholia means that one has little choice but to rely on Lentz's text (*GG* iii.ii: 129–65) and on the additional fragments provided by Ludwich (1891).

The Περὶ παθῶν, a work that now consists of numerous fragments from a variety of sources, presents particular problems. Lentz has incorrectly separated the remains into two works (Ἡρωδιανοῦ περὶ παθῶν, *GG* iii.ii: 166–388, and Ὑπόμνημα τῶν περὶ παθῶν Διδύμου, *GG* iii.ii: 389), as well as arranging the fragments in the wrong order and making some poor editorial decisions. There is nevertheless no good alternative to Lentz for this work.

The Περὶ κλίσεως ὀνομάτων is preserved primarily in fragments found in Choeroboscus' commentary on Theodosius; the edition of this commentary in *GG*

---

4. Erbse marks scholia probably derived from Herodian with the marginal notation "Hrd.," so they are not difficult to find; one can also use his index of words whose accentuation is discussed in the scholia (1969–88: vii. 5–15).

iv. i–ii is far superior to the texts on which Lentz's reconstruction (*GG* iii.ii: 634–777) was based. Some other sources for the treatise were not available to Lentz, including a fifth-century papyrus fragment of an epitome of the work, for which see Wouters (1973; 1979: 231–6).

For the Περὶ μονήρους λέξεως Lentz (*GG* iii.ii: 908–52) reprints Lehrs's (1848: 7–189) text, though without his detailed and useful commentary. Since the work is intact rather than a modern reconstruction, this edition is largely sound, but some important corrections to Lehrs's text can still be made; see Egenolff (1884: 62–70; 1900: 254–5).

Herodian's numerous doubtful and spurious works are omitted from Lentz's edition, but some of these are easier to consult than the genuine works. An Atticist glossary entitled Φιλέταιρος, originally composed sometime between the second and fourth centuries AD, survives in an abridgement that has been edited by Dain (1954 =*TLG*). A treatise Περὶ σχημάτων, composed of two independent works neither of which can be attributed to Herodian, is now available in a critical edition by Hajdú (1998); there are less good editions in Walz (1832–6: viii. 578–610) and Spengel (1856: 83–104 =*TLG*). An epitome of this treatise also exists and can be found only in Hajdú (1998). The Περὶ σολοικισμοῦ καὶ βαρβαρισμοῦ and the Περὶ ἀκυρολογίας have been edited by Nauck (1867: 294–312 =*TLG*, 313–20), and Vitelli (1889) has provided supplements to the latter. A transcript of a manuscript of the Σχηματισμοὶ Ὁμηρικοί has been published by Egenolff (1894 =*TLG*). The Περὶ παραγωγῶν γενικῶν ἀπὸ διαλέκτων and Περὶ τῶν ζητουμένων κατὰ πάσης κλίσεως ὀνόματος are edited by Cramer (1836: 228–36, 246–55 =*TLG*; some other fragments attributed to Herodian can also be found in this volume). The Περὶ αὐθυποτάκτων καὶ ἀνυποτάκτων is printed by Bekker (1814–21: iii.1086–8 =*TLG*), and a short metrical work called Περὶ τῆς λέξεως τῶν στίχων is carefully edited by Studemund (1867; superseded edition by De Furia 1814: 88 =*TLG*). The Παρεκβολαὶ τοῦ μεγάλου ῥήματος can be found in La Roche (1863 =*TLG*).

The only portions of Herodian's works that have been translated are the papyri, by Wouters (1979).

Discussion of Herodian's work, while less abundant than discussion of Apollonius Dyscolus, is not uncommon. It focuses on textual and interpretive problems, on the literary fragments to be found in the text, and on the sources (both immediate and ultimate) for Herodian's knowledge of classical and Homeric accentuation. Dyck (1993*a*) offers an excellent introduction and further bibliography, and other useful works include those of Dyck (1977, 1981), Argyle (1989), Erbse (1960: 344–406), Van der Valk (1963–4: i. 592–602), Martin Schmidt (1976: 32–5), Wackernagel (1893, 1914*a*, 1914*b*), and Laum (1928).

3.1.3 Dionysius Thrax

A short, simple grammatical introduction entitled Τέχνη γραμματική is traditionally attributed to Dionysius (*c*.170–*c*.90 BC), a pupil of Aristarchus. This handbook was enormously influential from late antiquity onwards[5] and is certainly one of the most important surviving grammatical works. If the attribution to Dionysius can be trusted, the handbook is also the only Hellenistic grammatical treatise to survive to modern times. Dionysius' authorship, however, has been doubted since antiquity and has recently been the focus of considerable discussion; some scholars maintain that the entire treatise is a compilation of the third or fourth century AD, while others defend its complete authenticity and date it to the end of the second century BC. There is also a range of intermediate positions, which in recent years have gained much ground against both the more extreme views: some portion of the beginning of the work could go back to Dionysius, while the rest was written later, or the entire work (or sections of it) could be originally Dionysius' but seriously altered (and perhaps abridged) by later writers. Some argue that if the Τέχνη is spurious, we must revise our whole view of the development of Greek grammatical thought, to put the creation of fully developed grammatical analysis in the first century BC. Others maintain that Aristarchus and his followers already possessed an advanced grammatical system and that the date of the Τέχνη therefore makes little difference to our view of the evolution of grammar.

The Τέχνη itself is relatively straightforward; it consists of a concise explanation of the divisions of grammar and definitions of the main grammatical terminology. Because of its extreme brevity, it accumulated a large body of explanatory commentary (this material is all traditionally known as "scholia," but it includes continuous commentaries as well as marginal scholia), which is in many ways more interesting and informative than the text itself, though clearly later. The Τέχνη is also traditionally accompanied by four supplements, which are probably old but later than the text itself: Περὶ προσῳδιῶν (De prosodiis), Περὶ τέχνης (Definitio artis), Περὶ ποδῶν καὶ περὶ τοῦ ἡρωϊκοῦ μέτρου (De pedibus et de metro heroico), and a paradigm of the declension of τύπτω derived from the Κανόνες of Theodosius. Some of these supplements are the subjects of additional commentaries. Both "scholia" and supplements contain valuable information about other ancient grammatical writings, particularly the lost works of Apollonius Dyscolus, and cover a wide variety of topics.

Dionysius also wrote a number of other works that survive only in fragments, including various grammatical works and a commentary on Homer. As unquestioned testimonia to Dionysius' grammatical ideas, these 59 short fragments (47 of them on Homer) are important for the debate over the authenticity of the Τέχνη as well as for studies of Hellenistic grammatical thought.

The standard text of the Τέχνη is that of Uhlig in Grammatici Graeci (vol. i.i =TLG), with a thorough discussion of the textual tradition, extensive apparatus, and superbly detailed indices that include much information on the meanings and usage of Greek terms; this text is reprinted in Lallot (1998) and Swiggers and Wouters (1998). A more recent text by Pecorella (1962) has not superseded Uhlig's edition (see Lallot 1998: 15), and the older edition by Bekker (1814–21: vol. ii)

5. Arguably even to the present day; see Wouters (1979: 35).

should be used only as a last resort. Translations of the Τέχνη abound; there is an English version by Kemp (1986), a German one by Kürschner (1996), and a Dutch one by Swiggers and Wouters (1998) in addition to the important French translation by Lallot (1998).

The supplements and "scholia" are best consulted in *Grammatici Graeci* (supplements on pp. 103–32 of vol. i.i, "scholia" in vol. i.iii (=*TLG*), good indices in both volumes); the first three supplements can also be found in Pecorella's edition (1962). None of the translations of the Τέχνη include these works, but the commentaries by Lallot (1998) and Robins (1993) include translations or summaries of many of the most important "scholia." Uhlig, in his introduction to *GG* i.i, offers an excellent discussion of the content, sources, and textual tradition of both "scholia" and supplements; a more detailed treatment of the "scholia" is provided by Hilgard in the introduction to *GG* i.iii, and a shorter overview can be found in Lallot (1998: 31–6). The fragments do not appear in *Grammatici Graeci*; the best edition of them is that of Linke (1977 =*TLG*), who provides a good introduction and commentary. In the absence of this edition, Moritz Schmidt (1852) provides a poor substitute.

References to works that appear in *Grammatici Graeci* are usually made by work, page, and line number of that edition, though references to the Τέχνη are sometimes given by the pages of Bekker's edition, which Uhlig prints in the margins, or simply by chapter numbers (though this is unkind, especially in the longer chapters). Older works, including cross-references within the *Grammatici Graeci* editions, use Bekker's numeration for both Τέχνη and "scholia."

The best introductions to the Τέχνη are those of Lallot (1998) and Swiggers and Wouters (1998). The work has recently been the subject of an enormous amount of scholarly attention, much of it devoted to the questions of the dating of the Τέχνη and whether Dionysius himself had a fully developed system of grammatical analysis; pieces on these issues include those of Erbse (1980), Kemp (1991: 307–15), Di Benedetto (1990, 2000), Blank (2000), Ax (1982), Schenkeveld (1983, 1994: 266–9), Law (1990), Ildefonse (1997: 447–59), and Law and Sluiter (1995). Works that deal with other issues include those of Lallot (1995), Wouters (1975, 1979, 1991–3, 2000), Swiggers and Wouters (1994, 1995*a*, 1995*b*), Robins (1986, 1993: 41–86, 1996), Pecorella (1962), Fuhrmann (1960: 29–34, 144–56), Siebenborn (1976), and Pantiglioni (1998). Treatments of the "scholia" and supplements are much rarer than those of the Τέχνη itself, but still not uncommon; they include the works of Caujolle-Zaslawsky (1985), Lallot (1985: 70–4), Rijksbaron (1986), Robins (1993: 41–86), Wouters (1994), Erbse (1960: 213–29), R. Schneider (1874), Hoerschelmann (1874), and Moritz Schmidt (1853: 243–7). For further bibliography see Lallot (1998) and Swiggers and Wouters (1994, 1998).

The Τέχνη was translated into both Armenian and Syriac in the fifth to sixth century AD; these translations, and commentaries on the Τέχνη in those languages, are discussed by Adontz (1970), Clackson (1995), Sgarbi (1990), Merx (*GG* i.i, pp. lvii–lxxiii), and Uhlig (*GG* i.i, pp. xliii–xlvi). The Armenian translation in

particular is sometimes useful in establishing the Greek text, since it represents a
tradition divergent from that of all our extant manuscripts.

3.1.4 Choeroboscus

George Choeroboscus,[6] who lived in the eighth and ninth centuries AD,[7] was a
Byzantine teacher and author of a number of grammatical works. Choeroboscus'
works were not intended as contributions to the advancement of grammatical theory;
they are clearly part of his teaching materials and were often intended for fairly elementary students. Their significance lies in three areas: the light they shed on grammatical teaching in the ninth century, the influence they exerted on later scholars
(including Eustathius and the compiler of the *Etymologicum genuinum*), and their
extensive use of earlier grammatical treatises (Choeroboscus is for example responsible for much of the preservation of Herodian's Περὶ κλίσεως ὀνομάτων).

The longest and most important of Choeroboscus' works is a gigantic commentary on the Κανόνες of Theodosius (see 3.1.7), evidently composed as a teaching
tool, which survives both intact and drastically excerpted in a short collection of
extracts on accents entitled Περὶ τόνων. Choeroboscus also produced a commentary on the Τέχνη of (ps.-) Dionysius Thrax that is preserved in extracts under
the name of Heliodorus.[8] Closely related is Περὶ προσῳδίας, a commentary on
the Περὶ προσῳδιῶν supplement to the Τέχνη, which survives both under Choeroboscus' own name and in a longer version rewritten by Porphyry.[9] From a discussion of correct spelling, Περὶ ὀρθογραφίας, we have both an epitome under that
name, in which difficult words are listed and their correct spellings explained and
justified, and an extract Περὶ ποσότητος "On quantity." Choeroboscus also left
us a commentary on the *Encheiridion* of Hephaestion (discussing Greek meter)
and a set of epimerismi on the Psalms that contain both religious and scholarly
information, and his work is one of the sources of the Περὶ πνευμάτων, a Byzantine collection of extracts on breathings.

6. Sometimes identified by the epithets "diakonos" or "chartophylax."

7. Choeroboscus' dating was long disputed, and in many older books he is put as much
as 200 years earlier, but the later date has recently been definitely established by recog-
nition of Choeroboscus' citations of other late authors; see e.g. Theodoridis (1980) and
N. Wilson (1983a: 70).

8. Until the redating of Choeroboscus, this Heliodorus was thought to be a grammarian of probably the 7th cent. who made the excerpts from Choeroboscus' work. Now it is
unclear when Heliodorus lived and what his exact connection with the excerpts was. There
are a number of known writers of the same name with whom he is probably not to be
identified, including the author of the novel *Aethiopica*; the Homerist; the metrician
mentioned in the scholia to Aristophanes; a Neoplatonist philosopher who was the son
of Hermeias and brother of Ammonius; a bishop of Tricca; Heliodorus Periegeta the
antiquarian; and Heliodorus Arabius the sophist.

9. This Porphyry is not the 3rd-cent. Neoplatonist who left works on Homer, Plato,
Aristotle, and Ptolemy, nor either of the Latin writers Publilius Optatianus Porfyrius and
Pomponius Porphyrio, but an otherwise unknown later scholar; see *GG* i.iii, pp. xxi–xxii.

There are also a number of extant works of uncertain authorship that are sometimes attributed to Choeroboscus. These include the *Epimerismi Homerici* (see 2.1.1.3) and a short work on poetical figures of speech entitled Περὶ τρόπων ποιητικῶν.

The *Grammatici Graeci* collection contains Choeroboscus' most important grammatical works: the intact version of the commentary on Theodosius (iv.i: 101–iv.ii: 371 =*TLG*), the extracts from the commentary on the Τέχνη (i.iii: 67–106 =*TLG*; cf. i.i, p. xxxiv, and i.iii, pp. xiv–xviii), and both versions of the Περὶ προσῳδίας commentary (i.iii: 124–50 =*TLG*; cf. i.i, pp. l–li, iv.ii (original, = iv.i in reprint), pp. lxx–lxxii). Other works are scattered through older publications; the Περὶ ὀρθογραφίας epitome can be found in Cramer[10] and the Περὶ ποσότητος extract from it is in the same volume.[11] The commentary on Hephaestion has been edited by Consbruch (1906: 175–254 =*TLG*), the Περὶ πνευμάτων by Valckenaer (1822: 188–215 =*TLG*), and the epimerismi on the Psalms by Gaisford (1842: vol. iii =*TLG*). The Περὶ τόνων extracts are given by Koster (1932 =*TLG*), the *Epimerismi Homerici* have been edited by Dyck (1983–95 =*TLG*), and the Περὶ τρόπων ποιητικῶν can be found in Walz (1832–6: viii. 799–820) and Spengel (1856: 244–56 =*TLG*).

In addition to the works mentioned above, discussion of Choeroboscus is provided by Hilgard (*GG* iv.ii (original) or iv.i (reprint): esp. pp. lxi–xc), Kaster (1988: 394–6), F. Montanari (1997*a*), Cohn (1899), N. Wilson (1983*a*: 69–74), Erbse (1960: 213–29), Richard (1950: 202–3), M. L. West (1965*b*: 232), Rijksbaron (1986: 435–7), Hunger (1978: ii. 11, 13–14, 19, 23, 50), and Egenolff (1887, 1888). Kaster (1988), F. Montanari (1997*a*), and Cohn (1899) provide further bibliography.

3.1.5 Philoponus

The sixth-century philosopher Ioannes Philoponus of Alexandria,[12] who is known primarily for his heretical Christian theology and for his commentaries on Aristotle (for which see 2.2.3), is also credited with several grammatical works, three of which survive. One, the Τονικὰ παραγγέλματα, was originally an epitome of Herodian's Περὶ καθολικῆς προσῳδίας. The surviving work is very brief and seems to be an epitome of Philoponus' epitome, which was used in a fuller form by Eustathius. It is useful because Herodian's original work has been lost.

---

10. Cramer (1835: 167–281 =*TLG*); cf. R. Schneider (1887: 20–9) and *GG* iv.ii (orig.) or iv.i (repr.), pp. lxxviii–lxxx.

11. Cramer (1835: 283–330); cf. R. Schneider (1887: 29–33) and *GG* iv.ii (orig.) or iv.i (repr.), pp. lxxx–lxxxi.

12. Often called John of Alexandria and occasionally Joannes Grammaticus, but to be distinguished from the John of Alexandria who produced commentaries on Galen and Hippocrates in the 6th/7th cent.; from the 5th-cent. Joannes Grammaticus of Antioch; and from the 9th-cent. iconoclast Joannes Grammaticus.

Philoponus also produced a treatise on homonyms that are distinguished only by their accents, which survives (probably in abbreviated form) in many manuscripts but for which there is no established title. The work is probably based to some extent on Herodian, but the extent of its dependence on Herodian and the degree of interpolation it underwent between Philoponus' time and our earliest manuscripts are both matters of debate. The treatise consists of pairs of words with a short definition of each; some pairs, such as βίος "life" and βιός "bow," are genuinely homonyms apart from the accent, but others, such as ἕτερος and ἑταῖρος, are spelled very differently and were homophonous only in postclassical Greek pronunciation.

Philoponus is also credited with a Περὶ διαλέκτων, which was an important source for Gregory of Corinth and of which some abbreviated extracts survive directly. The remains are short and basic and rarely considered useful today, though they have some value for the history of the Greek perception of dialects.

The grammatical works of Philoponus are not easy to consult. The only edition of the Τονικὰ παραγγέλματα is the very rare text of W. Dindorf from 1825, and the Περὶ διαλέκτων was last edited by Hoffmann (1893: 204–22). The work on homonyms has recently been edited by Daly (1983 =TLG), who found it impractical to reconstruct a common text from the disparate manuscript tradition and so gives five separate versions; there is also an earlier edition by Egenolff (1880) that reproduces only one of the forty-four manuscripts. The most thorough discussion is that of Kroll (1916, with further references), but see also Koster (1932).

3.1.6 Gregory of Corinth

Gregorios (or Georgios) Pardos, bishop of Corinth probably in the eleventh to twelfth centuries,[13] was the author of a number of extant scholarly works, as well as some religious and rhetorical writings. His most famous work is the Περὶ διαλέκτων ("On dialects"), which discusses the Greek literary dialects (Attic, Doric, Ionic, and Aeolic). Although this treatise is not very accurate, it is useful for understanding the Greeks' perception of their own dialect situation, and it preserves some earlier scholarship, for it is based on lost dialectological works of Trypho and Philoponus. Gregory's other productions include the Περὶ συντάξεως λόγου, a work of less than the highest quality that is the third oldest Greek syntactic work we possess (after those of Apollonius Dyscolus and Michael Syncellus); its attribution to Gregory has been questioned but is now accepted as correct (Donnet 1967: 16–19). A short treatise Περὶ τρόπων, discussing rhetorical figures, has been attributed to Gregory but certainly predates him; it may have been written by Trypho (M. L. West 1965b). A long commentary on the Περὶ μεθόδου δεινότητος ("On the method of forcefulness") attributed to Hermogenes is a teaching tool and discusses various passages in classical literature as well as rhetorical

---

13. Gregory's dating has been debated; he used to be put in the 12th–13th cents., and while most now believe that he was bishop after 1092 and before 1156, some place him in the 10th cent. See Laurent (1963), Becares (1988), and Montana (1995: pp. xlviii–xlix).

issues; this work may be based partly on lost ancient sources, but it is now generally neglected.

Most of Gregory's works can be consulted in only one edition. For the Περὶ διαλέκτων, this edition is that of G. Schaefer (1811); for the Περὶ συντάξεως λόγου that of Donnet (1967); and for the Hermogenes commentary that of Walz (1832–6: vii. 1088–1352). The best edition of the misattributed Περὶ τρόπων is that of M. L. West (1965b), but it can also be found in Walz (1832–6: viii. 761–78) and Spengel (1856: 215–26). Only the Περὶ συντάξεως λόγου has been translated, into French by Donnet (1967).

Discussions of Gregory's works include those of Kominis (1960), Donnet (1966, 1967), N. Wilson (1983a: 184–90), Bolognesi (1953), Glucker (1970), Montana (1995), Robins (1993: 163–72), and Hunger (1982); for further bibliography see Montana (1995), Donnet (1967), and Kominis (1960).

3.1.7 Theodosius

Theodosius of Alexandria, who lived probably in the fourth and fifth centuries AD,[14] was the author of the Κανόνες, a set of rules and paradigms for declensions and conjugations. This long and detailed work was a teaching tool intended to supplement the Τέχνη of (ps.-) Dionysius Thrax and appears to be the ancestor of the fourth supplement to that work. It gives all theoretically possible forms of the words it illustrates (most famously in an ultra-complete paradigm of τύπτω), thus producing a large number of forms unattested in actual usage. Partly as a result of this inclusiveness, the Κανόνες are not highly respected today, but for many centuries they exerted an important influence on Greek textbooks.

Two lengthy commentaries on the Κανόνες survive; that of Choeroboscus (eighth–ninth century) is intact, and that of Joannes Charax (sixth–eighth century) is preserved in an excerpted version by Sophronius (ninth century). These commentaries, particularly that of Choeroboscus (see 3.1.4), are now considered more important than the Κανόνες themselves.

The best text of the Κανόνες is that of Hilgard (GG iv.i =TLG); this work offers not only a critical edition, detailed introduction, and indices, but also texts of the commentaries of Choeroboscus and Charax / Sophronius.

Theodosius is also credited with short treatises entitled Περὶ κλίσεως τῶν εἰς ῶν βαρυτόνων and Περὶ κλίσεως τῶν εἰς ῶν ὀξυτόνων (text of both in Hilgard 1887: 16–22, 22–4 =TLG) and he may be responsible for the Περὶ προσῳδιῶν supplement to (ps.-) Dionysius Thrax's Τέχνη (q.v.; text in GG i.i. 105–14 =TLG). Spurious works include a long Περὶ γραμματικῆς (text in Goettling 1822: 1–197 =TLG), and shorter works entitled Περὶ διαλέκτων (text in R. Schneider 1894 =TLG), and Περὶ τόνου (text in Goettling 1822: 198–201 =TLG).

---

14. This Theodosius is to be distinguished from a number of emperors with the same name, one of whom was responsible for the Theodosian Code, and from Theodosius of Bithynia, an astronomer and mathematician who wrote c.100 BC.

Discussion of Theodosius' works is not extensive, but information can be found in Kaster (1988: 366–7), N. Wilson (1983a: 42–3), Robins (1993: 111–15), Hunger (1978: ii. 11–12), Oguse (1957), and Wouters (1979, esp. 271–2). Kaster (1988: 366–7) provides further bibliography.

3.1.8 Trypho

Trypho(n) son of Ammonius, a scholarly "grandchild" of Aristarchus who worked in Rome in the second half of the first century BC,[15] is a somewhat elusive figure who probably made crucial contributions to the development of Greek grammatical thought, though little of his work survives. His name carried great authority for later writers, especially Apollonius Dyscolus, and much of what we know about him comes from their citations.

The surviving portions of Trypho's work amount to 109 fragments, most of them short, and several extant treatises; all the latter are of doubtful authenticity and, if descended from Trypho's own work at all, were probably severely altered in transmission. A treatise on rhetorical figures entitled Περὶ τρόπων is preserved under Trypho's name, and another treatise of the same name, misattributed in modern times to Gregory of Corinth, is ascribed to Trypho in the manuscripts and may in fact descend (with alterations) from his work. The Περὶ παθῶν τῆς λέξεως, which classifies linguistic changes, irregularities, and dialect forms, probably contains at least some authentic work of Trypho and could be simply an abridgement of his work on that topic. A Byzantine collection of excerpts on breathings, Περὶ πνευμάτων, claims Trypho's treatise of that name as one of its sources. A substantial fragment of a Τέχνη γραμματική, attributed to Trypho in a papyrus of c.300 AD, is probably not the work of this grammarian but could be by a later scholar of the same name, and the Περὶ μέτρων ("On meters") and Περὶ τοῦ ὥς ("On the particle ὥς") are not by Trypho.

Editions of Trypho's work are almost all very old. The standard edition of the fragments is that of Velsen (1853 =TLG), which omits the extant treatises and a more recently discovered fragment (the latter published by Pasquali in 1910). The Περὶ τρόπων attributed to Trypho can be found in Walz (1832–6: viii. 726–60) and Spengel (1856: 189–206 =TLG), and the Περὶ τρόπων attributed to Gregory of Corinth is best consulted in M. L. West (1965b =TLG) but also available in Walz (1832–6: viii. 761–78) and Spengel (1856: 215–26). R. Schneider (1895 =TLG) provides a text of the Περὶ παθῶν, and Valckenaer (1822: 188–215) one of the Περὶ πνευμάτων compilation. A good edition of the Τέχνη γραμματική fragment, with translation and commentary, is provided by Wouters (1979: 61–92), but the original edition by Kenyon (1891) is also usable. Matthaios (forthcoming) is expected to provide a complete re-edition of all Trypho's works.

Trypho has not been much studied in recent years, but there are some useful discussions. Probably the most helpful is Wendel (1939b); others include Sieben-

---

15. There is also a second and probably later grammarian named Trypho, about whose work little is known.

born (1976: 48–9, 89, 150–1, 161–2), Fraser (1972: i. 474, ii. 687–8), Wackernagel (1876: 26–32), and Bapp (1885). For further bibliography see Wendel (1939*b*) and Baumbach (2002).

3.1.9 Tyrannio and Diocles

These two grammarians tend to be treated together because they are impossible to distinguish completely. Tyrannio(n), also known as Tyrannio the Elder, was a pupil of Dionysius Thrax and lived from *c*.100 to *c*.25 BC, first in Pontus and then in Rome, where he had a distinguished career that included tutoring Cicero's son and (at least according to some sources) discovering the manuscripts from which our texts of Aristotle ultimately descend. Diocles[16] (first century BC to first century AD) was a pupil of Tyrannio, whose name he adopted, with the result that he is also known as Tyrannio the Younger. It is possible that there was another scholar named Diocles who cannot now be distinguished completely from this Diocles, and in addition Tyrannio the Younger / Diocles cannot be completely distinguished from Tyrannio the Elder. The works of both authors are largely lost; we have a total of 67 fragments of their works, of which 55 come from Tyrannio's Περὶ τῆς Ὁμηρικῆς προσῳδίας, a treatise on Homeric accentuation, and the rest come from a wide variety of other works of both authors.

The standard edition of the fragments of Tyrannio and Diocles is that of Haas (1977 =*TLG*); most of the fragments are from the scholia to the *Iliad* and therefore can also be found in Erbse (1969–88). Discussions are neither common nor extensive; they include those of Haas (1977), Wendel (1948*a*, 1948*b*), Lehmann (1988), Pfeiffer (1968: 272–3), F. Montanari (1997*b*), Chroust (1965: 44–6), Tolkiehn (1915), and Düring (1957). For further bibliography see Haas (1977) and Wendel (1948*a*).

3.1.10 Philoxenus

Philoxenus[17] of Alexandria, a grammarian who worked in Rome in the first century BC, wrote a variety of works that now exist only in fragments. His main work, Περὶ μονοσυλλάβων ῥημάτων, was etymological (probably in the synchronic rather than the historical sense) and concerned with deriving the Greek vocabulary from a core of monosyllabic verbs (as opposed to the Stoic view that the base words were nouns). The surviving fragments therefore come principally from Orion and the etymologica, though scholia are also a major source.

The fragments have been well edited by Theodoridis (1976*a* =*TLG*), with further suggestions by Dyck (1982*c*) and Koniaris (1980), and discussed by Lallot (1991) and Heller (1962).

---

16. This Diocles is to be distinguished from a host of better-known men with the same name, including Diocles of Carystus (a medical writer of the 4th cent. BC), Diocles of Magnesia (a historian of philosophy from the 1st cent. BC), Diocles of Peparethos (a historian probably of the 3rd cent. BC), a mathematician, a comic poet, and several Syracusans.

17. Not to be confused with several poets of the same name.

3.1.11 Theognostus

Theognostus,[18] a Byzantine grammarian of the ninth century AD, has left us a work on correct spelling entitled Περὶ ὀρθογραφίας or Κανόνες. This treatise consists of more than a thousand rules for producing the correct ancient spellings of sounds that had merged in Byzantine Greek, with lists of words illustrating each rule. It is useful today not only for an understanding of Byzantine scholarship but also because it preserves elements of the ancient Greek vocabulary not attested in earlier works. Theognostus' sources were earlier works of scholarship, including Cyrillus and lost works of Herodian.

The best edition of Theognostus, that of Alpers (1964), contains only the beginning of the work; for the rest one must rely on Cramer's text (1835: 1–165 =*TLG*), which was published before the discovery of an important manuscript. For discussion see Alpers (1964), Kambylis (1971), and Bühler (1973).

3.1.12 Michael Syncellus

Between AD 810 and 813 Michael, Syncellus of the Patriarch of Jerusalem, composed a textbook on Greek syntax entitled Μέθοδος περὶ τῆς τοῦ λόγου συντάξεως ("Treatise on the syntax of the sentence"). This work, which makes use of the writings of (ps.-) Dionysius Thrax, Apollonius Dyscolus, and Herodian, is less theoretical than these earlier works and more didactic. It preserves little in the way of fragments of lost works and is primarily of interest as the first Byzantine work on syntax; as such it documents a key stage in the evolution of Greek linguistic thought from antiquity into the Middle Ages.

The treatise is thorough and systematic, covering the syntax of all parts of speech but largely ignoring morphological issues; clearly its author expected his readers to know basic Greek already but to need help in forming correct constructions. The presentation is generally straightforward and the style fairly clear.

The standard edition of Michael's treatise, and the only usable one, is that of Donnet (1982), who provides a good introduction to the work, a detailed description of the complex and abundant manuscript tradition, the complete text with apparatus criticus, facing French translation, and commentary. Discussion of Michael and of the treatise can be found in Robins (1993: 149–62), M. Cunningham (1991), Donnet (1987), and Hunger (1978: ii. 15); further bibliography in Donnet (1982) and M. Cunningham (1991).

3.1.13 Other Grammatical Writers

While the grammarians discussed here are those whose surviving works are the most substantial and significant, there are many other remains as well. Some Byzantine works of considerable dimensions are preserved intact, though these

---

18. This Theognostus is not to be confused with Theognostus of Alexandria, who lived in the 3rd cent. AD, nor with Theognostus the monk, a political opponent of Photius in the 9th century.

do not on the whole preserve significant amounts of ancient scholarship. In addition, numerous fragments, short epitomes, and minor works survive from older writers, primarily but not exclusively those of the late antique and Roman periods. Some of these remains have been collected and published in modern editions, for example Lesbonax by Blank (1988), Comanus of Naucratis by Dyck (1988), and Agathocles, Hellanicus, Ptolemaeus Epithetes, Theophilus, Anaxagoras, Xenon by F. Montanari (1988a), and Epaphroditus by Braswell and Billerbeck (forthcoming). Most, however, have received only non-critical editions with little systematic study, usually in dissertations or *Programmschriften*; these texts are hard to use but offer excellent opportunities for future research. There is good information on late antique and Byzantine grammarians and their editions in Hunger (1978: ii. 3–83), and the list of editions in Erbse's edition of the *Iliad* scholia (1969–88)[19] is a good key to the works of grammarians of all periods; many editions are also listed in the *TLG Canon*.[20]

There is also a substantial body of grammatical papyri, containing doctrine that is often anonymous but usually of considerable antiquity. These papyri have been collected and discussed by Wouters (1979 =TLG), but more have been published since, including by Wouters (1997). Further discussions include those of Holwerda (1983), Swiggers and Wouters (1995b), and Wouters (1993, 2000).

3.2 LEXICA

A large number of ancient and Byzantine lexica survive intact or abbreviated. These are the source of our knowledge of many elements of Greek vocabulary and of much of our information on lost works of literature, and much still remains to be learned from them. They must, however, be used with care, as they are usually poorly transmitted and often inadequately edited. Moreover, the Byzantine lexica are mostly interrelated; the most significant of those relationships are indicated in this chapter, but others exist as well. When using Byzantine lexica it is important to find out whether entries in two lexica that bear on the same topic are independent witnesses to ancient information or not; very often they are not. Those needing to use multiple Byzantine lexica should learn as much as they can about the history of the works involved; a good place to start is I. Cunningham (2003).

19. Found at the front of each volume as part of the list of abbreviations, though works that Erbse did not cite in every volume appear only in the list in the volume where they are cited. Erbse's list is in general an excellent guide to editions of any type of ancient scholarship, since he can be trusted to cite the best text that had been published by c.1960 (and usually, in the later volumes, the best published up to c.1975) and to reproduce the bibliographical information correctly; it is, however, not complete.

20. Either via Berkowitz and Squitier (1990) or at http://www.tlg.uci.edu. This list is more comprehensive than Erbse's, and somewhat more up to date, but it cannot be relied upon to cite the best editions or to give correct bibliographic information, and it is not complete.

3.2.1 Hesychius

Hesychius of Alexandria[21] composed in the fifth or sixth century AD[22] a lexicon of
obscure words of which an abridged and interpolated version still survives. Hesychius
based his work on the lexicon of Diogenianus,[23] which he claims to have supplemented from the works of Aristarchus, Heliodorus, Apion, and Herodian; such
claims are now difficult to verify or refute, but the work clearly contains material
from lost sources much earlier than Hesychius himself.

The lexicon consists of a list of poetic and dialectal words, phrases, and short
proverbs. The words are often in inflected forms (as they appeared in the original
texts from which Hesychius' predecessors extracted them), rather than the dictionary forms used today. They are alphabetized (usually by the first three letters)
under the actual form of the lemma, so that, for example, augmented verbal forms
are listed under ϵ, and prepositional phrases are listed under the preposition. Most
entries are followed by one or more equivalents more intelligible to later Greeks
(and usually, though not always, to us); the entry is separated from the gloss simply by a high point. In some cases the gloss is not in fact an equivalent, but the
abridged remains of Hesychius' originally more complex explanation. Some longer
explanations survive, but even these tend to be extremely compressed.

Hesychius' lexicon is useful for several reasons. It is the only source for a large
number of rare words that occur nowhere else in extant literature (particularly
dialect forms). It also preserves, and provides information on, many words that
would be omitted from a modern dictionary for being proper names (thus, for
example, it is one of our main sources for the names of Attic γένη); in some ways
an ancient lexicon fulfilled the function of a modern encyclopedia as well as that
of a modern dictionary. In some cases Hesychius' entries can be used as independent witnesses to the texts of extant authors and can supply correct readings of
words corrupted in the transmission of those texts. Because of problems with the
textual tradition, however, all words and readings taken from Hesychius must be
treated with caution; the accentuation in particular is thoroughly unreliable.
Hesychius also tells us what ancient scholars thought his obscure words meant;
this information can be useful both as a guide to the actual meanings of the words
and as a source of insight into the ways that ancient scholars understood and in-
terpreted literature.

21. Not to be confused with Hesychius of Jerusalem, Hesychius of Miletus (also
known as Hesychius Illustrius and sometimes confused with our Hesychius in antiquity,
cf. schol. rec. to Aristophanes' *Clouds* 540), or any of a large number of other Hesychii.

22. The work is often dated to the 5th cent. on the assumption that the Eulogius
addressed in the dedicatory epistle can be identified with a Eulogius Scholasticus thought
to have lived in the 5th cent., but Latte (1953–66: i, pp. vii–viii) rejects this identification and dates the lexicon to the 6th cent.

23. This work, itself a compilation of earlier lexica, was composed in the 2nd cent.
AD; the author was not the Epicurean Diogenianus. The lexicon is now lost.

The lexicon in its current form is substantially different from the one Hesychius wrote. Not only was his work severely abridged in transmission (a process that eliminated, among other things, most of Hesychius' indications of his sources for the various words), but it has been heavily interpolated as well. About a third of "Hesychius'" entries are Biblical glosses from a lexicon attributed to Cyrillus (see 3.2.14), and material from paraphrases of Homer and Euripides, from the *Onomasticum sacrum*, and from Epiphanius has also been added to Hesychius' original core. The status of some other material, including Latin and Atticist glosses, is disputed. The interpolations must have occurred rather early, for material from Cyrillus was already in Hesychius' work by the eighth century.

A further complication is the state of the text. Only one manuscript of Hesychius survives, and it is late (fifteenth century), damaged, and seriously corrupt. The best edition, that of K. Latte (1953–66 =*TLG*) and P. Hansen (2005), covers only A–Σ;[24] for the rest of the alphabet the standard text is Moritz Schmidt's editio maior (1858–68 =*TLG*), which covers the whole alphabet and is very different from Latte's. Though generally less good, Schmidt's edition has some advantages over Latte's, including excellent critical material and indices. It is sometimes useful to supplement consultation of Schmidt's edition with examination of Alberti's text (1746–66). Moritz Schmidt's editio minor (1867) is more commonly available than his editio maior but should be avoided, for it is the result of an attempt to reconstruct Diogenianus' lexicon by removing all other material. As this other material had not been correctly identified by 1867, the result not only includes many of the interpolated glosses, but also omits a number that probably do go back to Diogenianus.

A number of fragments of Diogenianus' work survive independently of Hesychius. These include *PSI* viii. 892, *P.Oxy.* xlvii. 3329, a fragment on dialect glosses (κατὰ πόλεις) published by Latte (1924), and numerous fragments preserved in scholia.

Major studies of Hesychius are less common than one would expect, given the acknowledged importance of his work, but there are hundreds of discussions of minor points, many of which represent the best work on the text of specific entries. The best overall introduction is the introduction to Latte's edition (in very readable Latin); other useful sources include Tosi (1988), Latte (1942), Blumenthal (1930), H. Schultz (1913*b*), and the discussions in Moritz Schmidt (1858–68: iv, pp. i–cxcii). Hesychius' own introductory letter is also worth reading. Textual and exegetic notes on specific entries include those of Perilli (1990–3), Degani (1998), Bossi (2000), Spanoudakis (2000), and a long series of articles by Casadio, Curiazi, Funaioli, Dettori, Marzullo, and others in *Museum Criticum* from 1980 to 2000. For further bibliography see Tosi (1998).

References to Hesychius are often given without any numeration, simply by citing the word; as the lexicon's alphabetical order is not exact, persistence may be needed to track down one of these references. Those scholars with more sympathy for their readers give a numerical reference, such as "α 4430" or (even better)

---

24. The rest of the alphabet is to be covered by I. Cunningham (forthcoming).

"α 4430 Latte," which means that the word in question is the 4,430th word beginning with α (in Latte's edition). If the name of the editor is not given it is important to find out which edition of Hesychius the scholar in question was using, since although both Latte and Schmidt number their entries in this way, any given word has a different number in each edition.

3.2.2 *Suda*

The *Suda* is a huge dictionary/encyclopedia compiled in the late tenth century. From the twelfth until the mid-twentieth century the work was referred to as *Suidae lexicon*, the "Lexicon of Suidas," but now it is generally thought that the Σοῦδα in manuscripts is the work's title, not the author's name, and in consequence the work is usually called the *Suda* and considered to be anonymous.[25] The *Suda* may have been compiled by a group of scholars, but authorship by an individual cannot be ruled out.

The *Suda* consists of *c*.30,000 entries of varying types; some lemmata are followed by short definitions as in a lexicon, and others by detailed articles resembling those in a modern encyclopedia. They are arranged in a form of alphabetical order adapted to Byzantine Greek pronunciation (i.e. vowels not distinguished in pronunciation are alphabetized together). Sources are transcribed largely intact and are usually identifiable. The work is obviously related to Photius' *Lexicon*, and there has been much debate over the nature of the relationship, but the latest evidence suggests that the compiler of the *Suda* simply drew directly on Photius' work.

Despite its late date, the *Suda* is of great importance for our knowledge of antiquity, since it is based to a large extent on lost sources. Most of the immediate sources were lexica and other scholarly compilations of the Roman and late antique periods, such as Harpocration, Diogenianus, and scholia (though some pieces of classical literature, particularly the plays of Aristophanes, seem to have been consulted directly), but as these compilations were based on earlier work, the ultimate sources of the *Suda* include a significant amount of Alexandrian scholarship and historical material reaching back to the classical period. The plays of Aristophanes and scholia to them are particularly well represented, appearing in more than 5,000 entries. The *Suda* is especially useful for information about classical and later writers (indeed, it is our main source for the titles of lost literary works and the original extent of each author's output) because it includes material from a lost dictionary of literary biography composed by Hesychius of Miletus. It is also the source of important poetic and historical fragments, not to mention countless fragments of ancient scholarship.

25. The arguments about the word and its meaning are many, and not everyone is convinced that "Suidas" is not a name; for an example of dissent see Hemmerdinger (1998), and for summaries of the different variations on the standard view see Tosi (2001) and Hunger (1978: ii. 40–1).

There is an excellent edition of the *Suda* by Ada Adler (1928–38 =*TLG*), and some of the entries have been translated into English and provided with annotations by the Suda On Line project.[26] Discussions are numerous: N. Wilson (1983*a*: 145–7) provides a good introduction, and more detailed studies include those of Adler (1931), Theodoridis (1988; 1993; 1982–: ii, pp. xxvii–xl, li–ci), and the essays in Zecchini (1999).

3.2.3 Etymologica

A number of enormous, anonymous Byzantine etymological lexica have survived more or less intact and preserve much valuable ancient scholarship. Though traditionally referred to as etymologica, they are by no means strictly concerned with etymologies. They consist of lemmata (in alphabetical order) followed by some type of explanation, such as a definition, an etymology, and/or further information on usage, often including quotations from literature.

The oldest and most important of these is the *Etymologicum genuinum*, which was compiled in the ninth century, though our only witnesses to it are two tenth-century manuscripts of unusually poor quality. From the original version of this work, with various excisions and additions, are descended almost all the other etymologica, of which the most important are the *Etymologicum magnum* from the twelfth century, the *Etymologicum Gudianum* from the eleventh century, and the *Etymologicum Symeonis* from the twelfth century. The *Etymologicum (Florentinum) parvum*, for which we have only entries from the first half of the alphabet, is somewhat older but much less useful because of its small scale and lack of quotations.

The sources of the etymologica vary but generally date to the second century AD and later; major sources include Herodian, Orus, Orion, Theognostus, Choeroboscus, scholia, and the *Epimerismi Homerici*. But since these works were themselves usually based on earlier scholarship, the etymologica are indirect witnesses to a considerable amount of Hellenistic scholarly work, as well as preserving numerous fragments of classical literature otherwise lost.

The etymologica are difficult to use because editions are scattered, mostly elderly, and woefully incomplete. The primary edition is that of Lasserre and Livadaras (1976– =*TLG*), which offers synoptic texts of the *Etymologicum genuinum*, the *Etymologicum magnum*, and the *Etymologicum Symeonis*, but this edition has so far reached only as far as the letter β; its first volume is partially duplicated by Sell's edition (1968) of some entries beginning with α from the *Etymologicum Symeonis*, and its second volume by Berger's edition (1972) of entries beginning with β from the *Etymologicum genuinum* and *Etymologicum Symeonis*. For the rest of the alphabet the *Etymologicum magnum* can be consulted only in Gaisford's

---

26. Available at www.stoa.org/sol/. The translations must be used with careful attention to the notes that indicate whether or not they have been checked by the editors, as many are the uncorrected work of people with no expertise in the subject.

edition (1848 =*TLG*), and the *Etymologicum Symeonis* remains unpublished.[27]
The *Etymologicum genuinum* has received some piecemeal publications: apart
from Lasserre and Livadaras's edition of the beginning, we have Miller's partial
text of one manuscript (1868: 1–318), which covers the whole alphabet but includes only a few of the entries for each letter; an edition of the entries beginning
with the letter ζ (Funaioli 1983), two editions of the entries beginning with the
letter λ (Alpers 1969 (=*TLG*) and Colonna 1967), an edition of the entries beginning with μ, ν, ξ, and ω (Curiazi, Funaioli, *et al.* 1980–2), and a series of articles
containing annotated editions of some (but not all) of the entries beginning with
γ (Casadio 1986–7), δ (Casadio 1988–9), and ε (Casadio 1990–3). The *Etymologicum Gudianum* has been separately edited: De Stefani (1909–20 =*TLG*) covers letters α–ζ only, and the rest must be consulted in Sturz's text (1818 =*TLG*).
The *Etymologicum parvum* has been edited by Pintaudi (1973 =*TLG*), and several other Byzantine etymologica exist in unpublished form (but note Parlangèli
1953–4 for publication of a fragment of the *Etymologicum Casulanum*).

Discussions include those of Reitzenstein (1897), Erbse (1960: 123–73), Pintaudi (1975), Hunger (1978: ii. 45–8), Cellerini (1988), Maleci (1995), and the
introductions to the various editions; for further references see Cellerini (1988).
There have also been numerous short publications making textual suggestions and
reporting discoveries of new fragments of classical literature from the etymologica,
including Curiazi (1983), Perilli (1990–3), Massimilla (1990), and Calame (1970).

3.2.4 Aristophanes of Byzantium

Aristophanes of Byzantium (*c*.257–*c*.180 BC) was one of the most important
Alexandrian scholars and the teacher of Aristarchus; his works survive only in
fragments. Aristophanes produced editions of Homer, Hesiod, the lyric poets
(including Pindar), and Aristophanes the comedian (and perhaps other authors of
Old Comedy), and he seems to have worked on Sophocles, Euripides, and Menander
as well. Most scholars believe that he produced only texts, not commentaries, but
others maintain that he left at least some sort of notes to explain his texts.
Aristophanes' work also forms the basis for some of the "hypotheses" or introductions attached to tragedies and comedies; these hypotheses contain valuable information about the circumstances of each play's production, and Aristophanes
is thought to have based them on the work of Callimachus and of Dicaearchus,
the pupil of Aristotle.[28] He also composed some monographs on subjects such as

---

27. But Gaisford (1848) reports in his apparatus the readings of a manuscript (V) that
is actually a witness to the *Etymologicum Symeonis*.

28. Some plays have two or three hypotheses: a scholarly one that could be derived
from the works of Aristophanes, a popular one descended from Hellenistic works but
offering a summary of the play rather than scholarly information, and a longer Byzantine
one (13th–14th cent. AD). Clearly none of Aristophanes' hypotheses survive unaltered,
and it is difficult to tell which of the scholarly hypotheses descend from his work and
how different our versions of these hypotheses are from the ones he produced.

proverbs, and an important glossary entitled Λέξεις, which contained sections such as Περὶ τῶν ὑποπτευομένων μὴ εἰρῆσθαι τοῖς παλαιοῖς "On words suspected of not having been said by the ancients" (i.e. post-classical words), Περὶ ὀνομασίας ἡλικιῶν "On the names of ages" (i.e. terms used to designate men, women, and animals of different ages), and Περὶ συγγενικῶν ὀνομάτων "On kinship terms."[29] Aristophanes seems to have been the first editor of lyric poetry to divide the text into verse lines, rather than writing it out as prose, and to note the metrical structure of the poems; his input was also important in establishing the canonical corpus of classical works. In addition, he made crucial contributions to the history of diacritical signs: Aristophanes is credited with inventing the symbols for Greek accents that we still use today, as well as a system of critical signs for commenting upon texts.

Of this prodigious output we have only fragments. Some hypotheses survive, though variously altered, and comments in the scholia to the texts Aristophanes edited preserve a few of his readings. The critical signs are largely lost, but the accent marks are still in use. Hundreds of fragments of the Λέξεις exist, most gathered from sources such as Eustathius, Erotian, Pollux, and the scholia to Lucian but some also surviving in a direct manuscript tradition. A few fragments of the other monographs survive by indirect transmission.

The standard text of the fragments is that of Slater (1986); an older edition by Nauck (1848 =TLG) is excellent but lacks some of the most important sources, which were discovered after its publication. Slater's edition, however, omits the hypotheses, a few of which (i.e. the ones Nauck believed to be genuine) can be found in Nauck's edition. The other hypotheses can be found in editions of the texts of the dramatists concerned. Slater also omits the full version of the testimonia to Aristophanes' invention of the marks for accents and breathings, which are best consulted in Lameere (1960: 90–2), though they can also be found in Nauck (1848: 12–15). In addition, Slater confines to an appendix with little discussion the numerous and important fragments of Aristophanes' edition of Homer, on the grounds that these fragments, which come from the Homer scholia, are best consulted in editions of those scholia; Nauck gives these fragments pride of place and accords them substantial discussion. Both editions have excellent indices. A few more recently discovered fragments are absent from both editions but can be found in Lasserre (1986–7) and Roselli (1979).

Discussions of Aristophanes are numerous. The best general introduction is that of Pfeiffer (1968: 171–209), and the most detailed study that of Callanan (1987), though both editions also provide significant discussion. Much recent work has attempted to recover Aristophanes' ideas of grammatical analysis and determine how sophisticated his system was, but some focuses on his methods of textual criticism or attempts to reconstruct his monographs. A good survey of important work on Aristophanes up to the 1980s is given by Callanan (1987: 9–20; see also

---

29. A few scholars think that these sections were self-standing works and maintain that the overall title Λέξεις is a fiction (see Slater 1976: 237 n. 11).

the bibliography in Slater 1986); more recent discussions include those of Ax
(1990; 2000: 95–115), Schenkeveld (1990, 1994), Slater (1982), Blank and Dyck
(1984), Rengakos (1993: 89–96), Van Thiel (1992: 14–15), Porro (1994: 3–12,
223–4, 238), Longo (1987), and Tosi (1990–3, 1997). The hypotheses are treated
by Zuntz (1955: 129–52), Meijering (1985), Koster (1962), O. Montanari (1970–
2), and Achelis (1913–16).

3.2.5 Harpocration

Valerius Harpocration produced a glossary to the Attic orators, Λέξεις τῶν δέκα
ῥητόρων, in the later second century AD. The glossary is particularly important as
a source of fragments of lost works and of historical information on classical Athens; the information it contains is notably more accurate than the average of ancient scholarship. The work is also significant in the history of ancient lexicography,
as it is one of the earliest surviving glossaries. Unusually for a work of this period,
Harpocration's glossary follows complete alphabetical order (i.e. words are not
merely grouped together by their first letters, or by their first two or three letters,
but fully alphabetized as in a modern dictionary); there is, however, some debate
about whether this feature can be traced to Harpocration himself or was added at
a later stage of transmission.

The work survives, in a contaminated and somewhat abridged form, in a number of late manuscripts; this version is known as the "full version" in contrast to
our other main witness to the text, an epitome dating probably to the early ninth
century. There is also an early papyrus fragment of the glossary, from the second
or third century AD, as well as extracts from Harpocration preserved in Photius
and in scholia to the orators.

There is no consensus on the best text of Harpocration. Keaney's text (1991)
is an important edition and cannot be ignored, but it is too full of errors to be
safely usable by itself (see Otranto 1993), while the previous edition, that of
W. Dindorf (1853 =TLG) is not without its own problems, with the result that some
scholars prefer to rely on Bekker's text (1833b). The safest method is usually consultation of at least two of these editions. The papyrus is published as P.Ryl. iii. 532 and
supplemented by Naoumides (1961). Discussions include those of Hemmerdinger
(1959), Keaney (1973, 1995), Whitehead (1997, 1998), and H. Schultz (1912). Some
examples of the way Harpocration has recently been used are provided by Kinzl (1991),
C. Gibson (1997), Thompson (1983), and Keaney (1967).

3.2.6 Ammonius / Herennius Philo

A lexicon entitled Περὶ ὁμοίων καὶ διαφόρων λέξεων (De adfinium vocabulorum
differentia) is preserved in late manuscripts under the name of Ammonius, but it
is generally agreed not to have been composed by any of the known bearers of
that name.[30] The work is closely related to a number of other lexica that survive

30. The main contenders would be Ammonius of Alexandria (pupil and successor of
Aristarchus, and author of many scholarly works now lost), Ammonius Saccas (an Alex-

only as epitomes, of which the most significant are the Περὶ διαφορᾶς λέξεων attributed to Ptolemaeus[31] and the Περὶ διαφόρους σημασίας (*De diversis verborum significationibus*) of Herennius Philo.[32] It is thought that the ancestor of all these works was probably a lexicon composed by Herennius Philo in the early second century AD, which was severely epitomized both with and without its author's name and preserved (probably still in a reduced form, but one of substantial size) with the substitution of Ammonius' name.[33]

The lexicon consists primarily of pairs of words that are similar or identical in some way, with an explanation of the difference between them. It is often called a lexicon of synonyms, and in the majority of cases the paired words are in fact synonyms (e.g. πόλις and ἄστυ, or εὖ and καλῶς), but in other cases they are homonyms, similar or identical in form but different in meaning (e.g. ἐκεῖ and ἐκεῖσε, or δῆμος "populace" and δημός "fat"). Some are similar in both form and meaning, and occasionally an entry consists of a single word followed by a list of synonyms. The sources include classical literature, Alexandrian scholarship, and scholarship of the early Roman period, most now lost; sometimes literary quotations are included to exemplify the meaning or usage of a particular word. While the vast majority of the entries contain information that is correct by the standards of classical usage, and some of them preserve really valuable scholarly information, there are also a few mistakes and a certain amount of banality.

The standard edition of Ammonius' work is that of Nickau (1966 =*TLG*), who provides in an appendix entries missing from manuscripts of Ammonius but recoverable from the epitomes. Since the publication of this edition some more manuscripts of Ammonius have been discovered and findings from them published by Bühler (1972) and Nickau (1978), but they do not greatly alter our understanding of the text. There are separate editions and discussions of the epitomes attributed to Herennius (Palmieri 1981, 1988, both =*TLG*) and Ptolemaeus (Heylbut 1887; Palmieri 1981–2; Nickau 1990), as well as of a number of other fragments

andrian Platonist of the 3rd cent. AD and the teacher of Plotinus), and Ammonius son of Hermeias (an Alexandrian Neoplatonist of the 6th cent. AD, some of whose commentaries on Aristotle are still extant); none of these lived at the right time to be the author of the lexicon.

31. The Ptolemy in question is presumably intended to be the 1st-cent. grammarian Ptolemy of Ascalon, who cannot be the author of the work (nor can the scientist Ptolemy of Alexandria or any other known Ptolemy); probably the attribution is simply false, but Ptolemaeus could be the name of a later epitomator.

32. Also known as Erennius Philo and as Philo of Byblos, but not to be confused with Philo Judaeus (Philo of Alexandria), author of numerous extant religious works. Herennius Philo was a prolific antiquarian writer of the late 1st and early 2nd cent. AD; most of his work was not concerned with language and is in any case lost, but his most famous work, the *Phoenician history*, survives in substantial fragments.

33. The name could indicate that someone named Ammonius (who might or might not be one of the famous Ammonii) abridged the work or was otherwise involved in its transmission, but it could also have been attached simply in order to lend the work more authority by associating it with a more famous scholar.

of related work (e.g. Palmieri 1984, 1986, both =*TLG*), but these are useful primarily for understanding the transformations that the lexicon underwent between the time of Herennius and the late Byzantine period. The most important discussions of the lexica are those of Erbse (1960: 295–310) and Nickau (1966: preface; 2000); because these scholars changed our understanding of the lexica significantly, earlier studies are not normally useful.

3.2.7 Pollux

Julius Pollux (or Polydeuces) of Naucratis, a rhetorician of the latter part of the second century AD, was the author of the *Onomasticon*, a wide-ranging lexicon in ten books. The work now survives only in the form of an epitome that has suffered interpolation as well as abridgement, but it is still of considerable bulk and primarily Pollux's own work. It is based on works of classical literature and Alexandrian scholarship, including many no longer extant; among these sources are Aristophanes of Byzantium and Eratosthenes.

The *Onomasticon* is organized not in alphabetical order like other surviving ancient lexica, but by topic; in this it preserves a very early method of organization that originally predominated in Greek scholarship and was only gradually replaced by alphabetical ordering. Some entries are very brief, but others are complex and detailed, offering much more than a simple definition. Perhaps the most famous section is Pollux's discussion of the classical theater and its paraphernalia, including a description of seventy-six different types of mask for different characters in tragedies, comedies, and satyr plays, which is an invaluable source of information on the ancient stage. Much other historical information can also be found in the *Onomasticon*, as can fragments of lost works, better readings of extant works, and definitions (including some earliest attestations) of obscure words.

The standard edition of the *Onomasticon* is that of Bethe (1900–37 =*TLG*), which also includes the scholia found in some manuscripts (printed below the text). Numerous textual suggestions have been made since the appearance of this edition, such as those of Marzullo (1995–6). For further information see Bethe (1917) and Tosi (1988: 87–113), and for examples of recent use of Pollux see Poe (1996, 2000), Theodorides (1976*b*), and Vinson (1996). Wieseler (1870) can be helpful in understanding Pollux's unusual vocabulary.

3.2.8 Phrynichus

Phrynichus Arabius,[34] a rhetorician and lexicographer of the later second century AD, was one of the strictest of the Atticists. Unlike many Atticists of his period, he sought examples of usage from tragedy and Old Comedy, and he was prepared to censure even words appearing in standard Attic prose authors if they did not be-

---

34. This Phrynichus, who is also identified as being from Bithynia, is not to be confused with Phrynichus the tragedian or Phrynichus the comedian, both of whom belong to the classical period.

long to fifth-century usage. Two of his works survive, both concerned with the nuances of correct Attic usage.

Phrynichus' major work was the Σοφιστικὴ προπαρασκευή (*Praeparatio sophistica*), a lexicon of Attic words originally in thirty-seven books but now surviving only in a substantial epitome and a collection of fragments. The entries, which are alphabetized by first letters only, consist of obscure words, often collected from lost tragedies or comedies, with definitions and sometimes specific attributions to classical authors. The work was extensively discussed by Photius, who is the source of many of the fragments.

Phrynichus' other work, the Ἐκλογὴ Ἀττικῶν ῥημάτων καὶ ὀνομάτων (*Ecloga*), used to be considered an epitome but is now thought to be more or less complete; it is in two books, with a certain amount of repetition between them, and two short epitomes are also preserved. The work consists of a series of pronouncements on different aspects of Attic and non-Attic usage, arranged in the form of a lexicon (but not in alphabetical order, except for a few sets of entries taken over from alphabetizing sources). Many entries consist of a non-Attic word, usually but not always from the koiné (e.g. δυσί), an injunction against using it, and the appropriate Attic replacement (e.g. δυοῖν), while others give the proper Attic syntax of the lemma (e.g. τυγχάνω must be accompanied by ὤν when it means "happen to be") or the difference between easily confused words (e.g. a μεῖραξ is female, but a μειράκιον is male). Phrynichus' sources include the Antiatticista (see 3.2.9) and several lost works of ancient scholarship, and his work is valuable both for preserving such fragments and for the light it sheds on the way the Atticists worked and on the type of mistakes that Greek speakers trying to write classical Attic were likely to make in the second century.

The standard edition of the *Praeparatio* is that of Borries (1911 =*TLG*), and for the *Ecloga* that of Fischer (1974 =*TLG*). Discussions include the introductions to the editions, Slater (1977), Rutherford (1881), Bossi (1980–2), and Blanchard (1997).

3.2.9 Antiatticista

The anonymous composition normally referred to as the work of the Antiatticista is not, as this designation might seem to suggest, a polemic against Atticism, but rather a second-century (AD) Atticist lexicon that is "Antiatticist" only in having a broader definition of "Attic" than did the strict Atticists like Phrynichus. The Antiatticist admitted a larger group of authors into his canon and apparently held that the use of a word by any Attic author made it acceptable as Attic, even if a more recherché alternative existed. Until recently it was believed that the Antiatticist was a contemporary of Phrynichus who wrote in response to the first book of Phrynichus' *Ecloga* and against whom the second book of the *Ecloga* was then directed, but now some hold that Phrynichus attacked the Antiatticist throughout the *Ecloga*, and others that Phrynichus used the Antiatticist's work rather than attacking it, suggesting that the Antiatticist may have been a predecessor rather than a contemporary.

The lexicon seems to have originally consisted of a list of Attic words, with definitions and references to the words' occurrences in classical texts; many of the words listed were ones whose claim to be considered properly Attic had been disputed by the stricter Atticists, and the Antiatticist seems to have made a point of showing that those words were indeed attested, often by quoting the relevant passage. Unfortunately the work survives only in the form of a drastically reduced epitome from which most of the quotations have been excised, leaving only tantalizing references to lost works. Enough remains, however, that the work is useful for information on lost literary works, historical details about classical Athens, and fragments of Hellenistic scholarship, as well as for understanding the controversies of the Second Sophistic period.

The epitome has been published by Bekker (1814–21: i. 75–116 =*TLG*) and discussed by Latte (1915), Fischer (1974), Slater (1977), and Arnott (1989); Jacoby (1944) and Tosi (1997) provide examples of its uses.

3.2.10 Moeris

The Atticizing lexicographer Moeris has left us an intact work entitled Λέξεις ’Αττικῶν καὶ ‘Ελλήνων κατὰ στοιχεῖον, or ’Αττικιστής. Moeris' date is uncertain, but it was clearly late enough to allow him to use all the other Atticists; the third century AD is a likely possibility. His lexicon consists of almost a thousand entries, alphabetized by their first letters, most of which involve Attic/non-Attic pairs. Many appear in a formula that juxtaposes ’Αττικοί and ‘Ελληνες, as ὀμνύναι ’Αττικοί· ὀμνύειν ‘Ελληνες “The Attic speakers [used as the infinitive of ὄμνυμι] ὀμνύναι, but the [other, i.e. later] Greeks [use] ὀμνύειν.” Sometimes κοινόν or κοινῶς (or the name of a different dialect) appears instead of ‘Ελληνες, sometimes no non-Attic equivalent is given, and sometimes a reference to a classical author supports the claim of Attic usage. Moeris' Attic canon excluded tragedy and New Comedy but included, in addition to prose and Old Comedy, Homer and Herodotus.

The standard edition and study of Moeris is that of D. Hansen (1998), who provides ample further bibliography.

3.2.11 Philemon

Two Greek glossographers bore the name Philemon.[35] The first, living in the third and second centuries BC, wrote a work called Περὶ ’Αττικῶν ὀνομάτων ἢ γλωσσῶν; it is lost, but fragments are preserved in the works of later writers, particularly Athenaeus and “Ammonius.”

The second Philemon was an Atticist who around AD 200 composed in iambics a work entitled Περὶ ’Αττικῆς ἀντιλογίας τῆς ἐν ταῖς λέξεσιν. This piece survives only in two brief extracts, both of which are essentially alphabetic lists of non-

---

35. They are not to be confused with the 3rd-cent. Latin grammarian of the same name, nor with several comic poets named Philemon. The two discussed here are numbers 13 and 14 in *RE*.

Attic words and their Attic equivalents. One covers the whole alphabet and has been published by Reitzenstein (1897: 392–6), while the other, which has more entries beginning with each letter and gives more detail on each entry, covers only the first four letters of the alphabet; this one has been edited by Osann (1821).

The Philemons have been discussed by Cohn (1898), but much remains to be done.

3.2.12 Aelius Dionysius and Pausanias

Aelius Dionysius of Halicarnassus and Pausanias,[36] both from the early second century AD, were the founders of Attic lexicography. Both produced lexica of Attic words and phrases in alphabetical order, respectively entitled Ἀττικὰ ὀνόματα and Ἀττικῶν ὀνομάτων συναγωγή, that had a great influence on later lexicographers and survived at least until the twelfth century. Their sources included Alexandrian scholarship such as the works of Aristophanes of Byzantium. Both lexica are now lost, but a substantial body of fragments can be recovered from the works of later scholars, particularly Eustathius; these have been collected by Erbse (1950 =TLG), though this collection also contains a number of items not specifically attributed to Aelius Dionysius or Pausanias in the sources but assigned to them by Erbse on various grounds. Erbse (1950) also provides the main discussion of the lexica. See also Van der Valk (1955) and Heinimann (1992).

3.2.13 Orus and Orion

These two grammarians of the fifth century AD are confused with one another in Byzantine and early modern works, but their respective surviving works have now been separated. Orus, who was born in Alexandria and worked in Constantinople,[37] produced numerous grammatical and lexicographical works, of which only four survive to any significant extent: an Attic lexicon, a manual on orthography, and short treatises on words with multiple meanings and on ethnic names. Orio(n) of Thebes[38] wrote a number of scholarly works, of which we now have only one, an etymological lexicon, plus the fragments of a florilegium (see Haffner 2001).

Orus' Attic lexicon, entitled Ἀττικῶν λέξεων συναγωγή, is probably the best known of his works, but all we have of it is a large group of fragments, collected primarily from the lexicon of Zonaras. The work, which is concerned more with distinguishing classical from koiné Greek than with identifying peculiarities of the Attic dialect, was written in opposition to Phrynichus and is based on classical sources. There is a good edition of the fragments with discussion by Alpers (1981 =TLG).

---

36. This Pausanias is to be distinguished both from the Spartan kings of that name and from the author of the Periegesis or Description of Greece.

37. He is also, for unknown reasons, associated with Miletus and so may be identified by reference to any of these three cities.

38. The Egyptian Thebes. He was born there but worked in Alexandria, Constantinople, and Caesarea.

From Orus' manual on orthography ('Ορθογραφία) we possess a substantial excerpt concerning the use of the iota subscript. This consists of a list of words in alphabetical order (only entries from the second half of the alphabet are preserved), with indication of whether or not each is written with the iota. Entries are often accompanied by evidence in the form of quotations from classical literature, thus sometimes preserving fragments of lost works, and some fragments of earlier scholarship can be found as well. The excerpt has been published by Rabe (1892 =TLG, 1895) and discussed by Reitzenstein (1897: 289–316) and Erbse (1960: 274–80).

Orus' treatise on ethnics was called Περὶ ἐθνικῶν or ῞Οπως τὰ ἐθνικὰ λεκτέον; from it we have a set of fragments gathered from Stephanus and the *Etymologicum genuinum*. Of the treatise on words with multiple meanings, entitled Περὶ πολυσημάντων λέξεων, we have substantial excerpts, preserved independently in the manuscript tradition. Both have been edited and discussed by Reitzenstein (1897: 316–35, 335–47).

The Ἐτυμολογικόν or Περὶ ἐτυμολογίας of Orion survives in three abbreviated versions, one of which is still of considerable bulk; the smaller versions are known as the Werfer excerpts and the Koës excerpts after their first transcribers. The work is an etymological lexicon that combines material from other scholars in alphabetical order and so preserves much earlier scholarship, including portions of Aristonicus' work on Homer. All three versions have been published by Sturz (1818: 611–17 =TLG; 1820 =TLG), and one of them re-edited by Micciarelli Collesi (1970*a* =TLG). The lexicon has been discussed by Erbse (1960: 280–94), Reitzenstein (1897: 309–11, 347–50), Wendel (1939*a*), Garzya (1967), Theodoridis (1976*a*: 16–41), and Micciarelli Collesi (1970*b*), but much remains to be done.

3.2.14 Cyrillus

A substantial lexicon compiled in the fifth century AD is attributed to Cyrillus.[39] It consists primarily of Biblical glosses, but there is also some material from the ancient scholarly tradition, including Atticist writings and scholia. Entries from this lexicon have been heavily interpolated into our version of Hesychius, but Cyrillus' lexicon also exists independently in numerous manuscripts.

Unfortunately most of the lexicon is unpublished. The most important study, that of Drachmann (1936), provides an edition of only a few sections (words beginning with βα-, θα-, θε-, λα-, and λε-), and Cramer's text (1839–41: iv. 177–201) contains a drastically abbreviated version. Selected glosses from individual manuscripts have been edited by Naoumides (1968), Burguière (1961–2), and Moritz Schmidt (1858–68: iv, e.g. 365–8). Discussions include those of Latte (1953–66: i, pp. xliv–li), I. Cunningham (2003: esp. 43–9), Burguière (1970),

---

39. Or Cyril. The attribution probably refers to St. Cyril of Alexandria—though St. Cyril of Jerusalem and Cyril of Scythopolis are also candidates—and the person so designated may well have had something to do with the lexicon, but the work as it stands cannot be simply the composition of any of these Cyrils.

Henrichs (1971–3: 112–16), Reitzenstein (1888), and Lucà (1994), but much remains to be done. A new edition is expected from N. Wilson and H. van Thiel.

3.2.15 Stephanus

Stephanus of Byzantium,[40] a grammarian who taught in Constantinople in the sixth century AD, composed a gigantic geographical lexicon in more than fifty books. The work, called *Ethnica*, originally contained detailed linguistic, geographical, historical, and mythological information about hundreds of place-names and the ethnic adjectives corresponding to them. Its sources included Herodian, Orus, Pausanius, Strabo, and some ancestors of the Homer scholia, as well as many lost works of scholarship. We now have an epitome, in which the amount of information given about each entry is drastically reduced (in many cases to a mere listing of place-names and their adjectives); eight pages of the original that survive in a separate manuscript; and several fragments preserved in the work of later Byzantines, notably Constantine Porphyrogenitus. Though these remains are only a fraction of the original work, their bulk is still impressive.

The *Ethnica* have been edited by Meineke (1849 =*TLG*), though this text is not entirely satisfactory; a new edition is in preparation by Margarethe Billerbeck. Studies include those of Diller (1938, 1950), Erbse (1960: 251–69), and Whitehead (1994).

3.2.16 Photius' *Lexicon*

Photius (*c.*810–*c.*893), patriarch of Constantinople, is now known chiefly for his *Bibliotheca* (see 3.3.1), but he also composed a lexicon. The work is huge and concerned chiefly with prose words, though a number of items from Old Comedy also appear. Most entries are short, consisting only of the lemma and a one- or two-word definition, but some are substantial paragraphs with citations of authors who use a word, and sometimes with quotations. The lexicon's immediate sources are other late lexica, particularly that of Cyrillus (see 3.2.14), but it indirectly preserves much earlier scholarship (particularly material from the lost lexica of Diogenianus, Aelius Dionysius, and Pausanias) and is a source of fragments of lost literary works.

Significant portions of the lexicon were unknown until 1959, when the only complete manuscript of the work was discovered. A new edition incorporating this material is in progress (Theodoridis 1982– =*TLG*) and is by far the best; until

---

40. This Stephanus is to be distinguished from Stephanus of Alexandria / Stephanus of Athens / Stephanus the philosopher, who wrote commentaries on Hippocrates, Galen, and Aristotle (and who may himself be more than one person); from the 7th-cent. grammarian Stephanus who is responsible for some of the "scholia" to Dionysius Thrax; and from the 16th-cent. scholar and publisher Henri Estienne, often known by his Latinized name Stephanus; this last Stephanus is the one responsible for the gigantic dictionary called *Thesaurus Graecae Linguae* or *Stephani Thesaurus*, as well as for the Stephanus numeration of Plato.

it is complete, however, Porson's edition (1823 =*TLG*) remains the best choice for the rest of the lexicon (rather than Naber's 1864–5 edition). Discussions of the work are numerous; N. Wilson (1983*a*: 90–3) provides a good introduction, and Theodoridis' edition includes important, comprehensive studies (in the second volume as well as in the first). There is a series of critical notes in Casadio *et al.* (1984–5). For further bibliography see Theodoridis (1982–).

3.2.17 Συναγωγὴ λέξεων χρησίμων

This lexicon, also known as *Lexicon Bachmannianum* and as *Lexicon Bekkeri VI*, was composed in the late eighth or early ninth century AD, though a substantial body of material was added later. Its original basis was the lexicon of Cyrillus, which is still extant (see 3.2.14), and many of the other sources are also extant. It is therefore often ignored, but the fact that we can trace the growth of the work over several centuries and know its contents at each point makes it useful for understanding Byzantine lexicography. The best text of and source of information on the Συναγωγή is I. Cunningham's edition (2003).

3.2.18 *Lexicon* αἱμωδεῖν

A small lexicon dating to the ninth or tenth century is known as the *Lexicon* αἱμωδεῖν after the lemma of the first entry. This work has fairly detailed entries and is sometimes useful for its preservation of earlier scholarship, since it is based in part on lost scholarly material. There is a good edition and study in Dyck (1983–95: ii. 825–1016).

3.2.19 Zonaras

An enormous lexicon compiled in the first half of the thirteenth century carries the name of Zonaras, a historian who lived in the eleventh and twelfth centuries and so cannot have written it. The lexicon draws freely on the works of a wide variety of earlier (late antique and early Byzantine) scholars and so preserves much scholarship that is otherwise lost, including many of the fragments of Orus' lexicon. It is organized first alphabetically (to two letters) and then by grammatical category. Entries range in length from two words (lemma and definition) to long paragraphs including quotations from ancient literature.

The only edition of the lexicon is that of Tittmann (1808 =*TLG*), whence it is sometimes called the *Lexicon Tittmannianum*. The work has been little studied, and some of what has been done is unusable; for the best available see Alpers (1972; 1981: 3–55).

3.2.20 Other Lexica

The works mentioned above are by no means all the lexica that preserve ancient scholarship. A number of important lexica to the works of individual authors survive: Apollonius Sophista's and Apion's works on Homer (see 2.1.1.3), Erotian's and Galen's glossaries of Hippocratic words (see 2.2.1), Timaeus' lexicon to Plato (see 2.2.2), and some anonymous lexica to Herodotus (see 2.2.6). In addition, there is a substantial body of other lexicographical material surviving on papyrus or via the manuscript tradition; these works and fragments are too numerous and too obscure to be discussed individually here but are nevertheless useful on occasion.

A number of minor lexica from the late antique and Byzantine periods have survived in manuscripts, and of these a few are reasonably accessible. There is a good edition by Naoumides (1975 =*TLG*) of a little school lexicon related to the scholia on Aristophanes, Pindar, and Demosthenes and perhaps dating to the late antique period. Suetonius, the Roman biographer, wrote two Greek works Περὶ βλασφημιῶν and Περὶ παιδιῶν, of which lexicon-like epitomes survive (Περὶ βλασφημιῶν in its present form can be fairly described as a dictionary of insults) and have been edited by Taillardat (1967 =*TLG*). Thomas Magister's Attic lexicon has been edited by Ritschl (1832), and Nauck (1867 =*TLG*) has edited the *Lexicon Vindobonense*, a compilation of the early fourteenth century ascribed to Andreas Lopadiotes (see Guida 1982). A number of additional lexica can be found in Latte and Erbse (1965), Bachmann (1828), and the "Anecdota Bekker" (Bekker 1814–21), but others are confined to obscure dissertations or *Programmschriften* or remain entirely unpublished. For references to these and to the scattered fragments of and testimonia to earlier lexica, see general discussions of Greek lexicography; particularly good ones with extensive further references are Degani (1995) and Hunger (1978: ii. 33–50), and useful lists of editions can also be found in Erbse (1969–88) and in the *TLG Canon*.[41]

There are also numerous fragments of older lexica surviving on papyrus. Most of these lexica appear to be focused on the works of a particular author or group of authors, but more general lexica are not unknown. Naoumides (1969) offers a list of papyrus lexica with discussion of their characteristics, but more have been published since, including *P. Oxy.* xlv. 3239 and xlvii. 3329. The collection *Commentaria et Lexica Graeca in Papyris reperta*, to be published by K. G. Saur, is expected eventually to include texts and discussions of papyrus lexica.

3.3 OTHER TYPES OF WORK

3.3.1 Photius' *Bibliotheca*

Photius, patriarch of Constantinople in the ninth century, was the most important of the Byzantine scholars. His influence was responsible for the preservation of many ancient texts that would otherwise have been lost, and his own work drew on, and thus preserves fragments from, many other works that subsequently disappeared.

---

41. Erbse gives a list of editions as part of his list of abbreviations at the front of each volume; this list is a reliable guide to the best editions that had been published by *c.*1960 (and a mostly reliable guide up to 1975), but it is not complete, and some new editions have since appeared. The *Canon* can be found in Berkowitz and Squitier (1990) or at http://www.tlg.uci.edu; it too is incomplete and somewhat out of date, and in addition neither the choice of editions nor the bibliographical information given there is completely trustworthy.

Two of his works concern classical scholarship: the *Lexicon* (for which see 3.2.16) and the *Bibliotheca*.[42] The latter, which is sometimes called the *Myriobiblos*, is an enormous literary encyclopedia covering a wide range of authors from the classical to the early Byzantine periods. It contains summaries and discussions of the books Photius had read, ostensibly prepared for his brother's use when Photius was departing on an embassy. The *Bibliotheca* consists of 280 entries, known as *codices* ("books"), each of which is concerned with a different work or set of works; some are only a few lines in length, but others stretch to many pages. The works discussed come from many different subjects and genres, both Christian and pagan, with two major restrictions: technical scientific works and poetry are both excluded.

The entries contain not only summaries but also critical commentary of various types, with an emphasis on style. From Photius' perspective one of the main reasons for reading ancient literature was the improvement of one's own prose style, so he frequently offered stylistic judgements of the works included; interestingly, his highest praise was reserved not for any of the classical writers, but for Atticists of the Roman period. He also discussed textual issues and questions of authenticity, using both his own judgement and ancient scholarly materials.

Many of the works Photius discussed are now lost, so that his summaries provide all or most of what we know about them. Even when the originals have survived, Photius' comments can be very useful to modern scholars, for apart from the fact that he was an intelligent and perceptive scholar, he often had access to better or more complete texts than we do, and he sometimes provides information on the age of the manuscript he used or on how many manuscripts of a work he found. In addition, his discussions tell us much about the history of the transmission of ancient literature by indicating how much survived into the ninth century and was then lost.

The standard text of the *Bibliotheca* is that of Henry (1959–77 =*TLG*), who provides a facing French translation, and some of the more interesting entries have been translated into English with notes by N. Wilson (1994). Good introductions to the work can be found in N. Wilson (1983*a*: 93–111; 1994), and significant studies include those of Schamp (1987, 2000), Treadgold (1980), Hägg (1975), Lemerle (1971: 177–204), and Ziegler (1941); there is also a collection of articles in Menestrina (2000).

3.3.2 Hephaestion

Hephaestion of Alexandria,[43] who lived in the second century AD, was the author of the most important ancient metrical treatise and is now our main source for ancient metrical theory, analysis, and terminology. His treatise originally comprised forty-eight books, but after repeated epitomizing, much of it conducted by the author himself, we now have an epitome in one book, known as the *Handbook* or

---

42. For Photius' other works see N. Wilson (1983*a*: 111–19).
43. Not to be confused with Hephaestion of Thebes, author of the *Apotelesmatica*.

Encheiridion. There are also some fragments of disputed authorship that could be excerpts from fuller versions of the work, entitled Περὶ ποιήματος, Περὶ ποιημάτων, and Περὶ σημείων.

The most important of these survivals is the *Encheiridion*, which discusses and explains different metrical structures, illustrating them with extensive quotations from ancient poetry. The two fragments on poems, the contents of which overlap to a great extent, concern the analysis of poetic texts by metrical structure, and the Περὶ σημείων discusses the use of the coronis, diple, asteriskos, and other diacritic marks in different types of meter.

Though not designed as an introduction to the field, the *Encheiridion* soon became a textbook because of its straightforward, systematic presentation and was used as such for much of the Byzantine period. In consequence it accumulated an extensive body of scholia and commentary, including a detailed and informative commentary by Choeroboscus (early ninth century). A reworking in verse by John Tzetzes is also extant. Hephaestion continued to be the basis of metrical theory until the nineteenth century, and while modern work on meter has tended to move away from Hephaestion's theories, his terminology is still standard in the field.

Recently Hephaestion has been used chiefly in work on ancient metrical theory, for which Hephaestion's own work is crucial and the ancient commentary on it is also valuable. The collection is however also very important as a source of fragments of lost poetry, and for our understanding of Byzantine classical scholarship.

Hephaestion's exposition has a parallel in the first book of Aristides Quintilianus' three-book *De musica*, which devotes considerable attention to meter. Aristides cannot be securely dated, but he probably wrote between the second and the fourth centuries AD and so is likely to be somewhat later than Hephaestion. His and Hephaestion's treatises are frequently discussed together, as each aids greatly in the interpretation of the other.

The standard text of all Hephaestion's surviving work, Choeroboscus' commentary, and the scholia is that of Consbruch (1906 =*TLG*); for Aristides Quintilianus one uses the text of Winnington-Ingram (1963) and A. Barker (1989) for translation and discussion. The *Encheiridion* has been translated into English, with extensive commentary, by Van Ophuijsen (1987). The two fragments on poems have been translated into German by Nehrling (1989–90), and Van Ophuijsen (1993*b*) gives an English translation of most portions of these fragments, together with the parallel passages from Aristides Quintilianus. Aristides' complete work has been translated into English by Mathiesen (1983) and into German by Schäfke (1937). Other works on Hephaestion include those of Palumbo Stracca (1979) and Consbruch (1889), and examples of recent work using Hephaestion include Lomiento (1995), Gentili (1983), Gentili and Perusino (1999), Wouters (1991–3), and Fowler (1990).

3.3.3 Stobaeus

Ioannes Stobaeus, or John of Stobi, was a writer of the fifth century AD from Stobi in Macedonia. He compiled an anthology of Greek literature from Homer to the fourth century AD, consisting of a set of excerpts ranging in length from a single line to several pages, grouped by theme. The themes involved are primarily (but not exclusively) ethical ones, and the more than five hundred authors represented come from a range of genres in both poetry and prose; Neoplatonic sources tend to predominate, and Christian texts are conspicuously absent. Stobaeus' sources seem to have been primarily earlier anthologies, rather than the original texts themselves.

Stobaeus' work is useful to modern scholars because he preserves numerous extracts from works that are otherwise lost; even when the originals survive, Stobaeus offers an independently (though not necessarily more accurately) transmitted text and so can be useful for textual criticism. Because the anthology was influential in the Byzantine world, it is also helpful for understanding the Byzantine reception of classical literature.

The anthology is in four books and has survived almost intact, though the first book in particular seems to have been somewhat abbreviated. There is an edition by Wachsmuth and Hense (1884–1912 =*TLG*), and an introduction with references to further discussion can be found in Piccione and Runia (2001); Campbell (1984) and Sider (2001) offer some cautions and insights about his quotation and citation processes.

4

Introduction to Scholarly Greek

THE DIFFICULTIES ANCIENT SCHOLARSHIP PRESENTS TO the reader are very different from those involved in reading literary authors such as Demosthenes, Sophocles, Lucian, or Aristophanes. Sentences in lexica, grammars, and scholia tend to be fairly short, and grammatical and syntactic complexities are relatively rare. These works are largely free of obscure, archaic, and dialectal forms, and the vocabulary is in many ways more limited and more manageable than that of most literary texts. Yet scholarly Greek is not easy to read until one becomes familiar with the genre, because it employs a set of space-saving conventions and numerous technical words pertaining to scholarly disciplines. In addition, it sometimes happens (though not as often as one would expect) that the late date of the writer betrays itself in the use of post-classical words or constructions, and a grasp of the Greek numeral systems and the use of various editorial symbols is not infrequently required to get the full meaning of a passage.

4.1 CONVENTIONS AND CHARACTERISTICS OF SCHOLARLY WRITING

4.1.1 Introduction
Scholarly Greek makes use of certain syntactic conventions rarely encountered in classical literature. These allow many words to remain unexpressed and so permit highly compact, very efficient writing, but they require some adjustment on the part of readers more familiar with other types of Greek. Though many such conventions are restricted to particular types of scholarship, others are found more generally.

4.1.2 Basic Formula
In scholia and lexica each entry consists of two parts: the lemma (word or words to be explained) and the definition or comment. The lemma always comes first and in modern editions is usually separated from the comment upon it by an extra space, a change in type font, or a symbol such as a high point or Roman colon. The material that follows the lemma may be any type of comment—a variant reading, a note on spelling or punctuation, a discussion of interpretation, etc.—but if

no indication is given to the contrary, it is usually assumed to consist of, or at least to begin with, a definition or paraphrase. Thus Hesychius' entry γοῖνος· οἶνος (Γ 784 Latte) can be translated "γοῖνος[1] [means] 'wine'," and the T scholion to *Iliad* 12. 6 ἤλασαν: ἐξέτειναν, ἀπὸ τῶν σιδήρων can be translated "ἤλασαν [means] 'they stretched out,' from iron things" [i.e. from the word's use in iron-work], or simply "ἤλασαν: 'they stretched out,' from iron things."[2]

4.1.3 Bracketed Lemmata

Often the lemmata of scholia are bracketed in modern editions; this means that they are absent from the manuscripts and have been supplied from the text commented on. Thus a T scholion to *Iliad* 12. 13 reads ‹κατὰ μὲν Τρώων θάνον:› Ἰακὴ διαίρεσις, that is, "κατὰ μὲν Τρώων θάνον [is an example of] Ionic separation [i.e. tmesis]." A few editions of scholia lack lemmata altogether, forcing the reader to supply them from an edition of the text, but this practice is rare.

4.1.4 Multiple Definitions

In both scholia and lexica a single lemma may be followed by multiple definitions or comments, and in composite works these different definitions or comments may have separate sources. They may be separated only by punctuation, but the addition of words meaning "or," "and," or "alternatively" is not uncommon. Thus one of Hesychius' entries (Α 7280 Latte) reads ἄρκος· ἄρκεσμα. βοήθεια. ἢ τὸ παιόνιον. καὶ τὸ ζῷον. καὶ ἱέρεια τῆς Ἀρτέμιδος, which could be translated "ἄρκος [means] 'aid' [or] 'help,' or the medicine, and the animal,[3] and a priestess of Artemis." In such a passage there is often no difference between "and" and "or."

4.1.5 ἄλλως

In scholia multiple explanations are often separated by ἄλλως, a word indicating that the material after the ἄλλως comes from a different source from that of the material preceding it. Thus the scholia to Pindar's *Pythian* 3. 97 (or 3.173a; really on the sentence ἐν δ᾽ αὖτε χρόνῳ / τὸν μὲν ὀξείαισι θύγατρες ἐρήμωσαν πάθαις / εὐφροσύνας μέρος αἱ τρεῖς, 96–8) read in part τὸν μὲν ὀξείαισι: τὸν μὲν Κάδμον αἱ θυγατέρες ἀπολλύμεναι τὸ τῆς εὐφροσύνης μέρος ἠρήμωσαν. ἐν σχήματι δὲ εἶπεν, ἀντὶ τοῦ εὐφροσύνης ἔρημον ἐποίησαν. b. ἄλλως· τὸν μὲν Κάδμον αἱ τρεῖς θυγατέρες ταῖς ὀξείαις συμφοραῖς τὸ τῆς εὐφροσύνης

---

1. Hesychius uses gamma for digamma here.

2. i.e. this usage of the term is derived from iron-working. ἐλαύνω usually means "drive" in Homer, but that meaning is inappropriate in this passage, since the reference is to the process of creating the ditch the Greeks had dug around their protective wall. The scholiast is both explaining how to understand the verb here and suggesting a source for the odd meaning by connecting it with a rare Homeric usage of ἐλαύνω for "to hammer out [metal]" (see *Iliad* 7. 223): metal is stretched out by hammering it.

3. i.e. the bear (which had a particular connection to Artemis); this entry mixes meanings of ἄρκος, -εος, τό with those of ἄρκ(τ)ος, -ου, ὁ and ἡ.

μέρος ἠρήμωσαν καὶ ἀφείλαντο· . . . This could be translated "τὸν μὲν ὀξείαισι: 'his daughters, by dying, deprived Cadmus of his share of happiness.' For [the poet] said it in a figure, instead of 'they made him destitute of happiness.' Alternatively: 'his three daughters, with sharp misfortunes, deprived Cadmus of his share of happiness and took [it] away'. . . ." In this case (though by no means always) the two entries are very similar and may well have the same ultimate source, but certain scribes were nonetheless scrupulous in distinguishing them. A number of other scribes who copied this same set of scholia were less scrupulous and conflated the two, jumping from the end of the first entry to the end of the section quoted here and thereby making it appear that the information that follows (an explanation of who Cadmus' daughters were and what happened to them) originally went with the first entry rather than the second. Such conflations are common and need to be taken into account in arguments about the original source of a scholion.

4.1.6 Abbreviated Lemmata

The lemma of a scholion may, especially if it is original, be only a part of the passage explained by the scholion. This is the case in the scholion just quoted, for which the lemma makes no sense independently and is simply the beginning of the line[4] whose meaning is discussed; it acts as a link enabling one to find the correct place in the text, like the symbols that were sometimes employed instead of lemmata in ancient hypomnemata. Such abbreviated lemmata are common, with the result that the most important aid to reading scholia is often the text commented on.

4.1.7 Form of Lemmata

The lemmata of scholia and commentaries normally appear in the same form as in the text. The lemmata of lexica vary in form, even within individual lexica; some are in what we think of as the citation form of the word concerned (nominative singular, first-person active indicative), but others, taken over from commentaries, occur in inflected forms.[5] Definitions normally appear in the same form as the lemma; that is, if the lemma is an accusative singular, the definition is in the accusative singular as well, in order to identify the form of the lemma concisely. Thus one of Hesychius' entries (B 647 Latte) reads βλάβεν· ἐσφάλησαν. ἐστέροντο. ἐβλάβησαν; this informs us that βλάβεν is an alternative third-person plural aorist passive of βλάπτω and yields the translation "βλάβεν [means] 'they were overthrown' [or] 'they lost' [or] 'they were harmed'." Similarly a T scholion to *Iliad* 11. 308 reads ἰωῆς: ὁρμῆς, παρὰ τὸ ἴω, which could be translated "ἰωῆς [means] 'of a rush,' [and it comes] from ἴω" (for ἴω see 4.1.22).

---

4. Note that it is not the beginning of the sentence, which starts at the end of 96.

5. This feature is very useful, as sometimes it allows us to trace these lemmata to their original sources in literary texts. However, on occasion lemmata are inflected to fit the syntax of their new contexts, so not all inflected lemmata can be assumed to be original.

4.1.8 Form of Definition

Definitions, especially in lexica, are not necessarily self-standing, that is, they are not always comprehensible without reference to the lemma. Rather the lemma is taken as a basis that remains syntactically available, and from which elements can be understood at any point in the explanation. Thus one of Hesychius' entries (B 1269 Latte) reads βρυχήσασθαι· ὡς λέων, which means "βρυχήσασθαι [means to roar] like a lion."

4.1.9 Nominatives: Definitions

Definitions may be given anywhere in an entry, not only at the beginning, and such definitions often follow the convention that the word to be defined comes first, without an article, and the definition follows it, with the article. The general syntactic rule that of two Greek nominatives the one with the article is the subject and the other the predicate indicates that in such cases the definition is actually the subject and the word to be defined the predicate. Strictly speaking, therefore, the verb to be understood is "is called" rather than "means," and the proper English order would be the reverse of the Greek order. Thus when Hesychius says ἀσαλεῖν· ἀφροντιστῆσαι. Σάλα γὰρ ἡ φροντίς (A 7616 Latte), the literal translation is "ἀσαλεῖν [means] 'to be heedless.' For thought [is called] σάλα" rather than ". . . for σάλα [means] 'thought'." The reverse in order, however, causes a regrettable shift of emphasis, and in some cases the definition is so long and complex that such a reversed order is impractical. Scholars do not agree about whether it is better to be faithful to the grammar or the word order when translating Greek definitions, though readers of this book will observe that I personally tend to follow the grammar.

4.1.10 Nominatives: Sources

Often scholia and entries in lexica contain words in the nominative that are clearly not definitions but govern no expressed verb. Such nominatives are usually sources: most often sources of a particular reading, interpretation, or usage, but potentially sources of anything asserted by the writer of the entry (see below for examples). The type of source can normally be determined by the context, and a verb must usually be added in order to translate the entry unambiguously into English.

4.1.11 Sources: Scholars and Texts

In scholia, when a nominative is the name of a scholar or a group of texts, the meaning is usually that another word or phrase given in the scholion (usually immediately after the nominative) was read instead of (part of) the lemma by that scholar, or that it was found instead of the lemma in that group of texts. Thus an A scholion to *Iliad* 10. 79 reads ‹ἐπέτραπεν:› ᾿Αρίσταρχος "ἐπέτρεπε," which could be translated "ἐπέτραπεν: Aristarchus [reads] ἐπέτρεπε [instead]," and a T scholion to *Iliad* 10. 38 reads ‹ὀτρύνεις:› αἱ ᾿Αριστάρχου "ὀτρυνέεις" διῃρημένως, which means "ὀτρύνεις: the [texts⁶] of Aristarchus [have] ὀτρυνέεις separately [i.e. without contraction]." An A scholion to *Iliad* 11. 632 makes the interesting statement ‹ἦγ’ ὁ γεραιός:› διχῶς Ἀρίσταρχος, ἦγ’ ὁ γεραιός καὶ "εἶχ’ ὁ γεραιός," that is, "ἦγ’ ὁ γεραιός: Aristarchus [reads the text of this passage] in two ways, ἦγ’ ὁ γεραιός and εἶχ’ ὁ γεραιός." The source may also be less precisely identified, as in a T scholion to *Iliad* 12. 142: ‹ἐόντας:› "ἐόντες" αἱ πλείους, which means "ἐόντας: most [texts have] ἐόντες." Similarly a T scholion to *Iliad* 11. 652 reads πάλιν ἄγγελος: τινὲς ὑφ’ ἕν "παλινάγγελος", οὐχ ὑγιῶς, that is, "πάλιν ἄγγελος: some [texts have (or perhaps 'some scholars read') this] as a single word, παλινάγγελος, [but] not well [i.e. it should be two words]." Sometimes, however, the meaning is that the scholar or texts named is the source of the lemma; in such cases no alternative reading is given and the name of the source is usually preceded by οὕτω(ς), as in another (A) scholion to *Iliad* 12. 142, which reads ‹ἐόντες:› οὕτως Ἀρίσταρχος ἐόντες κατὰ τὴν εὐθεῖαν, that is, "ἐόντες: so Aristarchus [reads], ἐόντες in the nominative."⁷

4.1.12 Sources: Authors

In lexica, the sources mentioned are normally not sources of readings, but rather authors or dialects in which the lemma occurs. When the source is an author, the work in which the lemma is found may be given in the dative, as in Hesychius' entry ἄσεπτον· ἀσεβές. Σοφοκλῆς Αἰχμαλωτίσιν (A 7644 Latte) would be translated "ἄσεπτον [means] 'unholy.' Sophocles [uses this word] in the *Aechmalotides*." Dialects are usually indicated by a masculine plural form designating the speakers of a given dialect, so that Hesychius' entry βίώρ· ἴσως. σχεδόν. Λάκωνες (B 645 Latte) can be translated "βίώρ [means] 'perhaps' [or] 'almost.' The Laconians [use this form]." This type of source designation can also be found in scholia, for example in a T scholion to *Iliad* 12. 77 that reads πρυλέες: οὕτω Γορτύνιοι and means "πρυλέες: so the people of Gortyn [call foot-soldiers]," indicating that the word belongs to a Cretan dialect.

4.1.13 Sources: Imprecise

A source can also be the source of a definition or interpretation. A bT scholion to *Iliad* 10. 23 reads ‹δαφοινόν:› λίαν φονευτικόν. τινὲς δὲ πυρρόν, which means "δαφοινόν [means] 'very deadly,' but some [say it means] 'yellowish-red'." Similarly Apollonius Sophista's entry on πολύαινε (133. 14 Bekker) reads πολύαινε: Ἀρίσταρχος πολλοῦ ἐπαίνου ἄξιε. οἱ δὲ πολύμυθε, which could be translated

---

6. The word implied here is ἐκδόσεις; Didymus cites two Aristarchean ἐκδόσεις, which do not always have the same readings (see M. L. West 2001: 61–2).

7. Note that in both the scholia to *Iliad* 12. 142 quoted here, the lemmata have been supplied by the editor. He was able to work out that one scholion presupposed the lemma ἐόντας and the other presupposed ἐόντες because of the convention that if οὕτω(ς) precedes the nominative, the source named is the source of the lemma, but if there is an alternative and no οὕτω(ς), the source named is the source of the alternative.

"πολύαινε: Aristarchus [says it means] 'worthy of much praise,' but others [say it means] 'much talked about'." Occasionally it is difficult to distinguish this type of source from the others, as in Hesychius' entry βλᾶκα καὶ βλακεύειν· τὸν ἀργὸν καὶ ἀργεῖν 'Αθηναῖοι. ἔνιοι προβατώδη (B 664 Latte), where the first part clearly means that βλᾶκα and βλακεύειν are words from the Athenian dialect meaning "idler" and "to do nothing." The second part could conceivably mean either that some scholars think the words mean "sheep-like" (i.e. simple-minded), or that some speakers of other dialects used these words with this meaning (either "[But] some [say it means] 'sheeplike'" or "[But] some [use it with the meaning] 'sheeplike'"), though in this case the first possibility is much more likely.

4.1.14 Sources: Other

Occasionally other kinds of sources are indicated in the same way. Thus for example an A scholion to *Iliad* 12. 205 states ἰδνωθείς: ψιλωτέον τὸ ι. οὕτως καὶ 'Αλεξίων καὶ οἱ ἄλλοι, which since Alexion was a grammarian means "ἰδνωθείς: the ι must have a smooth breathing. Thus both Alexion and the other [grammarians say that this word should be written/pronounced]."

4.1.15 Non-nominative Sources

Of course, nominatives without expressed verbs are not the only kind of source designation found in scholia and lexica. Verbs are not infrequently expressed, and the origin of a lemma or an alternative can also be indicated in other ways that pose less difficulty to English-speaking readers. Thus an A scholion to *Iliad* 12. 179 reads ‹θυμόν:› ἐν ἄλλῳ "θυμῷ," which means "θυμόν: in another [copy/manuscript there is the word] θυμῷ [instead]."

· · · ·

4.1.16 Articles: Paradigms

The article plays a vital role in scholarly Greek, where it has several distinct uses not found in literary texts. When the complete declension of a noun or adjective is given, or when a single case form other than the nominative singular is considered, the article is often used to indicate gender, number, and case.[8] (In the vocative, the particle ὦ substitutes for the article.[9]) This convention relieves the author of having to produce the kind of verbose descriptions of a form that we often use. Thus to decline χαρίεις in the masculine dual, one simply says "Τὼ χαρίεντε,

8. For these purposes the article's feminine dual forms are τά (nom.-acc.) and ταῖν (gen.-dat.), rather than the classical Attic τώ and τοῖν, which would not distinguish gender effectively.

9. Many ancient grammarians considered ὦ to be the vocative of the article; though this view is false from the standpoints of etymology and of classical usage and was recognized as false in antiquity (see Apollonius Dyscolus, *Synt.* 62. 6–74. 3), this particle does function as the vocative of the article in grammatical works.

τοῖν χαριέντοιν, ὦ χαρίεντε" (*GG* iv.i: 11. 15), which is the equivalent of "Nominative-accusative masculine-neuter dual, χαρίεντε; genitive-dative masculine-neuter dual, χαριέντοιν; vocative dual, χαρίεντε."

4.1.17 Articles: Quotation Marks (i)

The article is also frequently used with a word or phrase that is the topic of discussion; phrases normally take neuter articles (as do letters of the alphabet, verb forms, and other words with no gender of their own), and words with their own gender can take either neuter articles or ones corresponding their own gender. These articles serve two important purposes: they show the case that the word has in the syntax of the sentence discussing it, thus making it possible to use a verb form, or even a noun form in an inappropriate case, as the subject of a sentence or as the object of a verb or preposition, and they function like quotation marks in showing that a word is the topic of discussion rather than simply part of a sentence. (Although modern editions may set off such words with quotation marks, letter-spacing, capital letters, or different fonts, no such devices were used in ancient times, and therefore it was essential for Greek writers to make their meaning clear by purely syntactic means.)

4.1.18 Articles: Quotation Marks (ii)

Thus one sees sentences like Περὶ δὲ τοῦ Αὐγούστα λέγουσιν ὅτι ὤφειλεν Αὐγούστη εἶναι ἡ εὐθεῖα διὰ τοῦ η̄ ... , which means "About the [word] Αὐγούστα [fem. nom. sg., modified by an article in the neut. gen. sg.] they say that the nominative should be Αὐγούστη with an η ..." (*GG* iv.i: 305. 7). Similarly, an A scholion to *Iliad* 10. 10 concludes ἐλέγχεται δὲ ὁ Ζηνόδοτος ἁμαρτάνων ἐκ τοῦ "ὣς δ᾽ αὔτως Μενέλαον ἔχε τρόμος," which means "but Zenodotus is shown to be in error by the [phrase] ὣς δ᾽ αὔτως Μενέλαον ἔχε τρόμος," i.e. by the fact that Homer a few lines later says ὣς δ᾽ αὔτως Μενέλαον ἔχε τρόμος. Occasionally such articles, rather than being in the neuter, agree in gender with an understood noun such as a part of speech: thus an A scholion to *Iliad* 10. 18 notes Πάμφιλος τὴν ἐπί ἀναστρέφει ("Pamphilus puts the [preposition] ἐπί into anastrophe," i.e. accents it ἔπι), where the feminine article agrees with an understood πρόθεσιν "preposition." Such articles are usually omitted when translating into English, as they are not needed if the word or phrase so marked remains in Greek.

4.1.19 Order: Paradigms

The order in which elements are given can also convey important information. Since the Greeks normally presented paradigms in a fixed order, context sometimes permitted them to omit the article in declension, as we sometimes omit the verbal description of gender, number, and case. Nominal paradigms without articles assume the following order:[10] nominative singular, genitive singular, dative singular, accusative singular, vocative singular; nominative-accusative dual, genitive-dative dual, vocative dual; nominative plural, genitive plural, dative plural, accusative plural, vocative plural. For gender, the order is masculine, feminine, neuter. Verbs are conjugated in the order first person, second person, third person, with singular preceding plural, and active preceding middle and passive (whose position relative to each other is not consistent).

4.1.20 Order: Derivations

In etymological works, a series of forms is often given to illustrate the steps by which one word is derived from another. The order here is one of progression from the original word to the derivative via intermediate steps that break down the differences between them into one difference per step, and no assertion that the intermediate forms necessarily exist is implied by their presentation in such a context. Such derivations are often simply the way an oblique form relates to its nominative or present indicative, as in the *Etymologicum Gudianum*'s explanation of εἵμαρμαι (ed. De Stefani, vol. ii, p. 420. 7–11): πόθεν; φαμὲν ἀπὸ τοῦ μείρω, μερῶ, μέμαρκα, μέμαρμαι, καὶ κατὰ τοὺς 'Αττικοὺς ἀποβολῇ τοῦ συμφώνου καὶ προσελεύσει τοῦ ι᾽ εἵμαρμαι, ὡς τὸ λέληφα εἴληφα. This could be translated "Where [does it come] from? We say [that it comes] from μείρω, [via the future] μερῶ [which gets rid of the ι], [the perfect active] μέμαρκα [which changes the ε in the root to α], [the perfect passive] μέμαρμαι [which changes the ending to -μαι], and according to Attic speakers [i.e. in Attic] with loss of the consonant and addition of the ι [we get] εἵμαρμαι, as λέληφα [becomes] εἴληφα [in Attic]." In this example the intermediate steps also indicate what grammatical form εἵμαρμαι is, namely the Attic perfect passive of μείρω, but such information is not always provided. Thus the entry for ἡρῴδης in the *Etymologicum magnum* comments (ed. Gaisford, 437. 56–438. 2): ἔστι γὰρ ἥρως, ἥρωος, ἥρωϊ· καὶ γίνεται ἡρωΐδης· καὶ κατὰ συναίρεσιν τοῦ ω καὶ ι εἰς τὴν ωι δίφθογγον, ἡρῴδης. That is, "for there is [as the base form] [nom. sg.] ἥρως, [from which we get the stem ἡρω- from the gen. sg.] ἥρωος, [and the ι from the dat. sg.] ἥρωϊ; and it becomes ἡρωΐδης; and by synaeresis of the ω and ι into the diphthong ῳ [we get] ἡρῴδης."

.   .   .   .   .

4.1.21 Post-Classical Features

Since most Greek scholarship was written well after the end of the classical period, scholarly Greek often shares many of the characteristics of post-classical Greek. Late Greek (especially that of the Byzantine period) normally differs markedly from the classical language, but such differences are less noticeable in scholarly texts than in

---

10. This ancient order of the cases is still followed by many of today's Greek textbooks, though British textbooks are more likely to use a revised order inspired partly by Sanskrit grammatical order; see Allen and Brink (1980).

some other types of literature, since most scholars were well trained in classical Greek usage and made great efforts to write like the classical authors. Nevertheless, even the best grammarians use non-classical constructions on occasion, and in some texts post-classical language is rampant. It is thus useful to be aware of some of the main characteristics of late Greek when reading scholarly texts.[11]

4.1.22 Regularization

One of the most common grammatical features of late Greek is regularization of irregular paradigms. Even grammarians can make the aorists of ἄγω, λείπω, δίδωμι, and τίθημι into ἦξα, ἔλειψα, ἔδωσα, and ἔθησα, or use ἡδύτατος as the superlative of ἡδύς. There is also a tendency for prefixes to be augmented (or even reduplicated) where a classical writer would augment the verb after the prefix. Verbs that normally lack certain forms in the classical period often acquire those forms later; thus the verb τύπτω, for which perfect and aorist forms are very rare in classical writers and which therefore has suppletive principal parts in modern grammars, appears without difficulty in those tenses in later authors.[12] Similar to this general regularization in effect, but distinct from it in cause, is a tendency among grammarians to cite a simple, one-syllable base form for a verb that normally has a more complex citation form: thus we consider βῶ to be the aorist subjunctive of βαίνω, but on occasion an ancient scholar can use βῶ as an equivalent of βαίνω, viewing the shorter form as a kind of underlying base form. Thus a T scholion to *Iliad* 11. 308 reads ἰωῆς: ὁρμῆς, παρὰ τὸ ἴω, which could be translated "ἰωῆς [means] 'of a rush,' [and it comes] from ἴω." Here ἴω (technically the subjunctive of εἶμι *ibo*) is being used as an alternative citation form for εἶμι.[13]

4.1.23 Loss of Distinctions

Some classical Attic distinctions, such as those between οὐ and μή, between ἄλλος and ἕτερος, and between οὗτος "the former" and ὅδε "the latter," are often ignored by later authors (scholiasts, for example, nearly always use οὕτως both where classical authors would have used οὕτως and where they would have used ὧδε). The perfect and aorist tenses may be used interchangeably. Comparative forms

---

11. Late Greek, which has already been thoroughly described elsewhere, is really a separate phenomenon from scholarly Greek. These sections are therefore far more cursory and derivative than the rest of Ch. 4.1; they are intended only to provide the most essential information needed by readers of scholarly Greek that contains late features. Readers are encouraged to consult Gignac (1976–81) or Blass and Debrunner (1979) for more detailed information.

12. Because of its relevance to the students' classroom experience, τύπτω was the standard paradigm verb in elementary Greek grammars for many centuries and was therefore provided with all theoretically possible forms. Not until the modern period did a change in educational philosophy result in the replacement of τύπτω with alternatives like παιδεύω.

13. For such shortened base forms see Dyck (1983–95: ii. 647, s.v. πάτος).

of adjectives are sometimes used as positives (as Δωρικώτερος for "Doric"), and sometimes μᾶλλον is then added to comparatives to make their comparative force clear (as μᾶλλον καταλληλότερος for "more correct"). Neuter plural subjects very often take plural verbs rather than singular ones. Indirect interrogatives such as ὁπότερος and ὅστις may be used in direct questions where classical usage would require the direct interrogatives πότερος and τίς. The subjunctive and the indicative may be confused (not only within each tense, but also to the extent that the aorist subjunctive can be used as a future), and uncertainty occurs in the use of ἄν, leading to confusion between εἰ/ὅτε and ἐάν/ὅταν and to potential optative constructions that lack ἄν and so look like wishes. Conditional sentences can undergo not only confusion of moods and in the use of ἄν, but also some other changes in conjunctions: both ὅτι μή and χωρὶς εἰ μή are equivalent to εἰ μή.

4.1.24 New Formations

Many of the tendencies of late Greek are found in the classical period as well but greatly increase in frequency later. For example, new adjectives are freely formed (especially with -ικός) and used instead of genitives; thus an idea of Aristarchus' is Ἀριστάρχειος "Aristarchean," while the syntax of the adverb is ἐπιρρηματικὴ σύνταξις "adverbial syntax." On the other hand, one sometimes finds prepositional phrases with ἐκ, ἀπό, or κατά where such an adjective (or a plain possessive genitive) might seem more natural to us (e.g. ἡ διάβασις ἡ ἀπὸ τῆς ἐνεργείας at Apollonius Dyscolus, *Adv.* 119. 10, where one could have written ἡ ἐνεργητικὴ διάβασις "active force.")

4.1.25 Periphrasis

There is also a tendency toward periphrasis,[14] including periphrastic verb forms such as ἔστιν ἔχον "is having" for ἔχει "has" or παρεπόμενόν ἐστιν "is following" for παρέπεται "follows" (and, since the verb "be" can be omitted in Greek, such forms sometimes occur without the ἐστί). Certain authors, particularly but not exclusively Apollonius Dyscolus, often use a neuter article with the partitive genitive where a classical writer would use the noun alone (e.g. τὰ τοῦ τόνου "the [things] of the accent" for ὁ τόνος "the accent," or τὸ τῆς συντάξεως "the [thing] of the construction" for ἡ σύνταξις "the construction"); they may also use the same construction with a prepositional phrase instead of the genitive (e.g. τὰ ἐν τῇ ποιότητι "the [things] in the quality" for ἡ ποιότης "quality," or τὸ κατὰ τὸ λευκώλενος "the [thing] about the [word] 'white-armed'" for τὸ λευκώλενος "the [word] 'white-armed'"). Apollonius also has a tendency to use an article with a relative clause to show the case of an omitted antecedent; thus τῶν οἷς ὑπετάγη "of the [things] to which they are subordinated" (*Synt.* 81. 5) or τῷ πρὸς ὅν "to the [person] towards whom" (*Synt.* 156. 2).[15]

14. For which see Aerts (1965).
15. Apollonius' language is idiosyncratic; for more information on it see Schneider's excellent explanation in *GG* ii.iii: 141–61.

4.1.26 Substantivization

Instead of nouns, substantivized adjectives in the neuter are very often used; while for Euripides it may have been true that τὸ σοφὸν οὐ σοφία (*Bacch.* 395), for some grammarians there is clearly no difference between καταλληλότης "correctness" and τὸ κατάλληλον "the correct [thing]."

.   .   .   .   .

4.1.27 Prepositions

The use of prepositions in scholarly writing is particularly tricky. In post-classical Greek prepositions are used more often and in new ways, and the meanings of some prepositions are unpredictable and must simply be gathered from the context. At the same time, however, there are specifically scholarly uses of certain prepositions that are fixed and must be borne in mind whenever those prepositions occur in scholarly contexts. And it is always possible for a preposition to be used in its normal classical sense, even in close proximity to late or technical uses.

4.1.28 Prepositions: παρά

The preposition παρά has a number of common scholarly uses. παρά with the dative is used to indicate authors who employ a term or usage under discussion, and in such contexts is translatable as "in the works of" or simply "in," as περὶ τῶν παρ' Ὁμήρῳ Κυκλώπων καὶ Λαιστρυγόνων (scholion to Thucydides 6. 2. 1), which means "about the Cyclopes and Laestrygonians in Homer", or τὸ γὰρ ὁ ἕτερος διὰ τοῦ ου οὕτερος, ὡς παρὰ Ἡροδότῳ (scholion to Theocritus 7. 36a, p. 88. 10–11 Wendel), which could be translated "for the [phrase] ὁ ἕτερος [when brought together in crasis is written] with an ου, [that is] οὕτερος, as in Herodotus." παρά with dative can also be used with the name of a group of speakers to designate a dialectal or foreign word, as in Hesychius' entry βύβλιοι· οἱ τῶν τάφων φύλακες, παρὰ Κυπρίοις (B 1290 Latte), meaning "βύβλιοι [are] the guardians of tombs, among [i.e. in the dialect of the] Cyprians."[16] With accusative, oddly, παρά often means "from," in the sense of "derived from." Thus a typical entry in the *Etymologicum magnum* (580. 25) states Μερμήριξε: παρὰ τὸ μείρω, that is, "Μερμήριξε [is derived] from μείρω," and Apollonius Sophista comments (107. 24–6 Bekker) λειριόεντα . . . παρὰ τὸ λίαν, meaning "λειριόεντα . . . [is derived] from λίαν." (The same idea, however, is also frequently expressed with ἐκ or ἀπό + genitive, as Λάξ: ἀπὸ τοῦ λήγω ῥήματος (*Etymologicum magnum* 556. 14), which means "Λάξ [is derived] from the verb λήγω.") With genitive, like a number of prepositions, παρά in late texts can mean "by" in a genitive of agent construction, as in a bT scholion to *Iliad* 1. 545 that mentions τὰ παρὰ Ἀγαμέμνονος πρὸς Ὀδυσσέα λεγόμενα "the things said by Agamemnon to Odysseus."

---

16. Greek παρά + dative thus has almost exactly the same scholarly meanings as French *chez* and Latin *apud*; it is English that is difficult here.

4.1.29 Prepositions: εἰς

The preposition εἰς is often used, with or without the verb λήγω "end," to group words by their terminations, in which situations it is best translated "(ending) in." Thus τῶν δὲ εἰς μι ληγόντων ῥημάτων συζυγίαι εἰσὶ τέσσαρες (GG i.i: 59.3) means "and there are four conjugational types of the verbs ending in -μι [i.e. the mi-verbs]," and τὰ εἰς ος ἔχοντα ῥῆμα ἀντιπαρακείμενον διὰ τοῦ ευω (Etymologicum magnum, ed. Gaisford 462. 10–11) means "[nouns ending] in -ος that have a corresponding verb in -ευω." εἰς can also be used in lexica (especially the later ones) to indicate a cross-reference. The Etymologicum Gudianum has a fairly typical entry (p. 195. 8 De Stefani) Ἀριθμητικά· εἰς τὸ Εἴκοσι καὶ Ἑβδομήκοντα, which could be translated "'Ἀριθμητικά: see Εἴκοσι and Ἑβδομήκοντα." When the cross-reference is in addition to some information given under the original heading, it often appears in the form καὶ εἰς, "see also," as in the same etymologicum's entry on Γελοίιος, which concludes (p. 303. 16 De Stefani) καὶ εἰς τὸ Σκῶμμα, that is, "see also Σκῶμμα." Sometimes the formula occurs in a fuller form with ζήτει that gives a hint as to its origin: thus the entry on Οἰδίπους in the Etymologicum magnum concludes (617. 3) with ζήτει εἰς τὸ Εἰδίπους, which means "see (also) Εἰδίπους." Occasionally only the first letter of the cross-reference is given, as εἰς τὸ Θ, which can be translated "see in the section for words beginning with the letter Θ."

4.1.30 Prepositions: διά

Discussions of spelling normally use the formula διά + genitive "with." Thus one finds phrases like διὰ τοῦ ᾱ γράφεται meaning "it is written with an α" (T scholion to Iliad 10. 29) and διὰ τοῦ ν ἀνστήσων ("ἀνστήσων with a ν," A scholion to Iliad 10. 32). Sometimes, when it refers to the spelling of the end of a word, this type of διά is almost indistinguishable from εἰς, as in the second example quoted in 4.1.29.

4.1.31 Prepositions: ἐπί

ἐπί + genitive can often be translated "applied to" or "with reference to," as in Apollonius Sophista's entry (4. 32–4 Bekker) ἀγάασθαι· ἐπὶ μὲν τοῦ θαυμάζειν "ὥς σὲ γύναι ἄγαμαι τέθηπά τε δείδιά τ' αἰνῶς," ἐπὶ δὲ τοῦ φθονεῖν "ἐξείπω, καὶ μήτι κότῳ ἀγάσησθε ἕκαστος," which could be translated "ἀγάασθαι [is] applied on the one hand to being amazed, [as in the line] ὥς σὲ γύναι ἄγαμαι τέθηπά τε δείδιά τ' αἰνῶς, and on the other hand to envying, [as in the line] ἐξείπω, καὶ μήτι κότῳ ἀγάσησθε ἕκαστος."[17] With accusative or dative, ἐπί can mean "after," as in διασταλτέον ἐπὶ τὸ πρόσθε (A scholion to Iliad 12. 446–7), "it is necessary to distinguish [i.e. punctuate] after πρόσθε."

---

17. The lines quoted here are Odyssey 6. 168 and Iliad 14. 111; it is amusing to compare them to these lines as they now appear in texts of Homer.

4.1.32 Prepositions: κατά

The preposition κατά develops such a wide range of meanings in late texts that they are almost beyond classification, and sometimes the meaning must simply be gathered from the context. One often finds phrases like κατὰ πλεονασμὸν τοῦ ε̄ (A scholion to *Iliad* 11. 201) "by addition of an extra ε"; κατὰ τήν εὐθεῖαν (A scholion to *Iliad* 12. 142) "in the nominative"; κατὰ κρᾶσιν (A scholion to *Iliad* 11. 88) "with crasis"; γράφεται γὰρ κατ᾿ ἀμφότερα (scholion to Lucian, *Phalaris* 1. 2) "it is written both ways."

4.1.33 Prepositions: ἐν

ἐν may be found with datives that in classical usage would not need a preposition at all, such as after verbs that take the dative, and both ἐν ᾧ and ἐν οἷς can mean "because." But ἐν is also a common way to give references to specific works, as ὅταν δὲ λέγῃ ἐν τῇ Τ τῆς ᾿Οδυσσείας, which means "when [Homer] says in [book] 19 of the *Odyssey*" (Apollonius Sophista 68. 11 Bekker). When the article τῇ or an ordinal numeral in the feminine (πρώτῃ, πέμπτῃ, etc.) is found alone after ἐν, as here, the noun to be understood is usually βίβλῳ; when the article or number is neuter, the noun understood is βιβλίῳ, but the meaning "book" is the same in either case.

4.1.34 Prepositions: περί

περί commonly has an inclusive use when preceded by a form of οἱ, so that οἱ περὶ Ζηνόδοτον (literally "those around Zenodotus," i.e. Zenodotus' followers) means "Zenodotus and his followers" (e.g. bT scholion to *Iliad* 1.1). Sometimes this construction is even used periphrastically for a single individual, so that τῶν περὶ Τρύφωνα (Apollonius Dyscolus, *Pronouns* 65. 20) equals Τρύφωνος and παρὰ τοῖς περὶ τὸν ᾿Αλκαῖον (Apollonius, *Adverbs* 177. 5) is equivalent to παρὰ ᾿Αλκαίῳ.[18]

·   ·   ·   ·   ·

4.1.35 Other Special Words: λείπει

A number of other words also have notable uses in scholarly writings. When the original text leaves a word to be understood, the scholia often supply that word and indicate it with λείπει or ἐλλείπει meaning "is lacking," "is omitted," or "is understood," as in the A scholion on *Iliad* 15. 432 κατέκτα Κυθήροισι. This scholion begins ὅτι ἐλλείπει ἡ ἔν· ἔστιν γὰρ ἐν Κυθήροις, which means "the [preposition] ἐν is omitted; for [the meaning of the phrase] is ἐν Κυθήροις" (for ὅτι see 4.1.44).

4.1.36 σεσημείωται

The perfect passive of σημειόω "note," σεσημείωμαι, developed in grammatical texts the specialized meaning "be a (noted) exception." It is thus used for exceptions to

18. These constructions have been much discussed; see Gorman (2001).

rules even when not previously noted in the work at hand. So Herodian says (in Schmidt's edition of [Arcadius'] epitome, 39. 4–6) τὰ εἰς χις ὀξύνεται, εἰ μὴ ὀνόματα πόλεων ἢ νήσων εἴη· Κολχίς 'Αντιοχίς παννυχίς. τὸ δὲ ῥάχις σεσημείωται, which means "[words ending] in -χις are oxytone, unless they be names of cities or islands: Κολχίς, 'Αντιοχίς, παννυχίς. But ῥάχις is an exception."

4.1.37 πρόσκειται

As in classical Greek, κεῖμαι and its compounds regularly function as the perfect passive of τίθημι and its compounds. πρόσκειμαι is therefore the perfect passive of προστίθημι "add." It is employed, among other ways, in explanations of grammatical rules: the rule is first stated, and then particular provisions of it, introduced by πρόσκειται, are justified. Thus the *Etymologicum magnum* entry for θυσία contains the rule τὰ διὰ τοῦ ια θηλυκὰ μονογενῆ πρὸ μιᾶς ἔχοντα τὸν τόνον ὑπερδισύλλαβα, μὴ ὄντα ... διὰ τοῦ ι γράφεται (461.36–43) "feminine [words] in -ια, having only one gender [i.e. being nouns not adjectives], of more than two syllables, having the accent one syllable before the end, if they are not . . . [a long list of exceptional categories follows here], are written with ι [i.e. are spelled -ια not -εια]." This rule is followed by a clause-by-clause explanation, beginning πρόσκειται "μονογενῆ" διὰ τὸ Πολυδεύκεια . . . (461.44) "[the specification] μονογενῆ has been added because of Πολυδεύκεια [which would otherwise be an exception to the spelling rule] . . ."

4.1.38 τὸ ἑξῆς

Difficult passages are often explained in scholia and commentaries by paraphrases in which as many as possible of the original words are retained but the sense is clarified by changing their order (and sometimes adding additional words, as in the Pindar scholion quoted in 4.1.5). Such rearrangements may be introduced by τὸ ἑξῆς (ἐστι) "the sequence in which the words are to be taken is." Thus *Iliad* 10. 19, εἴ τινά οἱ σὺν μῆτιν ἀμύμονα τεκτήναιτο, is explained by an A scholion with εἰσὶν οἳ ἀνέγνωσαν καθ᾽ ἓν μέρος λόγου ὡς εὔμητιν, κακῶς· δύο γάρ ἐστι μέρη λόγου, σὺν καὶ μῆτιν. τὸ δὲ ἑξῆς ἐστι συντεκτήναιτο μῆτιν, which could be translated "There are those who read [this] in one word, like εὔμητιν, [but they do this] wrongly; for there are two words, σύν and μῆτιν. And the sequence in which the words are to be taken is συντεκτήναιτο μῆτιν." τὸ ἑξῆς in this meaning should be carefully distinguished from τὰ ἑξῆς, which means "et cetera," and from the adverbial usage of ἑξῆς, in which it means "following, later" as διὸ καὶ ἑξῆς λέγει "wherefore he also says later" (A scholion to *Iliad* 10. 23, mentioning *Iliad* 10. 34).

4.1.39 ὁ δεῖνα

The expression ὁ δεῖνα is used for "someone" to designate an indeterminate person when giving examples; its meaning partially overlaps with that of τις. Thus a scholion on Lucian's *Phalaris* 1. 1 reads in part πάρεδροι: πάρεδρος τοῦ δεῖνος, παρεδρεύει δὲ τῷ δεῖνι· τὸ ὄνομα μετὰ γενικῆς, τὸ δὲ ῥῆμα μετὰ δοτικῆς, which means "πάρεδροι: [one is a] πάρεδρος of someone, but [one] acts as a πάρεδρος to someone; the noun [is construed] with the genitive, but the verb with the dative."

4.1.40 οἷον

The neuter οἷον is used adverbially in grammatical, syntactic, and etymological discussions with the meaning "such as," "as," "e.g." to introduce examples pertaining to a rule that has just been stated. Thus in the Τέχνη attributed to Dionysius Thrax one finds statements like Τύποι δὲ τῶν πατρωνυμικῶν ἀρσενικῶν μὲν τρεῖς, ὁ εἰς δης, ὁ εἰς ων, ὁ εἰς αδιος, οἷον Ἀτρείδης, Ἀτρείων, καὶ ὁ τῶν Αἰολέων ἴδιος τύπος Ὑρράδιος ... (GG i.i: 26. 1–3), which could be translated "And [there are] three types of masculine patronymic: the one in -δης, the one in -ων, [and] the one in -αδιος, such as Ἀτρείδης, Ἀτρείων, and the Ὑρράδιος type [that is] unique to the Aeolians." The example introduced may be a single word, a phrase, or a whole quotation, as in the *Etymologicum magnum* entry on ὅς, which reads in part σημαίνει καὶ ἀντωνυμίαν ἰσοδυναμοῦσαν τῇ οὗτος· οἷον, Ὅς γὰρ δεύτατος ἦλθεν Ἀχαιῶν χαλκοχιτώνων (635. 14–15), that is, "it also has the force of a pronoun having the same meaning as the [pronoun][19] οὗτος, as [in the line] Ὅς γὰρ δεύτατος ἦλθεν Ἀχαιῶν χαλκοχιτώνων."

4.1.41 εἶδος

The formula εἶδος + genitive is often used in definitions to mean "a kind of," as in an A scholion to *Iliad* 10. 30 that reads στεφάνη εἶδος περικεφαλαίας and means "στεφάνη [is] a kind of helmet"; or as in Hesychius' entry (Δ601 Latte) δελφίνιον· εἶδος βοτάνης, which means "δελφίνιον [is] a kind of plant."

4.1.42 ὁ ποιητής

If a reference is given to ὁ ποιητής, and the context does not indicate which poet is involved, Homer is normally meant.[20] Thus Erotian, in his glossary of Hippocratic words (A 31 Nachmanson), uses διδάσκει δὲ καὶ ὁ ποιητής "and the poet also teaches us" to introduce a quotation from Homer in an entry where not only has Homer not been previously mentioned, but Euripides has just been named. In some texts there is a similar usage of ὁ τεχνικός ("the grammarian") to mean Apollonius Dyscolus or Herodian.

4.1.43 Omitted Subject

The particular poet or other author who is the subject of commentary need not be designated by any noun at all, since he is assumed to be the subject of any appropriate verb for which no other subject is expressed. Thus an A scholion on

---

19. The noun implied by τῇ is ἀντωνυμία "pronoun."

20. This rule is not absolute, and other poets are occasionally so designated by Byzantine writers.

Iliad 10. 326 states ‹μέλλουσιν·› ὅτι ἀντὶ τοῦ ἐοίκασι. καὶ οὕτως ἀεὶ κέχρηται τῇ λέξει, which means "μέλλουσιν [is] instead of ἐοίκασι. And [Homer] always uses the word in this way."[21]

4.1.44 ὅτι etc.

ὅτι is sometimes used redundantly at the beginnings of scholia, as in the passage just quoted and that in 4.1.35. This usage may go back to Alexandrian marginal signs and have originally meant something like "the sign is there because" or "Aristarchus put a sign there because." Sometimes such a ὅτι can be translated with "because" or "note that," but often it is best treated as an introductory marker (and omitted in translation). In this function it can be useful for separating several comments that appear in the same scholion, since it can appear at the start of each one. διότι, καθότι, and καθό can all mean "because." ὅτι, ὡς, and sometimes καθό and διότι can mean "that" and introduce indirect statements, which are much less likely to use the accusative and infinitive or accusative and participle constructions than are indirect statements in classical Attic.

4.1.45 ὡς

Apollonius can use ὡς with participles to mean "because," even when it is accompanied by ἄν or is in the compound forms ὡσεί, ὡσανεί, or ὡσπερεί; thus we find not only οὐχ ὡς ἐγκειμένου τοῦ πύσματος "not because there is an interrogative in [it]" (*Synt.* 455. 15–16), but also ὡς ἂν αὐτοῦ προϋφεστῶτος "because it existed previously" (*Synt.* 19. 4) and ὡσεὶ λελησμένοι "because having forgotten" (*Synt.* 392. 9–10). When used with conjugated verbs, ὡσεί can be the equivalent of either ὡς or ὅτι, and with adjectives ὡς can mean "quasi-" or "used like."

．　　　　．　　　　．　　　　．　　　　．

4.1.46 Horizontal Bar

Certain typographical conventions widely used in editions of scholarly texts are also helpful to the reader. The most important of these is that when groups of letters that do not form a complete word are discussed, a horizontal line is normally placed over them to indicate that they are not to be read as a word, as "τὰ εἰς θαι λήγοντα" meaning "words ending in -θαι" (A scholion to *Iliad* 10. 67). The same applies to discussions of individual letters, as in another A scholion to *Iliad* 10. 67, which comments καὶ δῆλον ὅτι μεταβέβληται τὸ γ̄ εἰς τὸ χ̄ ἐν τῷ ἄνωχθι διὰ τὸ θ̄, that is, "and it is clear that the γ has been changed to χ in ἄνωχθι on account of the θ." As such use of horizontal bars is usual in manu-

---

21. The accuracy of this statement as it stands may be debatable, but it contains the remains of an important point made by Aristonicus, for this fundamental meaning of μέλλω (cf. LSJ s.v.) is more common in Homer than in later texts.

scripts as well as in modern editions, an editor's practice in this respect may well have manuscript authority (though such authority cannot be safely presumed).

4.1.47 Accentuation

When a whole word is being discussed, it is not so marked, but its separation from the syntax of the sentence may still be indicated by its accentuation, if it is naturally oxytone. Since a word under discussion is not really part of the sentence in which it is mentioned, a final acute accent on such a word is not changed to a grave, and these anomalous-looking acute accents can give the reader valuable hints about how to read a sentence. Thus in the Τέχνη attributed to Dionysius Thrax one finds the statement τοῦ δὲ ὀνόματος διαθέσεις εἰσὶ δύο, ἐνέργεια καὶ πάθος, ἐνέργεια μὲν ὡς κριτή ς ὁ κρίνων, πάθος δὲ ὡς κριτός ὁ κρινόμενος (GG i.i: 46. 1–2), which could be translated "and there are two voices of the noun, active and passive; active like κριτής 'the one who judges,' and passive like κριτός 'the one who is judged'." This convention is not followed in all texts.

4.1.48 Spacing

Words that are the topic of discussion are sometimes marked by wider spacing between the letters than is found in other words, as κ ρ ι τ ή ς and κ ρ ι τ ό ς in the example just given. This spacing, which is a substitute for quotation marks, is not always easy to spot and can be used inconsistently. Therefore the absence of such extra spacing, even in an edition where it occurs elsewhere, does not necessarily show that the word in question should be read as a grammatical part of the sentence. The same type of spacing can also be used for quotations from texts, for proper names, or for other words the editor wishes to set apart from the rest of the text.

4.2 TECHNICAL VOCABULARIES

4.2.1 Introduction

Our own system of grammatical analysis is a direct descendant of that developed by the Greeks, so most Greek concepts in these areas are ones with which we are familiar. Moreover, most of our grammatical terminology comes from Latin terms that were themselves calques of Greek grammatical terminology (e.g. "case" from Latin *casus* "fall," which was derived from the Greek use of πτῶσις "fall" for a grammatical case). As a result most of the Greek grammatical vocabulary can be assimilated fairly easily by Classicists: one need only learn the Greek words for those familiar concepts, for example that δοτική means "dative case." The difficulties come in two areas. One is that our system of grammatical analysis is not identical to that of the Greeks, and therefore some of the concepts expressed by their terminology are not familiar to us: for example, we tend to say that Greek had three genders, but many Greek grammarians thought there were four or five (see 4.2.11 below), giving us some words for genders that are not immediately equivalent to anything currently in use.

4.2.2 Fluidity of Usage

The second difficulty is that there is a certain fluidity in Greek technical terminology, so that the same word can have a number of different uses in different passages. Often these differences are the result of the evolution of grammatical theory during the thousand or so years in which ancient scholarship developed. Our own grammatical analyses and terminology are not the same as those current in 1000 AD, nor even, in some cases, are the Greek grammatical analyses standard in the English-speaking world the same as those now used in France or Germany, so it is not surprising that different ancient grammarians could have different terminology from one another. Sometimes, however, a single word can have a variety of uses even within one grammatical treatise; for example Dionysius Thrax uses ἀόριστος both to mean "aorist tense" and to mean "indefinite." The root of this problem is the fact that Greek grammatical terms were often common words that had non-technical as well as technical meanings (e.g. even after it came to be used for "case," πτῶσις continued to mean "fall," to grammarians as well as to other Greeks), and even the less common ones were usually formed by a transparent process of derivation that gave them a basic meaning obvious to all (e.g. ἀόριστος is clearly derived from the alpha privative and ὁρίζω "divide, define," with the result that the basic meaning "indefinite" is always available). Thus the basic, etymological meanings of grammatical terms continued to be present in the minds of writers and readers, and words could be used both in those senses and in more developed technical uses (such as "case" or "aorist") without any more discomfort than an English speaker would feel about a sentence like "It is certainly not the case that Greek words could be used in random order because of the syntactic information conveyed by their cases." It is therefore important to look carefully at the context of an ambiguous term and consider all its possible uses before deciding on a translation.

4.2.3 Limitations

Greek grammatical terminology is a complex issue that has been much discussed, and fuller information about the different terms can be found in the Glossary below (Ch. 6). The following summary, which is based on the classifications of Dionysius Thrax, is something of an oversimplification but should suffice for dealing with most scholarly texts from the Hellenistic, Roman, and later periods. It does not, however, necessarily apply to the grammatical discussions of Aristotle and the Stoics, since early Greek grammar employed different concepts from those found in the later system.

4.2.4 Vowels etc.

A λόγος (sentence; note that while λόγος has many meanings in grammatical writings, it cannot mean "word" in such texts) is made up of λέξεις (words; sometimes ὄνομα, μόριον, μέρος λόγου, or other terms are also used for our "word," all with slightly different meanings), which in turn are composed of συλλαβαί (syllables, lit. "takings together") made up of στοιχεῖα (sounds/letters, lit. "elements" of language) written with, and often not clearly distinguished from, γράμματα (written letters). στοιχεῖα can be φωνήεντα (vowels, lit. "things sounding") or σύμφωνα (consonants, lit. "things sounding with," because they often cannot be pronounced without a vowel). φωνήεντα may be μακρά (long), βραχέα (short), or δίχρονα/κοινά (capable of being either long or short); δίφθογγοι (diphthongs, lit. "two sounds") are formed by combining a προτακτικὸν φωνῆεν (a vowel that comes first in a diphthong) with a ὑποτακτικὸν φωνῆεν (one that comes second, i.e. ι or υ).

4.2.5 Consonants

σύμφωνα may be ἡμίφωνα (lit. "semivowels," but the sounds so designated are continuants, i.e. ζ, ξ, ψ, λ, μ, ν, ρ, and σ, since these can be pronounced on their own almost like vowels; therefore this category corresponds to our liquids, nasals, and sibilants, not our semivowels), or ἄφωνα (stops, lit. "not sounding [on their own]"), which are further divided into ψιλά (bare, i.e. without aspiration; applied to the voiceless unaspirated stops κ, π, τ), δασέα (hairy, i.e. aspirated; applied to θ, φ, χ), and μέσα (middle, used for the voiced stops β, γ, δ). Other groups of consonants include the διπλᾶ (double: ζ, ξ, ψ) and the ἀμετάβολα or ὑγρά ("unchanging" or "fluid," used for the liquids and nasals: λ, μ, ν, ρ).

4.2.6 Diacritics and Punctuation

In addition to the στοιχεῖα there are προσῳδίαι (diacritic marks, or features of pronunciation so indicated). These include πνεύματα (breathings), which may be δασέα (rough) or ψιλά (smooth, lit. "bare"; note that this terminology corresponds to that used for aspirated and unaspirated stops), and a variety of στιγμαί (punctuation marks, lit. "dots"). The most commonly mentioned στιγμαί are the τελεία (period/full stop, lit "complete"), διαστολή (lit. "separation," used for a type of comma), and ὑποστιγμή (lit. "dot underneath," used for another type of comma).

4.2.7 Accents (i)

The most frequently mentioned προσῳδίαι are the τόνοι (accents), which are more often discussed with verbs than with the nouns and adjectives we tend to use. ὀξύνειν and ὀξύτονος (oxytone, lit. "sharp-toned") are used for syllables having an ὀξεῖα [προσῳδία] (acute accent), and for words with such an accent on the final syllable. Words with an ὀξεῖα on the penult could be designated by παροξύνειν/παροξύτονος (paroxytone), and those with an ὀξεῖα on the antepenult by προπαροξύνειν/προπαροξύτονος (proparoxytone), though they were often called βαρύτονος (see 4.2.9 below) instead.

4.2.8 Accents (ii)

The second main accentual group consists of words having a περισπωμένη (circumflex accent, lit. one "drawn around"). These are designated by περισπᾶν and περισπώμενος (perispomenon), used for syllables bearing a περισπωμένη and for words with a περισπωμένη on the final syllable, and προπερισπᾶν/προπερισπώμενος (properispomenon), used for those with a περισπωμένη on the penult.

4.2.9 Accents (iii)

Unaccented syllables are designated by βαρύνειν and βαρύτονος (lit. "heavy-toned"). When referring to whole words, these terms were in antiquity defined as designating those with no accent on the final syllable,[22] but in practice they were normally used for words with a recessive accent (i.e. one as close to the beginning of the word as the normal rules of Greek accentuation allow), thus providing a convenient cover term for the προπαροξύτονοι, most of the παροξύτονοι, and many of the προπερισπώμενοι.[23] Only rarely do ancient writers use these terms for words having a βαρεῖα (grave accent) on the last syllable.[24] Enclitics are ἐγκλιτικοί (lit. "leaning on [a word with an accent]").

4.2.10 Parts of Speech

The μέρη λόγου (parts of speech) are not divided exactly as in modern grammars. Most, but not all, ancient grammarians divided words into eight parts of speech. They are the ὄνομα (noun, lit. "name," used for both nouns (substantives) and adjectives), ῥῆμα (verb), μετοχή (participle, lit. "participation [in the character-istics of both nouns and verbs]"), ἄρθρον (article, lit. "joint," used for both articles

---

22. See Philoponus, τονικὰ παραγγέλματα, ed. W. Dindorf (1825: 6. 15–17).

23. All proparoxytone words are necessarily recessive; paroxytone ones are recessive unless the final syllable has a short vowel, and properispomena are recessive if composed of only two syllables; thus ἔλιπον, ἀπολείπω, and λεῖπε are all recessive and would be called βαρύτονα, but ἀπόδος and ἀποδοῦναι are not. By modern definitions, a monosyl-lable may be recessive even if it is accented (e.g. Ζεῦ), but the ancients did not use the term βαρύτονος for monosyllables. Thus the only words in which the ancient definition (unaccented final syllable) and the ancient practice (recessive accent) do not coincide are those with three or more syllables, of which the last is short, with an accent on the penultimate (e.g. ἀπόδος and ἀποδοῦναι); and even these are occasionally called βαρύτονα (see Arcadius' epitome of Herodian, Moritz Schmidt 1860: 100. 13, 15).

24. Accent marks almost never occur in inscriptions but are present from the early Hellenistic period in some papyri; they were invented by Aristophanes of Byzantium (see Lameere 1960: 90–2). Originally they were applied sporadically as aids to reading, par-ticularly to indicate the division of words (between which no spaces were left in ancient texts). The acute and circumflex marked accented syllables, while the grave could be used to indicate any unaccented syllable; it was particularly helpful in alerting the reader to long compounds by showing that the syllable that would have been accented in the sim-plex form had no accent (e.g. ὀρεὶχάλκωι for our ὀρειχάλκῳ). During the Roman period the grave came to be used to mark the suppression of a final acute before another word (as in modern texts). See Moore-Blunt (1978).

and relative pronouns), ἀντωνυμία (pronoun,[25] lit. "name-replacement,"), πρόθεσις (preposition, lit. "putting before," designating both prepositions and preverbs), ἐπίρρημα (adverb, lit. "on the verb," usually applied to adverbs but also to some words we classify as conjunctions, particles, and interjections), and σύνδεσμος (conjunction, lit. "binding together," usually applied to conjunctions but also to some adverbs and particles).

4.2.11 Nouns (i)

ὀνόματα have γένος (gender), which can be ἀρρενικόν/ἄρρεν (masculine), θηλυκόν/θῆλυ (feminine), οὐδέτερον (neuter), κοινόν (common, i.e. capable of being either masculine or feminine, as ὁ or ἡ ἵππος), or ἐπίκοινον (epicene, i.e. a word with a fixed gender used for both masculine and feminine beings, as ἡ χελιδών "swallow," which is used for swallows of either sex). ὀνόματα also have ἀριθμός (number), which can be ἑνικός (singular), δυϊκός (dual), or πληθυντικός (plural); and πτῶσις (case, lit. "fall"): εὐθεῖα, ὀρθή, or ὀνομαστική (nominative, lit. "straight," "upright," or "for naming"); γενική, κτητική, or πατρική (genitive, lit. "of the γένος," "possessive," or "of the father"); δοτική or ἐπισταλτική (dative, lit. "for giving" or "epistolary"[26]); αἰτιατική (accusative[27]); and κλητική or προσαγορευτική (vocative, lit. "for calling" or "for addressing"). Those πτώσεις that are not ὀρθαί can be grouped together as πλάγιαι (oblique, lit. "sideways"); the process of putting a noun into such a case is κλίνειν (to decline, lit. "cause to slope").

4.2.12 Nouns (ii)

ὀνόματα are also characterized by εἶδος (derivational status, lit. "form"), i.e. πρωτότυπον (primary, underived, lit. "original") or παράγωγον (derived, lit. "led aside"); this latter term includes among other derivational types πατρωνυμικόν (patronymic), κτητικός (possessive), συγκριτικόν (comparative, lit. "for comparing"), ὑπερθετικόν (superlative, lit. "for putting higher"), and ὑποκοριστικόν (diminutive, lit. "for calling endearing names"). The term εἶδος is also used for a completely different classification of ὀνόματα that includes κύρια (proper names), προσηγορικά (common nouns), ἐπίθετα (adjectives, lit. "put on [a noun]"), ὁμώνυμα (homonyms), συνώνυμα (synonyms), ἐθνικά (ethnics), ἐρωτηματικά or πευστικά (interrogative adjectives), ἀόριστα (indefinite adjectives), and πεποιημένα (onomatopoeic words); some of these categories are not mutually exclusive. ὀνόματα are also classified by σχῆμα (compositional status), by which a word can be ἁπλοῦν

25. Including the pronominal adjectives known both as "possessive pronouns" and as "possessive adjectives" in English (ἐμός, ἡμέτερος, etc.).
26. This last term comes from the use of the dative for the addressee in letter headings, e.g. Πλάτων Διονυσίῳ χαίρειν "Plato to Dionysius, greetings" (*Epistle* 3).
27. The literal meaning of this term is disputed; see Lallot (1998: 146–8), Dalimier (2001: 345–6), De Mauro (1965).

(simplex, i.e. uncompounded), σύνθετον (compounded, lit. "put together"), or παρασύνθετον (derived from a compound).

4.2.13 Verbs

ῥήματα are characterized by ἔγκλισις (mood), διάθεσις (voice), πρόσωπον (person, lit. "face"), χρόνος (tense), and συζυγία (conjugation, lit. "yoking together [into classes]"), in addition to the ἀριθμός, εἶδος (in the first sense, i.e. primary or derived), and σχῆμα that they share with ὀνόματα. The ἐγκλίσεις are ὁριστική or ἀποφαντικός (indicative, lit. "for defining" or "for declaring"), προστακτική (imperative, lit. "for commanding"), εὐκτική (optative, lit. "for wishing/praying"), ὑποτακτική (subjunctive, lit. "for putting under/after"), and ἀπαρέμφατος (infinitive, lit. "with [person, number, etc.] not indicated"); the μετοχή (participle) is not an ἔγκλισις but a μέρος λόγου. The διαθέσεις are ἐνέργεια (active, lit. "activity"), πάθος (passive, lit. "experience"), and μεσότης (middle), while the πρόσωπα are πρῶτον (first), δεύτερον (second), and τρίτον (third). The χρόνοι are ἐνεστώς (present, lit. "standing in [our time]"), παρεληλυθώς or παρῳχημένος (past, lit. "having gone past"), and μέλλων (future, lit. "yet to happen"); παρεληλυθώς is further divided into παρατατικός (imperfect, lit. "continuing"), παρακείμενος[28] (perfect, lit. "lying beside," "at hand"), ὑπερσυντέλικος (pluperfect, lit. "beyond completed"), and ἀόριστος (aorist, lit. "without boundaries"). Classified by συζυγία, a verb can be βαρύτονος (ordinary ω-verbs, because these have a recessive accent), περισπώμενος (contract verbs, because these usually have a circumflex accent), or εἰς μι λήγων (μι-verbs, lit. "ending in -μι").

4.2.14 Others

ἄρθρα are divided into προτακτικόν (the definite article, because it is put before the noun) and ὑποτακτικόν (the relative pronoun, because it is put after its antecedent), while ἀντωνυμίαι can be ἀσύναρθροι (pronouns, because these do not take an article) or σύναρθροι (possessive adjectives, because these usually take an article in Greek). σύνδεσμοι include συμπλεκτικοί (lit. "twining together," used for copulative conjunctions, i.e. those meaning "and" or "but"), διαζευκτικοί (lit. "separating," used for disjunctive conjunctions, i.e. those meaning "or"), συναπτικοί (lit. "joining together," used for conditional conjunctions, i.e. those meaning "if"), αἰτιολογικοί (causal, used for conjunctions meaning "since" or "because"), and παραπληρωματικοί (lit. "filling out," used for particles such as δή or γε).

.   .   .   .   .

4.2.15 Further Information

The foregoing discussion includes only a few of the most common elements of grammatical Greek. Some more are included in the Glossary (Ch. 6 below), and one can also consult LSJ and Bécares Botas (1985). The scholarly literature on

---

28. Some grammarians agree with modern classifications in considering the perfect a type of present tense.

this type of Greek, however, is not always adequate to explain everything one finds in texts, and sometimes one is reduced to working out a word's meaning for one-self. The best way to do this is to examine parallel passages, by collecting as much data as possible on the way the word in question is used by the author concerned, or at least in texts from the same genre and date. An effective way to collect such data is to search the author's works electronically for the word in question. If the text involved is a scholion, the word index to Erbse's edition of the *Iliad* scholia (1969–88) is another good source of information on usage. Some editions of other scholarly texts also have indices that can be useful for this purpose, and occasion-ally (as in the case of Apollonius Dyscolus) editors even provide a glossary. Such specialized glossaries must be treated with caution when used for texts other than the ones for which they were designed, but they may still be a valuable resource in emergencies.

4.2.16 Other Specialized Vocabularies

Grammatical terminology forms only one of the specialized vocabularies that may be encountered in scholarly texts. It is the only one explained here because it is the most common in the type of works covered by this book and the hardest to master with existing resources, but rhetoric, philosophy, metrical analysis, and literary criticism all have their own technical terminology, which is not infrequently encountered in scholia. Readers with particular interest in scholia on these top-ics should consult modern scholarship in these areas for the detailed nuances of specific terms, but for ordinary purposes the definitions in LSJ often suffice. Scholia and commentaries on works on technical subjects, such as medicine, astronomy, or geometry, often use the technical terminology of the discipline concerned as well as scholarly vocabularies; here again consultation of subject-specific works is necessary when one wishes to go beyond the information given in LSJ. The procedures mentioned in 4.2.15 are also useful.

4.3 NAMES AND TITLES

There are two difficulties with the personal or place-names and book titles that occur in scholarly texts: determining what is a name or title and what is not, and identifying the bearers of names. In many modern editions the first problem is partially solved by the editors, who often capitalize names and at least the first word of a title; quotation marks are occasionally used for titles as well. Such indi-cations do not however normally have manuscript authority, and they are not al-ways completely trustworthy, so it is useful to keep an open mind about what is and is not a title. With many editions the open mind is encouraged by the fact that capitalization and quotation marks are used sporadically or not at all.

Determining whether a mention of an ancient work is giving a title or simply a description can be difficult. Many ancient titles begin with the word περί "about," and therefore a comment such as λέγει ἐν τῷ περὶ Ὁμήρου could in theory mean either "says in his [book] about Homer" or "says in his [book] *About Homer.*" The situation is complicated by the fact that the concept of a book title was not as well established in antiquity as it is today: ancient titles often seem not to go back to the authors themselves, and particularly at early periods works might have had no title at all (being known by their opening words) or several (being known sometimes by one and sometimes by another; see Nachmanson 1941 and Schröder 1999). The modern practice is that when a reference to an ancient work could contain a title, it is usually assumed to do so. Thus ὡς καὶ Φιλοξένῳ ἐν τῷ Περὶ προσῳδιῶν δοκεῖ (from an A scholion to *Iliad* 1. 231) would be printed with a capitalized Περί and translated "as Philoxenus also decides in his *About Diacritics.*"

Names of people and places are usually easier to recognize than titles. It is not, however, always simple to find out who or what the referent was. Pauly–Wissowa (*RE*) has entries on most obscure authors and is often the fullest source of information, but some information there is out of date, and finding the right entry when there are many with the same name requires patience. The *Neue Pauly* (*NP*) often omits obscure authors, though it is usually worth checking anyway for recent bibliography. The *TLG Canon* (Berkowitz and Squitier 1990) can be useful if the person mentioned left any extant writings (including fragments that have been edited as a collection), and the distinguishing epithets it provides can then be used to identify the relevant entry in Pauly–Wissowa. If the name is that of a place rather than an author, Pauly–Wissowa can still be helpful, but there are various geographical dictionaries as well that are often useful. Mythological figures, likewise, can sometimes be located in specialized works.

4.4 REFERENCES

When a quotation or other type of citation occurs in a work of ancient scholarship, most modern editors add to the text a reference to the work cited. Sometimes the reference is to a work that is still extant, and under those circumstances the references are normally familiar to most readers and easy to follow up (e.g. line numbers for tragedies, Stephanus numbers for Plato).

Often, however, the citation involves a lost work, and in that case the references are usually harder to use. Such references refer to collections of fragments, and usually all one finds if one looks in the collection is a reprinting of the source one is already using. Sometimes, however, useful information can be found in the collection (either because there is information from other sources that bears on the fragment concerned, or because the editor of the collection has re-edited the source of the fragment). This is particularly likely to be the case if the collected fragments have been edited more recently than the source text.

Precisely in such circumstances, however, it is often difficult to use editors' references to find the right collection. Editors inevitably refer to collections that predate their own work, and yet it is particularly important for modern readers to check collections that postdate the edition of the source text. In addition, the abbreviations used can make it difficult to find even the collection to which the editor was referring once it has become obsolete and obscure.

There are three large collections of fragments that between them cover more than half the citations in most scholarly texts: tragic fragments are found in Snell, Kannicht, and Radt's *Tragicorum Graecorum Fragmenta*, abbreviated "*TrGF*" (except fragments of Euripides, for which one must still use the older collection: Nauck's *Tragicorum Graecorum Fragmenta*, abbreviated "*TGF*"), comic fragments are in Kassel and Austin's *Poetae Comici Graeci*, abbreviated "K–A" or "*PCG*," and many types of prose fragments can be found in Jacoby's *Fragmente der griechischen Historiker*, abbreviated "*FGrHist*" or sometimes "Jacoby". Each of these collections contains concordances enabling one to find the fragment number that corresponds to a number in an older edition, so if one needs to follow up an outdated reference to a lost work in one of these genres, the best way to proceed is to skip the work to which the editor refers altogether and use the concordances to find the fragment in the modern collection.

If the fragment concerned is not in any of these collections, information on the best place to look for it can often be obtained by looking up the author in Berkowitz and Squitier (1990), *NP*, *RE*, or (for fragments of relatively well-known authors) *OCD*, and using the editions listed in those works. Usually once one has found the best edition it will contain a concordance to enable one to convert fragment numbers belonging to an earlier collection. If one needs to follow up an editor's reference to the actual outdated source cited, and the abbreviation used is not in the editor's list of abbreviations, it can often be found by looking in older reference works, especially *RE*.

4.5 NUMBER SYSTEMS

There are several ancient Greek numeral systems, all of which use letters as numbers. The different systems use many of the same letters but assign them different values, requiring alertness on the part of the reader. By far the most common system in scholarly (and literary and scientific) Greek texts is one based on the order of letters in the alphabet, which closely resembles the numeral system of Biblical Hebrew. This system uses the letters (normally, but not always, followed by a small diagonal mark to indicate that they are to be read as numbers rather than letters) as follows:

α΄ = 1	ι΄ = 10	ρ΄ = 100	͵α΄ = 1000
β΄ = 2	κ΄ = 20	σ΄ = 200	͵β΄ = 2000, etc.
γ΄ = 3	λ΄ = 30	τ΄ = 300	
δ΄ = 4	μ΄ = 40	υ΄ = 400	
ε΄ = 5	ν΄ = 50	φ΄ = 500	
Ϝ΄ or ϛ΄ = 6	ξ΄ = 60	χ΄ = 600	
ζ΄ = 7	ο΄ = 70	ψ΄ = 700	
η΄ = 8	π΄ = 80	ω΄ = 800	
θ΄ = 9	ϟ΄ = 90	ϡ΄ = 900	

These letters are strung together from left to right, in decreasing order of magnitude, with the diagonal mark occurring only after the last one: thus νδ΄ is 54, ψξε΄

is 765, and ‚ητγ´ is 8,303. In this numeral system the letters are virtually never capitalized, at least in modern editions. Such letters can represent ordinal as well as cardinal numbers.

In referring to books of the *Iliad* and *Odyssey*, a different alphabetic system is used, employing only letters of the classical Ionic alphabet. In this system:

α = 1	η = 7	ν = 13	τ = 19
β = 2	θ = 8	ξ = 14	υ = 20
γ = 3	ι = 9	ο = 15	φ = 21
δ= 4	κ = 10	π = 16	χ = 22
ε = 5	λ = 11	ρ = 17	ψ = 23
ζ= 6	μ = 12	σ = 18	ω = 24

In this system no numeral consists of more than one letter, and diagonal marks are not normally added. The letters may be capitalized or not; when no work is specified, most editors follow the convention that capital letters refer to books of the *Iliad* and lower-case ones to books of the *Odyssey*.

The third numeral system has nothing to do with alphabetic order but follows an acrophonic principle, so that I = 1, Γ = 5, Δ = 10, H = 100, X = 1,000, and M = 10,000.[29] These letters are always capitalized and are strung together from left to right in decreasing order of magnitude, so that XHHΔΔΔΔΓΙ is 1,246. They can also be combined with each other and with monetary symbols such as Σ (stater) and T (talent) in certain prescribed patterns, such as Ϝ (50), Ϝ (5,000), or Δ(10 talents), leading to numerals like MXXϜHHϜΔΓΙΙΙ (12,768). This numeral system is common in classical inscriptions but very rare in works of scholarship.[30]

The third system is unlikely to cause difficulties, both because its distinctive strings of capital letters make it easy to identify and because it is so rarely found in scholarly works. The first two, however, are easily confused. An ancient scholar referring to book ζ will mean *Odyssey* 6 if he is discussing Homer but book 7 if he is discussing Thucydides, and one referring to book λ will mean *Odyssey* 11 if he is discussing Homer but book 30 if he is discussing Polybius.

Thus the scholion to the beginning of Pindar's first *Pythian* comments ἐνίκησε δὲ ὁ Ἱέρων τὴν μὲν κς´Πυθιάδα καὶ τὴν ἑξῆς κέλητι, τὴν δὲ κθ´ἅρματι, i.e. "and Hieron won the 26th Pythiad and the following one with a racehorse, but the 29th with a chariot," while that to the beginning of the second *Pythian* states τῆς δευτέρας ᾠδῆς ἡ μὲν στροφὴ καὶ ἀντίστροφος κώλων ιε´. τὸ α´δίμετρον τροχαϊκὸν καταληκτικὸν . . . , which means "the strophe and antistrophe of the second ode [are] of 15 cola. The 1st [is] a trochaic dimeter catalectic . . ." Hesychius says βίσταξ· ὁ β´⟨μετὰ⟩ βασιλέα παρὰ Πέρσαις (B 632 Latte), which can be

---

29. From πέντε (the symbol Γ is Π written in the old Attic alphabet), δέκα, ἑκατόν (written in the old Attic alphabet where H indicated a rough breathing rather than the letter we know as eta), χίλιοι, and μύριοι. The sign for "one" is not acrophonic.

30. For more complete information on the acrophonic numeral system see works on Greek epigraphy, e.g. Woodhead (1959: 109).

translated "βίσταξ [means] the 2nd [man] after the king, among the Persians [i.e. in the Persian language]." But the A scholion to *Iliad* 15. 525 reads in part οὗτος Τρωϊκὸς Δόλοψ, Λάμπου υἱὸς τοῦ ἀδελφοῦ Πριάμου, ὁμώνυμος τῷ ἐν τῇ Λ Δόλοπι, which means "this Trojan Dolops, son of Lampos the brother of Priam, [is] homonymous with the Dolops in [*Iliad*] 11" (τῇ agrees with an understood βίβλῳ, see 4.1.33).

4.6 BRACKETS AND OTHER SYMBOLS

Because of their difficult textual tradition, works of ancient scholarship are more likely than most works of ancient literature to be decorated with brackets, obeli, and other symbols in modern texts. A correct understanding of such symbols can be important for successful reading of the text.

The key to the understanding of symbols such as brackets is realization that there are no universal rules for their use, and thus when confronted with an unfamiliar text one should never jump to conclusions about what the brackets mean. In some texts, the notation [καί] means that the word καί is present in the manuscript(s) but the editor thought it ought not to be, while in others the same notation means that καί was not present but the editor thought it should be. Most editors include a list of symbols at the front of their texts, or failing that a verbal description in the preface, and it is important to find this list before making any assumptions.

Editions of papyri often do not list symbols, however, because almost all papyri published since 1931 (and many published earlier) follow the "Leiden conventions." If a papyrus was published after that date and does not contain an explicit statement to the contrary, the editor can be assumed to be following these principles when using brackets, dots, and other symbols. The Leiden conventions can be found in almost all papyrological handbooks.[31]

The most important of these symbols are as follows. Square brackets mark a break in the papyrus, and any writing within them is an editor's conjecture: for example φιλ[. . . .] means that the letters φιλ are visible on the papyrus and after them there is a hole wide enough to contain four letters, while φίλ[τατε] represents the same situation on the papyrus but indicates that the editor thinks the letters τατε originally stood in the gap. Parentheses (round brackets) are used to expand abbreviations, so φιλ(τατε) means that the letters φιλ are visible, and they are all of that word that ever appeared on the papyrus, but the editor believes that they are an abbreviation for φίλτατε.

Some other brackets show erasures and insertions by scribes: φίλ⟦τα⟧τατε means that the writer originally produced φίλτατατε but the extra τα was later erased, and φίλ`τα´τε means that the writer originally wrote φιλτε but this was then corrected to φίλτατε by writing the τα over the line. Others indicate corrections by the editor: φίλ{τα}τατε means that the scribe wrote φιλτατατε and did

---

31. e.g. Turner (1980: 70, 203), Rupprecht (1994: 18, 26); the original publication is in *Chronique d'Égypte*, 7 (1932), 285–7 (cf. also 262–9).

not try to change it, but the editor believes that the extra τα was a mistake, while φίλ‹τα›τε means that the scribe wrote φίλτε but the editor thinks the word should have been φίλτατε. Dots indicate doubtful letters, so that φίλτα̣τε̣ means that the letters φιλ are indubitable, and they are followed by traces of four other letters that can no longer be securely identified but that the editor thinks were originally τατε. φιλ.... means that the letters φιλ are followed by traces of four other letters that can no longer be securely identified and of the restoration of which the editor is uncertain. (Often in such cases there are only a few real possibilities, usually discussed in notes or an apparatus criticus.)

Some recent editors of non-papyrological texts use variants of this Leiden system as well, but many editions of such texts do not follow the Leiden conventions and frequently use the same symbols with opposite meanings. The only symbol whose meaning is securely established among editors of non-papyrus texts is the obelus or dagger (†), which indicates corruption in the word following the obelus, or in the words between the obeli if two are used.[32]

When an edition based on medieval manuscripts does not have a list of symbols, the meaning in each individual case can usually be extracted from the apparatus. Erbse's edition of the *Iliad* scholia (1969–88), for example, has no list of symbols, but every time a bracket is used the reason is given in the apparatus. Erbse's conventions are essentially the same as the Leiden conventions, with the following additions: / indicates a line break within a lemma, | separates two different sources within a single scholion, and ——— indicates omission by Erbse (equivalent of . . . in English, and used primarily for the D scholia, of which Erbse normally prints only a few words).

Editions of scholia often give, at the end of each entry, an indication of which manuscripts contain that entry, in the form of a series of sigla. The ultimate source of the entry (as determined by the editor's researches) may also be indicated in the margin; for example Erbse's edition of the *Iliad* scholia (1969–88) uses the following marginal signs: *ex.* = exegetical tradition (usually applied to bT scholia, but also to some A scholia), *Did.* = traceable to Didymus' portion of VMK, *Ariston.* = traceable to Aristonicus' portion of VMK, *Nic.* = traceable to Nicanor's portion of VMK, *Hrd.* = traceable to Herodian's portion of VMK, *D* = D-scholion.

4.7 THE APPARATUS

When dealing with scholarly texts one cannot afford to ignore the material at the bottom of the page. In many editions two distinct sets of material are located there. The upper one, which may or may not be present, is a register (or "apparatus") of sources, parallels, and testimonia. In this section are given, in condensed form, references to related, similar, or relevant passages in other scholarly works; sometimes such information is instead put into the text itself or in the margins. These parallels are important; often one of them turns out to be a better source of the

---

32. M. L. West (1973: 80–8) gives a useful explanation of many of the symbols used by editors, but not all editions follow these recommendations.

information in question than is the passage one is consulting, and sometimes one of them is the direct source of that passage. When using scholarly literature for its factual information, one must take care to track down the different versions given in the parallel passages and consider their variations. It is also important to consider the textual traditions and historical interrelationships of the works involved before drawing conclusions about how many independent witnesses to a given piece of information a list of six or seven parallels actually provides.

The lowest (or only, if there is only one) apparatus on the page is normally the apparatus criticus, an indication (in extremely abbreviated form) of what is found in the sources on which the edition is based, at least in those places where the editor had to make choices. Because the transmission of scholarly texts is often so much more problematic than that of literary texts, readers of ancient scholarship need to be able to understand an apparatus criticus.[33] The base language of an apparatus is Latin, but most frequently used words are abbreviated. Abbreviations used in particular editions may be, but often are not, listed in the preface. Ones it is useful to be aware of are listed below.

a. c., a. corr.	*ante correctionem, ante correcturam* "before correction"
abiud.	*abiudicavit* "rejected" (in the sense of showing that something does not belong, e.g. of an interpolation)
absc.	*abscissus* "torn off"
acc.	*accedente* "with (name of modern scholar) agreeing" (as ablative absolute)
add.	*addidit* "added"
adi.	*adiunxit* "joined"
agn.	*agnoscit* "recognizes" or *agnovit* "recognized"
al.	*alii* "others" or *alibi* "elsewhere"
approb.	*approbante* "with (name of modern scholar) agreeing" (as ablative absolute)
archet.	*archetypus* "archetype"
arg.	*argumentum* "argument" (in the sense of a summary)
attr.	*attribuit* "attributed"
cett.	*ceteri* "others"
cf.	*confer* "compare"
ci., cj.	*coniecit* "conjectured"
cl.	*collato* "with (the following pertinent passage) being compared" (as ablative absolute)
cod.	*codex* "manuscript"; plural *codd.* is often used to indicate the reading of all or the majority of the manuscripts

---

33. For a more comprehensive discussion of the apparatus criticus and its conventions see M. L. West (1973: 82–94); this work is also very helpful for anyone editing a text and therefore constructing his or her own apparatus criticus.

coll.	*collato* "with (the following pertinent passage) being compared" (as ablative absolute)
comm.	*commentarius* "commentary"
coni., conj.	*coniecit* "conjectured," *coniectura* "conjecture," or *coniunxit*, *coniunctus* "joined"
coniung.	*coniungunt* "join"
corr.	*correxit, correctus* "corrected"
cp.	*compendium* "abbreviation" or *compara* "compare"
damn.	*damnavit* "condemned"
def.	*defendit* "defended" or *deficit* "is lacking, is missing"
del.	*delevit* "deleted"
deprec.	*deprecatur* "deprecates, rejects"
det.	*deterior (codex)* "worse (manuscript)"; plural *dett.* is often used to indicate the reading of a group of inferior manuscripts (usually identified in the preface)
detr.	*detritus* "rubbed away"
dist.	*distinxit* "separated, distinguished," used particularly of adding punctuation and of redividing words
dub.	*dubitanter* "doubtingly" or *dubitat* "doubts, queries"
ed. pr.	*editio princeps* "first edition"
em.	*emendavit* "emended"
evan.	*evanuit* "disappeared"
ex., exp.	*expunxit* "rejected, crossed out"
expl., explic.	*explicavit* "explained, resolved (an abbreviation, misdivision, etc.)" or *explicatio* "explanation, resolution"
flag.	*flagitavit* "demanded"
fort	*fortasse* "maybe"
gl.	*glossema, glossa* "gloss"
γρ.	γράφεται "gives as a variant reading" (the use of this abbreviation in an apparatus is derived from its use by scribes, who sometimes noted the readings of other manuscripts in the margin and used γρ(άφεται) to indicate that the reading was an actual variant found elsewhere, rather than a gloss or their own conjecture. Some editors use γρ. in their apparatus not only when the manuscript actually has the note γρ., but also for equivalent notations such as τινες δέ.)
hab.	*habet, habuit* "has, had"
hyp.	*hypomnema* "ancient commentary" or *hyparchetypus* "hyparchetype"
i. r., in ras.	*in rasura* "written over an erasure"
ib., ibid.	*ibidem* "in the same place"
in.	*initium* "beginning"
indic.	*indicavit* "pointed out"
init.	*initium* "beginning"

ins.	*inseruit, insertus* "inserted"
l.	*linea* "line"
l. c.	*loco citato* "in the place cited"
lac.	*lacuna* "lacuna"
le.	*lemma* "lemma"
m. al.	*manus alia, manus altera* "another hand," i.e. a different person writing
m. pr.	*manus prima, manus prior* "first hand"
m. rec.	*manus recens, recentior* "a (more) recent hand"
m. sec.	*manus secunda* "second hand"
mg., marg.	*margo* "margin" or *in margine* "in the margin"
mg. ext.	*margo exterior* "outer margin"
mg. inf.	*margo inferior* "lower margin"
mg. sup.	*margo superior* "upper margin"
ms.	*liber manu scriptus* "manuscript"
n.	*nota* "note" (imperative)
n. pr., nom. pr.	*nomen proprium* "proper noun"
negl.	*neglexit* "neglected"
nov.	*novit* "knew"
om.	*omisit* "left out"
p. c., p. corr.	*post correctionem, post correcturam* "after correction"
pap.	*papyrus* "papyrus"
par.	*paraphrasis* "paraphrase"
pot. qu.	*potius quam* "rather than"
pr.	*primus, prior* "first"
praef.	*praefatio* "preface"
prob.	*probavit* "approved"
propos.	*proposuit* "proposed"
ras.	*rasura* "erasure"
rec.	*recens, recentior* "(more) recent"
rell.	*reliqui* "the remainder, others"
resp.	*respicit* "refers to, alludes to"
rest.	*restituit* "restored"
rubr.	*rubricator* "rubricator" (the person who supplies initial letters left by the scribe to be added in a more decorative fashion)
Σ	"scholion"
s.	*saeculum* "century"
s. v.	*sub voce* "under the entry for the word"
sc.	*scilicet* "in other words"
sch.	*scholium* "scholion" or *scholiasta* "scholiast"
scr.	*scripsit* "wrote" or *scriptus* "written"
sec.	*secundum* "according to"
secl.	*seclusit* "regarded as an intrusion" (used to justify an editor's placing square brackets around words or letters)

sim.	*similia* "similar", *similiter* "similarly," *vel similiter* "or similarly"
sp.	*spatium* "(empty) space"
sq.	*sequens* "following"
ss.	*supra scriptus* "written above" or *superscripsit, suprascripsit* "wrote above"
stat.	*statuit* "posited"
suppl.	*supplevit* "supplied"
susp.	*suspectus, suspicatus est (falsum esse)* "suspected (of being wrong)"
test.	*testimonia* "testimonia"
transp.	*transposuit* "transposed, moved"
trib.	*tribuit* "assigned"
trsp., trps.	*transposuit* "transposed, moved"
u. v., uv.	*ut videtur* "as it seems"
v.	*vox, verbum* "word," *versus* "line," or *vide* "see"
v. l.	*varia lectio* "variant reading"
v. l. ant.	*varia lectio antiqua* "ancient variant reading"
vet.	*vetus, veteres* "old" (plural *vett.* is sometimes used for the consensus of the older manuscripts)
vid.	*videtur* "seems"
vs.	*versus* "line"
vulg.	the vulgate (the main group of manuscripts)

Plurals of nouns and adjectives are often indicated by doubling the last letter of an abbreviation, as *sqq.* for *sequentes*, *cll.* for *collatis*, or *mss.* for "manuscripts." Other changes of ending are not normally reflected in the abbreviation; thus all the verb abbreviations given above with singular definitions can also be used for the corresponding plurals, and the noun abbreviations given with nominative definitions for all the oblique cases; often verb abbreviations given in one tense are also used in other tenses. Thus, in *lac. stat. Allen et Bekker, approb. West et Smith, lac.* would stand for *lacunam, stat.* for *statuerunt,* and *approb.* for *approbantibus,* for a final meaning of "Allen and Bekker posited a lacuna, with West and Smith agreeing."

Individual manuscripts are identified by single letters, for which a key (entitled "sigla") is given at the start of the edition; often capital Roman letters are used for extant manuscripts and lower-case and/or Greek letters for lost archetypes reconstructed on the basis of extant manuscripts. Superscript numbers usually (but not always) indicate different hands in a single manuscript. The readings of previous editors and others who have worked on the text are also commonly mentioned, often with the scholars' names abbreviated; these abbreviations may not be listed anywhere but can be decoded from the discussion of previous editions in the preface.

Thus a sentence like παιδίσκη καὶ θεράπαινα διαφέρει might be accompanied in the apparatus by notations such as "καί *om.* AB," meaning that manuscripts A and B do not have καί at this point (but implying that the other manuscripts do have it), or "καί AB," meaning that manuscripts A and B have καί at this point (but implying that the other manuscripts do not have it), or "καί *addidi*," meaning that none of the manuscripts have καί at this point but the editor has added it because he thinks it was originally there (in such cases καί may be bracketed in the text, but it may well not be), or "καί *Iri.*," meaning that καί is in none of the manuscripts but was added by Irigoin, a previous editor of the text, whose reading the current editor is following. Other possibilities include "καί *corr. m. pr. e* κατά," meaning that the scribe originally wrote κατά but then changed it to καί (i.e. καί *correxit manus prima e* κατά), and "καί *m. alt. in mg. inf.* A," meaning that in manuscript A a second scribe added καί in the bottom margin (i.e. καί (*scripsit*) *manus altera in margine inferiore*). Often the reading of more than one manuscript is reported in the apparatus, as "καὶ θεράπαινα A: θεραπαίνης B: θεράπαινά τε c," which would mean that manuscript A read παιδίσκη καὶ θεράπαινα διαφέρει, manuscript B read παιδίσκη θεραπαίνης διαφέρει, and manuscript family c read παιδίσκη θεράπαινά τε διαφέρει.

When an emendation replaces words found in the manuscripts (rather than being an addition to them as in the example above), both the emendation and the manuscript reading(s) are given in full in the apparatus, with the reading that is printed in the main text normally coming first. Thus in the apparatus to a text reading παιδίσκη καὶ θεράπαινα διαφέρει one might find "καὶ θεράπαινα *Iri.*: θεραπαίνης ABc" or "καὶ θεράπαινα *Iri.*: θεραπαίνης *codd.*," both of which would mean that the manuscripts (*codices*) had θεραπαίνης but that this had been emended to καὶ θεράπαινα by Irigoin and that that emendation was accepted by the current editor. If however the abbreviation *corr.* (*correxit*) is used, the manuscript readings are listed first in the apparatus even though the emendation is printed in the text: thus "θεραπαίνης *codd.*: *corr. Iri.*" means that Irigoin is responsible for the words printed in the text (and one cannot tell what those are from the apparatus alone), but the manuscripts had something different, namely θεραπαίνης. If the emendation was made by the current editor rather than by a predecessor, the formula used is "θεραπαίνης *codd.*: *correxi.*"

Often emendations not printed in the text are mentioned in the apparatus, along with other information on the opinions of scholars who have worked on the text. For example "καὶ θεράπαινα Bc: θεράπαινα δέ A (*def. Iri.*): *fort. legend.* θεράπαινά τε" would mean that the reading of this text, καὶ θεράπαινα, was supported by manuscript B and manuscript family c, that manuscript A had θεράπαινα δέ and Irigoin thought this reading was correct, and that the current editor is not so sure and suggests that perhaps the correct reading is θεράπαινά τε (i.e. θεράπαινα δέ A (*defendit Irigoin*): *fortasse legendum* θεράπαινά τε).

By no means all variations are indicated in an apparatus; the thoroughness with which different readings are reported depends on the individual editor, but in general obvious mistakes that occur in only one or two manuscripts are passed over without discussion. (Often an editor's preface gives information on the principles on which his or her apparatus is based.) Sometimes even major deviations are ignored, because the point behind an apparatus is normally to indicate genuine alternative possibilities in the reconstruction of the author's original text. Modern editions use modern conventions regarding diacritics, often without any discussion or indication in the apparatus; thus the accents and breathings in most editions cannot be assumed to be those of the particular manuscripts on which the editions are based, and in the case of papyri accents, breathings, and word divisions are usually editorial additions.

5

Reader

T‍HE PURPOSE OF THIS CHAPTER IS TO PROVIDE PRACTICE in reading scholarly Greek. In order to derive maximum benefit from it, readers are advised to work systematically through one or more of the four sections, writing out a translation of each selection and checking it against the key in 5.2 before proceeding to the next selection. Extracts are arranged here by the type of skills required to read them, not by the criteria governing the arrangement of Chapters 2 and 3, and the sections have been arranged in ascending order of difficulty: lexica are on the whole the easiest ancient scholarship to read, while grammatical treatises are the most difficult. Further selections from each group, without key, are provided in 5.3 for use as class assignments or for extra practice.

Not all texts discussed in Chapters 2 and 3 are represented here. Owing to space limitations, all that has been attempted is inclusion of some selections from each major type of scholarly material. Some classes of material, however, have been systematically excluded: in addition to fragmentary, lacunose, or corrupt texts, commentary that is primarily philosophical, mathematical, or scientific in nature has been omitted, on the grounds that reading such material requires different skills from the ones it is the purpose of this book to provide. Metrical commentary is likewise omitted, because Hephaestion's treatise and Van Ophuijsen's translation of it (1987) already offer a good introduction to reading Greek metrical work. The selections presented here aim to provide a representative view of the type of material found in each category, and therefore some of them contain ancient scholars' errors. No attempt has been made to select the most important or profound passages from each text; these are rarely self-explanatory enough to be appropriate here and have in any case usually been discussed and translated elsewhere.

Examples are presented in exactly the form in which they appear in the editions cited, and there is consequently no consistency in the use of symbols, abbreviations, types of sigma, etc.[1] Any symbols or notations the editors added to the text itself have been included, although those in the margins and apparatus

---

1. Except that typographical customs now completely obsolete, such as the use of ligatures or the use of final sigma within certain words, have been suppressed in the interests of legibility.

are omitted. Some editors followed conventions of accentuation different from those now in use (particularly as regards the accentuation of enclitics and the use of the grave accent before punctuation), and others produced typographical errors, but these have generally not been altered or corrected, because dealing with the vagaries of editions is part of the task of reading scholarly Greek.[2] When errors or editorial practices could be misleading, however, or when the absence of the apparatus poses a problem, further information is given in the notes. Unless the notes specify otherwise, all Greek material printed should be taken as part of the passage, regardless of the type of brackets in which it may be enclosed.

Scholia quoted here have also been selected for their ability to be understood without reference to more of the text commented on than is given in the lemma. Many scholia do not meet this criterion, so readers should be aware that the impression given by this selection that scholia can be read without reference to the text is largely false; the most useful aid to reading many scholia is a copy of the text commented on.

When translating scholarly texts one is faced with a question about how much to translate. If the words under discussion are themselves put into English, passages that discuss their spelling or textual history may no longer have any meaning. On the other hand, if lemmata are not understood, passages that discuss their meaning become incomprehensible. The same goes for quotations embedded in scholarly works: if their purpose is to attest to the use of a word in a particular form, the point will be lost in translation, but if the reason they are quoted has to do with their meaning, the point will be lost if the quotation is not understood. Obviously, it is always best to understand everything in a passage, whether or not one ultimately translates it; in practice, however, it can be a poor use of time to struggle with the translation of a syntactically incomplete quotation, in a very different kind of Greek, that is irrelevant to the point of the exercise at hand.

I recommend, therefore, the following procedure for those whose purpose in translating these exercises is to learn how to read scholarly Greek: (1) initially, leave the lemma in Greek; (2) translate all the scholarly material, except words or phrases that are the focus of discussion (those preceded by an article and/or marked by quotation marks) and quotations, which may be left in Greek; (3) put any references added by the editor into the translation, changing them into a familiar format (this is necessary practice because when actually using scholarly texts one usually needs to follow up the references); (4) assess the situation—Is it absolutely clear what the lemma means and what the author is saying? Is it certain that any quotations still untranslated are given purely as attestations of a word's use? If so, no more translation is necessary; if not, translate whatever is needed to make the passage maximally comprehensible. (Some hints about what should be

---

2. A very few typographical errors have been silently corrected because they were too awful to retain and too embarrassing to explain in a note, but this procedure has been adopted only as a last resort.

translated can be found in the commentary: if notes are given on a quotation, it needs to be translated.)

Because of the extent to which essential information tends to be left understood in ancient scholarly texts, it is easy to translate the words of such texts without producing any meaning. While some scholarly texts are indeed meaningless in the form we now have them, no such texts have been included in this reader. Therefore, an important part of the translation exercise is to supply the missing information correctly: no translation is finished until it makes sense.

5.1 TEXTS WITH KEY

5.1.1 Lexica

Contents. Hesychius 1–15; Ammonius 16–20; Timaeus 21–3; Apollonius Sophista 24–5; Etymologica 26–35; Suda 36.

1. Hesychius, ed. Latte, A 1307
   ἀείρομαι· ἄνω αἴρομαι. Σοφοκλῆς Τραχινίαις (216)
   Notes: cf. 4.1.2, 4.1.12. The line number has been added by the editor.

2. Hesychius, ed. Latte, A 1346
   ἀελλάδων ἵππων· ταχέων. Σοφοκλῆς Οἰδίποδι Τυράννῳ (466)
   Notes: cf. 4.1.2, 4.1.7, 4.1.12.

3. Hesychius, ed. Latte, A 7284
   ἀρκτοῦρος· βοτάνης εἶδος. καὶ ἄστρον
   Notes: βοτάνη "plant"; cf. 4.1.4.

4. Hesychius, ed. Latte, B 642
   βιῳ· τῷ τόξῳ. ἢ τῇ ζωῇ
   Note that βίος means "life" and βιός means "bow"; this entry is accented βιῷ in the manuscript, but Latte has omitted the accent because Hesychius' gloss depends on an ambiguity of accent.

5. Hesychius, ed. Latte, A 7274
   ἀρκεῖ· προσαρκεῖ. βοηθεῖ. Εὐριπίδης Πηλεῖ (fr. 624)
   Notes: cf. 4.1.4; προσαρκέω "give aid." The reference is to TGF.

6. Hesychius, ed. Latte, A 1357
   ἄεπτοι· δεινοί. καὶ ἄαπτοι. Αἰσχύλος Πρωτεῖ (fr. 213)
   Notes: ἄαπτος "invincible." The reference is to TGF and would now be fr. 213 TrGF.

7. Hesychius, ed. Latte, B 1277
   βρύτιχοι· βάτραχοι μικροὶ ἔχοντες οὐράς
   Notes: βάτραχος "frog"; οὐρά "tail."

8. Hesychius, ed. Latte, A 7607
   ἀρῶς· ἀριθμοῦ ὄνομα, παρὰ Πέρσαις
   Notes: παρά: cf. 4.1.28.

9. Hesychius, ed. Latte, A 7630

 ἄσβεσε· διέφθειρε. Κρῆτες

 Notes: cf. 4.1.7, 4.1.12.

10. Hesychius, ed. Latte, A 7617

 ἀσαλαμίνιος· ἄπειρος θαλάσσης. οἱ δὲ οὐ κεκοινωνηκὼς ὑπὲρ
 Σαλαμινίων (Ar. Ran. 204)

 Notes: ἄπειρος "without experience"; οἱ δέ: cf. 4.1.13; κοινωνέω "take part in (the
 battle)"; Σαλαμίνιος "Salaminian, from Salamis." The reference, which indicates
 where the lemma occurs in extant literature, has been added by the editor.

11. Hesychius, ed. Latte, A 7305

 ἁρματροχιή· ἡ τῶν τροχῶν ἀποχάραξις (Ψ 505)

 Notes: τροχός "wheel"; ἀποχάραξις "incision, track."

12. Hesychius, ed. Latte, Γ 759

 γογγρύζειν· τονθρύζειν. τὸ ὡς ὗς φωνεῖν, ὅπερ ἔνιοι γογγύζειν.
 τὸ αὐτὸ καὶ γρυλίζειν λέγεται

 Notes: τονθρύζω "mutter"; γογγύζω "murmur"; γρυλίζω "grunt."

13. Hesychius, ed. Latte, A 6404

 ἀποκορσωσαμέναις· ἀποκειραμέναις· κόρσας γὰρ τρίχας.
 Αἰσχύλος Ὑψιπύλη (fr. 248)

 Notes: ἀποκείρω "cut", esp. of hair: middle, "cut off one's hair." The second part
 would have the same meaning if the accusatives were nominatives. The reference gives the fragment number in *TGF*, which is the same as its number in
 TrGF (cf. 4.4).

14. Hesychius, ed. Latte, A 7619

 ἀσαλγάνας· φοβερός. εἴρηκε δὲ οὕτως παραβαρβαρίζων

 Notes: εἴρηκε: cf. 4.1.43; παραβαρβαρίζω "speak somewhat like a barbarian," i.e.
 imitate barbarians.

15. Hesychius, ed. Latte, B 1262

 βρύττος· εἶδος ἐχίνου πελαγίου, ὥς φησιν ᾿Αριστοτέλης (h. an.
 4,530b5) οἱ δὲ ἰχθύν. οἱ δὲ τρισυλλάβως·‘‹ἄμ›βρυττον, ἤν, Λάχης
 ποιεῖ’

 Notes: ἐχῖνος "hedgehog, sea-urchin"; πελαγίου indicates which kind of ἐχῖνος
 is intended; οἱ δέ: cf. 4.1.13; ἤν is an exclamation, "see there!"; ποιέω can mean
 "get for oneself." The last four words are probably a comic fragment (frag. adesp.
 com. 296 K–A); see Latte (1942: 85).

16. Ammonius, ed. Nickau, 30

 ἄλλος καὶ ἕτερος διαφέρει. ἕτερος μὲν γὰρ ἐπὶ δυοῖν, ἄλλος δὲ
 ἐπὶ πλείονων.

 Notes: ἐπί "applied to" (cf. 4.1.31). Our version of Ammonius seems to use the
 singular διαφέρει interchangeably with the plural in such contexts.

17. Ammonius, ed. Nickau, 26

ἀληθές καὶ ἄληθες διαφέρει. ἀληθὲς μὲν γὰρ ὀξυτόνως τὸ ἐναντίον τῷ ψεύδει, ἄληθες δὲ προπαροξυτόνως τὸ κατ' ἐπερώτησιν λεγόμενον.

Notes: cf. 4.1.9; ἄληθες means "really?" as a skeptical response; ὀξυτόνως and προπαροξυτόνως: cf. 4.2.7; κατ' can be translated "as" here.

18. Ammonius, ed. Nickau, 386

πελαστὴς καὶ Πενέστης διαφέρει. πελαστὴς μὲν γὰρ ὁ πρόσφυξ, Πενέστης δὲ παρὰ Θεσσαλοῖς ὁ κατὰ πόλεμον διουλωθεὶς ὡς παρὰ Λάκωσιν οἱ Εἵλωτες.

Notes: cf. 4.1.9; πρόσφυξ "one who seeks protection"; παρά: cf. 4.1.28; κατά "in the course of."

19. Ammonius, ed. Nickau, 180

ἐπίκουροι καὶ σύμμαχοι διαφέρουσιν. ἐπίκουροι μὲν γάρ εἰσιν οἱ τοῖς πολεμουμένοις βοηθοῦντες καὶ συλλαμβανόμενοι, σύμμαχοι δὲ οἱ τῶν πολεμούντων. Ὅμηρος δι' ὅλης ἐφύλαξε τῆς ποιήσεως τὴν διαφοράν· οὐκ ἔστιν οὖν παρ' αὐτῷ ἐπικούρους Ἑλλήνων λεγομένους ιεὑρεῖνι, ἀλλὰ Τρώων.

Notes: πολεμέω "make war (on)"; συλλαμβάνω + dat. "take the part of"; ἔστιν "it is possible"; the statement about Homer is essentially correct.

20. Ammonius, ed. Nickau, 334

νῆες πλοίων διαφέρουσιν. Δίδυμος (p. 321 Schmidt) ἐν ἑνδεκάτῳ ῥητορικῶν ὑπομνημάτων φησὶν οὕτως· ὅτι διαφέρουσιν αἱ νῆες τῶν πλοίων. τὰ μὲν γάρ ἐστι στρογγύλα, αἱ δὲ κωπήρεις καὶ στρατιώ,τιδες. Ἀριστοτέλης δὲ (fr. 614 Rose) ἱστορεῖ ἐν Δικαιώμασι τῶν πόλε{μ}ων οὕτως· "Ἀλέξανδρος ὁ Μολοττὸς ὑπὸ ταὐτὸν χρόνον, Ταραντίνων αὐτὸν μεταπεμψαμένων ἐπὶ τὸν πρὸς τοὺς βαρβάρους πόλεμον, ἐξέπλευσε ναυσὶ μὲν πεντεκαίδεκα, πλοίοις δὲ συχνοῖς ἱππαγωγοῖς καὶ στρατιωτικοῖς'.

Notes: ἑνδεκάτῳ: sc. βιβλίῳ (cf. 4.1.33); ὑπόμνημα "commentary"; οὕτως: see 4.1.23; ὅτι: see 4.1.44; τὰ μέν and αἱ δέ can be translated "the latter" and "the former" respectively, and their genders indicate the references; στρογγύλος "round"; κωπήρης "oared"; στρατιῶτις "military"; ἱστορέω "relate" (as a result of research); δικαίωμα "justification"; ὑπό + acc. "at about"; συχνός "many"; στρατιωτικός "for soldiers," i.e. troop transports. The Aristotle reference could also be given as fr. 407.1 Gigon.

21. Timaeus' Platonic lexicon, ed. Ruhnken, 190. 2–3.

Πύθιοι. δ̄ ἄνδρες αἱρετοὶ παρὰ Λάκωσιν, δύο καθ' ἕκαστον βασιλέα σύσσιτοι.

Notes: δ̄ is the equivalent of δ' here; αἱρετός "chosen"; σύσσιτος "messmate."

22. Timaeus' Platonic lexicon, ed. Ruhnken, 78. 1–2.

Ἑαυτῷ. ἐπὶ τρίτου προσώπου. οἱ ᾿Αττικοὶ δὲ ἐπὶ δευτέρου κέχρηνται.

Notes: Attic authors do indeed sometimes use forms of ἑαυτόν for σαυτόν, e.g. at Plato, *Lysis* 209c; ἐπί: see 4.1.31.

23. Timaeus' Platonic lexicon, ed. Ruhnken, dedicatory epistle, pp. 3–4.

ΤΙΜΑΙΟΣ ΓΕΝΤΙΑΝΩΙ
εὖ πράττειν.

᾿Επιστάμενος ἀκριβῶς τὴν γνώμην καὶ τὴν περὶ Πλάτωνα σπουδὴν καὶ φιλοκαλίαν, εἰωθώς τε τῇ Κρονίων ἑορτῇ τῶν ἐμαυτοῦ τοῖς φίλοις ἀπάρχεσθαι· παιδιᾷ τε ἅμα καὶ τῇ τῆς παιδιᾶς ἀδελφῇ σπουδῇ χρησάμενος ἐξέλεξα τὰ παρὰ τῷ φιλοσόφῳ γλωσσηματικῶς ἢ κατὰ συνήθειαν ᾿Αττικὴν εἰρημένα, οὐχ ὑμῖν μόνοις τοῖς ῾Ρωμαίοις ὄντα ἀσαφῆ, ἀλλὰ καὶ τῶν ῾Ελλήνων τοῖς πλείστοις, τάξας τε ταῦτα κατὰ στοιχεῖον καὶ μεταφράσας ἀπέστειλά σοι, νομίσας καὶ αὐτὸν ἕξειν σε παιδιὰν οὐκ ἄμουσον. ῎Ερρωσο.

Notes: εὖ πράττειν with the nominative of the sender and dative of the addressee is one of the standard ways of beginning a letter and can be roughly translated "X to Y, greetings"; Κρόνια "Saturnalia"; ἀπάρχομαι + gen. "offer some of" (with the connotations of an offering of first fruits); παιδιά "amusement"; σπουδή "seriousness"; ἐκλέγω "pick out"; ὁ φιλόσοφος refers to Plato; παρά cf. 4.1.28; γλωσσηματικός "with unusual words"; κατὰ στοιχεῖον "in alphabetical order"; μεταφράζω "paraphrase".

24. Apollonius Sophista, ed. Bekker, 4. 8–11

ἀγλαΐας τὰς καλλονὰς καὶ τοὺς κόσμους· "ἀγλαΐας τῆς νῦν γε μετὰ δμωῇσι κέκασται." καὶ ἑνικῶς "ἀγλαΐην γὰρ ἔμοιγε θεοὶ οἳ ᾿Ολυμπον ἔχουσιν ὤλεσαν." ἔστι δὲ καὶ ᾿Αγλαΐη κύριον ὄνομα· "Νηρεὺς ᾿Αγλαΐης υἱὸς Χαροποῖο ἄνακτος."

Notes: καλλονή "beauty"; the quotations are *Od.* 19. 82 (in a distorted form, and not comprehensible as it stands), *Od.* 18. 180–1, and *Il.* 2. 672 (with a τ' missing between the last two words).

25. Apollonius Sophista, ed. Bekker, 106. 4–6.

κώδειαν ἰδίως ἡ τῆς μήκωνος κεφαλή. ὅταν δὲ λέγῃ "ὁ δεφη κώδειαν ἀνασχών," παρέλειπεν τὸ ὥς, ἵν' ᾖ τὴν τοῦ ἀνθρώπου κεφαλὴν ὡς τὴν τῆς μήκωνος ἀνέσχεν. τῶν ἅπαξ εἰρημένων.

Notes: μήκων "poppy"; the quotation is from *Il.* 14. 499, apparently with the expectation that the second word would be divided δ' ἔφη rather than into the δὲ φή (φή meaning "like") preferred by Zenodotus and modern scholars; παραλείπω "omit"; a ἅπαξ εἰρημένον is what we call a *hapax legomenon*, and strictly speaking κώδεια is not one, though it occurs only once in Homer.

26. *Etymologicum Gudianum*, ed. De Stefani, vol. ii, p. 356. 16

Δίαιτα· δαῖς δαιτός δαῖτα καὶ δίαιτα.

Notes: cf. 4.1.20; δίατα "way of living"; δαῖς for δαίς "meal."

27. *Etymologicum genuinum*, ed. Lasserre and Livadaras, A 131

    ἀθέμιστος (I 63)· ἄδικος, ἄνομος· θέμιστος καὶ ἀθέμιστος B, Sym.
    197, EM 364.

    Notes: θέμιστος "righteous, lawful"; the reference after the lemma indicates where
    the word occurs in Homer, and the letters at the end indicate sources and parallels.

28. *Etymologicum genuinum*, ed. Lasserre and Livadaras, A 500

    Ἀλκάος· ὃν γὰρ τρόπον οἱ Ἴωνες ἐκβάλλουσι τὸ ῑ τῶν κτητικῶν,
    ἤγουν τῆς ε͞ι διφθόγγου, τὸν αὐτὸν τρόπον καὶ οἱ Αἰολεῖς τῆς α͞ι
    διφθόγγου ἐκβάλλουσιν τὸ ῑ, οἷον Θηβαῖος Θηβάος, ἀρχαῖος ἀρχάος,
    Ἀλκαῖος Ἀλκάος. οὕτως Ἡρωδιανὸς Περὶ παθῶν (II 276,26) AB,
    Sym. 602, EM 885. Hdn. l.c.

    Notes: relative-correlative construction; ἐκβάλλω "drop"; ῑ cf. 4.1.46; κτητικός
    "possessive"; ἤγουν "or rather"; modern studies of Greek dialectology describe these
    phenomena somewhat differently. The letters at the end indicate sources and
    parallels.

29. *Etymologicum magnum*, ed. Gaisford, 556. 23–4

    Λαοδίκη· Ὄνομα κύριον· ἐκ τοῦ λαὸς καὶ τοῦ δίκη. Τὰ δὲ εἰς ΟΣ
    ὀκταχῶς συντίθενται. Ζήτει εἰς τὸ Θ.

    Notes: ὄνομα κύριον "proper name"; note the use of a neuter article with the femi-
    nine δίκη to indicate that it is the word under discussion; τὰ εἰς ΟΣ "nouns end-
    ing in -ος"; ὀκταχῶς "in eight ways"; ζήτει εἰς τό: cf. 4.1.29.

30. *Etymologicum magnum*, ed. Gaisford, 605. 42–5

    Νίζε: Σημαίνει τὸ νίπτε. Οἱ Αἰολεῖς τὰ εἰς ΠΤΩ ῥήματα εἰς δύο
    ΣΣ μεταβάλλουσι, νίπτω, νίσσω. Ταραντίνων δὲ φωνῇ γίνεται νίζω·
    παρὰ τὸ νίζω γίνεται νίτρον, ὡς μάσσω, μάκτρον· καὶ πλήσσω,
    πλῆκτρον.

    Notes: νίπτω "wash"; φωνή "speech," i.e. dialect; παρά + acc. "from" (cf. 4.1.28);
    νίτρον "sodium carbonate" (used with oil as soap); μάσσω "wipe" (here); μάκτρον
    "towel"; πλῆκτρον "instrument for striking a lyre."

31. *Etymologicum genuinum*, ed. Lasserre and Livadaras, A 557

    ἀλφηστής· ὁ εὑρετικός· οἱ μὲν γὰρ ἐπίθετον τοῦ ἀνθρώπου, οἱ
    δὲ αὐτὸν τὸν ἄνθρωπον. παρὰ τὸ ἄλφειν, τὸ εὑρίσκειν· μόνος γὰρ
    ὁ ἄνθρωπος εὑρετικός. ἐξ οὗ ἡ γενικὴ τῶν πληθυντικῶν ἀλφηστῶν
    καὶ (ζ 8)

        ἀλφηστάων·

    ὅθεν καὶ ἄλφα τὸ στοιχεῖον ὠνόμασται, παρὰ τὸ ἄλφω, τὸ εὑρίσκω·
    πρῶτον γὰρ τῶν ἄλλων στοιχείων εὑρέθη. ἢ ἀπὸ τοῦ κατὰ ἀμοιβὰς
    πολιτεύεσθαι· ἄλφειν γὰρ τὸ ἀμείβειν, ὅθεν καὶ (Σ 593)

        ἀλφεσίβοιαι

    AB, Sym. 642, EM 967, Et. Gud. (c) a 882, Eust. 1224,44; 1422,33;
    1788,34. *Methodius.

    Notes: ἀλφηστής is a Homeric word now thought to mean "bread-eating"; εὑρετικός "inventive"; ἐπίθετον "adjective"; παρά: cf. 4.1.28; ἄλφειν and ἄλφω are unattested elsewhere but must be present forms derived from the second aorist of ἀλφάνω, ἦλφον; τὸ εὑρίσκειν is a gloss on τὸ ἄλφειν; μόνος γάρ . . . is an explanation of the views expressed in the previous clauses (or perhaps just of the second view); γενική, πληθυντικῶν: cf. 4.2.11; στοιχεῖον "letter"; ὀνομάζομαι "be named"; τὸ ἄλφω: cf. 4.1.17–18; the story about the name of the letter alpha is wrong, since "alpha" comes from the Phoenician name for the first letter in the alphabet; πρῶτον . . . ἄλλων "first, before the others"; ἢ ἀπό introduces an alternate (and incorrect) explanation of ἀλφηστής; κατὰ ἀμοιβάς "in turn"; ἀμείβω "exchange"; πολιτεύομαι "govern"; ἀλφεσίβοιος "bringing in oxen."

32. *Etymologicum genuinum*, ed. Lasserre and Livadaras, A 584

ἀμάμαξυς· ἡ ἀναδενδράς· παρὰ τὸ ἀμμίξαι, ἡ συνδεδεμένη· ἀναδεσμοῦνται γὰρ αἱ ἀναδενδράδες· ἀμμιξύς, καὶ ἐν πλεονασμῷ καὶ τροπῇ ἀμάμαξυς· Ἐπίχαρμος ἐν Γᾷ καὶ θαλάσσᾳ (fr. 24 Kaibel):

 οὐδ' ἀμαμάξυας φέρει·

Σαπφὼ δὲ διὰ τοῦ δ̄ (fr. 173 Lobel–Page):

ἀμαμάξυδες

λέγει. Μεθόδιος AB, Sym. 725, EM 1012. Methodius.

Notes: ἀμάμαξυς "vine trained on two poles"; ἀναδενδράς "vine that grows up trees"; παρά: cf. 4.1.28; ἀμμίξαι is an aorist infinitive of ἀναμείγνυμι "mix"; understand something like "therefore" before συνδεδεμένη, which is a further gloss on ἀμάμαξυς; ἀναδεσμέω "tie up"; ἀμμιξύς is a hypothetical intermediate form; ἐν (here) "with"; πλεονασμός "addition of a letter"; τροπή "change of one letter into another one"; διά + gen. "with" (cf. 4.1.30); τοῦ: cf. 4.1.17–18. The reference given with "fr. 24 Kaibel" is to an outdated collection of comic fragments; the new reference would be "fr. 21 K–A" (cf. 4.4). The Sappho reference is still good; it refers to E. Lobel and D. Page, *Poetarum Lesbiorum Fragmenta* (Oxford 1955).

33. *Etymologicum magnum*, ed. Gaisford, 512. 37–43

Κιανίς:

Ἀφίκοντο Κιανίδος ἤθεα γαίης.

Κίος πόλις Μυσίας, ἀπὸ Κίου τοῦ ἡγησαμένου τῶν Μιλησίων τῆς ἀποικίας. Τὸ ἐθνικόν, Κιανός·

Τοὔνεκεν εἰς ἔτι νῦν περ Ὕλαν ἐρέουσι Κιανοί.

Κατῴκισαν δὲ αὐτὴν Μυσοί, εἶτα Κάρες· καὶ τρίτον, Μιλήσιοι. Ἔστι δὲ καὶ ποταμὸς ὁμωνύμως τῆς Μυσίας παραρρέων τῇ γῇ. Ἡ δὲ Κίος ἔστι πόλις, ἡ νῦν Προυσίοις ἡ Προῦσα.

Notes: ἐθνικόν "ethnic"; ἔστι: Gaisford's accentuation does not follow modern conventions, so this means both "there is" and "is" in this passage; Κάρες for Κᾶρες; παραρρέω "flow past"; τῆς Μυσίας is best taken after τῇ γῇ; πόλις ἡ is equivalent to "the city that." The quotations are from Apollonius Rhodius 1. 1177 and 1. 1354.

34. *Etymologicum Gudianum*, ed. De Stefani, vol. i, p. 39. 14–19

Ὄϊ["Άϊδι ⟨A3⟩· οἱ μέν φασιν· παρὰ τὸ εἴδω, τὸ βλέπω, ὁ μέλλων

εἴςω, ὄνομα ῥηματικὸν ἵς διὰ τοῦ ῑ· πολλὰ γάρ εἰσιν ὀνόματα—·
καὶ μετὰ τοῦ στερητικοῦ ᾱ "Ἄϊς, ἐν ᾧ οὐδέν ἐστιν ὁρᾶν, καὶ ἡ γενικὴ
"Ἄϊδος καὶ "Ὅμηρος ‹Γ322› "δῦναι δόμον "Ἄϊδος εἴςω", καὶ ἡ δοτικὴ
"Ἄϊδι. οἱ δέ φασι κατὰ μεταπλασμὸν ἀπὸ τοῦ 'Άϊδης 'Άϊδου 'Άϊδη
καὶ "Ἄϊδι.

Notes: the symbol at the start shows that the lemma is a Homeric word, as is con-
firmed by the reference to *Iliad* 1. 3; παρά: cf. 4.1.28; εἴδω: cf. 4.1.22; βλέπω is a
gloss on εἴδω; ὄνομα ῥηματικόν "verbal noun"; διά: 4.1.30; the dash indicates a
lacuna; ᾱ στερητικός "alpha privative"; οὐδέν ἐστιν for οὐδὲν ἔστιν; γενική: cf.
4.2.11; μεταπλασμός "metaplasm" (change in declension, esp. the formation of
oblique cases from a non-existent nominative).

35. *Etymologicum magnum*, ed. Gaisford, 749. 5–22

Ταών· Πόθεν; Παρὰ τὸ τείνειν τὴν οὐράν· τὸ γὰρ ζῷον ἐναβρυνόμενον
τῷ ἑαυτοῦ κάλλει τοῖς ὁρῶσι τὴν οὐρὰν ἐξαπλοῦν ἀποδεικνύει. Τινὲς
δὲ ἀπὸ τοῦ ταὸς βούλονται εἶναι κατ' ἔκτασιν τοῦ Ο εἰς τὸ Ω, καὶ
ἐναλλαγῇ τοῦ τόνου. 'Αλλ' οὐκ ἔστιν· ἐπειδὴ τὸ ταὸς, ὡς φησιν
Ἡρωδιανὸς, διὰ τοῦ Ο μικροῦ, οὐκ ἔστι σύνηθες τοῖς "Ελλησι. Καὶ
λέγουσι τινὲς, ὅτι ὤφειλεν εἶναι τεὼς, ὡς λαὸς λεώς· πρὸς οὓς ἔστιν
εἰπεῖν, ὅτι συνεσταλμένον ἔχει τὸ Α· καὶ τούτου χάριν οὐκ ἐγένετο
παρὰ 'Αττικοῖς τροπῇ τοῦ Α εἰς Ε, ὥσπερ τὸ Οἰνόμαος. "Ἄξιον δὲ
ζητῆσαι, διατί οὐ κλίνεται ταῶς ταῶτος, καὶ Τυφὼς Τυφῶτος, ὡς
τὸ ἱδρὼς ἱδρῶτος. Καὶ ἔστιν εἰπεῖν, ὅτι ἐκεῖνα ὀξύνεται, ταῦτα δὲ
περισπᾶται· καὶ ὅτι ταῦτα εἰς Ν λήγει. Μηδεὶς δὲ οἰέσθω ταῦτα
δικατάληκτα εἶναι· τὰ γὰρ δικατάληκτα τὴν αὐτὴν κλίσιν φυλάττει,
ῥὶν καὶ ῥὶς ῥινός· ταῦτα δὲ οὐκ ἔχει τὴν αὐτὴν κλίσιν· Τυφῶν γὰρ
τυφῶνος, καὶ ταῶν ταῶνος· καὶ τυφῶς τυφῶ, καὶ ταῶς ταῶ. Χοιροβοσκός.

Notes: ταών is an alternate form of ταώς/ταῶς "peacock," but in order for this
passage to make sense one must assume that the original writer considered the
lemma to be ταῶν (which is probably the correct accentuation—see Chandler
1881: 175–6); οὐρά "tail"; ἐναβρύνομαι "pride oneself on"; ἐξαπλόω "unfold, spread
out"; ταός is another variant of ταώς/ταῶς but may not actually have existed;
ἔκτασις "lengthening"; ἐναλλαγή "change"; τόνος "accent"; ἔστι: Gaisford's accentuation does not follow modern conventions, so this means both "is possible"
and "is" in this passage; διά: cf. 4.1.30; συνήθης "customary"; συστέλλω "shorten";
ἱδρώς for ἱδρὼς; ἐκεῖνα and ταῦτα are being used in the opposite of their classical meanings, so that ἐκεῖνα refers to ἱδρώς and other words of a similar type,
while ταῦτα refers to ταώς and Τυφώς (which must be accented ταῶς and Τυφῶς
for this passage to make sense); δικατάληκτος "having a double ending" (in this
passage, though not always, restricted to words that have two alternative forms in
the nominative but only one form for other cases); κλίσις "declension."

36. *Suda*, ed. Adler, Π 1617

Πίνδαρος, Θηβῶν, Σκοπελίνου υἱός, κατὰ δέ τινας Δαϊφάντου· ὃ
καὶ μᾶλλον ἀληθέϲ· ὁ γὰρ Σκοπελίνου ἐϲτὶν ἀφανέϲτεροϲ καὶ

προσγενὴς Πινδάρου, τινὲς δὲ καὶ Παγωνίδου ἱστόρησαν αὐτόν.
μαθητὴς δὲ Μυρτίδος γυναικός, γεγονὼς κατὰ τὴν ξε΄ ὀλυμπιάδα καὶ
κατὰ τὴν Ξέρξου στρατείαν ὢν ἐτῶν μ΄. καὶ ἀδελφὸς μὲν ἦν αὐτῷ
ὄνομα Ἐρωτίων καὶ υἱὸς Διόφαντος, θυγατέρες δὲ Εὔμητις καὶ
Πρωτομάχη. καὶ συνέβη αὐτῷ τοῦ βίου τελευτὴ κατ᾿ εὐχάς· αἰτήσαντι
γὰρ τὸ κάλλιστον αὐτῷ δοθῆναι τῶν ἐν τῷ βίῳ ἀθρόον αὐτὸν ἀποθανεῖν
ἐν θεάτρῳ, ἀνακεκλιμένον εἰς τὰ τοῦ ἐρωμένου Θεοξένου αὐτοῦ γόνατα,
ἐτῶν νε΄. ἔγραψε δὲ ἐν βιβλίοις ιζ΄ Δωρίδι διαλέκτῳ ταῦτα·
Ὀλυμπιονίκας, Πυθιονίκας, Προσόδια, Παρθένια, Ἐνθρονισμούς,
Βακχικά, Δαφνηφορικά, Παιᾶνας, Ὑπορχήματα, Ὕμνους, Διθυράμβους,
Σκολιά, Ἐγκώμια, Θρήνους, δράματα τραγικὰ ιζ΄, ἐπιγράμματα ἐπικὰ
καὶ καταλογάδην παραινέσεις τοῖς Ἕλλησι, καὶ ἄλλα πλεῖστα.

Notes: ἀφανής "obscure"; προσγενής "kinsman"; ἱστορέω "record"; κατά "during";
ἀθρόον "all at once"; ἀποθανεῖν understand something like "it is said that"; ἀνακλίνω
εἰς "cause to lean on"; Ὀλυμπιόνικος "[ode] celebrating an Olympian victory";
προσόδιον "processional hymn"; παρθένιον i.e. song for a chorus of girls; ἐνθρονισμός
"enthroning [song]"; ὑπόρχημα "song for dancing"; σκολιόν "drinking-song"; θρῆνος
"lament"; καταλογάδην "in prose"; παραίνεσις "exhortation."

5.1.2 Scholia and Commentaries

Contents. Poetry: Homer 37–53; Euripides 54; Aeschylus 55–9; Pindar 60–4;
Aristophanes 65–6. Prose: Plato 67–9; Aeschines 70–5; Hippocrates 76–8. Post-
classical: Lucian 79–81; Apollonius Rhodius 82–6; Aratus 87–8.

37. Homer scholia, ed. Erbse, Iliad 15. 739a (from Didymus?)
⟨Τρώων πεδίῳ:⟩ ἐν ἄλλῳ "Τρώων ὁμάδῳ" (= Ο 689). Aⁱᵐ
Notes: cf. 4.1.3, 4.1.15; understand ἀντιγράφῳ "copy" with ἄλλῳ. The notation at
the end indicates the manuscript source: a note written in A between the text and
the main body of marginal scholia.

38. Homer scholia, ed. Erbse, Iliad 15. 395b (from Aristonicus)
⟨τεῖχος:⟩ ὅτι ἐλλείπει ἡ ἐπί, ⟨ἐπὶ⟩ τεῖχος. Aⁱⁿᵗ
Notes: ὅτι: cf. 4.1.44; ἡ: cf. 4.1.17–18; ἐλλείπω "be lacking" (cf. 4.1.35). The notation at the end indicates the manuscript source: a note written in the inside
margin of A.

39. Homer scholia, ed. Erbse, Iliad 15. 459 (from Didymus)
⟨μάχης:⟩ Ζηνόδοτος μάχης, ἄλλοι δὲ "μάχην". καὶ Ἀριστοφάνης
δὲ "μάχην". Aⁱᵐ
Note: cf. 4.1.11

40. Homer scholia, ed. Erbse, Iliad 15. 394b¹ (from Didymus)
⟨ἀκήματα:⟩ ἔν τισιν "ἀκέσματα"· οὕτως δὲ καὶ Ἀρίσταρχος.
⟨δι⟩χῶ⟨ς⟩ οὖν. Aⁱᵐ
Notes: cf. 4.1.11, 4.1.15; understand ἀπογράφοις "copies" after τισιν, διχῶς "in
two ways."

41. Homer scholia, ed. Erbse, *Iliad* 15. 437 (from Nicanor)

Τεῦκρε πέπον, ‹δὴ νῶϊν ἀπέκτατο πιστὸς ἑταῖρος›: ἄξιον
ἀποδέξασθαι τὴν συνήθειαν μετὰ τὸ πέπον στίξασαν, καὶ μὴ μετὰ
τὸν δή σύνδεσμον. **A**

Notes: cf. 4.1.47; συνήθεια "customary practice"; στίζω "punctuate"; σύνδεσμος
"conjunction."

42. Homer scholia, ed. Erbse, *Iliad* 15. 729 (exegetical)

θρῆνυν: τὴν τῶν κωπηλατῶν καθέδραν **b**(BCE³E⁴) **T** ἢ τὴν τοῦ
κυβερνήτου. Ἀττικοὶ δὲ θρᾶνον τὸ τοῦ κωπηλάτου φασὶ καὶ θρανίτας
αὐτούς. **b**(BCE³) **T**

Notes: κωπηλάτης "rower"; καθέδρα "seat"; κυβερνήτης "steersman"; Ἀττικοί
"speakers of the Attic dialect"; τό understand "seat." The groups of letters in the
middle and at the end indicate the manuscript sources: T and four members of
the b family, one of which contains only the first part of the scholion.

43. Homer scholia, ed. Erbse, *Iliad* 15. 444b (exegetical)

ἰοδόκον: προπαροξυτόνως τινὲς τὸν δεχόμενον ἰούς, "ξεινοδόκον"
(Γ 354) δὲ τὸν ξενίζοντα παροξυτόνως ἢ τὸν ξένους δοκεύοντα.
"Ατταλος δὲ παροξύνει. **A T**

Notes: the understood verb with τινές is something like "say that it should be pronounced . . . and means . . ." (cf. 4.1.13–14); προπαροξυτόνως and παροξύνω: cf.
4.2.7; ἰός "arrow"; ξενίζω "receive guests"; δοκεύω "watch for." This is one of the
passages mentioned in 4.1.9 in which subject and predicate need to be reversed
to produce a comprehensible English translation.

44. Homer scholia, ed. Erbse, *Iliad* 15. 468 (exegetical)

ὅ τέ μοι βιὸν ‹ἔκβαλε χειρός›: ὅ τε ἀντὶ τοῦ ὅστις. οἱ δὲ
‹ἀντὶ τοῦ› ὅτι· "ὅτε με βροτοὶ οὔτι τίουσιν" (ν 129) ἀντὶ τοῦ ὅτι. **T**
Notes: there were no spaces between words at the time that most of the commentaries on which scholia are based were composed, so there would be no visible
difference between ὅ τε and ὅτε; τοῦ: cf. 4.1.17–18; οἱ δέ: cf. 4.1.13.

45. Homer scholia, ed. Erbse, *Iliad* 15. 601b (from Aristonicus)

‹ἔμελλε› παλίωξιν παρὰ νηῶν: ὅτι ὑγιῶς παλίωξιν, πάλιν
δίωξιν, ὅταν ἐξ ὑποστροφῆς διώκωσιν οἱ διωκόμενοι. καὶ πρὸς τὸ
ἔμελλεν, ὅτι ἀντὶ τοῦ ἐῴκει. **A**

Notes: ὅτι: cf. 4.1.44; ὑγιῶς "correctly" (modifying an understood verb like "the
text reads"); ὑποστροφή "turning around"; πρός "regarding"; τοῦ: cf. 4.1.17–18.

46. Homer scholia, ed. Erbse, *Iliad* 15. 417a¹ and a² (from Didymus)

νῆας: Ἀρίσταρχος χωρὶς τοῦ σ̄ γράφει "νῆα"· προεῖπε γὰρ ʽτὼ δὲ
περὶ μιᾶς νηὸς ἔχον πόνον' (cf. O 416). **A**
Ἀρίσταρχος "νῆα", ἄλλοι δὲ νῆας. **A**int

Notes: these two notes must go back to the same source, but they have clearly
undergone different developments before ultimately finding their way to different

places in the same manuscript. The subject of προεῖπε is the poet (cf. 4.1.43); the quotation appears as τὼ δὲ μιῆς περὶ νηὸς ἔχον πόνον in our texts of Homer.

47. Homer scholia, ed. Erbse, *Iliad* 15. 2c (from Herodian)

{πολλοὶ δὲ} δάμεν: ὁμοίως τῷ "πολλοὶ δ᾽ Ἀργείων οἱ μὲν δάμεν, οἱ δ᾽ ἐλίποντο" (Μ 14) καὶ τῷ "φάνεν δέ οἱ εὑρέες ὦμοι" (σ 68) ἀνεγνώσθη κατὰ ἀφαίρεσιν τοῦ ἄρχοντος χρόνου. ἔφαμεν δέ (sc. ad A 464a) τὰ τοιαῦτα ἀδιαφόρως εὑρεθῆναι παρὰ τῷ ποιητῇ. **A**

Notes: the brackets around πολλοὶ δέ indicate that it should not be part of the lemma. The topic of discussion is the lack of an augment on δάμεν (aor. pass. 3rd pl. of δαμάζω) so the quotations are examples of other unaugmented verbs. The cross-reference indicated by ἔφαμεν δέ comes from Herodian's work before it was converted into scholia, but the passage referred to survives as another scholion, hence Erbse's note. φάνεν is the unaugmented aor. pass. 3rd pl. of φαίνω; ὦμος "shoulder"; ἀναγιγνώσκω "read"; ἀφαίρεσις is the removal of a letter or letters at the beginning of a word; χρόνος "augment" (here); ἀδιαφόρως "without distinction"; παρά: cf. 4.1.28; ὁ ποιητής is Homer (cf. 4.1.42).

48. Homer scholia, ed. Erbse, *Iliad* 15. 1b¹ (exegetical)

διά τε σκόλοπας ‹καὶ τάφρον ἔβησαν›: ἢ ἀντὶ τοῦ διὰ σκολόπων καὶ τάφρου, ὡς "διά τ᾽ ἔντεα καὶ μέλαν αἷμα" (Κ 298), ἢ τὸ ἑξῆς διέβησαν. ἡ δὲ διακοπὴ τῆς λέξεως τὸ ταλαίπωρον καὶ δυσδιόδευτον ἐμφαίνει· οὐ γὰρ ἔφυγον "τῇ περ Ἀχαιοί / ἐκ πεδίου νίσοντο" (Μ 118–9), ἀλλὰ διὰ τῆς τάφρου ἔφευγον. b(BCE³E⁴) **T** | ἡ αὐτὴ διακοπὴ καὶ ἐν τοῖς "κατὰ πυρὸν ἄλεσσαν" (υ 109). **T**

Notes: the point of the first sentence is that either διά means "through" despite being followed by the accusative rather than the genitive, or the verb is διέβησαν by tmesis; σκόλοψ "stake"; τάφρος "ditch"; τὸ ἑξῆς "sequence in which the words are to be taken" (cf. 4.1.38); διακοπή "tmesis"; λέξις "word"; δυσδιόδευτον "difficulty of passing through [the Greek barricades]"; the subject of ἔφυγον is the Trojans; νίσομαι "come back"; the groups of letters indicate that the last sentence of the scholion is found only in manuscript T, but the rest is also found in four manuscripts of the b family; πυρός "wheat"; ἀλέω "grind."

49. Homer scholia, ed. Erbse, *Iliad* 15. 735b (from Herodian)

{ἠέ τινας} φαμέν {εἶναι}: τὸ φαμέν ἐντελές ἐστι καὶ ἐνεστῶτα χρόνον σημαίνει· διὸ τὰς δύο συλλαβὰς βαρυτονητέον. εἰ μέντοι παρατατικὸς γίνοιτο, δῆλον ὅτι ἀποβολὴν χρόνου τοῦ κατ᾽ ἀρχὴν πάσχει καὶ ἐπὶ τὴν φα συλλαβὴν ἡ ὀξεῖα τάσις ἔσται, ὅμοιον ὡς τὸ ἔφαμεν ἐντελές, ὥσπερ ἐπ᾽ ἐκείνου "φάμεν δέ οἱ οὐ τελέεσθαι" (δ 664), ὅπερ οὐκ ἐπιζητεῖ νῦν ἡ διάνοια. **A**

Notes: the brackets in the lemma mean that the lemma should be simply φαμέν; the discussion concerns the distinction between the present φαμέν and the unaugmented imperfect φάμεν. The conditional clause is in meaning fundamentally a future less vivid (remote future), despite the abandonment of the optative for the present indicative and then for the future indicative. ἐντελής "complete"; ἐνεστὼς χρόνος and παρατατικός: cf. 4.2.13; διό "on account of which"; βαρυτονέω "leave unaccented" (cf. 4.2.9); δῆλον ὅτι = δηλονότι, an adverbial unit meaning "clearly"; ἀποβολή "dropping," i.e. loss; χρόνος "augment"; ὀξεῖα τάσις "acute accent"; ὅπερ i.e. the interpretation of φάμεν as an imperfect; ἐπιζητέω "require"; νῦν i.e. in this passage; διάνοια "meaning."

50. Homer scholia, ed. Erbse, *Iliad* 15. 4a (from Herodian)
χλωροὶ ὑπαὶ δείους ‹πεφοβημένοι›: ἡ ὑπό πρόθεσις ὑπαί ἐγένετο ὁμοίως τῇ "ὑπαὶ πόδα νείατον "Ἴδης" (B 824). καὶ ἔστι τὸ ἑξῆς ὑπὸ δέους. οὕτω καὶ 'Αρίσταρχος· διὸ παραιτητέον τὸν Τυραννίωνα (fr. 35 P.) βαρύνοντα τὴν ὑπαί καὶ ἡγούμενον ἀπὸ τοῦ ὕπαιθα εἶναι πάθος τὸ τῆς ἀποκοπῆς. ἕως δὲ τοῦ ὑπαὶ δείους ὀφείλομεν ἀναπαύεσθαι· οὐ γὰρ πιθανὸν ἕως τοῦ χλωροί, εἶτα πεφοβημένοι, τουτέστι φεύγοντες. ἔστι μέντοι καὶ ἡ ἑτέρα ἀνάπαυσις οὐκ ἀδόκιμος. **A**
Notes: cf. 4.1.47. The γάρ clause is very parenthetical, so the εἶτα clause continues the thought before the γάρ. The point of the last sentence is that although the writer prefers one punctuation, the other is also possible. πρόθεσις "preposition"; ἔστι = ἐστι; τὸ ἑξῆς "normal equivalent" (cf. 4.1.38, but this use is unusual because it does not involve a change of word order); διό "on account of which"; παραιτητέον "it is necessary to reject the view of"; βαρύνω "accent recessively" (cf. 4.2.9); εἶναι i.e. "happen" (the subject is πάθος); πάθος "transformation" (in ancient grammatical theory, words changed from one form to another only via certain clearly defined types of transformations known collectively as πάθη); ἕως + gen. "until" i.e. after; ἀναπαύομαι "pause" i.e. put a comma; ἀδόκιμος "unconvincing." The reference is to M. Planer, *De Tyrannione grammatico* (Berlin 1852) and would now be expressed as "fragment 37 Haas."

51. Eustathius' commentary on the *Iliad*, ed. Van der Valk, 600. 32–3
Λέγει δὲ ἐκφραστικῶς ὁ ποιητὴς καὶ τὸ "κρατὶ δ' ἐπ' ἀμφίφαλον κυνέην θέτο τετραφάληρον, χρυσείην, ἑκατόν", ἤτοι πολλῶν, "πόλεων πρυλέεσιν", ὅ ἐστι πεζοῖς ὁπλίταις, "ἀραρυῖαν".
Notes: discussing *Iliad* 5. 743–4. ἐκφραστικῶς "descriptively," i.e. in an ecphrasis; ἀμφίφαλος "with two ridges"; κυνέη "helmet"; τετραφάληρος is an obscure word meaning something like "with four bosses"; ἤτοι is equivalent here to "i.e."; ἀραρυῖα "fitted with" here means that the helmet is decorated with human figures.

52. Eustathius' commentary on the *Iliad*, ed. Van der Valk, 893. 34–42
Πρυλέες δὲ οἱ ἐν μάχη πεζοὶ κατὰ γλῶσσαν Γορτυνίων, ὥς φασιν οἱ παλαιοί. ἡ δὲ τῆς λέξεως παραγωγὴ προγέγραπται. νῦν δὲ τοσοῦτον ῥητέον ὡς, εἰ μὲν ὀξύτονος ἡ ταύτης εὐθεῖα, ἑτέρου τοῦτο λόγου, εἰ δὲ βαρύτονος, συνηγορηθείη ἂν ἐντεῦθεν εἶναι τὸ παρὰ Λυκόφρονι κύριον ὄνομα ἐν τῷ "τῶν αὐθομαίμων συγκατασκάπτην Πρύλιν". οὕτω καὶ 'Ιππότης ἐν 'Οδυσσείᾳ κύριον ὄνομα ὁμώνυμον τῷ ἱππεύοντι.

Notes: discussing *Iliad* 12. 77. γλῶσσα i.e. dialect; παραγωγή "derivation"; ὀξύτονος: cf. 4.2.7; εὐθεῖα: cf. 4.2.11, but here probably referring to the nominative singular; ταύτης and τοῦτο both refer to Πρυλέες; ἑτέρου λόγου "of another reason," i.e. it should be explained differently (not via the Πρύλιν that is about to be mentioned); βαρύτονος: cf. 4.2.9; συνηγορέω "advocate"; ἐντεῦθεν i.e. from Πρυλέες; παρά: cf. 4.1.28; κύριον ὄνομα "proper noun"; ὁμώνυμος "homonymous with"; τῷ ἱππεύοντι i.e. the ἱππότης that means "cavalryman"; αὐθόμαιμος "blood relative"; συγκατασκάπτης "co-destroyer." Van der Valk's notes inform us that the reference in προγέγραπται is to 601. 2–8, that the Lycophron reference is to line 222, and that the name Ἱππότης is not directly attested in the *Odyssey* but was inferred from the patronymic Ἱπποτάδης (10. 2).

53. Eustathius' commentary on the *Iliad*, ed. Van der Valk, 600. 45–601. 8

Τινὲς δὲ τὸ "ἑκατὸν πόλεων πρυλέεσσιν ἀραρυῖα" οὕτως ἔφρασαν· ἑκατὸν πόλεων ἀριστεῖς ἔχουσαν, ἢ κεκοσμημένην τοῖς τῆς Κρήτης ὁπλίταις, τουτέστι τὰ τῶν Κορυβάντων ἔργα ἔχουσαν ἐντετυπωμένα. Ὅτι δὲ ἑκατόμπολις ἡ Κρήτη, καὶ ἐν Ὀδυσσείᾳ δηλοῦται. ὡς δὲ καὶ Κρῆτες οἱ Κορύβαντες, δῆλον καὶ αὐτό. Εὐθεῖαν δέ φασί τινες τοῦ πρυλέεσσι πρύλις, γινομένην ἐκ τοῦ περῶ περύω, τὸ ὁδεύω, περύσω, πέρυλις καὶ πρύλις, ὡς δαμάσω δάμαλις. [Ἴσως δὲ συντελεῖ τι πρὸς τὴν τοιαύτην κλίσιν καὶ τόνωσιν καὶ τὸ κύριον ὁ Πρύλις, ὁ παρὰ Λυκόφρονι.] Καὶ μὴν ἄλλοι, ἐν οἷς καὶ Ἡρῳδιανός, πρυλής γράφουσιν ὀξυτόνως καὶ κλίνουσι κανονικῶς πρυλέος, πρυλοῦς, ὡς που καὶ προείρηται. [Καὶ ἔστιν ἀσφαλέστερον τοῦτο. ἀπὸ γάρ τοι τοῦ πρύλις πρύλεες ὤφειλεν εἶναι ὡς ὄφεες, ἀλλὰ μὴν εὕρηται πρυλέες ὡς εὐσεβέες.]

Notes: discussing *Iliad* 5. 744. The brackets enclose additions made by Eustathius after writing the rest of the entry. οὕτως: see 4.1.23; φράζω "explain"; ἀριστεῖς is acc. pl. of ἀριστεύς, "chief"; ἐντυπόω "carve, mold"; ἑκατόμπολις "having a hundred cities"; καὶ αὐτό "[that] itself [is] also"; εὐθεῖα: cf. 4.2.11; περύω is not attested (nor is its assumed future περύσω, nor is the πέρυλις assumed to be the link between περύσω and πρύλις) but is being taken to be an intermediate form between περῶ and πρύλις; τὸ ὁδεύω ("travel") is a gloss on περῶ; συντελέω "contribute" (subject is τὸ κύριον ὁ Πρύλις); κλίσις "inflection"; τόνωσις "accentuation"; κύριον is short for κύριον ὄνομα; καὶ μήν "but"; ὀξυτόνως: cf. 4.2.7; κανονικῶς "regularly"; ἀσφαλής "sound."

54. Euripides scholia, ed Schwartz, *Hecuba* 13

ἦν ἀντὶ τοῦ ἤμην φησίν. ἔστιν Ἀττικόν:—Mᵍ

νεώτατος δ' ἦν: ἀντὶ τοῦ ἤμην φησίν. Ἀττικῶς δὲ ἦν. καὶ χωρὶς δὲ τοῦ ῡ ἦ, ἀντὶ τοῦ ἔα. οὕτω Δίδυμος. ἐν μέντοι τοῖς ἀντιγράφοις ἦν φέρεται καὶ κοινὴ ἀνάγνωσις ἦν:—Vat. 1345

Notes: Here there are notes from two different manuscripts (M (g = interlinear gloss) and Vatican 1345) with overlapping content. Some editors accept Didymus' reading into the text on the authority of this scholion. ἤμην "I was" (late Greek imperfect of εἰμί); καὶ χωρὶς δέ: the presence of both καί and δέ shows that καί means "also," so understand something like "there is a reading here"; ἔα "I was" (Ionic imperfect of εἰμί); ἀντίγραφον "copy, manuscript"; φέρομαι "be transmitted."

55. Aeschylus scholia, ed. Smith, *Choephori* 973
ἀνοίγεται ἡ σκηνὴ καὶ ἐπὶ ἐκκυκλήματος ὁρᾶται τὰ σώματα ἃ λέγει διπλῆν τυραννίδα.

Notes: σκηνή "stage-building"; ἐκκύκλημα is a type of wheeled platform whose exact nature is much debated; the subject of λέγει could be Aeschylus or Orestes, the character who speaks the last two words.

56. Aeschylus scholia, ed. Herington, *Prometheus Vinctus* 397b
Mediceus: Τὸ στάσιμον ᾄδει ὁ χορὸς ἐπὶ τῆς γῆς κατεληλυθώς.

Note: "Mediceus" indicates the manuscript in which the scholion is found.

57. Aeschylus scholia, ed. Wecklein, *Persae* 34–5
τινὲς διαιροῦσι Σουσισκάνης (Σοῦσις καὶ Κάνης Blomf.) καὶ Πηγάς καὶ Ταγών. τὰ γὰρ ὀνόματα πέπλακε καὶ οὐκ ἔστιν Αἰγυπτιακά.

Notes: the text on which the scholion comments is Σουσισκάνης Πηγασταγὼν Αἰγυπτογενής; the material in parentheses is a suggested emendation by the nineteenth-century scholar C. J. Blomfield; διαιρέω "divide"; πλάσσω "fabricate" (for the subject cf. 4.1.43); ἔστιν = ἐστιν. This scholion is considered to be important evidence for the Alexandrian origins of the Aeschylean scholia, since it must have been written by someone with knowledge of Egypt.

58. Aeschylus scholia, ed. Smith, *Agamemnon* 503a (Triclinian)
Τινὲς μέμφονται τῶι ποιητῆι ὅτι αὐθήμερον ἐκ Τροίας ποιεῖ τοὺς Ἕλληνας ἥκοντας.

Note: αὐθημερόν "on the same day."

59. Aeschylus scholia, ed. Herington, *Prometheus Vinctus* 561d
Ἡ δὲ ἱστορία τοιαύτη· Ἰὼ ἡ τοῦ Ἰνάχου θυγάτηρ, ἐρασθεῖσα παρὰ τοῦ Διός, ἐπεὶ τοῦτο ἔγνω ἡ Ἥρα καὶ ἔμελλε καταλαμβάνεσθαι παρ' αὐτῆς, μετεβλήθη παρὰ τοῦ Διὸς εἰς βοῦν, ἵνα μὴ γνωσθῇ τίς εἴη. ἡ Ἥρα δὲ προσελθοῦσα τῷ Διὶ ἐζήτησε ταύτην καὶ ἔλαβε δῶρον παρ' αὐτοῦ, καὶ δέδωκεν Ἄργῳ τῷ πανόπτῃ φυλάττειν αὐτήν. ὁ δὲ Ζεὺς πάλιν ἐρασθεὶς αὐτῆς ἔπεμψε τὸν Ἑρμῆν ἀφελέσθαι ταύτην τοῦ Ἄργου καὶ διακομίσαι αὐτῷ. καὶ ἐπεὶ ἄλλως λαθεῖν Ἄργον τὸν παντόπτην οὐκ ἦν, διὰ βολῆς λιθείας τοῦτον ἀνήρηκεν· οὗ τὸ φάσμα ἡ Ἥρα τῇ Ἰοῖ καὶ μετὰ τὸν αὐτοῦ θάνατον παρεδείκνυεν ἐπὶ τῷ μάλιστα ἐκφοβεῖν αὐτήν. ἡ δὲ πολλὰ πλανηθεῖσα κατὰ διαφόρους τόπους, τελευταῖον ἀπῆρε καὶ πρὸς τὸν Καύκασον ὀψομένη τὸν Προμηθέα. A.

Notes: ἱστορία i.e. background; ἐρασθείς has passive meaning the first time it occurs, but active meaning ("having become enamored") the second time; ἔμελλε has Io as its subject; μεταβάλλω "change"; παρά + gen. "by" (cf. 4.1.28); δῶρον "as a gift"; δέδωκεν: cf 4.1.23 for tense; πανόπτης "all-seeing"; φυλάττειν is an infinitive expressing purpose; οὐκ ἦν "it was not possible"; ἀναιρέω "kill, destroy"; φάσμα "phantom"; ἐπὶ τῷ + inf. is equivalent to a purpose clause; πλανάομαι "wander"; τελευταῖον "finally"; ἀπαίρω "go away."

60. Pindar scholia, ed. Drachmann, *Pythian* 2. 106

κύριε: κυρωτικὲ καὶ τελεστικὲ, τουτέστι πάντων ἔχων τὴν κυριότητα.

Notes: κυρωτικός "sovereign"; τελεστικός "completely powerful"; κυριότης "dominion"; κύριε was a very common word from the first century AD onwards, but at that period it did not have the same meaning as it does here (this is its only attestation in classical literature), so the scholion serves not to gloss an unfamiliar word but to alert readers to its archaic meaning.

61. Pindar scholia, ed. Drachmann, *Pythian* 8. 107

τὰ δ᾽ οὐκ ἐπ᾽ ἀνδράσι κεῖται: ταῦτα δὲ οὐκ ἔστιν ἐν ἀνθρώποις, τὸ ἐκ περινοίας κτήσασθαι· τὸ δαιμόνιον δὲ ἑκάστῳ παρέχει.

Notes: the first part (up to the comma) is a paraphrase of the lemma, in which the τά referred to blessings available to humans, and these blessings are also the understood object of κτήσασθαι; περίνοια "deliberation" (i.e. acting with forethought). The last clause paraphrases the rest of the line that begins with the lemma, δαίμων δὲ παρίσχει.

62. Pindar scholia, ed. Drachmann, *Pythian* 4. 1c

σὺν 'Αρκεσίλᾳ: τὸ σύν πρὸς τὸ αὔξῃς, ἵν᾽ ᾗ συναύξῃς. κωμάζοντι δὲ, κώμους ἄγοντι· κώμους δὲ ἄγουσιν οἱ νικῶντες κατὰ τὴν ἑαυτῶν πατρίδα.

Notes: πρός is equivalent to "goes with"; ἵνα is probably consecutive not final; κωμάζοντι is a second lemma; κῶμος "victory procession"; κατά "in" (cf. 4.1.32).

63. Pindar scholia, ed. Drachmann, *Pythian* 6 title

Inscr. Γέγραπται Ξενοκράτει 'Ακραγαντίνῳ νενικηκότι κατὰ τὴν κδ' Πυθιάδα. φανερὸν δὲ, ὅτι αἱ ᾠδαὶ οὐ κατὰ χρόνον διάκεινται· ἡ γὰρ πρὸ ταύτης ᾠδὴ 'Αρκεσιλάῳ γέγραπται νικήσαντι λα' Πυθιάδα.

Notes: Inscr(iptio) refers to the title of the ode, which reads Ξενοκράτει 'Ακραγαντίνῳ ἅρματι; κατά: cf. 4.1.32; Πυθιάς "Pythiad" (celebration of the Pythian games and the interval of time between games, like "Olympiad"); κατὰ χρόνον i.e. in chronological order; διάκειμαι "be arranged".

64. Pindar scholia, ed. Drachmann, *Pythian* 3 title

Inscr. b. ῎Ηθελον Χείρωνά κε Φιλλυρίδαν: 'Ιέρωνι Πύθια νικήσαντι τὴν κζ' Πυθιάδα· μέμνηται δὲ καὶ τῆς πρὸ ταύτης Πυθιάδος, ὥστε ἐπὶ ταῖς δύο νίκαις τὴν ᾠδὴν συντετάχθαι. συνᾴδει δὲ καὶ τὰ ἀπὸ τῶν χρόνων. ὡς γὰρ ἤδη βασιλεύοντός φησιν (Vs. 70)· ὃς Συρακόσσαισιν ἄρχει πραῢς ἀστοῖς. καθίσταται δὲ ὁ 'Ιέρων βασιλεὺς κατὰ τὴν ος' 'Ολυμπιάδα, τῆς κη' Πυθιάδος τῇ προκειμένῃ 'Ολυμπιάδι συγχρόνου οὔσης, ὥστε πάντη τε καὶ πάντως μετὰ

τὴν ὕστερον Πυθιάδα, ἥτις γέγονε περὶ τὴν οε΄ Ὀλυμπιάδα,
συντετάχθαι τόνδε τὸν ἐπίνικον. πρὸς δὲ τὴν παροῦσαν τύχην
τοῦ Ἱέρωνος ἁρμοσάμενος εὔχεται ἐν ταῖς πτυχαῖς τοῦ Πηλίου
διάγειν τὸν Χείρωνα ὑπὲρ τοῦ δύνασθαι τὸν Ἱέρωνα θεραπείας
τυχεῖν ὑπ᾽ αὐτοῦ· λιθιάσει γὰρ νόσῳ κατείχετο. τὸν δὲ Χείρωνα
μιᾶς τῶν Ὠκεανίδων καὶ Κρόνου γενεαλογοῦσιν.

Notes: Inscr(iptio) b indicates that this is the second scholion on the title, though
the lemma that immediately follows is from the first line rather than the title, and
the scholion covers both title and lemma; Πύθια "Pythian games"; Πυθιάς "Pythiad";
μέμνημαι (here) "mention" (the subject is Pindar); συντάσσω "compose"; δύο is
indeclinable here; συνᾴδω "be in accord [with this]"; τὰ ἀπὸ τῶν χρόνων "chronological information [in the ode]"; ὡς + gen. absolute i.e. "implying that";
βασιλεύοντος understand Ἱέρωνος; πραΰς "mild"; κατά "during" (cf. 4.1.32);
προκείμενος "aforementioned"; πάντη = πάντῃ "in every way"; ὕστερον could be
adverbial or perhaps a mistake for ὑστέραν; ἁρμοσάμενος πρός "fitting with"; παρών
"contemporary" i.e. to the dating just discussed; εὔχεται "pray for": the subject is
Pindar (cf. 4.1.43); διάγω "live on"; θεραπεία "medical treatment"; λιθίασις "kidney stones"; γενεαλογέω "trace a pedigree, say that [someone] is born from." In
the fifth century both Pythiads and Olympiads lasted four years (the Pythian games
took place in the third year of each Olympiad); the former were counted from 582
BC and the latter from 776.

65. Aristophanes scholia, ed. Koster and Holwerda, *Pax* 782b
ἐν τῷ ἀντιγράφῳ παροξύτονον εὗρον τὸ Καρκίνος. ἴσως οὖν
συνέστειλεν αὐτό, ὡς καὶ Ἄρατος. RVΓ
Notes: τῷ i.e. "my"; ἀντίγραφον "copy"; παροξύτονος: cf. 4.2.7; Καρκίνος is the
word being discussed; συστέλλω "shorten" (understood subject is Aristophanes);
the statement about Aratus is true, e.g. *Phaenomena* 147.

66. Aristophanes scholia, ed. Koster and Holwerda, *Pax* 1244c
κότταβος: Ἀθήναιος ἐν τῷ ιε΄ φησὶν ὅτι σικελική τις ἐστὶ παιδιὰ
πρώτων εὑρόντων Σικελῶν, ὥς φησι Κριτίας VΓ ὁ Καλλαίσχρου V
ἐν τοῖς ἐλεγείοις
   κότταβος ἐκ σικελῆς ἐστι χθονός, ἐκπρεπὲς ἔργον.
Δικαίαρχος δὲ ὁ Μεσσήνιος, Ἀριστοτέλους μαθητής, ἐν τῷ περὶ
Ἀλκαίου καὶ τὴν λάταγα αὐτὴν εἶναί φησι σικελικὸν ὄνομα. λατάγη
δέ ἐστι τὸ ὑπολειπόμενον ἐκ τοῦ ἐκποθέντος ποτηρίου ὑγρόν, ὃ
συνεστραμμένῃ τῇ χειρὶ ἄνωθεν ἔρριπτον οἱ παίζοντες εἰς τὸ
κοττάβιον. κότταβος δὲ ἐκαλεῖτο καὶ τὸ τιθέμενον ἄθλον τοῖς
νικῶσιν ἐν τῷ πότῳ καὶ τὸ ἄγγος εἰς ὃ ἐνέβαλλον τὰς λάταγας,
ὡς Κρατῖνος ἐν Νεμέσει δείκνυσιν. ὅτι δὲ καὶ χαλκοῦν ἦν, Εὔπολις
Βάπταις λέγει·
   χαλκῷ περὶ κοττάβῳ.
Πλάτων δὲ ἐν Διὶ κακουμένῳ παιδιᾶς εἶδος παροίνιον τὸν κότταβον
εἶναι ἀποδίδωσιν, ἐν ᾗ ἐξίσταντο καὶ τῶν σκευαρίων οἱ

διακυβεύοντες. ἐκάλουν δὲ ἀγκύλην τὴν τοῦ κοττάβου πρόεσιν διὰ τὸ ἐπαγκυλοῦν τὴν δεξιὰν χεῖρα ἐν τοῖς ἀποκοτταβισμοῖς. καὶ ἀγκυλητοὺς ἔλεγον κοττάβους. ὅτι δὲ ἆθλον προέκειτο τῷ προεμένῳ, προείπομεν.

ἐλέγοντο δέ τινες καὶ κατακτοὶ κότταβοι. ἦν δὲ λύχνιον ἀγόμενον πάλιν τε συμπῖπτον ὑψηλόν, ἔχον τὸν μάνην καλούμενον, ἐφ' ᾧ τὴν καταβαλλομένην ἐπιπεσεῖν πλάστιγγα, ἐντεῦθεν δὲ ἐμπίπτειν εἰς λεκάνην ὑποκειμένην πληγεῖσαν τῷ κοττάβῳ. καί τις ἦν ἀκριβὴς εὐχέρεια τῆς βολῆς. τοῦ δὲ μάνου πολλοὶ μέμνηνται.

ἦν δὲ ἕτερον εἶδος παιδιᾶς τῆς ἐν λεκάνῃ. αὕτη δὲ ὕδατος πληροῦται. ἐπέκειτο δὲ ἐπ' αὐτῇ ὀξύβαφα κενά, ἐφ' ἃ βάλλοντες τὰς λάταγας ἐκ καρχησίων ἐπειρῶντο καταδύειν. ἀνῃρεῖτο δὲ τὰ κοττάβια ὁ πλείω καταδύσας.

ὅτι δὲ τῶν ἐρωμένων ἐμέμνηντο ἀφιέντες ἐπ' αὐτοῖς τοὺς λεγομένους κοττάβους, δῆλον ποιεῖ ᾿Αχαιὸς VΓ ἐν Λίνῳ V καὶ Καλλίμαχος·

> πολλοὶ δὲ φιλέοντες ἀκόντιον ἧκον ἔραζε
> οἰνοπόται σικελὰς ἐκ κυλίκων λάταγας.

σικελὰς δὲ αὐτὰς οὐκ ἀπεικότως ὠνόμασεν, ἐπεί, ὡς προείπομεν, Σικελῶν τὸ εὕρημα, καὶ ἐσπούδασται σφόδρα παρ' αὐτοῖς ὁ κότταβος. VΓ

Notes: insight into the development of scholia can be gained by comparing this note to the fuller version in the passage of Athenaeus from which it is derived (15. 665–8); ἐν τῷ ιε΄ "in book 15" i.e. of the *Deipnosophistai*; ἐκπρεπής "remarkable"; λάταξ and λατάγη "wine-dregs" (the latter form is the Sicilian dialectal variant); αὐτήν "itself"; ὄνομα "word" (predicate, because it does not have the article); ἐκπίνω "drink up, drain"; ποτήριον "drinking-cup"; ὑγρόν "wet substance"; συστρέφω "close [a fist]"; ἄνωθεν "from above"; κοττάβιον "*kottabos*-basin"; ἄγγος "vessel"; the Plato mentioned here is the comic poet, not the philosopher; κακόω "distress"; εἶδος "type"; παροίνιος "suitable for a drinking party"; ἀποδίδωμι "explain"; ἐξίσταμαι + gen. "abandon"; σκευάριον refers to a small utensil, including those used for dice games; διακυβεύω "play dice"; the point is probably that this version of *kottabos* was a gambling game so alluring that the players gambled away even their basic implements; ἀγκύλη "bend of the arm"; πρόεσις "throwing forth"; ἐπαγκυλόω "bend"; ἀποκοτταβισμός "action of hurling out the last drops"; ἀγκυλητός "thrown from the bent arm"; προίεμαι "throw out"; κατακτός "to be let down"; λύχνιον "lamp"; ἀγόμενον "[capable of] being drawn up"; συμπίπτω "descend"; μάνης is a small bronze figure; πλάστιγξ "disk on top of the *kottabos* staff"; λεκάνη "basin"; πληγεῖσαν (from πλήσσω "strike") is probably a temporal participle agreeing with πλάστιγγα; εὐχέρεια "skill"; μέμνημαι "mention"; ὀξύβαφον "saucer"; καρχήσιον "drinking-cup"; ἀναιρέομαι "take"; κοττάβιον "*kottabos*-prize"; αὐτοῖς i.e. the saucers; the quotation is *Aetia* fragment 69 (from the story of Acontius and Cydippe), and its text is debated; ἀκόντιον: Acontius; ἧκον "threw"; ἔραζε "to the ground"; οἰνοπότης "wine-drinker"; κύλιξ "wine-cup";

ἀπεικότως "unreasonably." The fragments are Critias fr. B 2 in M. L. West, *Iambi et Elegi Graeci* (2nd edn., Oxford 1992) vol. ii; Dicaearchus fr. 95 in F. Wehrli, *Die Schule des Aristoteles* (2nd edn., Basle 1967) vol. i; Cratinus fr. 124 K–A; Eupolis fr. 95 K–A; Plato fr. 46 K–A; *TrGF* Achaeus I fr. 26 (vol. i, p. 123); Callimachus fr. 69 in Pfeiffer (1949–53).

67. Plato scholia vetera, ed. Greene, *Symposium* 194b
ὀκρίβαντα.

τὸ λογεῖον ἐφ᾽ οὗ οἱ τραγῳδοὶ ἠγωνίζοντο. τινὲς δὲ καλλίβαντα (sic) τρισκελῆ φασίν, ἐφ᾽ οὗ ἵστανται οἱ ὑποκριταὶ καὶ τὰ ἐκ μετεώρου λέγουσιν.

Notes: λογεῖον "speaking-place"; τραγῳδός "tragic actor"; καλλίβαντα is not otherwise attested (hence the editor's "sic"), but it must be related to κιλλίβας "stand or pedestal"; τρισκελής "three-legged"; μετέωρος "aloft."

68. Plato scholia vetera, ed. Greene, *Republic* 338c
Πουλυδάμας.

οὗτος ὁ Πουλυδάμας ἀπὸ Σκοτούσσης ἦν, πόλεως Θεσσαλίας, διασημότατος παγκρατιαστής, ὑπερμεγέθης, ὃς ἐν Πέρσαις παρ᾽ Ὤχῳ γενόμενος τῷ βασιλεῖ λέοντας ἀνεῖλεν καὶ ὡπλισμένους γυμνὸς κατηγωνίσατο.

Notes: παγκρατιαστής "pancration fighter"; ὑπερμεγέθης "extremely large"; παρά + dat. "at the court of"; ἀναιρέω "kill"; καταγωνίζομαι "defeat"; ὁπλίζω "arm"; γυμνός "unarmed."

69. Plato scholia vetera, ed. Greene, *Philebus* 66d
τὸ τρίτον τῷ σωτῆρι.

ἐκ μεταφορᾶς εἴρηται τοῦ ἐν ταῖς συνουσίαις ἔθους· Σοφοκλῆς ἐν Ναυπλίῳ καταπλέοντι (fr. 425 Pearson). ἐκιρνῶντο γὰρ ἐν αὐταῖς κρατῆρες τρεῖς, καὶ τὸν μὲν πρῶτον Διὸς Ὀλυμπίου καὶ θεῶν Ὀλυμπίων ἔλεγον, τὸν δὲ δεύτερον ἡρώων, τὸν δὲ τρίτον σωτῆρος, ὡς ἐνταῦθά τε καὶ δὴ ἐν Πολιτείᾳ (583b). ἔλεγον δὲ αὐτὸν καὶ τέλειον, ὡς Εὐριπίδης Ἀνδρομέδᾳ (TGF fr. 148) καὶ Ἀριστοφάνης Ταγηνισταῖς (fr. 526 Kock).

Notes: ἐκ μεταφορᾶς "metaphorically"; τοῦ i.e. based on the; συνουσία "social gathering"; Σοφοκλῆς: cf. 4.1.12; καταπλέω "sail back"; κιρνάω "mix wine with water"; σωτήρ i.e. Zeus Soter (see E. Fraenkel 1950: iii. 652). The reference to Pearson is to an outdated collection, but the fragment is still numbered 425 in *TrGF*; the Kock reference is now fragment 540 K–A (in vol. iii.ii).

70. Aeschines scholia, ed. Dilts, 1. 182
365 ἀνὴρ εἷς τῶν πολιτῶν] Ἱππομένης ἀπὸ Κόδρου καταγόμενος, ἡ δὲ θυγάτηρ Λειμωνίς. οὕτω Καλλίμαχος. amgVxLS

Notes: κατάγομαι "be descended from"; for the Callimachus reference see fr. 94 in Pfeiffer (1949–53).

71. Aeschines scholia, ed. Dilts, 1. 39

83 πρὸ Εὐκλείδου] Εὔμηλος ὁ περιπατητικὸς ἐν τῷ τρίτῳ περὶ τῆς ἀρχαίας κωμῳδίας φησὶ Νικομένη τινὰ ψήφισμα θέσθαι μηδένα τῶν μετ᾽ Εὐκλείδην ἄρχοντα μετέχειν τῆς πόλεως, ἂν μὴ ἄμφω τοὺς γονέας ἀστοὺς ἐπιδείξηται, τοὺς δὲ πρὸ Εὐκλείδου ἀνεξετάστους ἀφεῖσθαι. amgVxLS

Notes: περιπατητικός "Peripatetic" (Aristotelian philosopher); τρίτῳ: cf. 4.1.33; Νικομένη is acc. subject of θέσθαι ("made"); μηδένα is subject of μετέχειν; Εὐκλείδην ἄρχοντα i.e. the archonship of Eukleides; ψήφισμα "decree"; πόλεως i.e. citizenship; ἄν = ἐάν; ἀστός "citizen"; ἀνεξέταστος "unexamined."

72. Aeschines scholia, ed. Dilts, 3. 95

213 σύνταγμα] οἱονεὶ πλῆθος χρημάτων. λέγεται δὲ καὶ ἀλλαχοῦ τὸ σύνταγμα καὶ ἐπὶ τοῦ τάγματος τῶν στρατιωτῶν. ὅθεν καὶ παρὰ Μενάνδρῳ ἀνέγνωμεν τὸ 'σύνταγμα τῆς ἀρχῆς'. τὸ δὲ λεγόμενον περὶ βιβλίου παρά τινων οὐ λέγεται σύνταγμα παρὰ τοῖς ἀρχαίοις, ἀλλὰ μᾶλλον σύγγραμμα. VxLSf

Notes: σύνταγμα "arrangement"; οἱονεί "that is" (introducing a paraphrase); πλῆθος "sum"; ἀλλαχοῦ "elsewhere"; ἐπί: cf. 4.1.31; τάγμα "arrangement"; ὅθεν i.e. for this reason; ἀναγιγνώσκω "read"; τὸ λεγόμενον goes with an understood σύνταγμα; παρά: cf. 4.1.28; σύγγραμμα "written work."

73. Aeschines scholia, ed. Dilts, 3. 160

366a εἰς αἰτίαν] οἱονεὶ κατηγορίαν, ἐπειδὴ ἡ βουλή, ἀναπεισθεῖσα παρ᾽ αὐτοῦ, ἔθυσε θεοῖς χάριν ὁμολογοῦσα ὑπὲρ τοῦ Φιλίππου θανάτου. ἕνεκα τούτου Ἀθηναίοις ὕστερον ἐπιστέλλων Ἀλέξανδρος οὕτως ἔγραψεν· ''Ἀλέξανδρος τῷ μὲν δήμῳ χαίρειν, τῇ δὲ βουλῇ οὐδέν'. xLSf

366b ἡ σύνταξις δέ· 'εἰς αἰτίαν δὲ τὴν βουλὴν κατέστησεν ὑπὲρ τῆς θυσίας τῶν εὐαγγελίων'. xL

Notes: οἱονεί "that is"; αὐτοῦ i.e. Demosthenes; ἐπιστέλλω "send a message"; οὕτως: see 4.1.23; σύνταξις "construction"; καθίστημι εἰς αἰτίαν "bring into blame"; εὐαγγέλιον "good news."

74. Aeschines scholia, ed. Dilts, 1. 59

135b ἀστραγάλους τέ τινας διασείστους] πολλάκις τινὲς κώδωνας ἀργυροῦς ἢ χαλκοῦς ἐξῆπτον ἔνδον αὐτῶν, ἵνα ἀφιέμενοι ἦχόν τινα ἀποτελῶσι καὶ τέρψιν ἐν τῇ παιδιᾷ. οὗτοι οὖν ἐλέγοντο διάσειστοι. 'φιμοὺς' δὲ ἀλλαχοῦ μὲν σημαίνει εἰς οὓς ἐμβάλλονται αἱ ψῆφοι, ἐνταῦθα δὲ ἃ νῦν καλοῦσιν οἱ κυβευταὶ πυργία. amgVxLSf

Notes: ἀστράγαλοι "dice"; διάσειστος "shaken about"; κώδων "bell"; ἐξάπτω "fasten"; ἦχος "sound"; ἀποτελέω "produce"; παιδιά "game"; φιμός "dice-cup"; ἀλλαχοῦ "elsewhere"; σημαίνει: subject is φιμούς; ψῆφος "pebble"; ἐνταῦθα: understand 'φιμοὺς' σημαίνει; κυβευτής "dice-player"; πυργίον diminutive of πύργος "dice-box."

75. Aeschines scholia, ed. Dilts, 2. 10

27 τῆς ἱερείας ἐνύπνιον] περὶ τὴν γραφὴν ἡμάρτηται· δεῖ γὰρ γεγράφθαι Ἱμεραίας. Τίμαιος γὰρ ἐν τῇ ἕκτῃ ἱστορεῖ γυναῖκά τινα τὸ γένος Ἱμεραίαν ἰδεῖν ὄναρ ἀνιοῦσαν αὐτὴν εἰς τὸν οὐρανὸν καὶ πρός τινος ἄγεσθαι θεασομένην τὰς τῶν θεῶν οἰκήσεις. ἔνθα ἰδεῖν καὶ τὸν Δία καθεζόμενον ἐπὶ θρόνου, ἐφ᾽ ᾧ ἐδέδετο πυρρός τις ἄνθρωπος καὶ μέγας ἁλύσει καὶ κλοιῷ. ἐρέσθαι οὖν τὸν περιάγοντα ὅστις ἔστιν, τὸν δὲ εἰπεῖν· ἀλάστωρ ἐστὶ τῆς Σικελίας καὶ Ἰταλίας, καὶ ἐάνπερ ἀφεθῇ, τὰς χώρας διαφθερεῖ᾽. περιαναστᾶσαν δὲ χρόνῳ ὕστερον ὑπαντῆσαι Διονυσίῳ τῷ τυράννῳ μετὰ τῶν δορυφόρων, ἰδοῦσαν δὲ ἀνακραγεῖν ὡς οὗτος εἴη ὁ τότε ἀλάστωρ δειχθείς, καὶ ἅμα ταῦτα λέγουσαν πεσεῖν εἰς τὸ ἔδαφος ἐκλυθεῖσαν· μετὰ δὲ τρίμηνον οὐκέτι ὀφθῆναι τὴν γυναῖκα, ὑπὸ Διονυσίου διαφθαρεῖσαν λάθρα. οὗτος δὲ ἱερείάν φησιν εἶναι τὴν γυναῖκα, μηδενὸς τοῦτο ἱστορήσαντος. amgVxLSiD

Notes: Ἱμεραίας i.e. instead of ἱερείας; ἕκτῃ: cf. 4.1.33; ἱστορέω "record"; ὄναρ is adverbial ("in a dream"); ἀνιοῦσαν is participial indirect statement (after ἰδεῖν), but this construction quickly gives way to the infinitive, hence the καί connecting ἀνιοῦσαν to ἄγεσθαι; πρός + gen. "by"; θεάομαι "view"; οἴκησις "dwelling"; πυρρός "red-haired"; ἄλυσις "chain"; κλοιός "collar"; ἀλάστωρ "scourge"; περιανίστημι "wake up"; ὑπαντάω "encounter"; ἀνακράζω "shout out"; ἔδαφος "ground"; ἐκλύομαι "faint"; τρίμηνος "period of three months"; οὗτος i.e. Aeschines (or perhaps the copyist who made the mistake pointed out at the beginning of this note).

76. Erotian's Hippocratic glossary, ed. Nachmanson, introduction (31–2 = pp. 4–5)

παρὰ ταύτην γέ τοι τὴν αἰτίαν πολλοὶ τῶν ἐλλογίμων οὐκ ἰατρῶν μόνον, ἀλλὰ καὶ γραμματικῶν ἐσπούδασαν ἐξηγήσασθαι τὸν ἄνδρα καὶ τὰς λέξεις ἐπὶ τὸ κοινότερον τῆς ὁμιλίας ἀγαγεῖν. Ξενόκριτος γὰρ ὁ Κῷος, γραμματικὸς ὤν, ὥς φησιν ὁ Ταραντῖνος Ἡρακλείδης, πρῶτος ἐπεβάλετο τὰς τοιαύτας ἐξαπλοῦν φωνάς. ὡς δὲ καὶ ὁ Κιτιεὺς Ἀπολλώνιος ἱστορεῖ, καὶ Καλλίμαχος ὁ ἀπὸ τῆς Ἡροφίλου οἰκίας. μεθ᾽ ὃν φασι τὸν Ταναγραῖον Βακχεῖον ἐπιβαλεῖν τῇ πραγματείᾳ καὶ διὰ τριῶν συντάξεων πληρῶσαι τὴν προθεσμίαν, πολλὰς παραθέμενον εἰς τοῦτο μαρτυρίας ποιητῶν, ᾧ δὴ τὸν ἐμπειρικὸν συγχρονήσαντα Φιλῖνον διὰ ἑξαβίβλου πραγματείας ἀντειπεῖν, καίπερ Ἐπικλέους τοῦ Κρητὸς ἐπιτεμομένου τὰς Βακχείου λέξεις διὰ . . συντάξεων, Ἀπολλωνίου τε τοῦ Ὄφεως ταὐτὸ ποιήσαντος, καὶ Διοσκορίδου τοῦ Φακᾶ πᾶσι τούτοις ἀντειπόντος δι᾽ ἑπτὰ βιβλίων, Ἀπολλωνίου τε τοῦ Κιτιέως ὀκτωκαίδεκα πρὸς τὰ τοῦ Ταραντίνου τρία πρὸς Βακχεῖον διαγράψαντος, καὶ Γλαυκίου τοῦ ἐμπειρικοῦ δι᾽ ἑνὸς πολυστίχου πάνυ καὶ κατὰ στοιχεῖον πεποιημένου ταὐτὸ ἐπιτηδεύσαντος πρός τε τούτοις Λυσιμάχου τοῦ Κῴου κ΄ βιβλίων ἐκπονήσαντος πραγματείαν μετὰ τοῦ τρία μὲν γράψαι πρὸς Κυδίαν τὸν Ἡροφίλειον, τρία δὲ πρὸς Δημήτριον. τῶν δὲ γραμματικῶν οὐκ ἔστιν ὅστις ἐλλόγιμος φανεὶς παρῆλθε τὸν ἄνδρα.

Notes: παρά + acc. "for"; ἐλλόγιμος "highly regarded"; τὸν ἄνδρα means Hippocrates but refers to his writings; ὁμιλία "speech"; γραμματικὸς ὤν is for γραμματικὸς ὤν; ἐπιβάλλομαι "undertake"; ἐπιβάλλω "throw self into"; ἐξαπλόω "explain"; φωνή "phrase"; πραγματεία "treatment of a subject"; σύνταξις "treatise"; προθεσμία "allotted time"; παρατίθεμαι "apply"; ἐμπειρικός i.e. a member of the Empiricist school of medicine; ἐπιτέμνω "abridge"; διὰ . . συντάξεων is missing only a number; φακᾶς "having a birthmark" (gen. sing. here); πολύστιχος "with many lines"; κατὰ στοιχεῖον "in alphabetical order"; ἐπιτηδεύω "practice"; παρῆλθε i.e. did not write about.

77. Galen, commentary on Hippocrates' *Aphorisms* 4. 48 (Kühn xvii.ii. 727)
τὸ δ᾽ ἐπὶ τῇ τελευτῇ τοῦ ἀφορισμοῦ διχῶς εὑρίσκεται γεγραμμένον, ἔν τισι μὲν ὡς προγέγραπται, ἢν δὲ μή τι τῶν συμφερόντων ἐκκρίνηται, ἔν τισι δὲ χωρὶς τοῦ μὴ, κατὰ τόνδε τὸν τρόπον, ἢν δέ τι τῶν συμφερόντων ἐκκρίνηται· κατὰ μὲν τὴν προτέραν γραφὴν ὁ λόγος ἔσται τοιοῦτος, ἢν δέ τι τῶν μὴ συμφερόντων ἐκκρίνεσθαι φαίνηται κενούμενον, οὐκ ἀγαθόν ἐστι· κατὰ δὲ τὴν δευτέραν, ἢν δέ τι τῶν συμφερόντων τῷ ζώῳ καὶ οἰκείων ἐκκρίνηται, οὐκ ἀγαθόν ἐστι. βελτίων οὖν ἡ προτέρα γραφή.

Notes: the difficulty here is to distinguish Galen's own words from quotations and paraphrases of Hippocrates; διχῶς "in two ways"; προγέγραπται i.e. at the beginning of the passage, which is not quoted here, and in the quotation from Hippocrates that begins immediately after this word; ἐκκρίνω "excrete"; λόγος "meaning"; κενόω "evacuate [from the bowels]."

78. Galen, commentary on Hippocrates' *On fractures* 1 (Kühn xviii.ii. 323–5)
περὶ δὲ τῶν καταγμάτων ἄξιον ἐπισημήνασθαι τοσοῦτον, ὡς πλειστάκις ὀνομάζων οὕτως αὐτά, σπανιάκις δέ που γράψας ἀγμὸς τὴν ἐπιγραφὴν ἐποιήσατο κατὰ τὸ σπάνιον. ὅθεν ἔνιοί φασιν οὐδὲ διῃρῆσθαι πρὸς Ἱπποκράτους αὐτοῦ τὰ συγγράμματα, γραφῆναι δὲ ἓν ὅλον ἄμφω προσκειμένου τῷ νῦν ἡμῖν προκειμένῳ βιβλίῳ τοῦ περὶ ἄρθρων ἐπιγεγραμμένου, διαιρεθῆναι δὲ ὕστερον ὑπό τινος εἰς δύο διὰ τὸ μέγεθος, ἡνίκα δὲ ἦν ἓν ἄμφω, κοινὸν καὶ τὸ ἐπίγραμμα αὐτοῖς εἶναι τὴν κατ᾽ ἰητρεῖον φωνήν. καὶ τούτου δ᾽ αὐτοῦ πειρῶνται φέρειν μαρτυρίαν κακῶς, ἅτε ἓν εἶναι σύγγραμμα τὸ κατ᾽ ἰητρεῖον παλαιὸν ἄνδρα λέγοντες, τοῦ Ἱπποκράτους τοῦ Γνωσιδίκου υἱέως· οὐ γὰρ δὴ τὸ νῦν γε οὕτως ἐπιγεγραμμένον βιβλίδιον μικρόν, ὅπερ ὁ μέγας Ἱπποκράτης ἔγραψεν, ὃς ἔδοξεν ἐν αὐτοῖς Ἕλλησιν ἄριστος ἰατρός τε καὶ συγγραφεύς· ἀλλ᾽ ἐπειδὴ περὶ τῶν κατ᾽ ἰητρεῖον πραττομένων ἐν τούτοις δύο βιβλίοις ὁ λόγος αὐτῷ γίνεται, διὰ τοῦτ᾽ ἐπιγραφῆναι κατ᾽ ἰητρεῖον αὐτά

φασι, διὰ ταὐτὸ δὲ τοῦτο καὶ τὴν τῆς διδασκαλίας τάξιν οὐκ ἀκριβῶς ἔχειν. ἔν τε γὰρ τούτῳ τῷ βιβλίῳ τῷ περὶ τῶν καταγμάτων ἐξαρθρημάτων τινῶν μνημονεύειν αὐτὸν κἀν τῷ μετ' αὐτὸ περὶ τῶν ἐξαρθρημάτων ἀναμεμίχθαι τινὰ περὶ καταγμάτων οὐκ ὀλίγον λόγον. οἷς δ' οὐ διηρῆσθαι πρός τινος, ἀλλ' ἐξ ἀρχῆς δύο γεγράφθαι δοκεῖ τὰ βιβλία, κατὰ τὸ πλειστοδυναμοῦν φασιν. οὕτω γὰρ νομίζουσιν αὐτοὶ τὰς ἐπιγραφὰς αὐτῶν πεποιῆσθαι, κἀντεῦθεν ἀρξάμενοι μακρὸν ἀποτείνουσι λόγον, ἀποδεικνύντες τὰ πλεῖστα τῶν βιβλίων αὐτοῦ κατὰ τοῦτον ἐπιγεγράφθαι τὸν τρόπον. ἐγὼ δ' εἰ μὲν αὐτὸς Ἱπποκράτης ἔγραψεν ὑφ' ἕν ἢ οὐχ ὑφ' ἕν ἀμφότερα τὰ βιβλία λέγειν οὐκ ἔχω . . .

Notes: Galen discusses the title of Hippocrates' Περὶ ἀγμῶν; watch for titles not marked off from the surrounding text except by their Ionic dialect. ἐπισημαίνομαι "note [in addition]"; κάταγμα "fracture"; ὥς with ἐποιήσατο, of which the understood subject is Hippocrates; οὕτως i.e. with the term κάταγμα; σπανιάκις "rarely"; ἀγμός "fracture"; ἐπιγραφή "title"; διαιρέω "divide"; πρός + gen. "by"; προσκειμένου . . . ἐπιγεγραμμένου gen. absolute (the second participle is substantivized and is the subject of the gen. abs.); προστίθημι "add"; ἐπιγράφω "entitle"; ἡνίκα "when"; ἄμφω is the suject of ἥν; ἐπίγραμμα "title"; κατ' ἰητρεῖον "in the doctor's office"; φωνή "phrase"; παλαιὸν ἄνδρα requires emendation, probably to παλαιοῦ ἀνδρός; the point is that the famous Hippocrates was the later of two physicians of that name; οὐ γάρ: understand something like "this Hippocrates wrote"; διδασκαλία "teaching" is the subject of ἔχειν; ἐξάρθρημα "dislocation"; αὐτόν is Hippocrates; κἀν = καὶ ἐν; οἷς is governed by δοκεῖ and has as its antecedent the understood subject of φασιν; understand something like "that they were given titles" to introduce κατὰ τὸ πλειστοδυναμοῦν; πλειστοδυναμέω "be the greater part" (of the contents of each book); αὐτοῦ refers to Hippocrates; ὑφ' ἕν "in one."

79. Lucian scholia, ed. Rabe, *Apologia* 12
    ἀπαξαπάντων· ὑφ' ἕν· ἀντὶ γὰρ τοῦ παντάπασιν. Ἀριστοφάνης Εἰρήνη [247]
        "ἀπαξάπαντα καταμεμυττωτευμένα." ~ ECVφΔ
    Notes: ὑφ' ἕν "as one," i.e. with one accent, to be read as one word; καταμυττωτεύω "make mincemeat of"; the symbols at the end refer to manuscripts.

80. Lucian scholia, ed. Rabe, *Phalaris* 1. 3
    ἐφήβων] ἔφηβοι λέγονται οἱ μέχρι τῶν ιε΄ χρόνων τυγχάνοντες. ~ Φ
    Notes: μέχρι + gen. "up to" (i.e. in age); χρόνος "year."

81. Lucian scholia, ed. Rabe, *Soloecista* 5
    πατρῷα*] πατρικὰ ὅταν εἴπωμεν, τὰ τοῦ πατρὸς λέγομεν ζῶντος τοῦ πατρός, ὅταν δὲ τὰ πατρῷα, τεθνηκότος. ~ ΓΥΜΟUΩ
    Note: the asterisk indicates that although there is no lemma, at least one manuscript had a sign linking this scholion to the word πατρῷα.

82. Apollonius Rhodius scholia, ed. Wendel, end of book 4

Παράκειται τὰ σχόλια ἐκ τῶν Λουκίλλου Ταρραίου καὶ Σοφοκλείου καὶ Θέωνος. [Τάρρα πόλις Κρήτης, ὥς φησι Λογγῖνος ἐν τοῖς Φιλολόγοις (fg philol. 18 Vauch. 307).] L

Notes: this is the subscription, the note at the very end of the scholia stating where they come from. The second part has been added later to explain the first part, a scholion on a scholion. παράκειμαι "be written beside [the text]"; σχόλια "scholia"; τῶν understand "works." The reference is to L. Vaucher, *Études critiques sur le traité du sublime* (Geneva 1854), but the fragment is easier to find on p. 92 of O. Jahn and J. Vahlen, *Dionysii vel Longini de sublimitate libellus* (1910, repr. Stuttgart 1967); both are editions of *On the Sublime* with collections of fragments at the end.

83. Apollonius Rhodius scholia, ed. Wendel, 1. 1081

ὧλλοι μέν ῥα: ἡ τοιαύτη συναλοιφὴ τῆς νεωτέρας Ἰάδος ἐστί. διὸ μέμφονται Ζηνοδότῳ εἰπόντι ‹δεῖν ἀναγινώσκειν› (B 1) ’ὧλλοι μέν ῥα θεοί τε καὶ ἀνέρες‘· οὐ κέχρηται γὰρ ταύτῃ Ὅμηρος.

Notes: συναλ(ο)ιφή "crasis"; Ἰάς [γλῶττα] "Ionic [dialect]"; διό "on account of which"; ἀναγι(γ)νώσκω "read."

84. Apollonius Rhodius scholia, ed. Wendel, 1. 985

ἠοῖ δ’ εἰσανέβαν: ἡ εἰς πρόθεσις περιττή. Δίνδυμον δὲ ὄρος Κυζίκου ἱερὸν τῆς Ῥέας, διὰ τὸ διδύμους μαστοὺς ἐν αὐτῷ ἀνήκειν, ὥς φησι Φιλοστέφανος (fg 2 M. III 29), οὕτω προσαγορευθέν· σύμπασα δὲ ἡ Φρυγία ἱερὰ τῇ θεῷ. ἢ διὰ τὸ δύο ἔχειν ἄκρας οὕτω καλεῖται.

Notes: πρόθεσις "preposition"; περισσός "superfluous"; μαστός "breast, hill"; ἀνήκω "reach up"; ἄκρα "top"; προσαγορεύω "call." The reference is to the collection of historical fragments that preceded *FGrHist*: C. (or K.) Müller, *Fragmenta Historicorum Graecorum* (Paris 1841–70, repr. Frankfurt 1975), where this fragment appears in vol. iii, p. 29; the reference is still valid, as this fragment is not in *FGrHist*.

85. Apollonius Rhodius scholia, ed. Wendel, 1. 1085–87b

λῆξιν ὀρινομένων: τὴν κατάπαυσιν καὶ λώφησιν τῆς τῶν ἀνέμων βίας. ‹ἀκταίης:› τὸ γὰρ ὄρνεον θαλάσσιον καὶ ἐν τοῖς αἰγιαλοῖς βιοῦν. λέγεται δὲ καὶ ὁ Ζεὺς ἐφεξῆς ιε΄ ἡμέρας ἤ, ὥς τινες, ιδ΄ εὐδιεινὰς ποιεῖν, ἵνα ἀποκυήσῃ παρὰ τοῖς αἰγιαλοῖς, αἳ ἀλκυονίδες ἡμέραι καλοῦνται, ζ΄ πρὸ τοῦ τόκου καὶ ζ΄ μετὰ τὸν τόκον. εἴληφε δὲ τὰ περὶ τῶν ἀλκυόνων παρὰ Πινδάρου ἐκ Παιάνων (fg 62 Schr.). εὐλόγως δὲ ὄσσαν εἶπε τὴν τῆς ἀλκυόνος φωνήν· ὑπὸ γὰρ Ἥρας ἦν ἀπεσταλμένη, ὥς φησι Πίνδαρος.

Notes: κατάπαυσις "stopping"; λώφησις "cessation"; ἀκταίης ("coastal") is a second lemma, supplied by the editor because the explanation following it is a note on a different word; ὄρνεον "bird"; αἰγιαλός "seashore"; ἐφεξῆς "successively, in a row"; εὐδιεινός "clear, fine"; ἀποκυέω "bear young"; ἀλκυονίς is the adjective from ἀλκυών "halcyon" (a kind of bird); ὄσσα "omen-bearing cry." The reference would now be given as fr. 62 Snell–Maehler, referring to H. Maehler, *Pindari carmina cum fragmentis,* ii (Leipzig 1989).

86. Apollonius Rhodius scholia, ed. Wendel, 1. 1089a

ἀφλάστοιο: Ἀπολλόδωρος ἐν ταῖς Λέξεσι (cf. 244 fg 240 J.) ἀποδέδωκεν ἄφλαστον τὸ ἀκροστόλιον. οὐκ εὖ, ἐπειδὴ τὸ ἀκροστόλιόν ἐστι τὸ ἄκρον τοῦ στόλου, στόλος δὲ λέγεται τὸ ἐξέχον ἀπὸ τῆς πτυχῆς καὶ διῆκον ἄχρι τῆς πρώρας ξύλον· πτυχὴ δὲ λέγεται, ὅπου τὸ τῆς νεὼς ἐπιγράφεται ὄνομα. ἔστιν οὖν ἄφλαστον ‹οὐ› τὸ ἀκροστόλιον ‹τὸ› κατὰ τὴν πρώραν, ἀλλ' ὁ ποιητὴς αὐτὸ παραδίδωσιν ἐπὶ τῆς πρύμνης λέγων (Ο 716 sq.)·

"Ἕκτωρ δὲ πρύμνηθεν ἐπεὶ λάβεν, οὔτι μεθίει
ἄφλαστον μετὰ χερσὶν ἔχων.'

καὶ εἴρηται ἄφλαστον κατὰ συγγένειαν τοῦ φ πρὸς τὸ θ, ἄθλαστον· κατὰ ἀντίφρασιν, ἐπεὶ εὔθλαστόν ἐστιν. ἔστιν οὖν ἄφλαστον σανίδιον κατὰ τὴν πρύμναν.

Notes: ἄφλαστον "stern-ornament"; ἀποδίδωμι "define"; ἀκροστόλιον "terminal ornament"; ἄκρον "top (of)"; στόλος "prow"; ἐξέχω "project from"; πτυχή "fold" (part of a ship); διήκω "extend, reach"; ἄχρι "as far as"; πρώρα for πρῷρα "front of a ship"; ξύλον "beam"; ἐπιγράφω "inscribe"; ὁ ποιητής: Homer (cf. 4.1.42); παραδίδωμι "teach"; πρύμνα "stern"; ἄθλαστος "undentable"; ἀντίφρασις "antiphrasis" (the replacement of a negative word by its opposite, as εὔξεινος for ἄξεινος); εὔθλαστος "easily dented"; σανίδιον "small board." The reference is to *FGrHist* = Jacoby 1929.

87. Hipparchus' commentary on Aratus, 1. 2. 1–5

Ὅτι μὲν οὖν τῇ Εὐδόξου περὶ τῶν φαινομένων ἀναγραφῇ κατηκολούθηκεν ὁ Ἄρατος, μάθοι μὲν ἄν τις διὰ πλειόνων παρατιθεὶς τοῖς ποιήμασιν αὐτοῦ περὶ ἑκάστου τῶν λεγομένων τὰς παρὰ τῷ Εὐδόξῳ λέξεις. οὐκ ἄχρηστον δὲ καὶ νῦν δι' ὀλίγων ὑπομνῆσαι διὰ τὸ διστάζεσθαι τοῦτο παρὰ τοῖς πολλοῖς. ἀναφέρεται δὲ εἰς τὸν Εὔδοξον δύο βιβλία περὶ τῶν φαινομένων, σύμφωνα κατὰ πάντα σχεδὸν ἀλλήλοις πλὴν ὀλίγων σφόδρα. τὸ μὲν οὖν ἕν αὐτῶν ἐπιγράφεται "Ἔνοπτρον", τὸ δὲ ἕτερον "Φαινόμενα". πρὸς τὰ Φαινόμενα δὲ τὴν ποίησιν συντέταχεν.

Notes: φαινόμενα "things that appear [in the sky], [celestial] phenomena"; ἀναγραφή "description"; κατακολουθέω "follow, imitate"; πλειόνων: understand something like "passages"; παρατίθημι "compare"; λέξις "prose expression"; ἄχρηστος "without profit"; ὑπομιμνήσκω "mention"; διστάζω "doubt"; ἀναφέρω "attribute"; σύμφωνος "agreeing"; ἐπιγράφομαι "be entitled"; ἔνοπτρον "mirror"; πρός i.e. following; συντάσσω "compose" (the subject is Aratus).

88. Hipparchus' commentary on Aratus, 1. 3. 1–4

Ὅτι μὲν οὖν Εὐδόξῳ ἐπακολουθήσας ὁ Ἄρατος συντέταχε τὰ Φαινόμενα, ἱκανῶς οἶμαι δεικνύναι διὰ τῶν προειρημένων. ἐν οἷς δὲ διαπίπτουσιν οὗτοί τε καὶ οἱ συνεπιγραφόμενοι αὐτοῖς, ὧν ἐστι καὶ ὁ Ἄτταλος, νῦν ὑποδείξομεν. ἐκθησόμεθα δὲ εὐθέως καὶ ἐν οἷς ἰδίᾳ ἕκαστος αὐτῶν διαμαρτάνει.

Προδιαληπτέον δέ, διότι Ἄτταλος πᾶσι σχεδὸν τοῖς ὑπὸ τοῦ Ἀράτου λεγομένοις περὶ τῶν οὐρανίων συνεπιγράφεται ὡς συμφώνως τοῖς φαινομένοις ὑπ᾽ αὐτοῦ λεγομένοις, πλὴν ἐφ᾽ ἑνὸς καὶ θατέρου, ἃ δὴ καὶ ὑποδείξομεν ἐν τοῖς ἑξῆς. λέγει γοῦν ἐν τῷ προοιμίῳ τὸν τρόπον τοῦτον· "διὸ δὴ τό τε τοῦ Ἀράτου βιβλίον ἐξαπεστάλκαμέν σοι διωρθωμένον ὑφ᾽ ἡμῶν καὶ τὴν ἐξήγησιν αὐτοῦ, τοῖς τε φαινομένοις ἕκαστα σύμφωνα ποιήσαντες καὶ τοῖς ὑπὸ τοῦ ποιητοῦ γεγραμμένοις ἀκόλουθα." καὶ πάλιν ἑξῆς φησι· "τάχα δέ τινες ἐπιζητήσουσι, τίνι λόγῳ πεισθέντες φαμὲν ἀκολούθως τῇ τοῦ ποιητοῦ προαιρέσει τὴν διόρθωσιν τοῦ βιβλίου πεποιῆσθαι· ἡμεῖς δὲ ἀναγκαιοτάτην αἰτίαν ἀποδίδομεν τὴν τοῦ ποιητοῦ πρὸς τὰ φαινόμενα συμφωνίαν." τοιαύτην οὖν ἔχοντος τοῦ Ἀττάλου τὴν διάληψιν, ὅσα ἂν ἀποδεικνύωμεν τῶν ὑπὸ τοῦ Ἀράτου καὶ Εὐδόξου κοινῶς λεγομένων διαφωνοῦντα πρὸς τὰ φαινόμενα, δεῖ διαλαμβάνειν καὶ τὸν Ἄτταλον περὶ τῶν αὐτῶν διημαρτημένως συναποφαινόμενον.

Notes: ἐπακολουθέω "follow closely"; ἐν οἷς: in both cases, understand antecedents ταῦτα (objects of ὑποδείξομεν and of ἐκθησόμεθα); διαπίπτω "err"; συνεπιγράφομαι "assent"; ὑποδείκνυμι "show"; ἐκτίθεμαι "set forth, expound"; εὐθέως "straightaway"; ἰδίᾳ "individually"; διαμαρτάνω "err"; προδιαλαμβάνω "explain beforehand"; διότι "that"; ἐφ᾽ ἑνὸς καὶ θατέρου "on one [point] and the other," i.e. on one or two points; ἑξῆς "following, later"; προοίμιον "preface"; διό "on account of which"; τό understand "copy"; ἐξαποστέλλω "dispatch"; διορθόω "correct"; ἐξήγησις "explanation, commentary"; ἀκόλουθος "conforming to"; τάχα "perhaps"; ἐπιζητέω "inquire further"; προαίρεσις "purpose"; ἀποδίδωμι "give in explanation"; διάληψις "judgement"; διαφωνέω "disagree"; διαλαμβάνω "assume"; συναποφαίνομαι "agree in asserting."

5.1.3 Grammatical Treatises

Contents: Theodosius 89; Choeroboscus 90; Michael Syncellus 91; Trypho 92; Gregory of Corinth 93–4; Dionysius Thrax 95–8; Herodian 99–101; Apollonius Dyscolus 102–4.

89. Theodosius, *Canons* (from *GG* iv.i), 7. 6ff.

Κανὼν ε´.

Ἑνικά. Ὁ Δημοσθένης τοῦ Δημοσθένους: τὰ εἰς ης ὀνόματα παρ᾽ οὐδετέρων συντεθειμένα πάντως εἰς ους ἔχει τὴν γενικήν, γένος εὐγενὲς εὐγενοῦς, ἦθος κακόηθες κακόηθους· σεσημείωται τὸ ἀγκυλοχείλης ἀγκυλοχείλου. Εἰδέναι δὲ δεῖ ὅτι πᾶσα γενικὴ εἰς ους λήγουσα συνηρημένη ἐστίν· δεῖ οὖν τὸν κλίνοντα πρότερον λαμβάνειν τὸ ἐντελὲς καὶ οὕτως ποιεῖν τὴν συναίρεσιν, τοῦ

Δημοσθένεος τοῦ Δημοσθένους. τῷ Δημοσθένεϊ τῷ Δημοσθένει, τὸν Δημοσθένεα τὸν Δημοσθένη, ὦ Δημόσθενες· τὰ εἰς ης εἰς ους ἔχοντα τὴν γενικὴν εἰς ες ποιεῖ τὴν κλητικήν, Δημοσθένης Δημοσθένους ὦ Δημόσθενες.

Δυϊκά. Τὼ Δημοσθένεε τὼ Δημοσθένη, τοῖν Δημοσθενέοιν τοῖν Δημοσθενοῖν, ὦ Δημοσθένεε ὦ Δημοσθένη.

Πληθ. Οἱ Δημοσθένεες οἱ Δημοσθένεις, τῶν Δημοσθενέων τῶν Δημοσθενῶν, τοῖς Δημοσθένεσι μόνως, τοὺς Δημοσθένεας τοὺς Δημοσθένεις ὦ Δημοσθένεες ὦ Δημοσθένεις.

Notes: The dual and plural forms, though theoretically possible, are unlikely for practical reasons; the editor's use of extra spacing for examples follows the principle that each element of the paradigm is spaced out the first time it occurs, but not in later occurrences; cf. 4.1.16, 19 and for vocabulary 4.2.11; κανών "rule," i.e. paradigm; εἰς: cf. 4.1.29; παρά "from"; συντίθημι "compound"; πάντως i.e. always; σημειόω cf. 4.1.36; ἀγκυλοχείλης "with crooked beak"; συναιρέω "contract"; κλίνω "decline"; ἐντελής "full"; συναίρεσις "contraction"; πληθ. = πληθυντικά.

90. Choeroboscus, Commentary on Theodosius (from *GG* iv.i), 307. 5ff.

Ἰστέον ὅτι τὰ εἰς η λήγοντα θηλυκὰ προσθέσει τοῦ ς ποιοῦσι τὴν γενικήν, οἷον καλή καλῆς, Ἀφροδίτη Ἀφροδίτης, τιμή τιμῆς, μελέτη μελέτης· ὅθεν τὴν γυναικός γενικὴν ἀπὸ τῆς γύναιξ εὐθείας κεκλίσθαι φαμὲν καὶ οὐκ ἀπὸ τῆς γυνή, ἐπεὶ τῆς γυνῆς εἶχεν εἶναι· ὅτι δὲ τῆς γυναικός γενικῆς γύναιξ ἐστὶν ἡ εὐθεῖα, ἐν τῇ διδασκαλίᾳ τῆς κλητικῆς τοῦ θώραξ μεμαθήκαμεν. Ταῦτα μὲν ἐν τούτοις.

Ἄξιον δέ ἐστι ζητῆσαι, διατί τὸ γυνή ἄκλιτόν ἐστιν, οὐδὲ γὰρ λέγομεν τῆς γυνῆς· καὶ ἔστιν εἰπεῖν ταύτην τὴν ἀπολογίαν, ὅτι τὰ εἰς υη λήγοντα δισύλλαβα τῷ υ παραληγόμενα ἐκτεταμένον ἔχουσι τὸ υ, οἷον μύνη (ἡ προτροπὴ καὶ ἡ πρόφασις) Βύνη (οὕτως ἐκλήθη ὕστερον ἡ Ἰνώ) Φρύνη (ὄνομα κύριον)· τὸ δὲ γυνή συστέλλει τὸ υ· εἰκότως οὖν ὡς μονῆρες ἄκλιτον ἔμεινε. Ταῦτα μὲν ἐν τούτοις.

Notes: cf. 4.2.11–12 for vocabulary; πρόσθεσις "addition"; οἷον: cf. 4.1.40; κλίνω "decline"; εἶχεν [ἂν] εἶναι "would have had to be"; ταῦτα μέν: understand something like "suffice"; διατί "why"; ἄκλιτος "indeclinable"; ἀπολογία "defence"; δισύλλαβα "disyllabic [nouns]"; παραλήγομαι "to have in the penultimate syllable" (+ dat.); ἐκτείνω "lengthen"; προτροπή "incitement"; πρόφασις "excuse"; συστέλλω "have short"; εἰκότως "reasonably"; μονήρης "exceptional."

91. Michael Syncellus, ed. Donnet 1982, 11. 69ff.

Περὶ κυρίων καὶ προσηγορικῶν κοινῶν τε καὶ ἐπικοίνων.

Κατὰ σημασίαν τοίνυν τῶν ὀνομάτων διαιρουμένων εἰς κύριά τε καὶ προσηγορικὰ καὶ ἐπίθετα, τὰ μὲν κύρια ἀεὶ μονογενῆ ἐστιν, ἢ ἀρσενικὰ μόνον, ἢ θηλυκὰ μόνον οἷον "ὁ Ὅμηρος", "ἡ Καλλιόπη." Τῶν δὲ προσηγορικῶν, ὅσα μὲν ζώων ἐστὶ σημαντικὰ ὡς ἐπὶ τὸ πλεῖστον κοινὰ τῷ γένει καθέστηκεν, εἴτουν ἀρσενικὰ καὶ θηλυκά, ἔνια δέ ἐστιν ἐπίκοινα.

Κοινὰ μὲν οὖν ἐστιν ὅταν ἡ αὐτὴ φωνὴ μετὰ διαφόρου ἄρθρου προφέρηται, οἷον "ὁ ἄνθρωπος" καὶ "ἡ ἄνθρωπος", "ὁ ἵππος" καὶ "ἡ ἵππος."

Ἐπίκοινα δὲ ὅταν ἡ αὐτὴ φωνὴ μετὰ τοῦ αὐτοῦ ἄρθρου, οἷον "ἡ χελιδών" ἐπὶ τοῦ ἀρσενικοῦ καὶ θηλυκοῦ προφέρηται· διαστέλλοντες δὲ τὸ ἄρσεν ἀπὸ τοῦ θήλεος, λέγομεν "ἡ χελιδὼν ὁ ἄρσην," καὶ "ἡ χελιδὼν ἡ θήλεια"· καὶ ὁ ἀετός ἐπὶ τοῦ ἀρσενικοῦ καὶ θηλυκοῦ, διαστέλλοντες δὲ τὸ θῆλυ ἀπὸ τοῦ ἄρσενος, λέγομεν "ὁ ἀετὸς ἡ θήλεια" καὶ "ὁ ἀετὸς ὁ ἄρσην."

Notes: an explanation of the types of noun gender; cf. 4.2.10–12 for vocabulary; κύριον sc. ὄνομα; προσηγορικόν sc. ὄνομα; σημασία "meaning"; διαιρέω "divide"; μονογενής "having only one gender"; ζῷον "living being"; σημαντικός "indicative of [i.e. referring to]"; ὡς ἐπὶ τὸ πλεῖστον "for the most part"; καθέστηκα "be correctly"; εἴτουν "i.e."; φωνή "word"; προφέρω "utter"; χελιδών "swallow"; διαστέλλω "distinguish"; ἀετός "eagle."

92. Trypho, treatise Περὶ τρόπων attributed to Gregory of Corinth, ed. M. L. West 1965b, p. 238

Κατάχρησις

Κατάχρησίς ἐστι μέρος λόγου ⟨ἀπὸ τοῦ⟩ κυρίως καὶ ἐτύμως κατονομασθέν⟨τος⟩ λεγόμενον ἐπί τινος ἑτέρου ἀκατονομάστου κατὰ τὸ οἰκεῖον, οἷον πυξὶς χαλκῆ καὶ τριήραρχος. καὶ ἡ μὲν πυξὶς κυρίως καὶ ἐτύμως ἐστὶν ἡ ἐκ {ξύλου} πύξου κατεσκευασμένη, ⟨καταχρηστικῶς δὲ⟩ καὶ τὰ μολίβδινα ⟨καὶ τὰ⟩ χαλκᾶ πυξ⟩ίδας προσαγορεύομεν· καὶ τριήραρχον οὐ μόνον τὸν τριήρους ἄρχοντα, ἀλλὰ καὶ πεντήρους καὶ ἐξήρους. καὶ τὸν ἀνδριάντα καὶ γυναικὸς λέγομεν. καὶ Ὅμηρος
νέκταρ ἐῳνοχόει,
οὐ κατὰ τὸ οἰκεῖον, ἀλλ' ἀκατανόμαστόν ἐστι.

Notes: μέρος λόγου i.e. word; ἀπό "[by transference] from"; ἐτύμως "etymologically"; κατονομάζω "name"; ἐπί: cf. 4.1.31; ἑτέρου = ἄλλου; ἀκατονόμαστος "nameless"; κατὰ τὸ οἰκεῖον "properly speaking"; πυξίς "box"; πύξος "box tree"; μολίβδινος "leaden"; προσαγορεύω "call"; πεντήρης "quinquereme" (ship with five rows of oars); ἐξήρης "ship with six rows of oars"; ἀνδριάς "statue"; οἰνοχοέω "pour wine"; ἀκατανόμαστον: for ἀκατονόμαστον. The Homer quotation is from Iliad 4. 3.

93. Gregory of Corinth, On Dialects, ed. Schaefer, 23–9

Καὶ τὸ ὁμοῖος προπερισπωμένως ἐκφέρουσιν, ὡς καὶ παρ' Ὁμήρῳ·
Ὡς αἰεὶ τὸν ὁμοῖον ἄγει θεὸς ὡς τὸν ὁμοῖον.
καὶ ἔστι καὶ τοῦτο ἀνάλογον· τὰ γὰρ διὰ τοῦ οιος ὑπὲρ δύο συλλαβὰς, μὴ ὄντα προσηγορικά, ἅπαντα προπερισπῶνται, οἷον γελοῖος, ἀλλοῖος, ἑτεροῖος, παντοῖος, οὕτω καὶ ὁμοῖος. τὸ μέντοι ὑπὲρ δύο συλλαβὰς εἴρηται διὰ τὸ γλοιὸς, φλοιὸς, κλοιός· προστέθειται δὲ τὸ μὴ ὄντα προσηγορικὰ διὰ τὸ κολοιὸς, ὄνομα ὀρνέου. τὸ δὲ ὁμοῖος προπαροξύνεται κατὰ τὴν κοινὴν συνήθειαν.

Τρέπει ἡ Ἀτθὶς τὸ σ πῆ μὲν εἰς τ, πῆ δὲ εἰς ξ· τὴν γὰρ θάλασσαν
θάλατταν λέγει, καὶ τὸ σεῦτλον τεῦτλον, καὶ τὴν συμφορὰν ξυμφορὰν,
καὶ τὸ σύμβολον ξύμβολον. τρέπει δὲ τὸ σ εἰς ξ ἐπὶ τῶν ἀπὸ τῆς
σὺν προθέσεως ἀρχομένων καὶ συντεθειμένων λέξεων μόνων. καὶ
αὐτὴ δὲ ἡ σὺν καθ᾽ ἑαυτὴν εἰς ξὺν τρέπεται, ὡς τό·
— — —Ἀρτέμιδι ξύν.

Notes: accentuation does not follow modern practice; cf. 4.2.7, 8, 10 for vocabulary; the understood subject of the first sentence is the speakers of Attic (in this
case specifically old Attic, as later Attic had ὅμοιος); ἐκφέρω "pronounce"; ἀνάλογος
"regular"; τὰ διὰ τοῦ οιος "those [ending] with -οιος"; ὑπέρ "more than"; μή signals conditional participle; προσηγορικόν "common noun" (a designation that in
this passage excludes adjectives); ὄρνεον "bird"; κοινός i.e. koiné; συνήθεια "usage";
Ἀτθίς "Attic dialect"; πῆ ... πῆ "in some places ... in other places"; λέγει the
subject is still Ἀτθίς; συντίθημι "compound"; λέξις "word"; συντεθειμένων i.e.
with σύν. The quotations are from *Odyssey* 17. 218 and the *Homeric hymn to Apollo*
165.

94. Gregory of Corinth, *On Syntax*, ed. Donnet, 33. 192ff.

Πρόσεχε οὖν καί, κατὰ τοὺς ἀριθμούς, τὰ οἰκεῖα τοῖς ὀνόμασι
ῥήματα σύναπτε, πλὴν τῶν τοιούτων "τὰ παιδία γράφει, τὰ ὦτα
ἀκούει, τὰ ῥήματα λαλεῖται." Ἐνταῦθα γὰρ τοῖς πληθυντικοῖς, ὡς
ὁρᾷς, οὐδετέροις ὀνόμασιν ἑνικὰ ἐπιφέρονται ῥήματα καὶ εἴωθεν
οὕτω γράφεσθαί ποτε ἐν μόνοις τοῖς οὐδετέροις.

Σημείωσαι καὶ τὰ λεχθησόμενα· "ὁ σύλλογος γράφουσιν, ὁ χορὸς
ἀναγινώσκουσιν, ἡ πληθὺς θορυβοῦσιν, τὸ συνέδριον σκέπτονται."
Ἐνταῦθα γὰρ τοῖς ἑνικοῖς, ὡς ὁρᾷς, ὀνόμασι πληθυντικὰ ἐπιφέρονται
ῥήματα, διὰ τὸ τὰ λεχθέντα ὀνόματα πλήθους εἶναι σημαντικά·
καὶ γὰρ ὁ σύλλογος καὶ ὁ χορός καὶ τὰ τοιαῦτα ἄθροισμά εἰσι
πολλῶν· ἐπὶ μόνων γοῦν τῶν τοιούτων ὀνομάτων ἑνικῶν ὄντων,
δυνατὸν τίθεσθαι ῥήματα πληθυντικά.

Notes: cf. 4.2.10–11 for vocabulary; προσέχω [τὸν νοῦν] "pay attention"; οἰκεῖος
"suitable"; συνάπτω "attach"; ἐπιφέρομαι "follow" (note that Gregory fails here to
follow the rule he is expounding); εἴωθα "be accustomed"; σημειόω "note [as ex-
ceptions]"; συνέδριον "council"; σημαντικός "indicative [of]"; σύλλογος "assembly"; ἄθροισμα "gathering."

95. Dionysius Thrax, Τέχνη, ch. 12 (from *GG* i.i), 24. 3ff.

Ὄνομά ἐστι μέρος λόγου πτωτικόν, σῶμα ἢ πρᾶγμα σημαῖνον, σῶμα
μὲν οἷον λίθος, πρᾶγμα δὲ οἷον παιδεία κοινῶς τε καὶ ἰδίως
λεγόμενον, κοινῶς μὲν οἷον ἄνθρωπος ἵππος, ἰδίως δὲ οἷον
Σωκράτης.—Παρέπεται δὲ τῷ ὀνόματι πέντε· γένη, εἴδη, σχήματα,
ἀριθμοί, πτώσεις.

Γένη μὲν οὖν εἰσι τρία· ἀρσενικόν, θηλυκόν, οὐδέτερον. ἔνιοι δὲ
προστιθέασι τούτοις ἄλλα δύο, κοινόν τε καὶ ἐπίκοινον, κοινὸν μὲν
οἷον ἵππος κύων, ἐπίκοινον δὲ οἷον χελιδών ἀετός.

Εἴδη δὲ δύο, πρωτότυπον καὶ παράγωγον. πρωτότυπον μὲν οὖν
ἐστι τὸ κατὰ τὴν πρώτην θέσιν λεχθέν, οἷον Γῆ. παράγωγον δὲ τὸ
ἀφ’ ἑτέρου τὴν γένεσιν ἐσχηκός, οἷον Γαιήϊος <η 324>.

Εἴδη δὲ παραγώγων ἐστὶν ἑπτά· πατρωνυμικόν, κτητικόν,
συγκριτικόν, ὑπερθετικόν, ὑποκοριστικόν, παρώνυμον, ῥηματικόν.
Notes: cf. 4.2.10–12 for vocabulary, but note that εἶδος also has the meaning "type"
in this passage; πτωτικός "declinable"; σῶμα ("concrete thing") and πρᾶγμα ("incorporeal item") are objects of σημαῖνον; οἷον "such as" (cf. 4.1.40); ἰδίως "particularly"; παρέπομαι "be an accident of"; προστίθημι "add"; θέσις "formation";
παρώνυμον "derived from a noun"; ῥηματικόν "derived from a verb."

96. Dionysius Thrax, Supplement Περὶ προσῳδιῶν (from GG i.i), 107. 6ff.
Ἡ ὀξεῖα τόπους ἔχει τρεῖς· ὀξύτονον, παροξύτονον, ὃ καὶ βαρύτονον
‹λέγεται, καὶ προπαροξύτονον, ὃ καὶ βαρύτονον› παρατέλευτον
λέγεται. ὀξύτονον ὄνομα καλεῖται τὸ ἐπὶ τοῦ τέλους ἔχον τὴν
ὀξεῖαν, οἷον καλός σοφός δυνατός. παροξύτονον ὄνομα καλεῖται
τὸ πρὸ μιᾶς συλλαβῆς τοῦ τέλους ἔχον τὴν ὀξεῖαν, οἷον Ἰωάννης
Πέτρος. προπαροξύτονον ὄνομα καλεῖται τὸ πρὸ δύο συλλαβῶν
τοῦ τέλους ἔχον τὴν ὀξεῖαν, οἷον Γρηγόριος Θεόδωρος.

Ἡ περισπωμένη τόπους ἔχει δύο, περισπώμενον καὶ προπερισπώμενον.
περισπώμενον ὄνομα καλεῖται τὸ ἐπὶ τοῦ τέλους ἔχον τὴν
περισπωμένην, οἷον Θωμᾶς Λουκᾶς. προπερισπώμενον ὄνομα
καλεῖται τὸ πρὸ μιᾶς συλλαβῆς τοῦ τέλους ἔχον τὴν περισπωμένην,
οἷον κῆπος δῆμος.

Ἡ γὰρ βαρεῖα συλλαβικὸς τόνος ἐστί, τουτέστιν εἰς τὴν συλλαβὴν
τὴν μὴ ἔχουσαν τὸν κύριον τόνον † ἐπὶ τέλους ἐτίθετο. ἀλλ’ ἵνα
μὴ καταχαράσσωνται τὰ βιβλία, τοῦτο νῦν οὐ γίνεται, ἀλλ’ εἰς
τὸν τόπον τῆς ὀξείας ἐν τῇ συνεπείᾳ τίθεται· οἷον ἄνθρωπος
καλός. ἰδοὺ ἐνταῦθα εἰς τὸ λος ἐτέθη ἡ ὀξεῖα, ὅτι ἐπὶ τέλους
εὑρέθη. ἐὰν δὲ εἴπῃς καλὸς ἄνθρωπος, ἰδοὺ ὧδε εἰς τὸ λος ἐτέθη
ἡ βαρεῖα, ὅτι μετὰ ταῦτα ἐτέθη τὸ ἄνθρωπος.
Notes: one learns something about the author's date and background from the clearly
Christian orientation of the examples; cf. 4.2.7–9 for vocabulary; παρατέλευτος
"penultimate"; οἷον: cf. 4.1.40; συλλαβικὸς τόνος i.e. a mark indicating the normal pitch of an unaccented syllable; κύριος "principal"; the ἐπὶ τέλους marked †
is corrupt and is best omitted; καταχαράσσω "scratch all over"; i.e. "cover with
marks"; συνέπεια "continuous text"; ἰδού "behold"; some of the aorists near the
end are equivalent to perfects (cf. 4.1.23).

97. Dionysius Thrax, "Scholia" (from GG i.iii), 391. 23ff.
Πολλὰ δὲ τῶν ἀντιγράφων ἔσφαλται· ἡ γὰρ ὀρθότης τοῦ ῥητοῦ
αὕτη ἐστίν· "διώνυμον δέ ἐστι", φησίν, "ὀνόματα δύο κύρια καθ’
ἑνὸς τεταγμένα"· οὐχ οὕτως δὲ ἔχει τὰ πλεῖστα τῶν ἀντιγράφων,
ἀλλὰ "καθ’ ἑνὸς κυρίου", πάνυ ἀνοήτως.

Notes: cf. 4.2.12 for vocabulary; ἀντίγραφον "copy, manuscript"; σφάλλομαι "to err," pf. "to be incorrect"; ὀρθότης "correct form"; ῥητός "expression"; διώνυμον "double name"; τάττω κατά "apply to."

98. Dionysius Thrax, "Scholia" (from *GG* i.iii), 160. 24ff.

Περὶ δὲ τοῦ εἰ ἔcτι γνήcιον τὸ παρὸν cύγγραμμα Διονυcίου τοῦ Θρᾳκὸc ἠμφιcβήτηται· ἐπεχείρηcαν γάρ τινεc οὕτωc εἰπόντεc, ὡc οἱ τεχνικοὶ μέμνηνται Διονυcίου τοῦ Θρᾳκὸc καὶ λέγουcιν, ὅτι διεχώριζε τὴν προcηγορίαν ἐκεῖνοc ἀπὸ τοῦ ὀνόματὸc καὶ cυνῆπτε τῷ ἄρθρῳ τὴν ἀντωνυμίαν· ὁ δὲ παρὼν τεχνικὸc τὴν προcηγορίαν καὶ τὸ ὄνομα ἓν μέροc λόγου οἶδεν ἐν οἷc φηcιν <p. 23, 2 Uhl> "ἡ γὰρ προcηγορία ὡc εἶδοc τῷ ὀνόματι ὑποβέβληται", καὶ τὸ ἄρθρον καὶ τὴν ἀντωνυμίαν δύο μέρη λόγου γινώcκει, καὶ οὐχὶ ἕν. Ἔcτιν οὖν εἰπεῖν, ὡc ἐκεῖνοc ὁ Διονύcιοc ἄλλοc ἦν· ἐκεῖνοc μὲν γὰρ μαθητὴc ἦν Ἀριcτάρχου, ὃc καὶ τὸν ἑαυτοῦ διδάcκαλον ζωγραφήcαc ἐν τῷ cτήθει αὐτοῦ τὴν τραγῳδίαν ἐζωγράφηcε διὰ τὸ ἀποcτηθίζειν αὐτὸν πᾶcαν τὴν τραγῳδίαν· οὗτοc δέ ἐcτιν ὁ λεγόμενοc ὁ τοῦ Πηροῦ· ἐλέγετο δὲ καὶ οὗτοc Θρᾷξ, ἢ διὰ τὸ τραχὺ ἴcωc τῆc φωνῆc, ἢ διότι καὶ τῇ ἀληθείᾳ Θρᾷξ ἦν· εἰκὸc δὲ καὶ κατὰ πλάνην κληθῆναι αὐτὸν Θρᾷκα. Ὅτι δὲ ἄλλοc ἐcτὶν ἐκεῖνοc καὶ ἄλλοc οὗτοc, δηλοῖ καὶ ὁ παρ' ἀμφοτέρων ὁριcμὸc τοῦ ῥήματοc· οὗτοc μὲν γὰρ οὕτωc τὸ ῥῆμα ὁρίζεται, <p. 46, 4 Uhl> "ῥῆμά ἐcτι λέξιc ἄπτωτοc, ἐπιδεικτικὴ χρόνων τε καὶ προcώπων καὶ ἀριθμῶν, ἐνέργειαν ἢ πάθοc παριcτῶcα"· ὁ δὲ Διονύcιοc ὁ Θρᾷξ, ὥc φηcιν Ἀπολλώνιοc ἐν τῷ Ῥηματικῷ, οὕτωc ὁρίζεται τὸ ῥῆμα, "ῥῆμά ἐcτι λέξιc κατηγόρημα cημαίνουcα."

Notes: this scholion is part of the still ongoing debate over the authenticity of the Τέχνη. Cf. 4.2.10–13 for vocabulary; τοῦ goes with the whole clause that begins with εἰ (cf. 4.1.17–18); γνήcιος "authentic"; ἐπιχειρέω "attack"; τεχνικός "grammarian"; μέμνημαι "mention"; διαχωρίζω "distinguish"; προcηγορία "appellative," i.e. common noun or adjective, not a proper name; ὑποβάλλω "subordinate"; ἐν οἷς i.e. "when"; ζωγραφέω "paint" (a picture of); ἀποcτηθίζω "repeat by heart"; κατὰ πλάνην "by mistake"; παρά: cf. 4.1.28; ὁριcμός "definition"; ὁρίζομαι "define"; ἄπτωτος "indeclinable"; παρίcτημι "present to the mind," i.e. "express"; the Ῥηματικόν is a lost work of Apollonius Dyscolus, so this is fr. 55 Linke; κατηγόρημα "predicate." There is a distinction between οὗτος for the author of the present treatise and ἐκεῖνος for the pupil of Aristarchus, and an assumed etymological connection between Θρᾷξ "Thracian" and τραχύς "rough" (cf. 4.1.26). The references are to *GG* i.i.

99. Herodian, Περὶ μονήρους λέξεως, ed. Lentz (*GG* iii.ii), 950. 14ff., with corrections from Egenolff (1884)

Ἦν. οὐδὲν ῥῆμα ὁριcτικὸν ἑνικὸν πρῶτον πρόcωπον κατὰ τὸν αὐτὸν χρόνον ὁρᾶται πρῶτον πρόcωπον ἑνικοῦ καὶ τρίτον ἑνικοῦ καὶ πρῶτον

καὶ τρίτον πληθυντικοῦ, ὅτι μὴ μόνον τὸ ἦν. ἦν γὰρ ἐγὼ 'Αττικοὶ
λέγουσι καὶ ἦν ἐκεῖνος· καὶ πληθυντικῶς Cιμωνίδης ἐπὶ πρώτου
προσώπου, ὥσπερ καὶ ἐν ἐπιγράμμασιν·

ἦν ἑκατὸν φιάλαι, δίχα δέ cφισιν

ἀντὶ γὰρ τοῦ ἦμεν ἦν.

τῆc δ᾽ ἦν τρεῖc κεφαλαί (Hes. Theog. 321).

καὶ

κωφοὶ δ᾽ ἦν προπάροιθεν.

οὐκ ἀγνοῶ δὲ ὅτι ἄλλως ποικίλως λέγεται τὸ ῥῆμα.

Notes: cf. 4.2.10–13 for vocabulary; κατά "in" (cf. 4.1.32); understand ὄν after
ὁρᾶται; ὅτι μή "except"; 'Αττικοί "speakers of the Attic dialect"; ἐπί: cf. 4.1.31;
ὥσπερ καί i.e. "as for example"; ἐπίγραμμα "epigram"; κωφός "blunt";
προπάροιθεν "in front." The first quotation is odd, as it is difficult to believe that
ἦν is a first-person verb here, but in the absence of context such an interpretation is not impossible. The point of the second and third quotations is that there
ἦν is used for ἦσαν.

100. Herodian, Περὶ καθολικῆς προσῳδίας, from Schmidt's edition of
[Arcadius'] epitome, 58. 5ff.

Τὰ εἰς ΚΟΣ ὑπερδισύλλαβα εἰ παραλήγοιτο Ι μακρῷ βαρύνεται·
"Ανικος (κύριον) Κάικος Γρήνικος Φίλικος εἰ δὲ τῇ ΕΙ
διφθόγγῳ, ὀξύνεται· δαρεικός βοεικός Δεκελεικός Κεραμεικός.
σεσημείωται τὸ Καμικός ὀξύτονον καὶ ἔχον τὸ Ι μακρόν, ὡς τὸ
Παλικός.

Τὰ εἰς ΙΚΟΣ κτητικὰ ἐπιθετικὰ καὶ θηλυκὸν ἔχοντα ὀξύνεται·
Γαλατικός 'Ιταλικός Πυθαγορικός. τὸ δὲ ἄδικος οὐ κτητικόν.
τὸ δὲ ἡλίκος καὶ πηλίκος παροξύνονται· οὐ γὰρ κτητικά.

Notes: cf. 4.2.4, 7, 9, 11–12 for vocabulary; cf. 4.1.17–18 for the use of the article; εἰς: cf. 4.1.29; ὑπερδισύλλαβος "of more than two syllables"; παραλήγομαι
"have in penultimate syllable" (+ dat.), σημειόω cf. 4.1.36; θηλυκὸν ἔχοντα i.e.
not being two-termination adjectives.

101. Herodian, Περὶ μονήρους λέξεως, ed. Lentz (GG iii.ii), 929. 26ff.

Εἰμί. οὐδὲν εἰς πτ λῆγον ὁριστικὸν ῥῆμα κατὰ τὴν ἡμετέραν
διάλεκτον διφθόγγῳ παραλήγεται, ἀλλὰ μόνον τὸ εἰμί, ὃ σημαίνει
τὸ ὑπάρχω. οὐκ ἀγνοῶ δὲ ὅτι καὶ τὸ βαρυνόμενον ἡ παράδοσις
διὰ τῆς ΕΙ διφθόγγου γράφει· οὐχ ὑγιῶς μέντοι οὔτε κατὰ τὸ
κίνημα αὐτοῦ οὔτε κατὰ τὴν Αἰολίδα διάλεκτον, ὡς δέδεικταί
μοι ἐν τοῖc περὶ ὀρθογραφίας. πρόσκειται δὲ κατὰ τὴν ἡμετέραν
διάλεκτον, ἐπεὶ Αἰολεῖς πάλαιμι καὶ γέλαιμί φασι καὶ πλάναιμι,
Βοιωτοὶ δὲ τάρβειμι καὶ ποίειμι καὶ φίλειμι.

Notes: cf. 4.2.4, 13 for vocabulary; λήγω εἰς: cf. 4.1.29; κατά: cf. 4.1.32; παραλήγομαι
"have in the penultimate syllable" (+ dat.); σημαίνω "mean"; ὑπάρχω "be"; τὸ
βαρυνόμενον "[the εἰμι] that has a recessive accent," i.e. εἶμι ibo; παράδοσις
"tradition"; διά: cf. 4.1.30; ὑγιῶς "correctly"; κίνημα "inflection"; the point is

that a verb conjugated 1st sing. -μι, 3rd sing. -σι is a true μι-verb (and thus should not have a diphthong before the -μι) rather than an Aeolic reworking of a contract verb into a μι-verb, which would be conjugated 1st sing. -μι, 3rd sing. no ending (and would usually have a diphthong before the -μι)—see Choeroboscus at *GG* iv.i. 320. 33–322. 12; ὀρθογραφία "orthography"; πρόσκειμαι: cf. 4.1.37 (the subject is κατὰ τὴν ἡμετέραν διάλεκτον).

102. Apollonius Dyscolus, ed. Uhlig (*GG* ii.ii), *Syntax* 273. 9ff.

Οὐδὲ ἐκεῖνο δέ με λέληθεν, ὥς τινες ἐπετάραξαν τὴν παρὰ πᾶσιν συμφώνως πιστευθεῖσαν δόξαν, ὡς μιᾶς λέξεως κακία ἐστὶν ὁ βαρβαρισμός, ἐπιπλοκῆς δὲ λέξεων ἀκαταλλήλων ὁ σολοικισμός, αὐτοὶ εἰσηγησάμενοι τὸ καὶ ἐν μιᾷ λέξει καταγίγνεσθαι σολοικισμόν, εἰ κατὰ θηλείας φαίη τις οὗτος ἢ πλήθους ὑπόντος, παραθέμενοι καὶ ἄλλα τῆς αὐτῆς ἐχόμενα εὐηθείας. τὸ πρῶτον, ὅτι οὐδεμία εὐθεῖα συνίσταται δίχα ῥήματος εἰς αὐτοτέλειαν, καὶ ῥήματος τοῦ μὴ ἀπαιτοῦντος ἑτέραν πλαγίαν. ἔστιν γὰρ τὸ οὗτος περιπατεῖ αὐτοτελές, οὐ μὴν τὸ βλάπτει· λείπει γὰρ τὸ τίνα. ἀλλ' εἰ καὶ οὕτως φαίημεν, τίς σε ἔτυψε; τὸ ἀνθυπαγόμενον οὗτος κοινὸν ἔχει παραλαμβανόμενον τὸ ῥῆμα· τίς καλεῖται Αἴας; οὗτος. οὐκ ἄρα ἀληθὲς τὸ ἐν μιᾷ λέξει σολοικισμὸν γίνεσθαι.... Τὸ οὖν κατὰ θηλείας λεγόμενον οὗτός με ἔτυψεν οὐχ ἁμάρτημα τοῦ λόγου· τὸ δέον γὰρ τοῦ καταλλήλου ἀνεδέξατο. εἰ γοῦν ὑπούσης θηλείας φαίη τις αὕτη με ἔτυψαν, ὁμολόγως σολοικιεῖ διὰ τὸ ἀκατάλληλον τῶν λέξεων, κἂν ἀληθεύει τὸ γένος.

Notes: Apollonius defends the usual distinction between barbarism and solecism (cf. Quintilian, *Inst.* 1.5), arguing that because it is possible for a statement to be factually wrong without being ungrammatical, lack of concord with the reality outside a sentence does not constitute a one-word solecism. ἐπιταράσσω "to trouble," i.e. "argue against"; παρά "among," here = "by"; συμφώνως "harmoniously," i.e. "unanimously"; λέξις "word"; ἐπιπλοκή "combination"; ἀκατάλληλος "lacking in concord"; εἰσηγέομαι "introduce [the idea that]" (the object is the articular infinitive); καταγίγνομαι "exist in" (articular infinitive with subject σολοικισμόν); κατά "about" (cf. 4.1.32); ὕπειμι "to be the subject of discussion"; παρατίθεμαι "offer"; ἔχομαι "to pertain to"; εὐήθεια "silliness"; ὅτι: supply something like "it is clear" to govern this; εὐθεῖα: cf. 4.2.11; συνίστημι εἰς "to form into"; δίχα + gen. "without"; αὐτοτέλεια "complete sentence"; μή signals a generic participle; ἀπαιτέω "to require"; πλαγία "oblique case"; αὐτοτελής "complete in itself"; λείπω: cf. 4.1.35; ἀνθυπάγω "to say in reply"; κοινὸν ἔχει "has in common" (with the τίς); παρακαταλαμβάνω "use"; λόγος "sentence"; τὸ κατάλληλον "agreement"; ἀναδέχομαι "receive" (understood subject is the sentence); ὁμολόγως "agreed-ly," i.e. "it is agreed that"; σολοικίζω "to commit a solecism"; γένος "gender."

103. Apollonius Dyscolus, ed. Uhlig (*GG* ii.ii), *Syntax* 389. 13ff.

Πῶς οὖν οὐ γελοῖοι καὶ οἱ ἀφορισάμενοι ὡς Δωριεῖς οὐ περισπῶσι τοὺς ὑποτακτικοὺς μέλλοντας, καὶ οἱ ἐπιζητήσαντες κατὰ τί οὐ περισπῶσιν; ὁ γὰρ λόγος αὐτῶν ἐξ ἀσυστάτου λήμματος συνέστηκεν. ἦν δὲ τὸ δελεάσαν τὴν τούτων ἄγνοιαν ἡ γενομένη ὁμοφωνία ἐκ τοῦ εἰς ᾱ λήγοντος ἀορίστου, ἔχουσα οὕτως. ὁ προσγενόμενος χρόνος ἐν τοῖς ὁριστικοῖς ἅμα τῷ μεταστῆναι τὴν ὁριστικὴν ἔγκλισιν περιγράφεται· παρὰ γὰρ τὸ ἔλεξα εὐκτικὸν μὲν γίνεται τὸ λέξαιμι, ἀπαρέμφατον δὲ τὸ λέξαι, προστακτικὸν δὲ τὸ λέξον. καὶ δὴ οὖν ἐν τῇ ὑποτακτικῇ ἐγκλίσει ταὐτὸν παρείπετο μεταποιουμένου τοῦ τέλους εἰς τὸ ῶ. καθότι καὶ ἐπὶ τῶν ἄλλων παρῳχημένων ταὐτὸν συνέβαινεν· ἔφαγον–ἐὰν φάγω, ἔδραμον–ἐὰν δράμω, καὶ οὕτως τὸ ἔλεξα–ἐὰν λέξω γίνεται ὅμοιον ὁριστικῷ μέλλοντι τῷ λέξω. ὅτι γὰρ οὐχ ἡ σύνταξίς ἐστιν τοῦ μέλλοντος τοῦ ἀχωρίστου, σαφὲς ἐκ τῆς προκειμένης συντάξεως· ἧς εἰ μὴ μεταλάβοιεν οἱ ἐντελέστερον τῶν λόγων κατακούοντες, δυσπειθέστερον ἀναστρέφουσιν.

Notes: Apollonius ridicules those who think there is such a thing as the future subjunctive; cf. 4.2.13 for vocabulary. ἀφορίζομαι "determine"; περισπάω i.e. treat as contracted forms (cf. 4.2.8); λόγος "reasoning"; ἀσύστατος "incoherent"; λῆμμα "premise"; συνίσταμαι "arise"; δελεάζω "to lure [into]"; εἰς: cf. 4.1.29; ἔχω + adverb = εἰμί + adjective; προσγενόμενος χρόνος "augment"; περιγράφω "remove"; παρά: cf. 4.1.28; παρέπομαι "occur in consequence"; καθότι "because" (cf. 4.1.44); by "other past tenses" Apollonius must mean second aorists (and perhaps aorist passives) here; ἐάν (which always takes the subjunctive) is used with these examples to make it clear that they are subjunctive; σύνταξις first "construction," then the title of the work from which this passage is taken; ἀχώριστος "indistinguishable" (i.e. from the aorist subjunctive); προκειμένης i.e. "in front of you"; ἧς i.e. the views expressed in this book (governed by μεταλάβοιεν); μεταλαμβάνω "share"; ἐντελέστερον "completely"; κατακούω "listen" (+ gen.); δυσπειθέστερον "stubbornly"; ἀναστρέφω "to turn things upside down."

104.   Apollonius Dyscolus, ed. Uhlig (GG ii.ii), Syntax 434. 1ff.

Μετὰ τὰς τῶν ῥημάτων συντάξεις, ἃς ἐν τῷ πρὸ τούτου ἀνεπληρώσαμεν, ὄντι τρίτῳ τῆς ὅλης πραγματείας, μέτιμεν καὶ ἐπὶ τὰς τῶν προθέσεων συντάξεις, δεομένας ἀποδείξεως πάνυ ἀκριβεστάτης, καθὸ δοκεῖ τὰ μόρια οἷς μὲν μέρεσι τοῦ λόγου δόκησιν παρέχειν συνθέσεως, οἷς δὲ παραθέσεως, ἔσθ' ὅτε οὐ βοηθούμενα τόνων ἰδιώμασι, καθάπερ τὰ πλεῖστα τῶν μερῶν τοῦ λόγου διὰ τῆς ἑνώσεως τοῦ τόνου τὸ μοναδικὸν τῆς λέξεως ὑπαγορεύει, τουτέστι τὸ ἓν μέρος λόγου εἶναι, ἢ διὰ τῆς μονῆς τῆς καθ' ἕκαστον μόριον τὸ δισσὸν ἐμφαίνει τῶν λέξεων. Τὸ γὰρ Διὸς κόρος παροξυνόμενον μὲν τὴν γενικὴν ἔχει ἰδίᾳ νοουμένην, ὅμοιον ὂν τῷ Διὸς υἱός, προπαροξυνόμενον δὲ ὅμοιόν ἐστιν τῷ Διόγνητος, Διόδοτος· τό τε εὖ νοῷ δύο ἔχον περισπωμένας ὁμολογεῖ τὴν ἐξ ἐπιρρήματος καὶ ῥήματος παράθεσιν, καὶ τὸ Ἕλλης πόντος κατὰ τὴν ἀρχὴν ἔχον τὴν ὀξεῖαν, καὶ τὸ ἐμοῦ αὐτοῦ δὶς ἔχον τὴν περισπωμένην. ταῦτα

γὰρ καὶ τὰ τούτοιc ὅμοια, ἄπειρα ὄντα, cυνελθόντα μὲν κατὰ
τὸν λόγον τῆc cυνθέcεωc ἔχει καὶ τὸν τόνον cυνηρημένον, οὐχ
οὕτωc δὲ ἔχοντα καὶ τὰ τοῦ τόνου ἔχει ἀcυνέλευcτα, καθάπερ
δὲ εἴπομεν, ἐν τῇ καθ' ἕκαcτον μόριον μονῇ τοῦ τόνου τὸ κατὰ
παράθεcιν ὁμολογεῖ.

Notes: This section provides a transition between the discussion of verbs in the
third book and that of prepositions in the fourth book; the need to identify by
accentuation what makes a word is caused partly by the lack of word division in
ancient written texts. Cf. 4.2.7–8, 10 for vocabulary; ἀναπληρόω "to complete";
πραγματεία "treatise"; μέτειμι ἐπί "go after," i.e. "turn to"; καθό "because" (cf.
4.1.44); μόριον "word"; οἷς μὲν μέρεσι τοῦ λόγου . . . οἷς δέ "with some parts
of speech . . . but with others"; δόκησις "appearance"; σύνθεσις "composition"
(i.e. the formation of compound words); παράθεσις "juxtaposition"; ἔσθ' ὅτε
"sometimes"; ἰδίωμα "individual feature"; ἕνωσις "combination into one," i.e.
"oneness"; μοναδικόν "single[ness]"; ὑπαγορεύω "imply"; μονή "retention [of the
accent]"; δισσόν "two[ness]"; ἐμφαίνει subject is τὰ πλεῖστα τῶν μερῶν τοῦ
λόγου above; γενικὴ νοουμένη "genitive meaning"; ἰδίᾳ "by itself"; ὁμολογέω
i.e. "demonstrate"; ἄπειρος "innumerable"; λόγον "rule"; συναιρέω "combine";
οὕτως i.e. compounded; τὰ τοῦ τόνου = τὸν τόνον (cf. 4.1.25); ἀσυνέλευστος
"uncompounded." The point at the end is that εὖ νοῶ, Ἕλλης πόντος, and ἐμοῦ
αὐτοῦ all have doubles (εὐνοῶ, Ἑλλήσποντος, ἐμαυτοῦ) that are compounds
and distinguished from the uncompounded forms only by their accents.

5.2 KEY TO 5.1

5.2.1 Lexica

1. ἀείρομαι [means] "I rise up." Sophocles [uses this word] in the *Trachiniae*
   (line 216).

2. ἀελλάδων ἵππων [means] "of swift [horses]." Sophocles [uses this word]
   in the *Oedipus Rex* (line 466).

3. ἀρκτοῦρος [is] a kind of plant, and a star.

4. βιῷ [means] "with the bow." Or "with life."

5. ἀρκεῖ [means] "he gives aid" [or] "he helps." Euripides [uses this word] in
   the *Peleus* (*TGF* fr. 624).

6. ἄεπτοι [means] "terrible." And "invincible." Aeschylus [uses this word]
   in the *Proteus* (*TrGF* fr. 213).

7. βρύτιχοι [are] little frogs that have tails.

8. ἀρῶς [is] the name of a number among the Persians [i.e. in the Persian
   language].

9. ἄσβεσε [means] "he destroyed." The Cretans [use this word].

10. ἀσαλαμίνιος [means] "without experience of the sea." But others [say that it means] "not having taken part in [the battle] on behalf of the Salaminians" [i.e. the battle of Salamis]. (Aristophanes, *Frogs* 204)

11. ἁρματροχιή [means] the track of the wheels. (*Iliad* 23. 505)

12. γογγρύζειν [means] "mutter" [or] "make a sound like a pig." [It is] the same thing that some [call] γογγύζειν ["murmur"]. The same thing is also called γρυλίζειν ["grunt"].

13. ἀποκορσωσαμέναις [means] "having cut off their hair." For κόρσαι [means] "hair." Aeschylus [uses this word in the] *Hypsipyle* (*TrGF* fr. 248).

14. ἀσαλγάνας [means] "fearful", and [the author] spoke thus imitating barbarians.

15. βρύττος [is] a kind of sea-urchin, as Aristotle says (*Historia animalium* 4. 530b5). But others [say it is] a fish. And others [take it] trisyllabically [i.e. as ἄμβρυττον], [as in] "See, Laches is getting himself a sea-urchin."

16. ἄλλος and ἕτερος are different. For ἕτερος [is] applied to two, but ἄλλος [is] applied to more [than two].

17. ἀληθές and ἄληθες are different. For the opposite of false [is called] ἀληθές with oxytone accent, but what is said as a question [is called] ἄληθες with proparoxytone accent.

18. πελαστής and Πενέστης are different. For one who seeks protection [is called] a πελαστής, but one who was enslaved in the course of war, among [i.e. in the dialect of] the Thessalians, [is called] a Πενέστης, like the Helots among the Spartans.

19. ἐπίκουροι and σύμμαχοι are different. For those coming to help the people on whom war is made [i.e. who are attacked] and taking their part are ἐπίκουροι, but the [allies] of those who make the war are σύμμαχοι. Homer preserved the difference through his whole poetry; therefore it is not possible to find in his works [anyone] called ἐπίκουροι of the Greeks, but [only] of the Trojans.

20. νῆες are different from πλοῖα. Didymus (see Moritz Schmidt 1854: 321) in the eleventh [book] of his rhetorical commentaries says thus: νῆες are different from πλοῖα. For the latter are round, and the former are oared and military. And Aristotle (fr. 614 in Rose's edition) relates as follows in his *Justifications of wars*: "at about the same time Alexander the Molossian, when the men of Tarentum had summoned him to the war against the barbarians, sailed out with fifteen νῆες and many horse-transport and troop-transport πλοῖα."

21. Πύθιοι [refers], among the Spartans, [to] four chosen men, two messmates for each king.

22. Ἑαυτῷ [is] applied to the third person. But Attic speakers [also] use it applied to the second person.

23. Timaeus to Gentianus, greetings. Understanding accurately your judgement and your seriousness and love of beauty concerning Plato, and being accustomed at the festival of Saturnalia to offer to my friends some of my own [work], making use of amusement and at the same time of the sister of amusement, seriousness, I picked out the things in the works of the philosopher that are said with unusual words or according to Attic usage, as [these things] are unclear not only to you Romans, but also to most of the Greeks, and having arranged these things in alphabetical order and paraphrased them I sent them off to you, thinking that it too would provide you with a not inelegant amusement. Farewell.

24. ἀγλαΐας [means] beauties and ornaments, [as in] ἀγλαΐας τῆς νῦν γε μετὰ δμωῇσι κέκασται; and in the singular, [as in] ἀγλαΐην γὰρ ἔμοιγε θεοὶ οἳ Ὄλυμπον ἔχουσιν ὤλεσαν ("for the gods who hold Olympus destroyed my beauty"). And Ἀγλαΐη is also a proper name, [as in] Νηρεὺς Ἀγλαΐης υἱὸς Χαροποῖο ἄνακτος ("Nereus son of Aglaia [and] of lord Charopos").

25. κώδειαν [is] properly the head of the poppy. But when [Homer] says ὁ δεφη κώδειαν ἀνασχών ("and he spoke lifting up the poppy head"), he left out ὡς ("like"), so that [i.e. if the ὡς is supplied] it would be [i.e. mean] "he lifted up the head of the man like that of a poppy." [And it is one] of the hapax legomena.

26. Δίαιτα ["way of living"] [comes from] δαίς, [genitive] δαιτός ["meal"], [via the accusative singular] δαῖτα.

27. ἀθέμιστος (Iliad 9. 63) [means] unjust, lawless; [the opposition / the derivation is] θέμιστος and ἀθέμιστος.

28. Ἀλκάος: in the way that the Ionians drop the ι of possessives, or rather from the ει diphthong, in the same way the Aeolians too drop the ι of the αι diphthong, as [in the Aeolic forms] Θηβάος [for] Θηβαῖος, ἀρχάος [for] ἀρχαῖος, [and] Ἀλκάος [for] Ἀλκαῖος. Thus Herodian [says in his] Περὶ παθῶν (2. 276. 26).

29. Λαοδίκη [is] a proper name; from λαός and δίκη. And the [nouns ending] in -ος are compounded in eight ways. [For more information] look in the [section of words beginning with the letter] θ.

30. Νίζε means "wash" (imperative). The Aeolians change verbs in -πτω into two sigmas [i.e. into an ending in -σσω], [so in this case from] νίπτω, [they

have] νίσσω. But in the speech of the Tarentines it becomes νίζω; [and] from νίζω comes νίτρον, as μάκτρον [comes from] μάσσω and πλῆκτρον [comes from] πλήσσω.

31. ἀλφηστής [means] an inventive person. For some [say that it is] an adjective applied to a human and others [say that it means] the human being himself. [It is] from ἄλφειν, [which means] to find; for only a human [is] inventive. From which the [i.e. Its] genitive plural is ἀλφηστῶν and (in *Odyssey* 6. 8) ἀλφηστάων. Whence also the letter alpha is named, from ἄλφω [meaning] to find; for it was invented first, [before] the other letters. Or [ἀλφηστής could be] from governing in turn; for ἄλφειν [means] to change, from which also [comes] ἀλφεσίβοιαι (in *Iliad* 18. 593).

32. ἀμάμαξυς [is] a vine that grows up a tree; from ἀμμίξαι, [therefore a vine] that is tied [to something]; for vines that grow up trees are tied up; [from ἀμμίξαι one could get the form] ἀμμιξύς, and with addition of a letter and change of one letter into another one [one gets] ἀμάμαξυς; Epicharmus in "Earth and Sea" (fr. 21 K–A) [says] οὐδ' ἀμαμάξυας φέρει; but Sappho (fr. 173 in Lobel and Page's edition) says [the word] with a δ, ἀμαμάξυδες.

33. Κιανίς [occurs in the quotation] Ἀφίκοντο Κιανίδος ἤθεα γαίης. Cius [is] a city of Mysia, [named] from Cius, the man who led the colony of Milesians. The ethnic [for Cius] is Κιανός, [as in the quotation]: Τοὔνεκεν εἰς ἔτι νῦν περ" Ὑλαν ἐρέουσι Κιανοί. And Mysians settled it, then Carians, and thirdly Milesians. And there is also a river with the same name flowing past the land of Mysia. And Cius is the city that [is] now Prusa for the Prusians [i.e. that its current inhabitants, the Prusians, call Prusa].

34. Ἄϊδι (*Iliad* 1. 3): some say: from εἴδω, [meaning] see, [from which one can get] the future εἴσω [and thence] the verbal noun ἴς with an ι. For there are many nouns . . . ; and with alpha privative [it becomes] Ἄϊς, [that is, the place] in which it is not possible to see anything, and the genitive [is] Ἄϊδος and Homer [says] "δῦναι δόμον Ἄϊδος εἴσω" (*Iliad* 3. 322) and the dative [is] Ἄϊδι. But others say [that Ἄϊδι arises] by metaplasm from Ἀΐδη, dative of Ἀΐδης.

35. Ταών [i.e. ταῶν]: where [does it come] from? From extending the tail; for the creature priding himself on his own beauty shows off his tail to those watching, spreading it out. But some want [ταῶν to be] from ταός, by lengthening of the o to ω, and by change of the accent. But it is not possible; since ταός with omicron, as Herodian says, is not customary for Greeks. And some say that [ταῶν] should have been τεώς, as [Homeric] λαός [is in Attic] λεώς; to whom it is possible to reply that [ταῶν] has a shortened α; and on account of this it did not become [τεώς] among Attic speakers by the change of α to ε, just like Οἰνόμαος [which also preserves an ending in -αος because the α is short]. And it is worth inquiring why it

is not declined [nom.] ταῶς, [gen.] ταῶτος, and [why] Τυφῶς [is not declined with genitive] Τυφῶτος, like ἱδρώς [which has the genitive] ἱδρῶτος. And it is possible to say that those words [i.e. ones like ἱδρώς] are oxytone; and that these [i.e. ταῶς and Τυφῶς] have a circumflex; and that these end in ν [i.e. have alternate nominative forms ταῶν and Τυφῶν]. But let no-one think that these [i.e. ταῶς and Τυφῶς] are words with a double ending; for words with a double ending keep the same declension, [as] ῥίν and ῥίς [both sharing the genitive] ῥινός; but these [i.e. ταῶς and Τυφῶς] do not have the same declension; for Τυφῶν [has the genitive] τυφῶνος, and ταῶν [has the genitive] ταῶνος; and τυφῶς [has the genitive] τυφῶ, and ταῶς [has the genitive] ταῶ. [Information from] Choeroboscus.

36. Pindar, of Thebes, son of Scopelinus, but according to some [son] of Daïphantus, which also [is] more true; for the [son] of Scopelinus is more obscure and a kinsman of Pindar's. But some also recorded that he [was the son] of Pagonides. And [he was] a disciple of the woman Myrtis, having been born in the sixty-fifth Olympiad and being 40 years [old] during the campaign of Xerxes. And there was to him a brother [i.e. he had a brother], Erotion by name and a son Diophantus, and daughters Eumetis and Protomache. And the end of his life happened to him according to [his] prayers; for [it is said that] having asked for the best [thing] of the [things] in life to be given to him, all at once he died in the theater, leaning on the knees of Theoxenus, his beloved, [at the age] of 55 years. And he wrote in seventeen books in the Doric dialect the following: Olympian victory odes, Pythian victory odes, Prosodia, Parthenia, Enthronismoi, Bacchica, Daphnephorica, Paeans, Hyporchemata, Hymns, Dithyrambs, drinking-songs, Encomia, Threnoi, seventeen tragedies, epic epigrams, and prose exhortations to the Greeks, and very many other [books].

5.2.2 Scholia and Commentaries

37. Τρώων πεδίῳ: in another [copy there is instead] Τρώων ὁμάδῳ (which is the phrase found at *Iliad* 15. 689).

38. τεῖχος: [the sign is there] because the [preposition] ἐπί is lacking, [so the phrase is equivalent to] ἐπὶ τεῖχος.

39. μάχης: Zenodotus [reads] μάχης, but others [read] μάχην. And Aristophanes [of Byzantium] too [reads] μάχην.

40. ἀκήματα: in some [copies the word is] ἀκέσματα; and Aristarchus also [reads the text] this way. So [the text is read] in two ways.

41. Τεῦκρε πέπον, ‹δὴ νῶϊν ἀπέκτατο πιστὸς ἑταῖρος›: [it is] worth accepting the customary practice which punctuates after the πέπον, and not after the conjunction δή.

42. θρῆνυν: the seat (in the accusative) of the rowers, or the [seat] of the steersman. But speakers of the Attic dialect call the [seat] of the rower θρᾶνος and the [rowers] themselves θρανῖται.

43. ἰοδόκον: some [say that it should be pronounced] with proparoxytone accent [and means] the one that receives arrows, but ξεινοδόκον (*Iliad* 3. 354), with paroxytone accent, [means] the one who receives guests or the one who watches for guests. And Attalus gives [this word] a paroxytone accent.

44. ὅ τέ μοι βιὸν ἔκβαλε χειρός: ὅ τε [is used] instead of ὅστις. But others [say it is] instead of ὅτι, [as in] ὅτε με βροτοὶ οὔτε τίουσιν (*Odyssey* 13. 129), [where ὅτε is used] instead of ὅτι.

45. ‹ἔμελλε› παλίωξιν παρὰ νηῶν: [the sign is there] because [the text reads] παλίωξιν correctly, [παλίωξιν meaning] a pursuit back again, when out of a turning around the pursued pursue [their former pursuers]. And regarding the ἔμελλεν, that [it is] instead of ἐῴκει.

46. νῆας: Aristarchus writes [this] without the σ, [as] νῆα. For [the poet] said earlier τὼ δὲ περὶ μιᾶς νηὸς ἔχον πόνον ("they were laboring around one ship") (*Iliad* 15. 416, i.e. the preceding line). Aristarchus [writes] νῆα, but others [have] νῆας.

47. δάμεν: in the same way as πολλοὶ δ' Ἀργείων οἱ μὲν δάμεν, οἱ δ' ἐλίποντο (*Iliad* 12. 14) and φάνεν δέ οἱ εὐρέες ὦμοι (*Odyssey* 18. 68) [the verb] was read with aphaeresis (loss) of the initial augment. And we said (in a passage that is now scholion *a* to *Iliad* 1. 464) that such forms are found without distinction in the works of the poet.

48. διά τε σκόλοπας καὶ τάφρον ἔβησαν: either for διὰ σκολόπων καὶ τάφρου, as in διά τ' ἔντεα καὶ μέλαν αἷμα (at *Iliad* 10. 298), or the sequence in which the words are to be taken [is] διέβησαν. And the tmesis of the word shows the pathos and the difficulty of passing through [the Greek barricades]; for [the Trojans] did not flee τῇ περ Ἀχαιοί / ἐκ πεδίου νίσοντο ("by the same way as the Achaeans used to come back from the plain," *Iliad* 12. 118–19), but they were fleeing through the ditch. The same tmesis also [occurs] in κατὰ πυρὸν ἄλεσσαν ("they ground down wheat," *Odyssey* 20. 109).

49. φαμέν: φαμέν is complete and indicates the present tense, on account of which it is necessary to leave the two syllables unaccented [i.e. the word is enclitic]. If, however, it should be [in the] imperfect, it is clear that it undergoes a loss of the augment at the beginning and an acute accent will be on the syllable φα, like the complete [form] ἔφαμεν, as in that φάμεν δέ οἱ οὐ τελέεσθαι (*Odyssey* 4. 664), which [interpretation] the meaning in this passage does not require.

50. χλωροὶ ὑπαὶ δείους πεφοβημένοι: the preposition ὑπό became ὑπαί in the same way as in ὑπαὶ πόδα νείατον Ἴδης (*Iliad* 2. 824). And the normal equivalent is ὑπὸ δέους. Aristarchus also [interprets this word] in this way; on account of which it is necessary to reject the view of Tyrannion (fr. 37 Haas), who accented ὑπαί recessively (i.e. as ὕπαι) and considered that the transformation of apocope happened from ὕπαιθα [i.e. ὕπαιθα lost its final syllable]. And we ought to pause after the ὑπαὶ δείους—for it is not plausible [to put the pause] after the χλωροί—and then [have in isolation] πεφοβημένοι, that is, "fleeing." However, the other pause [i.e. putting the pause after χλωροί] is also not unconvincing.

51. And the poet says in an ecphrasis also "and he put on his head a golden helmet with two ridges and four bosses, fitted with the πρυλέεσιν," which is foot-soldier hoplites, "of a hundred," i.e. many, "cities."

52. And "πρυλέες" are those in battle on foot [i.e. foot soldiers] in the dialect of the people of Gortyn, as the ancients say. And the derivation of the word has already been given. But now [we] should just say that if the nominative [singular] of this [word] has an acute on the final syllable, it should be explained differently, but if it has an unaccented final syllable, it could be advocated that from this is the proper name [found] in Lycophron in the [phrase] "τῶν αὐθομαίμων συγκατασκάπτην Πρύλιν." In this way too Hippotes in the *Odyssey* is a proper name homonymous with the [ἱππότης that means] "cavalryman."

53. But some explained the "fitted with the πρυλέεσσιν of a hundred cities" thus: having the chiefs of a hundred cities, or decorated with the hoplites of Crete, that is, having the deeds of the Corybantes molded [on it]. And that Crete has a hundred cities is shown in the *Odyssey* too. And that the Corybantes were also Cretans, [that] itself [is] also clear. And some say that the nominative [singular] of πρυλέεσσι is πρύλις, coming from περῶ [hence] περύω, [meaning] to travel, [hence the future] περύσω, [hence] πέρυλις and πρύλις, as δαμάσω [future of δαμάζω "to subdue"] [produces] δάμαλις ["heifer"]. And perhaps the proper [noun] Πρύλις, [found] in Lycophron, also contributes something toward [its having] this sort of inflection and accentuation. But others, including Herodian, write πρυλής with an acute accent on the final syllable and decline it regularly [so that the genitive is] πρυλέος [or] πρυλοῦς, as has also already been said. And this is sounder. For indeed from πρύλις [the nominative plural] ought to be πρύλεες, like ὄφεες [which comes from ὄφις], but in fact πρυλέες is found, like εὐσεβέες [from εὐσεβής].

54. He says ἦν instead of "I was"; it is Attic.
    νεώτατος δ' ἦν: he says [ἦν] instead of "I was"; and it is Attic. And also [there is a reading here] without the ν, ἦ, instead of [i.e. contracted

from] "I was"; thus Didymus [read the text]. However, in the manuscripts ἦν is transmitted, and the usual reading is ἦν.

55. The stage-building is opened and on an *ekkuklema* are seen the bodies that he calls "double tyranny."

56. The chorus sings the stasimon having come down to earth.

57. Some divide Σουσισκάνης [into Σοῦσις and Κάνης] and [Πηγαστάγων into] Πηγάς and Ταγών. For he has fabricated the names, and they are not Egyptian. (Or, following the suggested emendation: some divide [these words into] Σοῦσις and Κάνης and Πηγάς and Ταγών.)

58. Some blame the poet because he makes the Greeks arrive from Troy on the same day [as they left Troy].

59. And the background is like this. Io the daughter of Inachus, having been loved by Zeus, since Hera [had] discovered this and she [Io] was about to be caught by her [Hera], was changed by Zeus into a cow, in order that she might not be recognized [for] who she was. But Hera coming to Zeus sought her and received [her as] a gift from him, and she gave her to Argos the all-seeing to guard. But Zeus having again become enamored of her sent Hermes to take her away from Argos and bring [her] to him. And since there was no other way to escape Argos the all-seeing, [Hermes] killed him with a stone blow [i.e. a blow from a stone]. Hera used to show the phantom of him to Io even after his death in order to frighten her particularly. And she, having wandered much through different places, finally went away even to the Caucasus in order to see Prometheus.

60. κύριε: sovereign and completely powerful [in the vocative], that is, having dominion over everything.

61. τὰ δ' οὐκ ἐπ' ἀνδράσι κεῖται: this is not possible, among men, to obtain [blessings] from deliberation; but the divinity provides [them] to each [man].

62. σὺν 'Αρκεσίλᾳ: the σύν goes with the αὔξῃς, so as to be συναύξῃς. And κωμάζοντι [means] leading victory processions; and those who win lead victory processions in their own country.

63. Title. It has been written for Xenocrates of Acragas when he won in the 24th Pythiad. And it is clear that the odes are not arranged in chronological order; for the ode before this one was written for Arcesilaus when he won [in] the 31st Pythiad.

64. Title b. Ἤθελον Χείρωνά κε Φιλλυρίδαν: to Hieron when he won the Pythian games during the 27th Pythiad; and he mentions also the Pythiad before that one, so that the ode was composed for the two victories. And the chronological information [in the ode] also accords with [this dating].

For he says, implying that [Hieron] is already king, ὃς Συρακόσσαισιν ἄρχει πραῢς ἀστοῖς (line 70). And Hieron became king during the 76th Olympiad, the 28th Pythiad being at the same time as the aforementioned [i.e. 76th] Olympiad, so that this epinician ode was composed in every way and entirely after the later [i.e. 27th] Pythiad, which was about [i.e. in] the 75th Olympiad. And fitting with the contemporary fortune of Hieron [Pindar] prays for Chiron to be living on in the folds of Pelion for the sake of Hieron's being able to obtain medical treatment by him; for he was gripped by kidney stones. And they say that Chiron was born from one of the Oceanids and Cronus.

65. In my copy I found Καρκίνος with paroxytone accent. So perhaps [Aristophanes] shortened it, as Aratus also [did].

66. κότταβος: Athenaeus in book 15 [of the *Deipnosophistae*] says that it is a Sicilian game, since the Sicels first invented [it], as Critias the son of Callaeschrus says in his elegies: κότταβος ἐκ σικελῆς ἐστι χθονός, ἐκπρεπὲς ἔργον ("*kottabos* is from the Sicilian land, a remarkable thing"). And Dicaearchus the Messenian, student of Aristotle, in his *On Alcaeus* also says that "wine-dregs" itself is a Sicilian word. And wine-dregs is the wet substance left behind from the drained drinking-cup, which the players used to throw from above into the *kottabos*-basin with a closed fist. And the prize set for the winners in the drinking was also called "*kottabos*," and [so was] the vessel into which they used to throw the dregs, as Cratinus shows in the *Nemesis*. And that it was also [made of] bronze, Eupolis says in the *Baptae*: χαλκῷ περὶ κοττάβῳ ("around a bronze *kottabos*"). And Plato in the *Distressed Zeus* explains that *kottabos* is a type of game suitable for a drinking party, [a game] in which the dice-players abandon even their small utensils. And they used to call the throwing forth of the *kottabos* ἀγκύλη ("bend of the arm") because of the bending the right hand in the action of hurling out the last drops. And they called the *kottaboi* ἀγκυλητοί ("thrown from the bent arm"). And that a prize used to be set out for the one throwing out [the *kottabos*], we have already said.

And some [i.e. some kinds of] *kottaboi* also used to be called to-be-let-down. And there was [as part of these games] a high lamp [capable of] being drawn up and descending again, having the so-called μάνης, on which the disk fell when it was thrown down, and from there it fell into the basin lying underneath, when it was struck by the *kottabos*. And there was a certain precise skill of the throw. And many have mentioned the μάνης.

And there was another type of game in the basin. And this [the basin] is filled with water. And on it lay empty saucers, onto which throwing the dregs from the drinking-cups [the players] tried to sink [the saucers]. And the one who sank more [than the other players] used to take the *kottabos*-prize.

And that the ones throwing the so-called *kottaboi* at them [the saucers] made mention of their beloveds, Achaeus makes clear in the *Linus*, and Callimachus: πολλοὶ δὲ φιλέοντες ἀκόντιον ἧκον ἔραζε / οἰνοπόται σικελὰς ἐκ κυλίκων λάταγας. ("And many wine-drinkers, loving Acontius, threw to the ground the Sicilian dregs out of their cups"). And he called them Sicilian not unreasonably, since, as we said before, the invention [is] of the Sicels, and the *kottabos* was especially valued among them.

67. ὀκρίβαντα: the speaking-place on which the tragic actors used to compete. But some say [that it is] a three-legged stand, on which the actors stand and say the things [that come] from aloft.

68. Πουλυδάμας: this Polydamas was from Scotussa, a city of Thessaly, [and was] a very famous pancration fighter, extremely large, who when he was among the Persians at the court of King Ochus killed lions and unarmed defeated armed men.

69. τὸ τρίτον τῷ σωτῆρι: [the expression] has been said metaphorically, based on the custom in social gatherings; Sophocles [uses this phrase] in his *Nauplius sailing back* (*TrGF* fr. 425). For in them [social gatherings] three craters [of wine] used to be mixed, and they used to say that the first one [was] of [i.e. dedicated to] Olympian Zeus and the Olympian gods, and the second one [was] of the heroes, and the third [was] of Zeus Soter, as both here and indeed in [Plato's] *Republic* (583b). And they also used to call it [i.e. the third crater] "final," as Euripides [does in his] *Andromeda* (*TGF* fr. 148) and Aristophanes [does in his] *Tagenistae* (fr. 520 K–A).

70. ἀνὴρ εἷς τῶν πολιτῶν ("one of the citizens"): Hippomenes, descended from Codrus. And the daughter [was] Leimonis. Thus Callimachus [says].

71. πρὸ Εὐκλείδου ("before Euclides"): Eumelus the Peripatetic in his third [book] about Old Comedy says that a certain Nicomenes made a decree that no one of those after the archonship of Euclides was to have a share in the city [i.e. have citizenship], if he did not show [that] both his parents [were] citizens, but that those before Euclides be passed unexamined.

72. σύνταγμα: that is, a sum of money. And elsewhere too σύνταγμα is also used with reference to the arrangement of the soldiers [i.e. military formations]. Whence also in Menander we read the "σύνταγμα of the rule." But the [σύνταγμα] said by some about a book is not called σύνταγμα among the ancients, but rather "written work."

73. εἰς αἰτίαν: that is, "[into] accusation", since the council, having been persuaded by him [Demosthenes], sacrificed to the gods acknowledging gratitude for the death of Philip. On account of this Alexander later sending a message to the Athenians wrote thus: "Alexander [sends] greetings to the people, but none to the council." And the construction is: "he brought the council into blame for the thank-offering for good news."

74. ἀστραγάλους τέ τινας διασείστους ("and some shaken dice"): often some people used to fasten silver or bronze bells within them [the dice], so that when thrown they might produce a certain sound and [produce] enjoyment in the game. These then were called "shaken." And elsewhere "dice-cups" [means the things] into which the pebbles are cast, but here [that word means the things] which the dice-players now call little dice-boxes.

75. τῆς ἱερείας ἐνύπνιον ("the dream of the priestess"): there has been a mistake about the writing; for what ought to have been written is "[the dream of the] Himeraean woman". For Timaeus in his sixth [book] records that a certain woman, Himeraean by birth, saw in a dream that she was going up to heaven and being led by someone to view the dwellings of the gods. There she saw Zeus too [i.e. among others] sitting on his throne, on which a big and red-haired man was bound with a chain and a collar. So she asked the one leading her around who [the bound man] was, and he said: "He is the scourge of Sicily and of Italy, and if he is released, he will destroy the countries." And having woken up, later in time she encountered the tyrant Dionysius with his bodyguards, and when she saw him she shouted out that he was the man who had been shown [to her] then as the scourge, and as she said this she fell to the ground having fainted. And after three months the woman was no longer seen, having been secretly killed by Dionysius. But he [Aeschines] says that the woman was a priestess, although no one has recorded this.

76. For this reason many of the highly regarded men, not only among the doctors but also among the grammarians, have made an effort to explain the man['s writings] and to bring his words to a more common [type] of speech. For Xenocritus the Coan, being a grammarian, as Heraclides the Tarentine says, was the first to undertake to explain phrases of this type. And as the Citian Apollonius also relates, Callimachus from the household of Herophilus also [undertook to explain them]. After whom, they say, Bacchius the Tanagran threw himself into the treatment of the subject and filled up his allotted time with three treatises, applying to this [purpose] many pieces of evidence from the poets; in response to whom indeed Philinus the Empiricist, who was a contemporary, produced a treatment of the subject in a six-book work, although Epicles the Cretan abridged Bacchius' glossary in . . . treatises, and Apollonius the son of Ophis did the same thing, and Dioscurides, the one with the birthmark, responded to all these in seven books, and Apollonius the Citian wrote eighteen [books] against [Heraclides] the Tarentine's three books against Bacchius, and Glaucon the Empiricist practiced the same thing in one [book] of very many lines and made in alphabetical order, and in addition to these Lysimachus the Coan laboriously produced a treatment in twenty books after writing three [books on this topic] against Cydias the follower

of Herophilus and three against Demetrius. And of the grammarians there is none of high repute who passed by the man.

77. But the [part] at the end of the aphorism is found written in two ways, in some [manuscripts] as was written earlier, ἢν δὲ μή τι τῶν συμφερόντων ἐκκρίνηται ("and if not any of those things that are useful is excreted") and in others without the μή, in this way, ἢν δέ τι τῶν συμφερόντων ἐκκρίνηται ("and if any of the things that are useful is excreted"); according to the first writing the meaning will be of this sort: "and if any of the things that are not useful to be excreted is clearly evacuated [from the bowels], it is not good"; but according to the second [the meaning will be]: "and if any of the things that are useful to the animal and proper [to it] is excreted, it is not good." So the first writing is better.

78. And concerning fractures it is worth noting this much, that although [Hippocrates] very often names them thus [i.e. κατάγματα], and rarely writes ἀγμός, he made the title with the rare [form]. Whence some say that the writings were not divided by Hippocrates himself, but that both were written as one entire [work], with the book entitled "On joints" added to the book that is now before us, and that they were divided later by someone into two on account of their bulk, but when they were both one, they had also as title the phrase "In the doctor's office" in common. And they try to supply evidence of this very thing badly, because they say that there is one work [called] "In the doctor's office," of [i.e. by] an ancient man, Hippocrates the son of Gnosidicus; for indeed [this Hippocrates did] not [write] the present tiny little book thus entitled, which the great Hippocrates wrote, who seemed the best doctor and writer among the Greeks themselves; but since he has a discussion in these two books about the things that are done in the doctor's office, for this reason they say that they were entitled "In the doctor's office," and that for this same reason also the order of the teaching is not clear. For in this book, the one about fractures, he mentions some dislocations, and in the one after it, [which is] about dislocations, some not inconsiderable discussion about fractures has been mixed in. And those to whom the books seem not to have been separated by someone, but to have been written as two from the beginning, say [that they were given titles] according to the [subject-matter] that forms the greater part [of the contents of each book]. For thus they themselves think that their [i.e. these books'] titles have been made, and beginning from there they stretch out a long discussion, showing that most of his [Hippocrates'] books were given titles in this way. And I am not able to say if Hippocrates himself wrote both the books in one or not in one . . .

79. ἀπαξαπάντων: [to be read] as one [word]; for it is instead of "altogether." Aristophanes [in his] *Peace* [line 247] [says] "altogether made into mincemeat".

80. ἐφήβων: those who happen (to be) up to 15 years [old] are called ephebes.

81. πατρῷα: when we say πατρικά ("paternal"), we are talking about the things of the father when the father is living, but when [we say] πατρῷα, [we are talking about the things of the father when the father is] dead.

82. The scholia from the works of Lucillus Tarrhaeus and Sophocleius and Theon are written beside [the text]. Tarra is a city of Crete, as Longinus says in his *Philological writings*. (ed. Jahn and Vahlen p. 92)

83. ὦλλοι μέν ῥα ("the others on the one hand"): the crasis is [characteristic] of the more recent Ionic [dialect]. On account of which they blame Zenodotus because he said that it is necessary to read (at *Iliad* 2. 1) ὦλλοι μέν ῥα θεοί τε καὶ ἀνέρες. For Homer does not use this [type of crasis].

84. ἠοῖ δ᾽ εἰσανέβαν: the preposition εἰς [is] superfluous. And Dindymus [is] a mountain of Cyzicus sacred to Rhea, having been called thus on account of the twin hills reaching up in it, as Philostephanus says (ed. Müller, vol. iii, p. 29); and all Phrygia is sacred to the goddess. Or it is called thus because it has two tops.

85. λῆξιν ὀρινομένων: the stopping and cessation of the force of the winds. ἀκταίης: for the bird [is] of the sea and living on the seashores. And Zeus too is said to make fifteen days in a row fine, or, as some [say], fourteen, in order that it may bear its young along the shores, which [days] are called halcyon days, seven before the birth and seven after the birth. And he has taken the [material] about the halcyons from Pindar, from the Paeans (fr. 62 Snell–Maehler). And reasonably he called the voice of the halcyon an omen-bearing cry, for it had been sent by Hera, as Pindar says.

86. ἀφλάστοιο: Apollodorus in his *Lexeis* (FGrHist 244 F 240) has defined ἄφλαστον as the ἀκροστόλιον (terminal ornament). Not well [did he so define it], since the ἀκροστόλιον is the top (ἄκρον) of the prow (στόλος), and the beam projecting from the fold and extending as far as the front of the ship is called "prow"; and [the part] where the name of the ship is inscribed is called "fold". Therefore the terminal ornament on the front of the ship is not the ἄφλαστον, but the poet [Homer] teaches that it [the ἄφλαστον] is on the stern, saying "And Hector when he seized it by the stern, was not at all letting go, having the ἄφλαστον between his hands" (*Iliad* 15. 716–17). And ἄφλαστον has been said by the kinship of the φ to the θ: ἄθλαστον ("undentable"); by antiphrasis, since it is easily dented. Therefore ἄφλαστον is a small board on the stern.

87. Thus, that Aratus has imitated Eudoxus' description concerning [celestial] phenomena, someone could learn from many [passages] if he compared the prose expressions in Eudoxus to his [Aratus'] verses concerning each of the things that are said. And it [is] not without profit now too in a

few [words] to mention [this], because this is doubted by the multitude. And to Eudoxus are attributed two books about [celestial] phenomena, agreeing with each other in nearly everything except a very few things. The one of these is entitled *Mirror* and the other *Celestial phenomena*. And [Aratus] has composed his poem following the *Celestial phenomena*.

88. Thus that Aratus has composed the *Phaenomena* having closely followed Eudoxus, I think I showed sufficiently through the things previously said. But now we shall reveal [the things] in which these men [Eudoxus and Aratus] and those who assent to them, among whom is also [i.e. among others] Attalus, err. And straightaway we shall also set forth in what things each one of them individually errs.

But it must be explained beforehand that Attalus assents to nearly all the things said by Aratus about the heavenly [bodies] as [being] in agreement with the phenomena discussed by him, except on one or two points, which indeed we shall also show in the following. At least, he speaks this way in the preface: "On account of which indeed we have dispatched to you both [a copy of] the book of Aratus corrected by us and the commentary on it, having made each thing [in it] both agreeing with the phenomena and conforming to the things written by the poet [i.e. having brought everything in it into conformity with . . .]." And again later he says: "Perhaps some will inquire further: persuaded by what argument do we say that the correction of the book has been made in conformity with the purpose of the poet?; but we give in explanation as the most necessary cause the agreement of the poet with the phenomena." Since Attalus had this sort of judgement, however many of the things said in common by Aratus and Eudoxus as we show [to be] disagreeing with the phenomena, it is necessary to assume that Attalus too agreed (with them) in asserting erroneously concerning those same things.

5.2.3 Grammatical Treatises

89. Rule 5. Singular: nom. Δημοσθένης, gen. Δημοσθένους. The nouns in -ης compounded from neuters always have their genitive in -ους, [as] εὐγενής, εὐγενοῦς [from] γένος [and] κακοήθης, κακοήθους [from] ἦθος; ἀγκυλοχείλης, ἀγκυλοχείλου is a (noted) exception. And it is necessary to know that every genitive ending in -ους is contracted; therefore it is necessary for the one declining [such nouns] to take the full [form] first and make the contraction thus: Δημοσθένεος, Δημοσθένους. [The other forms are] dat. Δημοσθένεϊ, Δημοσθένει, acc. Δημοσθένεα, Δημοσθένη, voc. Δημόσθενες: the [nouns] in -ης having their genitive in -ους form their vocative in -ες, [as] Δημόσθενες [from] Δημοσθένης, Δημοσθένους. Dual: nom./acc. Δημοσθένεε, Δημοσθένη, gen./dat. Δημοσθενέοιν, Δημοσθενοῖν, voc. Δημοσθένεε, Δημοσθένη. Plural: nom. Δημοσθένεες, Δημοσθένεις, gen. Δημοσθενέων, Δημοσθενῶν, dat. only Δημοσθένεσι, acc. Δημοσθένεας, Δημοσθένεις, voc. Δημοσθένεες, Δημοσθένεις.

90. It is necessary to know that the feminine [nouns and adjectives] ending in -η make their genitive by the addition of σ, as καλή καλῆς, 'Αφροδίτη 'Αφροδίτης, τιμή τιμῆς, μελέτη μελέτης; whence we assert that the genitive γυναικός is declined from the nominative γύναιξ and not from γυνή, since it would have had to be γυνῆς [if it had been from γυνή]; and that the nominative of the genitive γυναικός is γύναιξ, we have learned in the teaching of the vocative of θώραξ. These [comments suffice] on these [points]. And it is worthwhile to investigate why γυνή is indeclinable, for we do not say γυνῆς [i.e. we do not form the other cases from this stem]; and it is possible to give this defense, that disyllabic [nouns] ending in -νη [and] having υ as penultimate have the υ lengthened, as μύνη (both [in the sense of] "incitement" and [in the sense of] "excuse"), Βύνη (thus was Ino called later), and Φρύνη (a proper noun); but γυνή has a short υ; reasonably therefore, as being exceptional, it remained indeclinable. These [comments suffice] on these [points].

91. Concerning proper and common nouns of common and of epicene gender.
    Moreover, when nouns are divided according to meaning into proper nouns, common nouns, and adjectives, the proper nouns are always of a single gender, either masculine only, or feminine only, such as ὁ "Ομηρος [or] ἡ Καλλιόπη. But of the common nouns, however many are indicative of living beings are for the most part correctly common in gender, i.e. [both] masculine and feminine, but some are epicene.
    [They] are common whenever the same word is uttered with a different article, such as ὁ ἄνθρωπος and ἡ ἄνθρωπος, [or] ὁ ἵππος and ἡ ἵππος.
    But [they are] epicene whenever the same word [is uttered] with the same article, as ἡ χελιδών ("the swallow") is uttered with reference to [both] masculine and feminine; and when we distinguish the male from the female, we say ἡ χελιδὼν ὁ ἄρσην ("the male swallow") and ἡ χελιδὼν ἡ θήλεια ("the female swallow"); ὁ ἀετός ("eagle") [is] also applied to [both] the masculine and the feminine, and when we distinguish the female from the male, we say ὁ ἀετὸς ἡ θήλεια ("the female eagle") and ὁ ἀετὸς ὁ ἄρσην ("the male eagle").

92. Κατάχρησις: Catachresis is a word that, [by transference] from the thing named [by it] properly and etymologically, is spoken with regard to something else [that is], properly speaking, nameless, as πυξὶς χαλκῆ ("bronze box") and τριήραρχος ("trierarch"). And a box properly and etymologically is one fashioned from boxwood, but by catachresis we call also leaden and bronze [containers] boxes; and [we call] τριήραρχος not only the one ruling a trireme, but also [those ruling] a quinquereme and a ship with six rows of oars. And we say ἀνδριάς ("statue of a man") also of a [statue of a] woman. And Homer [says] νέκταρ ἐῳνοχόει ("he wine-poured nectar") not properly speaking, but it [i.e. the act of pouring nectar] is nameless.

93. And [Attic speakers] pronounce ὁμοῖος with a circumflex on the penult, as also in Homer: Ὡς αἰεὶ τὸν ὁμοῖον ἄγει θεὸς ὡς τὸν ὁμοῖον. And this too is regular; for [words] of more than two syllables ending in -οιος, if they are not common nouns, are all circumflexed on the penult, as γελοῖος, ἀλλοῖος, ἑτεροῖος, παντοῖος, and thus also ὁμοῖος. But the "more than two syllables" was said because of γλοιός, φλοιός, [and] κλοιός; and the "not being common nouns" was added because of κολοιός, the name of a bird. But ὁμοῖος is accented with an acute on the antepenult according to the koiné usage.

Attic turns σ into τ in some places, and in other places into ξ. For it calls θάλασσα θάλαττα, and σεῦτλον τεῦτλον, and συμφορά ξυμφορά, and σύμβολον ξύμβολον. And it turns σ into ξ only in words beginning with the prefix σύν and compounded [with it]. And [sometimes] even σύν itself, by itself, is turned into ξύν, as — — — Ἀρτέμιδι ξύν.

94. So pay attention and, according to their numbers, attach the verbs suitable to the nouns [i.e. make your verbs agree in number with the nouns], except those of this sort: τὰ παιδία γράφει, τὰ ὦτα ἀκούει, τὰ ῥήματα λαλεῖται. For here singular verbs follow the plural neuter nouns, as you see, and it is customary [for them] to be written thus in [the case of] neuters only [i.e. the only plural nouns that can take a singular verb are neuter ones].

Note also (as exceptions) the things that are about to be said: ὁ σύλλογος γράφουσιν, ὁ χορὸς ἀναγινώσκουσιν, ἡ πληθύς θορυβοῦσιν, τὸ συνέδριον σκέπτονται. For here plural verbs follow singular nouns, as you see, because the nouns spoken are indicative of a multitude; for the σύλλογος ("assembly") and χορός ("chorus") and things of that sort are a gathering of many; to nouns only of this sort, when they are singular, is it possible to attach plural verbs [i.e. it is possible to attach plural verbs to singular nouns only if the nouns are of this type].

95. A noun is a declinable part of speech designating a concrete thing or an incorporeal item (a concrete thing such as λίθος, and an incorporeal item such as παιδεία), used generally or particularly (generally such as ἄνθρωπος [or] ἵππος, and particularly such as Σωκράτης)—and [there] are five accidents of the noun: genders, derivational statuses, compositional statuses, numbers, cases.

Now the genders are three: masculine, feminine, neuter. But some add to these two others, common and epicene; common such as ἵππος [or] κύων, and epicene such as χελιδών ("swallow") [or] ἀετός ("eagle").

And the derivational statuses are two, underived and derived. So an underived [noun] is one spoken according to its first formation, such as γῆ. But a derived [noun is] one having had its origin from another [word], such as γαιήϊος ("earth-born") (attested at *Odyssey* 7. 324).

And the types of derived [nouns] are seven: patronymic, possessive, comparative, superlative, hypocoristic, derived from a noun, derived from a verb.

96. The acute [accent] has three places: oxytone, paroxytone, which is also called barytone, and proparoxytone, which is also called penultimate barytone. A [noun] having the acute on the end, such as καλός, σοφός, [or] δυνατός, is called an oxytone noun. A [noun] having the acute one syllable before the end, such as Ἰωάννης [or] Πέτρος, is called a paroxytone noun. A [noun] having the acute two syllables before the end, such as Γρηγόριος [or] Θεόδωρος, is called a proparoxytone noun.

The circumflex [accent] has two places, perispomenon and properispomenon. A [noun] having the circumflex on the end, such as Θωμᾶς [or] Λουκᾶς, is called a perispomenon noun. A [noun] having the circumflex one syllable before the end, such as κῆπος [or] δῆμος, is called a properispomenon noun.

For the grave [accent] is a syllabic accent, that is, it used to be put on a [i.e. any] syllable not having the principal accent. But in order that the books not be covered with marks, this does not happen now, but [the grave] is put in the place of the acute in continuous text: such as ἄνθρωπος καλός. Behold, here the acute has been put on the -λος, because it was found at the end. But if you say καλὸς ἄνθρωπος, behold in that case the grave has been put on the -λος, because the ἄνθρωπος was put after those [letters].

97. But many of the manuscripts are incorrect; for the correct form of the expression is this: "And a double name," he says, "is two proper nouns applied to one [person]"; but most of the manuscripts are not thus, but "[applied] to one proper noun," utterly senselessly.

98. And there has been a debate about whether the present work is authentic[ally] of Dionysius Thrax; for some [scholars] have attacked [it] speaking thus, that the grammarians mention Dionysius Thrax and say that he distinguished the appellative from the noun and joined the pronoun to the article; but the present grammarian knows the appellative and the noun [to be] one part of speech when he says, "For the appellative is subordinated to the noun as a type [of noun]" (GG i.i. 23. 2), and he recognizes the article and the pronoun [to be] two parts of speech and not one. So it is possible to say that that Dionysius was another one: for that [Dionysius] was a student of Aristarchus, [the Dionysius] who also when he painted a picture of his own teacher painted Tragedy in his heart, because he [Aristarchus] [could] repeat every tragedy by heart; but this [Dionysius] [i.e. the author of the Τέχνη] is the one called the son of Perus. And he too used to be called "Thrax," either perhaps because of the roughness of his voice or because he was also really a Thracian; and [it is] probable that he was called "Thrax" also by mistake. And the definition of the verb by both of them also shows that that [Dionysius] is one and this one is an-

other [i.e. that they are different people]. For this [Dionysius] defines the verb thus, "A verb is an indeclinable word, showing tenses and persons and numbers, [and] expressing activity or passivity" (GG i.i. 46. 4); but Dionysius Thrax, as Apollonius says in his *Verbal treatise*, defines the verb thus: "A verb is a word signifying a predicate."

99. Ἦν. No first-person singular indicative verb is seen [to be], in the same tense, the first person of the singular and the third person of the singular and the first and third [persons] of the plural, except only ἦν. For Attic speakers say ἦν ἐγώ and ἦν ἐκεῖνος [i.e. they use ἦν both for "am" and for "is"]; and Simonides [uses ἦν] in the plural with reference to the first person, as for example in epigrams: ἦν ἑκατὸν φιάλαι, δίχα δέ σφισιν, for [here] ἦν [is] instead of ἦμεν. [And in the following we have ἦν for ἦσαν:] τῆς δ' ἦν τρεῖς κεφαλαί (Hesiod, *Theogony* 321) and κωφοὶ δ' ἦν προπάροιθεν. And I am not unaware that the verb is spoken [i.e. used] in a variety of other ways.

100. [Words] of more than two syllables [ending] in -κος, if they have long ι in the penultimate syllable, are accented recessively: Ἄνικος (proper name) Κάικος Γρήνικος Φίλικος. But if [they have] the ει diphthong [in the penultimate syllable], they are oxytone: δαρεικός βοεικός Δεκελεικός Κεραμεικός. [But] Καμικός, [which is] oxytone and has the long ι, like Παλικός, is a (noted) exception.

   Possessive adjectives [ending] in -ικος and having a [distinct] feminine [form] are oxytone: Γαλατικός Ἰταλικός Πυθαγορικός. But ἄδικος is not possessive [and therefore it is not an exception to this rule]. And ἡλίκος and πηλίκος have an acute on the penult; for they are not possessives.

101. Εἰμί. No indicative verb ending in -μι in our dialect has a diphthong in the penultimate syllable, but only the εἰμί that means "to be." And I am not unaware that the tradition writes the [εἶμι] that has a recessive accent with the ει diphthong too; but not correctly, neither according to its inflection nor according to the Aeolic dialect, as has been shown by me in [my writings] on orthography. And [the words] "in our dialect" is added [in the explanation above] since the Aeolians say πάλαιμι and γέλαιμι and πλάναιμι, and the Boeotians [say] τάρβειμι and ποίειμι and φίλειμι [i.e. since in other dialects there are other mi-verbs with a diphthong in the penultimate syllable].

102. Nor has it escaped me, that some people argued against the opinion believed unanimously by all, that a barbarism is a flaw [in] one word , and a solecism [is a flaw in] the combination of words lacking in concord. They [i.e. the "some people"] themselves [argued by] introducing [the idea that] a solecism [can] exist even in one word, if someone should say οὗτος about a female or a multitude that is the subject of discussion, offering also other [examples] pertaining to the same silliness [i.e.

other equally silly examples]. In the first place, [it is clear] that no nominative is formed into a complete sentence without a verb, that is to say, a verb that does not require another oblique case [i.e. the minimum that must be added to a nominative to form a complete sentence is an intransitive verb]. For οὗτος περιπατεῖ ("this man walks") is complete in itself, but not βλάπτει ("he harms"); for the whom is omitted [i.e. it does not say whom he harms]. But even if we were to speak thus, τίς σε ἔτυψε; ("Who beat you?") the οὗτος that is said in reply has in common [with the preceding question] the verb used: [thus] τίς καλεῖται Αἴας; οὗτος ("Who is called Ajax?" "This man [is]"). [i.e. even when a nominative like οὗτος does seem to function as a sentence by itself, a verb must be understood.] Therefore it is not true that a solecism [can] occur in one word. . . . Thus οὗτός με ἔτυψεν ("This man beat me") said about a female is not an error of the sentence [i.e. a grammatical error], for it [the sentence] received the necessary thing of the agreement [i.e. it has the necessary agreement]. Yet at least if, with a female being the subject of discussion, someone should say αὕτη με ἔτυψαν ("She they beat me"), it is agreed that he will commit a solecism because of the lack of agreement of the words, even if he speaks correctly as regards gender.

103.   So how are they not ridiculous, both those who determined that the Dorians [i.e. those speaking/writing in the Doric dialect] do not treat future subjunctives as contracted forms, and those who investigated why they do not treat [these forms] as contracted? For their reasoning [i.e. the reasoning of people who make such claims] has arisen from an incoherent premise. And the thing that lured [them into] their ignorance was the homophony [of the putative future subjunctive] that occurred with the aorist ending in -α [i.e. with the first aorist subjunctive], which is like this: the augment in [aorist] indicatives is removed at the same time as the changing of the indicative mood [i.e. is removed when the mood is changed to something other than indicative]. For from ἔλεξα comes the optative λέξαιμι, and the infinitive λέξαι, and the imperative λέξον. Thus indeed also in the subjunctive mood the same thing occurred in consequence when the ending is altered to -ω, because also in the other past [tenses] [i.e. second aorists] the same thing happened: [from] ἔφαγον [2nd aor. indic.] [comes] ἐὰν φάγω [aor. subj.], [from] ἔδραμον [2nd aor. indic.] [comes] ἐὰν δράμω [aor. subj.] and in the same way [from] ἔλεξα [1st aor. indic.] comes ἐὰν λέξω [aor. subj.], [which is] similar to the future indicative λέξω. For that the construction is not that of the indistinguishable future [i.e. that the subjunctive λέξω we have here is not the future that in terms of form is indistinguishable from it] [is] clear from the *Syntax* in front of you. In which if those listening completely to the arguments do not share [i.e. if those listening completely to my arguments do not share the views expressed in this *Syntax*], they are stubbornly turning things upside down.

104. After the constructions of verbs, which we completed in the [book] before this one, which is the third [book] of the whole treatise, we will also
turn to the constructions of prepositions/preverbs, which need a most
precise demonstration, because the[se] words seem with some parts of
speech to provide the appearance of composition [i.e. they seem to form
compounds], but with others [they seem to provide the appearance of]
juxtaposition, sometimes not being helped by the individual features of
the accents, since most parts of speech imply the singleness of the word,
that is the being one part of speech, through the accent's oneness [i.e.
with most parts of speech you can tell that something is a single word by
the fact that it has a single accent]; or they show the twoness of the words
through the retention [of the accent] on each word. For Διὸς κόρος
with an acute accent on the penult has its genitive meaning by itself [i.e.
Διός is a genitive], being similar to Διὸς υἱός, but when it has an acute
accent on the antepenult it is similar to Διόγνητος and Διόδοτος [i.e. it
is a compound, Διόσκορος]; and εὖ νοῶ when it has two circumflexes
demonstrates the juxtaposition of an adverb and a verb, and Ἕλλης
πόντος having the acute at the beginning, and ἐμοῦ αὐτοῦ having the
circumflex twice [are each juxtapositions, not compounds]. For these
and the [words] that are similar to these, which are innumerable, when
they come together according to the rule of composition also have the
accent combined [i.e. εὐνοῶ, Ἑλλήσποντος, ἐμαυτοῦ], but when they
are not thus [i.e. compounded] they have the accent uncompounded as
well [i.e. they have two accents], and, as we said, they demonstrate a
juxtaposition in [i.e. by] the retention of the accent on each word [i.e.
the two accents show that these words are a phrase not a compound].

5.3 TEXTS WITHOUT KEY

5.3.1 Lexica

Contents. Hesychius 105–21; Ammonius 122–6; Timaeus 127–8; Apollonius
Sophista 129–30; Etymologica 131–8; Suda 139.

105. Hesychius, ed. Latte, Γ 781
γοίδημι· ἐπίσταμαι
Notes: cf. 4.1.2; γ is for digamma.

106. Hesychius, ed. Latte, Γ 778
γοί· αὐτῷ
Notes: cf. 4.1.2, 4.1.7; γ is for digamma.

107. Hesychius, ed. Latte, Α 7643
ἄσεν· ἐνέδησεν (λ 61)
Notes: cf. 4.1.7; ἐνδέω "bind in"; the reference indicates that the entry can be
traced to the Odyssey.

108. Hesychius, ed. Latte, A 7279
   ἀρκόν· σχολήν. Μακεδόνες
   Note: cf. 4.1.12.

109. Hesychius, ed. Latte, Γ 770
   γοᾶναι· κλαίειν. Κύπριοι
   Note: cf. 4.1.12.

110. Hesychius, ed. Latte, Γ 756
   γόβαλα· τὸ ὅριον. Φοίνικες
   Note: ὅριον "boundary."

111. Hesychius, ed. Latte, A 7307
   Ἀρμεθεῖς· οἱ εὐπατρίδαι ἐν Κύπρῳ
   Note: εὐπατρίδης "noble."

112. Hesychius, ed. Latte, B 685
   βλάσταν· βλάστησιν, Κύπριοι
   Note: βλάστησις "sprouting."

113. Hesychius, ed. Latte, A 1330
   ἀειφόρος· ἀειθαλής. Σοφοκλῆς Τηλέφῳ (fr. 522)
   Notes: cf. 4.1.12; ἀειθαλής "ever-blooming." The reference is to *TGF* and would
   now be fr. 580 *TrGF*.

114. Hesychius, ed. Latte, A 7273
   Ἀρκὰς κυνῆ· Ἀρκαδικὸς πῖλος. Σοφοκλῆς Ἰνάχῳ (fr. 250)
   Notes: cf. 4.1.12; πῖλος "cap." The reference is to *TGF* and would now be
   fr. 272 *TrGF*.

115. Hesychius, ed. Latte, Γ 753
   γνωτή· ἀδελφή: (Ο 350) Σp ἢ ἐρωμένη
   Notes: the reference indicates that the entry can be traced to the *Iliad*, and the
   Σp shows that the first part of this entry is also in the manuscript designated *p*
   of the Συναγωγὴ λέξεων χρησίμων.

116. Hesychius, ed. Latte, A 1318
   ἀείσιτος· ὁ ἐφ᾽ ἑκάστῃ ἡμέρᾳ ἐν τῷ Πρυτανείῳ δειπνῶν

117. Hesychius, ed. Latte, A 7267
   *Ἀρίων· ὁ ἵππος, Ποσειδῶνος υἱὸς καὶ μιᾶς τῶν Ἐρινύων AS
   Notes: the asterisk indicates that the entry comes from Cyrillus' lexicon, and the
   letters AS refer to the two manuscripts of Cyrillus that contain this entry.

118. Hesychius, ed. Latte, Γ 736
   γνύπωνες· στυγνοί. κατηφεῖς. ἄτολμοι. παρειμένοι. καὶ μαλακοί,
   ἀπὸ τοῦ εἰς γόνυ πεπτωκέναι
   Notes: στυγνός "gloomy"; κατηφής "downcast"; παρειμένος (pf. part < παρίημι)
   "slack."

119. Hesychius, ed. Latte, E 6383

ἔστη· στολή. Κύπριοι. ἠγέρθη, ἵστατο (E 108)

Notes: στολή "garment"; ἐγείρομαι "wake up."

120. Hesychius, ed. Latte, E 6397

Ἑστίας χῶρος· μέρος τοῦ ἥπατος ἐν θυτικῇ

Notes: ἥπαρ "liver"; θυτική "art of divination."

121. Hesychius, ed. Latte, E 6402

ἑστιᾶχος· οἰκουρός. οἰκῶναξ. καὶ Ζεὺς παρ' ᾽Ιωσιν

Notes: οἰκουρός "housekeeper"; οἰκῶναξ "master of the house" ᾽Ιων "Ionian."

122. Ammonius, ed. Nickau, 329

ναὸς καὶ σηκὸς διαφέρει. ὁ μὲν γὰρ ναός ἐστι θεῶν, ὁ δὲ σηκὸς ἡρώων.

Notes: σηκός "sacred enclosure."

123. Ammonius, ed. Nickau, 144

διδάσκαλος καὶ ἐπιστάτης διαφέρει. διδάσκαλος μὲν γάρ ἐστι λόγων, ἐπιστάτης δὲ ἔργων.

124. Ammonius, ed. Nickau, 140

διδάξω καὶ διδάξομαι διαφέρει. 'διδάξω' μὲν γὰρ δι' ἑαυτοῦ, 'διδάξομαι' δὲ δι' ἑτέρου· ὡς 'οἰκοδομήσω' μὲν δι' ἑαυτοῦ, οἰκοδομήσασθαι δὲ δι' ἑτέρου.

Notes: understand something like "is said of something that is done" with each verb discussed; ἑτέρου: cf. 4.1.23; the use of the infinitive οἰκοδομήσασθαι rather than the first person singular used for the other verbs is not meaningful.

125. Ammonius, ed. Nickau, 480

τύραννον οἱ ἀρχαῖοι καὶ ἐπὶ βασιλέως ἔτασσον. Ἡρόδοτος (1, 6, 1) ἐπὶ Κροίσου 'τυράννου δ' ἐθνέων', καὶ προβὰς (1, 26, 1) 'τελευτήσαντος δ' Ἀ‹λ›υ‹άτ›τεω διεδέξατο τὴν βασιλείην'. καὶ Ἀριστοφάνης (II p. 1098 M. = fr. 357 K.) ἐν Λημνίαις·

ἐνταῦθ' ἐτυράννευεν Ὑψιπύλης πατὴρ
Θόας, βραδύτερος τῶν ἐν ἀνθρώποις δραμεῖν'.

ἔσθ' ὅτε καὶ τὸν τύραννον βασιλέα ἔλεγον, ὡς Εὔπολις ἐν Δήμοις (II p. 474 M. = fr. 123 K.) ἐπὶ τοῦ Πεισιστράτου.

Notes: βασιλεύς, in the writer's own time, referred to a king by legitimate inheritance, while τύραννος referred to a king who had seized power; τάσσω "apply"; ἐπί: cf. 4.1.31; προβαίνω "continue on"; ἔσθ' ὅτε "sometimes." The references would now be expressed as fr. 373 K–A and fr. 137 K–A respectively.

126. Ammonius, ed. Nickau, 451

συμμαχεῖν καὶ ἐπιμαχεῖν διαφέρει. συμμαχεῖν μὲν γὰρ λέγουσι τὸ σὺν ἑαυτοῖς, φησὶ Δίδυμος (p. 334 Schmidt), εἴτ' αὐτοῖς ἐπίοιεν πολέμιοι ‚εἴτε αὐτοὶ‚ ἑτέροις‚ ἐπιστρατεύοιεν. ἐπιμαχεῖν δὲ ὅταν τοὺς ἐπιόντας ἀμύνωνται μόνον. διέσταλκε Θουκυδίδης ἐν τῇ πρώτῃ (1, 44, 1) λέγων Κερκυραίοις ᾿Αθηναίους συμμαχίαν μὲν οὐ ποιήσασθαι, ἐπιμαχίαν δέ.

Notes: ἀμύνομαι "defend self against"; διαστέλλω "distinguish"; πρώτῃ: cf. 4.1.33; συμμαχία i.e. an agreement to συμμαχεῖν.

127. Timaeus' Platonic lexicon, ed. Ruhnken, 79. 1–3.

᾿Εδίδαξα. ἐπαίδευσα αὐτὸς δι᾿ ἑαυτοῦ. ᾿Εδιδαξάμην, ἐπαιδευσάμην δι᾿ ἑτέρου, αὐτὸς ἐπιμεληθεὶς τούτου.

Notes: there are two lemmata here, and the point of the note is the distinction between them; we would expect ἐμαυτοῦ instead of ἑαυτοῦ; ἐπιμελέομαι "have the charge or management of."

128. Timaeus' Platonic lexicon, ed. Ruhnken, 163. 4–6

᾿Ορχήστρα. τὸ τοῦ θεάτρου μέσον χωρίον, καὶ τόπος ἐπιφανὴς εἰς πανήγυριν, ἔνθα ῾Αρμοδίου καὶ ᾿Αριστογείτονος εἰκόνες.

Notes: ἐπιφανής "prominent"; πανήγυρις "festival assembly"

129. Apollonius Sophista, ed. Bekker, 107. 3–4

λαοσσόος ἡ τοὺς λαοὺς σοοῦσα, ὅ ἐστι σοβοῦσα καὶ ἐπὶ πόλεμον ὁρμῶσα. ὁ δὲ ᾿Απίων ἡ τοὺς λαοὺς σώζουσα.

Notes: σοέω = σεύω "chase"; σοβέω "drive off".

130. Apollonius Sophista, ed. Bekker, 106. 15–19.

λαβρεύεται ὁ μὲν ᾿Απίων προγλωσσεύει· ἔστι γὰρ κυρίως λάβρον μέγα κατὰ τὴν βοράν· τὸ γὰρ λᾶ μέγα δηλοῖ. μεταφορικῶς οὖν κεῖται ἐπὶ τοῦ μεγάλα βουλομένου διὰ τὸν λόγον ἐμφαίνειν. πρὸ καιροῦ πολυλογεῖς καὶ λάλος γίνῃ, καὶ οἷον ἀθρόως λέγεις, ἀμέτρως, καὶ μεγαληγορεῖς.

Notes: λαβρεύεται is a corruption of λαβρεύεαι (Il. 23. 474, 478), a second-person form that was altered in the transmission of the glossary because the definition looked like a third-person form; προγλωσσεύομαι "be hasty of tongue" (2nd sing. middle, although it looks like 3rd sing. active); λάβρος "eager"; βορά "food" (the idea is that this word is etymologically present in the second half of λάβρος); κεῖμαι "is applied to"; ἐπί cf. 4.1.31; λάλος "loquacious"; the last sentence consists of a string of translations of the lemma, in its original second-person form.

131. *Etymologicum magnum*, ed. Gaisford, 617. 30

Οἰκῆας· Οἰκείους, οἰκέτας, δούλους· οἶμαι ἀπὸ τοῦ οἰκεὺς, ὡς ᾿Αχιλλεύς.

Notes: τοῦ: cf. 4.1.17–18; οἰκεύς is the nominative singular of which οἰκῆας is the accusative plural; understand "declined" before ὡς.

132. *Etymologicum Gudianum*, ed. De Stefani, vol. ii, p. 362. 2–3

Δίε· παρὰ τὸ δείω ὁ δεύτερος ἀόριστος ἔδιον ἔδιες ἔδιε, καὶ δίε τὸ προστακτικόν.

Notes: παρά: cf. 4.1.28; τό: cf. 4.1.17–18; δείω is apparently the verb we know as δείδω; προστακτικόν: cf. 4.2.13; the writer's point is that δίε is a second aorist imperative, though in fact it is an unaugmented third-person singular aorist indicative (= ἔδιε), at least where it occurs in Homer.

133. *Etymologicum Gudianum*, ed. De Stefani, vol. ii, p. 329. 1–2

Δαιμόνιος· τὸ ΠΤ τ ὡς ἐπίθετον· τὸ ΠΟ μικρὸν ὡς κοινόν. ἐκ τοῦ δαίμων δαίμονος.

Notes: understand something like "is written with" after νι, and something like "usual for" after ὡς; though ἐπίθετον is best translated "adjective" and κοινόν "common noun," the two categories overlap in Greek because common nouns are any type of noun or adjective that is not a proper name; μικρόν i.e. written with omicron.

134. *Etymologicum Gudianum*, ed. De Stefani, vol. i, p. 117. 1–3

Ἀμορραίων· γενικῆς τῶν πληθυντικῶν· ὄνομα ἔθνους· ὁ Ἀμορραῖος, τοῦ Ἀμορραίου. ὁ δὲ τόπος τὸ ΠΟ μέγα καὶ ἐν ρ, οἷον τὸ Ἀμώριον.

Notes: cf. 4.2.11 for vocabulary; understand something like "is the base form" after Ἀμορραίου and "has" after τόπος; μέγα i.e. written with omega; οἷον: cf. 4.1.40.

135. *Etymologicum genuinum*, ed. Lasserre and Livadaras, A 515

ἄλλιξ (Call. fr. 253,11)· σημαίνει δὲ κατὰ Θετταλοὺς τὴν χλαμύδα· Καλλίμαχος (l.c.)·

ἄλλικα χρυσείῃσιν ἐπεργομένην ἐνέτῃσιν.

ἀλλάσσω ἄλλαξ καὶ ἄλλιξ AB, Sym. 611, EM 902. *Methodius.

Notes: χλαμύς "cloak"; ἀλλάσσω "change"; ἄλλαξ "reversely"; the point of the last line is that ἄλλιξ is derived from ἀλλάσσω via the intermediate form ἄλλαξ (cf. 4.1.20); the letters at the end indicate sources and parallels. The reference is to Pfeiffer (1949–53: vol. i, fr. 253, line 11).

136. *Etymologicum magnum*, ed. Gaisford, 635. 4–7

Ὀρχομενός· Δύο εἰσὶ, Βοιωτικὸς καὶ Ἀρκαδικός· ἀλλ' ὁ μὲν Βοιωτικὸς, Μινύειος καλεῖται· ὁ δὲ Ἀρκαδικὸς, πολύμηλος· καὶ τοῖς ἐπιθέτοις διαστέλλεται ἡ ὁμωνυμία.

Notes: Ὀρχομενός is the name of several cities; πολύμηλος "rich in flocks"; ἐπίθετον "adjective"; διαστέλλω "distinguish"; ὁμωνυμία "homonymy, ambiguity."

137. *Etymologicum Gudianum*, ed. De Stefani, vol. ii, p. 302. 12–14

Γείνω· τὸ γεννῶ· τὸ ΓΕΙ δίφθογγον· διὰ τί; διότι ἔχει ἐν τῷ μέλλοντι τὸ ε. ὁ παθητικὸς γείνομαι, τὸ τρίτον γείνεται. καὶ εἰς τὸ Γίνομαι καὶ Γυνή.

Notes: γεννάω "beget"; understand something like "is written with" after γει; δίφθογγον: cf. 4.2.4; παθητικός "passive"; τρίτον "third (person)"; εἰς: cf. 4.1.29; the point is that because the future is γενήσομαι, with an ε in the first syllable, the ε must also be present in the other tenses, and therefore the present, which from its pronunciation could be spelled either γείνω or γίνω, must have the ει diphthong (γείνω) rather than the ι alone (γίνω).

138. *Etymologicum genuinum*, ed. Lasserre and Livadaras, A 122

ἀηδών· παρὰ τὸ ἀείδω ἀειδών, καὶ τροπῇ Αἰολικῇ τῆς ει διφθόγγου εἰς η ἀηδών. ἄλλοι δὲ τροπὴν μόνον λέγουσι γεγονέναι τοῦ ε εἰς η καὶ μένει τὸ τ προσγεγραμμένον B, Sym. 188, EM 361. Orio 28,1+

Notes: ἀηδών "nightingale"; παρά: cf. 4.1.28; ἀείδω "sing"; ἀειδών is a hypothetical intermediate form, (though it is possible that in an originally unaccented form of this entry there was a conflation of ἀειδών, the form necessary to give ἀηδών, with ἀείδων, the present participle of ἀείδω); τροπή "sound change"; τ προσγεγραμμένον "iota subscript." The view of the ἄλλοι is that the correct form is ἀηδών.

139. *Suda*, ed. Adler, T 1115

Τρύφων, Ἀμμωνίου, Ἀλεξανδρεύς, γραμματικὸς καὶ ποιητής, γεγονὼς κατὰ τοὺς Αὐγούστου χρόνους καὶ πρότερον. Περὶ πλεονασμοῦ τοῦ ἐν τῇ Αἰολίδι διαλέκτῳ βιβλία ζ', Περὶ τῶν παρ' Ὁμήρῳ διαλέκτων καὶ Cιμωνίδῃ καὶ Πινδάρῳ καὶ Ἀλκμᾶνι καὶ τοῖς ἄλλοις λυρικοῖς, Περὶ τῆς Ἑλλήνων διαλέκτου καὶ Ἀργείων καὶ Ἱμεραίων καὶ Ῥηγίνων καὶ Δωριέων καὶ Cυρακουσίων, Περὶ τῆς ἐν κλίσεσιν ἀναλογίας α', Περὶ τῆς ἐν εὐθείᾳ ἀναλογίας, Περὶ ὀνομάτων συγκριτικῶν α', Περὶ τῆς ἐν μονοσυλλάβοις ἀναλογίας, Περὶ ὀνομάτων χαρακτήρων α', Περὶ ῥημάτων ἀναλογίας βαρυτόνων α', Περὶ ῥημάτων ἐγκλιτικῶν καὶ ἀπαρεμφάτων καὶ προστακτικῶν καὶ εὐκτικῶν καὶ ἁπλῶς πάντων, Περὶ ὀρθογραφίας καὶ τῶν αὐτῇ ζητουμένων, Περὶ πνευμάτων καὶ τρόπων· καὶ ἄλλα.

Notes: cf. 4.2.11–13 for vocabulary; κατά "during"; the capitalization of Περί means that the editor considers these to be the titles of the books, not simply descriptions of their contents; πλεονασμός "redundancy"; παρά: cf. 4.1.28; λυρικός "lyric poet"; κλίσις "declension"; ἀναλογία "analogy, regularity"; α': sc. βιβλίον; though ὄνομα is usually translated "noun" it also includes adjectives; χαρακτήρ "declensional category"; αὐτῇ ζητουμένων "inquired about in it" (i.e. its difficulties), or perhaps "sought by means of it" (i.e. its goals); πνεῦμα: cf. 4.2.6; τρόπος "trope."

5.3.2 Scholia and Commentaries

Contents. Poetry: Homer 140–57; Euripides 158–9; Aeschylus 160–2; Pindar 163–6; Aristophanes 167–8. Prose: Plato 169–70; Aeschines 171–5; Hippocrates 176–8. Post-classical: Lucian 179–82; Apollonius Rhodius 183–6; Aratus 187.

140. Homer scholia, ed. Erbse, *Iliad* 15. 467a (from Didymus?)

⟨ὦ πόποι:⟩ ἐν ἄλλῳ "ὦ πέπον". A^{im}

Notes: understand ἀντιγράφῳ "copy" after ἄλλῳ. The notation at the end indicates the manuscript source: a note written in A between the text and the main body of marginal scholia.

141. Homer scholia, ed. Erbse, *Iliad* 15. 388 (exegetical)

⟨ξυστοῖσι:⟩ λείπει δόρασιν. **T**il

Notes: λείπω: cf. 4.1.35. The notation at the end indicates that the scholion comes from T, where it was written over a verse of the text.

142. Homer scholia, ed. Erbse, *Iliad* 15. 427b (exegetical)

⟨μιν:⟩ ἀντὶ τοῦ αὐτοῦ, Ἀττικῶς. **T**il

Note the broad definition of "Attic" to include a word that we might think of as Ionic; τοῦ: cf. 4.1.17–18. The point is that the scholiast interprets μιν as a genitive here.

143. Homer scholia, ed. Erbse, *Iliad* 15. 450a¹ (from Didymus)

⟨ἱεμένων:⟩ διχῶς Ἀρίσταρχος, καὶ "ἱεμένῳ" καὶ ἱεμένων. **A**im

Notes: cf. 4.1.11; διχῶς "in two ways."

144. Homer scholia, ed. Erbse, *Iliad* 15. 737a² (from Didymus)

⟨οὐ μέν τι:⟩ οὕτως Ἀρίσταρχος χωρὶς τοῦ σ. τινὲς δὲ "οὐ μέν τις". **T**il

Note: cf. 4.1.11.

145. Homer scholia, ed. Erbse, *Iliad* 15. 554 (from Herodian)

⟨ἀνεψιοῦ:⟩ τὴν ΨΙ συλλαβὴν ἐκτατέον διὰ τὸ μέτρον. **A**im **T**il

Notes: ἐκτατέον "it is necessary to lengthen"; this word is interesting because its failure to scan results from contraction of the earlier genitive ending -οο to -ου: if the -οο is restored, the ι need not be lengthened.

146. Homer scholia, ed. Erbse, *Iliad* 15. 363b (from Nicanor)

⟨νηπιέῃσιν:⟩ βέλτιον μετὰ τὸ νηπιέῃσιν ὑποστικτέον. **A**int

Note: ὑποστίζω "put a comma."

147. Homer scholia, ed. Erbse, *Iliad* 15. 639a (exegetical)

Κοπρῆος: Κοπρεὺς Πέλοπος παῖς τοῦ Ἠλείου. ἔστι δὲ καὶ ἄλλος Βοιώτιος, Ἀλιάρτου παῖς. **T**

Notes: Ἠλεῖος "Elean"; understand Κοπρεύς with ἄλλος.

148. Homer scholia, ed. Erbse, *Iliad* 15. 488 (from Nicanor)

νῆας ἀνὰ γλαφυράς: βέλτιον τοῦτο τοῖς ἄνω συνάπτειν. προτρέπει γὰρ αὐτοὺς ἐπὶ τὰς ναῦς ὁρμᾶν. **A**

Notes: the lemma occurs at the beginning of a line, so the question addressed by this scholion is whether to punctuate before it and take it with the other material in its own line, or to punctuate after it and take it with the preceding line. τοῖς ἄνω i.e. the words in the preceding line, προτρέπω "urge forward" (the subject here is the speaker of the lines, Hector).

149. Homer scholia, ed. Erbse, *Iliad* 15. 626b (from Aristonicus)

δεινὸς ἀήτη: ὅτι ἀρσενικῶς δεινὸς ἀήτη, ἀλλ' οὐ δεινή, ὡς "κλυτὸς Ἱπποδάμεια" (B 742). ἔνιοι δὲ ἀγνοοῦντες ποιοῦσι "δεινὸς ἀήτης". ἀλλ' οὐ δεῖ γράφειν οὕτως. **A**

Notes: ὅτι: cf. 4.1.44; ἀρσενικῶς "in masculine form."

150. Homer scholia, ed. Erbse, *Iliad* 15. 563a¹ (from Didymus)

αἰδομένων δ' ἀνδρῶν: χωρὶς τοῦ συνδέσμου ἔγραφεν 'Αρίσταρχος, πάντως ἵνα ἀσυνδέτως γενόμενος ὁ λόγος πλέον τε διαστῇ καὶ μᾶλλον ἐμφήνῃ. **A**

Notes: σύνδεσμος: cf. 4.2.10; πάντως "certainly"; ἀσύνδετος "without conjunctions"; λόγος "sentence"; διΐστημι "separate"; ἐμφαίνω i.e. stand out.

151. Homer scholia, ed. Erbse, *Iliad* 15. 414a¹, a² (from Aristonicus)

ἄλλοι δ' ἀμφ' ἄλλῃσι μάχην ‹ἐμάχοντο νέεσσιν›: ὅτι ἐκ τούτου διεσκεύασται ὁ τῆς τειχομαχίας στίχος (M 175): "ἄλλοι δ' ἀμφ' ἄλλῃσι μάχην ἐμάχοντο πύλῃσιν". **A**

ὅτι ἐντεῦθεν ὁ ἐν τῇ τειχομαχίᾳ μεταπεποίηται στίχος· ἀρέσκει γὰρ 'Αριστάρχῳ μίαν εἶναι πύλην. **Tⁱˡ**

Notes: these two notes, from different manuscripts, must go back to the same source, and neither is fully comprehensible without the other. The point is that because there is (in Aristarchus' view) one gate but many ships, the line with the plural is more at home here than in book 12 and therefore must have originated here. ὅτι: cf. 4.1.44; διασκευάζω "prepare"; μεταποιέω "remake"; the στίχος in the second note should be taken before μεταπεποίηται.

152. Homer scholia, ed. Erbse, *Iliad* 15. 382a, b¹ (first from Herodian, second D scholion and exegetical)

νηὸς ὑπὲρ τοίχων: οὐκ ἀναγκαῖόν ἐστιν ἀναστρέφειν τὴν πρόθεσιν, ἀλλὰ συντάσσειν τῇ τοίχων γενικῇ. **A**

‹νηὸς ὑπὲρ τοίχων:› ἀντὶ τοῦ ὑπὲρ τοὺς τοίχους. | ὑψηλότερον γενόμενον τὸ κῦμα τῶν τοίχων τῆς νεώς. **Tⁱˡ**

Notes: These two scholia show the development of interpretation of a passage. The earliest section is probably the first part of the second scholion (up to the |), which is a D scholion. Both the A scholion (from Herodian) and the T scholion build upon that information, but in different ways. Cf. 4.2.10–11 for vocabulary; ἀναστρέφω "take in anastrophe" (i.e. move the accent to the first syllable and assume that the preposition is following its object); συντάσσω "take together"; τοῖχος "side."

153. Homer scholia, ed. Erbse, *Iliad* 15. 365b (exegetical)

ἤϊε: 'Αρίσταρχος δασύνει, παρὰ τὴν ἔσιν τῶν βελῶν· ὁ δὲ Ἡρωδιανὸς (2, 95, 26) ψιλοῖ· ἀεὶ γὰρ τὸ ἦ πρὸ φωνήεντος ψιλοῦται. οἱ δὲ παρὰ τὴν ἴασιν ἢ παρὰ τὸ ἰέναι· ἥλιος γάρ ἐστιν. ἔστι δὲ περιπαθὴς ἡ ἀναφώνησις καὶ ἐμφαντικὴ τῆς δυνάμεως τοῦ θείου. **b** (BCE³) **T**

Notes: δασύνω "write with a rough breathing"; παρά: cf. 4.1.28; ἔσις "throwing"; ψιλόω "write with a smooth breathing"; φωνῆεν: cf. 4.2.4; ἴασις "healing"; the point of ἥλιος γάρ ἐστιν (of which ἥλιος is the predicate) is that ἤϊος is an epithet of Phoebus, who is the sun-god, and the sun is always in motion and involved in healing; ἔστι = ἐστι; περιπαθής "passionate"; ἀναφώνησις "appellation."

154. Homer scholia, ed. Erbse, *Iliad* 15. 545a[1] (from Aristonicus)

{συλήσειν. ἕκτωρ δὲ} κασιγνήτοισι: ὅτι κασίγνητοι κοινότερον οἱ συγγενεῖς· | σημειοῦνται γάρ τινες ὅτι τοὺς ἀνεψιοὺς κασιγνήτους ἐκάλουν· ὁ γὰρ Μελάνιππος ἀνεψιὸς ἦν Ἕκτορος. ἀνεψιοὶ δέ εἰσιν οἱ τῶν ἀδελφῶν παῖδες, ὥσπερ Αἴας καὶ Ἀχιλλεύς, ὁ μὲν Τελαμῶνος, ὁ δὲ Πηλέως. A

Notes: the brackets indicate that the lemma should be only κασιγνήτοισι, and the vertical line marks the point from which this A scholion is paralleled by a D scholion that may also descend from Aristonicus. κοινότερον "in a more general form," i.e. in the koiné form; ἀνεψιός "cousin"; σημειόομαι "note."

155. Homer scholia, ed. Erbse, *Iliad* 15. 619a[1] (from Herodian)

ἠλίβατος {μεγάλη}: ψιλῶς· ἀπὸ γὰρ τοῦ ἀλιτεῖν ἐσχημάτισται· καὶ ὤφειλεν ὅμοιον εἶναι τῷ "ἠλιτόμηνος" (cf. T 118), συγκοπὴν δὲ ἔπαθεν. διδάσκει δὲ καὶ τὸ τῆς συναλιφῆς ὅτι ψιλοῦται· "τὸν μέν τ᾽ ἠλίβατος πέτρη" (O 273). οἱ μέντοι δασύνοντες ἐτυμολογοῦσι παρὰ τὸν ἥλιον, τὴν ἡλίῳ βατὴν οὖσαν μόνῳ. οὐκ ἐπείσθη δὲ ἡ παράδοσις, ὡς πρόδηλον ἐγένετο ἐκ τῆς συναλιφῆς. A

Notes: the brackets in the lemma indicate that the comment is purely about ἠλίβατος, an epithet of rocks whose meaning is unknown. The point of the quotation is that the τ᾽ is not aspirated into θ᾽. ψιλῶς etc.: cf. 4.2.6; σχηματίζω "form," i.e. "derive"; συγκοπή "syncope" (in this case loss of -το-); τό understand something like "results"; συναλ(ο)ιφή "elision"; ἐτυμολογέω "derive"; παρά: cf. 4.1.28; βατός "accessible"; τὴν ἡλίῳ βατὴν οὖσαν μόνῳ is a definition of ἠλίβατος according to those who would write it ἡλίβατος and is in the feminine accusative because it agrees with an understood ἡλίβατον πέτραν, object of δασύνοντες and ἐτυμολογοῦσι; παράδοσις "tradition" (i.e. the main group of manuscripts).

156. Homer scholia, ed. Erbse, *Iliad* 15. 741a (from Nicanor)

τῶ ἐν χερσὶ φόως, ⟨οὐ μειλιχίη πολέμοιο⟩: Ἀρίσταρχος κατὰ δοτικὴν ἔγραφεν, συνάπτων δηλονότι ὅλον τὸν στίχον· ἔσται δὲ οὕτως τὸ ἑξῆς, τῷ ἐν χερσίν, οὐ μειλιχίη, τέλος πολέμοιο, οἷον ἐν τῷ δόρατι, οὐκ ἐν προσηνείᾳ οὐδ᾽ ἐν ἀργίᾳ κεῖται ἡ τοῦ πολέμου σωτηρία. Διονύσιος δὲ ὁ Θρᾷξ (fr. 20 Schm.) κατ᾽ εὐθεῖαν πτῶσιν, ᾧ ἀκόλουθόν ἐστι στίζειν ἐπὶ τὸ φόως τελείᾳ στιγμῇ· καὶ ἔσται καθ᾽ ἑαυτὸ ἑκάτερον ἡμιστίχιον. ὁ δὲ λόγος· διόπερ ἐν χερσὶν ἡ σωτηρία, προσήνεια δὲ οὐκ ἔστι πολέμου. A

Notes: κατὰ δοτικήν "in the dative case"; the understood object of ἔγραφεν is μειλιχίη "gentleness"; δηλονότι i.e. "clearly"; στίχος "line"; τὸ ἑξῆς: cf. 4.1.38; the distinction between τῶ in the lemma and τῷ in the paraphrase is not relevant to the import of the scholion but comes from a divergent textual tradition: both τῶ and τῷ are attested for the text of Homer here; οἷον introduces a second, looser paraphrase of the same line; προσήνεια "softness"; εὐθεῖα πτῶσις: cf. 4.2.11 and understand something like "puts the μειλιχίη"; ἀκόλουθος "in accordance with"; στίζω "punctuate"; ἐπί: cf. 4.1.31; τελεία στιγμή "period"; καθ᾽

ἑαυτό "by itself"; ἡμιστίχιον "half line"; λόγος "sense" (introducing another paraphrase); ἔστι = ἐστι; πολέμου "suitable to war, belonging to war." The reference is to Moritz Schmidt (1852) and would now be expressed as fr. 17 in Linke
(1977).

157. Eustathius' commentary on the *Iliad*, ed. Van der Valk, 1084. 19–21

Τὸ δὲ "οὐδὲ δὴν χάζετο" τὸ τῆς βολῆς γενναῖον πιθανολογεῖ. ὁ
γὰρ μὴ χαζόμενός τινος, ἀλλ᾽ ἐγγὺς δηλαδὴ γεγονώς, δύναιτ᾽
ἂν καὶ γενναίαν ἐκείνῳ ἐντινάξαι πληγήν.

Notes: this passage (*Iliad* 16. 736) is important because the scholia and all the
major manuscripts have ἄζετο here rather than χάζετο, but χάζετο could well
be the correct reading (though it is not without its own problems); δήν "for long";
χάζομαι "withdraw from"; βολή "stroke, blow"; τὸ γενναῖον "excellence" (cf.
4.1.26); πιθανολογέω "speak persuasively about"; δηλαδή "clearly"; ἐντινάσσω
"hurl against."

158. Euripides scholia, ed. Schwartz, *Hecuba* 847

καὶ τὰς ἀνάγκας οἱ νόμοι διώρισαν: μεταλλακτέον τὰς
πτώσεις· ἔστι γάρ· καὶ αἱ ἀνάγκαι τοὺς νόμους διώρισαν. ὁ δὲ
νοῦς· δεινὸν ὅτι πάντα συνέρχεται τὰ κακὰ κατὰ ταὐτὸν τοῖς
ἀνθρώποις, καὶ αἱ ἀνάγκαι τὰ νενομισμένα τοῖς ἀνθρώποις
μετήλλαξαν. ἐδέδοκτο γὰρ πολέμιον εἶναι τῇ Ἑκάβῃ τὸν
Ἀγαμέμνονα, ἀλλ᾽ ἡ ἀνάγκη τὸ νενομισμένον τῇ Ἑκάβῃ
μετήλλαξεν:—MB

καὶ ἄλλως· ἐναντίως εἶπεν. ἔδει γάρ· καὶ τοὺς νόμους αἱ ἀνάγκαι
διορίζουσιν· αὗται γὰρ καὶ νόμων ἐπικρατέστεραι, οὐ τὸ ἐναντίον,
διότι οἱ νόμοι τὰ ἑκούσια τιμωροῦνται, οὐχὶ τὰ ἐξ ἀνάγκης
δρώμενα· ὡς καὶ νῦν ἡ γραῦς ἐξ ἀνάγκης φίλον ποιεῖται τὸν
πολέμιον:—MB

ὁ δὲ Δίδυμος οὕτως· μᾶλλον ὤφειλεν εἰπεῖν ὅτι τοὺς νόμους αἱ
ἀνάγκαι διορίζουσιν· αἱ γὰρ ἀνάγκαι καὶ τῶν νόμων ἐπικρατέστεραι,
οὐχ οἱ νόμοι τῶν ἀναγκῶν. καὶ νῦν οὖν τοὐναντίον εἶπεν:—M

Notes: the unexpressed subject of the verbs of saying is Euripides (cf. 4.1.43);
μεταλλακτέον "it is necessary to transpose" (from μεταλλάσσω "change, transpose");
διορίζω "determine, define"; νοῦς "sense, meaning"; κατὰ ταὐτόν "at the same time";
ἄλλως: cf. 4.1.5; ἐπικρατέστερος "stronger"; ἑκούσιον "voluntary [acts]."

159. Euripides scholia, ed. Schwartz, *Orestes* 331

ἵνα μεσόμφαλοι λέγονται: ὀμφαλὸς κέκληται ἡ Πυθὼ παρὰ
τὰς ὀμφὰς τὰς ὑπὸ τοῦ θεοῦ χρηστηριαζομένας.   ἢ παρὰ
τὸ εἶναι ἐν μέσῳ τῆς οἰκουμένης τὴν Πυθώ. λέγεται γὰρ τὸν
Δία μαθεῖν βουλόμενον τὸ μέσον τῆς γῆς δύο ἀετοὺς ἰσοταχεῖς
ἀφεῖναι, τὸν μὲν ἀπὸ δύσεως, τὸν δὲ ἀπὸ ἀνατολῆς, καὶ ἐκεῖσε
αὐτοὺς ἀπαντῆσαι, ὅθεν ὀμφαλὸς ἐκλήθη. ἀνακεῖσθαί τε χρυσοῦς
ἀετοὺς φασι τῶν μυθευομένων ἀετῶν ὑπομνήματα:—MTAB

Notes: Πυθώ Pytho, the region in which Delphi is located; παρά: cf. **4.1.28**; ὀμφή "voice"; χρηστηριάζω "prophesy"; οἰκουμένη "inhabited world"; ἀετός: "eagle"; δύσις "west"; ἀνατολή "east"; ἀπαντάω + dat. "meet"; ἀνακεῖμαι is perfect passive of ἀνατίθημι "dedicate"; ὑπόμνημα "memorial"; μυθεύω "tell about in a myth."

160. Aeschylus scholia, ed. Smith, *Choephori* 899

μετεσκεύασται ὁ ἐξάγγελος εἰς Πυλάδην ἵνα μὴ δ' λέγωσιν.

Notes: μετασκευάζω "transform"; ἐξάγγελος "messenger coming from indoors"; the reason four characters could not speak is that most tragedies used only three speaking actors.

161. Aeschylus scholia, ed. Herington, *Prometheus Vinctus* 472b

πέπονθας κ. τ. λ.] Τοῦτο διὰ τὸ φιλονεικῆσαι Διί. μεσολαβοῦσι δὲ αἱ τοῦ χοροῦ τὴν ἔκθεσιν τῶν κατορθωμάτων, διαναπαύουσαι τὸν ὑποκριτὴν Αἰσχύλου.

Notes: the scholiast is attempting to justify the insertion of a few lines of sympathetic comment from the chorus in the midst of Prometheus' long recitation of his woes; φιλον(ε)ικέω "engage in rivalry"; μεσολαβέω "interrupt"; ἔκθεσις "exposition"; κατόρθωμα "success"; διαναπαύω "allow to rest awhile."

162. Aeschylus scholia, ed. Smith, *Septem* 311a

Τηθύος δὲ παῖδες· πάλιν τοὺς ποταμοὺς ὀνομάζει· μυθεύεται γὰρ ὅτι ὁ Οὐρανὸς συμμιγεὶς τῇ Γῇ ἀπέτεκε τὸν Ὠκεανὸν καὶ τὴν Τηθὺν καὶ ἄλλους οὐκ ὀλίγους παῖδάς τε καὶ θυγατέρας. ὁ δὲ Ὠκεανὸς μιγεὶς τῇ Τηθύι τῇ αὐτοῦ ἀδελφῇ ἐγέννησε τοὺς ποταμοὺς καὶ τὰς πηγὰς τὰς οὔσας ἐν τῷ κόσμῳ, καὶ οὕτως λέγονται οἱ ποταμοὶ παῖδες Τηθύος.
CNaNcNdP²PdSjVWXaXcYYa

Note: μυθεύω "relate (fabulously)."

163. Pindar scholia, ed. Drachmann, *Pythian* 2. 107

εὐστεφάνων: ἤτοι ὑψηλῶν, ἢ εὖ τετειχισμένων. στέφανος γὰρ πόλεως τὸ τεῖχος.

Notes: ἤτοι "either"; ὑψηλός "high."

164. Pindar scholia, ed. Drachmann, *Pythian* 8. 91

τόθι χαρμάτων: ὡς τοῦ Ἀριστομένους, πρὶν λαβεῖν τὰ Πύθια, νενικηκότος ἐν οἴκῳ, τουτέστιν ἐν Αἰγίνῃ ἀγῶνα ἱερὸν Ἀπόλλωνος πένταθλον. ἄγεται δὲ ἐν Αἰγίνῃ Δελφίνια Ἀπόλλωνι.

Notes: the lemma, which literally translated would be "there of joys," is only a key to the larger section of text to which this comment applies: τὸ μὲν μέγιστον τόθι χαρμάτων / ὤπασας, οἴκοι δὲ πρόσθεν ἁρπαλέαν δόσιν / πενταεθλίου σὺν ἑορταῖς ὑμαῖς ἐπάγαγες (64–6) (cf. **4.1.6**); Ἀριστομένης is the dedicatee of the ode, which celebrates his Pythian victory; λαμβάνω i.e. "win"; Πύθια "Pythian games"; ἐν οἴκῳ "at home"; ἄγομαι "be held"; Δελφίνια "Delphinian games"; the point of the last sentence is only to give the name of the games where Aristomenes had his earlier victory.

165. Pindar scholia, ed. Drachmann, *Pythian* 6. 15

πατρὶ τεῷ Θρασύβουλε: ὦ τοῦ Ξενοκράτους παῖ. τοῦτον δὲ ὡς φιλοπάτορα καὶ προεστῶτα τῆς ἱππικῆς ἐπαινεῖ, οὐχ ὥς τινες ἐβουλήθησαν, ἡνίοχον. ὁ γὰρ ἡνίοχος Νικόμαχός ἐστιν, ὡς ἐκ τῶν Ἰσθμιονικῶν (II 22) δῆλός ἐστιν.

Notes: φιλοπάτωρ "devoted to one's father"; προΐστημι "be outstanding in"; ἱππική "horsemanship"; ἐπαινεῖ· cf. 4.1.43; ἡνίοχος "charioteer"; the Ἰσθμιονῖκαι are the group of odes we call the *Isthmians*, so the reference is to *Isth.* 2. 22.

166. Pindar scholia, ed. Drachmann, *Pythian* 6. 35

a. Μεσσανίου δὲ γέροντος· Μεσσήνιον τὸν Νέστορά φασιν οὗτοι, ὅσοι ὑπέλαβον τὴν Πύλον τῆς Μεσσήνης εἶναι, ἀλλ' οὐχὶ τῆς κατὰ τὴν Ἀρκαδίαν Τριφυλίας. ὁ μέντοι Ὅμηρος οἶδεν ὑποτεταγμένην τῇ Λακωνικῇ τὴν Μεσσήνην. φησὶ γάρ (φ 13. 15)·

δῶρα τά οἱ ξεῖνος Λακεδαίμονι δῶκε τυχήσας·
τὼ δ' ἐν Μεσσήνῃ ξυμβλήτην ἀλλήλοιϊν.

b. ὁ δὲ νοῦς· τοῦ δὲ Μεσσηνίου γέροντος ταραχθεῖσα ἡ φρὴν ἐβόα τὸν παῖδα.   c. ἄλλως· καὶ Πίνδαρος τὸν Νέστορα ἐκ τῆς Μεσσηνιακῆς Πύλου φησὶν εἶναι. τριῶν γὰρ ὄντων τῶν ἐν Πελοποννήσῳ Πύλων εἷς μέν ἐστιν ὁ περὶ τὸν Ἀλφειὸν ποταμὸν ἐν Ἤλιδι Πύλος, ὃν καὶ ὑφ' Ἡρακλέος πεπορθῆσθαί [φασιν]· ἕτερος δὲ ὁ Τριφυλιακὸς Πύλος, ἐν ᾧ ὁ Ἀμαθόεις ποταμός· τρίτος ἐν Μεσσήνῃ περὶ τὸ Κορυφάσιον. εἰσὶ δὲ οἵ φασι τοὺς τρεῖς Πύλους περὶ τὸ Κορυφάσιον ὑπὸ τὸν Νηλέα εἶναι· δοκεῖ δὲ τῷ Διδύμῳ ἐκ τοῦ Τριφυλιακοῦ Πύλου εἶναι τὸν Νέστορα, ἔνθα καὶ Ἀμαθόεις ἐστὶ ποταμὸς καθ' Ὅμηρον.

Notes: ὑπολαμβάνω "suppose"; κατά "in"; Τριφυλία is a place; ὑποτάττω "subordinate, subject"; νοῦς "meaning"; ἄλλως: cf. 4.1.5; πορθέω "destroy, sack"; ὑπό + acc. "subject to"; Neleus was Nestor's father. There were indeed three ancient towns named Pylos, all of which claimed to be the home of Homer's Nestor (in part because the information given by Homer about Pylos matches none of them perfectly), but only the Messenian one was near the Coryphasium (a promontory). The Mycenean palace now called "Nestor's," from which come Linear B tablets identifying the place as Pylos, is near (but not identical with) the Messenian Pylos of the classical period.

167. Aristophanes scholia, ed. Koster and Holwerda, *Pax* 755a

ἀπ' ὀφθαλμῶν Κύννης R: Ἐρατοσθένης ἀγνοήσας τὰ κατὰ τὴν Κύνναν "κυνὸς" γράφει, RVΓ

κυνὸς ὡς ἀκτῖνες ἔλαμπον. VΓ

Κύννα δὲ καὶ Σαλαβακχὼ πόρναι Ἀθήνησιν. RVΓ

Notes: τὰ κατά "the facts about"; the indented line is a quotation of the second half of *Pax* 755 according to the text of Eratosthenes; 'Αθήνησιν "at Athens." The groups of letters indicate that there are three manuscripts from which this scholion is drawn, but none of them contains all of it: the lemma is only in R, and the quotation only in V and Γ.

168. Aristophanes scholia, ed. Koster and Holwerda, *Pax* 123d

καὶ κόνδυλον R: Δημήτριος ὁ ζηνοδότειος μεταγράφει "κάνδυλον"· V εἶδος δέ ἐστι πλακοῦντος. ἀλλὰ διὰ τὸ "ὄψον" περιττὴ ἡ μεταγραφή. RV

Notes: the context of the lemma is ἢν δ' ἐγὼ εὖ πράξας ἔλθω πάλιν, ἕξετ' ἐν ὥρᾳ / κολλύραν μεγάλην καὶ κόνδυλον ὄψον ἐπ' αὐτῇ, "but if I come back having done well, you will soon have a big bread-roll and κόνδυλον relish on it"; thus Aristophanes made a pun by putting the word κόνδυλον ("knuckle," i.e. thrashing) where a word for food was expected, Demetrius removed the pun, and the present scholiast defends the original; ζηνοδότειος "Zenodotean," i.e. student of Zenodotus; μεταγράφω "change the reading to"; εἶδος "type"; πλακοῦς "cake"; ὄψον "relish"; περιττός "superfluous"; the letters R and V are manuscript designations, and when they come in the middle of the text they indicate that individual parts of it are found only in one or the other manuscript.

169. Plato scholia vetera, ed. Greene, *Apologia* 22a

νὴ τὸν κύνα.

῾Ραδαμάνθυος ὅρκος οὗτος ὁ κατὰ χηνὸς ἢ κυνὸς ἢ πλατάνου ἢ κριοῦ ἢ τινος ἄλλου τοιούτου.

οἷς ἦν μέγιστος ὅρκος
ἅπαντι λόγῳ κύων, ἔπειτα χήν, θεοὺς δ' ἐσίγων.

Κρατῖνος Χείρωσι (fr. 231 Kock). τοιοῦτοι δὲ καὶ οἱ Σωκράτους ὅρκοι.

Notes: κατά "by"; χήν "goose"; πλάτανος "plane-tree"; κριός "ram." The reference would now be expressed as fr. 249 K–A.

170. Plato scholia vetera, ed. Greene, *Philebus* 60d

οἱ.

οἳ περισπωμένως ἑαυτῷ, ὡς νῦν· ὀξυτόνως δὲ οὗτοι. σημαίνει δὲ καὶ τὸ ὅπου.

Notes: cf. 4.2.7–8 for vocabulary; νῦν i.e. in this passage. Note the way the definitions indicate the different cases of οἳ and οἵ.

171. Aeschines scholia, ed. Dilts, 2. 157

339 τοὺς Καρίωνας καὶ Ξανθίας] ἀντὶ τοῦ 'δούλους'· τοιαῦτα γὰρ τὰ τῶν δούλων πρόσωπα εἰσάγεται ἐν τῇ κωμῳδίᾳ, Ξανθίου καὶ Καρίωνος καὶ ἄλλων τινῶν. mgVxLSfi

Notes: πρόσωπον "character"; εἰσάγω "introduce." The point is that Xanthias and Carion are standard slave names in comedy.

172. Aeschines scholia, ed. Dilts, 1. 29

66 τὰ ὅπλα μὴ τίθεσαι] τὸ τίθεσθαι λέγεται καὶ ἐπὶ τοῦ ἀποτίθεσθαι
τὰ ὅπλα καὶ ἐπὶ τοῦ περιτίθεσθαι καὶ ἐνδύεσθαι, ὡς ἔγνωμεν ἐν
τοῖς Θουκυδιδείοις ἐν τῷ δευτέρῳ (2). ἐνταῦθα οὖν ἐπὶ τοῦ
περιτίθεσθαι λέγει. amgVxLSf

Notes: ἐπί: cf. 4.1.31; ἀποτίθεμαι "take off"; περιτίθεμαι "put on"; ἐνδύομαι
"get into"; γιγνώσκω "determine"; Θουκυδίδειος i.e. a commentary or work on
Thucydides; δευτέρῳ: cf. 4.1.33; ἐνταῦθα i.e. in this passage; λέγει: cf. 4.1.43.
The reference is to a scholion on Thucydides 2. 2.

173. Aeschines scholia, ed. Dilts, 1. 157

315 πόρνους μεγάλους Τιμαρχώδεις] τοῦτο Παρμένων ὁ κωμικὸς
ἔσκωψεν εἰς Τίμαρχον τοῦτον τὸν ῥήτορα. ἦν δὲ καὶ ἕτερος
Τίμαρχος Τισίου μὲν υἱὸς τοῦ Ῥαμνουσίου, Ἰφικράτους δὲ
ἀδελφιδοῦς τοῦ στρατηγοῦ. amgVxLS

Note: ἀδελφιδοῦς "nephew."

174. Aeschines scholia, ed. Dilts, 3. 222

485a Πόλλιν] στρατηγὸν Λακεδαιμονίων, περὶ οὗ καὶ ὁ Ἀριστείδης
(2, 232 Di.) λέγει ἐν τῷ ὑπὲρ τῶν τεσσάρων ὅτι οὗτος ἐπώλησε
τὸν Πλάτωνα. xLSf

485b. κατεναυμάχησε δὲ αὐτὸν Χαβρίας περὶ Νάξον τὴν νῆσον. LS

Notes: ὑπὲρ τῶν τεσσάρων is a title; πωλέω "sell"; καταναυμαχέω "defeat in a
sea battle." According to legend, the philosopher Plato spent a period as a slave,
having been sold to the Aeginetans while in Sicily. The reference is to G. Dindorf,
Aristides (Leipzig 1829), vol. ii, speech 46, marginal number 232; now that reference would be expressed as speech 3, marginal number 379, in F. W. Lenz
and C. A. Behr, P. Aelii Aristidis opera quae exstant omnia (Leiden 1976).

175. Aeschines scholia, ed. Dilts, 1. 64

147 Κρωβύλος] Κρωβύλον καλεῖ τὸν ἀδελφὸν τοῦ Ἡγησάνδρου τὸν
Ἡγήσιππον τὸν μισοφίλλιπον, καθὸ αὐτὸς ἀλείφει τὴν κεφαλὴν
καὶ φιλοκαλεῖ τὰς τρίχας. κρωβύλος γάρ ἐστιν εἶδος ἐμπλέγματος
πρῴην γενομένου παρὰ τοῖς παλαιοῖς τῶν Ἀθηναίων, ὡς ἔγνωμεν
ἐν τοῖς Θουκυδιδείοις (1, 6). amgVxLSf

Notes: κρωβύλος "top-knot"; μισοφίλλιπον from μισοφίλιππος "hating Philip";
καθό: cf. 4.1.44; ἀλείφω "anoint with oil"; φιλοκαλέω "beautify"; εἶδος: cf. 4.1.41;
ἔμπλεγμα "plait"; πρῴην "formerly"; γιγνώσκω "determine." The reference is to
a scholion on Thucydides 1. 6. 3.

176. Erotian's Hippocratic glossary, ed. Nachmanson, introduction (35 = p. 8)

διόπερ ἡμεῖς καθ' ἑκάστην γραφὴν ἐκλεξάμενοι τὰς καταγεγραμμένας
λέξεις διὰ μὲν τοῦ συγγράμματος δηλώσομεν, ὁποῖαι τυγχάνουσι
κείμεναι ἐν ὅσαις τε βίβλοις ἱστοροῦνται αἱ μὴ συνήθεις, διὰ
δὲ τῆς ἐξαπλώσεως ἐμφανίσομεν πόσα σημαίνουσι, μιμνησκόμενοι

καὶ τῶν ἅπαξ εἰρημένων καὶ τὰς ἀνακεχωρηκυίας διδύμοις
πιστούμενοι μαρτυρίαις, τὰς δὲ οὐχ οὕτως ἀσαφεῖς εἰς τὸ ⟨ἕν⟩
ἀνθ' ἑνὸς δηλούμενον ὑπάγοντες, προσεξαπλοῦντες δὲ καὶ τὰς παρὰ
τοῖς ἄλλοις τέλεον παραλελειμμένας. τό τε γὰρ τέρθρον τοῦ πάθους
οὐδεὶς αὐτῶν ἐξηγεῖται καὶ τὰς αἰθόλικας καὶ τὸ κερχνῶδες καὶ
τὰς τερμίνθους τό τε θηριῶδες καὶ τὸ σκορδίνημα καὶ τὸν σκῖρον
καὶ τὴν ἐκνυπὴν μήτραν καὶ τὸ ἐπηλυγάζεσθαι τά τε αἱμόκερχνα
καὶ τὸ φολλικῶδες καὶ τὸ ἔναιμον νεῦρον καὶ τὸ ἴκταρ καὶ ἄλλας
πλείους λέξεις, ὑπὲρ ὧν ἐν τοῖς κατὰ μέρος ἐροῦμεν.

Notes: ἐκλέγω "pick out"; σύγγραμμα "treatise"; ἐξάπλωσις "explanation"; κεῖμαι
"be attested"; ἱστορέω "record"; a ἅπαξ εἰρημένον is what we call a *hapax legomenon*; ἀνακεχωρικώς "obsolete"; πιστόομαι "guarantee," i.e. cite attestations
of; τὸ ⟨ἕν⟩ ἀνθ' ἑνὸς δηλούμενον i.e. a regime of one explanation or citation per
word; ὑπάγω εἰς "bring under"; προσεξαπλόω "explain additionally"; τέλεον "completely"; τέρθρον "crisis"; αἰθόλιξ "pustule"; κερχνώδης "rough"; τέρμινθος "terebinth," i.e. a swelling like the fruit of the terebinth tree; θηριώδης "malignant";
σκορδίνημα "stretching"; σκῖρος "hardened tumor"; ἐκνυπός "distended" (perhaps);
μήτρα "womb"; ἐπηλυγάζομαι "be suppressed"; αἱμόκερχνον "cough with blood-
spitting"; φολλικώδης "scabby"; ἔναιμον νεῦρον "vein"; ἴκταρ "female genitalia."

177. Galen, commentary on Hippocrates' *Aphorisms*, 5. 13 (Kühn xvii.ii.
       797–8)
       Ὁκόσοι αἷμα ἀφρῶδες πτύουσι, τουτέοισιν ἐκ τοῦ πνεύμονος ἡ
       ἀναγωγὴ γίνεται.

————————

Καὶ τῶν ἀντιγράφων τὰ πολλὰ καὶ τῶν ἐξηγησαμένων τὸ βιβλίον
οὐκ ὀλίγοι ἴσασι κατὰ τήνδε τὴν λέξιν τὸν ἀφορισμὸν γεγραμμένον,
ὁκόσοι ἀφρῶδες αἷμα ἐμέουσι. καί τινές γε τὴν ἐξήγησιν αὐτοῦ
ποιούμενοι πλῆθος ἐνδείκνυσθαί φασι τοὔνομα καὶ διὰ τοῦτο ἀπὸ
τοῦ κυρίου μετενηνέχθαι. προδήλως δ' οὗτοι καταψεύδονται τοῦ
φαινομένου. πολλάκις γὰρ ὦπται πτύσις αἵματος ἀφρώδους ἄνευ
πλήθους γεγενημένη. εἰ μὲν οὖν ὄντως ὑφ' Ἱπποκράτους οὕτως
ἐγράφη, κατακεχρῆσθαι τῇ προσηγορίᾳ φήσομεν αὐτόν.

Notes: the first sentence is Hippocrates' aphorism and is therefore in literary Ionic,
the dialect in which Hippocrates wrote; the material below the horizontal line is
Galen's commentary, in Attic—but watch for unmarked quotations from Hippocrates. The problem the note addresses is the precise difference in meaning
between ἐμέω and πτύω, and whether Hippocrates was aware of that difference.
ὁκόσος = ὁπόσος; ἀφρώδης "foamy"; ἀναγωγή "bringing up" (of the blood); ἀντίγραφον
"copy"; ἐξηγέομαι "explain," "write a commentary on"; ἀφορισμός "aphorism" (a short
pithy maxim, in this case the one appearing as the lemma), τήνδε i.e. ἐμέουσι; ἐμέω
"vomit"; πλῆθος i.e. a large quantity of blood; ἐνδείκνυμαι "indicate"; κύριος "proper
meaning"; μεταφέρω "use metaphorically"; καταψεύδομαι "speak falsely of"; οὕτως
i.e. with ἐμέουσι; καταχράομαι "misuse"; προσηγορία "word."

178. Galen, glossary, introduction (Kühn xix. 63–5)

ὅθεν ἔμοιγε καὶ θαυμάζειν ἐπῆλθε τῶν ἅπασαν ἐξηγεῖσθαι τὴν
Ἱπποκράτους λέξιν ἐπαγγειλαμένων, εἰ μὴ συνίασιν ὅτι πλείω
παραλείπουσιν ὧν διδάσκουσι. πολλὰ γοῦν βιβλία Διοσκουρίδης
γράψας, οὐχ ὁ ἐπικληθεὶς Φακᾶς, ὁ Ἡροφίλειος, ἀλλ' ὁ νεώτερος
ὁ κατὰ πατέρας ἡμῶν οὐχ ὅπως τὸ ἥμισυ μέρος, ἀλλ' οὐδὲ
τὸ τρίτον ἢ τέταρτον ἐξηγήσατο τῆς ὅλης λέξεως· τούτῳ μέν
γε πρὸς τοῖς ἄλλοις καὶ δύο ταῦτα ἐξ ἐπιμέτρου καθ' ὅλον
πεπλημμέληται τὸν λόγον· ὀνομάτων τε σαφεστάτων μνημονεύειν
μὴ ὅτι πολλῆς, ἀλλὰ μηδὲ ἐλαχίστης ἐξηγήσεως δεομένων καὶ
τούτων αὐτῶν πλεονάκις. ταῦτά τε οὖν ἡμεῖς περιίδομεν καὶ πρὸς
τούτοις ἔτι τὸ διηγεῖσθαι τὴν ἰδέαν ἑκάστου φυτοῦ καὶ βοτάνης
καὶ τῶν μεταλλευομένων· ἤδη δὲ καὶ τῶν ἰχθύων καὶ τῶν ζώων
ὅλων ὅσων ἂν ἑκάστοτε τύχῃ μεμνημένος ὁ Ἱπποκράτης, ἅπερ ὁ
Διοσκουρίδης οὐκ αἰδεῖται μεταγράφων ἐκ τῶν Νίγρου τε καὶ
Παμφίλου καὶ Διοσκουρίδους τοῦ Ἀναζαρβέως καὶ πρὸ τούτων
Κρατεύα τε καὶ Θεοφράστου καὶ Ἡρακλείδου τοῦ Ταραντίνου καὶ
ἄλλων μυρίων· οὕτως δὲ καὶ πόλεων ὀνόματα διηγεῖται γνωριμωτάτων
καὶ ἄστρων ὁμοίως ἐπιφανεστάτων, ἃ μηδὲ ἂν παῖς ἀγνοήσειε·
ταῦτα δὲ καὶ ἄλλοι πολλοὶ τῶν ἐξηγησαμένων ἁμαρτάνουσιν. εἰ
τοίνυν ταῦτά τις περιέλοι πάντα, τὰς γλώττας ἂν ἐξηγήσατο
μόνας, ὥσπερ ὁ Ἡρόφιλος ἐποίησε καὶ Βακχεῖος, Ἀριστάρχου
τοῦ γραμματικοῦ τὸ πλῆθος αὐτῷ τῶν παραδειγμάτων ἀθροίσαντος,
ὥς φασιν.

Notes: λέξις "vocabulary"; ὧν attracted relative pronoun with omitted antecedent in genitive of comparison; ἐπικαλέομαι "be surnamed"; φακᾶς "having a birthmark"; Ἡροφίλειος "follower of Herophilus"; κατά + acc. "around the time of";
οὐχ ὅπως … ἀλλ' οὐδέ "not only not … but not even"; ἐξ ἐπιμέτρου "in addition"; πλημμελέομαι "be done wrongly"; ὄνομα "word"; μὴ ὅτι … ἀλλὰ
μηδέ "not only not … but not even"; πλεονάκις "frequently"; φυτόν "plant";
βοτανή "herb"; μεταλλευώ "mine" (as for ore or crystals); ἰχθύων is gen.
after ἰδέαν; μεταγράφω "copy out"; Κρατεύα is gen. sing.; μυρίοι "countless";
τῶν understand βιβλίων; περιαιρέω "strip away"; αὐτῷ refers to Bacchius
and makes the gen. absolute equivalent to a relative clause; παράδειγμα
"example."

179. Lucian scholia, ed. Rabe, *Pro lapsu* 5

τὸ * πεντάγραμμον] ὅτι τὸ ἐν τῇ συνηθείᾳ λεγόμενον πένταλφα
σύμβολον ἦν πρὸς ἀλλήλους Πυθαγορείων ἀναγνωριστικὸν καὶ
τούτῳ ἐν ταῖς ἐπιστολαῖς ἐχρῶντο· ὅ ἐστι τοῦτο ☆. ~ VCφ

Notes: the asterisk in the lemma indicates that although the scholion had no
lemma, in at least one manuscript it was linked by a sign to the τό; ὅτι: cf. 4.1.44;
πένταλφα "pentagram"; συνήθεια "ordinary usage"; ἀναγνωριστικός "for rec-
ognition"; the symbols at the end refer to manuscripts.

180. Lucian scholia, ed. Rabe, *Apologia* 2

ῥήτραν] ῥῆτραι· συνθῆκαι, ὁμολογίαι. Ταραντῖνοι δὲ νόμους καὶ οἷον ψηφίσματα. παρὰ Λακεδαιμονίοις δὲ ῥήτρα Λυκούργου νόμος ὡς ἐκ χρησμοῦ τιθέμενος. οἱ δὲ ῥήτρας ὁμολογίας, οἱ δὲ συγγράμματα, καὶ ῥητροφύλακας τοὺς συγγραμματοφύλακας. ~ Δ

Notes: συνθήκη "treaty"; οἷον "as it were"; συγγραμματοφύλαξ "keeper of books." The definitions given here fit the main usages of the word, but not the particular passage of Lucian in question here, where ῥήτρα means "speech."

181. Lucian scholia, ed. Rabe, *Soloecista* 5

πατριώτης*] ὁμοήθης γὰρ ἔδει εἰπεῖν, ὁμόγλωσσος, ὁμόνομος. τὸ δὲ πατριώτης ἐπὶ βαρβάρων· οἱ βάρβαροι γὰρ οὕτως ἀλλήλους φασὶν ἀντὶ τοῦ πολίτης, καὶ ἴσως ὅτι μὴ κατὰ πόλεις οἰκοῦσιν. Πλάτων μέντοι καὶ ἐφ' Ἑλλήνων ἐν τοῖς Νόμοις [VI 771 D] τῷ πατριώτης ἐχρήσατο. ~ Γ2CVMOUΩ

Notes: the point of this scholion, like most of those to the *Soloecista*, is to explain the grammatical errors that Lucian deliberately committed in this piece; μή is probably for οὐ.

182. Lucian scholia, ed. Rabe, *Phalaris* 1. 7

τυράννους σοφούς] περὶ Περιάνδρου τοῦ Κυψέλου λέγει, ὃς τῶν ἑπτὰ μὲν παρ' Ἕλλησι σοφῶν εἷς, Κορίνθου δὲ τῆς πρὸς τῷ Ἰσθμῷ Πελοποννήσου τύραννος ἦν. τούτου καὶ ἀπόφθεγμα ἐν Δελφοῖς ἀνέκειτο τοῦτο 'θυμοῦ κράτει'. ἦσαν δὲ καὶ τῶν ἄλλων σοφῶν ἀποφθέγματα, ἃ καὶ αὐτὰ Πυθοῖ ἀνέκειτο, ταῦτα· Κλεοβούλου Λινδίου 'μέτρον ἄριστον', Χείλωνος Λακεδαιμονίου 'γνῶθι σαυτόν', Πιττακοῦ δὲ τοῦ Μιτυληναίου 'μηδὲν ἄγαν', Σόλωνος Ἀθηναίου 'τέλος ὅρα μακροῦ βίου', Βίαντος δὲ Πριηνέως 'οἱ πλέονες κακοί', Θάλητος Μιλησίου 'ἐγγύα, πάρα δ' ἄτα'. ~ BφNOSUΩΔ

Notes: ἀπόφθεγμα "saying"; Πυθοῖ "at Delphi"; κρατέω + gen. "control"; note the fluctuation between ἦσαν and ἀνέκειτο in the number of a verb with a neuter plural subject; ἐγγύα (= ἐγγύη) "pledge"; πάρα = πάρεστι; ἄτα = ἄτη.

183. Apollonius Rhodius scholia, ed. Wendel, 1. 436

θηεύμενος: τὸ θηεῖσθαι Ὅμηρος ἐπὶ τοῦ θαυμάζειν τίθησιν (κ 180)· 'θήσαντ' ἔλαφον· ὁ δὲ Ἀπολλώνιος ἐπὶ τοῦ βλέπειν. L

Notes: θηέομαι = θεάομαι "behold"; understand punctuation before Ὅμηρος; ἐπί: cf. 4.1.31.

184. Apollonius Rhodius scholia, ed. Wendel, 2. 896

‹Ἐργῖνος:› Ἡρόδωρος (31 fg 55 J.) Ἐργῖνόν φησι κυβερνῆσαι τὴν Ἀργὼ μετὰ τὸν θάνατον Τίφυος.

Notes: κυβερνάω "steer." The reference is to *FGrHist* author 31, fr. 55.

185. Apollonius Rhodius scholia, ed. Wendel, 1. 936–49q

ἐν δ' ἥρως Αἰνήιος: ὅτι Αἰνεὺς Θετταλὸς ὢν τὸ γένος ᾤκησεν ἐν Ἑλλησπόντῳ. γήμας δὲ Εὐσώρου βασιλέως τῶν Θρακῶν Αἰνήτην,

γεννᾷ Κύζικον, ἀφ' οὗ ἡ πόλιc. Εὐcώρου δὲ υἱὸc 'Ακάμαc, ὃν
"Ομηροc ἐν τῇ Βοιωτίᾳ (Β 844) ἡγεῖcθαι Θρᾳκῶν ἅμα τῷ Πείρῳ
‹φηcίν›.

Notes: Αἰνήτη is a woman's name; ἡ πόλις i.e. Cyzicus, understand "is named."

186. Apollonius Rhodius scholia, ed. Wendel, 1. 1207b

τόφρα δ' "Υλαc: τὸν "Υλαν ὁ μὲν 'Απολλώνιοc Θειοδάμαντόc
φηcιν υἱὸν εἶναι, 'Ελλάνικοc (4 fg 131 b J.) δὲ Θειομένουc.
'Αντικλείδηc δὲ ἐν Δηλιακοῖc (140 fg 2 J.) ἱcτόρηcεν οὐ τὸν "Υλαν
εἰc τὴν ὑδρείαν ἐξεληλυθέναι, ἀλλὰ τὸν "Υλλον, καὶ ἀνεύρετον
γενέcθαι. ἐγένοντο δὲ πολλοὶ ἐρώμενοι 'Ηρακλέουc· "Υλαc,
Φιλοκτήτηc καὶ Δίομοc καὶ Πέρινθοc καὶ Τρίγξ, ἀφ' οὗ πόλιc
τῆc Λιβύηc. Cωκράτηc δὲ ἐν τῷ Πρὸc Εἰδόθεόν (fg 9 M. IV 498)
φηcι τὸν "Υλαν ἐρώμενον Πολυφήμου καὶ οὐχ 'Ηρακλέουc γενέcθαι.
" Οναcοc δὲ ἐν α' 'Αμαζονικῶν (41 fg 1 a J.) ἀληθέcτερον τὴν ἱcτορίαν
ἐκτίθεται, οὐχ ἡρπάcθαι αὐτὸν ὑπὸ νυμφῶν, ἀλλὰ κατηνέχθαι
αὐτὸν εἰc κρήνην καὶ οὕτωc ἀποθανεῖν.

ἀπρεπὲc δὲ νεανίαν ὑδρίαν βαcτάζειν· "Ομηροc (η 20) δὲ πρεπόντωc
παρθένον. πιθανώτερον δὲ ἦν ἀμφορέα εἰπεῖν, ὡc Καλλίμαχοc
(fg 546 Schn.).

Notes: τόφρα "meanwhile"; ἱστορέω "record"; ὑδρεία "water-drawing"; ἀνεύρετος
"undiscovered, lost"; ἀφ' οὗ understand "is named"; Σωκράτης: not the philosopher, but a later writer (probably Socrates of Argos, who lived in the Hellenistic
period); πρός "against"; α' i.e. book 1; ἐκτίθεμαι "set forth"; καταφέρω "draw
down"; κρήνη "well, spring"; ἀπρεπής "unseemly"; ὑδρία "water jar"; βαστάζω
"carry"; παρθένον understand something like "had carry a water jar"; πιθανός
"plausible"; ἦν sc. ἄν; ἀμφορεύς "amphora"; the point is that since a hydria was
a girl's tool (because carrying water was girls' work), if a male had to be made to
carry water (as was necessary for the all-male Argonaut expedition) he ought to
use a more manly container for it. The references are to FGrHist author 4, fr.
131b; FGrHist author 140, fr. 2, Müller (see notes to exercise 84 above), now
replaced by FGrHist author 310, fr. 15; FGrHist author 41, fr. 1a; and an outdated edition of Callimachus now cited as fr. 596 in Pfeiffer (1949–53).

187. Hipparchus' commentary on Aratus, 1. 2. 5–7

Πρῶτον μὲν οὖν ὁ "Αρατοc ἀγνοεῖν μοι δοκεῖ τὸ ἔγκλιμα τοῦ
κόcμου νομίζων ἐν τοῖc περὶ τὴν 'Ελλάδα τόποιc τοιοῦτον εἶναι,
ὥcτε τὴν μεγίcτην ἡμέραν λόγον ἔχειν πρὸc τὴν ἐλαχίcτην τὸν
αὐτὸν, ὃν ἔχει τὰ ε' πρὸc τὰ γ'. λέγει γὰρ ἐπὶ τοῦ θερινοῦ τροπικοῦ·

497 τοῦ μέν, ὅcον τε μάλιcτα, δι' ὀκτὼ μετρηθέντοc
πέντε μὲν ἔνδια cτρέφεται καὶ ὑπέρτερα γαίηc,
τὰ τρία δ' ἐν περάτῃ.

cυμφωνεῖται δή, διότι ἐν μὲν τοῖc περὶ τὴν 'Ελλάδα τόποιc ὁ
γνώμων λόγον ἔχει πρὸc τὴν ἰcημερινὴν cκιάν, ὃν ἔχει τὰ δ'
πρὸc τὰ γ'. ἐκεῖ δὴ τοίνυν ἡ μεγίcτη ἡμέρα ἐcτὶν ὡρῶν ἰcημερινῶν

ιδ΄ καὶ τριῶν ἔγγιστα πεμπτημορίων, τὸ δὲ ἔξαρμα τοῦ πόλου
μοιρῶν λζ΄ ὡς ἔγγιστα. ὅπου δὲ ἡ μεγίστη ἡμέρα λόγον ἔχει
πρὸς τὴν ἐλαχίστην, ὃν ἔχει τὰ ε΄ πρὸς τὰ γ΄, ἐκεῖ ἡ μὲν μεγίστη
ἡμέρα ἐστὶν ὡρῶν ιε΄, τὸ δὲ ἔξαρμα τοῦ πόλου μοιρῶν μα΄ ὡς
ἔγγιστα. δῆλον τοίνυν ὅτι οὐ δυνατὸν ἐν τοῖς περὶ τὴν Ἑλλάδα
‹τόποις› τὸν προειρημένον εἶναι λόγον τῆς μεγίστης ἡμέρας πρὸς
τὴν ἐλαχίστην, ἀλλὰ μᾶλλον ἐν τοῖς περὶ τὸν Ἑλλήσποντον τόποις.

Notes: ἀγνοέω "be in error about"; ἔγκλιμα "inclination, tilt"; τοιοῦτον for τοιοῦτο;
λόγος "ratio"; the Greeks said "has the same ratio that *x* has to *y*" where we would
say "has a ratio of x : y"; ἐπί: cf. 4.1.31; θερινὸς τροπικός "summer solstice";
τοῦ μέν supply "circle" here; ὅσον τε μάλιστα "as closely as possible"; δι᾽ ὀκτώ
"into eight [parts]"; μετρέω "measure"; ἔνδιος "in the sky"; περάτη "opposite
side"; συμφωνέω "agree"; διότι "that" (cf. 4.1.44); γνώμων "gnomon" (pointer
on a sundial); ἰσημερινός "equinoctial"; τοίνυν "therefore"; ἔγγιστα "approxi-
mately"; πεμπτημόριον "fifth"; ἔξαρμα "elevation"; πόλος "pole" (i.e. North pole);
μοῖρα "degree (of arc)."

5.3.3 Grammatical Treatises
Contents. Theodosius 188; Choeroboscus 189; Michael Syncellus 190; Trypho
191; Gregory of Corinth 192–3; Dionysius Thrax 194–7; Herodian 198–200;
Apollonius Dyscolus 201.

188. Theodosius, *Canons* (from *GG* iv.i), 68. 1ff.
Περὶ εὐκτικῶν
Εὐκτικὰ ἐνεργητικά.
Χρόνου ἐνεστῶτος καὶ παρατατικοῦ.
Ἑνικά. Τύπτοιμι: πᾶσα μετοχὴ ἐνεργητική, τὸ τέλος τῆς
γενικῆς τρέψασα εἰς μ̅ι̅ καὶ πρὸ τοῦ μ̅ δεξαμένη τὸ τ̅ παραιτησαμένη
τε τὰ μὴ δυνάμενα σὺν αὐτῷ ἀκουσθῆναι στοιχεῖα, τὸ εὐκτικὸν
ἐνεργητικὸν ποιεῖ, τύπτων τύπτοντος τύπτοιμι, τετυφὼς τετυφότος
τετύφοιμι· εἰ μέντοι εἴη εἰς σ̅ ὀξύτονος ἡ μετοχὴ διὰ τοῦ ν̅τ̅
κλινομένη, τὸ τέλος τῆς γενικῆς οὐκ εἰς μ̅ι̅ ἀλλ᾽ εἰς η̅ν̅ τρέπεται,
δοθείς δοθέντος δοθείην, στάς στάντος σταίην. τύπτοις: πᾶν ῥῆμα
εἰς μ̅ι̅ λῆγον τροπῇ τῆς μ̅ι̅ εἰς σ̅ τὸ δεύτερον ποιεῖ, λέγοιμι λέγοις,
τίθημι τίθης.
Notes: cf. 4.2.7, 10, 11, 13 for vocabulary; παραιτέομαι "reject" (i.e. dropping
any part of the genitive stem that cannot easily precede ι, e.g. the φιλού-ιμι from
φιλοῦντος becomes φιλοῖμι); στοιχεῖον "letter"; δεύτερον [πρόσωπον] "second
person."

189. Choeroboscus, commentary on Theodosius (from *GG* iv.i), 333. 5ff.
Ἰστέον ὅτι τὰ εἰς ω̅ς̅ ὀξύτονα θηλυκὰ δύο ταῦτά εἰσι, τὸ αἰδώς
καὶ ἠώς, καὶ εἰς ου̅ς̅ ἔχουσι τὴν γενικήν, οἷον αἰδοῦς καὶ ἠοῦς, καὶ

δι᾽ ὅλου κλίνονται ὥσπερ τὰ εἰς ω θηλυκὰ ἐν ἁπάσαις ταῖς πτώσεσι·
τὸ δὲ δώς, ὃ σημαίνει τὴν δόσιν, ὡς παρ᾽ Ἡσιόδῳ <Opp. 356>
δὼς ἀγαθή, ἅρπαξ δὲ κακή, θανάτοιο δότειρα, ὀξύνεται
καὶ θηλυκόν ἐστιν, ἔστι δὲ ἄκλιτον, ὡς μαθησόμεθα· ἰστέον δὲ
ὅτι τὸ αἰδώς Φιλητᾶς ὁ διδάσκαλος Θεοκρίτου χωρὶς τοῦ ϲ
προηνέγκατο, εἰπὼν ἀγαθὴ δ᾽ ἐπὶ ἤθεσιν αἰδώ. Τὰ δὲ βαρύτονα
ἀποβολῇ τοῦ ϲ ποιοῦσι τὴν γενικήν, ὁμοίως δὲ καὶ τὰ περισπώμενα,
καὶ ἐπιδέχονται κλίσιν ὁμοίαν τοῖς εἰς ωϲ Ἀττικοῖς ἐν ἁπάσαις
ταῖς πτώσεσιν, οἷον ἡ Κῶς τῆς Κῶ, ἡ Τλῶς τῆς Τλῶ, ἡ Κρῶς τῆς
Κρῶ (εἰσὶ δὲ ταῦτα ὀνόματα πόλεων), ἡ ἅλως τῆς ἅλω· τὸ γὰρ
ἅλωος πταῖσμα νεωτερικόν ἐστι ...

Notes: cf. 4.2.7–9, 11 for vocabulary; ὅλου "the whole paradigm"; Opp. is a reference to the *Works and Days*; δόσις "giving"; ἄκλιτος "indeclinable" (here designating a word that does not occur in oblique cases, rather than one that keeps
its nominative form in other cases); Φιλητᾶς (nom.) was an important pre-
Alexandrian scholar and poet; προφέρομαι "use, cite"; ἀποβολή "dropping";
Ἀττικά probably refers here to words like λεώς and νεώς that belonged to the
"Attic declension" only in Attic and followed the normal second-declension paradigm (λαός, ναός) in the koiné; πταῖσμα "error"; νεωτερικός "more recent."

190. Michael Syncellus, ed. Donnet (1982), 15. 96ff.

Τοίνυν τὰ ἐπίθετα ὁμοιογενῶς καὶ ὁμοιοπτώτως τοῖς κυρίοις τε
καὶ προσηγορικοῖς συντάσσονται δι᾽ ὅλων τῶν πτώσεων καὶ ἀριθμῶν·
ἐὰν γὰρ ὦσι τὰ κύρια ἢ τὰ προσηγορικὰ ἀρσενικὰ ἢ θηλυκὰ ἢ
οὐδέτερα, ὁμοίως καὶ τὰ ἐπίθετα σχηματίζονται, οἷον· ἀρσενικὸν
μέν "ὁ σοφὸς Ὅμηρος, τοῦ σοφοῦ Ὁμήρου, τῷ σοφῷ Ὁμήρῳ, τὸν
σοφὸν Ὅμηρον, ὦ σοφὲ Ὅμηρε"· καὶ ἄχρι τῶν δυϊκῶν καὶ πληθυντικῶν,
ὡς ἔφαμεν· θηλυκὸν δὲ οἷον "ἡ σοφὴ Καλλιόπη, τῆς σοφῆς Καλλιόπης,
τῇ σοφῇ Καλλιόπῃ, τὴν σοφὴν Καλλιόπην, ὦ σοφὴ Καλλιόπη"· καὶ
ἐπὶ οὐδετέρων ὡσαύτως, οἷον "τὸ σοφὸν παιδίον, τοῦ σοφοῦ παιδίου,
τῷ σοφῷ παιδίῳ, τὸ σοφὸν παιδίον, ὦ σοφὸν παιδίον." ...

Εἰσὶ δέ τινα διγενῆ μόνον ἃ ποτὲ μὲν ὡς προσηγορικὰ λαμβάνονται,
ποτὲ δὲ ὡς ἐπίθετα, οἷον "ὁ φυγάς, καὶ ἡ φυγάς, ὁ ἐθάς, καὶ ἡ
ἐθάς, ὁ πολίτης, καὶ ἡ πολῖτις, ὁ ἄναξ καὶ ἡ ἄνασσα, ὁ βασιλεύς
καὶ ἡ βασίλισσα, καὶ ἡ βασιλίς"· καὶ ταῦτα πρὸς μὲν τὰ προσηγορικὰ
ἢ κύρια τασσόμενα τάξιν ἐπιθετικὴν ἔχει, οἷον "ὁ ἄναξ ἀνήρ, ἡ
ἄνασσα γυνή, ὁ βασιλεὺς Κωνσταντῖνος, ἡ βασίλισσα καὶ ἡ βασιλὶς
Ἑλένη, ὁ προφήτης ἄνθρωπος καὶ ἡ προφῆτις γυνή, ὁ προφήτης
Σαμουὴλ καὶ ἡ προφῆτις Ἄννα"· ἐπιθέτοις δὲ συμπλεκόμενα
προσηγορικὰ γίνονται, οἷον "ὁ καλὸς βασιλεύς καὶ ἡ καλὴ βασίλισσα
καὶ βασιλίς, ὁ εὐκλεὴς πολίτης καὶ ἡ εὐκλεὴς πολῖτις"·

Notes: cf. 4.2.11–12 for vocabulary; ὁμοιογενῶς i.e. agreeing in gender; σχηματίζω
"form"; ἄχρι "as far as"; διγενής "of two genders"; ποτὲ μέν i.e. sometimes; τάξις

ἐπιθετική "adjectival position" i.e. between the article and its noun (often called "attributive position" now).

191. Trypho, Περὶ παθῶν, from *TLG* version of Schneider, 1. 1ff.

Τὰ τῆς λέξεως πάθη εἰς δύο γενικώτατα διαιροῦνται, ποσόν τε καὶ ποιόν. εἴδη τοῦ μὲν ποσοῦ ἔνδεια καὶ πλεονασμός, τοῦ δὲ ποιοῦ μετάθεσις καὶ μετάληψις. ἀμφοτέρων δὲ συνελθόντων ὁμοῦ τμῆσις γίνεται. ἔστι δέ, ὡς ἐν κεφαλαίῳ, πάθη πέντε· αʹ πλεονασμός, βʹ ἔνδεια, γʹ μετάθεσις, δʹ μετάληψις, εʹ τμῆσις. Πλεονασμὸς μὲν οὖν ἐστι περισσότης χρόνων ἢ χρόνου, στοιχείων ἢ στοιχείου. Ἔνδεια δὲ τοὐναντίον χρόνου ἢ χρόνων, στοιχείου ἢ στοιχείων ἐλάττωσις. Μετάθεσις δὲ στοιχείου ἐστὶ μετακίνησις ἐκ τῆς ἰδίας τάξεως ἐφ᾽ ἑτέραν τάξιν, οἷον ὡς ὅταν τὰ δαρτά δρατά λέγωμεν καὶ τὸν προθμόν πορθμόν, ὁμοίως καὶ τὴν καρδίαν κραδίαν καὶ τὸ κράτος κάρτος. καλεῖται δὲ καὶ ἐναλλαγὴ καὶ ὑπέρθεσις. Μετάληψις δέ ἐστι στοιχείων μετακίνησις ἐπ᾽ ἀντίστοιχον ἄλλο, οἷον ἀπεδανός, ἠπεδανός, αἱμοπόται αἱμηπόται, μέλαξ μάλαξ καὶ τὰ ὅμοια. τμῆσις δέ ἐστι συνθέτου λέξεως διάλυσις εἰς δύο λέξεις, οἷον ἀκρόπολις πόλις ἄκρα, αἴγαγρον ἄγριον αἶγα.

Notes: Trypho's initial explanation of his subject, containing the definitions of some of his key terms; note the numerals. πάθος "modification"; γενικώτατα "very general [categories]"; διαιρέω "divide"; εἶδος: cf. 4.1.41; μετάληψις "substitution"; ὡς ἐν κεφαλαίῳ "to summarize, in short"; περισσότης "excess"; χρόνος "[vocalic] quantity"; στοιχεῖον "letter"; ἐλάττωσις "diminution"; μετακίνησις "dislocation, change"; ἐναλλαγή "interchange"; ὑπέρθεσις "transposition"; ἐπ᾽ ἀντίστοιχον ἄλλο "into another corresponding one" [i.e. into one of its corresponding letters; in ancient theory letters like π and φ or τ and θ were ἀντίστοιχος to each other]; σύνθετος "compound"; διάλυσις "separation."

192. Gregory of Corinth, *On Dialects*, ed. Schaefer, pp. 9–12

Διάλεκτός ἐστιν ἰδίωμα γλώσσης, ἢ διάλεκτός ἐστι λέξις ἴδιον χαρακτῆρα τόπου ἐμφαίνουσα. Ἰὰς ἐκλήθη ἀπὸ τοῦ Ἴωνος, τοῦ υἱοῦ τοῦ Ἀπόλλωνος, καὶ Κρεούσης, τῆς Ἐρεχθέως θυγατρὸς, ᾗ ἔγραψεν Ὅμηρος. Ἀτθὶς ἀπὸ τῆς Ἀτθίδος, τῆς Κραναοῦ θυγατρὸς, ᾗ ἔγραψεν Ἀριστοφάνης. Δωρὶς ἀπὸ Δώρου, τοῦ Ἕλληνος, ᾗ ἔγραψε Θεόκριτος. Αἰολὶς ἀπὸ Αἰόλου, τοῦ Ἕλληνος, ᾗ ἔγραψεν Ἀλκαῖος. Κοινὴ δὲ, ᾗ πάντες χρώμεθα, καὶ ᾗ ἐχρήσατο Πίνδαρος, ἤγουν ἡ ἐκ τῶν δ συνεστῶσα. Ἑκάστη δὲ διάλεκτος ἔχει οἰκεῖον ἰδίωμα.

Notes: ἰδίωμα "peculiarity"; Ἰάς "Ionic dialect"; ᾗ "in which [dialect]"; Ἀτθίς "Attic dialect"; Δωρίς "Doric dialect"; Ἕλλην is a man's name here; Αἰολίς "Aeolic"; Κοινή "common dialect" [supply "is the dialect"]; ἤγουν "or rather," "i.e."; δ̄ is equivalent to δʹ here.

193. Gregory of Corinth, *On Dialects*, ed. Schaefer, pp. 179–82

Τὰ πρῶτα πρόσωπα τῶν πληθυντικῶν ἐνεργητικῶν, οἷον τύπτομεν, ποιοῦμεν, τύπτομες καὶ ποιοῦμες λέγουσι.

Τῶν παρατατικῶν παθητικῶν ὁριστικῶν καὶ τῶν ἐνεστώτων τὰ πρῶτα πρόσωπα τῶν πληθυντικῶν, οἷον τυπτόμεθα, ποιούμεθα, ἐτυπτόμεθα, ἐποιούμεθα, ποιούμεσθα λέγουσι καὶ τυπτόμεσθα, καὶ ἐποιούμεσθα, ἐτυπτόμεσθα. ὡς Θεόκριτος·

Οἳ θνατοὶ πελόμεσθα, τὸ δ’ αὔριον οὐκ ἐσορῶμες. τοῦτο ἔστι καὶ Ἰωνικόν.

Τὸ η εἰς α μακρὸν τρέπουσι, τὴν σελήνην σελάναν λέγοντες, καὶ τὸν ἥλιον ἄλιον, καὶ τὸ σήμερον σάμερον.

Notes: the unexpressed subject is the speakers of Doric; cf. 4.2.11, 13 for vocabulary; ἐνεργητικός "active"; παθητικός "passive." The quotation is from Theocritus 13. 4.

194. Dionysius Thrax, Τέχνη, ch. 15 (from *GG* i.i), 60. 1ff.

Μετοχή ἐστι λέξις μετέχουσα τῆς τῶν ῥημάτων καὶ τῆς τῶν ὀνομάτων ἰδιότητος. Παρέπεται δὲ αὐτῇ ταὐτὰ ἃ καὶ τῷ ὀνόματι καὶ τῷ ῥήματι δίχα προσώπων τε καὶ ἐγκλίσεων.

Notes: cf. 4.2.4, 10, 13 for vocabulary; μετέχω "have a share of"; ἰδιότης "individual nature"; παρέπομαι + dat. "be an accident of"; δίχα + gen. "apart from."

195. Dionysius Thrax, Supplement Περὶ προσῳδιῶν (from *GG* i.i), 105. 1ff.

Προσῳδίαι εἰσὶ δέκα· ὀξεῖα ´, βαρεῖα `, περισπωμένη ~, μακρά –, βραχεῖα ˘, δασεῖα ῾, ψιλή ᾿, ἀπόστροφος ᾿, ὑφέν ‿, ὑποδιαστολή „. [τούτων εἰσὶν σημεῖα τάδε· ὀξεῖα οἷον Ζεύς, βαρεῖα οἷον Πὰν, περισπωμένη οἷον πῦρ, μακρὰ οἷον Ἥρα, βραχεῖα οἷον γὰρ, δασεῖα οἷον ῥῆμα, ψιλὴ οἷον ἄρτος, ἀπόστροφος οἷον ὣς ἔφατ’, ὑφέν ὣς πασι‿μέλουσα <μ 70>, ὑποδιαστολή "Δία δ’ οὐκ ἔχεν, ἥδυμος ὕπνος" <Β 2 >.]

Notes: cf. 4.2.6–9 for vocabulary; the adjectives in the first sentence are feminine because they modify an understood προσῳδία; ἀπόστροφος "apostrophe"; ὑφέν "hyphen" (a sign written below two consecutive letters to show that they belong to the same word); ὑποδιαστολή "mark showing word division"; note that in the example given a word divider is needed because ἔχε νήδυμος is also possible (and indeed is the reading of this line in modern texts).

196. Dionysius Thrax, "Scholia" (from *GG* i.iii), 239. 14ff.

Εἰς τὸ αὐτὸ καὶ ἄλλως.—Στεφάνου.—Διαφέρει πευστικὸν ἐρωτηματικοῦ· τῷ γὰρ ἐρωτηματικῷ ἀποχρήσει τὸ ναί ἢ τὸ οὔ, καὶ ἀνάνευσις ἢ ἐπίνευσις, τῷ δὲ <πευστικῷ> πάντως ἀποκρίσεως δεῖ· καὶ ἡ μὲν ἐρώτησις ἐπὶ παντὸς μέρους λόγου <γίνεται>, ἡ δὲ πεῦσις ἐπ’ ὀνομάτων ἢ ἐπιρρημάτων.

Notes: the formula at the beginning does not mean "see . . ." but indicates that this is the second scholion (cf. 4.1.5) on a lemma given earlier (Ἐρωτηματικὸν δέ ἐστιν, ὃ καὶ πευστικὸν καλεῖται, τὸ κατ᾽ ἐρώτησιν λεγόμενον, οἷον τίς ποῖος πόσος πηλίκος) and gives the source of the information (in the genitive); πευστικόν and ἐρωτηματικόν refer to words used in questions and could both be translated "interrogative" in English, while πεῦσις and ἐρώτησις refer to questions asked with those words and could both be translated "interrogation"; ἀποχράω "suffice"; ἀνάνευσις i.e. upward nod, meaning "no"; ἐπίνευσις i.e. downward nod, meaning "yes"; ἐπί: cf. 4.1.31; μέρος λόγου: cf. 4.2.10; understand "only" at the end. The point of the last section is that questions that are not yes/no questions can begin only with pronouns (e.g. τίς; ὄνομα here is clearly to be taken in its most general sense, which includes pronouns) or adverbs (e.g. πῶς).

197. Dionysius Thrax, "Scholia" (from GG i.iii), 250. 26ff.

Εἰς τὸ αὐτὸ καὶ ἄλλως.—Cτεφάνου.—Τὸν ἐνεστῶτα οἱ Cτωϊκοὶ ἐνεστῶτα παρατατικὸν ὁρίζονται, ὅτι παρατείνεται καὶ εἰς ‹παρεληλυθότα καὶ εἰς› μέλλοντα· ὁ γὰρ λέγων "ποιῶ" καὶ ὅτι ἐποίησέ τι ἐμφαίνει καὶ ὅτι ποιήσει· τὸν δὲ παρατατικὸν παρῳχημένον παρατατικόν· ὁ γὰρ ‹λέγων› "ἐποίουν" ὅτι τὸ πλέον ἐποίησεν ἐμφαίνει, οὔπω δὲ πεπλήρωκεν, ἀλλὰ ποιήσει μέν, ἐν ὀλίγῳ δὲ χρόνῳ· εἰ γὰρ τὸ παρῳχημένον πλέον, τὸ λεῖπον ὀλίγον· ὃ καὶ προσληφθὲν ποιήσει τέλειον παρῳχηκότα, τὸν γέγραφα, ὃς καλεῖται παρακείμενος διὰ τὸ πλησίον ἔχειν τὴν συντέλειαν τῆς ἐνεργείας· ὁ τοίνυν ἐνεστὼς καὶ παρατατικὸς ὡς ἀτελεῖς ἄμφω συγγενεῖς, διὸ καὶ τοῖς αὐτοῖς συμφώνοις χρῶνται, οἷον τύπτω ἔτυπτον.

Notes: this scholion (which continues beyond the portion quoted here) is famous as being the foundation for our understanding of the Stoic analysis of tenses; see Lallot (1998: 174–9), Caujolle-Zaslawsky (1985), and Wouters (1994: 98–102). It is the second scholion on the lemma ὧν συγγένειαί εἰσι τρεῖς, ἐνεστῶτος πρὸς παρατατικόν, παρακειμένου πρὸς ὑπερσυντέλικον, ἀορίστου πρὸς μέλλοντα. cf. 4.2.13 for vocabulary; ὁρίζομαι "define"; παρατείνω "extend"; ἐμφαίνω "reveal"; πληρόω i.e. finish; ἐν + dat. for genitive of time; understand ἐστί before πλέον and ὀλίγον; ὃ is the subject of ποιήσει; προσλαμβάνω "take in addition"; παρῳχηκώς "past"; τὸν γέγραφα: understand χρόνον; πλησίον (adverb) "near"; συντέλεια "completion"; ἐνέργεια "action"; ἀτελής "incomplete"; διό "on account of which."

198. Herodian, Περὶ μονήρους λέξεως, ed. Lentz (GG iii.ii), 931. 20ff.

"Απαξ. τὰ εἰς αξ̄ λήγοντα ἐπιρρήματα ὀξύνεcθαι θέλει, ὀκλάξ, ὀδάξ, ἐναλλάξ, εὐράξ, αὐτοδάξ, ἐπιτάξ· ἀλλὰ μόνον τὸ ἄπαξ βαρύνεται. ὅπερ ἐν cυντάξει τοῦ ἄπαντες ἢ τοῦ ἁπλῶς ἐκκλίνει τὸν τόνον ὡcεὶ ὀξύνοιτο τὸ ἄπαξ. ἀπαξάπαντας γὰρ λέγομεν καὶ ἀπαξάπλῶς ἐν τῇ ἀνὰ χεῖρα ὁμιλίᾳ.

Notes: cf. 4.1.29, 4.2.7, 9, 10 for vocabulary; θέλω i.e. "have a tendency to"; σύνταξις + gen "combination with"; ἐκκλίνω "turn away" (i.e. lose); τόνος "accent"; ἀνὰ χεῖρα "current, everyday"; ὁμιλία "conversation." Ἀπαξάπαντας and ἀπαξάπλῶς must be written as ἅπαξ ἅπαντας and ἅπαξ ἁπλῶς in modern notation to capture the sense of the passage.

199. Herodian, Περὶ καθολικῆς προσῳδίας, from Schmidt's edition of [Arcadius'] epitome, 162. 11ff.

> Πᾶν ἐγκλινόμενον μόριον ἢ ὀξύνεται ἢ περισπᾶται, οὐδὲν δὲ βαρύνεται. ὀκτὼ δὲ ὄντων τῶν μερῶν τοῦ λόγου τὰ πέντε ἐγκλίνονται· ὄνομα ῥῆμα ἀντωνυμία ἐπίρρημα σύνδεσμος. πάλιν τῶν ἐγκλινομένων τὰ μὲν χάριν κόσμου ἐγκλίνονται, ὡς τὰ ῥήματα καὶ οἱ σύνδεσμοι, τὰ δὲ σημασίας, ὡς τὰ λοιπά. ἐν μὲν οὖν ὀνόμασι τὸ ΤΙΣ μόνον ἐγκλίνεται καὶ αἱ τούτου πτώσεις καὶ οἱ ἀριθμοὶ καὶ τὸ οὐδέτερον· ἄνθρωπός τις, ἤκουσά τινος, ἔδωκά τινι, ἐδίδαξά τινα καὶ ἐπὶ τῶν λοιπῶν ὡσαύτως. καὶ τὰ ἰσοδυναμοῦντα τούτοις ΤΟΥ καὶ ΤΩΙ· ἤκουσά του, ἔδωκά τῳ. ταῦτα δὲ ἐγκλινόμενα, ὡς πρόκειται, ἀόριστά εἰσι. Τὸν δὲ κατὰ φύσιν τόνον ἔχοντα πυσματικὰ γίνονται· τίς τίνος τίνι τίνα.

Notes: cf. 4.2.7–11 for vocabulary; ἐγκλίνομαι "be enclitic," "be able to be enclitic"; μόριον "word"; χάριν κόσμου "for decoration"; σημασία "meaning"; ἐπί: cf. 4.1.31; ὡσαύτως "in the same way"; ἰσοδυναμέω "be equivalent" (here = be the alternate forms of τινος and τινι), ὡς πρόκειται = "as we said earlier"; ἀόριστος "indefinite"; κατὰ φύσιν τόνος "natural [i.e. non-enclitic] accent"; πυσματικός "interrogative."

200. Herodian, Περὶ καθολικῆς προσῳδίας, from Schmidt's edition of [Arcadius'] epitome, 198. 18ff.

> Πᾶς παρῳχημένος ὁριστικὸς ἀπὸ φωνήεντος ἀρχόμενος καὶ ἀπὸ φύσει μακρᾶς τὸν αὐτὸν φυλάττει τόνον καὶ ἐν τῇ συνθέσει· εἶχον κατεῖχον, ἦψα συνῆψα, εἶπον ἐξεῖπον, εὗρον ἐξεῦρον, πλὴν τοῦ εἶξεν ὑπόειξεν, εἶκον ἐπίεικον. τὸ δὲ οἶδα σύνοιδα Αἰολικόν· χαίρουσι γὰρ οἱ Αἰολεῖς ἀναβιβάζειν τοὺς τόνους, ὥσπερ ἐπὶ τοῦ Ἀτρεύς Ἄτρευς. πρόσκειται "ἀπὸ φωνήεντος ἀρχόμενα" διὰ τὸ σχές περίσχες, κεῖτο κατέκειτο. πρόσκειται "ἀπὸ φύσει μακρᾶς" διὰ τὸ ἵζε ἔφιζε. πρόσκειται "ὁριστικὸς" διὰ τὸ εἰπέ ἔξειπε, εὑρέ ἔφευρε.

Notes: cf. 4.2.4, 7, 13 for vocabulary; ἀπὸ φύσει μακρᾶς "from [a syllable] long by nature," i.e. beginning with a long vowel; φυλάττω "preserve"; σύνθεσις "composition"; ἀναβιβάζω "retract"; πρόσκειμαι: cf. 4.1.37; ἵζε: the argument requires ἵζε with short ι, and this form is found here in the manuscripts, but the editor has substituted ἵζε, presumably because it is the more common form (ἵζε is the unaugmented imperfect and ἵζε the augmented one). Nowadays the rule given in this passage is expressed differently, by saying that if a verb form has the augment, the accent cannot go further back than the syllable with the augment.

201. Apollonius Dyscolus, ed. Uhlig (*GG* ii.ii), *Syntax* 51. 1ff.

> Προφανῶν οὐσῶν τῶν τοιούτων συντάξεων οἰήσονταί τινες, κἂν μὴ παραλάβωσι τὸν λόγον, διασῴζειν τὰ τῆς συντάξεως. οὗτοι

δὲ ὅμοιόν τι πείcονται τοῖc ἐκ τριβῆc τὰ cχήματα τῶν λέξεων παρειληφόcιν, οὐ μὴν ἐκ δυνάμεωc τῶν κατὰ παράδοcιν τῶν Ἑλλήνων καὶ τῆc cυμπαρεπομένηc ἐν αὐτοῖc ἀναλογίαc· οἷc παρακολουθεῖ τὸ εἰ διαμάρτοιεν ἔν τινι cχήματι μὴ δύναcθαι διορθοῦν τὸ ἁμάρτημα διὰ τὴν παρακολουθοῦcαν αὐτοῖc ἀπειρίαν.

καθάπερ οὖν πάμπολλόc ἐcτιν ἡ εὐχρηcτία τῆc κατὰ τὸν Ἑλληνιcμὸν παραδόcεωc, κατορθοῦcα μὲν τὴν τῶν ποιημάτων ἀνάγνωcιν τήν τε ἀνὰ χεῖρα ὁμιλίαν, καὶ ἔτι ἐπικρίνουcα τὴν παρὰ τοῖc ἀρχαίοιc θέcιν τῶν ὀνομάτων, τὸν αὐτὸν δὴ τρόπον καὶ ἡ προκειμένη ζήτηcιc τῆc καταλληλότητοc τὰ ὁπωcδήποτε διαπεcόντα ἐν λόγῳ κατορθώcει.

Notes: Apollonius explains why even native speakers of Greek need to study the rules of syntax. προφανής "clear"; σύνταξις "construction"; κἄν "even if"; παραλαμβάνω "grasp"; λόγον "theory" (i.e. the theory behind the construction); διασώζω "preserve"; i.e. "use correctly"; τὰ τῆς συντάξεως = τὴν σύνταξιν (cf. 4.1.25); πείσονται is from πάσχω here; τριβή "use, practice"; σχῆμα "form"; λέξις "word"; τῶν κατὰ παράδοσιν τῶν Ἑλλήνων ("of the things to do with the tradition of the Greeks," cf. 4.1.25) here refers to the written tradition of Greek; συμπαρέπομαι ἐν "to be attached to"; αὐτοῖς i.e. the forms; ἀναλογία "morphological regularity"; παρακολουθέω "to befall" (the subject here is an articular infinitive); διορθόω "correct"; καθάπερ "just as"; εὐχρηστία "utility"; Ἑλληνισμός "correct Greek usage"; κατορθόω "to correct"; ποιήματα i.e. ancient poems; ἀνάγνωσις "reading"; ἀνὰ χεῖρα "current, everyday"; ὁμιλία "usage"; ἐπικρίνω "to determine"; θέσις "application" (i.e. meaning); ὄνομα "word"; προκείμενος "present"; καταλληλότης "grammatical regularity"; διαπίπτω "to be wrong"; λόγος "speech."

6

Glossary of Grammatical Terms

THIS SECTION IS NOT A COMPLETE DICTIONARY, BUT A glossary giving in most cases only the grammatical meanings of the words included; these words are also used by scholarly writers in their non-technical senses on occasion. For such meanings and fuller information on these words, including citations of passages in which they occur, see LSJ and Bécares Botas (1985). A selection of references is given here to other works in which individual terms are discussed; such references are normally given only once but should be understood to apply to closely related words as well (e.g. a discussion of ἀμφιβολία will normally be useful for understanding ἀμφίβολος as well).

The state of scholarship on Greek grammatical terminology is not one that would make it possible for a glossary of this type to be completely reliable. The only specialized dictionary (Bécares Botas 1985) is full of errors, the information in LSJ is seriously incomplete, and other discussions are widely scattered, incomplete, and often unreliable. There is a great need for a thorough, accurate study of this vocabulary—and this glossary is not intended to address that need, only to help learners to get through texts. For lack of anything better, the information given here is based on that in Bécares Botas (1985) and LSJ, corrected and supplemented from a wide range of other sources.

ἀβαρβάριστος, -ον   without barbarisms
ἄγμα, -ατος, τό   velar nasal (the sound represented by γ in words like ἄγκυρα)
ἀγράμματος, -ον   inarticulate, indistinct, incapable of being written
ἀγωγή = παραγωγή
ἄδεια, -ας, ἡ (ποιητική)   poetic license; see Lallot (1997: ii. 40, cf. 170)
ἀδιάβατος, -ον   intransitive
ἀδιαβίβαστος, -ον   intransitive
ἀδιαίρετος, -ον   undivided, contracted, without διαίρεσις
ἀδιάκριτος, -ον   indistinguishable
ἀδιάπταιστος, -ον = ἀδιάπτωτος
ἀδιάπτωτος, -ον   not using cases at random; uninflected
ἀδιάστατος, -ον   inseparable (of iota in diphthongs, not forming a separate syllable)

ἀδιάστολος, -ον   not distinguished

ἀδιάστροφος, -ον   strictly accurate

ἀδιαφορέω   to make or have no difference, not to agree

ἀδιαφορία, -ας, ἡ   equivalence (of signification, of metrical quantity)

ἀδιάφορος, -ον   having/making no difference; common (in meter), anceps

ἀδιαχώριστος, -ον   inseparable, undistinguished

ἀδίπλ(ασι)αστος, -ον   not doubled (of letters)

ἀδίπλωτος, -ον   not doubled (of letters)

ἀδόκιμος, -ον   not approved, not accepted

ἀήθης, -ες   unused, unusual

ἄθροισις, -εως, ἡ   collection

ἀθροιστικός, -ή, -όν   collective (of nouns), copulative (of conjunctions); see Lallot
   (1997: ii. 104)

αἰολίζω   to speak in Aeolic dialect, use Aeolic forms

αἰτέω   to require, postulate

αἰτιατικός, -ή, -όν   causal; accusative, αἰτιατική (πτῶσις) the accusative case;
   see Lallot (1998: 146–8), Dalimier (2001: 345–6), De Mauro (1965)

αἰτιολογικός, -ή, -όν   causal (of conjunctions, clauses, etc.); see Lallot (1998:
   247–9)

αἰτιώδης, -ες   causal (of conjunctions, etc.)

ἀκαταλληλία, -ας, ἡ   incorrect agreement

ἀκατάλληλος, -ον   ungrammatical, lacking in concord

ἀκαταλληλότης, -ητος, ἡ   incorrect agreement

ἀκατάστατος, -ον   irregular, unstable

ἀκατάχρηστος, -ον   unused

ἀκινητίζω   to remain uninflected

ἀκίνητος, -ον   not inflected, unmodified (of a noun in the nom. sing. or a verb
   in the first-person sing.), invariable

ἀκλισία, -ας, ἡ   indeclinability

ἄκλιτος, -ον   indeclinable; (as neut. subst., a term for adverbs, prepositions, and
   conjunctions as a class)

ἀκοινώνητος, -ον   having no share of; incompatible; distinct

ἀκόλλητος, -ον   incombinable

ἀκολουθέω   to follow analogy of, follow logically

ἀκολουθία, -ας, ἡ   consequence, analogy, agreement

ἀκόλουθος, -ον   regular, consistent with, in accordance with, analogical; see
   Sluiter (1990: 84)

ἀκυρ(ι)ολέκτητος, -ον   incorrectly used

ἀκυρολεξία, -ας, ἡ   incorrect phraseology

ἀκυρολογέω   to speak incorrectly

ἀκυρολογία, -ας, ἡ   incorrect phraseology

ἄκυρος, -ον   used in improper sense

ἄληκτος, -ον   without ending

ἀλλεπαλληλία, -ας, ἡ   accumulation, succession (lit. one-on-anotherness) ἀλλεπάλληλος, -ον   successive, cumulative, varied (of style)

ἀλλόγλωσσος, -ον   foreign

ἀλλοίωσις, -εως, ἡ   difference, varied construction, change

ἀλλοπαθής, -ές   transitive (of verbs), non-reflexive (of pronouns)

ἄλλως   alternatively (used in scholia to introduce a second or subsequent note on a single lemma; cf. 4.1.5)

ἀλογέομαι   to be irregular

ἀλογία, -ας, ἡ   irregularity, irrationality (in meter); cf. ἄλογος

ἄλογος, -ον   irregular, irrational (= not able to be expressed by a simple ratio, of feet or syllables in meter); ἄλογος (γραμμή) critical sign marking corrupt or doubtful passages

ἀλφάβητος, -ου, ὁ   alphabet

ἀμάρτυρος, -ον   unattested

ἀμερής, -ές   indivisible

ἀμετάβατος, -ον   intransitive (of verbs), reflexive (of pronouns)

ἀμετάβλητος, -ον   unchanging, uninflected

ἀμετάβολος, -ον   immutable; unchanging (of pure vowels as opposed to diphthongs); without modulation (of music); ἀμετάβολον (γράμμα) liquid or nasal consonant (λ, ρ, μ, ν)

ἀμετάθετος, -ον   uninflected, unchanging

ἀμετάληπτος, -ον   not to be substituted; having no equivalent

ἀμετάπτωτος, -ον   unchanging

ἀμετάστατος, -ον   unchanging

ἀμετάφραστος, -ον   untranslatable, inexplicable, not etymologizable

ἀμοιβή, -ῆς, ἡ   change

ἀμοιρέω   to lack

ἀμφιβάλλομαι   to be doubtful, be in dispute, be ambiguous

ἀμφιβολία, -ας, ἡ   ambiguity, doubt

ἀμφίβολος, -ον   ambiguous, doubtful

ἀμφίγλωσσος, -ον   ambiguous

ἀμφίδοξος, -ον   ambiguous, doubtful

ἀμφίλεκτος, -ον   doubtful

ἀμφότερος, -α, -ον = ἐπίκοινος

ἀναβιβάζω   to retract (the accent)

ἀναβιβασμός, -οῦ, ὁ   retraction (of the accent)

ἀνάγνωσις, -εως, ἡ   reading (esp. in textual criticism), reading aloud; see Lallot (1997: ii. 268–9, 1998: 75–7, 83–6)

ἀνάγνωσμα, -ατος, τό = ἀνάγνωσις

ἀναγνωστέον   one must read

ἀναγραμματίζω   to transpose letters of one word to form another

ἀναγραμματισμός, -οῦ, ὁ   transpostion of letters of one word to form another

ἀνάγω   to derive, form

ἀναδίδωμι   to retract (the accent)

ἀναδιπλασιάζω   to reduplicate

ἀναδίπλασι(ασι)ς, -εως, ἡ   reduplication
ἀναδιπλασιασμός, -οῦ, ὁ   reduplication
ἀναδιπλόω   to reduplicate
ἀναδίπλωσις, -εως, ἡ   reduplication
ἀνάδοσις, -εως, ἡ   retraction (of the accent)
ἀναδρομή, -ῆς, ἡ   retraction (of the accent); transformation of (third-decl.)
    genitives in -ος into (second-decl.) nominatives in -ος.
ἀναίρεσις, -εως, ἡ   negation, privation, removal
ἀναιρετικός, -ή, -όν   negative, privative, adversative (of conjunctions)
ἀναιρέω   to annul, negate
ἀνακεφαλαιωτικός, -ή, -όν   for summary, recapitulative
ἀνακεχωρικώς, -υῖα, -ός   obsolete
ἀνάκλησις, -εως, ἡ   invocation
ἀνακολουθία, -ας, ἡ   anomaly
ἀνακόλουθος, -ον   irregular, anomalous
ἀνάκρισις, -εως, ἡ   inquiry
ἀνακριτικός, -ή, -όν   interrogative
ἀναλογ(ητ)ικός, -ή, -όν   analogical; teaching analogy
ἀναλογία, -ας, ἡ   analogy, regularity; see Lallot (1998: 80–1)
ἀναλογιστικός, -ή, -όν   analogical, judging by analogy; teaching analogy
ἀνάλογος, -ον   regular, analogical
ἀνάλυσις, -εως, ἡ   resolution, analysis
ἀναλύω   to resolve (into its elements), analyze; see Lallot (1997: ii. 55,
    127–8)
ἀναμερίζω   to distribute, distinguish; see Lallot (1997: ii. 169–70)
ἀναμερισμός, -οῦ, ὁ   redistribution
ἀναμφίβολος, -ον   certain, unambiguous
ἀναμφίλεκτος, -ον   indisputed, undoubted, unambiguous
ἀνανταπόδοσις, -εως, ἡ   suppressed apodosis
ἀνανταπόδοτος, -ον   without apodosis (of a protasis by itself)
ἀνάπαυσις, -εως, ἡ   pause; cadence (of a period)
ἀναπέμπω   to throw back (the accent, esp. of enclitics); to refer
ἀνάπεμψις, -εως, ἡ   throwing back (of the accent)
ἀναπληρόω   to complete
ἀναπληρωματικός, -ή, -όν   expletive (= used for filling up, for completing)
ἀναπλήρωσις, -εως, ἡ   completion
ἀναπόδοτος, -ον   without apodosis (of a protasis by itself)
ἀναπολέω   to repeat, refer
ἀναπόλησις, -εως, ἡ   repetition, relation, reference
ἀνάπτυξις, -εως, ἡ   insertion of a vowel between two consonants
ἄναρθρος, -ον   avoiding the use of the article
ἀναρτάομαι   to depend
ἀναστρέφομαι   to be subject to anastrophe

ἀναστροφή, -ῆς, ἡ   anastrophe (retraction of the accent, esp. in prepositions placed after their objects); inversion of a natural order; repetition of words that close one sentence at the start of another; see Lallot (1998: 217–18)

ἀνάτασις, -εως, ἡ   raising (of pitch of voice in acute accent)

ἀνατάσσω   to retract (the accent)

ἀνατρεπτικός, -ή, -όν   privative

ἀνατρέπω   to be irregular

ἀνατρέχω   to throw back (the accent)

ἀναττικός, -όν   not Attic

ἀναυξησία, -ας, ἡ   omission of the augment

ἀναύξητος, -ον   without augment

ἀναφορά, -ᾶς, ἡ   reference, repetition (of a word), relation, anaphora

ἀναφορικός, -ή, -όν   relative (of pronouns, etc.); see Dalimier (2001: 427–32)

ἀναφώνημα, -ατος, τό   interjection, exclamation

ἀναφωνητικός, -ή, -όν   exclamatory

ἀνέγκλιτος, -ον   not enclitic

ἀνειμένος, -η, -ον   unaccented

ἀνεκφώνητος, -ον   not pronounced (of iota subscript, etc.)

ἀνελλ(ε)ιπής, -ές   not defective

ἀνελλήνιστος, -ον   not Greek

ἀνενδοίαστος, -ον   unquestionably correct

ἀνεπέκτατος, -ον   not lengthened; parisyllabic (of declensions)

ἀνερμήνευτος, -ον   inexplicable

ἄνεσις, -εως, ἡ   relaxation of the voice (on unaccented syllables)

ἀνέτυμ(ολόγητ)ος, -ον   of unknown derivation

ἀνέφικτος, -ον   grammatically impossible, forbidden

ἀνθυπάγω   to reply; to substitute; (mid.) to correspond; see Lallot (1997: ii. 98)

ἀνθυπαγωγή, -ῆς, ἡ   reply

ἀνθυπαλλαγή, -ῆς, ἡ   substitution (of one case or mood for another)

ἀνθυπαλλάσσω   to substitute one case for another, change moods

ἀνθυπ(εισ)έρχομαι   to take the place of

ἀνθυποφέρω   to use (a word or phrase) in reply

ἀνθυποφορά, -ᾶς, ἡ   reply

ἀνομοιογενής, -ές   with different gender

ἀνομοιοκατάληκτος, -ον   with different ending

ἀνομοιόπτωτος, -ον   with different inflection, in a different case

ἀνομοιόχρονος, -ον   of dissimilar quantity

ἀνόξυντος, -ον   not to be written with an acute accent

ἀντανακλάομαι   to be reflexive (of pronouns)

ἀντανάκλασις, -εως, ἡ   use of a word in an altered sense

ἀντανακλασμός, -οῦ, ὁ   reciprocal or reflexive sense (of pronouns)

ἀντανάκλαστος, -ον   reciprocal, reflexive (of pronouns)

ἀνταναπληρόω   to fill up, complete

ἀνταποδίδομαι   to correspond with, be correlative to, make to correspond with; see Lallot (1997: ii. 302)

ἀνταπόδοσις, -εως, ἡ   correspondence; parallelism (of clauses in a period); correlation; correlative clause

ἀνταποδοτικός, -ή, -όν   correlative

ἀντέμφασις, -εως, ἡ   distinction; antithesis

ἀντεξέτασις, -εως, ἡ   distinction, comparison

ἀντί: ἀντὶ τοῦ,   instead of (i.e. x ἀντὶ τοῦ y can mean "x means y here," "y is what one would expect instead of x here," or "x is an alternate reading for y here"; see Slater 1989a: 53–4)

ἀντιβολή, -ῆς, ἡ   discussion, confrontation; see Dalimier (2001: 230)

ἀντιβραχύς, -εῖα, -ύ   functioning like a short vowel

ἀντίγραφον, -ου, τό   copy, manuscript

ἀντιδιασταλτικός, -ή, -όν   distinctive, opposed

ἀντιδιαστέλλω   to distinguish, oppose

ἀντιδιαστολή, -ῆς, ἡ   distinction, opposition

ἀντίθεσις, -εως, ἡ   antithesis (in rhetoric), transposition or change (of a letter)

ἀντίθετος, -ον   opposed; (as neut. subst.) antithesis

ἀντίκειμαι   to be opposed, be an exception, be in opposition

ἀντίληψις, -εως, ἡ   understanding, apprehension, intuition; see Lallot (1997: ii. 168)

ἀντιμεταβολή, -ῆς, ἡ   transposition (as a figure of speech)

ἀντιμεταλαμβάνω   to substitute (one form for another); to change

ἀντιμετάληψις, -εως, ἡ   interchange of forms

ἀντιμεταχώρησις, -εως, ἡ   interchange of letters

ἀντιπαθέω   to be affected

ἀντιπαραβάλλω   to compare

ἀντιπαραδέχομαι   to admit instead of

ἀντιπαράθεσις, -εως, ἡ   contrast, comparison

ἀντιπαράκειμαι   to correspond with, be correlative to, be opposed to

ἀντιπαραλαμβάνομαι   to be used in place of

ἀντιπαρατίθημι   to compare

ἀντιπαραχώρησις, -εως, ἡ   interchange of letters

ἀντιπεπονθώς, -υῖα, -ός   reflexive, reciprocal (of verbs)

ἀντιπεριποιέομαι   to express reciprocal action (of verbs)

ἀντιπίπτω   to be irregular

ἀντιπροηγέομαι   to precede instead of following

ἀντίπτωσις, -εως, ἡ   exchange of cases

ἀντιπτωτικός, -ή, -όν   pertaining to interchange of cases

ἀντιστοιχείωσις, -εως, ἡ   change of a letter

ἀντιστοιχέω   to correspond (of letters, as π to φ and τ to θ); see Lallot (1998: 104)

ἀντιστοιχία, -ας, ἡ   correspondence (of letters)

ἀντίστοιχος, -ον   corresponding (of letters)

ἀντιστρέφω   to be inverted

ἀντιστροφή, -ῆς, ἡ   antistrophe (in meter); rhetorical figure consisting of closing words repeated in successive members; inversion of letters

ἀντίστροφος, -ον   antistrophic, (as fem. subst.) antistrophe

ἀντιτυπέω   to be dissonant

ἀντιτυπία, -ας, ἡ   dissonance

ἀντίτυπος, -ον   dissonant

ἀντίφρασις, -εως, ἡ   antiphrasis (the use of words in a sense opposite to their proper meaning, e.g. in a euphemism such as "Eumenides"); κατ' ἀντίφρασιν expression by means of negation (e.g. *lucus a non lucendo*, in etymology)

ἀντιφραστικῶς   by way of antiphrasis

ἀντιχρονία, -ας, ἡ = ἀντιχρονισμός

ἀντιχρονισμός, -οῦ, ὁ   use of one tense for another

ἀντονομάζω   to use epithets or rhetorical figures; to use a pronoun

ἀντονομασία, -ας, ἡ   use of epithets, patronymics, etc. instead of a proper name; pronoun; use of a pronoun

ἀντωνυμία, -ας, ἡ   pronoun (including possessive adjectives like ἐμός); see Lallot (1998: 198–210, 1999)

ἀντωνυμικός, -ή, -όν   pronominal

ἀντώνυμον, -ου, τό   pronoun

ἀνυπόκριτος (ὑπο)στιγμή   punctuation mark used in a simple sentence; see Blank (1983*a*)

ἀνυπόστατος, -ον   not existing

ἀνυπότακτος, -ον   having no first aorist (of verbs); not subordinate

ἀνύπτιος, -ον   not passive

ἀνύω   to complete

ἀνωμαλία, -ας, ἡ   anomaly, irregularity, variety

ἀνώμαλος, -ον   anomalous, irregular; diversity (as neut. subst.)

ἀξίωμα, -ατος, τό   postulate, axiom; logical proposition; speech, sentence

ἀξιωματικός, -ή, -όν   declarative, not interrogative or hypothetical etc.

ἀορισταίνω = ἀοριστόομαι

ἀοριστόομαι   to be indefinite

ἀόριστος, -ον   indefinite (of pronouns, etc.); aorist, ἀόριστος (χρόνος) the aorist tense; see Lallot (1998: 157, 172–3, 177), Petrilli (1997)

ἀοριστώδης, -ες   indefinite

ἀπαγόρευσις, -εως, ἡ   prohibition

ἀπαγορευτικός, -ή, -όν   prohibitory (e.g. of particles)

ἀπαθής, -ές   not changed, unmodified (e.g. of uncontracted forms); free from metrical licenses

ἀπαιτέω   to require (e.g. a certain case)

ἀπαναγιγνώσκω   to read wrongly

ἀπανάγνωσμα, -ατος, τό   faulty reading

ἅπαξ   once, very rarely, only in isolated cases

ἀπαράδεκτος, -ον   inadmissible, unacceptable

ἀπαράθετος, -ον   without quoted authority (of words and phrases)

ἀπαράλλακτος, -ον   indistinguishable; unchanging (of the accent)

ἀπαρασχημάτιστος, -ον   not parallel in formation; not corresponding

ἀπαρέμφατος, -ον   infinitive; not determinative or indicative; see Lallot (1998: 165–6)

ἀπαρνητικός, -ή, -όν   denying

ἀπάρτησις, -εως, ἡ   separation

ἀπαρτίζω   to express completely, to coincide with a sentence (of a line of verse), correspond precisely, be complete

ἀπαρτισμός, -οῦ, ὁ   completion

ἀπεκδέχομαι   to understand a word from the context

ἀπεκθλίβω   to elide, suppress (a letter)

ἀπέλευσις, -εως, ἡ   dropping out, elimination (of a letter)

ἀπεμφαίνω   to be incongruous, be inconsistent, be absurd, be discordant; to distinguish

ἀπενεκτική (πτῶσις)   Latin ablative case

ἀπέριττος, -ον   simple

ἀπλεόναστος, -ον   without an extra letter

ἁπλοϊκός, -ή, -όν = ἁπλοῦς

ἁπλότης, -ητος, ἡ   simplicity; positive degree

ἁπλοῦς, -ῆ, -οῦν   simple, uncompounded (of words or consonants); in the positive degree; without the article

ἀποβάλλω   to lose, drop (a word or letter)

ἀποβλητικός, -ή, -όν   tending to throw off

ἀποβολή, -ῆς, ἡ   removal (of a word or letter), rejection

ἀπόγραφος, -ου, ὁ (or ἀπόγραφον, -ου, τό)   copy

ἀποδεικτικός, -ή, -όν   demonstrative

ἀποδίδωμι   to produce an apodosis or conclusion

ἀποδοκιμάζω   to reject

ἀπόδοσις, -εως, ἡ   explanation, interpretation; apodosis; conclusion

ἀποδοτικός, -ή, -όν   correlative

ἀποθετικός, -ή, -όν   deponent (of verbs)

ἀποθλίβω   to drop a letter in the middle of the word, or a word in the middle of the sentence

ἀποκομιστική (πτῶσις)   Latin ablative case

ἀποκοπή, -ῆς, ἡ   apocope (cutting off of one or more letters, especially at the end of a word); abruptness; elliptical expression

ἀπολείπων, -ουσα, -ον   incomplete

ἀπολελυμένος, -η, -ον   absolute; general; in the positive (as opposed to comparative); unaccented; (of meter) without strophic responsion; see Swiggers and Wouters (1995a), Wouters (1993)

ἀπολυτικός, -ή, -όν = ἀπόλυτος

ἀπόλυτος, -ον   absolute; (as neut. subst.) positive degree (as opposed to comparative); independent ἀποξενόομαι   to be foreign, outlandish

ἀποπίπτω   to drop out (of letters in a word)

ἀπορηματικός, -ή, -όν   expressing doubt; interrogative; see Lallot (1998: 249–52)

ἀπορητικός, -ή, -όν   dubitative (of adverbs, etc.)

ἀποσβεννύω   to quench, esp. to quench the accent (i.e. change acute to grave)

ἀπόστασις, -εως, ἡ   separation, asyndeton

ἀποστρέφω   to elide

ἀποστροφή, -ῆς, ἡ   apostrophe (address to an individual); elision

ἀπόστροφος, -ου, ἡ   apostrophe (mark of elision), elision

ἀπότασις, -εως, ἡ   reference

ἀποτείνω   to refer to

ἀποτελεσ(μα)τικός, -ή, -όν   final (having to do with purpose); having to do with result; see Dalimier (2001: 356–8)

ἀποτελεσμός, -οῦ, ὁ   purpose clause

ἀποτελέω   to form, produce

ἀποτερματίζω   to define, end

ἀποφαίνομαι   to declare; see Lallot (1997: ii. 207–8)

ἀποφαντικός, -ή, -όν   indicative (mood); not interrogative (of enclitic τις)

ἀπόφασις, -εως, ἡ   negation, negative particle, negative statement; see Lallot (1997: ii. 207–8)

ἀποφατικός, -ή, -όν   negative

ἀποφυγή, -ῆς, ἡ   opposition

ἀπρόσληπτος, -ον   not taking or admitting (a construction)

ἀπρόσωπος, -ον   impersonal (of verbs)

ἄπτωτος, -ον   indeclinable

ἀρθρικός, -ή, -όν   pertaining to the article

ἄρθρον, -ου, τό   article (προτακτικόν), relative pronoun (ὑποτακτικόν); see Lallot (1998: 191–4, 1999)

ἀριθμητικόν (ὄνομα)   cardinal number

ἀριθμός, -οῦ, ὁ   number; rhythm

᾽Αριστάρχειος, -α, -ον   of or pertaining to Aristarchus

ἀρκτικός, -ή, -όν   initial, placed at the beginning

ἁρμογή, -ῆς, ἡ   joining

ἄρνησις, -εως, ἡ   negation

ἀρνητικός, -ή, -όν   negative

ἄρροιζος, -ον   without the sound of the letter ρ

ἀρσενικός, -ή, -όν   masculine

ἄρσην, -εν   male, masculine

ἄρσις, -εως, ἡ   omission; (in rhythm) upbeat

ἀρτάομαι   to be construed with, depend on

ἀσήμαντος, -ον = ἄσημος

ἄσημος, -ον   without meaning

ἀσόλοικ(ιστ)ος, -ον   correct, without solecisms

ἀστιγής, -ές unpunctuated

ἀστιξία, -ας, ἡ lack of punctuation

ἀσύγκριτος, -ον without comparison, without the comparative form

ἀσύζυγος, -ον unique, without exact correspondence; not belonging to the same class or conjugation

ἀσυμβίβαστος, -ον not to be brought together, not to be harmonized

ἀσύμμικτος, -ον incapable of blending

ἀσυμφωνία, -ας, ἡ discord, anomaly

ἀσύμφωνος, -ον discordant, anomalous

ἀσυναίρετος, -ον uncontracted

ἀσυνάλειπτος, -ον without synaloephe (see συναλοιφή)

ἀσύναρθρος, -ον without an article

ἀσύνδετος, -ον without conjunctions

ἀσυνέγκλιτος, -ον not participating in enclisis, not entering into a chain of enclitics

ἀσυνέλευστος, -ον not forming a compound, not entering into composition

ἀσυνέμπτωτος, -ον not coinciding in form

ἀσύνετος, -ον unintelligible (probably also "ungrammatical" in Apollonius Dyscolus)

ἀσυνήθης, -ές not in use, not usual

ἀσυνθεσία, -ας, ἡ state of being uncompounded

ἀσύνθετος, -ον uncompounded, simplex

ἀσυντακτικός, -ή, -όν against the rules of syntax

ἀσύντακτος, -ον ungrammatical, irregular

ἀσυνταξία, -ας, ἡ error in construction, ungrammatical form; irregularity, incapacity of entering into construction

ἀσυνύπαρκτος, -ον unable to coexist

ἀσυστατέω not to exist (of forms), to be badly formed

ἀσύστατος, -ον irregular, inadmissible, not existing, badly formed

ἄτακτος, -ον irregular, anomalous

ἀτελής, -ές incomplete; ἀτελής (στιγμή) punctuation mark indicating less completion than the τελεία στιγμή; (of tense) the present and imperfect

'Ατθίς, -ίδος, ἡ Attic dialect

ἄτονος, -ον unaccented

ἄτρεπτος, -ον = ἀμετάβολος

ἀτριβής, -ές not in use

'Αττική (χρῆσις) Attic usage

'Αττικίζω to speak or write Attic or Atticizing Greek

'Αττίκισις, -εως, ἡ = 'Αττικισμός

'Αττικισμός, -οῦ, ὁ Attic style, Atticism

αὐθυπότακτος, -ον second aorist subjunctive; aorist subjunctive; independent subjunctive

αὐξάνω to augment, to take an augment

αὔξησις, -εως, ἡ augment, lengthening, intensification

αὐτενεργητικός, -ή, -όν = αὐτενέργητος

αὐτενέργητος, -ον   deponent (a verb active in meaning but passive in form)

αὐτοέκτατος, -ον   long because of containing a long vowel (of syllables "long by nature")

αὐτόθετος, -ον   self-placed, not derived

αὐτοπάθεια, -ας, ἡ   reflexivity, intransitivity

αὐτοπαθής, -ές   reflexive (of pronouns), intransitive (of verbs)

αὐτοπαθητικός, -όν = αὐτοπαθής

αὐτοσύστατος, -ον   not dependent

αὐτοτέλεια, -ας, ἡ   completeness, complete sentence; see Donnet (1967: 150–3)

αὐτοτελής, -ές   complete in itself (of clauses etc.); intransitive; see Lallot (1997: ii. 8)

αὐτουδέτερος, -ον   absolutely neuter, absolutely intransitive

αὐτόφωνον (γράμμα)   vowel

ἀφαίρεσις, -εως, ἡ   removal, aphaeresis (removal of a letter or letters, esp. at the beginning of a word)

ἀφαιρέω   to remove (a letter or letters, esp. at the beginning of a word)

ἄφθογγον = ἄφωνον

ἄφωνον (γράμμα)   stop consonant ("mute," i.e. β, γ, δ, κ, π, τ, θ, φ, χ); consonant

ἀχαρακτήριστος, -ον   without grammatical form (e.g. of indeclinable foreign words)

ἀχάσμητος, -ον   without hiatus

ἀχρηστεύω   not to be in use

ἀχρηστολογέω   to speak unprofitably or amiss

ἄχρηστος, -ον   obsolete, disused

ἀχώριστος, -ον   inseparable

βαθμός, -οῦ, ὁ   degree of comparison

βαρβαρίζω   to speak bad Greek, commit barbarisms

βαρβαρισμός, -οῦ, ὁ   use of bad Greek or of a foreign language; barbarism (incorrect use of individual words, as opposed to σολοικισμός, incorrect syntax); see Lallot (1997: ii. 161), Donnet (1967: 154–6)

βαρυντικός, -ή, -όν   tending to retract the accent (normally used to indicate recessive accentuation, i.e. an accent as close to the beginning of the word as possible)

βαρύνω   (of letters or syllables) to pronounce without an accent, mark with a grave accent; (of words) pronounce without an accent on the final syllable, mark the final syllable with a grave accent, (mid.) have no accent on the final syllable (in practice, normally restricted to recessive accentuation)

βαρύς, -εῖα, -ύ   low (of pitch), grave or unaccented (of accent), long/heavy (of syllables); βαρύς (τόνος) or βαρεῖα (προσῳδία) the grave accent (but see section 4.2.9 above); βαρέως with the accent thrown back, with recessive accent; see section 4.2.9 above, Moore-Blunt (1978), Probert (2003: 16–17), and Lallot (1998: 88–9) βαρύτης, -ητος, ἡ   grave accent, absence of accent; (of words) absence of accent on the final syllable

βαρυτονέω   (of letters or syllables) to pronounce without an accent, mark with a grave accent; (of words) pronounce without an accent on the final syllable, mark the final syllable with a grave accent

βαρυτόνησις, -εως, ἡ   accentuation further back than the final syllable (in practice, normally restricted to recessive accentuation)

βαρύτονος, -ον   (of syllables) having no accent; (of words) having no accent on the final syllable (in practice normally restricted to recessively accented words)

βεβαίωσις, -εως, ἡ   affirmation, confirmation

βιβλιακός, -ή, -όν   of books, based on books

βουστροφηδόν   (of writing) going from right to left and left to right in alternate lines, boustrophedon

βραχυκαταληκτέω   to end in a short syllable

βραχυκατάληκτος, -ον   ending in a short syllable, having an ending that is (too) short by one foot

βραχυκαταληξία, -ας, ἡ   a short ending

βραχύνω   to shorten

βραχυπαραληκτέω   to have a short penultimate syllable

βραχυπαράληκτος, -ον   having a short penultimate syllable

βραχυπαράληξις, -εως, ἡ   state of having a short penultimate syllable

βραχυπροπαραληκτέω   to have a short antepenultimate syllable

βραχύς, -εῖα, -ύ   short (of vowels or syllables)

βραχυσύλλαβος, -ον   of short syllables

γενικός, -ή, -όν   genitive, γενική (πτῶσις) the genitive case; generic; see Lallot (1998: 145), Swiggers and Wouters (1995a: 151–2), De Mauro (1965)

γένος, -ους, τό   gender

γλῶσσα, -ης, ἡ   dialect, language, obsolete or dialectal word; see Lallot (1998: 77–9)

γλώσσημα, -ατος, τό   obsolete or foreign word

γλωσσηματικός, -ή, -όν   full of rare words

γράμμα, -ατος, τό   letter (of the alphabet), piece of writing; see Lallot (1998: 96–8)

γραμματικός, -ή, -όν   pertaining to letters, grammar, literary or textual criticism, etc.; (as masc. subst.) grammarian, critic, teacher of grammar; γραμματική (τέχνη) grammar (including literary and textual criticism, etc.), scholarship, alphabet, writing system; see Lallot (1995, 1998: 69–73), Kaster (1988: esp. 453–4), Schenkeveld (1994: 263–5), Robins (1996)

γραμματιστής, -οῦ, ὁ   elementary teacher, grammarian; see Kaster (1988: 447–52)

γραφή, -ῆς, ἡ   writing, (manuscript) reading, lesson

δακτυλικός, -ή, -όν   dactylic

δασυντής, -οῦ, ὁ   one inclined to aspirate sounds

δασύνω   to aspirate

δασύς, -εῖα, -ύ   aspirated (of consonants or vowels), having a rough breathing, (as fem. subst.) rough breathing; see Lallot (1998: 102–4)

δασύτης, -ητος, ἡ   aspiration

δεικτικός, -ή, όν   demonstrative, deictic (used not only for our demonstrative pronouns, but also for personal and possessive pronouns; also certain nouns and adverbs)

δεῖνα, -ος, ὁ/ἡ/τό   (consistently used with an article, usually ὁ) so-and-so, some-one, John Doe; cf. 4.1.39

δεῖξις, -εως, ἡ   demonstrative force or reference

δεκάσημος, -ον   of the length of ten short syllables

δευτέρωσις, -εως, ἡ   repetition

δηλονότι   clearly (often introduces explanations)

δηλόω   to mean

διά   cf. 4.1.30

διάβασις, -εως, ἡ   transitive force

διαβατικός, -ή, -όν   transitive

διαβεβαιωτικός, -ή, -όν   affirmative (of conjunctions)

διαβιβάζομαι   to be transitive

διαβιβασμός, -οῦ, ὁ   transitive force

διαβιβαστικός, -ή, -όν   transitive

διάδοσις, -εως, ἡ   distribution; see Van Groningen (1963)

διαζεύγνυμι, -νύω   to disjoin, separate

διαζευκτικός, -ή, -όν   disjunctive (of conjunctions, ones with non-connective meanings like ἤ: more specifically used for ἤ when it distinguishes between two mutually exclusive alternatives); see Lallot (1998: 244–6)

διάζευξις, -εως, ἡ   separation, disjunction

διάθεσις, -εως, ἡ   voice (e.g. active); tense; force, function; mood?; see Lallot (1997: ii. 62, 254, 1998: 159–60, 167–8), Lambert (1978), Andersen (1989, 1993), Rijksbaron (1986), Van Ophuijsen (1993a), Pantiglioni (1998)

διαίρεσις, -εως, ἡ   separation; resolution of a diphthong into two syllables, or of a single word into two (i.e. tmesis); (in meter) diaeresis

διαιρετικός, -ή, -όν   separative; having a tendency to resolve diphthongs

διαιρέω   to divide, divide words, punctuate, resolve a diphthong or contracted form

διακοπή, -ῆς, ἡ   separation, tmesis

διακριτικός, -ή, -όν   separating, distinguishing

διακρουστικός, -ή, -όν   expressing deception

διαλαλία, -ας, ἡ   talking, language

διάλεκτος, -ου, ἡ   dialect, speech, language; see Morpurgo Davies (1987), Dalimier (2001: 225–6); Consani (1991)

διαλλαγή, -ῆς, ἡ   change, difference

διάλληλος, -ον   interchangeable (of word order)

διάλυσις, -εως, ἡ   separation, resolution (of a compound word into its original elements, of a word into letters, of a diphthong into two vowels, of a double consonant such as ξ into two single consonants); asyndeton; hyperbaton; solution

διαλύω   to separate, resolve into its component parts

διάνοια, -ας, ἡ   meaning

διαπίπτω   to be wrong

διαπόρησις, -εως, ἡ   doubt, question

διαπορητικός, -ή, -όν   dubitative, interrogative; see Dalimier (2001: 274–5)

διαρθρόω   to distinguish, articulate

διάρθρωσις, -εως, ἡ   articulation

διασαφητικός, -ή, -όν   affirmative, declarative, explanatory, making completely clear; see Sluiter (1988: 56–7, 62–4)

διασταλτικός, -ή, -όν   distinguishing

διάστασις, -εως, ἡ   separation (of vowels, not being a diphthong; of words, written as two, as ἡμῶν αὐτῶν)

διαστατικός, -ή, -όν   separate

διαστέλλω   to distinguish, separate, oppose

διάστημα, -ατος, τό   interval, distance

διαστηματικός, -ή, -όν   indicating distance; by intervals (of the pitch changes of the voice when singing)

διαστιγμή, -ῆς, ἡ   punctuation

διαστίζω   to punctuate, separate words

διαστολή, -ῆς, ἡ   pause; word division; comma; separation (e.g. of a diphthong into two vowels), opposition; see Lallot (1998: 85), Blank (1983a)

διατίθημι   to act; τὸ διατιθέν subject; τὸ διατιθέμενον object; see also διάθεσις

διαφορά, -ᾶς, ἡ   distinction, subset

διαφωνία, -ας, ἡ   discord

δίβραχυς, -εια, -υ   of two short syllables

δίγαμμα, τό   digamma (F)

διγενής, -ές   of doubtful gender, of two genders

δίγραμμ(ατ)ος, -ον   of two letters

διεγείρω   raise, make acute (of the accent)

διηγηματικός, -ή, -όν   descriptive, narrative

δικατάληκτος, -ον   having two endings

δικαταληξία, -ας, ἡ   state of having two endings

δίκωλος, -ον   with two members or sections

διορθόω   to correct

διόρθωσις, -εως, ἡ   correction, edition (of a text; i.e. a corrected, critical edition —but there is much dispute about exactly how critical such an edition was in ancient times)

διορθωτικός, -ή, -όν   pertaining to correction of texts

διορίζω   to distinguish, define

διπλ(ασι)άζω   to reduplicate; to double a consonant

διπλασίασις, -εως, ἡ = διπλασιασμός

διπλασ(ιασ)μός, -οῦ, -ὁ   reduplication; doubling of consonants (as in τόσσος) διπλασιολογία, -ας, ἡ   repetition of words

διπλόσημ(αντ)ος, -ον   with double meaning

διπλοῦς, -ῆ, -οῦν   double (of consonants ζ, ξ, ψ)

δίπλωσις, -εως, ἡ   doubling, reduplication

διπρόσωπος, -ον   denoting two persons (of possessive pronouns); see Lallot (1998: 208)

δίπτωτος, -ον   having one form for two cases, having two cases or endings

δίσημ(αντ)ος, -ον   of doubtful quantity (of α, ι, υ); having two meanings

δισσολογέω   to repeat; to pronounce in two ways

δισσολογία, -ας, ἡ   repetition of words; pronunciation in two ways

δισσός -ή, -όν   double; doubtful, ambiguous

δισταγμός, -οῦ, ὁ   doubt, ambiguity

διστάζω   to be in doubt

διστακτικός, -ή, -όν   expressing doubt; διστακτικὴ ἔγκλισις conditional subjunctive; see Schenkeveld (1982: 253–6, 264)

διστασμός, -οῦ, ὁ = δισταγμός

δισυλλαβέω   to be disyllabic

δισυλλαβία, -ας, ἡ   pair of syllables

δισύλλαβος, -ον   disyllabic

δισχιδόν   in two columns

δισώνυμος, -ον   with two names

διτονέω   to have two accents, have a double accent (of words that have different accents under different circumstances, e.g. σέ and σε)

διτονίζω   to accent in two ways

δίτονος, -ον   accented in two ways

διφθογγίζω   to write with a diphthong

διφθογγογραφέω   to write with a diphthong

διφθογγόομαι   to be written with a diphthong

δίφθογγος, -ον   with two sounds, diphthongal; (as fem. or neut. subst.) diphthong

διφορέομαι   to be spelled or pronounced in two ways

διφόρησις, -εως, ἡ   double mode of writing, double pronunciation

διχονοητικός, -ή, -όν   indicating doubt; discordant

διχρονία, -ας, ἡ   two short syllables

δίχρονος, -ον   capable of being either long or short (of α, ι, υ); consisting of two short syllables; common (in meter, i.e. having two possible quantities)

διωνυμία, -ας, ἡ   double name

διώνυμος, -ον   having two names; διώνυμον ὄνομα double name; see Lallot (1998: 155–6)

δόκιμος, -ον   approved, found in classical Attic

δοτικός, -ή, -όν   dative; δοτική (πτῶσις) the dative case; see Lallot (1998: 145–6), De Mauro (1965)

δουλεύω   to be construed with, to take (a certain case)

δρᾶσις, -εως, ἡ   action, active force of a verb

δραστήριος, -ον active
δραστικός, -ή, -όν active
δυϊκός, -ή, -όν dual
δύναμαι to mean
δύναμις, -εως, ή meaning (of words), phonetic value (of letters); see Dalimier
    (2001: 291–2)
δυνητικός, -ή, -όν potential (of ἄν and κεν)
δυσέκφορ(ητ)ος, -ον hard to pronounce
δυσεκφώνητος, -ον hard to pronounce
δυσήκοος, -ον ill-sounding
δυσκίνητος, -ον hard to decline
δύσκλιτος, -ον hard to inflect, irregular
δύσφραστος, -ον hard to say; badly expressed
δυσφωνία, -ας, ή roughness of sound
δύσφωνος, -ον ill-sounding, harsh
δυσωνυμέω to have a bad name
Δωρίζω to speak or write in the Doric dialect, use Doric forms
Δωρικός, -ή, -όν Doric
Δώριος, -α, -ον (or just -ον) Doric
ἐγγιγνομένη κλίσις an augment added to a compound verb (i.e. an augment
    that is added inside a word)
ἔγγραμμ(ατ)ος, -ον written, containing letters, descriptive of letters
ἐγείρω (τὸν τόνον) to wake up the accent (i.e. to accent with an acute accent
    the final syllable of an inherently oxytone word that had not been accented be-
    cause it was followed by another word in a sentence)
ἐγερτικός, -ή, -όν enclitic (i.e. causing a preceding oxytone word to wake up
    its accent); with a final acute accent woken up
ἐγκελευσ(μα)τικός, -ή, -όν hortatory
ἔγκλιμα, -ατος, τό inflected form; form with grave accent
ἐγκλιματικός, -ή, -όν = ἐγκλιτικός
ἐγκλίνω to inflect; to throw back the accent, pronounce as an enclitic, change
    an acute accent to grave; (mid.) to be enclitic
ἔγκλισις, -εως, ή verbal mood, inflection, enclitic form, throwing back of the
    accent, change of acute accent to grave; see Lallot (1997: ii. 281–2, 314–15,
    1998: 164–5), Sluiter (1990: 86–9), Dalimier (2001: 421)
ἐγκλιτέον one must use as enclitic
ἐγκλιτικός, -ή, -όν enclitic (a word that attaches for purposes of accentuation
    to the one preceding it, thereby causing various accentual complications)
ἔθιμος, -ον customary, in use
ἐθνικός, -ή, -όν dialectal, indicating nationality; (as neut. subst.) ethnic
ἔθος, -ους, τό usage; see Lallot (1997: ii. 177)
εἰδικός, -ή, -όν specific, not generic; see Swiggers and Wouters (1995a:
    151–2)

εἶδος, -ους, τό   type, species, derivational status (i.e. primitive or derived); see
    Lallot (1998: 131, 149–50, 170); cf. 4.1.41
εἰκασμός, -οῦ, ὁ   conjecture, guessing
εἰς   cf. 4.1.29
ἐκβάλλω   to elide, suppress
ἐκβολή, -ῆς, ἡ   elision, suppression
ἐκδέχομαι   to accept, receive
ἔκδοσις, -εως, ἡ   text, publication, edition; see M. L. West (2001: 50–73), Van
    Groningen (1963), Lallot (1997: ii. 7); Erbse (1959: 291–2), GG ii.ii. 1–2
ἐκδρομή, -ῆς, ἡ   elision, suppression
ἔκθεσμος, -ον   irregular
ἐκθηλύνω   to make feminine
ἐκθλίβω   to elide, suppress (a letter)
ἔκθλιψις, -εως, ἡ   elision (elimination of a final vowel before a word beginning
    with a vowel), suppression (of a letter), ecthlipsis (elision in Latin of final syl-
    lables ending in -m)
ἔκκειμαι   to be set forth
ἐκκόπτω   to cut out, mark out
ἐκλειπτικός, -ή, -όν   elliptical
ἐκλείπω = ἐλλείπω, cf. 4.1.35
ἐκπίπτω   to arise from, be produced from, be derived from
ἔκτασις, -εως, ἡ   lengthening (of a vowel, syllable), augment, long form (of vowels
    that can be long or short)
ἐκτατικός, -ή, -όν   having a tendency to lengthen (+ gen.)
ἐκτείνω   to lengthen (a vowel, syllable), augment
ἐκφέρω   to pronounce; (pass.) to be formed (with, + διά; from, + ἀπό)
ἐκφορά, -ᾶς, ἡ   pronunciation
ἐκφωνέω   to pronounce
ἐκφώνησις, -εως, ἡ   pronunciation, exclamation
ἐλλειπής, -ές = ἐλλιπής
ἐλλειπτικός, -ή, -όν   elliptical, defective
ἐλλείπω   to be lacking, cf. 4.1.35
ἔλλειψις, -εως, ἡ   ellipsis (omission of words that can be understood from the
    context), omission (of a letter); see Lallot (1997: ii. 20)
ἑλληνισμός, -οῦ, ὁ   use of pure Greek; use of the koiné dialect; see Schenkeveld
    (1994: 281–91)
ἐλλιπής, -ές   defective, elliptical
ἐμπαθής, -ές   modified, inflected
ἐμπεριεκτικός, -ή, -όν   including, inclusive
ἐμπεριλαμβάνω   to include
ἐμπεριληπτικός, -ή, -όν   including, inclusive
ἐμφαίνω   to indicate, mean
ἐμφαντικός, -ή, -όν   expressive, vivid

ἔμφασις, -εως, ἡ   meaning, emphasis; suggestion (as opposed to expression); see Van Ophuijsen (1993a)

ἐν   cf. 4.1.33

ἐναλλαγή, -ῆς, ἡ   change in order, interchange

ἐναντιότης, -ητος, ἡ   opposition

ἐναντιωματικός, -ή, -όν   adversative (marking opposition, of conjunctions, as ὅμως)

ἐναρκτικός, -ή, -όν   inchoative

ἐνδεής, -ές   defective

ἔνδεια, -ας, ἡ   lack, defectiveness

ἐνδιπλασιάζω   to reduplicate

ἐνέργεια, -ας, ἡ   active voice, action; see Swiggers and Wouters (1996: 143–5), Van Ophuijsen (1993a)

ἐνεργέω   to act; ὁ ἐνεργῶν the subject; ὁ ἐνεργούμενος the object

ἐνεργητικός, -ή, -όν   active

ἐνεστώς, -ῶσα, -ός   present; (as masc. subst.) the present tense; see Lallot (1998: 172)

ἔνθεσις, -εως, ἡ   insertion

ἐνικός, -ή, -όν   singular

ἔννοια, -ας, ἡ   meaning, sense; see Van Ophuijsen (1993a)

ἐντελής, -ές   complete

ἐνυπόκριτος (ὑπο)στιγμή   punctuation put after the protasis, dramatic pause; see Blank (1983a)

ἐξακολουθέω   to follow (an analogical rule)

ἐξαλλαγή, -ῆς, ἡ   alteration, variation

ἐξάπλωσις, -εως, ἡ   explanation, paraphrase

ἐξάπτωτος, -ον   having six cases

ἐξασύλλαβος, -ον   having six syllables

ἐξαττικίζω   to Atticize, express in Attic form

ἐξέγερσις, -εως ἡ   raising of the accent (to an acute) on the final syllable of an oxytone word

ἐξηγέομαι   to explain, interpret, write a commentary on

ἐξήγησις, -εως, ἡ   explanation, commentary; see Lallot (1998: 77)

ἐξηγητής, -οῦ, ὁ   interpreter, commentator

ἐξηγητικός, -ή, -όν   explanatory

ἐξῆς, τό   sequence in which words are to be taken, normal word order, grammatical sequence; (as indeclinable adj.) following, next; see Lallot (1997: ii. 68), Sluiter (1990: 68); cf. 4.1.38

ἐξομαλίζω   to form according to the rule

ἔξωθεν   from outside; ἔξωθεν προσλαμβάνω to supply or understand a word; ἔξωθεν (προσ)κλίνω/(προσ)λαμβάνω to augment (add an ε from outside); ἔξωθεν κλίσις/χρόνος/αὔξησις augment, addition of letters to a word (e.g. ἐ-κεῖνος)

ἐξώθησις, -εως, ἡ   expulsion (of a letter)

ἐπαγγελία, -ας, ἡ   meaning

ἐπαίρω   to raise, make acute (of the accent)

ἐπακολουθητικός, -ή, -όν   inclined to follow (of δέ when it follows μέν)

ἐπαλληλία, -ας, ἡ   sequence, continuous series

ἐπάλληλος, -ον   in succession, one after another

ἐπαλληλότης, -ητος, ἡ   repetition, duplication

ἐπαμφοτερίζω   to have two forms (e.g. acc. sing. ending in -ν or -α), to have doubtful quantity (of vowels)

ἐπαναδιπλασιασμός, -οῦ, ὁ   doubling, gemination

ἐπαναδίπλωσις, -εως, ἡ   reduplication, gemination

ἐπαπορη(μα)τικός, -ή, -όν   dubitative (expressing doubt or question); see Dalimier (2001: 275)

ἐπαυξάνω   to increase, lengthen

ἐπαύξησις, -εως, ἡ   lengthening (esp. of vowels)

ἐπείσοδος, -ου, ἡ   coming in from outside (of extra letters added to a word)

ἐπέκτασις, -εως, ἡ   lengthening (of a vowel or a word, especially lengthening at the end of a word)

ἐπεκτατικός, -ή, -όν   lengthening

ἐπεκτείνω   to lengthen (a syllable, or a word), pronounce as long

ἐπένθεσις, -εως, ἡ   insertion of a letter or word, epenthesis (the insertion of a sound to make a word easier to pronounce)

ἐπενθετικός, -ή, -όν   inserted

ἐπεντίθημι   to insert

ἐπεξηγέομαι   to explain besides

ἐπεξηγηματικός, -ή, -όν   epexegetical (providing further explanation)

ἐπεξήγησις, -εως, ἡ   explanation

ἐπηρμένη (ἔγκλισις)   subjunctive (from αἴρω, i.e. the mood with the magnified thematic vowel)

ἐπί   cf. 4.1.31

ἐπιζευκτικός, -ή, -όν   connective; taking the subjunctive; see Schenkeveld (1982), Lallot (1997: ii. 236), Dalimier (2001: 352–3)

ἐπίζευξις, -εως, ἡ   repetition, addition

ἐπιθετικός, -ή, -όν   added; adjectival, pertaining to an epithet, (as neut. subst.) adjective

ἐπίθετος, -ον   adjectival, (as neut. subst.) epithet, adjective; see Lallot (1998: 151–2)

ἐπίκοινος, -ον   epicene (of gender; there is a distinction between two types of what we might call common gender, κοινόν "common" and ἐπίκοινον "epicene," whereby the former term is used for nouns that can be masculine or feminine according to the sex of the referent (e.g. ὁ or ἡ ἵππος) and the latter is used for nouns that always have the same gender regardless of the sex of the referent, as ἡ χελιδών "swallow," which is used for both male and female swallows)

ἐπικοινωνέω   to be in common, share in common

ἐπικράτεια, -ας, ἡ   prevalence, authority

ἐπιλείπω   to be defective (lack certain forms)

ἐπιλογιστικός, -ή, -όν   inferential, illative (indicating motion into)

ἐπιμεριζόμενος, -η, -ον   distributive; partitive (of genitives)

ἐπιμερίζω   to distribute

ἐπιμερισμός, -ή, -όν   distribution; parsing; division of a sentence into words; analysis; classification

ἐπιπλοκή, -ῆς, ἡ   insertion (of letters); combination (e.g. of letters or phrases); (in meter) conversion of rhythms by change in order of syllables

ἐπίρρημα, -ατος, τό   adverb; see Lallot (1998: 221–30, 1999)

ἐπιρρηματικός, -ή, -όν   adverbial

ἐπισημασία, -ας, ἡ   marking, notation, indication

ἐπισταλτικός, -ή, -όν   epistolary; dative, ἐπισταλτική (πτῶσις) dative case

ἐπιστέρησις, -εως, ἡ   a second negation cancelling an earlier one

ἐπισυναλοιφή, -ῆς, ἡ   elision at the close of a verse; coalescence of two syllables into one

ἐπισυνέμπτωσις, -εως, ἡ   succession of words with similar-sounding endings and the same vowels

ἐπισύνθετος, -ον   compound (esp. of meters)

ἐπιταγματικός, -ή, -όν   subsidiary; appositive, postpositive; see Lallot (1997: ii. 157)

ἐπίτασις, -εως, ἡ   intensity, intensification; presence of the acute accent; see Lallot (1997: ii. 83)

ἐπιτάσσω   to place after

ἐπιτατικός, -ή, -όν   intensive, intensifying

ἐπιτείνω   to intensify

ἐπιτελεστικός, -ή, -όν   indicating purpose or result; see Dalimier (2001: 356–8)

ἐπιτεταμένος, -η, -ον   comparative (of degree); acute (of accent)

ἐπιφέρομαι   to follow (e.g. of letters in a word, or words in a sentence; + dat.); see Dalimier (2001: 259–60)

ἐπίφθεγμα, -ατος, τό   exclamation, interjection

ἐπιφορά, -ᾶς, ἡ   conclusion; act of following immediately; see Lallot (1998: 252), Dalimier (2001: 411–12)

ἐπιφορ(ητ)ικός, -ή, -όν   illative (indicating motion into), inferential, forming the second or subsequent clause

ἐπιφωνέω   to exclaim

ἐπιφώνημα, -ατος, τό   interjection, exclamation

ἐπιφώνησις, -εως, ἡ   interjection

ἐπιφωνητικόν, -οῦ, τό   an added word

ἐπιχωριάζω   to call or name in the local dialect or language

ἐπιχώριος, -α, -ον   native, in the local dialect or language

ἑπταγράμματος, -ον   of seven letters

ἐπῳδός, -οῦ, ἡ   epode (part of a lyric ode sung after the strophe and antistrophe)

ἐπῳδός, -οῦ, ὁ   refrain; shorter verse of a couplet

ἐπωνυμία, -ας, ἡ   name, additional name, nickname

ἐπώνυμον (ὄνομα)   epithet, additional name; see Lallot (1998: 155–6)

ἑρμηνεία, -ας, ἡ   expression, explanation, interpretation, translation
ἑρμηνευτικός, -ή, -όν   expressive, interpretive
ἐρώτημα, -ατος, τό   question (esp. one answered with "yes" or "no"); see Dalimier
    (2001: 274)
ἐρωτηματικός, -ή, -όν   interrogative
ἐρώτησις, -εως, ἡ   question
ἐσόμενος, -ον   future
ἔσωθεν   inside (of the internal augment and reduplication found in verbs com-
    pounded with a preposition, as κατέγραψα)
ἑτεράριθμος, -ον   of different number; (as neut. subst.) change of number (as
    a figure of speech)
ἑτερογενής, -ές   of different gender; (as neut. subst.) change of gender (in a
    constructio ad sensum)
ἑτερόζυγος, -ον   differently formed; (as adv.) in a different declension
ἑτεροίωσις, -εως, ἡ   alteration, change
ἑτερόκλιτος, -ον   irregularly inflected (of nouns)
ἑτεροπάθεια, -ας, ἡ   reflexivity, reciprocity
ἑτερόπτωτος, -ον   having cases formed from different stems (as μέγας, μεγάλου);
    (as neut. subst.) change of case (as a figure of speech)
ἑτεροσήμαντος, -ον   with different meaning
ἑτεροσχημάτιστος, -ον   differently formed; (as neut. subst.) change of gram-
    matical form (as a figure of speech)
ἑτεροφωνέομαι   to be different in sound
ἑτερόχρονος, -ον   (as neut. subst.) change of tense (as a figure of speech)
ἑτερωνυμία, -ας, ἡ   difference of name, lack of synonymy
ἑτερώνυμος, -ον   with different meaning, with different name
ἐτυμηγορέω   to derive
ἐτυμηγορία, -ας, ἡ   etymology, derivation
ἐτυμολογέω   to analyze a word and find its origin, argue from etymology
ἐτυμολογία, -ας, ἡ   etymology; see Lallot (1998: 79–80)
ἐτυμολογικός, -ή, -όν   etymological; (as masc. subst.) etymologist
ἔτυμον, -ου, τό   etymology, true sense of a word according to its origin
ἐτυμότης, -ητος, ἡ   true meaning of a word
εὐαστικός, -ή, -όν   Bacchanalian, exclamatory (of adverbs etc.)
εὐγραμματία, -ας, ἡ   calligraphy
εὐδιάθετος, -ον   easily affected, well-arranged
εὐεπέκτατος, -ον   naturally lengthened
εὐθετίζω   to be suitably employed
εὐθετισμός, -οῦ, ὁ   convenience, orderly arrangement
εὐθετός, -όν   well-arranged, easy to use
εὐθύνομαι = ὀρθοτονέομαι
εὐθύς, -εῖα, -ύ   nominative; εὐθεῖα (πτῶσις) nominative case
εὐκτικός, -ή, -όν   expressing desire (of adverbs and verbs); εὐκτική (ἔγλισις)
    optative mood

εὐμάλακτος, -ον   liquid (of consonants)

εὐπαράδεκτος, -ον   acceptable, admissible

εὐρυφωνία, -ας, ἡ   broadness of sound

εὐσυνθεσία, -ας, ἡ   good arrangement of words

εὐσύνθετος, -ον   easy to compound into a word

εὐσύντακτος, -ον   well-arranged, with good syntax, easy

εὐσυνταξία, -ας, ἡ   the state of being εὐσύντακτος

εὐφημητικός, -ή, -όν   with auspicious meaning

εὐφημισμός, -οῦ, ὁ   use of an auspicious word for an inauspicious one

εὐφωνία, -ας, ἡ   euphony

εὔφωνος, -ον   euphonious

εὐχή, -ῆς, ἡ   wish, prayer

εὐχρηστέομαι   to be in common use (of words)

ἐφελκυσμός, -οῦ, ὁ   affixation of nu-movable or a similar suffix (see ἐφελκυστικός)

ἐφελκυστικός, -ή, -όν   attracting, attracted, suffixed (esp. of the κ in οὐκ and of
   nu-movable, called ν ἐφελκυστικόν); see Lallot (1997: ii. 47)

ἐφερμηνευτικός, -ή, -όν   explanatory

ἐφετικός, -ή, -όν   expressing desire (of verbs)

ἐφθαρμένος, -η, -ον   corrupt

ζεῦγμα, -ατος, τό   connection, zeugma (figure of speech in which two subjects
   are used with a predicate that strictly belongs only to one of them)

Ζηνοδότειος, -α, -ον   of or pertaining to Zenodotus

ἠθικός, -ή, -όν   expressive

ἡμίβραχυς, -εια, -υ   lasting half a short syllable

ἡμίφωνος, -ον   continuant (consonant that is not a stop, i.e. that can be pronounced for an indefinite length of time (ζ, ξ, ψ, λ, μ, ν, ρ, σ); note that this is not
   the same as English "semivowel," which refers to w and y); see Lallot (1998: 102)

ἦχος, -ου, ο   sound, breathing

θαυμαστικός, -ή, -όν   exclamatory, expressing astonishment (of adverbs,
   interjections)

θειασμός, -οῦ, ὁ   inspiration, frenzy

θέμα, -ατος, τό   base form (primary, non-derived form); see Lallot (1997: ii. 45)

θεματίζω   to establish as a base form; assign a meaning or gender arbitrarily

θεματικός, -ή, -όν   pertaining to the base form, primary (not derivative); θεματικά
   elements; θεματικώτερος using several different base forms

θεματισμός, -οῦ, ὁ   arbitrary determination, conventional arrangement

θεματοποιέω   to make into a θέμα

θέσις, -εως, ἡ   convention, form (esp. original form or derived form), position
   (in meter, of syllables long by position), downbeat, stop (in punctuation); see
   Lallot (1998: 109–11)

θετικός, -ή, -όν   positive (degree); affirmative; expressing obligation (of forms
   in -τέον)

θηλυκός, -ή, -όν   feminine

θηλύνω   to make a feminine form

θηλυπρεπής, -ές   feminine

θηλύς, -εῖα, -ύ   female, feminine

θλῖψις, -εως, ἡ = ἔκθλιψις

θρην(ητ)ικός, -ή, -όν   pertaining to lament, interjection

Ἰακός, -ά, -όν   Ionic

Ἰάς, -άδος, ἡ   Ionic dialect

ἰδιάζω   to be peculiar, be specific to an individual, be proper (of nouns)

ἰδιασμός, -οῦ, ὁ   peculiarity; conversion to a proper name

ἰδικός, -ή, -όν = εἰδικός

ἰδιοπάθεια, -ας, ἡ   reflexivity, reciprocity

ἰδιοπαθής, -ές   reflexive, intransitive

ἴδιος, -α, -ον   proper, specific, not generic; (as neut. subst.) specificity

ἰδιότης, -ητος, ἡ   peculiarity, individuality, individual nature; εἰς ἰδιότητα as
   a proper name

ἰδιότυπος, -ον   of a peculiar form

ἰδίωμα, -ατος, τό   peculiarity of style, unique feature, (individual) style

ἰδιώτης, -ου, ὁ   layman, ignoramus

ἰδιωτίζω   to pronounce in the local manner

ἰδιωτικός, -ή, -όν   unskilled, unlearned

ἰδιωτισμός, -οῦ, ὁ   vulgar phrase; *ad hominem* argument

ἱκετικός, -ή, -όν   pertaining to supplication (of verbs)

ἰσάριθμος, -ον   having the same (grammatical) number

ἰσοδυναμέω   to be equivalent to, mean the same thing

ἰσοδυναμία, -ας, ἡ   equivalence in meaning

ἰσοδύναμος, -ον   equivalent in meaning

ἰσόζυγος, -ον   of the same number and person

ἰσοκατάληκτος, -ον   having the same ending

ἰσοστοιχέω = ἀντιστοιχέω

ἰσοστοιχία = ἀντιστοιχία

ἰσοσυλλαβέω   to have the same number of syllables

ἰσοσυλλαβία, -ας, ἡ   equality of syllables

ἰσοσύλλαβος, -ον   having the same number of syllables

ἰσοχρονέω   to have the same length, number of syllables, or number of time-
   units

ἰσόχρονος, -ον   the same length, consisting of the same number of time-units

ἱστορία, -ας, ἡ   the usage of the ancients; a story or piece of information alluded to by a poet that requires explanation

Ἰωνικός, -ή, -όν   Ionic

ἰωτ(ακ)ίζω   to write with iota

ἰωτακισμός, -οῦ, ὁ   doubling or repetition of iota (esp. in Latin)

ἰωτογραφέω   to write with iota

καθάρ(ε)ιος, -ον   pure, correct

καθαρ(ι)εύω   to be pure, be correct, be preceded by a vowel, contain a pure
   syllable

καθαρολογέω   to be precise or accurate in language
καθαρός, -ά, -όν   pure, unmixed, clear, simple, preceded by a vowel (rather than
   a consonant)
καθό   that (introducing indirect statements)
καθότι   because
καινοσχημάτιστος, -ον   newly or strangely formed
καινόσχημος, -ον   newly or strangely formed
καινοσχήμων, -ον   newly or strangely formed
καινόφωνος, -ον   new-sounding
καιρικός, -ή, -όν   temporal
καιριολεκτέω   to use (a word) appropriately
κακοσύνθετος, -ον   ill-composed
κακοσυνταξία, -ας, ἡ   bad grammar
κακοφωνία, -ας, ἡ   cacaphony
κακόφωνος, -ον   cacophonous, ill-sounding
καλλιφωνέω   to speak beautifully, pronounce euphoniously
καλλιφωνία, -ας, ἡ   euphony
κανονίζω   to prescribe rules, conjugate, give the rule or paradigm, parse; κανονίζεται
   the rule is . . .
κανονικός, -ή, -όν   regular
κανόνισμα, -ατος, τό   grammatical rule
κανών, -όνος, ὁ   rule, paradigm, metrical scheme
καρίζω   to speak like a Carian, speak barbarously
κατά   cf. 4.1.32
καταβιβάζω   to throw the accent forward to the following syllable or to the end
   of the word
καταβίβασις, -εως, ἡ = καταβιβασμός
καταβιβασμός, -οῦ, ὁ   act of throwing the accent forward to the following syllable or to the end of the word
καταγλωττίζω   to compose using rare words, speak in dialect
κατάγλωττος, -ον   full of rare words
καταλέγω (τὸν τόνον) = καταβιβάζω
καταλείπω   to lack, be defective
καταλήγω   to end
καταληκτικός, -ή, -όν   terminal; leaving off; catalectic (in meter, lacking one
   syllable in the last foot of a verse)
κατάληξις, -εως, ἡ   ending, final syllable; cadence or close of a period
καταλληλία, -ας, ἡ = καταλληλότης; see Donnet (1967: 153)
κατάλληλος, -ον   rightly constructed, congruent, agreeing
καταλληλότης, -ητος, ἡ   correct form, correct construction, agreement, grammatical regularity; see Lallot (1997: ii. 8), Sluiter (1990: 50–1), Blank (1982:
   27–31, 45–9, 55–7)
καταλογάδην   in prose
καταπεραιόω   to close, end with or together with (+ εἰς + acc.)

κατα̣ττικίζω   to speak Attic

κατάφασις, -εως, ἡ   affirmation, affirmative particle

καταφατικός, -ή, -όν   affirmative, emphatic

καταφορά, -ᾶς, ἡ   pronunciation, utterance

κατάχρησις, -εως, ἡ   improper use of words, catachresis (application of a term to a thing that it does not properly denote, perversion of a trope or metaphor)

καταχρηστικός, -ή, -όν   misused, misapplied

καταχρηστικῶς   by extension

κατηγορέω   to signify, be the predicate; see Sluiter (1990: 93–5), Lallot (1997: ii. 58–9)

κατηγόρημα, -ατος, τό   predicate

κατηγορικός, -όν   affirmative; predicative; infinitive; categorical (as opposed to hypothetical), (as neut. subst.) statement combining subject and predicate

κατηγορούμενον, -ου, τό   predicate; see Pfister (1976), Lallot (1994b), Ildefonse (1994)

κατορθόω   to correct, (pass.) be correct, follow the pattern

κατόρθωμα, -ατος, τό   correct usage

κατόρθωσις, -εως, ἡ   correction; see Dalimier (2001: 223–4)

κατωμοτικός, -ή, -όν   pertaining to affirmative oaths (of adverbs)

κεῖμαι   to appear, be attested, be correct

κελευστικός, -ή, -όν   hortatory

κεραία, -ας, ἡ   apex of a letter (the top of it, in the written form), (by extension) word

κεράννυμι, -ύω   to coalesce by crasis, contract

κεχηνός, -ότος, τό   gap, lacuna (from χάσκω)

κινέω   to inflect; alter (a manuscript reading)

κίνημα, -ατος, τό   inflection

κίνησις, -εως, ἡ   inflection

κιονηδόν   like a pillar, in vertical lines from top to bottom

κιρνάω   to mix, contract (of vowels)

κλῆσις, -εως, ἡ   calling, nominative, vocative

κλητικός, -ή, -όν   vocative, of calling or address; κλητική (πτῶσις) the vocative case; κλητικὸν ἐπίρρημα the particle ὦ; see Lallot (1998: 148)

κλίμα, -ατος, τό   inflected form, inflection

κλίνω   to inflect, decline, augment

κλίσις, -εως, ἡ   inflection, declension, augment, reduplication

κλιτικός, -ή, -όν   declinable, pertaining to inflection (esp. declension); κλιτικὸν μόριον augment

κοιμίζω   to put the accent to sleep (i.e. change an acute on a final syllable to grave)

κοίμισις, -εως, ἡ   putting the accent to sleep (i.e. changing an acute on a final syllable to grave)

κοιμισμός, -οῦ, ὁ = κοίμισις

κοινολεκτέω   to use ordinary language

κοινόλεκτος, -ον   in ordinary language

κοινολεξία, -ας, ἡ   ordinary language

κοινολογία, -ας, ἡ   koiné dialect, dialog, ordinary language

κοινός, -ή, -όν   colloquial or non-literary Greek; κοινή (διάλεκτος) koiné dialect, κοινοί writers using the koiné dialect; κοινὸν γένος common gender (see above s.v. ἐπίκοινος); capable of being long or short (of vowels α, ι, υ); κοινὴ συλλαβή anceps (syllable capable of being either long or short); of ambiguous or mixed meter (of poems); in the middle voice (of verbs); κοινὸν ὄνομα common noun; ἀπὸ κοινοῦ zeugma (a figure of speech using a verb or adjective with two nouns, to only one of which it is strictly applicable, while the word applicable to the other noun is omitted); see Lallot (1998: 115–17)

κοινότης, -ητος, ἡ   common gender; zeugma, sharing of a word by two clauses (esp. in phrase ἐν κοινότητι παραλαμβάνεσθαι)

κόππα, τό   koppa (Ϙ)

κορωνίς, -ίδος, ἡ   coronis (a sign, like a smooth breathing, used to indicate crasis; also a sign indicating the end of a book or other section of a literary work); end

κουφίζω   to elide

κουφισμός, -οῦ, ὁ   elision

κρᾶσις, -εως, ἡ   mixing, combination, crasis (combination of two vowels, often from two different words, into one, as τοὔνομα for τοῦ ὄνομα); occasionally also synaeresis (removal of diaeresis to create a diphthong, as παῖς from πάϊς); see Lallot (1997: ii. 109)

κρίσις, -εως, ἡ   judgement, literary criticism

κριτικός, -ή, -όν   critical; (as masc. subst.) scholar, literary critic, grammarian

κτητικός, -ή, -όν   possessive (of adjectives, pronouns, etc.); genitive, κτητική (πτῶσις) genitive case; see Lallot (1998: 133)

κυριολεκτέω   to use words in their proper or literal sense

κυριολεξία, -ας, ἡ   use of literal rather than figurative expressions, proper speech

κυριολογία, -ας, ἡ   proper meaning of a word, proper speech, use of literal rather than figurative expessions

κύριος, -α, -ον   proper; κύριον (ὄνομα) proper name; κυρίως properly; κύριος τόνος principal accent, high tone; see Lallot (1998: 150), Matthaios (1996)

κυριωνυμία, -ας, ἡ   proper name, use of a proper name

λαλιά, -ᾶς, ἡ   talk, conversation, dialect

λα(μ)βδακισμός, -οῦ, ὁ   defect in pronunciation, dissonance of repetition of lambda

λείπω   to be lacking, be incomplete, be omitted; (pass.) remain; cf. 4.1.35

λεῖψις, -εως, ἡ   omission

λεκτικός, -ή, -όν   prose, in colloquial style, stylistic, pertaining to expression, with the force of a word (of the ending -θεν)

λεκτός, -ή, όν   capable of being spoken; (as neut. subst.) expression, phrase, meaning λέξις, -εως, ἡ   word, phrase, speech, diction, style, peculiar word (hence λέξεις glossary), text of an author (as opposed to commentary); see Lallot (1998: 119–22), Swiggers and Wouters (1996: 129–31)

λήγω   to terminate, end in (+ dat.), have a final syllable in (+ dat.) (also middle)

ληκτικός, -ή, -όν   terminal, at the end

λῆμμα, -ατος, τό   base form, premise

λῆξις, -εως, ἡ   ending

λόγος, -ου, ὁ   phrase, sentence, complex term; analogy, rule, principle, oration, narrative, utterance, speech, language; section, division (of a speech); proverb, saying; prose, dialog (note that λόγος *never* means "word" in grammatical contexts); see Lallot (1998: 119–22), Wouters (1975)

λύσις, -εως, ἡ   resolution (metrical, of a long into two shorts; or of a long vowel into two vowels, as ἠέλιος for ἥλιος); looseness of structure in writing, esp. asyndeton

λύω   to resolve (a long into two shorts)

μακροκαταληκτέω   to end in a long syllable

μακροκατάληκτος, -ον   ending in a long syllable

μακροπαράληκτος, -ον   having a long penultimate syllable

μακροπεριόδευτος, -ον   verbose

μακροπερίοδος, -ον   making or having long periods

μακρός, -ά, -όν   long (of vowels or syllables); (as fem. subst.) mark indicating a long vowel

μακροσύλλαβος, -ον   consisting of long syllables

μακρότης, -ητος, ἡ   length

μακρύνω   to lengthen

μαμμωνυμικός, -ή, -όν   derived from the grandmother's name

μάχη, -ης, ἡ   conflict

μάχομαι   to be in conflict with; see Dalimier (2001: 257–8)

μεγαλογραφέω   to write with omega

μέγεθος, -ους, τό   (metrical) length, lengthening, augment

μεγεθύνω   to lengthen

μεθίσταμαι   to change into (+ εἰς + acc.)

μέλλων (χρόνος)   future (tense); see Lallot (1998: 172); μετ' ὀλίγον μέλλων future perfect tense; see Wouters (1994)

μερισμός, -οῦ, ὁ   division, classification, distribution, parsing, scansion, division of a line into feet or a sentence into words; see Lallot (1997: ii. 169–70), Ildefonse (1997: 276–9), Sluiter (1990: 106)

μέρος, -ους, τό (λόγου)   part of speech; word; see Lallot (1997: ii. 9, 30; 1998: 122–5), Schenkeveld (1994: 269–73), Householder (1981: 4), Egenolff (1879)

μεσάζομαι   to be inserted in the middle, intervene, occupy a central position

μεσόπτωτος, -ον   inflected in the middle (of words like ὅστις)

μέσος, -η, -ον: μέσον (γράμμα)   voiced consonant (β, γ, δ); μέση (στιγμή) middle stop (in punctuation, indicates a pause for breath greater than that of a comma but less than that of a period/full stop, signified by a low point); μέση προσῳδία: see Probert (2003: 17–18); μέση διάθεσις middle voice; see Collinge (1963), Lallot (1998: 91–2, 102–5, 168–70), Blank (1983a: 51–2)

μεσοσυλλαβία, -ας, ἡ   parenthesis

μεσότης, -ητος, ἡ   middle voice; pertaining to quality (of adverbs); see Collinge (1963), Lallot (1998: 168–70, 227), Rijksbaron (1986), Andersen (1989)

μεταβαίνω   to change

μετάβασις, -εως, ἡ   change, inflectional change, state of being transitive or not reflexive; see Dalimier (2001: 409–10)

μεταβατικός, -ή, -όν   not reflexive (of pronouns), transitive (of verbs), transitional or copulative (of conjunctions)

μεταβιβάζω   to transfer, translate

μεταβολή, -ῆς, ἡ   change

μεταβολικός, -ή, -όν   subject to change, mutable, doubtful (of the quantity of α, ι, υ)

μεταγραμματίζω   to transcribe in different orthography, transpose the letters of a word

μεταγραμματισμός, -οῦ, ὁ   transcription into a different orthography

μεταγραφή, -ῆς, ἡ   transcription, translation, change of text or reading

μεταγράφω   to copy, transcribe, alter or correct what one has written, translate

μετάγω   to translate, derive; (pass.) be borrowed

μετάθεσις, -εως, ἡ   transposition, metathesis (transposition of letters), change (of a letter), plagiarism

μετακινέω   to change

μετακλίνω   to change (esp. of case)

μετάκλισις, -εως, ἡ   change of case; = μετάληψις

μεταλαμβάνω   to change, change construction, use in place of, take words in another sense, parody, translate, interpret

μεταληπτικός, -ή, -όν   pertaining to μετάληψις

μετάληψις, -εως, ἡ   substitution; change, change of construction, change in dialect, change of name, translation; see Sluiter (1990: 111–17), Lallot (1997: ii. 93)

μεταλλαγή, -ῆς, ἡ   change, exchange

μεταλλάσσω   to change, transpose

μετάμειψις, -εως, ἡ   exchange, alteration

μεταμορφόω   to transform

μεταξύ   intermediate, neuter

μεταξύτης, -ητος, ἡ   middle position, interval

μεταπλασμός, -οῦ, ὁ   metaplasm (formation of case or tense forms from a non-existent nominative or present base form), transformation, poetic license

μεταπλάσσω   to change; (pass.) be formed by metaplasm

μεταπλαστικός, -ή, -όν   changed in form

μεταποιέω   to change, transpose

μεταποίησις, -εως, ἡ   change, alteration

μετάπτωσις, -εως, ἡ   change, inflection

μεταπτωτικός, -ή, -όν   liable to change; common (of the quantity of vowels α, ι, υ)

μετασυντίθημι   to change, alter the arrangement of a sentence

μετασύρω   to alter in form

μετασχηματίζω   to change form, inflect

μετασχηματισμός, -οῦ, ὁ   change of form, inflection

μετάταξις, -εως, ἡ   transposition, metathesis

μετατίθημι   to transpose, change

μετατύπωσις, -εως, ἡ   transformation, resolution of a compound into two simple words

μεταφέρω   to use metaphorically

μεταφορά, -ᾶς, ἡ   metaphor

μεταφορικός, -ή, -όν   metaphorical, apt at metaphors

μεταφράζω   to paraphrase, translate

μετάφρασις, -εως, ἡ   paraphrase

μεταχαρακτηρίζω   to change the orthography

μετουσιαστικός, -ή, -όν   indicating participation (of adjectives), derivative adjective; see Lallot (1998: 159)

μετοχή, -ῆς, ἡ   participle; see Lallot (1998: 187–90; 1999)

μετοχικός, -ή, -όν   participial

μετωνυμία, -ας, ἡ   metonymy (use of one word for another)

μηκύνω   to lengthen

μηκυσμός, -οῦ, ὁ   lengthening

μητρωνυμικός, -ή, -όν   metronymic, named after one's mother

μικρογραφέω   to write with a short vowel, esp. omicron

μοναδικός, -ή, -όν   unique, having a single form, having one ending for all three genders, single

μονάζω   to be unique

μονή, -ῆς, ἡ   preservation (of letters), persistence (of accent)

μονήρης, -ες   rare, peculiar, not analogical, anomalous

μονογενής, -ές   having only one gender

μονογράμματος, -ον   consisting of only one letter

μονόκλιτος, -ον   indeclinable

μονοπροσωπέω   to have only one person

μονοπρόσωπος, -ον   having reference to only one person (of pronouns, i.e. as opposed to possessive pronouns that refer to both possessor and possessed), having one person (of pronouns, i.e. ἐκεῖνος as opposed to ἵ (nom. of οὗ), which has corresponding first and second persons)

μονόπτωτος, -ον   with only one case, indeclinable

μονοσυλλαβέω   to be a monosyllable

μονοσυλλαβία, -ας, ἡ   the state of being monosyllabic

μονοσύλλαβος, -ον   monosyllabic (of words), dealing in monosyllables (of grammarians) μονοσχημάτιστος, -ον   of only one form, indeclinable

μονότονος, -ον   without elevation of the voice

μονόφθογγος, -ου, ἡ   monophthong, single vowel sound, single syllable or letter

μονόφωνος, -ον   of one sound, indeclinable

μονόχρονος, -ον   always of the same quantity, occupying only one time-unit, short (of vowels)

μόριον, -ου, τό   word, part of speech, prefix or suffix; see Dalimier (2001: 226–7, 392)

μυγμός, -οῦ, ὁ   utterance or sound of the letter μ

μυοτακισμός, -οῦ, ὁ   repeated μ sound

νοέω   to mean

νοητόν, -οῦ, τό   meaning; see Lallot (1997: ii. 10)

νόθος, -η, -ον   spurious (of literary works), hybrid (of foreign words partly adapted into the language)

νοῦς, -οῦ, ὁ   sense, meaning

νυγμή, -ῆς, ἡ   dot, punctuation mark

νυγμός, -οῦ, ὁ   sound of the letter ν

νώνυμος, -ον   having no name

οἰκειοτονέομαι   to have its own accent

οἰκειω(μα)τικός, -ή, -όν   possessive

οἰκτικός, -ή, -όν   expressing pity or lamentation (of verbs)

οἷον   as, such as (introducing examples of a previously stated rule); cf. 4.1.40

ὀλίγος: μετ’ ὀλίγον μέλλων   future perfect tense; see Wouters (1994)

ὀλιγοσύλλαβος, -ον   of few syllables

ὀλιγωρέω   to neglect, (pass.) be defective or badly formed; see Lallot (1997: ii. 225)

ὁλόκληρος -ον   complete, in its original form, not subject to πάθη

ὁμαλισμός, -οῦ, ὁ   lack of accentual elevation, lack of accent

ὁμιλία, -ας, ἡ   (current) usage

ὁμόγλωσσος, -ον   of the same language, speaking the same language

ὁμοείδεια, -ας, ἡ   sameness, similarity of form or accent

ὁμοειδής, -ές   of the same form, indeclinable, related; see Lallot (1997: ii. 166–7)

ὁμοιογενής, -ές   of the same gender

ὁμοιογραφέω   to write alike

ὁμοιόγραφος, -ον   written alike

ὁμοιοκαταληκτέω   to have similar endings

ὁμοιοκατάληκτος, -ον   ending alike

ὁμοιοκαταληξία, -ας, ἡ   similarity of endings

ὁμοιοπαράγωγος, -ον   similarly derived

ὁμοιοπρόσωπος, -ον   in the same person

ὁμοιοπρόφορος, -ον   similar in pronunciation

ὁμοιόπτωτος, -ον   with a similar inflection, with similar endings, in a similar case, in the same case

ὁμοιόσημος, -ον   meaning the same thing

ὁμοιόσχημος, -ον   of similar form, agreeing

ὁμοιοτέλευτος, -ον ending similarly; (as neut. subst.) homoeoteleuton (a rhetorical figure in which several cola have similar-sounding endings)

ὁμοιότης, -ητος, ἡ similarity

ὁμοιότονος, -ον with similar accent

ὁμοιόφθογγος, -ον sounding similar

ὁμοιοφωνέω to sound like

ὁμοιωματικός, -ή, -όν correlative, signifying resemblance or comparison, pertaining to a simile

ὁμοίωσις, -εως, ἡ resemblance, comparison, simile

ὁμοτικός, -ή, -όν related to swearing (of adverbs)

ὁμοτονέω to have the same accent

ὁμότονος, -ον having the same accent

ὁμοτυπία, -ας, ἡ sameness of form

ὁμοφωνέω to sound the same or similar, coincide in form

ὁμοφωνία, -ας, ἡ sameness of sound or form

ὁμόφωνος, -ον having the same sound

ὁμόχρονος, -ον of the same time, quantity, or duration

ὁμωνυμέω to have the same name as, have the same meaning as

ὁμωνυμία, -ας, ἡ homonymy, ambiguity, homonymous word

ὁμώνυμος, -ον homonymous, having the same name; (as neut. subst.) homonym

ὄνομα, -ατος, τό noun or adjective, word; see Lallot (1997: ii. 22; 1998: 127–8; 1999)

ὀνομάζω to name, utter

ὀνομασία, -ας, ἡ name, noun, language

ὀνομαστικός, -ή, -όν nominative; ὀνομαστική (πτῶσις) the nominative case; pertaining to naming; ὀνομαστικόν (βιβλίον) vocabulary

ὀνοματικός, -ή, -όν pertaining to nouns

ὀνοματοθέτης, -ου, ὁ namer

ὀνοματοθετικός, -ή, -όν prone to name-giving

ὀνοματοποιέω to coin words (by onomatopoeia)

ὀνοματοποιία, -ας, ἡ onomatopoeia (coining a word in imitation of a sound), neologism

ὀνοματουργέω = ὀνοματοποιέω

ὀξύνω (of syllables) to pronounce or accent with an acute; (of words) to pronounce or accent with an acute on the final syllable

ὀξύς, -εῖα, -ύ acute; having an acute accent; ὀξεῖα (προσῳδία) the acute accent

ὀξυτονέω (of syllables) to pronounce or accent with an acute; (of words) to pronounce or accent with an acute on the final syllable

ὀξύτονος, -ον (of syllables) having an acute accent; (of words) having an acute accent on the final syllable

ὀξυφωνέω to pronounce with an acute accent

ὀρεκτικός, -ή, -όν conative (of verbs)

ὀρθογραφία, -ας, ἡ correct writing, orthography

ὀρθοέπεια, -ας, ἡ correct pronunciation, diction

ὀρθοεπέω   to speak or pronounce correctly

ὀρθολογέω   to speak correctly

ὀρθόπτωτος, -ον   nominative

ὀρθός, -ή, -όν   nominative; ὀρθή (πτῶσις) the nominative case; active (of verbs); real or unmodified (of the accent); see Lallot (1998: 140–2)

ὀρθοτονέω   to pronounce with the unmodified accent

ὀρθοτόνησις, -εως, ἡ   use of the unmodified accent

ὀρθότονος, -ον   with the unmodified accent

ὁρίζω   to define

ὁρισμός, -οῦ, ὁ   definition; the idea expressed by the indicative

ὁριστικός, -ή, -όν   indicative; ὁριστική (ἔγκλισις) indicative mood

ὁρκικός, -ή, -όν   pertaining to oaths

ὁρκωμοτικός, -ή, -όν   used in oaths (of adverbs)

ὅρος, -ου, ὁ   definition

ὅτε: ἔσθ' ὅτε   sometimes

οὐδέτερος, -α, -ον   neuter

παθητικός, -ή, -όν   passive (of verbs)

πάθος, -ους, τό   passive voice (of verbs); transformation/modification in form (of words; πάθη are an important concept in ancient grammatical theory and occur in many types, such as addition of letters to a word, subtraction of letters, metathesis, and tmesis); diacritic signs other than accents and breathings; see Swiggers and Wouters (1996: 142–5), Wackernagel (1876), Andersen (1989)

παλιλλογέω   to repeat

παλιλλογία, -ας, ἡ   repetition

παντοῖον γένος   common gender

παππωνυμικός, -ή, -όν   derived from the grandfather's name

παρά   cf. 4.1.28

παράβασις, -εως, ἡ   song that accompanies the entrance of a chorus in drama; transgression, breaking a rule

παραβολή, -ῆς, ἡ   comparison

παραβολικός, -ή, -όν   expressing comparison (of adverbs)

παράγγελμα, -ατος, τό   precept, rule

παραγραμματεύω   to alter by changing a letter, make an alliterative pun

παραγραμματίζω   to alter by changing a letter, emend by change of letters

παραγραμματισμός, -οῦ, ὁ   change of letters, alliteration

παραγραφή, -ῆς, ἡ   marginal note or sign (esp. for indicating the end of a paragraph, but also for stage directions, spurious passages, end of sentence, change of speaker); parenthetical statement; see Dalimier (2001: 410)

παραγραφικός, -ή, -όν   in the form of a παραγραφή; forming a parenthetical statement

παράγραφος, -ου, ἡ   paragraphos (marginal sign indicating change of speaker in drama, corresponding sections in a chorus, or a division for other reasons between sections of text) παράγω   to derive, form, inflect

παραγωγή, -ῆς, ἡ   derivation, derived form, inflection, formation, addition to the end of a syllable

παραγωγός, -όν   derived; see Lallot (1998: 131–3)

παραδέχομαι   to accept (a transmitted form or explanation); signify

παραδιαζευκτικός, -ή, -όν   (of conjunctions) subdisjunctive (a type of "or" used where either alternative alone and the two together are alike admissible); see Lallot (1998: 245)

παράδοσις, -εως, ἡ   transmission, grammatical doctrine, tradition; see Van Groningen (1963)

παραδοχή, -ῆς, ἡ   acceptance, use; ἐν παραδοχῇ γίγνομαι (+ gen.) to admit the use of

παράθεσις, -εως, ἡ   juxtaposition (the state of being two separate words rather than a compound; also a type of word formation that joins words complete with their endings, as Διόσ-κοροι, as opposed to composition, which uses only the stem form of the first element, so Διο-γενής); apposition

παραινετικός, -ή, -όν   hortatory

παρακατηγόρημα, -ατος, τό = παρασύμβαμα

παράκειμαι   to be laid down, mentioned in books, cited, joined by juxtaposition (as opposed to composition), parallel, interpolated, derived; παρακείμενος (χρόνος) the perfect tense; see Lallot (1998: 173)

παρακέλευσις, -εως, ἡ   exhortation

παρακελευσματικός, -ή, -όν   hortatory

παρακελευστικός, -ή, -όν   hortatory (of adverbs)

παρακλίνω   to alter

παρακολουθέω   to follow logically

παραλαμβάνω   to use, (pass.) to be found, occur, be used

παράλειψις, -εως, -ἡ   omission, *praeteritio*

παραλήγω   to be penultimate, have a penultimate syllable in (+ dat.) (also middle)

παράληξις, -εως, ἡ   penultimate syllable

παράληψις, -εως, ἡ   tradition, usage

παραλλαγή, -ῆς, ἡ   interchange (e.g. of gen. sing. -ου to -οιο, or of cases or persons), variation, change of meaning

παραλληλία, -ας, ἡ   repetition of sounds or letters; pleonasm

παραλληλισμός, -οῦ, ὁ   repetition

παράλληλος, -ον   parallel, used pleonastically

παραλληλότης, -ητος, ἡ   repetition

παραλογία, -ας, ἡ   false form

παράλογος, -ον   irregular

παραναλίσκω   to obliterate, modify, absorb

παραπλασμός, -οῦ, ὁ   change of grammatical form

παραπληρόω   to fill up (of an expletive particle)

παραπλήρωμα, -ατος, τό   pleonasm, expletive, superfluous complement παραπληρωματικός, -ή, -όν   expletive (completing the sense or meter); see Lallot (1998: 252–4), Dalimier (1999; 2001: 380–2), Sluiter (1997*b*)

παρασημείωσις, -εως, ἡ   marginal note, passing mention

παράσημον, -ου, τό   sign, marginal mark or note

παραστατικός, -ή, -όν   indicative of, denotative

παρασύμβαμα, -ατος, τό   impersonal verb governing a dative

παρασυναπτικὸς σύνδεσμος   causal connective particle; see Lallot (1998: 246–7), Dalimier (2001: 313–17)

παρασυνάπτομαι   to be connected by a causal particle

παρασύνθετος, -ον   formed from a compound; (as neut. subst.) word derived from a compound; see Lallot (1998: 137–8)

παρασχηματίζω   to change form, decline, form a derivative, speak incorrectly, form similarly to (+ dat.)

παρασχηματισμός, -οῦ, ὁ   inflection, change of form

παράτασις, -εως, ἡ   duration, continuance, time of the imperfect tense

παρατατικός, -ή, -όν   continuing, incomplete; imperfect, παρατατικός (χρόνος) the imperfect tense; see Lallot (1998: 173)

παρατείνω   to extend, prolong, lengthen in pronunciation

παρατελευταῖος, -α, -ον   penultimate

παρατέλευτος, -ον   penultimate

παρατήρησις, -εως, ἡ   observation, note, observance of rules

παρατίθημι   to juxtapose, place side by side without forming a compound

παρατροπή, -ῆς, ἡ   deviation, alteration, error

παραύξησις, -εως, ἡ   increase, metrical lengthening

παραύξω   to increase, augment, lengthen

παραφθείρω   to corrupt; (pass.) be lost, become obsolete

παραφθορά, -ᾶς, ἡ   corrruption

παραφυλακή = παρατήρησις

παραφυλάσσω   to observe

παράχρησις, -εως, ἡ   abuse

παρεγγράφω   to write by the side, subjoin, interpolate

παρεδρεύω   to be penultimate, have in the penultimate syllable

παρεισδύ(ν)ω   to insert

παρεκβολή, -ῆς, ἡ   digression, compilation of a set of critical remarks, commentary

παρέκτασις, -εως, ἡ   lengthening, extension

παρεληλυθώς, -υῖα, -ός   past; παρεληλυθώς (χρόνος) past tense; see Lallot (1998: 172)

παρελκύω   to derive

παρέλκω   to continue, be redundant, append, be derived

παρέλλειψις, -εως, ἡ   loss of one of two similar consonants

παρεμπίπτω   to occur, be inserted, be included in one form

παρέμπτωσις, -εως, ἡ   insertion, parenthesis

παρεμφαίνω   to mean, signify; see Van Ophuijsen (1993*a*)

παρέμφασις, -εως, ἡ   meaning, perversion of meaning

παρεμφατικός, -ή, -όν   indicative, finite (of verbs)

παρένθεσις, -εως, ἡ   insertion, parenthesis, interjection

παρένθετος, -ον   interpolated

παρεντίθημι   to insert, interpolate

παρέπομαι   to accompany, follow; be an accident of (+ dat.; e.g. person and number are accidents of verbs); see Lallot 1997 (ii. 99)

παρετυμολογέω   to allude to the etymology of a word

παρηχέομαι   to resemble in sound, be derived from another word by such resemblance, alliterate

παρήχημα, -ατος, τό = παρήχησις

παρήχησις, -εως, ἡ   the use of words alike in sound but different in meaning

παρηχητικός, -ή, -όν   alliterative

παρίστημι   to express, establish

παρολκή, -ῆς, ἡ   redundancy, abundance, pleonasm

παρονομάζω   to form a derivative, name after

παρονομασία, -ας, ἡ   assonance, derivative, use of a word first in its proper and then in its derived sense (note the difference from the modern use of "paronomasia" for "pun")

παροξύνω   to pronounce or accent a word with an acute on the penultimate syllable

παροξυτονέω   to pronounce or accent a word with an acute on the penultimate syllable

παροξύτονος, -ον   having an acute accent on the penultimate syllable

παρορμητικός, -ή, -όν   denoting excitement or stimulation (of verbs)

παρυφιστάμενον, -ου, τό   joint (lexical and/or grammatical) meaning; see Lallot (1997: ii. 21)

παρωνυμιάζω   to call by a derived name

παρώνυμ(ι)ος, -ον   derivative, derived from a noun, Latin cognomen, agnomen; see Lallot (1998: 135–6)

παρῳχημένος (χρόνος)   past (tense)

πάσχω   to be passive (of verbs), to be subject to changes

πατρικός, -ή, -όν   genitive, πατρική (πτῶσις) genitive case

πατρωνυμέομαι   to have the patronymic formed

πατρωνυμία, -ας, ἡ   patronymic name

πατρωνυμικός, -ή, -όν   patronymic; see Lallot (1998: 133), Dalimier (2001: 387–8)

πεζός, -ή, -όν   in or of prose; (as fem. subst.) prose

πεντάπτωτος, -ον   having five cases (of nouns)

πεντασύλλαβος, -ον   having five syllables (of words)

πεποιημένον (ὄνομα)   neologism, onomatopoeia, onomatopoeic word

περατόομαι   to end, terminate (in, + εἰς)

περιαίρεσις, -εως, ἡ = ἀφαίρεσις

περιγραφή, -ῆς, ἡ   conclusion, end

περιγραφικός, -ή, -όν   indicating a conclusion (of conjunctions, as δή, γε)
περιγράφω   to enclose in brackets, reject as spurious, remove; conclude
περιεκτικός, -ή, -όν   comprehensive; having both active and passive meaning
     (of verb forms), denoting a place in which things are situated (of nouns); see
     Lallot (1998: 158)
περικλάζω = περισπάω
περίκλασις, -εως, ἡ   circumflex accent
περικλάω = περισπάω
περικοπή, -ῆς, ἡ   section, passage
περικράτησις, -εως, ἡ   prevailing significance, dominant meaning
περιληπτικός, -ή, -όν   collective (of nouns)
περίοδος, -ου, ἡ   clausula, (rhetorical) period
περιποιητικὰ ῥήματα   verbs of acquiring or benefitting
περισπασμός, -οῦ, ὁ   circumflex accent
περισπάω   (of syllables) to pronounce with a circumflex, accent with a circum-
     flex; (of words) to pronounce or write with a circumflex on the final syllable
περισπώμενος, -η, -ον   (of syllables) having a circumflex accent; (of words) hav-
     ing a circumflex accent on the final syllable; περισπωμένη (προσῳδία) the cir-
     cumflex accent; περισπώμενον ῥῆμα contract verb
περισσεύω = πλεονάζω
περισσός, -ή, -όν   superfluous
περισσοσυλλαβέω   to be one syllable longer, to be imparisyllabic
περισσοσύλλαβος, -ον   one syllable longer, imparisyllabic
περιστίζω   to mark with dots, punctuate
πεῦσις, -εως, ἡ   question
πευστικός, -ή, -όν   interrogative
πλαγιάζω   to inflect, decline
πλαγιασμός, -οῦ, ὁ   use of oblique cases, inflection
πλάγιος, -η, -ον   oblique (of cases), dependent (of constructions); πλαγία
     (πτῶσις) oblique case
πλάσμα, -ατος, τό   invention, fiction; see Papadopoulou (1999)
πλεονάζω   o be superfluous, be redundant, use redundantly, have an added letter;
     to augment, reduplicate, or geminate; to have added (+ dat.)
πλεονασμός, -οῦ, ὁ   addition of a letter; redundancy, pleonasm, use of redun-
     dant words or letters
πλεονοσυλλαβέω   to consist of many or more syllables
πληθυντικός, -ή, -όν   plural
πληθύνω   to use, (pass.) to have or form a plural
πληθυσμός, -οῦ, ὁ   pluralization
πνεῦμα, -ατος, τό   breathing (rough or smooth)
πνευματίζω   to write or pronounce with the breathing
πνευματικός, -ή, -όν   pertaining to breathings
πνευματώδης, -ες   pronounced with a strong breathing (of the consonants φ,
     ψ, σ, ζ)

ποιέω   to be active

ποιότης, -ητος, ἡ   quality

πολιτευομένη λέξις   cultured speech

πολύλεξις, -ι   containing many words

πολυσήμαντος, -ον   having many meanings

πολύσημος, -ον   having many meanings

πολυσύλλαβος, -ον   polysyllabic

πολυσύμφωνος, -ον   containing many consonants

πολυσύνδεσμος, -ον   using many conjunctions or connecting particles

πολυσύνθετος, -ον   compounded from many elements

πολυωνυμία, -ας, ἡ   polyonymy, state of having many names; synonymy

πολυώνυμος, -ον   synonymous

ποσότης, -ητος, ἡ   quantity (of vowels or syllables, or with reference to adverbs of quantity); number of letters or syllables

πρᾶγμα, -ατος, τό   action (esp. of verb); abstraction, object of thought; see Lallot (1997: ii. 206–7; 1998: 127–8), Swiggers and Wouters (1996: 131–4), Van Ophuijsen (1993a)

πραγματεία, -ας, ἡ   treatise

προάγω   to pronounce

προαιρετικός, -ή, -όν   pertaining to purpose or desire (of verbs, e.g. βούλομαι)

προαναφώνησις, -εως, ἡ   statement by anticipation, preface, proem

προεκδίδωμι   to publish previously

προέκκειμαι   to precede, be set forth previously, be cited above; προεκκείμενα πτωτικά case-forms presupposed by underlying adverbs

πρόθεσις, -εως, ἡ   preposition; prefixing; = πρόσθεσις; see Lallot (1998: 211–19; 1999)

προθετικός, -ή, -όν   prepositional, of or for prefixing

προκαταλέγομαι   to be described beforehand

πρόκειμαι   to be the topic of the current discussion; precede, be initial

προλημμάτιζω   to place before (esp. of the protasis in a condition)

προληπτικός, -ή, -όν   anticipatory, of prolepsis

πρόληψις, -εως, ἡ   anticipation, prolepsis

προπαραλήγω   to be antepenultimate, be in the antepenultimate syllable

προπαροξυντικός, -ή, -όν   given to placing an acute accent on the antepenultimate syllable

προπαροξύνω   to accent a word with an acute on the antepenultimate syllable

προπαροξυτονέω = προπαροξύνω

προπαροξυτόνησις, -εως, ἡ   accentuation with an acute on the antepenultimate syllable

προπαροξύτονος, -ον   having an acute accent on the antepenultimate syllable

προπερισπάω   to accent a word with a circumflex on the penultimate syllable

προπερισπώμενος, -η, -ον   having a circumflex accent on the penultimate syllable

πρός τι (ἔχον)   relational (of nouns implying a relationship, as πατήρ and φίλος);

relative, correlative; see Lallot (1998: 152), Swiggers (1997: 41–2), Swiggers and Wouters (1995*a*)

προσαγόρευσις, -εως, ἡ   address, greeting, vocative

προσαγορευτικός, -ή, -όν   vocative; of address, greeting; προσαγορευτική (πτῶσις) the vocative case; see Lallot (1998: 148)

προσαγορεύω   to call

προσανταποδίδωμι   to retort, rejoin

προσαφαιρέω   to remove letters repeatedly; (pass.) to suffer repeated aphaeresis

προσγραφή, -ῆς, ἡ   writing of iota subscript/adscript

προσγράφω   to write iota subscript/adscript; ι προσγεγραμμένον iota subscript/adscript

προσδιατίθημι   to affect in addition

προσδιορισμός, -οῦ, ὁ   further definition, determination, or specification

προσέλευσις, -εως, ἡ = πρόσθεσις

προσηγορία, -ας, ἡ   common noun or adjective (as opposed to proper nouns), common noun (as opposed to both proper nouns and adjectives), appellative, greeting, address; see Lallot (1998: 129)

προσηγορικός, -ή, -όν   appellative, generic, used in address; nominal, pertaining to a common noun; προσηγορικὸν ὄνομα common noun, common name, Latin *praenomen, cognomen*

πρόσθεσις, -εως, ἡ   addition (esp. of letters or sounds at the beginning of a word)

προσθήκη, -ης, ἡ   particle, epithet

πρόσκειμαι   cf. 4.1.37

προσλαμβάνω   to add, take in addition, assume

προσληπτικός, -ή, όν   assumptive, presumptive, belonging to the minor premise (of conjunctions); allowing one to introduce a second premise, conjunction formed with a copulative and an expletive; see Dalimier (2001: 398–406)

πρόσληψις, -εως, ἡ   addition, taking in addition

πρόσοδος, -ου, ἡ   addition

προσπάθεια, -ας, ἡ   close connection

πρόσπνευσις, -εως, ἡ   aspiration, rough breathing

προσπνέω   to pronounce with a rough breathing

προσσημαίνω   to signify in addition, connote

προστακτικός, -ή, -όν   imperative; προστακτική (ἔγκλισις) imperative (mood)

πρόσταξις, -εως, ἡ   command

προσυπακούω   to understand something not expressed, supply in thought

πρόσφθεγμα, -ατος, τό   address, greeting, epithet, interjection

προσφωνέω   to address, speak to, call by name, dedicate, pronounce

προσφώνησις, -εως, ἡ   address, dedication, interjection

προσφωνητικός, -ή, -όν   exclamatory; interjectory

προσχηματισμός, -οῦ, ὁ   addition of a syllable to the end of a word

προσῳδία, -ας, ἡ   variation in pitch, pronunciation with a certain pitch, accentuation, other aspects of pronunciation that were normally unwritten (quantity, aspiration), diacritics (marks to indicate those features of pronunciation); see Lallot (1998: 84–5)

προσωπικός, -ή, -όν   personal (having to do with grammatical person, as of verbs that are not impersonal)

πρόσωπον, -ου, τό   (grammatical) person; see Lallot (1998: 170–1)

προσωποποιία, -ας, ἡ   change of (grammatical) person

προτακτικός, -ή, -όν   used as a prefix; coming first or in front; being the first vowel of a diphthong; προτακτικὸν ἄρθρον definite article (as opposed to the relative pronoun)

πρόταξις, -εως, ἡ   prefixing, putting in front; see Lallot (1997: ii. 162)

πρότασις, -εως, ἡ   hypothetical clause, protasis (the subordinate or *if*-clause of a conditional sentence)

προτάσσω   to prefix, put before

προϋπάρχω = προϋφίσταμαι

προϋπόκειμαι = προϋφίσταμαι

προϋφίσταμαι   to be (an) antecedent, exist before, presuppose

προφέρω   to utter, pronounce, use, cite (also in middle)

προφορά, -ᾶς, ἡ   pronunciation, utterance

προφορικός, -ή, -όν   pronounced

πρωτόθετος, -ον = πρωτότυπος

πρῶτος, -η, -ον   first, primitive

πρωτοτυπέω   to be original or primitive

πρωτότυπος, -ον   original, primitive, not derived, personal pronoun (as opposed to possessive pronouns)

πτῶσις, -εως, ἡ   case, inflection; see Lejeune (1950), Hiersche (1956), Lallot (1998: 139–42)

πτωτικός, -ή, -όν   declinable, able to be inflected, connected with case; (as neut. subst.) nominal form (noun, adjective, pronoun, participle)

πύσμα, -ατος, τό   question (esp. one requiring an answer other than "yes" or "no"), interrogative word; see Dalimier (2001: 275)

πυσματικός, -ή, -όν   interrogative

ῥῆμα, -ατος, τό   verb, phrase, word, predicate; see Lallot (1998: 161–4; 1999)

ῥηματικός, -ή, -όν   of or for a verb, derived from a verb, verbal; see Lallot (1998: 135–6)

ῥητός, -ή, -όν   in common use (of words, etc.); capable of being spoken; (as neut. subst.) expression

ῥοῖζος, -ου, ὁ   hissing, sound of the letter ρ

ῥώννυμι   to wake up the acute accent on the final syllable of an oxytone word (i.e. change it from grave to acute)

ῥωτακίζω   to use the letter ρ wrongly or excessively

σαμπῖ   the sign ϡ, used for the numeral 900

σημαίνω   to signify, mean, be significant

σημαντικός, -ή, -όν   significant, indicative of, meaning

σημασία, -ας, ἡ   meaning
σημεῖον, -ου, τό   sign, critical mark, diacritic (accents, breathings, punctuation, etc.)
σημειόω   to note (also in middle), mark with a sign, note as an exception; (pf. pass.) be a (noted) exception
σιγματίζω   to write with sigma
σιγμός, -οῦ, ὁ   hissing, sound of sibilant consonants
σκεύη, -ῶν, τά   neuter (nouns)
σολοικίζω   to speak incorrectly, commit a solecism
σολοικισμός, -οῦ, ὁ   incorrectness in the use of language, solecism (incorrect syntax, as opposed to βαρβαρισμός, the incorrect use of individual words); see Lallot (1997: ii. 161), Donnet (1967: 154–6)
σόλοικος, -ον   speaking incorrectly, using bad Greek
στέρησις, -εως, ἡ   negation, privation
στερητικός, -ή, -όν   negative, privative (esp. ᾱ στερητικόν alpha privative)
στιγμή, -ῆς, ἡ   punctuation mark, esp. the period or full stop; see Blank (1983a), Lallot (1997: ii. 106)
στίζω   to punctuate
στοιχεῖον, -ου, τό   individual sound; letter of the alphabet; element; word; see Lallot (1997: ii. 9; 1998: 95–8), Sluiter (1990: 43–4); κατὰ στοιχεῖον in alphabetical order
στοιχείωσις, -εως, ἡ   (elementary) teaching; alphabet
στοιχειωτής, -οῦ, ὁ   grammarian; teacher or creator of letters or elements; Euclid (the creator of the *Elements*); see Lallot (1997: ii. 285–6)
συγγενικός, -ή, -όν   hereditary, of the family; συγγενικὸν ὄνομα Latin *nomen gentilicium*
συγγράφω   to write iota subscript/adscript
συγκατάθεσις, -εως, ἡ   affirmation; συγκαταθέσεως affirmative (of adverbs)
συγκαταθετικός, -ή, -όν   affirmative
σύγκειμαι   to be composed of
συγκλίνω   to inflect similarly
συγκοπή, -ῆς, ἡ   cutting a word short by removing one or more sounds; syncope (loss of a sound or sounds in the middle of a word)
συγκόπτω   to cut short a sound or a word, syncopate
σύγκρισις, -εως, ἡ   comparison
συγκριτικός, -ή, -όν   comparative
σύγκρουσις, -εως, ἡ   collision (of sounds, etc.), hiatus (collision of vowels)
συγχρονέομαι   to be in the same tense as
συγχρονίζω = συγχρονέομαι
σύγχυσις, -εως, ἡ   confusion, indistinctness
συζυγέω   to correspond
συζυγία, -ας, ἡ   group of words inflected similarly, conjugation, declension; combination; conjunction of words or things in pairs; syzygy (a grouping of two feet in meter); group of related words; syncope; see Lallot (1997: ii. 86–7; 1998: 181–5), Sluiter (1990: 84)

συλλαβή, -ῆς, ἡ syllable; (in plural) letters of the alphabet; see Lallot (1998: 107–8)

συλλαβίζω to join letters into syllables, pronounce letters together

συλλαβικός, -ή, -όν syllabic

σύλλεξις, -εως, ἡ contribution

συλληπτικός, -ή, -όν collective

σύλληψις, -εως, ἡ collection, inclusion; conjunction (of consonants); rhetorical figure by which a predicate belonging to one subject is attributed to several

συλλογιστικός, -ή, -όν inferential (of conjunctions); see Lallot (1998: 252), Dalimier (2001: 411–12)

συμβαρύνομαι to take the grave accent in addition

συμβολικός, -ή, -όν figurative, conventional

συμβουλευτικός, -ή, -όν hortatory, deliberative

συμμετασχηματίζομαι to change form along with

συμμονή, -ῆς, ἡ close connection

συμπάθεια, -ας, ἡ analogy

συμπαράκειμαι to be adjacent

συμπαραπληρωματικός, -ή, -όν completing, expletive (of conjunctions)

συμπερισπάω to circumflex in addition

συμπίπτω to coincide in form

συμπλεκτικός, -ή, -όν connecting, copulative (of conjunctions); see Lallot (1997: ii. 104; 1998: 242–4)

συμπλέκω to join together, combine

συμπληθύνω to put into a plural form in addition

συμπλοκή, -ῆς, ἡ combination, connection, copula (verb "be" connecting subject and predicate)

συμφέρομαι to be constructed with, to agree in form with

συμφράζομαι to be used in the same context with, to be synonymous with

σύμφρασις, -εως, ἡ continuous speech

συμφώνησις, -εως, ἡ = συνίζησις

σύμφωνον (γράμμα) consonant

συναίρεσις, -εως, ἡ contraction, synaeresis (joining two vowels to form a diphthong)

συναιρέω to contract

συναλειφή = συναλ(ο)ιφή

συναλείφω to unite two syllables into one

συναλλαγή, -ῆς, ἡ interchange, especially between long α and η

συναλ(ο)ιφή, -ῆ, ἡ stopping of hiatus by uniting two syllables through elision, crasis, contraction, or synaeresis; see Lallot (1997: ii. 109), Dalimier (2001: 275–6)

συναοριστέομαι to acquire indefiniteness at the same time

συναπτικός, -ή, -όν connective; hypothetical, conditional (of conjunctions); see Lallot (1998: 246–7), Dalimier (2001: 313–17), Schenkeveld (1982: 250, 261–3) συνάπτω   to connect

σύναρθρος, -ον   accompanied by the article; σύναρθρος ἀντωνυμία possessive pronoun or possessive adjective

συναρτάομαι   to be construed with

συνάρτησις, -εως, ἡ   combination, construction

συνάρχομαι   to begin in the same way

συνάφεια, -ας, ἡ   connection, combination; polysyndeton; (in meter) the continuous repetition of the same foot. (Note that this is not identical to the modern use of "synapheia" to refer to the status of a unit, e.g. a line of poetry, within which word divisions can be ignored in determining syllable boundaries for scansion.)

συναφής, -ές   connective, connected, construed with, next

σύνδεσις, -εως, ἡ   conjunctive construction; connection by conjunctions

συνδεσμικός, -ή, -όν   conjunctive

συνδεσμοειδής, -ές   of the form of conjunctions

σύνδεσμος, -ου, ὁ   conjunction; see Lallot (1998: 231–56, 1999); Schenkeveld (1982), Belli (1987), Baratin (1989c)

συνδετικός, -ή, -όν   connective, conjunctive

συνδέω   to connect, fill the role of a conjunction

συνδηλόω   to signify (in addition)

συνεγκλίνω   to write as an enclitic

συνεγκλιτικός, -ή, -όν   enclitic

συνεκδρομή, -ῆς, ἡ   analogy, following of the same rule; illegitimate analogical extension; see Lallot (1997: ii. 46)

συνεκτρέχω   to have the same ending by analogy; extend illegitimately by analogy

συνεκφαντικός, -ή, -όν   having or pertaining to connotations

συνεκφωνέω   to pronounce at the same time, pronounce

συνεκφώνησις, -εως, ἡ = συνίζησις

συνέλευσις, -εως, ἡ   contraction, crasis

συνεμπίπτω   to coincide in form

συνέμπτωσις, -εως, ἡ   similarity of form

συνενόω   to form a compound with

συνεξακολουθέω   to have the same ending by analogy

συνεξομοιόω   to assimilate

συνέπεια, -ας, ἡ   connection of words or verses, continuous text

συνέχεια, -ας, ἡ   connection, sequence, coherence, context

συνεχής, -ές   frequent, continuous

συνήθεια, -ας, ἡ   customary usage, normal language, ordinary speech, koiné dialect

σύνθεσις, -εως, ἡ   composition, combination, construction (applied to words, sounds, sentences, etc.); see Lallot (1997: ii. 114)

σύνθετος, -ον or -η, -ον   compound (of words, or of sounds (the sound of a syllable made up of several individual sounds), or of metrical elements); see Lallot (1998: 137–8) συνίζησις, -εως, ἡ   synizesis (scanning as one vowel two vowels that are not a diphthong, as when πόλεως is disyllabic); the merger of two vowels into one; syncope

συνίσταμαι   to hold together, be well formed (of phrases)

σύνοδος, -ου, ἡ   agreement, grouping, construction, contraction; see Lallot (1997: ii. 22)

σύνταγμα, -ατος, τό   syntactic element, word in a grammatical construction; treatise

σύνταξις, -εως, ἡ   syntax, construction, combination of words, compound form, rule for combination (of sounds or letters), rule for construction, systematic treatise, composite volume; see Swiggers and Wouters (1996: 137–8), Dalimier (2001: 217), Lallot (1997: ii. 7–8, 185)

συντέλεια, -ας, ἡ   completed action

συντελεστικός (χρόνος)   tense of completion, past tense (of perfect and aorist)

συντελικός, -ή, -όν   completed, (as neut. subst.) aorist; ἐνεστὼς συντελικός the perfect tense

συντονόω   to pronounce with the same accent

συνυπακούω   to supply (something not expressed) together

συνωνυμία, -ας, ἡ   synonym, synonymity

συνώνυμος, -ον   having the same name as, synonymous; (as neut. subst.) synonym; see Lallot (1997: ii. 317)

συριγμός, -οῦ, ὁ   hissing (of sibilants)

συρισμός = συριγμός

συσσημαίνω   to signify in addition; to acquire a meaning through its context; see Schenkeveld (1982: 253)

συστατικός, -ή, -όν   productive, capable of being formed

συστατός, -ή, -όν   capable of being formed

συστέλλω   to shorten, contract

σύστοιχος, -ον   co-ordinate, correlative, corresponding

συστολή, -ῆς, ἡ   short form (of vowels that can be long or short), shortening; contraction; pronouncing a long syllable as short; changing a long vowel into a short one

συσχηματίζω   to form similarly to, transform at the same time as

συσχηματισμός, -οῦ, ὁ   correspondence of formation

σφάλλομαι   to be wrong, err

σχέσις, -εως, ἡ   relation (of place, kinship, possession, etc.), form; see Lallot (1997: ii. 308)

σχετλιαστικός, -ή, -όν   expressing anger or pain

σχῆμα, -ατος, τό   form, figure, compositional status (simple or compound); see Lallot (1998: 137–8), Dalimier (2001: 221, 228–9)

σχηματίζω   to form

σχηματισμός, -οῦ, ὁ   formation, configuration, form

τακτικός, -ή, -όν   ordinal (of numbers)

τάξις, -εως, ἡ   order, series; position

τάσις, -εως, ἡ   pitch, tension, intensity, accent

ταυτίζω   to use as synonymous

ταυτογραφέω   to write in the same way

ταυτοδυναμέω   to have the same meaning, to be identical in meaning

ταυτόνοια, -ας, ἡ   identity of meaning

ταυτοπάθεια, -ας, ἡ   the state of having a reflexive meaning

ταυτοσήμαντος, -ον   of the same meaning

ταυτόσημος, -ον   of the same meaning

ταυτόφωνος, -ον   of the same sound

τέλειος, -α, -ον   (as neut. subst.) complete word; τελεία (στιγμή) high point (punctuation mark equivalent to our period/full stop); see Lallot (1998: 91–2), Blank (1983a)

τελικός, -ή, -όν   of or in the ending (of a word)

τετραγράμματος, -ον   of four letters

τετραμερής, -ές   quadripartite

τετράπτωτος, -ον   having four case-forms (of nouns, etc.)

τετρασύλλαβος, -ον   of four syllables

τετράχρονος, -ον   containing four morae or time-units (e.g. four short syllables, two long syllables)

τέχνη, -ης, ἡ   art, system, grammatical or rhetorical treatise

τεχνικός, -ή, -όν   technical, systematic; grammarian (as masc. subst., used esp. for Herodian and Apollonius Dyscolus)

τεχνογραφέω   to write a treatise on rhetoric, write grammatical rules

τεχνολογέω   to prescribe as a rule

τεχνολογία, -ας, ἡ   systematic treatment (of grammar)

τεχνολόγος, -ου, ὁ   writer on the art of rhetoric

τηρέω   to observe, keep, preserve

τήρησις, -εως, ἡ   observation, guarding, keeping (of usage)

τμῆσις, -εως, ἡ   separation, division, tmesis

τονίζω   to accentuate, furnish with an accent

τονικός, -ή, -όν   of, for, or resulting from accents

τόνος, -ου, ὁ   accent, pitch, measure, meter, key (in music); see Lallot (1998: 87–9)

τονόω   to accentuate, furnish with an accent

τόνωσις, -εως, ἡ   accentuation

τοπικός, -ή, -όν   of place (of adverbs); local (of dialect)

τραχύνω   to pronounce roughly (of aspirated ρ, etc.)

τραχυφωνία, -ας, ἡ   roughness (of aspirated ρ, etc.)

τρίβραχυς, -υ   consisting of three short syllables

τριγένεια, -ας, ἡ   the state of having forms for all three genders

τριγενής, -ές   having separate forms for each of the three genders (e.g. of pronouns like αὐτός as opposed to ἐγώ)

τριγράμματος, -ον   of or with three letters

τρίπτωτος, -ον   having three case-forms (e.g. of neuter nouns)

GLOSSARY OF GRAMMATICAL TERMS 263

τρισύλλαβος, -ον   trisyllabic
τρισύνθετος, -ον   compounded with three elements
τρίφθογγος, -ου, ἡ   a triple vowel-sound
τρίχρονος, -ον   of three morae (i.e. of three short syllables or of one short and one long syllable); in three tenses
τριώνυμος, -ον   having three names
τροπή, -ῆς, ἡ   change (of sounds or letters), changing one letter into another; rhetorical figure
τρόπος, -ου, ὁ   way, trope (figurative usage, expression difficult to understand); see Lallot (1998: 77)
τύπος, -ου, ὁ   type, pattern, general rule, model, form, outline, rough draft
ὑγιής, -ές   correct, sound
ὑγρός, -ά, -όν   liquid or nasal (of consonants, i.e. λ, ρ, μ, ν); sometimes long and sometimes short (of vowels, i.e. α, ι, υ)
ὑπαγορεύω   to imply
ὑπακούω   to understand something not expressed, supply in thought
ὑπαρκτικός, -ή, -όν   substantive
ὕπαρξις, -εως, ἡ   existence
ὕπειμι   to be the topic of discussion
ὑπέρβασις, -εως, ἡ   transposition
ὑπερβατικός, -ή, -όν   delighting in hyperbaton, abounding in hyperbaton
ὑπερβατόν, -οῦ, τό   hyperbaton (inversion of order, transposition of words or clauses)
ὑπερβατός, -ή, όν   transposed
ὑπερβιβάζω   to transpose (letters, words); to explain as hyperbaton
ὑπερβιβασμός, -οῦ, ὁ   transposition
ὑπερδισύλλαβος, -ον   of more than two syllables
ὑπέρθεσις, -εως, ἡ   superlative degree; transposition (of words, letters, accents, etc.)
ὑπερθετικός, -ή, -όν   superlative
ὑπερσυντέλικος (χρόνος)   pluperfect (tense); see Lallot (1998: 173)
ὑπερτίθεμαι   to be formed as a superlative
ὑπερτρισύλλαβος, -ον   of more than three syllables
ὑπόδειγμα, -ατος, τό   example
ὑποδιαζευκτικός, -ή, -όν   subdisjunctive (of conjunctions, used for ἤ when several alternatives are given and no distinction is made between them, as "give me gold or silver or precious stones")
ὑποδιαστολή, -ῆς, ἡ   mark to divide words from each other in writing; (mark showing a) slight pause in speaking; see Blank (1983a), Lallot (1998: 85)
ὑποζευκτικός, -ή, -όν   subordinating (of conjunctions)
ὑπόζευξις, -εως, ἡ   subjoining (a figure of speech), subordination
ὑποθετικός, -ή, -όν   hypothetical, conditional, hortatory; see Schenkeveld (1982)
ὑπόκειμαι   to come first, be assumed
ὑποκείμενον, -ου, τό   subject; see Pfister (1976), Lallot (1994b; 1997: ii. 44, 213, 243), Ildefonse (1994)

ὑποκορίζομαι   to take the diminutive form, to use diminutives or endearments, to call by a diminutive or endearment; (pass.) to become diminutive in form

ὑποκόρισις, -εως, ἡ   use of diminutives, euphemism

ὑποκόρισμα, -ατος, τό   diminutive, endearing name

ὑποκορισμός, -οῦ, ὁ   use of diminutives, use of endearing names

ὑποκοριστικός, -ή, -όν   endearment, diminutive; see Lallot (1998: 135)

ὑπόκρισις, -εως, ἡ   delivery (in oratory); see Lallot (1998: 84)

ὑποστέλλω   to remove; see Dalimier (2001: 227)

ὑποστιγμή, -ῆς, ἡ   comma; see Lallot (1998: 91–2), Blank (1983a)

ὑποστίζω   to put a comma

ὑποστολή, -ῆς, ἡ   omission (of a letter), removal

ὑποστρέφω   to throw back the accent

ὑποστροφή, -ῆς, ἡ   throwing back of the accent; see Lallot (1997: ii. 283–4)

ὑποσυναλείφομαι   to be fused (of vowels), undergo synaloephe or crasis; see Lallot (1997: ii. 109)

ὑποσύνθετος, -ον   formed from compounds

ὑπόσχεσις, -εως, ἡ   promise, profession; see Lallot (1997: ii. 102)

ὑποταγή, -ῆς, ἡ   postposition; construction with subjunctive

ὑποτακτικός, -ή, -όν   postpositive (of conjunctions etc.), which must come second (of the second vowel of a diphthong); subjunctive, taking the subjunctive (of conjunctions), ὑποτακτική (ἔγκλισις) subjunctive mood; ὑποτακτικὸν ἄρθρον relative pronoun

ὑπόταξις, -εως, ἡ   postposition; subordination

ὑποτάσσω   to put into the subjunctive, govern the subjunctive (of conjunctions); put after or in a subordinate position; see Lallot (1997: ii. 210)

ὑποτελεία (στιγμή)   punctuation mark almost as strong as a period/full stop; see Blank (1983a)

ὕπτιος, -α, -ον   passive; Latin supine

ὑστερογενής, -ές   late in origin

ὑφαίρεσις, -εως, ἡ   omission of a letter or sound

ὑφέν, ὑφ' ἕν   in one, as a single word; (as fem. subst.) hyphen (a sign written below two consecutive letters to show that they belong to the same word)

ὕφεσις, -εως, ἡ   subtraction (of a letter or sound)

φέρομαι   to be transmitted

φερώνυμος, -ον   (as neut. subst.) name occasioned by an event; see Lallot (1998: 154)

φράσις, -εως, ἡ   speech, style, expression, idiom, phrase, diction, expressiveness

φυλάσσω   to keep (the accent) in the same place

φύσει   by nature (of long syllables containing a long vowel)

φωνή, -ῆς, ἡ   sound, word, form, phrase, language, formula, vowel-sound; see Dalimier (2001: 222), Lallot (1997: ii. 7); ἀπὸ φωνῆς "taken from the oral teaching of" (indicating that a commentary so designated consists primarily of listeners' lecture notes), see Richard (1950)

φωνῆεν, -εντος, τό   vowel; see Lallot (1998: 98–101)

χαρακτήρ, -ῆρος, ὁ   style, type, character, (typical) form, declensional category

χασμωδέω   to write verses that have hiatus

χασμωδία, -ας, ἡ   hiatus

χείρ: ἀνὰ χεῖρα   current, everyday (of usage)

χρῆσις, -εως, ἡ   usage (of words); example of usage; passage cited

χρονικός, -ή, -όν   temporal (of adverbs, conjunctions, augments, etc.), quantitative

χρόνος, -ου, ὁ   tense (of verbs); length or quantity (of syllables, etc.); augment; see Lallot (1998: 171–9)

χωρισμός, -οῦ, ὁ   separation

ψελλισμός, -οῦ, ὁ   indistinctness

ψιλογραφέω   to write with a single vowel (rather than a diphthong); write with a smooth breathing

ψιλοποιέω   to write with a smooth breathing

ψιλός, -ή, -όν   unaspirated, with a smooth breathing (of vowels); voiceless unaspirated consonant (π, τ, κ); the letters ε and υ written simply (not as αι or οι); see Lallot (1998: 102–5)

ψιλότης, -ητος, ἡ   smooth breathing

ψιλόω   to write or pronounce with a smooth breathing or unaspirated consonant

ψίλωσις, -εως, ἡ   writing or pronouncing with a smooth breathing or unaspirated consonant

ψιλωτής, -οῦ, ὁ   one who writes or pronounces with a smooth breathing or unaspirated consonant

ψιλωτικός, -ή, -όν   fond of the smooth breathing

ὡρισμένος, -η, -ον   definite (cf. ὁρίζω)

ὡς πρός τι (ἔχον)   quasi-relational (of nouns belonging to a pair of opposites, as νύξ and ἡμέρα); see Lallot (1998: 152), Swiggers (1997: 41–2), Swiggers and Wouters (1995a)

Appendix A

Hints for Finding Works on Ancient Scholarship in Library Catalogs

WORKS THAT ARE OBSCURE, OLD, OR PUBLISHED ABROAD ARE OFTEN tricky to get hold of, not only because libraries are less likely to own them but also because they are much harder to locate in the catalogs of the libraries that do have them than are more mainstream works. At the same time, when working in this area it is more important than usual to get hold of publications, since their rarity makes it more likely that second-hand information concerning their contents is incorrect and since the importance of the apparatus criticus makes it most unsafe to base any serious research on the *TLG* text. The following hints are intended as a guide for dealing with the electronic catalogs of major libraries in English-speaking countries.

1. Never give up if your first attempt produces no results. Major libraries do have most of the works in the bibliography of this book, but they rarely yield them to a cursory search.

2. The fastest way to find such works is often to do a combined author/title keyword search, taking care to pick keywords that are not only distinctive but also, if possible, free of diacritics and other elements that could cause mismatches (see below). Editions are often best located by a combined author/editor search. If the author's name is problematic, a title-only keyword search may be the best bet.

3. If those possibilities yield no results or are not available, the next best option is a search by the author's name alone. (Some libraries have catalogs in which certain types of old or obscure works are not searchable by title, even though title searches are available for most works.) When searching for an author's name, consider all possible variations in spelling. For example, if the name contains diacritics, try it both with the diacritics simply omitted and with the substitution of ae for ä, oe for ö, ue for ü, and aa for å (the electronic catalogs at most English-language libraries are supposed to simply drop diacritics, but in most cases there are some entries that have been entered the other way);

if the name contains ae or another combination that can also be expressed by a single letter with a diacritic, try it both with the combination of letters and with the single-letter version. (i.e. both Fränkel and Fraenkel may be found either under Frankel or under Fraenkel. This is because some authors published under several different spellings of their names, some with diacritics written and some with diacritics resolved into two letters, and while most bibliographies will use the spelling found on the title page of the work cited, most libraries will put all an author's works together under one spelling of his name. Recent works are usually cross-referenced, but older works often are not.) Also consider Latinized spellings, especially for first names: most early works of classical scholarship were published with the author's name Latinized on the title page, and most library catalogs have de-Latinized them (e.g. Carolus > Karl, Guilielmus > Wilhelm, Ioannes > Johann, Victorius > Vittorio). I have given names in their de-Latinized form in the Bibliography to this book when I could verify the form normally used in the catalogs of major libraries, but not all catalogs use these forms, and many bibliographies simply give authors' names in the forms in which they occur on the title page. For this reason it is usually better to omit the first name altogether when searching by author.

4. Different bibliographers may make different determinations as to who the author of a work is. Ideally, a catalog entry should be accessible via any of the possible authors, but in practice this is not always the case, so it pays to search under all possibilities if the first yields no results. Note in particular that in bibliographies composed by Classicists (including the one in this book) editions of texts tend to be listed under the name of the modern editor, but in most library catalogs they are under the name of the ancient author. (Note also that the spelling of ancient authors' names is even more subject to variation than the spellings of modern names.)

5. Though a title keyword search can be very useful, a title-only search for the full title is a last resort, since in addition to the potential diacritic problems that they share with names, titles of older works are subject to a certain unclarity as to where they begin and end. Sometimes a bibliographer considers the title to begin with the first word on the title page (which may be insignificant), and sometimes it is thought to begin with the words in largest type (which are usually the key ones). Initial articles are supposed to be dropped when alphabetizing titles, but in practice this policy is applied consistently only to English "the"; French, German, and other foreign equivalents are sometimes included and sometimes not according to the competence of the individual who entered the title, so that one always has to check both possibilities if a non-English title begins with an article. (Sometimes a cataloger even forgets to discount English "the.") A decision about who the author of a work is may also affect a bibliographer's determination of what the title is: thus the work listed in the Bibliography of this book as "Diggle, James (1981–94), *Euripidis fabulae*" will be found in many catalogs with the author as "Euripides" and the title as "*Fabulae*."

6. Some libraries suffer from a problem known as "unanalysed series," in which works that are part of a series do not have an independent catalog entry and can be found only under the name of the series. Series that may be affected by this problem include the *Mnemosyne* supplements, the Oxford Classical Texts, the Teubner texts, the Budé texts, and the Loeb texts. Thus if a work that is part of a series does not appear in the catalog of a library that ought to have it, it is worth searching under the name of the series as well. Many bibliographies do not mention series, so if no series is given it can be useful to look

the book up in WorldCat (see paragraph 8 below) to see whether it belongs to a series and then to search in one's library catalog under the name of the series.

7. *Sitzungsberichte* and other proceedings of scholarly organizations may be found via title or journal title searches, but often the best way to locate them is to look up the name of the organization as an author. Sometimes it is necessary to be creative about how to phrase the name of the organization, which some catalogers rearrange to begin with the place-name (or an Anglicized version of the place-name). *Programmschriften* may likewise be found under the name of the school concerned, but because many libraries purchased these individually rather than as a series, they are often easier to find using the author and title of the specific contribution in question.

8. If following these hints does not yield results with the catalog of a major library, it is possible that the reference is incomplete or wrong in some way. I hope that none of the references in this book fall into this category, but those using reference works like *NP* will encounter this problem frequently. It can most easily be dealt with by trying to find the book in a union catalog such as WorldCat (available at a price at http://firstsearch .oclc.org, but often for free via one's library's own website); the entry there may give additional information such as that the book is part of a series, or it may allow one to correct wrong information in one's source. Wrong article references can often be similarly corrected by appeal to *Année philologique*. If a reference is so wrong that it cannot be found even in a union catalog or *Année philologique*, it is sometimes possible to find the correct version by looking at the bibliographies of works that can be expected to cite the book or article for which one is looking.

Appendix B

Hints for Using Facsimiles

$\mathcal{S}$OME FAMOUS MANUSCRIPTS WITH SCHOLIA HAVE BEEN PUBLISHED IN facsimile editions that can be obtained like books.[1] These include the tenth-century Venetus Marcianus 822 (formerly 454), known to Homerists as A and containing the *Iliad* (De Vries 1901); the tenth-century Ravennas 429 (formerly 137 4 A), known to Aristophanes scholars as R and containing all eleven plays;[2] the eleventh- or twelfth-century Venetus Marcianus 474, known to Aristophanes scholars as V and containing seven plays;[3] the tenth-century Laurentianus Mediceus Plut. 32.9, containing works of Aeschylus, Sophocles, and Apollonius Rhodius and known as M by Aeschylus scholars and L by those working on the other two authors;[4] the ninth-century Bodleianus Clarkianus 39, containing tetralogies 1–6 of Plato and known as manuscript B;[5] the ninth-century Parisinus 1807, containing tetralogies 8–9 of Plato and known as A;[6] the

1. The ones mentioned here are not the only published facsimiles that include scholia; others can be found in S. J. Voicu, *IMaGES: Index in manuscriptorum graecorum edita specimina* (Rome 1981).

2. *Aristophanes Comoediae undecim cum scholiis: Codex Ravennas 137, 4, A*, preface by J. van Leeuwen (Leiden 1904).

3. *Ἀριστοφάνους κωμῳδίαι: Facsimile of the Codex Venetus Marcianus 474*, preface by J. W. White and introduction by T. W. Allen (London and Boston 1902).

4. *Facsimile of the Laurentian Manuscript of Sophocles*, introduction by E. M. Thompson and R. C. Jebb (London 1885) for the Sophocles portions; *L'Eschilo laurenziano: Facsimile* (Florence 1896) for the Aeschylus portions.

5. *Codex Oxoniensis Clarkianus 39 phototypice editus: Plato*, preface by T. W. Allen (Leiden 1898–9).

6. *Œuvres philosophiques de Platon: Facsimilé en phototypie à la grandeur exacte de l'original du ms. grec 1807 de la bibliothèque nationale* (Paris 1908).

ninth-century Parisinus 2934 known as manuscript S of Demosthenes;[7] and the Jerusalem palimpsest of Euripides.[8]

There are a number of books on palaeography that are useful with the process of learning to read scholia in their original format.[9] It is, however, also surprisingly simple to teach
oneself to read most kinds of Greek handwriting. To do so, one needs a good photograph
or facsimile of the work one intends to read and an edition or transcription of some part
of it; if there is no transcription of any part of it, it is necessary to find another text *in
exactly the same script* that does have a transcription.[10] (Multiple scripts are sometimes
found within a single work, as when scholia are written in a different script from that of
the text they surround, so care must be taken to learn the right one.) Then one works out
the alphabet of the script in question by comparison with the transcription, making an
accurate drawing of each letter as it appears in the script and arranging these in alphabetical order to produce a complete key. Often a single letter has more than one repre-
sentation, in which case it is useful to figure out the rules governing which one appears
where (usually they are based on the letter's proximity to certain other letters or to a word
boundary). The hardest part is usually working out the abbreviations, but with enough
patience and a good transcription even this is not too difficult. At the end of this process
one has a complete list of the different letters and abbreviations, which one can use to
read those portions of one's chosen text that do not appear in the edition or transcription.

7. *Œuvres complètes de Démosthène: Facsimile du manuscrit grec 2934 de la bibliothèque nationale* (Paris 1892–3).

8. *The Jerusalem Palimpsest of Euripides*, commentary by S. G. Daitz (Berlin 1970);
this version of the scholia is not included in Schwartz's edition, but Daitz (1979) has provided a separate edition of it.

9. These include, for medieval manuscripts, E. M. Thompson, *Handbook of Greek
and Latin Palaeography* (New York 1893, repr. Chicago 1980); E. M. Thompson, *An In-
troduction to Greek and Latin Palaeography* (Oxford 1912); B. A. van Groningen, *Short
Manual of Greek Palaeography* (2nd edn. Leiden 1955, repr. 1963); for literary papyri,
F. G. Kenyon, *The Palaeography of Greek Papyri* (Oxford 1899, repr. Chicago 1970);
E. G. Turner, *Greek Manuscripts of the Ancient World*, (2nd edn. London 1987); E. G.
Turner, *Greek Papyri: An Introduction* (Princeton 1968; does not help with reading the
scripts but very useful for understanding many other things about papyri); and for abbre-
viations in both types of text, A. N. Oikonomides, *Abbreviations in Greek: Inscriptions,
Papyri, Manuscripts, and Early Printed Books* (Chicago 1974).

10. There are collections of photographs with transcription that can be useful for this
purpose; one that includes texts with scholia is G. Vitelli, *Collezione fiorentina di facsimili
paleografici greci e latini* (Florence 1884–97).

Annotated Bibliography

ABBREVIATIONS

Note: For editions of papyri not listed here, see the *Checklist of Editions of Greek Papyri and Ostraca* by J. F. Oates, R. S. Bagnall, *et al.*, available at http://scriptorium.lib.duke.edu/papyrus/texts/clist_papyri.html.

AC	*L'Antiquité classique.*
ACA	Ancient Commentators on Aristotle, ed. Richard Sorabji (London and Ithaca). Translations into English of texts (most, but not all, from *CAG*). Many of these volumes have multiple titles and multiple dates of publication, and thus they may appear in library catalogs in a very different form from that given here (in particular, wherever the American titles listed below have "Aristotle's," the British equivalents have "Aristotle"; Latin titles are also used on occasion). New volumes continue to appear.

Alexander of Aphrodisias, *On Aristotle's Prior Analytics 1.1–7*, trans. J. Barnes *et al.* 1992.

Alexander of Aphrodisias, *On Aristotle's Prior Analytics 1.8–13 (with 1.17,36b35– 37a31)*, trans. I. Mueller with J. Gould 1999.

Alexander of Aphrodisias, *On Aristotle's Prior Analytics 1.14–22*, trans. I. Mueller with J. Gould 1999.

Alexander of Aphrodisias, *On Aristotle's Prior Analytics 1.23–31*, trans. I. Mueller 2005.

Alexander of Aphrodisias, *On Aristotle's Metaphysics 1*, trans. W. E. Dooley 1989.

Alexander of Aphrodisias, *On Aristotle's Metaphysics 2–3*, trans. W. E. Dooley and A. Madigan 1992.

Alexander of Aphrodisias, *On Aristotle's Metaphysics 4*, trans. A. Madigan 1994.

Alexander of Aphrodisias, *On Aristotle's Metaphysics 5*, trans. W. E. Dooley 1994.

Alexander of Aphrodisias, *On Aristotle's Topics 1*, trans. J. M. van Ophuijsen 2001.

Alexander of Aphrodisias, *On Aristotle's Meteorology 4*, trans. E. Lewis 1995.

Alexander of Aphrodisias, *Quaestiones 1.1–2.15*, trans. R. W. Sharples 1992.

Alexander of Aphrodisias, *Quaestiones 2.16–3.15*, trans. R. W. Sharples 1994.

Alexander of Aphrodisias, *On Aristotle's On Sense Perception*, trans. A. Towey 1999.

Alexander of Aphrodisias, *Ethical Problems*, trans. R. W. Sharples 1990.

Alexander of Aphrodisias, *Supplement to On the Soul*, trans. R. W. Sharples 2004.

ACA   Alexander of Aphrodisias, *On Aristotle's On Coming to be and Perishing 2.2–*
(cont.)   5, trans. E. Gannagé 2005.
              Ammonius, *On Aristotle's Categories*, trans. S. M. Cohen and G. B. Matthews
                 1992.
              Ammonius, *On Aristotle's On Interpretation 1–8*, trans. D. Blank 1995.
              Ammonius, *On Aristotle's On Interpretation 9*, trans. D. Blank 1996. Also
                 contains Boethius, *On Aristotle's On interpretation 9*, trans. N. Kretzmann.
              Dexippus, *On Aristotle's Categories*, trans. J. M. Dillon 1988.
              Philoponus, *On Aristotle's Physics 1.1–3*, trans. C. Osbourne 1995.
              Philoponus, *On Aristotle's Physics 2*, trans. A. R. Lacey 1993.
              Philoponus, *On Aristotle's Physics 3*, trans. M. J. Edwards 1994.
              Philoponus, *On Aristotle's Physics 5–8*, trans. P. Lettinck and J. O. Urmson
                 1994. Includes Simplicius' *On Aristotle on the Void*, which is a transla-
                 tion of Simplicius' commentary on *Physics* 4.6–9.
              Philoponus, *On Coming-to-be and Perishing 1.1–5*, trans. C. J. F. Williams
                 1998.
              Philoponus, *On Coming-to-be and Perishing 1.6–2.4*, trans. C. J. F. Williams
                 1999.
              Philoponus, *On Aristotle's On Coming to be and Perishing 2.5–11*, trans. I.
                 Kupreeva 2005.
              Philoponus, *Against Aristotle on the Eternity of the World*, trans. C. Wildberg
                 1987.
              Philoponus, *Against Proclus' On the Eternity of the World 1–5*, trans. M. Share
                 2005.
              Philoponus, *Against Proclus' On the Eternity of the World 6–8*, trans. M. Share
                 2005.
              Philoponus, *On Aristotle On the Intellect (De anima 3.4–8)*, trans. W. Charlton
                 1992.
              Philoponus and Simplicius, *Place, Void, and Eternity* (1991). Contains Philo-
                 ponus, *Corollaries on Place and Void*, trans. D. Furley, and Simplicius,
                 Against Philoponus On the Eternity of the World, trans. C. Wildberg.
              Philoponus, *On Aristotle's On the Soul 2.1–6*, trans. W. Charlton 2005.
              Philoponus, *On Aristotle's On the Soul 2.7–12*, trans. W. Charlton 2005.
              [Philoponus], *On Aristotle's On the Soul 3.1–8*, trans. W. Charlton 1999.
              [Philoponus], *On Aristotle's On the Soul 3.9–13*, trans. W. Charlton 1999.
                 Also contains Stephanus' *On Aristotle's On Interpretation*.
              Porphyry, *On Abstinence from Killing Animals*, trans. G. Clark 1999.
              Porphyry, *On Aristotle's Categories*, trans. S. K. Strange 1992.
              Priscian, *On Theophrastus On Sense-perception*, trans. P. Huby 1997. Also
                 contains Simplicius, *On Aristotle's On the Soul 2.5–12*, trans. C. Steel.
              Proclus, *On the Existence of Evils*, trans. J. Opsomer and C. G. Steel 2003.
              Simplicius, *On Aristotle's On the Heavens 1.1–4*, trans. R. J. Hankinson 2002.
              Simplicius, *On Aristotle's On the Heavens 1.5–9*, trans. R. J. Hankinson 2004.
              Simplicius, *On Aristotle's On the Heavens 1.10–12*, trans. R. J. Hankinson
                 2005.
              Simplicius, *On Aristotle's On the Heavens 2.1–9*, trans. I. Mueller 2004.
              Simplicius, *On Aristotle's Physics 2*, trans. B. Fleet 1996.
              Simplicius, *On Aristotle's Physics 3*, trans. J. O. Urmson 2002.
              Simplicius, *On Aristotle's Physics 4.1–5, 10–14*, trans. J. O. Urmson 1993.
                 For 4. 6–9 see Philoponus on *Physics* 5–8, above.
              Simplicius, *Corollaries on Place and Time*, trans. J. O. Urmson 1992. Con-
                 tains commentary on *Physics* 4, pp. 601. 1–645. 19 and 773. 8–800. 25.

ACA *(cont.)*	Simplicius, *On Aristotle's Physics 5*, trans. J. O. Urmson 1997. Simplicius, *On Aristotle's Physics 6*, trans. D. Konstan 1988. Simplicius, *On Aristotle's Physics 7*, trans. C. Hagen 1994. Simplicius, *On Aristotle's Physics 8.6–10*, trans. R. McKirahan 2000. For Simplicius' commentary on *Physics* 8. 10, pp. 1326. 38–1336. 34 see Simplicius, *Against Philoponus on the Eternity of the World*, in *Place, Void, Eternity* above. Simplicius, *On Aristotle's Categories 1–4*, trans. M. Chase 2003. Simplicius, *On Aristotle's Categories 5–6*, trans. F. A. J. de Haas and B. Fleet 2001. Simplicius, *On Aristotle's Categories 7–8*, trans. B. Fleet 2002. Simplicius, *On Aristotle's Categories 9–15*, trans. R. Gaskin 1999. Simplicius, *On Aristotle's On the Soul 1.1–2.4*, trans. J. O. Urmson 1995. For *De anima* 2. 5–12 see Priscian above. Simplicius, *On Aristotle's On the Soul 3.1–5*, trans. H. J. Blumenthal 1999. Simplicius, *On Epictetus' Handbook 1–26*, trans. C. Brittain and T. Brennan 2002. Simplicius, *On Epictetus' Handbook 27–53*, trans. C. Brittain and T. Brennan 2002. Themistius, *On Aristotle's On the Soul*, trans. R. B. Todd 1996. Themistius, *On Aristotle's Physics 4*, trans. R. B. Todd 2003. Various, *Aspasius on Aristotle Nicomachean Ethics 8 with Anonymous Paraphrase of Aristotle Nicomachean Ethics 8 and 9 and Michael of Ephesus on Aristotle Nicomachean Ethics 9*, trans. D. Konstan 2001.
AHES	*Archive for History of Exact Sciences.*
AJP	*American Journal of Philology.*
ANRW	*Aufstieg und Niedergang der römischen Welt*, ed. W. Haase, H. Temporini, et al. (Berlin 1972–).
APF	*Archiv für Papyrusforschung.*
BASP	*The Bulletin of the American Society of Papyrologists.*
BCH	*Bulletin de correspondance hellénique.*
BKT	*Berliner Klassikertexte.* i: *Didymos: Kommentar zu Demosthenes* (Papyrus 9780), ed. H. Diels and W. Schubart (Berlin 1904). Original publication of the papyrus of Didymus' commentary on Demosthenes, with a good introduction; also includes fragments of Didymus on Demosthenes gathered from Harpocration, and re-edition of papyrus with Demosthenes lexicon (Blass 1882). Texts (alone) also printed as a Teubner volume (*Didymi de Demosthene commenta*, Leipzig 1904). ii: *Anonymer Kommentar zu Platons Theaetet* (Papyus 9782), ed. H. Diels and W. Schubart (Berlin 1905). Text and detailed discussion of anonymous Plato commentary. v.i: *Epische und elegische Fragmente*, ed. W. Schubart and U. von Wilamowitz-Moellendorff (Berlin 1907). Edition of Theocritus commentary fragment (13 lines) on p. 56.
BollClass	*Bollettino dei classici* (Accademia nazionale dei Lincei).
BPW	*Berliner philologische Wochenschrift.*
BZ	*Byzantinische Zeitschrift.*
C&M	*Classica et mediaevalia.*
CAG	*Commentaria in Aristotelem graeca* (Berlin 1882–1909) Standard texts of most surviving commentaries.
CLGP	*Commentaria et Lexica Graeca in Papyris reperta* (Munich 2004–). Collection of texts, with commentary, in multiple volumes in alphabetical order

by author commented on. Little has appeared so far, but the collection may in time become an invaluable resource.

CMG   *Corpus medicorum graecorum* (Leipzig and Berlin 1908–). Includes editions of many commentaries on medical writers, often with translations; volumes so far published that are relevant to ancient scholarship include:

v.i.ii: Galen, *On the Elements According to Hippocrates*, ed. and trans. P. de Lacy 1996.

v.iv.i.ii: Galen, *On the Doctrines of Hippocrates and Plato*, ed. and trans. P. de Lacy 1978–84.

v.ix.i: Galen, *In Hippocratis De natura hominis: In Hippocratis De victu acutorum: De diaeta Hippocratis in morbis acutis*, ed. J. Mewaldt, G. Helmreich, and J. Westenberger 1914.

v.ix.ii: Galen, *In Hippocratis Prorrheticum I: De comate secundum Hippocratem; In Hippocratis Prognosticum*, ed. H. Diels, J. Mewaldt, and J. Heeg 1915.

v.x: Galen, *In Hippocratis Epidemiarum . . . commentaria*, ed. and trans. (German) E. Wenkebach and F. Pfaff 1934–60.

xi.i.i: Apollonius of Citium, *Kommentar zu Hippokrates Ueber das Einrenken der Gelenke*, ed. and trans. (German) J. Kollesch *et al.* 1965.

xi.i.ii: Stephanus of Athens, *Commentary on the Prognosticon of Hippocrates*, ed. and trans. J. M. Duffy 1983.

xi.i.iii: Stephanus of Athens, *Commentary on Hippocrates' Aphorisms*, ed. and trans. L. G. Westerink 1992–8.

xi.i.iv: John of Alexandria, *In Hippocratis Epidemiarum librum VI commentarii fragmenta*, ed. and trans. J. M. Duffy 1997. Also contains John's commentary on Hippocrates' *De natura pueri*, ed. and trans. T. A. Bell.

xi.ii.i: [Galen], *Pseudogaleni In Hippocratis De septimanis commentarium ab Hunaino q. f. arabice versum*, ed. and trans. (German) G. Bergstraesser 1914.

CP   *Classical Philology*.

CPF iii   *Corpus dei papiri filosofici greci e latini III: Commentari* (Florence 1995). Offers re-editions, with commentary and bibliography, of papyrus fragments of commentaries on philosophical texts.

CQ   *Classical Quarterly*.

CR   *Classical Review*.

FGrHist   *Fragmente der griechischen Historiker*, ed. F. Jacoby (Berlin 1923–).

GG   *Grammatici Graeci* (Leipzig 1867–1910; repr. with slightly different volume numbers Hildesheim 1965). A vital work, the definitive edition of the texts included and with excellent critical apparatus and detailed discussions of the textual tradition. Volumes iii.i and iii.ii were originally published separately and only later incorporated into the *Grammatici Graeci* series.

i.i: *Dionysii Thracis Ars grammatica*, ed. G. Uhlig 1883. Τέχνη and supplements.

i.ii (repr: ii.i.ii): *Apollonii Dyscoli quae supersunt: Commentarium criticum et exegeticum in Apollonii scripta minora*, by R. Schneider 1902. Extensive commentary (with index) to texts in vol. ii.i; see Maas (1903) and Ludwich (1902*b*) for useful corrections, and Uhlig (1902) for amusing commentary.

i.iii: *Scholia in Dionysii Thracis Artem grammaticam*, ed. A. Hilgard 1901. Ancient commentaries, with detailed introduction and indices. See Ludwich (1902*a*) for useful corrections.

ii.i (repr: ii.i.i): *Apollonii Dyscoli quae supersunt: Apollonii scripta minora*, ed. R. Schneider 1878. Text of *Pronouns*, *Adverbs*, and *Conjunctions* with

GG   Latin summaries. See Egenolff (1878), Hoerschelmann (1880), and Ludwich
(*cont.*)   (1879) for useful corrections.

ii.ii: *Apollonii Dyscoli quae supersunt: Apollonii Dyscoli De constructione libri quattuor*, ed. G. Uhlig 1910. Text of the *Syntax* with detailed introduction, Latin paraphrase/summary, and index/glossary with Latin translations of Apollonius' terminology. See Maas (1911*a*, 1912) and Ludwich (1910) for some useful corrections.

ii.iii: *Apollonii Dyscoli quae supersunt: Librorum Apollonii deperditorum fragmenta*, ed. R. Schneider 1910. Numerous fragments embedded in Latin commentary, useful explanation of the difficulties of Apollonius' style, and indices to the whole of Apollonius' surviving work. See Maas (1912) and Ludwich (1910) for some useful corrections.

iii.i: *Herodiani technici reliquiae*, ed. A. Lentz, 1867. Contains introduction and a reconstruction of the Περὶ καθολικῆς προσῳδίας, with its appendix on the accentuation of words in sentences (Περὶ προσῳδίας τῆς κατὰ σύνταξιν τῶν λέξεων). Misleading edition that should only be used with the help of Dyck (1993*a*) and Egenolff (1900, 1902, 1903); see also Hiller (1871).

iii.ii: *Herodiani technici reliquiae*, ed. A. Lentz, 1868–70. Contains the rest of Herodian's works and a substantial index. Same cautions as for iii.i.

iv.i: *Theodosii Alexandrini canones, Georgii Choerobosci scholia, Sophronii Patriarchae Alexandrini excerpta*, ed. A. Hilgard 1889. Contains the Κανόνες of Theodosius and the first part of Choeroboscus' commentary on it, with (in the reprinted edition only) a detailed introduction. See Ludwich (1890) for some useful textual suggestions.

iv.ii: *Theodosii Alexandrini canones, Georgii Choerobosci scholia, Sophronii Patriarchae Alexandrini excerpta*, ed. A. Hilgard 1894. Contains the second part of Choeroboscus' commentary on the Κανόνες, the surviving portions of Sophronius' commentary, and detailed indices. In the original edition the introduction to Theodosius and Choeroboscus is in this volume, but in the reprint it is moved to volume iv.i. See Ludwich (1894) for some useful textual suggestions.

GRBS   *Greek, Roman, and Byzantine Studies.*
HL   *Historiographia linguistica.*
HSCP   *Harvard Studies in Classical Philology.*
ICS   *Illinois Classical Studies.*
JCP   *Jahrbücher für classische Philologie.*
JHS   *Journal of Hellenic Studies.*
K–A   *Poetae Comici Graeci*, ed. R. Kassel and C. Austin (Berlin 1983–).
LGGA   *Lessico dei grammatici greci antichi* (ed. F. Montanari, F. Montana, and L. Pagani). Online resource with detailed information on individual ancient grammarians (including ones whose works are lost), available at http://www .aristarchus.unige.it./lgga.
LSJ   H. G. Liddell, R. Scott, H. S. Jones, and R. McKenzie, *A Greek-English Lexicon*, 9th edn. (Oxford 1940).
MAL   *Atti della Accademia Nazionale dei Lincei: Memorie: Classe di scienze morali, storiche e filologiche.*
MCr   *Museum Criticum.*
MH   *Museum Helveticum.*
NJPP   *Neue Jahrbücher für Philologie und Paedagogik.*
NP   *Der neue Pauly: Enzyklopädie der Antike*, ed. H. Cancik and H. Schneider (Stuttgart 1996–2002). Despite its title, this in no way supersedes *RE*, as it

has much less information and many more mistakes (particularly in bibliographical details). It is, however, useful for recent bibliography and concise summaries. There is now an English translation of this work (*Brill's New Pauly*, Leiden 2002–), but that has significantly more mistakes than the original.

OCD   *Oxford Classical Dictionary*, ed. S. Hornblower and A. Spawforth (3rd edn., Oxford 1996). Handy source of clear, concise, up-to-date information, but too small to contain entries on many ancient scholars.

P.Amh. ii   *The Amherst Papyri, Being an Account of the Greek Papyri in the Collection of the Right Hon. Lord Amherst of Hackney*, ii: *Classical Fragments and Documents of the Ptolemaic, Roman and Byzantine Periods*, ed. B. P. Grenfell and A. S. Hunt (London 1901).

P.Ant. ii   *The Antinoopolis Papyri*, ii, ed. J. W. B. Barns and H. Zilliacus (London 1960).

P.Oxy.   *The Oxyrhynchus Papyri*, ed. B. P. Grenfell, A. S. Hunt, *et al.* (London 1898–).

P.Rain. i   *Mitteilungen aus der Papyrussammlung der Nationalbibliothek in Wien: Papyrus Erzherzog Rainer*, NS, erste Folge, ed. H. Gerstinger *et al.* (Vienna 1932).

P.Ryl. iii   *Catalogue of the Greek and Latin Papyri in the John Rylands Library, Manchester*, iii: *Theological and Literary Texts*, ed. C. H. Roberts (Manchester 1938).

PSI xii.ii   *Papiri greci e latini*, Pubblicazioni della società italiana per la ricerca dei papiri greci e latini in Egitto, vol. xii.ii, ed. V. Bartoletti (Florence 1951).

QUCC   *Quaderni urbinati di cultura classica.*

RE   *Real-Encyclopädie der classischen Altertumswissenschaft*, ed. A. Pauly, G. Wissowa, and W. Kroll (Stuttgart 1893–1972). The best, and sometimes the only, source of information on many obscure figures, but superseded on some points.

REA   *Revue des études anciennes.*

REByz   *Revue des études byzantines.*

REG   *Revue des études grecques.*

RhM   *Rheinisches Museum für Philologie.*

RPh   *Revue de philologie, de littérature et d'histoire anciennes.*

SCO   *Studi classici e orientali.*

SGLG   Sammlung griechischer und lateinischer Grammatiker.

SIFC   *Studi italiani di filologia classica.*

TAPA   *Transactions of the American Philological Association.*

TGF   *Tragicorum Graecorum Fragmenta*, ed. A. Nauck (2nd edn. Leipzig 1889, supplement by B. Snell 1964).

TLG   *Thesaurus Linguae Graecae* (see Preface at footnote 1).

TrGF   *Tragicorum Graecorum Fragmenta*, ed. B. Snell, R. Kannicht, and S. Radt (Göttingen 1971–85).

WKP   *Wochenschrift für klassische Philologie.*

ZPE   *Zeitschrift für Papyrologie und Epigraphik.*

REFERENCES

Abbenes, Jelle G. J.; Slings, Simon R.; and Sluiter, Ineke (1995) (edd.), *Greek Literary Theory After Aristotle: A collection of papers in honour of D. M. Schenkeveld* (Amsterdam). Contains several pieces on ancient scholarship.

Abel, Eugenius (*or* Ábel, Jenő) (1891), *Scholia recentiora in Pindari Epinicia* (Budapest; vol. iii of Abel's *Scholia in Pindari Epinicia*). Most recent edition of Triclinius' scholia.

Achelis, Thomas O. H. (1913–16), "De Aristophanis Byzantii argumentis fabularum," *Philologus*, 72: 414–41, 518–45; 73: 122–53. Finds traces of the work of Aristophanes of Byzantium in the tragic and comic hypotheses.

Adler, Ada (1928–38), *Suidae lexicon* (Leipzig; repr. Stuttgart 1967–71). Best edition.

——— (1931), "Suidas 1," *RE*, 2nd ser. iv.i (vii): 675–717. Important study.

Adontz, Nicolas (1970), *Denys de Thrace et les commentateurs arméniens* (Louvain). Translation (by René Hotterbeex) of 1915 St. Petersburg doctoral thesis; focuses on the Armenian commentaries on Dionysius Thrax rather than on the Greek version.

Aerts, Willem J. (1965), *Periphrastica: An Investigation into the Use of εἶναι and ἔχειν as Auxiliaries or Pseudo-auxiliaries in Greek from Homer up to the Present Day* (Amsterdam).

———, Lokin, J. H. A.; Radt, S. L.; and Van der Wal, N. (1985) (edd.), *Σχόλια: Studia ad criticam interpretationemque textuum graecorum et ad historiam iuris graeco-romani pertinentia viro doctissimo D. Holwerda oblata* (Groningen). Contains many useful articles on ancient scholarship.

Ahrens, Heinrich Ludolf (1859), *Bucolicorum graecorum Theocriti Bionis Moschi reliquiae*, ii (Leipzig). Good edition of Theocritus scholia; superseded by Wendel for old scholia but best for Byzantine scholia.

Alberti, Johann/Jo(h)annes (1746–66), *Hesychii Lexicon, cum notis doctorum virorum integris . . .* (Leiden). Old edition, but sometimes still useful. It is a compendium of earlier editions and not based on personal acquaintance with the manuscript; provides a brief commentary that can be very enlightening. But Alberti's views are often superseded, and his Greek type is now difficult to read.

Alexanderson, Bengt (1969), *Textual Remarks on Ptolemy's Harmonica and Porphyry's Commentary* (Gothenburg; Studia graeca et latina Gothoburgensia, 27). Important emendations to Düring (1932).

Allatius, Leo (or Allaci, Leone) (1635), *Procli diadochi paraphrasis in Ptolemaei libros IV. De siderum affectionibus* (Leiden). Text and Latin trans.

Allen, Thomas W. (1912), *Homeri opera*, v (Oxford). Includes some Homerica.

Allen, W. Sidney, and Brink, C. O. (1980), "The Old Order and the New: A Case History," *Lingua*, 50: 61–100. Explains the history of the order of the cases in ancient and modern times.

Alpers, Klaus (1964), *Theognostos περὶ ὀρθογραφίας: Überlieferung, Quellen und Text der Kanones 1–84* (Diss. Hamburg). Important study and best (but partial) edition.

——— (1969), *Bericht über Stand und Methode der Ausgabe des Etymologicum Genuinum* (Copenhagen; Det Kongelige Danske Videnskabernes Selskab, Historisk-filosofiske Meddelelser, 44.3). Useful discussion; includes edition of entries beginning with λ.

——— (1972), "'Zonarae' Lexicon," in *RE*, 2nd ser. x.i (xix): 732–63. Excellent, thorough study.

——— (1981), *Das attizistische Lexikon des Oros: Untersuchung und kritische Ausgabe der Fragmente* (Berlin; SGLG 4). Standard edition and good discussion.

Alt, Karin (1998), "Homers Nymphengrotte in der Deutung des Porphyrios," *Hermes*, 126: 466–87.

Ambühl, Annemarie (1995), "Callimachus and the Arcadian Asses: The Aetia Prologue and a Lemma in the London Scholia," *ZPE* 105: 209–13. Uses scholia to Callimachus.

Andersen, Paul Kent (1989), "Remarks on the Origin of the Term 'Passive'," *Lingua*, 79: 1–16. Argues that Greek had no passive and that πάθος means "middle." Not generally accepted.

——— (1993), "Zur Diathese," *Historische Sprachforschung*, 106: 177–231. Highly linguistic discussion of the Greek concept of voice; conclusions not generally accepted.

Andorlini, Isabella (2000), "Codici papiracei di medicina con scoli e commento," in Goulet-Cazé (2000): 37–52.

Antoniou, Perséphone (1997), "Sur les notes marginales des manuscrits de Ptolémée (*Géographie* 3.11–15)," *Scriptorium*, 51: 314–6.

Apthorp, M. J. (1980), *The Manuscript Evidence for Interpolation in Homer* (Heidelberg). Primarily on Aristarchus' edition.

Argoud, Gilbert, and Guillaumin, Jean-Yves (1998) (edd.), *Sciences exactes et sciences appliquées à Alexandrie* (Saint-Étienne). Collection of essays, including some on scientific commentary.

Argyle, Sonia (1989), "A New Greek Grammarian," *CQ*, NS 39: 524–35.

Argyropoulos (*or* Argyropoulou), Roxane D., and Caras, Iannis (1980), *Inventaire des manuscrits grecs d'Aristote et de ses commentateurs: Supplément* (Paris). Additions to Wartelle (1963).

Arnott, W. Geoffrey (1989), "A Note on the Antiatticist (98.17 Bekker)," *Hermes*, 117: 374–6.

Arrighetti, Graziano (1977), "Hypomnemata e scholia: Alcuni problemi," *Museum philologum Londiniense*, 2: 49–67. On the nature of ancient commentaries, with special reference to the papyrus of Didymus' commentary on Demosthenes.

—— (1987): *Poeti, eruditi e biografi: Momenti della riflessione dei Greci sulla letteratura* (Pisa). On pp. 194–204 discusses the papyrus of Didymus' commentary on Demosthenes.

—— ; Mariotti, Giovanna Calvani; and Montanari, Franco (1991), *Concordantia et Indices in Scholia Pindarica Vetera* (Hildesheim). Gigantic 2-vol. concordance; no explanatory material, but a useful list of editions.

Asheri, David, *et al.* (1977–98), *Erodoto: Le storie* (Milan). Each volume (except viii and ix) contains just before the commentary a text of the scholia and Λέξεις entries for that book, the former based on Stein's text (but with consultation of Rosén (1987–97) where that edition predates this one) and the latter on Rosén's text (1962). The scholia, but not the Λέξεις, are provided with an Italian translation.

Asulanus, Franciscus (1528), *Didymi antiquissimi auctoris interpretatio in Odysseam* (Venice). Edition of D scholia to *Odyssey*.

Aubreton, Robert (1949), *Démétrius Triclinius et les recensions médiévales de Sophocle* (Paris). Discusses Byzantine scholia.

Auroux, Sylvain (1989) (ed.), *Histoire des idées linguistiques, i: La Naissance des métalangages en orient et en occident* (Liège). Very general collection; contains some essays on Greco-Roman grammarians.

—— et al. (2000) (edd.), *History of the Language Sciences* (Berlin). Chapter 11 consists of essays dealing with linguistics in ancient and Byzantine Greece.

Austin, Colin (1973), *Comicorum Graecorum fragmenta in papyris reperta* (Berlin). Comprehensive listing of papyri with text, scholia, or commentaries on comedy; also lists publications about each papyrus, and sometimes prints the texts of the papyri.

Ax, Wolfram (1982), "Aristarch und die 'Grammatik'," *Glotta*, 60: 96–109 (repr. in Ax 2000: 128–39). Based on Apollonius Dyscolus' citations of Aristarchus; argues that Aristarchus had an advanced concept of grammatical divisions. Clear and convincing.

—— (1986), *Laut, Stimme und Sprache: Studien zu drei Grundbegriffen der antiken Sprachtheorie* (Göttingen). Considers the evolution of analytical grammar from the Greek classical period to the Romans, tracing the extent to which Aristotle, the Stoics, and the grammarians ultimately contributed to this development. See Schenkeveld (1990) for English summary and discussion.

—— (1990), "Aristophanes von Byzanz als Analogist: Zu Fragment 374 Slater (=Varro, de lingua Latina 9, 12)," *Glotta*, 68: 4–18 (repr. in Ax 2000: 116–27). Considers how much of an Analogist Aristophanes was; opposes on the basis of different evidence Callanan's (1987) diminution of the role traditionally assigned to Analogy in Aristophanes' thought.

—— (1991), "Sprache als Gegenstand der alexandrinischen und pergamenischen Philologie," in Schmitter (1991): 275–301 (repr. in Ax 2000: 95–115). Good overview of the theories of Aristophanes of Byzantium, Aristarchus, and Crates, in the context of a discussion about the extent to which the Alexandrians possessed a developed grammatical theory.

———— (2000), *Lexis und Logos: Studien zur antiken Grammatik und Rhetorik* (Stuttgart). Collection of reprinted articles on grammatical topics.

Bachmann, Ludwig (1828), *Anecdota Graeca* (Leipzig; repr. Hildesheim 1965). Includes only editions of some lexica.

Baiter, Johann Georg; Orelli, Johann Kaspar von; and Winckelmann, August Wilhelm (1839), *Platonis opera quae feruntur omnia* (Zürich). Includes Dübner's edition of Timaeus' lexicon, pp. 969–1010.

Baldwin, Barry (1980–1), "The Scholiasts' Lucian," *Helikon*, 20–1: 219–34. On sources of insults used for Lucian by Byzantine scholiasts.

Bapp, Karl Albert (1885), "De fontibus quibus Athenaeus in rebus musicis lyricisque enarrandis usus sit," *Leipziger Studien zur classischen Philologie*, 8: 85–160. Discusses Trypho, pp. 107–25, 134–9.

Baratin, Marc (1989*a*), "La constitution de la grammaire et de la dialectique," in Auroux (1989): 186–206. General discussion of the nature and origins of the Greco-Latin grammatical tradition and philosophical work on language.

———— (1989*b*), "La maturation des analyses grammaticales et dialectiques," in Auroux (1989): 207–27. General discussion of Greek and Latin grammar and philosophy of language.

———— (1989*c*), *La Naissance de la syntaxe à Rome* (Paris). Largely about Latin, but much incidental discussion of Greek, including a long section (pp. 19–47, 61–9) on the Greek theory of conjunctions.

Barker, Andrew (1989), *Greek Muscial Writings*, ii (Cambridge). Translation and discussion of Aristides Quintilianus, pp. 392–535.

Barker, Edmund Henry (1820), Ἀρκαδίου περὶ τόνων (Leipzig). Superseded edition of Arcadius' epitome of Herodian.

Barrett, W. S. (1964), *Euripides: Hippolytus* (Oxford). Contains clear summary of history of scholia.

———— (1965), "The Epitome of Euripides' *Phoinissai*: Ancient and Medieval Versions," *CQ*, NS 15: 58–71. Shows that Moschopulus' version of the hypothesis is closer to the ancient one than is the version in our other manuscripts, and that therefore Moschopulus had access to sources independent of and better than those of our surviving manuscripts.

———— (1973), "Pindar's Twelfth *Olympian* and the Fall of the Deinomenidai," *JHS* 93: 23–35. Uses scholia to solve historical problems.

Bartalucci, Aldo (1984), "Note critiche agli scolii a Germanico," *Giornale italiano di filologia*, NS 15 [36]: 283–300. Largely text-critical discussion of Germanicus scholia, which were translated from the Greek.

Baumbach, Manuel (2002), "Tryphon 3," in *NP* xii.i: 885–6.

Becares, V. (1988), "Ein unbekanntes Werk des Gregorios von Korinth und seine Lebenszeit," *BZ* 81: 247–8. Argues from a neglected work of Gregory dedicated to Leo VI (886–911) that Gregory must have lived earlier than is usually thought. Cf. Laurent (1963), Montana (1995, pp. xlviii–xlix).

Bécares Botas, Vicente (1985), *Diccionario de terminología gramatical griega* (Salamanca). Extensive but unreliable dictionary of grammatical terms.

———— (1987), *Apolonio Díscolo, Sintaxis: Introducción, traducción y notas* (Madrid). Spanish translation of the *Syntax*, based on the GG text (not reproduced), with a long introduction (to be treated with caution) but very little commentary and inadequate index; cf. Lallot (1997: i. 63–4).

Bechtle, Gerald (1999), *The Anonymous Commentary on Plato's "Parmenides"* (Bern). Text, trans., detailed discussion, bibliography. Text consists only of six medium-sized fragments.

———— and O'Meara, Dominic (2000) (edd.), *La Philosophie des mathématiques de l'Antiquité tardive* (Fribourg). Contains articles on a number of ancient commentaries on mathematical works.

Bednarski, Michał (1994), *Studia nad grecką terminologią gramatyczną Apolloniosa Dyskolosa* (Cracow). Study of Apollonius' terminology and the way he expresses certain key concepts; in Polish.

Behr, Charles Allison (1968), *Aelius Aristides and the Sacred Tales* (Amsterdam). Discusses prolegomena.

Bekker, Immanuel (1813), *Apollonii Dyscoli, grammatici Alexandrini, de Pronomine liber* (Berlin). Superseded edition.

―――― (1814–21), *Anecdota Graeca* (Berlin). First editions of many Greek scholarly works, some but not all superseded.

―――― (1817), *Apollonii Alexandrini de Constructione orationis libri quatuor* (Berlin). Superseded edition of Apollonius Dyscolus' *Syntax*.

―――― (1833*a*), *Apollonii Sophistae Lexicon Homericum* (Berlin; repr. Hildesheim 1967). Standard edition.

―――― (1833*b*), *Harpocration et Moeris* (Berlin). Editions of lexica, superseded for Moeris but not entirely for Harpocration.

Belardi, Walter (1985), *Filosofia, grammatica e retorica nel pensiero antico* (Rome). Discusses Aristotle and other philosophers; limited treatment of grammarians both Greek and Latin.

Belli, Giorgio (1987), "Aristotele e Posidonio sul significato del 'syndesmos'," *Aevum*, 61: 105–7. Arguments about the meaning of σύνδεσμος based on a passage in Apollonius Dyscolus' *Conjunctions*.

Berger, Günter (1972), *Etymologicum Genuinum et Etymologicum Symeonis (β)* (Meisenheim am Glan; Beiträge zur klassischen Philologie, 45). Integrated edition of these two etymologica, but only for words beginning with β; good introduction.

Berkowitz, Luci, and Squitier, Karl (1990), *Thesaurus Linguae Graecae: Canon of Greek Authors and Works* (Oxford; 3rd edn.). Almost complete listing of classical texts with an edition for each; bibliographical information is unreliable. Updated version available at http://www.tlg.uci.edu.

Bernard, Wolfgang (1990), *Spätantike Dichtungstheorien: Untersuchungen zu Proklos, Herakleitos und Plutarch* (Stuttgart; Beiträge zur Altertumskunde, 3). Discusses Heraclitus' work on Homer; bibliography.

Bernhardy, Gottfried (1828), *Dionysius Periegetes Graece et Latine, cum vetustis commentariis et interpretationibus* (Leipzig; = *Geographi Minores*, i). Usable edition of Eustathius' commentary and scholia on Dionysius Periegetes.

Bessone, Federica (1991), "Valerio Flacco e l'Apollonio commentato: proposte," *Materiali e discussioni*, 26: 31–46.

Betegh, Gábor (2004), *The Derveni Papyrus: Cosmology, Theology and Interpretation* (Cambridge).

Bethe, Erich (1900–37), *Pollucis Onomasticon* (Leipzig; repr. Stuttgart 1998; Lexicographi graeci 9). Standard edition.

―――― (1917), "Iulius (398) Pollux," in *RE* x.i (xix): 773–9. Useful introduction.

Beutler, Rudolf (1938), "Die Gorgiasscholien und Olympiodor," *Hermes*, 73: 380–90. Argues that main source of *scholia vetera* is not Olympiodorus but a common ancestor, perhaps a lost commentary of the Athenian Neoplatonist Plutarchus.

Bicknell, P. (1975), "Diomedon Cholargeus?," *Athenaeum*, 53: 172–8. Discusses Tzetzes' scholia on the execution of the generals after Arginusae. (In English)

Blanchard, Alain (1997), "Destins de Ménandre," *Ktema*, 22: 213–25. Argues that the loss of the plays of Menander was due to Phrynichus' censure.

Blank, David L. (1982), *Ancient Philosophy and Grammar: The Syntax of Apollonius Dyscolus* (Chico, Calif.). Important study of Apollonius' *Syntax*; argues that it was based closely on Stoic theory and is now our best representative of that theory and that it made no distinction between philosophical and technical grammar.

—— (1983a), "Remarks on Nicanor, the Stoics, and the Ancient Theory of Punctuation," *Glotta*, 61: 48–67. Examines Nicanor's theory of punctuation, reconstructed from the scholia to Homer, and argues that Nicanor's system was essentially that of his predecessors (with the addition of a few more distinctions), and that this system derived ultimately from Stoic theory.

—— (1983b), Review of Householder (1981), in *HL* 10: 339–47. Provides useful corrections.

—— (1988), *Lesbonax: Περὶ σχημάτων* (Berlin; SGLG 7; in one vol. with F. Montanari 1988a and Dyck 1988). Standard edition.

—— (1993), "Apollonius Dyscolus," in *ANRW* II 34.1: 708–30. Superb general introduction, with excellent commentary on modern scholarship on Apollonius.

—— (1994), "Analogy, Anomaly and Apollonius Dyscolus," in Everson (1994): 149–65. Argues that the Analogy/Anomaly controversy did not exist and that Apollonius' theories were more influenced by Stoic theory than is usually thought.

—— (2000), "The Organization of Grammar in Ancient Greece," in Auroux *et al.* (2000): 400–17. Summary of development of Greek grammatical tradition, including a reconstruction of the original contents of Dionysius Thrax's Τέχνη, with bibliography.

—— and Dyck, Andrew R. (1984), "Aristophanes of Byzantium and Problem-Solving in the Museum: Notes on a Recent Reassessment," *ZPE* 56: 17–24. Argues against Slater (1982).

Blass, Friedrich (1882), "Neue Papyrusfragmente im Ägyptischen Museum zu Berlin," *Hermes*, 17: 148–63. Publication of papyrus with lexicon to Demosthenes, with extensive discussion; re-edited in *BKT* i.

—— (1892), "Demosthenica aus neuen Papyrus," *NJPP* 145 (= *JCP* 38): 29–44. Text and detailed discussion of papyrus fragment with commentary on Demosthenes.

—— (1906), *Aischylos' Choephoren* (Halle). Beneath the text prints an edition (now superseded) of M scholia to *Choephori*.

—— (1907), *Die Eumeniden des Aischylos* (Berlin). Beneath the text prints an edition (now superseded) of M scholia to *Eumenides*.

—— and Debrunner, Albert (1979), *Grammatik des neutestamentlichen Griechisch* (15th edn., Göttingen). Reference grammar useful for points of postclassical usage.

Blum, Rudolf (1977), *Kallimachos und die Literaturverzeichnung bei den Griechen* (Frankfurt am Main). Important study of Callimachus' scholarly activity.

—— (1991), *Kallimachos: The Alexandrian Library and the Origins of Bibliography*, trans. Hans H. Wellisch (Madison). Translation of Blum (1977), with dumbed-down footnotes and Anglicized bibliography going up to 1982.

Blumenthal, Albrecht von (1930), *Hesychstudien: Untersuchungen zur Vorgeschichte der griechischen Sprache nebst lexicographischen Beiträgen* (Stuttgart).

Boer, Aemilia, and Weinstock, Stephan (1940), "Porphyrii philosophi Introductio in Tetrabiblum Ptolemaei," in S. Weinstock, *Catalogus Codicum Astrologorum Graecorum*, v.iv (Brussels): 185–228. Standard edition.

Bollack, Jean (1990), *L'Œdipe roi de Sophocle* (Lille). Contains useful summary of information on scholia, with further references.

Bolognesi, Giancarlo (1953), "Sul Περὶ διαλέκτων di Gregorio di Corinto," *Aevum*, 27: 97–120. Important study and key source for information on this work.

Bonelli, Maddalena (1997), "La lessicografia filosofica nell'antichità: Il lessico Platonico di Timeo Sofista," *Elenchos*, 18: 29–56.

Borries, Johann von / Ioannes de (1911), *Phrynichi sophistae Praeparatio sophistica* (Leipzig). Standard text.

Bossi, Francesco (1980–2), "Phryn. *Ecl.* 62 Fischer," *MCr* 15–17: 199–200. Suggests emendation.

———— (1998), "Nota ad Apione (fr. 86 Neitzel ~ *Gl. Hom.* 97,10ss. Ludw.)," *Eikasmos*, 9: 225–7.

———— (2000), "Sui περιεργοπένητες di Diogeniano," *Eikasmos*, 11: 267–8. Note on the meaning of a word in Hesychius.

Bowen, Alan C., and Goldstein, Bernard R. (1991), "Hipparchus' Treatment of Early Greek Astronomy: The Case of Eudoxus and the Length of Daytime," *Proceedings of the American Philosophical Society*, 135: 233–54. Interesting discussion of Hipparchus 1. 3. 5–10 (with English trans. of the passage).

Brandenburg, Philipp. (2005), *Apollonios Dyskolos: Über das Pronomen* (Leipzig). Text, German trans., and commentary; see review by R. Ferri (*BMCR* 2006.02.59, available at http://ccat.sas.upenn.edu/bmcr) for corrections and detailed summary.

Brandis, Christian A. (1836), *Scholia in Aristotelem*, = I. Bekker, *Aristoteles Opera*, iv (Berlin; 2nd edn. ed. Olof Gigon 1961). Not primarily scholia, but extracts from self-standing commentaries mixed with a few scholia. Now superseded by *CAG* (which gives much fuller versions of the texts) except for a few texts not included in *CAG*; see the tables at the front of the second edition to determine which these are. Difficult Greek font.

Braswell, Karl; Billerbeck, Margarethe; *et al.* (forthcoming), *The Grammarian Epaphroditus* (Bern). New edition with trans., introduction, and commentary.

Breysig, Alfred (1867), *Germanici Caesaris Aratea: Cum scholiis* (Berlin). The scholia given here are the standard edition of the Latin version of the Φ commentary to Aratus; note that the second edition of this text (Leipzig 1899) does not contain the scholia.

Brittain, Charles, and Brennan, Tad (2002), *Simplicius: Commentarius in Enchiridion Epicteti* (London). Translation into English.

Bröcker, Ludwig O. (1885), "Die Methoden Galens in der literarischen Kritik," *RhM* 40: 415–38.

Broggiato, Maria (2002), *Cratete di Mallo: I frammenti* (La Spezia). Best edition of fragments, with discussion.

Browning, Robert (1962–3), "The Patriarchal School at Constantinople in the Twelfth Century," *Byzantion*, 32: 167–202 and 33: 11–40. Study of this school, with much useful information on the individual teachers and their works.

———— (1992), "The Byzantines and Homer," in Lamberton and Keaney (1992): 134–48.

Budelmann, Felix (1999), "Metrical Scholia on Pindar," *Bulletin of the Institute of Classical Studies of the University of London*, 43: 195–201. Simple introduction to metrical scholia, both old and Byzantine.

Buffière, Félix (1962), *Héraclite: Allégories d'Homère* (Paris). Good text, very helpful introduction, and French trans.

Bühler (*or* Buehler), Winfried (1972), "Zur Überlieferung des Lexikons des Ammonios," *Hermes*, 100: 531–50. Information on several newly discovered manuscripts.

———— (1973), "Eine Theognosthandschrift aus der Zeit um 1000 auf Patmos," *Jahrbuch der Österreichischen Byzantinistik*, 22: 49–91.

———— (1977), "Die Philologie der Griechen und ihre Methoden," *Jahrbuch der Akademie der Wissenschaften in Göttingen*, 44–62. General introduction to ancient scholarship.

Bülow-Jacobsen, Adam, and Ebbesen, Sten (1982), "Vaticanus urbinas graecus 35: An edition of the scholia on Aristotle's Sophistici Elenchi," *Cahiers de l'institut du moyen-âge grec et latin*, 43: 45–120.

Burguière, Paul (1961–2), "Cyrilliana: Observations sur deux manuscrits parisiens du lexique de Cyrille," *REA* 63: 345–61 and 64: 95–108. Study of specific manuscripts of Cyrillus' lexicon, with edition of a few glosses.

——— (1970), "Cyrilliana (III): Remarques sur la composition du lexique de Cyrille," *REA* 72: 364–84. Study of Cyrillus' sources.

Bussemaker, U. Cats (1849), *Scholia et paraphrases in Nicandrum et Oppianum*, published as the second half of Fr. Dübner, *Scholia in Theocritum* (Paris). Latest edition of Oppian material, but superseded by Geymonat for Nicander. With notes.

Buttmann, Alexander (1877), *Des Apollonius Dyskolos vier Bücher über die Syntax, übersetzt und erlaütert* (Berlin). German translation of the *Syntax*, very unreliable.

Calame, Claude (1970), *Etymologicum genuinum: Les citations de poètes lyriques* (Rome). Edition of fragments.

Callanan, Christopher K. (1987), *Die Sprachbeschreibung bei Aristophanes von Byzanz* (Göttingen; Hypomnemata, 88). Important study of Aristophanes' grammatical ideas; includes a good summary of previous work on Aristophanes and detailed bibliography. See Schenkeveld (1990) for an English summary of the main arguments; discussion of them in that work, in Ax (1990), and in Slater (1989*b*).

Cameron, Alan (1990), "Isidore of Miletus and Hypatia: On the Editing of Mathematical Texts," *GRBS*, 31: 103–27. On ancient editions of Archimedes and Ptolemy.

——— (1995), *Callimachus and his Critics* (Princeton). Much good (but scattered) discussion of scholia and *diegeses*.

——— (2004), *Greek Mythography in the Roman World* (New York). Fascinating study of mythographical commentary in the Roman period.

Campbell, David A. (1984), "Stobaeus and Early Greek Lyric Poetry," in D. E. Gerber (ed.), *Greek Poetry and Philosophy: Studies in Honour of Leonard Woodbury* (Chico, Calif.): 51–7. Investigates how Stobaeus made his selections.

Carawan, Edwin M. (1990), "The Five Talents Cleon Coughed Up (Schol. Ar. Ach. 6)," *CQ*, ns 40: 137–47. On the scholia and Athenian history.

Carden, Richard (1974), *The Papyrus Fragments of Sophocles* (Berlin). Some fragments have minor marginal scholia. Does not contain *Ichneutae* papyrus or papyri of hypotheses.

Cardini, Maria Timpanaro (1978), *Proclo: Commento al I libro degli* Elementi *di Euclide* (Pisa). Italian trans. with (short) introduction and notes.

Carnuth, Otto (1869), *Aristonici περὶ σημείων Ὀδυσσείας reliquiae emendatiores* (Leipzig). Collection of fragments.

——— (1875), *Nicanoris περὶ Ὀδυσσειακῆς στιγμῆς reliquiae emendatiores* (Berlin; repr. Amsterdam 1967). Collection of fragments.

Casadio, Valerio (1986–7), "*Etym. Gen.* γ," *MCr* 21–2: 401–24. Edition and discussion of entries beginning with gamma.

——— (1988–9), "Note ad *Etym. Gen.* δ," *MCr* 23–4: 335–51. Edition and discussion of selected entries beginning with delta.

——— (1990–3), "Note ad *Etym. Gen.* ε," *MCr* 25–8: 379–408. Edition and discussion of selected entries beginning with epsilon.

——— Cavallini, Eleonora; Curiazi, Dalila; Lasserre, François; Marzullo, Benedetto; and Tosi, Renzo (1984–5), "Note a Fozio," *MCr* 19–20: 265–328. Series of articles with critical notes to the *Lexicon*, mostly in Italian.

Cataudella, Quintino (1972), "Sugli scoli A, B al *Partenio* I di Alcmane," in Q. Cataudella, *Intorno ai lirici greci: Contributi alla critica del testo e all'interpretazione* (Rome), 21–41. Interpretation of scholia.

Caujolle-Zaslawsky, Françoise (1985), "La Scholie de Stephanos: Quelques remarques sur la théorie des temps du verbe attribuée aux Stoiciens," *Histoire Epistémologie Langage*, 7.1: 19–46. Examines one of the scholia to Dionysius Thrax, which is key to our understanding of the Stoic theory of tenses, and gives more bibliography on this topic.

Cazzaniga, Ignazio (1976), "Note Nicandree," *SCO* 25: 317–19. Uses scholia to Nicander.

Ceccarelli, Paola, and Steinrück, Martin (1995), "A propos de schol. in Lycophronis Alexandram 1226," *MH* 52: 77–89. On text and interpretation of scholion relevant to dating of poem.

Cellerini, Alberto (1988), *Introduzione all'*Etymologicum Gudianum (Rome; *BollClass* suppl. 6). Useful study with good bibliography.

Chandler, Henry W. (1881), *A Practical Introduction to Greek Accentuation* (Oxford; repr. New Rochelle 1983).

Chantraine, Pierre (1956), Review of Dain (1954), *RPh*, 3rd ser. 30: 322–3. Offers some useful textual suggestions.

Christodoulou, Georgios Andreou (1977), Τὰ ἀρχαῖα σχόλια εἰς Αἴαντα τοῦ Σοφοκλέους (Athens). Best edition; in addition to old scholia contains some later material. Detailed introduction in modern Greek, apparatus in Latin.

Chroust, Anton-Hermann (1965), "The Organization of the Corpus Platonicum in Antiquity," *Hermes*, 93: 34–46. Argues that our traditional grouping of the dialogs may be very old; theories not universally accepted. On pp. 44–6 discusses Tyrannion's work on Aristotle.

Clackson, James Peter (1995), "The *Technè* in Armenian," in Law and Sluiter (1995): 121–33. Focuses on the Armenian translation of Dionysius Thrax; of little use for those interested in the Greek.

Cleary, John J. (2000), "Proclus' Philosophy of Mathematics," in Bechtle and O'Meara (2000): 85–101. On Proclus' commentary on Euclid.

Cohn, Leopold (1884), "Untersuchungen über die Quellen der Plato-Scholien," *JCP* suppl., NS 13: 771–864. Definitive explanation of the sources and history of the Plato scholia.

—— (1898), "Der Atticist Philemon," *Philologus*, 57: 353–67. Important study.

—— (1899), "Choiroboskos," in *RE* iii.ii: 2363–7. Good, clear explanation of the various works and sources, with bibliography.

—— (1912), "Gregorios 1," in *RE* vii.ii (xiv): 1848–52. Thorough treatment with useful bibliography.

Collart, Jean (1978) (ed.), *Varron, grammaire antique, et stylistique latine* (Paris). Collection of articles, some pertaining to Greek grammarians.

Collinge, N. E. (1963), "The Greek Use of the Term 'Middle' in Linguistic Analysis," *Word*, 19: 232–41. Considers the different grammatical meanings of μέσος and their relationship to one another.

Colonna, Aristide (1953), "I *Prolegomeni* ad Esiodo e la *Vita Esiodea* di Giovanni Tzetzes," *Bollettino del Comitato per la preparazione della edizione nazionale dei classici greci e latini* (Accademia nazionale dei Lincei), 2nd ser. 2: 27–39. Edition of some of Tzetzes' work on Hesiod.

—— (1967), *Etymologicum Genuinum littera* Λ (Rome). Edition superseded by Alpers (1969).

Colson, F. H. (1919), "The Analogist and Anomalist Controversy," *CQ* 13: 24–36.

Condos, Theony (1970), *The* Katasterismoi *of the Pseudo-Eratosthenes: A Mythological Commentary and English Translation* (Diss. University of Southern California).

Conrad, Nicola (forthcoming), *Scholia D in Homeri Odysseam* (Diss. Cologne). Should eventually be available online via http://www.uni-koeln.de/phil-fak/ifa/klassphil/vanthiel/index.html.

Consani, Carlo (1991), Διάλεκτος: *Contributo alla storia del concetto di "dialetto"* (Pisa; Testi linguistici, 18).

Consbruch, Maximilian (1889), *De Hephaestioneis qui circumferuntur* περὶ ποιήματος *commentariis* (Diss. Breslau). On texts and authorship of scholia to Hephaestion.

—— (1906), *Hephaestionis Enchiridion cum commentariis veteribus* (Leipzig). Standard text of Hephaestion's work, Choeroboscus' commentary, and scholia to Hephaestion.

Corcella, Aldo (1996), "A New Fragment of the Historian Theseus," *CQ*, NS 46: 261–6. Uses scholia to Herodotus.

Coulter, James A. (1976), *The Literary Microcosm: Theories of Interpretation of the Later Neoplatonists* (Leiden; Columbia Studies in the Classical Tradition, 2).

Cousin, Victor (1864), *Procli commentarium in Platonis Parmenidem*: Part III of *Procli philosophi Platonici opera inedita* (Paris, 2nd edn.; repr. Hildesheim 1961). Somewhat inadequate edition, but currently best available.

Couvreur, Paul (1901), *Hermiae Alexandrini in Platonis Phaedrum scholia* (Paris; repr. Hildesheim 1971). Text with introduction. Reprint adds long index by Clemens Zintzen.

Cramer, John Anthony (1835), *Anecdota Graeca e codd. manuscriptis bibliothecarum Oxoniensium II* (Oxford; repr. Amsterdam 1963). Contains the only editions of Choeroboscus' Περὶ ὀρθογραφίας and Περὶ ποσότητος, also Theognostus; not a critical text, no apparatus. See R. Schneider (1887).

——— (1836), *Anecdota Graeca e codd. manuscriptis bibliothecarum Oxoniensium III* (Oxford; repr. Amsterdam 1963). Contains editions of some obscure works of [ps.-]Herodian.

——— (1839–41), *Anecdota Graeca e codd. manuscriptis bibliothecae regiae Parisiensis* (Oxford; repr. Hildesheim 1967). First editions of some scholarly works, not all of them superseded.

Crugnola, Annunciata (1971), *Scholia in Nicandri Theriaka cum glossis* (Milan). Standard edition.

Cunningham, Ian C. (2003), *Synagoge: Συναγωὴ λέξεων χρησίμων: Texts of the Original Version and of MS. B* (Berlin; SGLG 10). Best text and explanation.

——— (forthcoming). *Hesychii Alexandrini Lexicon*, iv (Berlin). A continuation of Latte's and Hansen's text, to cover τ–ω.

Cunningham, Mary B. (1991), *The Life of Michael the Synkellos* (Belfast). Critical edition of an anonymous, undated Byzantine life of Michael Syncellus, with introduction, trans., commentary, and bibliography.

Curiazi, Dalila (1983), "Etym. gen. π 19," *MCr* 18: 297–301. Note.

——— Funaioli, Maria Paola; *et al.* (1980–2), "*Etym. Gen.*," *MCr* 15–17: 237–302. Series of very short articles constituting an edition of letters μ, ν, ξ, and ω, with discussion.

Dähnhardt, Oscar (1894), *Scholia in Aeschyli Persas* (Leipzig). Contains M (far right column) and Φ scholia (marginal scholia on left-hand pages, interlinear ones in left column of right-hand pages); still one of the best texts of Φ scholia, though many of these are simply omitted and though text relies on Dindorf for some manuscripts.

Dain, Alphonse (1954), *Le "Philétaeros" attribué à Hérodien* (Paris). Only edition of this glossary; good introduction and indices. See Chantraine (1956).

Daitz, Stephen G. (1979), *The Scholia in the Jerusalem Palimpsest of Euripides: A Critical Edition* (Heidelberg). Edition of the scholia in a manuscript not used by Schwartz; adds little new material.

Dalfen, Joachim (1978), "Scholien und Interlinearglossen in Marc Aurel-Handschriften," *SIFC* 50: 5–26. Studies use of scholia for establishing history of text and argues that many glosses have crept into main text. Pages out of order; read 7–10–9–8–11.

Dalimier, Catherine (1999), "Apollonios Dyscole sur la fonction des conjonctions explétives," *REG* 112: 719–30. Discusses the meaning of παραπλήρωμα in Apollonius and other authors, arguing that the usage in geometry can shed light on the grammatical meaning.

——— (2001), *Apollonius Dyscole: Traité des Conjonctions* (Paris). New text of this work, with facing French trans., thorough introduction, extensive commentary, and good bibliography.

Daly, Lloyd W. (1967), *Contributions to a History of Alphabetization in Antiquity and the*

Middle Ages (Brussels; Collection Latomus, 10). Fascinating but not always reliable history.

––––– (1983), *Iohannis Philoponi de vocabulis quae diversum significatum exhibent secundum differentiam accentus / On the Accent of Homonyms* (Philadelphia). Standard edition; text is given in five versions, so use of index is essential. Bibliographical information in introduction is unreliable.

Davies, Malcolm (1991), *Poetarum Melicorum Graecorum Fragmenta* (Oxford). Includes some ancient commentaries and marginalia.

Dawe, Roger D. (1973), *Studies on the Text of Sophocles*, i (Leiden). Discusses scholia, pp. 113–19.

––––– (1975), Review of Wartelle (1971), *Gnomon*, 47: 641–5. Suggests (pp. 642–3) that Didymus may not have written the ancestor of the Aeschylus scholia. In English.

Deas, Henry Thomson (1931), "The Scholia Vetera to Pindar," *HSCP* 42: 1–78. Good explanation of sources of old, non-metrical scholia.

De Clercq, Jan, and Desmet, Piet (1994) (edd.), *Florilegium Historiographiae Linguisticae: Études d'historiographie de la linguistique et de grammaire comparée à la mémoire de Maurice Leroy* (Louvain). Collection containing several good pieces on ancient grammarians.

Decorps-Foulquier, Micheline (1998), "Eutocius d'Ascalon éditeur du traité des *Coniques* d'Apollonios de Pergé et l'exigence de 'clarté'," in Argoud and Guillaumin (1998) 87–101. Discusses Eutocius' commentaries on Apollonius and Archimedes.

De Falco, Vittorio (1926), *Ioannis Pediasimi in Aristotelis Analytica scholia selecta* (Naples). Edition of some 13th–14th cent. scholia.

De Faveri, Lorena (2002), *Die metrischen Trikliniusscholien zur byzantinischen Trias des Euripides* (Stuttgart). Best edition of these scholia.

De Furia, Franciscus (1814), *Appendix ad Draconem Stratonicensem, complectens Trichae, Eliae Monachi, et Herodiani Tractatus de Metris* (Leipzig). Contains edition of obscure work of Herodian, superseded by Studemund (1867).

Degani, Enzo (1995), "La lessicografia," in G. Cambiano, L. Canfora, and D. Lanza (edd.), *Lo spazio letterario della grecia antica* (Rome): ii. 505–27. Clear, thorough overview with excellent bibliography.

––––– (1998), "Corolla Esichiana," *Rivista di cultura classica e medioevale*, 40: 85–90. Notes on various entries, in Italian.

Deicke, Ludwig (1901), *De scholiis in Apollonium Rhodium quaestiones selectae* (Diss. Göttingen). Good but now superseded.

Delatte, Armand (1939), *Anecdota Atheniensia*, ii (Liége: Bibliothèque de faculté de philosophie et lettres de l'université de Liége, 88). Contains (pp. 129–87) second version of the second book of Philoponus' commentary on Nicomachus.

Del Canto Nieto, José Ramón (1993), *Eratóstenes: Catasterismos* (Madrid). Spanish trans., with introduction and notes.

Delcourt, Marie (1933), "Biographies anciennes d'Euripide," *AC* 2: 271–90. Detailed explanation.

Dell'Era, Antonio (1974), *Una caeli descriptio d'età carolingia* (Palermo). Only edition of some late scholia to Aratus.

––––– (1979a), "Una miscellanea astronomica medievale: Gli 'Scholia Strozziana' a Germanico," *MAL*, 8th ser. 23: 147–267. Best edition of these scholia, which were translated from the Greek.

––––– (1979b), "Gli 'Scholia Basileensia' a Germanico," *MAL*, 8th ser. 23: 301–79. Best edition of these scholia, which were translated from the Greek, with introduction and some bibliography.

De Marco, Vittorio (1936), "Sulla tradizione manoscritta degli scolii Sofoclei," *SIFC* 13: 3–44.

—————— (1937), *De scholiis in Sophoclis tragoedias veteribus* (Rome; *MAL*, 6th ser. 6; published both separately as fasc. 2 and as pp. 105–228 of vol. 6).

—————— (1946), *Scholia minora in Homeri Iliadem, pars prior* (Vatican). Edition of D scholia, covers A–E only.

—————— (1952), *Scholia in Sophoclis Oedipum Coloneum* (Rome). Best edition; old scholia only.

De Mauro, Tullio (1965), "Il nome del dativo e la teoria dei casi greci," *Atti della Accademia Nazionale dei Lincei: Rendiconti: Classe di scienze morali, storiche e filologiche*, 8th ser. 20: 151–211. Considers the meaning of case-names (mainly δοτική, but also γενική and αἰτιατική); looks at Latin and Sanskrit as well as Greek.

De Stefani, Eduardo Luigi/Aloysius (1909–20), *Etymologicum Gudianum* (Leipzig; repr. Amsterdam 1965). Best edition, but covers first six letters of the alphabet only.

Devarius, Matthaeus (1828), *Index in Eustathii Commentarios in Homeri Iliadem et Odysseam* (Leipzig; repr. Hildesheim 1960). Index to Stallbaum (1825–6) and to Stallbaum (1827–30).

De Vries, Scato (1901), *Homeri Ilias cum scholiis: Codex Venetus A, Marcianus 454* (Leiden). Complete facsimile of Venetus A. No author; De Vries is the series editor, and there is a preface by Domenico Comparetti.

Di Benedetto, Vincenzo (1990), "At the Origins of Greek Grammar," *Glotta*, 68: 19–39. Argues against Erbse (1980) that Dionysius did not write the Τέχνη.

—————— (2000), "Dionysius Thrax and the *Tékhnē Grammatikḗ*," in Auroux *et al.* (2000): 394–400. Summarizes arguments against authenticity of Τέχνη, with bibliography.

Dickson, Keith (1998), *Stephanus the Philosopher and Physician: Commentary on Galen's Therapeutics to Glaucon* (Leiden; Studies in Ancient Medicine, 19). Edition and trans.

Diehl, Ernst (1903–6), *Procli Diadochi in Platonis Timaeum commentaria* (Leipzig; repr. Amsterdam 1965). Text with introduction, scholia, and index.

Diels, Hermann (1910), "Die Anfänge der Philologie bei den Griechen," *Neue Jahrbücher für das klassische Altertum*, 25: 1–25 (repr. in *Kleine Schriften zur Geschichte der antiken Philosophie* (Hildesheim 1969): 68–92). On pre-Alexandrian philology, especially Herodotus and the philosophers.

Dietz, Friedrich Reinhold (1834), *Apollonii Citiensis, Stephani, Palladii, Theophili, Meletii, Damascii, Ioannis, aliorum Scholia in Hippocratem et Galenum* (Königsberg; repr. Amsterdam 1966). Not an edition of scholia, but of self-standing commentaries, not all of them complete. Vol. i is superseded, but vol. ii mostly not.

Diggle, James (1981–94), *Euripidis fabulae* (Oxford). Best text of the hypotheses.

—————— (2003), Review of Haffner (2001), *CR* 53: 487–8. Useful corrections.

Di Gregorio, Lamberto (1975), *Scholia vetera in Hesiodi Theogoniam* (Milan). Best edition.

Diller, Aubrey (1938), "The Tradition of Stephanus Byzantius," *TAPA* 69: 333–48. Important study of manuscript tradition.

—————— (1950), "Excerpts from Strabo and Stephanus in Byzantine Chronicles," *TAPA* 81: 241–53.

—————— (1956), "Pausanias in the Middle Ages," *TAPA* 87: 84–97. Includes information on scholia and on Stephanus of Byzantium.

Dillery, John (2003), "Putting him Back Together Again: Apion Historian, Apion *Grammatikos*," *CP* 98: 383–90. On the connections between the different genres of Apion's writings.

Dillon, John M. (1973), *Iamblichi Chalcidensis in Platonis dialogos commentariorum fragmenta* (Leiden; Philosophia Antiqua, 23). Text, facing English trans., introduction, bibliography.

—————— (1993), *Alcinous: The Handbook of Platonism* (Oxford). No text, but trans., introduction, extensive commentary, and bibliography.

Dilts, Mervin R. (1983–6), *Scholia Demosthenica* (Leipzig). Standard edition.

—— (1984), "Editions of Scholia Demosthenica," *Sileno*, 10 (*Studi in onore Adelmo Barigazzi*): 197–205. Summary of the situation, with references to much earlier literature.

—— (1985), "Palaeologan Scholia on the Orations of Demosthenes," *C&M* 36: 257–9. On textual history.

—— (1992), *Scholia in Aeschinem* (Stuttgart and Leipzig). Standard text of these scholia.

Dindorf, Ludwig August (1855), *Xenophontis expeditio Cyri* (Oxford). Prints *Anabasis* scholia, pp. 381–96. There are many editions of this work, starting in 1825, but the scholia should only be used from editions of 1855 and later.

Dindorf, Wilhelm/Guilielmus (1825), Ἰωάννου Ἀλεξανδρέως τονικὰ παραγγέλματα (Leipzig). Only edition of one of the two epitomes on which Lentz's edition of Herodian's Περὶ καθολικῆς προσῳδίας is based.

—— (1829), *Aristides* (Leipzig; repr. Hildesheim 1964). Vol. iii contains the scholia; most untrustworthy.

—— (1851*a*), *Aeschyli tragoediae superstites et deperditarum fragmenta*, iii: *Scholia graeca ex codicibus aucta et emendata* (Oxford; repr. Hildesheim 1962). Superseded edition of M and A scholia.

—— (1851*b*), *Demosthenes ex recensione Gulielmi Dindorfii*, vols. viii and ix: *Scholia graeca ex codicibus aucta et emendata* (Oxford). Superseded edition.

—— (1852*a*), *Scholia Graeca in Aeschinem et Isocratem* (Oxford). Best edition of Isocrates scholia (pp. vii–viii, 101–24), but superseded for Aeschines.

—— (1852*b*), *Scholia in Sophoclis tragoedias septem*, ii (Oxford). Edition of Byzantine scholia, pp. 145–404; not good, but best available except for *Oedipus Rex*.

—— (1853), *Harpocrationis lexicon in decem oratores Atticos* (Oxford). Edition in vol. i, extensive discussion in ii. Not ideal, but not yet superseded.

—— (1855), *Scholia graeca in Homeri Odysseam* (Oxford). Not ideal, but standard text except for α 1–309.

—— (1863*a*), "Ueber die mediceische Handschrift des Aeschylus und deren Verhältniss zu den übrigen Handschriften, Dritter Artikel," *Philologus*, 20: 385–411. Superseded edition of part of T.

—— (1863*b*), *Scholia graeca in Euripidis tragoedias ex codicibus aucta et emendata* (Oxford). Superseded for old scholia and Triclinius' metrical scholia, but best text of other Byzantine scholia.

—— (1864), "Ueber die mediceische Handschift des Aeschylus und deren Verhältniss zu den übrigen Handschriften, Dritten Artikels zweiter Theil," *Philologus*, 21: 193–225. Superseded edition of part of T.

—— (1875–8), *Scholia graeca in Homeri Iliadem ex codicibus aucta et emendata* (Oxford). Vols. i–ii give scholia in A (glosses separately at end), iii–iv give scholia in B (schol. rec. separately at end); much but not all of this material is superseded by Erbse (1969–88).

Dodds, Eric R. (1959), *Plato: Gorgias* (Oxford). Useful introduction provides excellent overview of Olympiodorus and scholia (pp. 58–62).

Donnet, Daniel (1966), "Précisions sur les œuvres profanes de Grégoire de Corinthe," *Bulletin de l'institut historique belge de Rome*, 37: 81–97. Useful discussion of the scholarly works attributable to Gregory and the sources of our knowledge of those works.

—— (1967), *Le traité Περὶ συντάξεως λόγου de Grégoire de Corinthe* (Brussels). Only edition of Gregory's *Syntax*; contains a thorough introduction focusing on textual history, Greek text with detailed app. crit., facing French trans., commentary, scholia and related texts, excellent indices, and extensive bibliography.

—— (1982), *Le* Traité de la construction de la phrase *de Michel le Syncelle de Jérusalem* (Brussels). Standard edition of the first Byzantine syntax.

—— (1987), "Michel le Syncelle, *Traité de la construction de la phrase*: Les manuscrits de l'Athos," *Byzantion*, 57: 174–80. Discusses some MSS not included in his 1982 edition.

D'Ooge, Martin Luther (1926), *Nicomachus of Gerasa: Introduction to Arithmetic* (New York, repr. 1972). Contains overview of commentaries etc. pp. 125–32.

Dörrie, Heinrich, and Baltes, Matthias (1987–), *Der Platonismus in der Antike* (Stuttgart and Bad Cannstatt). Multivolume work presenting excerpts from Platonists with trans. and commentary, grouped by themes. Extensive bibliography.

Dover, Kenneth (1955), "The Patmos Scholia and the Text of Thucydides," *CR*, NS 5: 134–7.

—— (1993), *Aristophanes: Frogs* (Oxford). Discusses scholia, pp. 94–102.

Drachmann, Anders Bjørn (1903–27), *Scholia vetera in Pindari carmina* (Leipzig; repr. Amsterdam 1966–9). Best edition of most of the Pindar scholia; contains all the old scholia and Eustathius' introduction. Superseded for the metrical scholia and Eustathius.

—— (1925), *Isaac Tzetzae de metris Pindaricis commentarius* (Copenhagen; Det Kgl. Danske Videnskabernes Selskab, Historisk-filologiske Meddelelser, 9.3). Only modern edition.

—— (1936), *Die Überlieferung des Cyrillglossars* (Copenhagen; Det Kgl. Danske Videnskabernes Selskab, Historisk-filologiske Meddelelser 21.5). Important study and partial edition.

Dübner, J. Friedrich (1842), *Scholia graeca in Aristophanem* (Paris; repr. Hildesheim 1969). Was the standard edition of Aristophanes scholia until the publication of the Koster–Holwerda edition, and is still the best text of the scholia not yet covered by the new edition.

Duentzer, Heinrich (1848), *De Zenodoti studiis Homericis* (Göttingen; repr. Hildesheim 1981). Essays incorporating only complete edition of fragments.

Dunbar, Nan (1995), *Aristophanes: Birds* (Oxford). Good summary of ancient scholarship, pp. 31–49.

Düring, Ingemar (1932), *Porphyrios, Kommentar zur Harmonielehre des Ptolemaios* (Gothenburg; Göteborgs Högskolas Årsskrift, 38; repr. Hildesheim 1978). Standard edition, but see emendations in Alexanderson (1969).

—— (1957), *Aristotle in the Ancient Biographical Tradition* (Gothenburg; repr. New York 1987). On pp. 412–13 assembles all the ancient evidence for Tyrannio's involvement in the editing of Aristotle; see also notes on pp. 393–4.

Durling, R. J. (1993), *A Dictionary of Medical Terms in Galen* (Leiden). Useful tool for reading any work of Galen.

Dyck, Andrew R. (1977), "Herodian über die Etymologie von ἴφθιμος," *Glotta*, 55: 225–7. On Herodian Περὶ διχρόνων.

—— (1981), "Notes on the Epimerismoi attributed to Herodian," *Hermes*, 109: 225–35. On the history and authenticity of these works; adds some new fragments not in Lentz, and argues that Herodian's epimerismi were a source for the *Epimerismi Homerici*.

—— (1982a), "Did Eustathius Compose a Commentary on Oppian's *Halieutica*?" *CP* 77: 153–4. Uses scholia to Oppian.

—— (1982b), Review of Linke (1977) / Haas (1977) / Neitzel (1977), *CP* 77: 270–7. Provides useful corrections to all three editions, listed individually below but all contained in SGLG 3.

—— (1982c), "Zu Philoxenus von Alexandrien," *Philologus*, 126: 149–51. Textual suggestions.

Dyck, Andrew R. (1983–95), *Epimerismi Homerici* (Berlin; SGLG 5). Excellent edition, study (in English), bibliography; includes both epimerismi and *Lexicon* αἱμωδεῖν.

—— (1985), "Notes on Platonic Lexicography in Antiquity," *HSCP* 89: 75–88. Excellent discussion of Timaeus, Boethus, and Clement, with edition of fragments of latter two.

—— (1987), "The Glossographoi," *HSCP* 91: 119–60. On some pre-Aristarchean explications of Homeric words: edition of fragments, discussion.

—— (1988), *The Fragments of Comanus of Naucratis* (Berlin; SGLG 7; in one vol. with F. Montanari 1988*a* and Blank 1988). Standard edition.

—— (1989), Review of Slater (1986), *CP* 84: 256–60. Some useful corrections.

—— (1993*a*), "Aelius Herodian: Recent Studies and Prospects for Future Research," in *ANRW* II 34.1: 772–94. Excellent introduction to Herodian's works and modern scholarship on them, and invaluable guide for handling Lentz's edition.

—— (1993*b*), "The Fragments of Heliodorus Homericus," *HSCP* 95: 1–64. Edition with good discussion; Apollonius Sophista is a major source.

Dzielska, Maria (1995), *Hypatia of Alexandria* (trans. F. Lyra; Cambridge, Mass.) Interesting study of an interesting woman.

Ebbesen, Sten (1981), *Commentators and Commentaries on Aristotle's Sophistici Elenchi: A Study of Post-Aristotelian Ancient and Medieval Writings on Fallacies* (Leiden). Contains editions of scholia to Aristotle, Galen's *De captionibus*, and other relevant texts, with extensive discussion, bibliography, list of MSS with scholia or paraphrases to the *Elenchi*, Danish summary.

Edlow, Robert Blair (1977), *Galen on Language and Ambiguity* (Leiden). Text (repr. of 1903 edn.), trans., introduction, and commentary.

Egenolff, Peter (1878), Review of *GG* ii.i, *NJPP* 117 (= *JCP* 24): 833–48. Offers some useful corrections.

—— (1879), "Zu Apollonios Dyskolos," *NJPP* 119 (= *JCP* 25): 693–8. Discusses the term μέρος λόγου in Apollonius and others.

—— (1880), *Ioannis Philoponi collectio vocum, quae pro diversa significatione accentum diversum accipiunt* (Breslau; repr. in Latte and Erbse (1965) 359–72). Superseded edition.

—— (1884), "Bericht über die griechischen Grammatiker," *Jahresbericht über die Fortschritte der classischen Alterthumswissenschaft, begründet von Conrad Bursian*, 38: 43–98. Useful summary of scholarship from 1879–83; on pp. 62–70 gives corrections to Lentz's edition of Herodian's Περὶ μονήρους λέξεως.

—— (1887), *Die orthoepischen Stücke der byzantinischen Litteratur* (Leipzig). Discusses Choeroboscus.

—— (1888), *Die orthographischen Stücke der byzantinischen Litteratur* (Leipzig). Discusses Charax *passim* and Choeroboscus' Περὶ ὀρθογραφίας pp. 17–21.

—— (1894), "Zu Herodianos technikos," *NJPP* 149 (= *JCP* 40): 337–45. Edition of Herodian's Σχηματισμοὶ Ὁμηρικοί.

—— (1900), "Zu Lentz' Herodian I," *Philologus*, 59: 238–55. Important critique with corrections.

—— (1902), "Zu Lentz' Herodian II," *Philologus*, 61: 77–132, 540–76. Important critique with corrections.

—— (1903), "Zu Lentz' Herodian III," *Philologus*, 62: 39–63. Important critique with corrections.

Egger, Emile (1854), *Apollonius Dyscole: Essai sur l'histoire des théories grammaticales dans l'antiquité* (Paris; repr. Hildesheim 1987). Detailed general discussion of Apollonius' ideas.

Eide, Tormod (1995), "Aristotelian *topos* and Greek Geometry," *Symbolae Osloenses*, 70: 5–21. Uses Proclus' commentary on Euclid.

Elmsley, Peter (1825), *Scholia in Sophoclis tragoedias septem*, i (Oxford). Superseded edition; if must be used, n.b. additions and corrections by W. Dindorf (1852b: 31–133).

Erbse, Hartmut (1950), *Untersuchungen zu den attizistischen Lexika* (Berlin; Abhandlungen der deutschen Akademie der Wissenschaften zu Berlin, philosophisch-historische Klasse, Jahrgang 1949, Nr. 2). Study and edition of Aelius Dionysius and Pausanias fragments, with discussion of related lexica. Very useful.

—— (1959), "Über Aristarchs Iliasausgaben," *Hermes*, 87: 275–303.

—— (1960), *Beiträge zur Überlieferung der Iliasscholien* (Munich; Zetemata, 24). Comprehensive study of the transmission of the *Iliad* scholia, with discussion of evidence from many sources outside the scholia.

—— (1969–88), *Scholia graeca in Homeri Iliadem* (*scholia vetera*) (Berlin). Superb edition, but not complete.

—— (1980), "Zur normativen Grammatik der Alexandriner," *Glotta*, 58: 236–58. Argues that advanced grammatical ideas date to Aristarchus and that Dionysius Thrax wrote the Τέχνη; useful discussion of some of the fragments of Dionysius.

Erren, Manfred (1994), "Arat und Aratea 1966–1992," *Lustrum*, 36: 189–284, 299–301. Excellent bibliographical overview with some substantive discussion.

Everson, Stephen (1994) (ed.), *Language* (Cambridge). Good collection of essays on ancient philosophies of language, with extensive, classified bibliography that is of minimal use for ancient scholarship but excellent for linguistic philosophy.

Fajen, Fritz (1969), *Überlieferungsgeschichtliche Untersuchungen zu den Halieutika des Oppian* (Meisenheim am Glan). Contains explanation of scholia, pp. 32–3.

—— (1979), *Handschriftliche Überlieferung und sogenannte Euteknios-Paraphrase der Halieutika des Oppian* (Wiesbaden; Mainz, Akademie der Wissenschaften und der Literatur, Abhandlungen der Geistes- und Sozialwissenschaftlichen Klasse, Jahrgang 1979, Nr. 4). Uses the paraphrase for textual criticism of Oppian.

Faraggiana di Sarzana, Chiara (1978), "Il commentario procliano alle *Opere e i giorni* I," *Aevum*, 52: 17–40. On Proclus' commentary to Hesiod and his great indebtedness to Plutarch's lost commentary.

—— (1981), "Il commentario procliano alle *Opere e i giorni* II," *Aevum*, 55: 22–9. On the fate of Proclus' commentary to Hesiod in the Athenian Neoplatonic school.

—— (1987), "Le commentaire à Hésiode et la *paideia* encyclopédique de Proclus," in Pépin and Saffrey (1987): 21–41.

Fehling, Detlev (1956–7), "Varro und die grammatische Lehre von der Analogie und der Flexion," *Glotta*, 35: 214–70 and 36: 48–100. Argues that Varro confused and misrepresented the ideas of the Hellenistic grammarians, so that later writers are more reliable witnesses to those ideas; argues in particular against the existence of the Analogist/Anomalist controversy.

Festugière, André J. (1966–8), *Proclus: Commentaire sur le "Timée"* (Paris). French translation with notes.

—— (1970), *Proclus: Commentaire sur la République* (Paris). French trans. with notes.

Fischer, Eitel (1974), *Die Ekloge des Phrynichos* (Berlin; SGLG 1). Best text and important study; for English summary and discussion of findings see Slater (1977).

Flach, Hans (*or* Flach, Johannes Louis Moritz) (1876), *Glossen und Scholien zur Hesiodischen Theogonie, mit Prolegomena* (Leipzig; repr. Osnabrück 1970). Superseded for old scholia but latest edition of Byzantine material. Dangerous.

Follet, Simone (1992), "Une négation double chez Hésiode (*Travaux*, 516–18)," *RPh* 66: 7–14. Uses Hesiod scholia.

Fowler, Robert L. (1990), "Two More New Verses of Hipponax (and a Spurium of Philoxenus)?," *ICS* 15: 1–22. Discusses and uses commentary and scholia to Hephaestion.

Fraenkel, Eduard (1950), *Aeschylus: Agamemnon* (Oxford).

Fränkel, Hermann (1964), *Einleitung zur kritischen Ausgabe der Argonautika des Apollonios* (Göttingen). Contains much discussion of ancient scholarship.

—— (1968), *Noten zu den Argonautika des Apollonios* (Munich). Contains many corrections to Wendel (1935); see index, pp. 647–8.

Fraser, Peter M. (1972), *Ptolemaic Alexandria* (Oxford). Chapter 8 gives an overview of Alexandrian scholarship.

Frede, Michael (1977), "The Origins of Traditional Grammar," in R. E. Butts and J. Hintikka (edd.), *Historical and Philosophical Dimensions of Logic, Methodology, and Philosophy of Science* (Dordrecht): 51–79. Repr. in Frede (1987): 338–59. Argues that the Alexandrians borrowed many of their ideas from the Stoics, who were at least partly responsible for the beginnings of grammatical analysis.

—— (1978), "Principles of Stoic Grammar," in J. M. Rist (ed.), *The Stoics* (Berkeley/ Los Angeles): 27–75. Repr. in Frede (1987): 301–37. A standard account of Stoic grammatical thought.

—— (1987), *Essays in Ancient Philosophy* (Minneapolis).

Freyer, Theodorus (1882), *Quaestiones de scholiorum Aeschineorum fontibus* (Diss. Leipzig), = *Leipziger Studien zur classischen Philologie*, 5: 237–392. Partially superseded.

Friedlaender, Ludwig (1850), *Nicanoris περὶ Ἰλιακῆς στιγμῆς reliquiae emendatiores* (Königsberg; repr. Amsterdam 1967). Collection of fragments, based on superseded text of Homer scholia.

—— (1853), *Aristonici περὶ σημείων Ἰλιάδος reliquiae emendatiores* (Göttingen; repr. Amsterdam 1965). Collection of fragments, based on superseded text of Homer scholia.

Friedlein, Gottfried (1873), *Procli Diadochi in primum Euclidis Elementorum librum commentarii* (Leipzig; repr. Hildesheim 1992). Standard edition.

Frommel, Wilhelm (1826), *Scholia in Aelii Aristidis sophistae orationes Panathenaicam et Platonicas* (Frankfurt am Main). Best edition of scholia to Orations 1–3.

Fuhrmann, Manfred (1960), *Das systematische Lehrbuch: Ein Beitrag zur Geschichte der Wissenschaften in der Antike* (Göttingen). Examination of Greek and Roman τέχναι on a range of subjects, including the grammatical one attributed to Dionysius Thrax.

Funaioli, Maria Paola (1983), "Etym. gen. ζ," *MCr* 18: 305–12. Edition and discussion.

Gain, D. B. (1976), *The Aratus Ascribed to Germanicus Caesar* (London). Text of a translation of Aratus that used Hipparchus' commentary.

Gaisford, Thomas (1823), *Scholia ad Hesiodum*, = *Poetae minores Graeci*, vol. ii (Leipzig; also published in Oxford 1814). Most recent complete edition of Hesiod scholia, still best source for some Byzantine material.

—— (1842), *Georgii Choerobosci Dictata in Theodosii Canones, necnon Epimerismi in Psalmos* (Oxford). Vol. iii contains the only edition of Choeroboscus' *Epimerismi* on the Psalms; vols. i–ii contain a superseded edition of Choeroboscus' commentary on Theodosius.

—— (1848), *Etymologicon magnum* (Oxford; repr. Amsterdam 1962). Only edition for letters γ—ω.

Gallavotti, Carlo (1988), "La citazione di Eroda negli scoliasti di Nicandro," *BollClass*, 3rd ser. 9: 3–20. Uses scholia to Nicander.

Garzya, Antonio (1967), "Per la tradizione manoscritta degli *excerpta* di Orione," *Le parole e le idee*, 9: 216–21.

—— and Jouanna, Jacques (1999) (edd.), *I testi medici greci: Tradizione e ecdotica* (Naples). Contains many good pieces on commentaries, scholia, and glossaries to Hippocrates and Galen; this is the third volume in a series of international colloquia, and the first two (ed. Garzya in 1992 and 1996) also contain some useful material.

Geerlings, Wilhelm, and Schulze, Christian (2002) (edd.), *Der Kommentar in Antike und*

Mittelalter: Beiträge zu seiner Erforschung (Leiden; Clavis commentariorum antiquitatis et medii aevi, 2). Collection of essays.

Gelzer, Thomas (1976), "Sophokles' Tereus, eine Inhaltsangabe auf Papyrus," *Jahresbericht der schweizerischen Geisteswissenschaftlichen Gesellschaft*, 1976: 183–92.

Gentili, Bruno (1983), "L'Asinarteto nella teoria metrico-ritmica degli antichi," in P. Händel and W. Meid (edd.), *Festschrift für Robert Muth* (Innsbruck): 135–43. Uses Hephaestion and Aristides Quintilianus.

——— and Perusino, Franca (1999) (edd.), *La colometria antica dei testi poetici greci* (Pisa). Collection of articles on ancient colometry, with much discussion of metrical scholia and of Hephaestion.

Gersh, Stephen (1992), "Porphyry's Commentary on the Harmonics of Ptolemy and Neoplatonic Musical Theory," in S. Gersh and C. Kannengiesser (edd.), *Platonism in Late Antiquity* (Notre Dame, Ind.): 141–55.

Geus, Klaus (2002), *Eratosthenes von Kyrene: Studien zur hellenistischen Kultur- und Wissenschaftsgeschichte* (Munich). Only major study of Eratosthenes.

Geymonat, Mario (1970), "Spigolature Nicandree," *Acme*, 23: 137–43. Uses scholia to Nicander.

——— (1974), *Scholia in Nicandri Alexipharmaca cum glossis* (Milan). Standard edition.

——— (1976), *Eutecnii Paraphrasis in Nicandri Alexipharmaca* (Milan). Standard edition.

Giardina, Giovanna R. (1999), *Giovanni Filopono, matematico: Tra neopitagorismo e neoplatonismo* (Catania). Reproduces Hoche's Greek text, with Italian trans. and notes.

Gibson, Craig A. (1997), "P.Berol. inv. 5008, Didymus, and Harpocration Reconsidered," *CP* 92: 375–81.

——— (2002), *Interpreting a Classic: Demosthenes and his Ancient Commentators* (Berkeley). Good, detailed discussion; also texts, translations, and commentary on Demosthenes papyri. Bibliography.

Gibson, Roy K., and Kraus, Christina S. (2002) (edd.), *The Classical Commentary: Histories, Practices, Theory* (Leiden; *Mnemosyne* suppl. 232). Collection of essays on commentaries to classical texts, including a few on ancient commentaries.

Gignac, Francis Thomas (1976–81), *A Grammar of the Greek Papyri of the Roman and Byzantine Periods* (Milan). Reference grammar useful for points of late Greek usage.

Giuliani, Mariafrancesca (1997), "Il 'glossario ippocratico' di Galeno," *Rudiae*, 9: 95–136.

Glasner, Ruth (1992), "Proclus' Commentary on Euclid's Definitions I,3 and I,6," *Hermes*, 120: 320–33.

Glucker, J. (1970), "Thucydides I 29, 3, Gregory of Corinth and the *Ars Interpretandi*," *Mnemosyne*, 4th ser. 23: 127–49. In the course of examining how and why interpretation of a passage of Thucydides has been mishandled by modern scholars, discusses Gregory's treatment of that passage (in his commentary on Hermogenes) and his scholarly technique in general.

Goettling, Karl Wilhelm (1822), *Theodosii Alexandrini Grammatica* (Leipzig). Editions of spurious works of Theodosius.

Göransson, Tryggve (1995), *Albinus, Alcinous, Arius Didymus* (Gothenburg; Studia Graeca et Latina Gothoburgensia, 61). Good study, in English, with extensive bibliography.

Gorman, Robert (2001), "Οἱ περί τινα in Strabo," *ZPE* 136: 201–13. On the inclusive and periphrastic uses of this construction; not directly concerned with ancient scholarship but a good source of bibliography on the issue.

Goulet-Cazé, Marie-Odile (2000) (ed.), *Le commentaire: Entre tradition et innovation* (Paris; Actes du colloque international de l'institut des traditions textuelles). Contains a number of useful pieces on ancient and medieval Greek commentary, both format and substance.

Gow, Andrew S. F. (1952), *Theocritus* (Cambridge, 2nd edn.). Discusses scholia, pp. lxxx–lxxxiv.

Gow, Andrew S. F. and Scholfield, Alwyn F. (1953), *Nicander: The Poems and Poetical Fragments* (Cambridge). Discusses the scholia.

Grandolini, Simonetta (1984), "Sugli scolii del codice B di Pindaro," *Giornale italiano di filologia*, 36 (NS 15): 301–7.

Graziosi, Barbara (2002), *Inventing Homer: The Early Reception of Epic* (Cambridge).

Greene, William Chase (1937), "The Platonic Scholia," *TAPA* 68: 184–96. Explanation of history of scholia; largely summarizes Cohn (1884).

——— (1938), *Scholia Platonica* (Haverford, Penn.). Standard edition of Plato scholia, but by no means complete.

Grynaeus (or Grynäus), Simon, and Camerarius, Joachim (1538), *Claudii Ptolemaei Magnae constructionis, id est Perfectae coelestium motuum pertractationis, lib. XIII. Theonis Alexandrini in eosdem Commentariorum lib. XI* (Basle). Latest edition of Theon's commentary on books 5–13.

Gualandri, Isabella (1962), *Index nominum propriorum quae in scholiis Tzetzianis ad Lycophronem laudantur* (Milan). Index to Scheer's edition (1908).

——— (1965), *Index glossarum quae in scholiis Tzetzianis ad Lycophronem laudantur* (Milan). Index to Scheer's edition (1908).

——— (1968), *Incerti auctoris in Oppiani Halieutica paraphrasis* (Milan). Superseded but usable edition, with detailed study.

Gudeman, Alfred (1921), "Scholien," *RE*, 2nd ser. ii.i (iii): 625–705. Interesting but now fairly dated overview; discusses scholia in general and devotes separate sections to Homer, Hesiod, Alcman, Pindar, Aeschylus, Sophocles, Euripides, Aristophanes, Attic Prose, Thucydides, Plato, Xenophon, Isocrates, Aeschines, Demosthenes, and Aristotle. Some of these sections are still valuable, others not.

Guhl, Claus (1969), *Die Fragmente des alexandrinischen Grammatikers Theon* (Diss. Hamburg). Edition and discussion.

Guida, Augusto (1982), "Il dictionarium di Favorino e il lexicon Vindobonense," *Prometheus*, 8: 264–86. Useful discussion.

Gundel, Wilhelm, and Gundel, Hans Georg (1966), *Astrologumena: Die astrologische Literatur in der Antike und ihre Geschichte* (Wiesbaden; *Sudhoffs Archiv*, Beiheft 6). Contains information on commentaries to Ptolemy.

Güngerich, Rudolf (1927), *Dionysii Byzantii Anaplus Bospori* (Berlin; Diss. Freiburg). Contains scholia, pp. 36–40.

Günther, Hans-Christian (1995), *The Manuscripts and the Transmission of the Paleologan Scholia on the Euripidean Triad* (Stuttgart; *Hermes* Einzelschr. 68). Definitive study of this topic; with bibliography.

——— (1998), *Ein neuer metrischer Traktat und das Studium der pindarischen Metrik in der Philologie der Paläologenzeit* (Leiden; *Mnemosyne* suppl. 180). Text and discussion of a Byzantine treatise on Pindaric meters.

Haas, Walter (1977), *Die Fragmente der Grammatiker Tyrannion und Diokles* (Berlin; SGLG 3; in one vol. with Linke 1977 and Neitzel 1977). The standard edition of these fragments; see Dyck (1982*b*) for some useful corrections.

Hadot, Ilsetraut (1996), *Simplicius: Commentaire sur le Manuel d'Épictète* (Leiden; Philosophia antiqua, 66). Detailed introduction, critical edition, and bibliography.

Hadot, Pierre (1968), *Porphyre et Victorinus* (Paris). Includes text, French translation, and discussion of an anonymous commentary on the *Parmenides* that could be by Porphyry. Partial Italian version published 1993 as *Porfirio: Commentario al "Parmenide" di Platone* (Milan).

Haffner, Medard (2001), *Das Florilegium des Orion* (Stuttgart). Best edition, German trans., and discussion; see Diggle (2003) for corrections.

Hägg, Tomas (1975), *Photios als Vermittler antiker Literatur: Untersuchungen zur Technik des Referierens und Exzerpierens in der Bibliotheke* (Stockholm).

Hajdú, Kerstin (1998), *Ps.-Herodian, De Figuris* (Berlin; SGLG 8; in one vol. with D. Hansen 1998). Standard critical edition with good introduction (in clear German).

Hangard, J. (1983), "Zur Überlieferung der Lysistratescholien in den Handschriften G, Neapolitanus und Baroccianus," *ZPE* 53: 65–9. On the textual history of some Aristophanes scholia.

—— (1985), "Bemerkungen zum codex Baroccianus Oxon. Bodleian. 38B, Folia 63–84," in Aerts *et al.* (1985), 29–35. On the text of the scholia to Aristophanes' *Lysistrata* in a particular manuscript.

Hankinson, R. J. (1994), "Usage and Abusage: Galen on Language," in Everson (1994): 166–87.

Hansen, Dirk U. (1998), *Das attizistische Lexikon des Moeris* (Berlin; SGLG 9; in one vol. with Hajdú 1998). Standard critical edition with good introduction and bibliography.

Hansen, Mogens Herman (1993), "Was the Athenian Ekklesia Convened according to the Festival Calendar or the Bouleutic Calendar?," *AJP* 114: 99–113. Opposes Harris (1986).

Hansen, Peter A. (2005), *Hesychii Alexandrini Lexicon*, iii (Berlin; SGLG 11). A continuation of Late (1953–66), covering π–σ and offering the best text of that section of the lexicon.

Hanson, Ann Ellis (1998), "Galen: Author and Critic," in Most (1998): 22–53.

Harris, Edward M. (1986), "How Often did the Athenian Assembly Meet?," *CQ*, NS 36: 363–77. Uses historical information from scholia to Demosthenes. Cf. M. Hansen (1993).

Haslam, Michael W. (1990), "A New Papyrus of the Mythographus Homericus," *BASP* 27: 31–6. On *P.Oxy.* lvi. 3830 and the Mythographus in general.

—— (1994), "The Homer Lexicon of Apollonius Sophista," *CP* 89: 1–45 and 107–19. Excellent study; first part on composition of lexicon, second on transmission.

Havekoss, J. (1961), *Untersuchungen zu den Scholien des Sophokles* (Diss. Hamburg).

Heiberg, Johan Ludvig (1882), *Litterargeschichtliche Studien über Euklid* (Leipzig). Includes text and German trans. of Theon's introduction to the *Optica*, pp. 139–45.

—— (1888), *Om Scholierne til Euklids Elementer* (Copenhagen: Danske videnskabernes selskab, Skrifter, Historisk og philosophiske afdeling, 6. Række, II, 3). Important study of the Euclid scholia, in Danish with French summary.

—— (1891–3), *Apollonii Pergaei quae graece exstant* (Leipzig). Vol. ii contains standard edition of Eutocius' commentary, with Latin trans.

—— (1903), "Paralipomena zu Euklid," *Hermes*, 38: 46–74, 161–201, 321–56. Information on textual history of the scholia, and (pp. 328–52) edition of some new scholia.

—— (1914), *Heronis Alexandrini opera quae supersunt omnia*, v (Leipzig; repr. 1976). Edition of scholia, pp. 222–32.

—— (1915), *Archimedis opera omnia cum commentariis Eutocii*, iii (2nd edn.; Leipzig, repr. with corrections by E. S. Stamatis 1972). Good text of Eutocius, with Latin trans.; also (pp. 321–9) edition of scholia.

—— and Menge, Henricus (1883–1916), *Euclidis Opera Omnia* (Leipzig). Vol. v (1888) contains scholia to *Elements*, except for those added by Heiberg (1903); 2nd edn. ed. E. S. Stamatis (1977) is the same to the extent of still omitting those scholia. Vol. vi (1896) contains *Data* with scholia and Marinus' introduction. Vol. vii (1895) contains *Optica* with scholia and Theon's introduction and edition. Vol. viii (1916) contains *Phaenomena* with scholia.

Heinimann, Felix (1992), "Vergessene Fragmente des Attizisten Pausanias?," *MH* 49: 74–87. Finds some additional glosses, in Latin.

Heller, John L. (1962), "*Nepos* 'σκορπιστής' and Philoxenus," *TAPA* 93: 61–89. Uses Philoxenus for understanding Latin terminology.

Helm, Karl (1908), *De Luciani scholiorum fontibus* (Diss. Marburg). Important study.

Hemmerdinger, Bertrand (1959), "Deux notes papyrologiques," *REG* 72: 106–9. Useful for dating of Harpocration.

—— (1998), "Suidas, et non la *Souda*," *BollClass*, 3rd ser. 19: 31–2. Argues that Σουίδα/Σοῦδα is a Doric genitive.

Henrichs, Albert (1969), "Kallimachos fr. 17,8–10 und 18,8 Pf. (P.Mich. inv. 3688)," *ZPE* 4: 23–30. Publication of possible commentary on Callimachus.

—— (1970), "Apollonios Rhodios I 699–719 (P.Mil. 6 + P.Colon. inv. 522)," *ZPE* 5: 49–56, 6: 76–7. Combined text of these papyri with marginal scholia, and commentary.

—— (1971–3), "Scholia minora zu Homer," *ZPE* 7: 97–149 and 229–60, 8: 1–12, 12: 17–43. Important study and series of editions of papyri.

—— and Müller, Wolfgang (1976), "Apollonios Sophistes, Homerlexikon," in A. E. Hanson (ed.), *Collectanea Papyrologica: Texts Published in Honor of H. C. Youtie*, i (Bonn): 27–51. Edition and discussion of two fragments.

Henry, René (1959–77), *Photius: Bibliothèque* (Paris). Standard edition, with French trans. Indices in ninth volume by J. Schamp (1991).

Herington, C. J. (1972), *The Older Scholia on the Prometheus Bound* (Leiden; *Mnemosyne* suppl. 19). Standard edition of M and A scholia on the *Prometheus*, with excellent introduction.

Hermann, Karl Friedrich (1853), *Appendix Platonica* or 2nd part of vol. vi of *Platonis Dialogi* (Leipzig). Often reprinted with later dates, sometimes as a separate volume. Contains superseded editions of scholia, Albinus and Alcinous, Olympiodorus' life of Plato, and anonymous prolegomena to Plato; one of the usable editions of Timaeus' lexicon.

Herter, Hans (1955), "Bericht über die Literatur zur hellenistischen Dichtung seit dem Jahre 1921: II. Teil: Apollonios von Rhodos," *Jahresbericht über die Fortschritte der Klassischen Altertumswissenschaft, begründet von Conrad Bursian*, 285: 213–410. Good discussion of scholia, with substance as well as references, on pp. 239–46.

Heylbut, G. (1887), "Ptolemaeus περὶ διαφορᾶς λέξεων," *Hermes*, 22: 388–410. Edition of epitome of "Ammonius'" lexicon.

Hiersche, Rolf (1956), "Aus der Arbeit an einem historischen Wörterbuch der Sprachwissenschaftlichen Terminologie: Entstehung und Entwicklung des Terminus πτῶσις 'Fall'," *Sitzungsberichte der Deutschen Akademie der Wissenschaften zu Berlin, Klasse für Sprachen, Literatur und Kunst*, 1955.3: 5–19.

Hilgard, Alfred (1887), *Excerpta ex Libris Herodiani Technici* (Leipzig; Beilage zum Jahresbericht des Heidelberger Gymnasiums für das Schuljahr 1886/87). Contains editions of some minor works of Theodosius.

Hiller, Eduard (1871), Review of *GG* iii, *NJPP* 103 (= *JCP* 17): 505–32, 603–29. Useful discussion and cautions.

Hillgruber, Michael (1994–9), *Die pseudoplutarchische Schrift De Homero* (Stuttgart). Definitive commentary; bibliography.

—— (1996), Review of Dilts (1992), *Gnomon*, 68: 484–8. Provides some useful corrections.

Hobein, Hermann (1910), *Maximi Tyrii Philosophumena* (Leipzig). Prints scholia at bottom of page.

Hoche, Ricardus (1864–7), Ἰωάννου γραμματικοῦ Ἀλεξανδρέως τοῦ Φιλοπόνου ἐξήγησις εἰς τὸ πρῶτον (δεύτερον) τῆς Νικομάχου Ἀριθμητικῆς εἰσαγωγῆς (Wesel; Gymnasium zu Wesel, Programm; 3 vols.). Only edition of this commentary. Rare; repr. in Giardina (1999).

Hoerschelmann, Wilhelm (1874), *De Dionysii Thracis Interpretibus Veteris* (Leipzig). Discusses scholia to the Τέχνη.

—— (1880), "Kritische Bemerkungen zu Apollonius Dyscolus de pronomine," *RhM* 35: 373–89. Useful corrections to *GG* ii.i.

Hoffmann, Otto (1893), *Die griechischen Dialekte in ihrem historischen Zusammenhange*, ii (Göttingen). Contains edition of Philoponus "On dialects."

Holwerda, Douwe (1958), "De novo priorum Aristophanis Nubium indicio," *Mnemosyne*, 4th ser. 11: 32–41. On information in the scholia about the first production of the *Clouds*.

—— (1964), "De Heliodori commentario metrico in Aristophanem," *Menemosyne*, 4th ser. 17: 113–39. On textual corruptions and metrical vocabulary in Heliodorus fragments preserved in Aristophanes scholia.

—— (1967), "De Heliodori commentario metrico in Aristophanem II," *Mnemosyne*, 4th ser. 20: 247–72. On metrical vocabulary, lectional signs, layout of hypomnemata, and history of metrical studies on Aristophanes.

—— (1976), "Zur szenisch-technischen Bedeutung des Wortes 'ὑπόθεσις'," in J. M. Bremer, S. L. Radt, and C. J. Ruijgh (edd.), *Miscellanea tragica in honorem J. C. Kamerbeek* (Amsterdam): 173–98. On staging, Aristophanes of Byzantium's criticisms thereof, and the meaning of ὑποτίθημι in scholia.

—— (1983), "Ein verkanntes doxographisches Bruchstück (PSI 7.849 fragm. II)," *ZPE* 53: 60–4.

—— (1984), Review of Wouters (1979), *Mnemosyne*, 4th ser. 37: 199–202. Useful suggestions about the texts of the papyri.

Holzinger, Karl (1930), "Kritische Bemerkungen zu den spätbyzantinischen Aristophanes-scholien," in *Charisteria Alois Rzach zum achtzigsten Geburtstag dargebracht* (Reichenberg): 58–85. On text and textual history of *scholia recentiora* to Aristophanes; partly superseded.

Householder, Fred W. (1981), *The Syntax of Apollonius Dyscolus: Translated, and with Commentary* (Amsterdam). Complete English trans., based on Uhlig's text with a few variant readings. Controversial because of its attribution of the ideas and terminology of modern linguistic theory to Apollonius. Commentary consists of brief clarifications added in brackets in the text; interesting introduction concentrates on finding the modern syntactic concept of Deep Structure in Apollonius. See Blank (1983*b*) for some useful corrections.

—— (1989), "History of Linguistics in the Classical Period," *HL* 16: 131–48. Review of *HL* 13 / Taylor (1987).

Hovdhaugen, Even (1982), *Foundations of Western Linguistics: From the Beginning to the End of the First Millenium AD* (Oslo). Basic introduction to Greek linguistic thought (pp. 19–67); accurate, accessible, and excellent for those with no background in Classics. Provides numerous long quotations from relevant texts, in translation; this system of presenting the ancient writers in their own words offers a more exciting and less biased introduction than many others, but it gives little information to readers who already know the texts.

Hubbard, Thomas (1987), "Pindar and the Aeginetan Chorus: Nemean 3.9–13," *Phoenix*, 41: 1–9. Uses scholiasts' syntactic suggestions to reinterpret several passages.

Hubbell, Harry M. (1957), "A Papyrus Commentary on Demosthenes," *Yale Classical Studies*, 15: 181–93. Edition with detailed discussion of papyrus with commentary on Demosthenes.

Hübner, Wolfgang (1998), "Hipparchos [6] aus Nikaia," in *NP* v: 567–71. General information on Hipparchus.

Hude, Karl (1927), *Scholia in Thucydidem ad optimos codices collata* (Leipzig; repr. New York 1973). Standard text; corrections in Powell (1936).

Hultsch, Friedrich (1878), *Pappi Alexandrini Collectionis quae supersunt*, iii (Berlin; repr. Amsterdam 1965). Provides edition of two parts of an anonymous commentary on Ptolemy, pp. xvii–xix and 1138–65, the latter with Latin trans.

Hunger, Herbert (1967), "Palimpsest-Fragmente aus Herodians Καθολικὴ προσῳδία, Buch

5–7," *Jahrbuch der österreichischen byzantinischen Gesellschaft*, 16: 1–33. Only publication of the palimpsest and its many literary fragments.

—— (1978), *Die hochsprachliche profane Literatur der Byzantiner* (Munich; Handbuch der Altertumswissenschaft, 12.5.i and 12.5.ii). Detailed reference work with useful information on Byzantine scholars.

—— (1982), "Gregorios von Korinth, Epigramme auf die Feste des Dodekaorton," *Analecta Bollandiana*, 100: 637–51. Edition and study of some of Gregory's non-scholarly works, sometimes useful for background on Gregory.

Hunt, Arthur S., and Johnson, John (1930), *Two Theocritus Papyri* (London). Publication of substantial fragments with marginal scholia; good discussion.

Ihm, Sibylle (2002), *Clavis commentariorum der antiken medizinischen Texte* (Leiden; Clavis commentariorum antiquitatis et medii aevi, 1). Lists editions and studies of ancient and medieval commentaries on medical writers, including published scholia. Not totally complete, but generally good. Useful introduction (in German).

Ildefonse, Frédérique (1994), "Sujet et prédicat chez Platon, Aristote et les Stoïciens," *Archives et documents de la société d'histoire et d'épistémologie des sciences du langage*, 2nd ser. 10: 3–34. On the development of these ideas, offering a good collection of original sources. Cf. Pfister (1976).

—— (1997), *La naissance de la grammaire dans l'antiquité grecque* (Paris). More philosophical than linguistic; discusses Plato, Aristotle, the Stoics, and Apollonius Dyscolus, with an appendix arguing for a late date for (ps.-)Dionysius' Τέχνη. Extensive but unreliable bibliography. Cf. Schenkeveld (1999).

Invernizzi, Giuseppe (1976), *Il didaskalikos di Albino e il medioplatonismo* (Rome). Italian trans. with introduction and commentary; not based on best edition of text.

Irigoin, Jean (1952), *Histoire du texte de Pindare* (Paris). Includes good discussion of Alexandrian scholarship on Pindar; bibliography.

—— (1958), *Les scholies métriques de Pindare* (Paris). Excellent study with edition appended; bibliography.

—— (1994), "Les Éditions de textes," in F. Montanari (1994): 39–82. Good discussion of Hellenistic editions of ancient literary texts, and of the transition from roll to codex.

Irmer, Dieter (1977), *Palladius: Kommentar zu Hippokrates "De fracturis" und seine Parallelversion unter dem Namen des Stephanus von Alexandria* (Hamburg). Edition with German trans. and introduction.

Irwin, Elizabeth (1999), "Solecising in Solon's Colony," *Bulletin of the Institute of Classical Studies of the University of London*, 43: 187–93. Uses a variety of ancient scholarly sources.

Jackson, Robin; Lycos, Kimon; and Tarrant, Harold (1998), *Olympiodorus: Commentary on Plato's Gorgias* (Leiden). Trans. with introduction, notes, and good bibliography.

Jackson, Steven (1999), "Theocritus and Something Fishy," *Maia*, 51: 29–32. Uses scholia for interpretation of Theocritus.

Jacoby, Felix (1913), "Herodotos 7," *RE* suppl. ii: 205–520. Contains discussion of ancient scholarship, pp. 513–15, with further references.

—— (1929), *FGrHist* ii b (Berlin; repr. Leiden 1962). Fragments of Apollodorus of Athens (#244).

—— (1944), "Γενέσια: A Forgotten Festival of the Dead," *CQ* 38: 65–75. Uses historical information from the Antiatticist.

—— (1958), *FGrHist* iii c (Leiden). Fragments of Apion (#616).

Janko, Richard (1995), "Crates of Mallos, Dionysius Thrax and the Tradition of Stoic Grammatical Theory," in L. Ayres (ed.), *The Passionate Intellect: Essays on the Transformation of Classical Traditions Presented to Professor I. G. Kidd* (New Brunswick, NJ): 213–33. Much more about Crates than about Dionysius.

――― (2002), "The Derveni Papyrus: an Interim Text," *ZPE* 141: 1–62. Greek text, English trans., and index.

Joly, Henri (1986) (ed.), *Philosophie du langage et grammaire dans l'antiquité* (Brussels; CNRS, Cahiers de philosophie ancienne, 5, Cahiers du groupe de recherches sur la philosophie et le langage, 6 et 7). Useful collection of articles on philosophical linguistics in the ancient world.

Jones, Alexander (1990), *Ptolemy's First Commentator* (Philadelphia; Transactions of the American Philosophical Society, 80.7). Edition with trans. and commentary of a fragment of early commentary on the Handy Tables.

――― (1999), "Uses and Users of Astronomical Commentaries in Antiquity," in Most (1999): 147–72. Discusses Theon's commentaries on Ptolemy.

Jorsal, Finn; Jørgensen, Margaret Kill; and Smith, Ole L. (1970), "A Byzantine Metrical Commentary on Aristophanes' *Frogs*," *C&M*, 31: 324–38. Standard edition of these scholia.

Junge, Gustav, and Thomson, William (1930), *The Commentary of Pappus on Book X of Euclid's Elements* (Cambridge, Mass.; Harvard Semitic Series, 8). Arabic text, English trans., introduction, and notes.

Kambylis, Athanasios (1971), "Theognostea," *Glotta*, 49: 46–65. Textual suggestions and discussion based on Alpers (1964).

――― (1991a), *Eustathios von Thessalonike: Prooimion zum Pindarkommentar* (Göttingen). Definitive edition of Eustathius' work on Pindar, with detailed introduction and indices. Introduction, though very hard to read, is important.

――― (1991b), *Eustathios über Pindars Epinikiendichtung: Ein Kapitel des klassischen Philologie in Byzanz* (Hamburg). Difficult but important.

Kapetanaki, Sophia, and Sharples, Robert W. (2000), "A Glossary Attributed to Alexander of Aphrodisias," *Bulletin of the Institute of Classical Studies of the University of London*, 44: 103–43. Edition, trans., and discussion of Aristotelian glossary.

Kaster, Robert A. (1988), *Guardians of Language: The Grammarian and Society in Late Antiquity* (Berkeley and Los Angeles). Excellent study of Latin and Greek grammarians in the 4th and 5th cents. AD, including a prosopography of known grammarians from AD 250–565 and extensive bibliography.

Kazazis, J. N. (or Kazazes, I. N.) (1986), Φιλιππικῶν Ῥητορικαὶ Λέξεις: *Editio princeps* (Thessaloniki). Edition of a Demosthenic lexicon, with discussion. In English.

Kazhdan, Alexander, with Franklin, Simon (1984), *Studies on Byzantine Literature of the Eleventh and Twelfth Centuries* (Cambridge). Includes background on Eustathius.

Keaney, John J. (1967), "New Fragments of Greek Authors in Codex Marc. Gr. 444," *TAPA* 98: 205–19. Uses a manuscript of Harpocration.

――― (1973), "Alphabetization in Harpocration's *Lexicon*," *GRBS* 14: 415–23.

――― (1979), "Moschopoulos and the Scholia to the *Batrachomyomachia*," *CP* 74: 60–3. Argues that certain scholia should not be attributed to Moschopulus.

――― (1991), *Harpocration: Lexeis of the Ten Orators* (Amsterdam). Latest edition, but problematic; see Otranto 1993.

――― (1995), "The Earliest Byzantine Witnesses to Harpocration (pl)," *Revue d'histoire des textes*, 25: 255–7.

――― and Lamberton, Robert (1996), *[Plutarch], Essay on the Life and Poetry of Homer* (Atlanta; American Philological Association monographs, 40). Text (not the best, but okay), trans., discussion, bibliography.

Keil, Heinrich (1854), "Scholia in Apollonii Argonautica," in R. Merkel, *Apollonii Argonautica* (Leipzig), 299–536. Edition of L scholia, now superseded.

Keizer, Helena Maria (1995), *Indices in Eustathii archiepiscopi Thessalonicensis commentarios ad Homeri Iliadem pertinentes* (Leiden). Index to Van der Valk (1971–87).

Kemp, Alan (1986), "The *Tekhnē Grammatikē* of Dionysius Thrax translated into English," *HL* 13: 343–63. Repr. in Taylor (1987): 169–89.

——— (1991), "The Emergence of Autonomous Greek Grammar," in Schmitter (1991): 302–33. Discusses the ideas of (ps.-)Dionysius Thrax and Apollonius Dyscolus.

Kenyon, Frederic G. (1891), *Classical Texts from Papyri in the British Museum* (London). Includes first edition of [Trypho] fragment.

——— (1892), *Aristotle on the Constitution of Athens* (3rd edn., London). Pages 215–19 give text and brief discussion of Demosthenes commentary found on the *Athenaion politeia* papyrus.

Kidd, Douglas Alexander (1997), *Aratus: Phaenomena* (Cambridge). Edition of Aratus (without scholia) with useful discussion of ancient scholarship. In English.

Kindstrand, Jan Fredrik (1990), *[Plutarchi] De Homero* (Leipzig). Standard edition, with detailed introduction and bibliography.

Kinzl, Konrad H. (1991), "AP 22.4: The Sole Source of Harpocration on the Ostrakismos of Hipparkhos Son of Kharmos," *Klio*, 73: 28–45.

Kleinlogel, Alexander (1964), "Beobachtungen zu den Thukydidesscholien I," *Philologus*, 108: 233–46. On textual history.

——— (1965), *Geschichte des Thukydidestextes im Mittelalter* (Berlin). Includes extensive discussion of scholia.

Klibansky, Raymond, and Labowsky, Carlotta (1953), *Plato Latinus III: Parmenides, Procli commentarium in Parmenidem* (London; Corpus Platonicum Medii Aevi). Text, English trans., and discussion of medieval Latin version of commentary.

Knorr, Wilbur Richard (1989), *Textual Studies in Ancient and Medieval Geometry* (Boston). Much information on ancient commentaries to geometrical works.

Koller, Hermann (1958), "Die Anfänge der griechischen Grammatik," *Glotta*, 37: 5–40. Seeks roots of grammatical ideas in early philosophical, rhetorical, and musical works.

Kominis, Athanasios (Atanasio) (1960), *Gregorio Pardos, metropolita di Corinto, e la sua opera* (Rome/Athens). Most important work on Gregory of Corinth; in Greek. See Laurent (1963).

Koniaris, George Leonidas (1980), "Conjectures in the Fragments of the Grammarian Philoxenus," *Hermes*, 108: 462–76. Suggested emendations.

Kontos, Konstantinos S. (1877), "Διορθωτικὰ εἰς τὰς Λέξεις μεθ᾽ ἱστοριῶν," *BCH* 1: 177–81. Corrections to Patmos scholia on Demosthenes; in Greek.

Kopff, E. Christian (1976), "Thomas Magister and the Text of Sophocles' Antigone," *TAPA* 106: 241–66. Uses Byzantine scholia.

Koster, Willem J. W. (1927), *Scholia in Aristophanis Plutum et Nubes: Vetera, Thomae Magistri, Demetrii Triclinii nec non anonyma recentiora partim inedita* (Leiden). Superseded edition of scholia.

——— (1932), "De Accentibus Excerpta ex Choerobosco, Aetherio, Philopono, aliis," *Mnemosyne*, 2nd ser. 59: 132–64. Introduction to and critical edition of a short collection of extracts on accents, drawn primarily from extant works of Choeroboscus etc.

——— (1957), *Autour d'un manuscrit d'Aristophane écrit par Démétrius Triclinius* (Groningen). On Parisinus Suppl. Gr. 463, with extensive discussion of its scholia.

——— (1962), "De Aristophane Byzantio argumentorum metricorum auctore," in *Charisteria Francisco Novotný Octogenario Oblata* (Prague): 43–50. Argues for the attribution to Aristophanes of some hypotheses that Nauck and others do not think go back to his work.

——— (1964), "De priore recensione Thomana Aristophanis," *Mnemosyne*, 4th ser. 17: 337–66. Argues that Thomas Magister produced two editions of Aristophanes.

——— (1985), "Quaestiones ad prolegomenorum de comoedia traditionem pertinentes," in Aerts *et al.* (1985), 61–74. On the textual history of prolegomena traditionally printed with the scholia to Aristophanes.

——— and Holwerda, Douwe (1954), "De Eustathio, Tzetza, Moschopulo, Planude Aristophanis Commentatoribus," *Mnemosyne*, 4th ser. 7: 136–56. On Byzantine commentaries on Aristophanes.

——— ——— (1960–) (general editors), *Scholia in Aristophanem* (Groningen). Standard text of Aristophanes scholia; individual volumes as follows: i.i a: Prolegomena de comoedia (W. J. W. Koster, 1975); i.i b: *Acharnians* (N. G. Wilson, 1975); i.ii: *Knights* (D. M. Jones and N. G. Wilson, 1969); i.iii.i: old scholia to *Clouds* (D. Holwerda, 1977); i.iii.ii: scholia recentiora to *Clouds* (W. J. W. Koster, 1974); ii.i: *Wasps* (W. J. W. Koster, 1978); ii.ii: *Peace* (D. Holwerda, 1982); ii.iii: *Birds* (D. Holwerda, 1991); ii.iv: *Lysistrata* (J. Hangard, 1996); iii.i a: old scholia to *Frogs* (M. Chantry 1999); iii.i b: scholia recentiora to *Frogs* (M. Chantry 2001); iii.iv a: old scholia to *Plutus* (M. Chantry, 1994); iii.iv b: scholia recentiora to *Plutus* (M. Chantry, 1996); iv i: Tzetzes' prolegomena and *Plutus* (L. Massa Positano, 1960); iv.ii: Tzetzes' *Clouds* (D. Holwerda, 1960); iv.iii: Tzetzes' *Frogs, Birds*, and preface to *Knights* (W. J. W. Koster, 1962); iv.iv: indices to Tzetzes (var. edd. 1964).

Kougeas, Socrates V. (1985), *Arethas of Caesareia*, ed. P. A. Demetrakopoulos (Athens). Collection of Kougeas' articles on Arethas from the first half of the 20th cent., including discussion of his scholia.

Krevans, Nita (1986), "P.Oxy. 2258 B Fr. 2: A Scholion to Callimachus' Victoria Berenices?" *ZPE* 65: 37–8. Argues for reassignment of a Callimachus scholion.

Kroll, Wilhelm (1899–1901), *Procli Diadochi in Platonis Rem publicam commentarii* (Leipzig; repr. Amsterdam 1965). Text, brief discussion, indices.

——— (1916), "Ioannes 21 Philoponus," in *RE* ix.ii (xviii): 1764–95. Good study with further references.

Kuchenmüller, Wilhelm E. (1928), *Philetae Coi reliquiae* (Borna). Most complete edition of the scholarly fragments.

Kühn, Carolus Gottlob (1821–33), *Claudii Galeni opera omnia* (Leipzig; repr. Hildesheim 1964–5). Includes texts and Latin translations of Galen's glossary and commentaries on Hippocrates, but superseded for many by *CMG*. Both texts and translations may predate Kühn himself.

Kürschner, Wilfried (1996), "Die Lehre des Grammatikers Dionysios," in Swiggers and Wouters (1996): 177–215. German trans. of Τέχνη, with facing Greek text. Also in Swiggers and Wouters (1998).

Laks, André, and Most, Glenn W. (1997) (edd.), *Studies on the Derveni Papyrus* (Oxford). Offers a trans. and scholarly essays.

Lallot, Jean (1985), "La description des temps du verbe chez trois grammairiens grecs (Apollonius, Stephanos, Planude)," *Histoire Epistémologie Langage*, 7.1 (1985): 47–81. Discusses how the different grammarians handle the time/aspect issue in treating the tenses.

——— (1991), "L'Étymologie chez les grammairiens grecs: Principes et pratique," *RPh* 65: 135–48. Etymological theory, especially in Philoxenus.

——— (1994*a*), "La syntaxe des cas obliques chez Apollonius Dyscole," in B. Jacquinod (ed.), *Cas et prépositions en grec ancien: Actes du colloque international de Saint-Étienne* (Saint-Étienne): 11–19. On Apollonius' explanations for the use of the genitive, dative, and accusative cases; offers a good introduction to the way the Greeks described their case system.

——— (1994*b*), "Sujet / prédicat chez Apollonius Dyscole," *Archives et documents de la société d'histoire et d'épistémologie des sciences du langage*, 2nd ser. 10: 35–47.

——— (1995), "Qu'est-ce que la grammaire?," *Lalies*, 15: 73–82. Considers the meaning of γραμματική for Dionysius Thrax and other Greek writers.

——— (1997), *Apollonius Dyscole: De la construction* (Paris). Superb edition of the *Syntax*, with Greek text based on Uhlig (not identical, but all differences are indicated and justified), facing French trans., excellent introduction providing one of the best available guides to the *Syntax*, detailed commentary, and substantial (but not always reliable) bibliography. Easy to use; Uhlig's page numbers are in the margins and all conventions are explicitly stated (pp. 85–6). Cf. Patillon (1998) and Schenkeveld (1999).

――― (1998), *La grammaire de Denys le Thrace: Traduite et annotée* (Paris, 2nd edn.). Repr. of the standard text of (ps.-) Dionysius Thrax, with a facing French trans., good introduction, extensive commentary taking the scholia into account, and substantial bibliography. Currently the best edition of the Τέχνη. Cf. Patillon (1990), Swiggers and Wouters (1994), Schenkeveld (1999).

――― (1999), "Strates chronologiques dans le lexique technique des grammairiens grecs: L'exemple des noms des parties du discours," in *La terminologie linguistique* (Louvain; Mémoires de la société de linguistique de Paris, NS 6): 51–66. Discusses the development of the Greek names for the parts of speech.

Lambert, Frédéric (1978), "Le terme et la notion de διάθεσις chez Apollonius Dyscole," in Collart (1978): 245–52.

Lamberton, Robert, and Keaney, John J. (1992), *Homer's Ancient Readers: The Hermeneutics of Greek Epic's Earliest Exegetes* (Princeton). Collection of articles pertaining to Homer scholarship.

Lamberz, Erich (1987), "Proklos und die Form des philosophischen Kommentars," in Pépin and Saffrey (1987): 1–20, 369.

Lambin, Gérard (1986), "Trois refrains nuptiaux et le fragment 124 Mette d'Eschyle," *AC* 55: 66–85. Uses Pindar scholia to interpret a fragment of Aeschylus.

Lameere, William (1960), *Aperçus de paléographie Homérique: À propos des papyrus de l'Iliade et de l'Odyssée des collections de Gand, de Bruxelles et de Louvain* (Brussels). On pp. 90–2 gives an excellent presentation of the MSS evidence for Aristophanes of Byzantium's invention of accent marks etc.

Lange, Christian Conrad Ludwig (1852). *Das System der Syntax des Apollonios Dyskolos* (Göttingen). Excellent work explaining the underlying logic of Apollonius' *Syntax*, still important today.

La Roche, J. (1863), Παρεκβολαὶ τοῦ μεγάλου ῥήματος ἐκ τῶν Ἡρῳδιανοῦ: E Duobus *Codicibus Caes. Reg. biblioth. Vindobonensis* (Vienna; Jahresbericht über das königlich-kaiserliche akademische Gymnasium in Wien für das Schuljahr 1862–3). Only modern edition of a work of ps.-Herodian.

Larrain, Carlos J. (1992), *Galens Kommentar zu Platons Timaios* (Stuttgart). Edition of fragments with extensive commentary, good introduction, and bibliography.

Larsen, Bent Dalsgaard (1972), *Jamblique de Chalcis: Exégète et philosophe* (Aarhus). Appendix contains collection of fragments of Iamblichus, including those of lost commentaries to Aristotle.

Lascaris, Janus (or Laskaris, Andreas Joannes) (1517), *Homeri interpres pervetustus / Σχόλια παλαιὰ τῶν πάνυ δοκίμων εἰς τὴν Ὁμήρου Ἰλιάδα* (Rome). Edition of D scholia to the *Iliad*.

Lasserre, François (1966), *Die Fragmente des Eudoxos von Knidos* (Berlin). Collection of fragments, many from Hipparchus' commentary on Aratus.

――― (1986–7), "Aristoph. Byz. Fragm. Neglecta (Tzetz. *Exeg. in Hom. Il.* A 1 et 601)," *MCr* 21–2: 303–15. Reporting a passage of Tzetzes that preserves a new fragment of Aristophanes of Byzantium. In French.

――― and Livadaras, Nicholas (1976–), *Etymologicum magnum genuinum; Symeonis etymologicum una cum magna grammatica; Etymologicum magnum auctum* (Rome). Synoptic edition of these three etymologica; best edition, but so far only two volumes (i: α–ἀμωσγέπως, ii: ἀνά–βώτορες) published, and vol. ii (1992) is rare. Refers to *Etymologicum genuinum* as *Etymologicum magnum genuinum*, and to *Etymologicum magnum* as *Etymologicum magnum auctum*.

Latte, Kurt (1915), "Zur Zeitbestimmung des Antiatticista," *Hermes*, 50: 373–94. Repr. in *Kleine Schriften* (Munich 1968): 612–30. Discusses one of the sources for the fragments of Aristophanes of Byzantium.

──── (1924), "Glossographika," *Philologus*, 80: 136–75. Repr. in *Kleine Schriften* (Munich 1968): 631–66. Discussion of dialect glossaries, including edition of a fragment of Diogenianus.

──── (1942), "Neues zur klassischen Literatur aus Hesych," *Mnemosyne*, 3rd ser. 10: 81–96. Repr. in *Kleine Schriften* (Munich 1968): 667–79.

──── (1953–66), *Hesychii Alexandrini Lexicon* (Copenhagen). Best edition of Hesychius, but not complete.

──── and Erbse, Hartmut (1965), *Lexica Graeca Minora* (Hildesheim; repr. 1992). Provides reprints of a number of useful but obscure publications.

Laum, Bernhard (1928), *Das alexandrinische Akzentuationssystem* (Paderborn; Studien zur Geschichte und Kultur des Altertums, Ergänzungsband 4). Extremely thorough study using papyri and remnants of the ancient grammarians; conclusions about the grave accent are not generally accepted, but the information on specific ancient scholars is good.

Laurent, V. (1963), Review of Kominis (1960), *REByz* 21: 290–1. Makes some original contributions to the dating controversy. Cf. Becares (1988), Montana (1995, pp. xlviii–xlix).

Lausdei, Claudio (1981), "Nota a Cic. 'Arat.' XXXIII 24–6," *Giornale italiano di filologia*, NS 12 [33]: 221–6. Discusses Cicero's use of the Aratus scholia.

Lavelle, Brian M. (1989), "Koisyra and Megakles, the Son of Hippokrates," *GRBS* 30: 503–13. Uses evidence from scholia for Athenian history.

Law, Vivien (1990), "Roman Evidence on the Authenticity of the Grammar Attributed to Dionysius Thrax," in H.-J. Niederehe and K. Koerner (edd.), *History and Historiography of Linguistics* (Amsterdam), i: 89–96. Argues against the authenticity of the Τέχνη, using evidence from Latin grammarians.

──── and Sluiter, Ineke (1995) (edd.), *Dionysius Thrax and the Technē Grammatikē* (Münster). Collection of articles focusing on the issues of dating and authenticity. Most are in favor of a late date for at least portions of the Τέχνη.

Le Bœuffle, André (1975), *Germanicus: Les Phénomènes d'Aratos* (Paris). Good edition of Germanicus' trans. of Aratus (which uses Hipparchus and probably the scholia), with good introduction.

──── (1983), *Hygin: L'Astronomie* (Paris). Edition superseded by Viré (1992) but with a useful introduction.

Le Bourdellès, Hubert (1985), *L'Aratus Latinus: Étude sur la culture et la langue latines dans le nord de la France au VIIIe siècle* (Lille). On the late Latin trans. of the Φ edition of Aratus.

Le Corre, René (1956), "Le prologue d'Albinus," *Revue Philosophique de la France et de l'Étranger*, 81: 28–38. French trans. and discussion of Albinus' prologue to Plato.

Lefkowitz, Mary R. (1975a), "The Influential Fictions in the Scholia to Pindar's *Pythian* 8," *CP* 70: 173–85. Refutes some scholiasts' interpretations.

──── (1975b), "Pindar's Lives," in P. T. Brannan (ed.), *Classica et Iberica: A Festschrift in Honor of the Reverend Joseph M.-F. Marique, S.J.* (Worcester, Mass.), 71–93. Discusses fictional biographical details in scholia and ancient lives of Pindar.

──── (1985), "The Pindar Scholia," *AJP* 106: 269–82. Discusses basis and value of exegetical scholia, and their influence on other ancient poetry.

──── (1991), *First-Person Fictions: Pindar's Poetic "I"* (Oxford). Contains revised versions of Lefkowitz 1975a (72–88), 1975b (89–110), and 1985 (147–60).

Lehmann, Yves (1988), "Varron et le grammairien Tyrannion: L'apport doctrinal de l'aristotélisme," *Ktèma*, 13: 179–86.

Lehnus, Luigi (2000), *Nuova bibliografia callimachea (1489–1998)* (Alexandria). Lists works on scholia, pp. 339–40.

Lehrs, Karl (1848), *Herodiani scripta tria emendatiora* (Königsberg). Contains the editions of Περὶ 'Ιλιακῆς προσῳδίας and Περὶ μονήρους λέξεως repr. in *GG* iii (with the original commentary on the latter, which is not reprinted), and a superseded edition of Περὶ διχρόνων.

——— (1882), *De Aristarchi studiis Homericis* (Leipzig, 3rd edn.). Important but somewhat dated.

Lejeune, Michel (1950), "Sur le nom grec du 'cas' grammatical," *REG* 63: 1–7. Suggests that the grammatical use of πτῶσις may originally come from the terminology of dice-games.

Lemerle, Paul (1971), *Le Premier Humanisme byzantin* (Paris; English trans. Canberra 1986 with title *Byzantine Humanism: The First Phase*). Important study of Byzantine culture to the 10th cent.

Lentz, August (1867–70), *Herodiani Technici Reliquiae* (Leipzig). The original publication of the standard edition of Herodian; it was later incorporated into the *Grammatici Graeci* series as *GG* iii.i and iii.ii and can be freely substituted for those volumes. Misleading edition that should only be used with the help of Dyck (1993a) and Egenolff (1900, 1902, 1903); see also Hiller (1871).

Lenz, Friedrich Walther (1934), *Untersuchungen zu den Aristeidesscholien* (Berlin; Problemata, 8; repr. in *Aristeidesstudien* (Berlin 1964), 1–99). Definitive study.

——— (1959), *The Aristeides Prolegomena* (Leiden; *Mnemosyne* suppl. 5). Best edition and good study.

Leone, Pietro Luigi M. (1991), "La tradizione manoscritta degli 'Scholia in Lycophronem' 1," *Quaderni catanesi di cultura classica e medievale*, 3: 33–76. Study of text history.

——— (1992–3), "La tradizione manoscritta degli 'Scholia in Lycophronem' 2," *Quaderni catanesi di cultura classica e medievale*, 4–5: 45–58. Study of text history.

Leverenz, Lynn (1999), "Two Darmarios Manuscripts of Scholia on Oppian's *Halieutica*," *RhM* 142: 345–58. On textual history of scholia.

Lewis, A.-M. (1992), "The popularity of the *Phaenomena* of Aratus: A Reevaluation," in Carl Deroux, *Studies in Latin Literature and Roman History*, vi (Brussels), 94–118. Interesting but unreliable discussion of the *Phaenomena* in antiquity and the Middle Ages.

Linke, Konstanze (1977), *Die Fragmente des Grammatikers Dionysios Thrax* (Berlin; SGLG 3; in one vol. with Haas 1977 and Neitzel 1977). Only usable edition of these numerous fragments, providing a good introduction and commentary; see Dyck (1982b) for useful corrections and additions.

Lomiento, Liana (1995), "Il *colon* 'quadrupede': Hephaest. *Ench.* p. 63,1 Consbr., con alcune riflessioni sulla antica teoria metrica," *QUCC*, NS 49: 127–33. Discusses definitions of stichos, colon, and comma in Hephaestion's work on poems and in commentary to Hephaestion.

Long, A. A. (1992), "Stoic Readings of Homer," in Lamberton and Keaney (1992): 41–66. Includes discussion of Heraclitus (Allegoricus).

Longo, Oddone (1971), *Scholia Byzantina in Sophoclis Oedipum Tyrannum* (Padua). Best edition.

——— (1987), "Le denominazioni di parentela in Aristofane di Bisanzio," in G. Bolognesi and V. Pisani (edd.), *Linguistica e filologia: Atti del VII convegno internazionale di linguisti* (Brescia): 319–26. Examines Aristophanes' Περὶ συγγενικῶν ὀνομάτων.

Lossau, Manfred Joachim (1964), *Untersuchungen zur antiken Demosthenesexegese* (Bad Homburg; *Palingenesia*, 2). Important study of ancient scholarship and criticism on Demosthenes, with much information on Didymus and his predecessors. Difficult.

Lowe, N. J. (1998), "Thesmophoria and Haloa: Myth, Physics and Mysteries," in

S. Blundell and M. Williamson (edd.), *The Sacred and the Feminine in Ancient Greece* (London): 149–73. Uses historical information from the scholia to Lucian.

Lucà, Santo (1994), "Il lessico dello ps.-Cirillo (redazione VI): Da Rossano a Messina," *Rivista di studi bizantini e neoellenici*, NS 31: 45–80. Study of manuscripts.

Luck, George (1976), "Aratea," *AJP* 97: 213–34. Discussion of the scholia's contribution to our understanding of Aratus' prologue.

Ludwich, Arthur (1879), Review of *GG* ii.i, *Jenaer Literaturzeitung*, 16: 223–4.

——— (1884–5), *Aristarchs Homerische Textkritik nach den Fragmenten des Didymos* (Leipzig; repr. Hildesheim 1971). Important study and edition of fragments; at end of vol. ii are editions of paraphrases and other scholarly material from various sources.

——— (1888–90), *Scholia in Homeri Odysseae A 1–309 auctiora et emendatiora* (Königsberg; repr. Hildesheim 1966). Best edition; reprint has useful preface by Erbse.

——— (1890), Review of *GG* iv.i, *BPW* 10: 528–33. Provides useful textual suggestions.

——— (1891), *Herodiani Technici Reliquiarum Supplementum* (Königsberg). Provides additional fragments of the Περὶ Ὀδυσσειακῆς προσῳδίας omitted from Lentz's edition.

——— (1894), Review of *GG* iv.ii, *BPW* 14: 1411–18. Provides useful textual suggestions.

——— (1896), *Die Homerische Batrachomachia des Karers Pigres, nebst Scholien und Paraphrase* (Leipzig). Standard edition and study.

——— (1902*a*), Review of *GG* i.iii, *BPW* 22: 737–50. Provides useful corrections.

——— (1902*b*), Review of *GG* i.ii, *BPW* 22: 801–10. Provides useful corrections.

——— (1910), Review of *GG* ii.ii and ii.iii, *BPW* 30: 1369–78. Useful observations.

——— (1912–14), *Die Homerdeuterin Demo: Zweite Bearbeitung ihrer Fragmente* (Königsberg; Verzeichnis der auf der königlichen Albertus-Universität zu Königsberg im Winterhalbjahre vom 15. Oktober 1912/1913/1914 an zu haltenden Vorlesungen). Edition and good discussion of fragments of late antique, female Homer scholar.

——— (1917–18), "Ueber die Homerischen Glossen Apions," *Philologus*, 74: 205–47 and 75: 95–127; repr. in Latte and Erbse (1965): 283–358. Standard edition; text is probably not by Apion. Incorporates a papyrus (*P.Ryl.* i. 26) that may not belong with the rest of the material.

Lührs, Dietrich (1992), *Untersuchungen zu den Athetesen Aristarchs in der Ilias und zu ihrer Behandlung im Corpus der exegetischen Scholien* (Hildesheim).

Lundon, John (1997), "Σχόλια: Una questione non marginale," in *Discentibus obvius: Omaggio degli allievi a Domenico Magnino* (Como): 73–86. Enlightening investigation of the use of the word σχόλιον in antiquity.

——— (1999), "Lexeis from the Scholia Minora in Homerum," *ZPE* 124: 25–52. Index of Homeric words explained in papyrus scholia. An enlarged and updated version with bibliography and quotation of contexts is available, in provisional form, at http://www.gltc.leidenuniv.nl/index.php3?m=56&c=238.

Lundström, Vilhelm (1913), "Scholierna till Xenophons Anabasis i Cod. Vat. Gr. 1335," *Eranos*, 13: 165–88. Edition and discussion of scholia.

Luppe, Wolfgang (1978), "Zum Aristophanes-Kommentar P. Flor. 112 / Nr. 63 Austin," *ZPE* 28: 161–4. On the text of some papyrus fragments of commentary on Aristophanes.

——— (1982), "'Απεώσθη πάλιν εἰς τοὺς Ληναϊκούς," *ZPE* 46: 147–59. On the text and interpretation of the Aristophanes commentary in *P.Oxy.* xxxv. 2737; in German.

——— (1992), "Zu Dikaiarchos fr. 63 Wehrli," *RhM* 135: 94–5. Textual solutions in a scholion to Euripides bearing on the history of the Medea legend.

——— (1996), "Zur 'Lebensdauer' der Euripides-Hypotheseis," *Philologus*, 140: 214–24. On the history of the "Tales from Euripides" between the 3rd and 11th cents. AD.

——— (2002), "Σχόλια, ὑπομνήματα und ὑποθέσεις zu griechischen Dramen auf Papyri," in Geerlings and Schulze (2002): 55–77.

Luschnat, Otto (1954), "Die Thukydidesscholien: Zu ihrer handschriftlichen Grundlage, Herkunft und Geschichte," *Philologus*, 98: 14–58. Definitive study of Thucydides scholia.

—— (1958), "Der Titel der Patmos-Scholien zu Demosthenes und Thukydides," *Philologus*, 102: 144–8. Study of Patmos scholia.

Luzzatto, Maria Jagoda (1993), "Scholia tardoantichi: Il commentario di Marcellino a Tucidide," *Quaderni di storia*, 38: 111–15. On textual history of the Life of Thucydides prefixed to his works.

—— (1999), *Tzetzes lettore di Tucidide: Note autografe sul Codice Heidelberg Palatino Greco 252* (Bari). On Byzantine scholia to Thucydides.

Maas, Paul (1903), Review of *GG* i.ii, *WKP* 20: 57–70 (important section repr. in *Kleine Schriften* (Munich 1973): 114–24). Many good suggestions for text and interpretation of Apollonius.

—— (1907), "Zu den Interpolationen im Text des Apollonios Dyskolos," *Philologus*, 66: 468–71 (repr. in *Kleine Schriften* (Munich 1973): 124–7). Corrections to the text of Apollonius.

—— (1911a), "Zur Überlieferung des Apollonius Dyskolos," *WKP* 28: 25–7. Observations on the manuscript tradition, correcting *GG* ii.ii.

—— (1911b), *Apollonii Dyscoli de Pronominibus pars generalis* (Bonn; Kleine Texte für Vorlesungen und Übungen 82). "Student" edition of *Pronouns* 3.1–49.7; no notes or other aids.

—— (1912), Review of *GG* ii.ii and ii.iii, *WKP* 29: 5–16. Provides useful corrections to both volumes.

Maass, Ernst (1887–8), *Scholia graeca in Homeri Iliadem Townleyana* (Oxford). Edition of scholia from T, published as vols. v–vi of W. Dindorf (1875–8).

—— (1892), *Aratea* (Berlin). Important discussion of some of the ancient scholarship on Aratus.

—— (1898), *Commentariorum in Aratum Reliquiae* (Berlin; repr. 1958). The best text of much of the ancient scholarship on Aratus, though superseded in the case of the scholia; it omits some material, including Hipparchus, and the discussion is often superseded. For a reliable summary of what the various texts in this compilation actually are and where they have been more recently discussed, see Martin (1998: i, pp. clxxx–clxxxi).

MacDowell, Douglas M. (1993), Review of Dilts (1992), *CR*, NS 43: 245–6. Provides some useful corrections.

McNamee, Kathleen (1977), *Marginalia and Commentaries in Greek Literary Papyri* (Diss. Duke University, UMI #77-31,676). Comprehensive discussion of the papyrus evidence.

—— (1982), "The Long and Short of Callimachus *Aetia* fr. 1.9–12," *BASP* 19: 83–6. Uses scholia to Callimachus.

—— (1992), "Annotated Papyri of Homer," in M. Capasso (ed.), *Papiri letterari greci e latini* (Galatina; Papyrologica Lupiensia, 1): 13–51. List of all known to that date, with reprints of most.

—— (1995), "Missing Links in the Development of Scholia," *GRBS* 36: 399–414. Argues that the transition from self-standing commentaries to scholia began in the 5th cent. AD.

—— (1998), "Another Chapter in the History of Scholia," *CQ*, NS 48: 269–88. Adduces parallels from legal commentaries to show that the transition to scholia began for literary works in the 5th cent. AD, and provides an excellent overview of the issue.

—— (forthcoming), *Annotations in Greek Literary Papyri* (American Studies in Papyrology). Even more comprehensive discussion of the papyrus evidence than in McNamee 1977.

Maehler, Herwig (1992), "Der Streit um den Schatten des Esels," in A. H. S. El-Mosalamy (ed.), *Proceedings of the XIXth International Congress of Papyrology* (Cairo): 625–36. Publication and discussion of a papyrus with commentary on Demosthenes (*P.Berol.* inv. 21188).

—— (1994), "Die Scholien der Papyri in ihrem Verhältnis zu den Scholiencorpora der Handschriften," in F. Montanari (1994), 95–127. Discusses the differences between the content of papyrus scholia and those preserved in medieval MSS, and the date of transfer of scholia to the margins of texts. Focuses on Theocritus, Apollonius Rhodius, Euripides, Pindar, and Aristophanes. To be treated with caution.

—— (2000), "L'évolution matérielle de l'*hypomnèma* jusqu'à la basse époque," in Goulet-Cazé (2000): 29–36.

Maehler, Margaret (1980), "Der 'wertlose' Aratkodex P. Berol. inv. 5865," *APF* 27: 19–32. Re-edition and re-evaluation of a fragment of Aratus with commentary.

Maleci, Stefano (1995), *Il codice Barberinianus graecus 70 dell'Etymologicum Gudianum,* (Rome; *BollClass* suppl. 15). Discussion of an important manuscript.

Manetti, Daniela, and Roselli, Amneris (1994), "Galeno commentatore di Ippocrate," in *ANRW* II 37.2: 1529–1635, 2071–80.

Manfredini, Mario (1975), "Gli scolii a Plutarco di Areta di Cesarea," *Siculorum Gymnasium,* 28: 337–50. Identifies scholia to the *Lives* by Arethas.

—— (1979), "Gli scolî alle vite di Plutarco," *Jahrbuch der österreichischen Byzantinistik,* 28: 83–119. Edition with introduction.

Manitius, Karl (1894), *Hipparchi in Arati et Eudoxi Phaenomena Commentariorum libri tres* (Leipzig). Best edition of this rare survival of an ancient commentary, with notes and German trans.

Mansfeld, Jaap (1998), *Prolegomena Mathematica* (Leiden; Philosophia Antiqua, 80). Good discussion of ancient scholarship on mathematical works, with excellent bibliography. Reliable. In English.

—— (2000), "Cosmic Distances: Aëtius 2.31 Diels and Some Related Texts," *Phronesis,* 45: 175–204. Finds early version of a ps.-Plutarch text in scholia to Ptolemy.

Martin, Jean (1956), *Histoire du texte des Phénomènes d'Aratos* (Paris). Excellent work focusing on the different types of ancient scholarship on Aratus and their origins; a model of good scholarship and a pleasure to read.

—— (1974), *Scholia in Aratum Vetera* (Stuttgart). The best text of the scholia to Aratus.

—— (1998), *Aratos: Phénomènes* (Paris). Excellent introduction gives the best overview of the textual history; commentary provides useful discussion of many scholia and passages from Hipparchus.

Marzullo, Benedetto (1995–6), "Poll. I 7," "Poll. III 36 (διαπαρθένια)," *MCr* 30–1: 289–93. Critical notes, in Italian.

Massa Positano, Lydia (1963), *Demetrii Triclinii in Aeschyli Persas Scholia* (Naples). Good edition of T scholia to *Persae* (including those not by Triclinius himself); preface is moderately useful.

Massimilla, Giulio (1990), "I primi due libri degli Αἴτια di Callimaco nell'*Etymologicum Genuinum*," *SIFC* 8: 180–91.

Mathiesen, Thomas J. (1983), *Aristides Quintilianus: On Music in Three Books* (New Haven). English trans. with detailed introduction.

Matthaios, Stephanos (1996), "Κύριον ὄνομα: Zur Geschichte eines grammatischen Terminus," in Swiggers and Wouters (1996): 55–77. Mostly concentrates on Aristotle, Stoics, and other writers prior to Dionysius Thrax.

—— (1999), *Untersuchungen zur Grammatik Aristarchs: Texte und Interpretation zur Wortartenlehre* (Göttingen; Hypomnemata, 126). Edition and commentary for Aristarchus' fragments on the doctrine of parts of speech.

—— (forthcoming), *Die Fragmente des Grammatikers Tryphon: Edition und Kommentar*

(Berlin; SGLG). Expected to provide a complete re-edition of all works and fragments of Trypho, directly and indirectly transmitted.

Matthews, Peter (1994), "Greek and Latin Linguistics," in Giulio Lepschy (ed.), *History of Linguistics*, ii: *Classical and Medieval Linguistics* (London): 1–133. Accurate, balanced, and thoughtful overview of ancient grammatical thought; arranged by topic rather than period, mixing Latin and Greek writers. Good bibliography.

Maurer, Karl (1995), *Interpolation in Thucydides* (Leiden; *Mnemosyne* suppl. 150). Chapter 5 examines the contributions of scholia to Thucydidean textual criticism and gives much useful background on general and specific problems, as well as explaining and correcting the text of some individual scholia.

Meijering, Roos (1985), "Aristophanes of Byzantium and Scholia on the Composition of the Dramatic Chorus," in Aerts *et al.* (1985): 91–102. Discusses scholia on the nature and role of choruses in plays of Euripides, Aristophanes, and Sophocles, arguing that they continue a line of research that goes back to Aristophanes' hypotheses.

———— (1987), *Literary and Rhetorical Theories in Greek Scholia* (Groningen).

Meineke, J. A. F. August (1849), *Stephani Byzantii Ethnicorum quae supersunt* (Berlin; repr. Graz 1958 as *Stephan von Byzanz: Ethnika* and Chicago 1992 as Ἐθνικόν: *A Geographical Lexicon on Ancient Cities, Peoples, Tribes and Toponyms*). Standard edition, but not ideal.

Meliadò, Claudio (2004), "Scoli a Teocrito in *P.Oxy.* 2064 + 3458," *ZPE* 147: 15–26. Edition and discussion of marginal scholia from papyrus of 2nd cent. AD.

Menestrina, Giovanni (2000) (ed.), *Fozio: tra crisi ecclesiale e magistero letterario* (Brescia). Collection of articles.

Meritt, Benjamin D. (1974), "The Count of Days at Athens," *AJP* 95: 268:79. Uses Hesiod and Aristophanes scholia for historical information. See Pritchett (1976).

Mette, Hans Joachim (1938), Review of Thierfelder (1935), *Philologische Wochenschrift*, 58: 227–32. Offers some useful observations.

———— (1952), *Parateresis: Untersuchungen zur Sprachtheorie des Krates von Pergamon* (Halle). Important work on Crates of Mallos.

———— (1978), "Die 'kleinen' griechischen Historiker heute," *Lustrum*, 21: 5–43. Contains some additional fragments of Apollodorus of Athens.

Micciarelli Collesi, A. M. (1970*a*), "Nuovi excerpta dall'Etimologico di Orione," *Byzantion*, 40: 517–42. Re-edition of Koës excerpts.

———— (1970*b*), "Per la tradizione manoscritta degli Excerpta di Orione," *Bollettino della Badia greca di Grottaferrata*, 24: 107–13.

Michaux, Maurice (1947), *Le commentaire de Marinus aux* Data *d'Euclide. Étude critique* (Louvain: Université de Louvain, recueil de travaux d'histoire et de philologie, 3rd ser. 25). Study with French trans. of text; the translation is reprinted, along with the Greek original, in A. N. Oikonomides, *Marinos of Neapolis: The Extant Works* (Chicago 1977).

Miller, Emmanuel (1868), *Mélanges de littérature grecque* (Paris; repr. Amsterdam 1965). Contains editions of lexicographical material, some still useful; pp. 385–436 are repr. in Latte and Erbse (1965).

Mogenet, Joseph (1956), *L'Introduction à l'Almageste* (Brussels; Académie royale de Belgique: Classe des lettres et des sciences morales et politiques: Mémoires, 2nd ser. 51.2). Edition of part of a commentary to Ptolemy.

———— (1975), "Sur quelques scolies de l'Almageste," in J. Bingen, G. Cambier, and G. Nachtergael (edd.), *Le monde grec: pensée, littérature, histoire, documents: Hommages à Claire Préaux* (Brussels): 302–11. Study of unpublished scholia to Ptolemy.

———— and Tihon, Anne (1981), "Le *Grand commentaire* aux *Tables faciles* de Théon d'Alexandrie et le *Vat. Gr.* 190," *AC* 50: 526–34.

———— ———— (1985), *Le "Grand commentaire" de Théon d'Alexandrie aux Tables faciles de Ptolémée, Livre I* (Vatican; Studi e testi, 315). Detailed introduction, edition, trans., commentary, and bibliography.

Montana, Fausto (1995), *Gregorio di Corinto, Esegesi al canone giambico per la pentecoste attribuito a Giovanni Damasceno* (Pisa). Edition of a (religious, not scholarly) commentary by Gregory of Corinth on some religious poetry, with introduction, detailed apparatus, Italian trans., and bibliography. Introduction is useful as being a more recent discussion of Gregory than can be found in editions of his scholarly works.

—— (1996), *L'Athenaion Politeia di Aristotele negli* scholia vetera *ad Aristofane* (Pisa and Rome: Istituti editoriali e poligrafici internazionali). Detailed study of the Aristophanes scholia.

Montanari, Franco (1976), "Un nuovo frammento di commentario a Callimaco," *Athenaeum*, NS 54: 139–51. Edition and discussion.

—— (1979), *Studi di filologia omerica antica*, i (Pisa). Important study, particularly for D scholia.

—— (1984), "Gli Homerica su papiro: Per una distinzione di generi," in *Filologia e critica letteraria della grecità* (Pisa; Ricerche di filologia classica, 2). Divides papyri into hypomnemata, glossaries, anthologies, etc.

—— (1988a), *I frammenti dei grammatici Agathokles, Hellanikos, Ptolemaios Epithetes: In appendice i grammatici Theophilos, Anaxagoras, Xenon* (Berlin; SGLG 7; in one vol. with Blank 1988 and Dyck 1988). Standard edition.

—— (1988b), "Filologia omerica antica nei papiri," in *Proceedings of the XVIII International Congress of Papyrology* (Athens): i. 337–44.

—— (1992), "Hermippus 2T: *De Aristotele* I," in *Corpus dei papiri filosofici greci e latini* (Florence), i.i.ii. 258–64. Edition and commentary on *PSI* 1093, 24–31; contains substantial discussion of Didymus.

—— (1993a), "L'Erudizione, la philologia e la grammatica," in G. Cambiano, L. Canfora, and D. Lanza (edd.), *Lo spazio letterario della grecia antica* (Rome), i.ii: 235–81. Good general treatment of ancient scholarship.

—— (1993b), "Pergamo," in G. Cambiano, L. Canfora, and D. Lanza (edd.), *Lo spazio letterario della grecia antica* (Rome), i.ii: 639–55. Includes background on the library.

—— (1994) (ed.), *La philologie grecque à l'époque hellénistique et romaine* (Geneva; Fondation Hardt *Entretiens*, 40). Very useful collection of articles on ancient scholarship.

—— (1995), "The Mythographus Homericus," in Abbenes *et al.* (1995): 135–72. Good general introduction, with further references and list of relevant papyri, pp. 168–70.

—— (1996a), "Apion," in *NP* i: 845–7. Concise introduction with useful bibliography.

—— (1996b), "Apollonios (12) Sophistes," in *NP* i: 883–5. Concise introduction with useful bibliography.

—— (1997a), "Choiroboskos Georgios," in *NP* ii: 1139–40. Concise introduction with useful bibliography.

—— (1997b), "Diokles (11)," in *NP* iii: 614–15. Short but useful explanation of the different possible identifications for Diocles.

—— (1998), "Zenodotus, Aristarchus and the *Ekdosis* of Homer," in Most (1998): 1–21.

Montanari, Ornella (1970–2), "Note agli *Argumenta metrica* delle commedie di Aristofane," *MCr* 5–7: 128–45. Discussion of hypotheses that could be derived from the work of Aristophanes of Byzantium.

Moore-Blunt, Jennifer (1978), "Problems of Accentuation in Greek Papyri," *QUCC* 29: 137–63. Important study of the use of the grave.

Moraux, Paul (1967), "Le Parisinus graecus 1853 (Ms. E) d'Aristote," *Scriptorium*, 21: 17–41. Description of manuscript with scholia; discusses scholia, pp. 29–37.

—— (1979), *Le commentaire d'Alexandre d'Aphrodise aux "Seconds analytiques" d'Aristote* (Berlin). Edition of fragmentary commentary not in *CAG*; discusses scholia, pp. 7–8.

Moraux, Paul (1981), "Anecdota graeca minora IV: Aratea," *ZPE*, 42: 47–51. New and important fragment of Aratus commentary (see Erren 1994: 200–3 for discussion).

───── (1985), *Galien de Pergame: Souvenirs d'un médecin* (Paris). Selections with French trans.

Morocho Gayo, Gaspar (1989), *Scholia in Aeschyli Septem Adversus Thebas* (León). Slightly updated version of a 1975 dissertation; gives all marginal scholia (but no interlinear ones) in all manuscripts. Full of errors.

Morpurgo Davies, Anna (1987), "The Greek Notion of Dialect," *Verbum* (Revue de linguistique publiée par l'université de Nancy, II), 10: 7–28.

Morrow, Glenn R. (1992), *Proclus: A Commentary on the First Book of Euclid's Elements* (Princeton, 2nd edn.). English trans. with introduction.

───── and Dillon, John (1987), *Proclus' Commentary on Plato's* Parmenides (Princeton). English trans. with extensive introduction; bibliography. Translation is based on Cousin's text improved by unpublished emendations from Westerink.

Most, Glenn W. (1987), "Alcman's 'cosmogonic' fragment (fr. 5 Page, 81 Calame)," *CQ* 37: 1–19. Argues that the language of the papyrus commentary demonstrates typical literary rather than philosophical analysis.

───── (1998) (ed.), *Editing Texts: Texte edieren* (Göttingen). Collection of articles on editing classical texts, including a few on ancient editorial practices.

───── (1999) (ed.), *Commentaries—Kommentare* (Göttingen; Aporemata, 4). Collection of articles on commentaries of all periods.

Mugler, Charles (1958–9), *Dictionnaire historique de la terminologie géometrique des grecs* (Paris). Useful for reading mathematical commentaries. Definitions in French, Latin, English, and German.

───── (1964), *Dictionnaire historique de la terminologie optique des grecs* (Paris). Useful for reading some mathematical commentaries. Definitions in French, Latin, English, and German.

───── (1972), *Archimède*, iv: *Commentaires d'Eutocius et fragments* (Paris). Good text and French trans. Very short introduction, but information on textual history in vol. i.

Müller, Carl Friedrich Wilhelm (1861), *Geographi graeci minores*, ii (Paris). Edition of commentary and scholia on Dionysius Periegetes (pp. 201–457), largely reproducing text of Bernhardy (1828).

Naber, S. A. (1864–5), *Photii Patriarchae Lexicon* (Leiden; repr. Amsterdam 1965). Edition to be avoided.

Nachmanson, Ernst (1918), *Erotiani vocum Hippocraticarum collectio cum fragmentis* (Uppsala). Standard edition of lexicon to Hippocrates.

───── (1941), *Der griechische Buchtitel* (Gothenburg; Göteborgs Högskolas Årsskrift, 47.19; repr. Darmstadt 1969). Clear and enjoyable explanation of the use and non-use of titles in antiquity.

Nadal, Robert, and Brunet, J.-P. (1984), "Le 'Commentaire' d'Hipparque: I. La sphère mobile," *AHES* 29: 201–36. Useful discussion of Hipparchus' mathematics and his scientific instruments.

───── ───── (1989), "Le 'Commentaire' d'Hipparque: II. Position de 78 étoiles," *AHES* 40: 305–54. On Hipparchus' astronomy and his scientific instruments.

Naddei, Mirella Carbonara (1976), *Gli scoli greci al* Gorgia *di Platone* (Bologna). Text, facing Italian trans., and extensive commentary.

Nagy, Gregory (1997), "Homeric Scholia," in I. Morris and B. Powell (edd.), *A New Companion to Homer* (Leiden; *Mnemosyne* suppl. 163): 101–22. General introduction; repr. with some changes as chapter 1 of Nagy (2004).

───── (1998), "The Library of Pergamon as a Classical Model," in H. Koester (ed.), *Pergamon: Citadel of the Gods* (Harrisburg): 185–232. On scholarship in Pergamon with particular reference to the editing of Homer.

—— (2004), *Homer's Text and Language* (Champaign, Il.).

Naoumides, Mark N. (1961), "The Papyrus of the *Lexicon* of Harpocration," *TAPA* 92: 384–8. Suggests supplements and interpretations.

—— (1968), "New Fragments of Ancient Greek Poetry," *GRBS* 9: 267–90. Edition and discussion of some glosses interpolated into Cyrillus that contain fragments of literature.

—— (1969), "The Fragments of Greek Lexicography in the Papyri," in *Classical Studies Presented to Ben Edwin Perry* (Urbana): 181–202. Listing and discussion.

—— (1975), Ῥητορικαὶ Λέξεις: *Editio princeps* (Athens). Edition and good study (in English) of small lexicon.

Nauck, August (1848), *Aristophanis Byzantii grammatici Alexandrini fragmenta* (Halle; repr. Hildesheim 1963) A superb edition of Aristophanes' fragments embedded in a Latin discussion; now incomplete because of the discovery of new sources and superseded by Slater (1986). Note that the author of the fragments on pp. 163–80 is actually Suetonius (see Taillardat 1967).

—— (1867), *Lexicon Vindobonense* (St. Petersburg; repr. Hildesheim 1965). Standard edition of a Byzantine lexicon; also contains the only edition of several works of [ps?-]Herodian (pp. xl–xlii, 294–312, 313–20); see Vitelli (1889) for readings from another MS.

Nehrling, Hans (1989–90), "Die zwei Gedichtlehren bei Hephaistion," *Helikon*, 29–30: 5–24. German translations of Hephaestion's two fragments on poems, with good introduction and bibliography.

Neitzel, Susanne (1977), *Apions* Γλῶσσαι Ὁμηρικαί (Berlin; SGLG 3; in one vol. with Linke 1977 and Haas 1977). Standard edition. See Dyck (1982*b*) for some useful corrections and Theodoridis (1989) for an addendum.

Nelis, Damien (2001), *Vergil's Aeneid and the Argonautica of Apollonius Rhodius* (Leeds: Francis Cairns). Discusses Vergil's use of scholia to Apollonius.

Netz, Reviel (1999*a*), *The Shaping of Deduction in Greek Mathematics: A Study in Cognitive History* (Cambridge). Discusses the use of diagrams.

—— (1999*b*), "Proclus' Division of the Mathematical Proposition into Parts: How and Why was it Formulated?," *CQ*, NS 49: 282–303. Uses Proclus' commentary on Euclid.

—— (1999–2000), "Archimedes Transformed: The Case of a Result Stating a Maximum for a Cubic Equation," *AHES* 54: 1–47. Uses Eutocius' commentary.

—— (2004–), *The Works of Archimedes* (Cambridge). Vol. i includes trans. of Eutocius' commentary on *De sphaera et cylindro* and some notes on it; later vols. should cover the rest of Eutocius' commentaries.

Nickau, Klaus (1966), *Ammonii qui dicitur liber de adfinium vocabulorum differentia* (Leipzig). Standard edition and discussion.

—— (1977), *Untersuchungen zur textkritischen Methode des Zenodotos von Ephesos* (Berlin). Study based largely on Homer scholia.

—— (1978), "Die Hamburger Handschrift des Ammonioslexikons (Q)," *Scriptorium*, 32: 60–6. On a newly found manuscript.

—— (1990), "Zur Geschichte der griechischen Synonymica: Ptolemaios und die Epitoma Laurentiana," *Hermes*, 118: 253–6. On an epitome of "Ammonius."

—— (2000), "Schiffbruch in der Wüste des Sinai: Zur Herennios Philon, Neilos von Ankyra und dem Ammonioslexikon," *Hermes*, 128: 218–26.

Nicole, Jules (1891), *Les Scolies genevoises de l'Iliade* (Geneva). Edition of scholia in Geneva manuscript.

Norvin, William (1913), *Olympiodori philosophi in Platonis Phaedrum commentaria* (Leipzig). Text only, superseded by Westerink (1976).

—— (1936), *Olympiodori philosophi in Platonis Gorgiam commentaria* (Leipzig; repr. Hildesheim 1966). Text only; superseded by Westerink (1970).

Nünlist, René (2003), "The Homeric Scholia on Focalization," *Mnemosyne*, 4th ser. 56: 61–71. On narratology in the bT scholia.

Nüsser, Olaf (1991), *Albins Prolog und die Dialogtheorie des Platonismus* (Stuttgart). Text with detailed commentary and extensive discussion.

Oguse, A. (1957), "Le papyrus grec de Strasbourg 364 + 16," *Aegyptus*, 37: 77–88. On pp. 85–8 discusses papyrus evidence for the date and history of Theodosius' Κανόνες.

Olivieri, Alexander (1897), *Pseudo-Eratosthenis Catasterismi* (Leipzig; Mythographi Graeci, iii.i). Best text of this epitome.

O'Neill, William (1965), *Proclus: Alcibiades I* (The Hague). English trans. with notes.

Osann, Friedrich Gotthilf (1821), *Philemonis grammatici quae supersunt* (Berlin). Standard edition.

Otranto, Rosa (1993), Review of Keaney (1991), *Quaderni di storia*, 38: 225–44. Provides many warnings and corrections, including an entirely revised index locorum.

Paap, Anton Herman Reinier Everhard (1948), *De Herodoti reliquiis in papyris et membranis Aegyptiis servatis* (Leiden). Includes edition of fragment of Aristarchus' commentary on Herodotus, pp. 37–40, with further references.

Pack, Roger A. (1965), *The Greek and Latin Literary Texts from Greco-Roman Egypt* (Ann Arbor, 2nd edn.). Guide to editions of papyri containing literary fragments, including some ancient scholarship.

Page, Denys L. (1934), *Actors' Interpolations in Greek Tragedy* (Oxford). Lucid explanation of ancient scholarship on Euripides, but makes some assertions no longer generally accepted.

Palmieri, Vincenzo (1981), " 'Eranius' Philo, *De differentia significationis*," *Revue d'histoire des textes*, 11: 47–80. Edition of much of the epitome, with discussion.

—— (1981–2), "Ptolemaeus (Ambrosianus qui dicitur) De differentia vocabulorum in litteram," *Annali della Facoltà di Lettere e Filosofia dell'Università di Napoli*, 24: 155–233. Edition and discussion of a manuscript not used by Heylbut (1887).

—— (1984), "Anonimo excerptum Casanatense sinonimico inedito," *BollClass* 5: 150–68. Edition and discussion.

—— (1986), "Un'anonima raccolta di sinonimi greci nel cod. Par. suppl. Gr. 1238," *Koinonia*, 10: 193–209. Edition and discussion.

—— (1988), *Herennius Philo: De diversis verborum significationibus* (Naples). Edition with introduction and commentary.

Palumbo Stracca, Bruna M. (1979), *La teoria antica degli asinarteti* (Rome; BollClass suppl. 3). Texts and Italian translations of Hephaestion 43.5–56.3 Consbruch, relevant scholia, and relevant sections of some other authors, with commentary.

Pantiglioni, M. (1998), "Il termine διάθεσις nella linguistica classica e Dionisio Trace," *Athenaeum*, 86: 251–61. Discusses views of διάθεσις in Dionysius, Apollonius Dyscolus, and Choeroboscus.

Papadopoulou, Thalia (1999), "Literary Theory and Terminology in the Greek Tragic Scholia: The Case of πλάσμα," *Bulletin of the Institute of Classical Studies of the University of London*, 43: 203–10. On the meanings of πλάσμα in scholia.

Papageorgius, Petros N. (1888), *Scholia in Sophoclis tragoedias vetera* (Leipzig). Poor edition, but best available except for *Ajax* and *Oedipus at Colonus*.

Papathomopoulos, Manoles (1976), Ἀνωνύμου παράφρασις εἰς τὰ Ὀππιανοῦ Ἁλιευτικά (Ioannina). Standard edition.

Parlangèli, Oronco (1953–4), "Il frammento dell'Etymologicum Casulanum nel manoscritto Vat. gr. 1276," *Bollettino della Badia greca di Grottaferrata*, NS 7: 115–26, 8: 97–112. Edition.

Parsons, Peter J. (1977), "Callimachus: Victoria Berenices" *ZPE* 25: 1–50. Text and discussion of a papyrus (3rd cent. BC) with Callimachus and commentary; commentary is interspersed with the text and indented.

Pasquali, Giorgio (1908), *Procli Diadochi in Platonis Cratylum commentaria* (Leipzig). Text of surviving fragments. Repr. in Romano (1989).

―――― (1910), "Ein neues Fragment des Grammatikers Tryphon," *Hermes*, 45: 465–7. Publication of a fragment of Trypho not included in Velsen (1853).

―――― (1934), *Storia della tradizione e critica del testo* (2nd edn., Florence 1952; repub. 1988 with foreword by D. Pieraccioni, repr. 2003). Discusses ancient editions of literary texts (both Greek and Latin).

Patillon, Michel (1990), "Contribution à la lecture de la *Technê* de Denys le Thrace," *REG* 103: 693–8. Presents some disagreements with an earlier edition of Lallot (1998). Cf. Swiggers and Wouters (1994).

―――― (1998), "À propos d'une nouvelle édition d'Apollonius Dyscole, De la construction (Περὶ συντάξεως)," *REG* 111: 323–30. Offers useful observations, mostly on textual issues.

Payne, Mark (2001), "Ecphrasis and Song in Theocritus' Idyll 1," *GRBS* 42: 263–87. Discusses interpretive strategies in the scholia.

Pearson, Lionel, and Stephens, Susan (1983), *Didymi in Demosthenem Commenta* (Stuttgart). Best edition of papyrus with Didymus' commentary on Demosthenes; also contains fragments from Harpocration of Didymus' work on Demosthenes.

Pecorella, Giovan Battista (1962), *Dionisio Trace: Τέχνη Γραμματική: testo critico e commento* (Bologna). New text of the Τέχνη and its first three supplements, with a huge apparatus criticus (but not bigger than that in *GG* i.i), substantial introduction, and extensive commentary. The thoroughness with which this text has been ignored by the scholarly community is impressive, especially considering that it makes use of a manuscript unavailable to Uhlig. See Lallot (1998: 15) for some reasons why this text does not supersede Uhlig's version (*GG* i.i).

Pépin, Jean, and Saffrey, Henri D. (1987) (edd.), *Proclus lecteur et interprète des anciens* (Paris). Collection of essays on philosophical commentary.

Perilli, Lorenzo (1990–3), "Marginalia lexicographica," *MCr* 25–8: 373–8. Notes on Erotian, Hesychius, and the etymologica.

Pernot, Laurent (1981), *Les Discours siciliens D'Aelius Aristide (OR. 5–6)* (New York). Discusses scholia to Aristides.

Pertusi, Agostino (1955), *Scholia vetera in Hesiodi Opera et Dies* (Milan). Best edition.

Petrilli, Raffaella (1997), *Temps et détermination dans la grammaire et la philosophie anciennes* (Münster). Discusses the meaning of ἀόριστον in Aristotle, Theophrastus, the Stoics, and the grammarians (chiefly Apollonius Dyscolus). Cf. Schenkeveld (1999).

Pfeiffer, Rudolf (1949–53), *Callimachus* (Oxford). Includes scholia; see esp. i. 3, 7, 11, 13, 17, 19, 31, 47, etc.; ii. 41–79, discussion with further references ii. pp. lxxvi–lxxix.

―――― (1968), *History of Classical Scholarship: From the Beginnings to the End of the Hellenistic Age* (Oxford). Still the standard history of Greek scholarship; superbly learned, detailed, and accurate, though now superseded on a few points.

Pfister, Raimund (1976), "Zur Geschichte der Begriffe von Subjekt und Prädikat," *Münchener Studien zur Sprachwissenschaft*, 35: 105–19. Studies these ideas from the classical Greek philosophers through late Latin, arguing that there was considerable evolution over that period. Cf. Ildefonse (1994).

Piccione, Rosa Maria, and Runia, David T. (2001), "Stobaios," in *NP* xi: 1006–1010. Good introduction with bibliography.

Piccirilli, Luigi (1983), "Ebbe Cimone un figlio di nome Callia?," *Civiltà classica e cristiana*, 4: 7–14. Uses historical information from the scholia to Aelius Aristides.

Piccolomini, E. (1895), "Sugli scolii all'Anabasi di Senofonte," *SIFC* 3: 518–30. Finds a new and important manuscript with scholia to Xenophon.

Piérart, Marcel (1993), "De l'endroit où l'on abritait quelques statues d'Argos et de la vraie nature du feu de Phoroneus: Une note critique," *BCH* 117: 609–13. Uses historical information from Sophocles scholia.

Pinborg, Jan (1975), "Classical Antiquity: Greece," in Thomas A. Sebeok (ed.), *Current Trends in Linguistics*, 13 (The Hague and Paris): 69–126. Clear and concise overview of ancient Greek grammatical thought (Plato, Aristotle, Stoics, Dionysius Thrax, Apollonius Dyscolus, Analogy and Anomaly). Probably easier than Matthews as an introduction, but not as trustworthy.

Pintaudi, Rosario (1973), *Etymologicum parvum quod vocatur* (Milan). Standard edition.

——— (1975), "Gli epimerismi come fonti dell'*Etymologicum Parvum*," *Annali della scuola normale superiore di Pisa, classe di lettere e filosofia*, 3rd ser. 5: 167–75.

Pistelli, Ermengildo/Hermenegildus (1894), *Iamblichi in Nicomachi Arithmeticam introductionem liber* (Leipzig; repr. with extensive addenda and corrigenda by U. Klein, Stuttgart 1975). Standard edition; includes scholia to Iamblichus' commentary.

Poe, Joe Park (1996), "The Supposed Conventional Meanings of Dramatic Masks: A Re-Examination of Pollux 4.133–54," *Philologus*, 140: 306–28.

——— (2000), "Pollux and the Aulaia," *Hermes*, 128: 247–50. Uses Pollux for information on the ancient theater.

Poltera, Orlando (1997), "Simonide, Eumelos et la *Korinthiaka* (Simon. 545 *PMG*): Un fragment irrecuperable?," *Emerita*, 65: 311–19. Uses Euripides scholia to reconstruct verses of lost poems.

Porro, Antonietta (1994), *Vetera Alcaica: L'esegesi di Alceo dagli Alessandrini all'età imperiale* (Milan). Important discussion of ancient scholarship on Alcaeus.

Porson, Richard (1823), *Photii Lexicon e codice Galeano* (Leipzig). Best edition of those portions not yet covered by Theodoridis (1982–).

Powell, J. Enoch (1936), "The Bâle and Leiden Scholia to Thucydides" and "The Aldine Scholia to Thucydides," *CQ* 30: 80–93, 146–50. Corrections to Hude (1927).

Pritchett, William K. (1976), "The Athenian Count of Days," *California Studies in Classical Antiquity*, 9: 181–95. Response to Meritt (1974), uses Hesiod scholia.

Probert, Philomen (2003), *A New Short Guide to the Accentuation of Ancient Greek* (London).

Rabe, Hugo (1892), "Lexicon Messanense de iota ascripto," *RhM* 47: 404–13. Edition of fragment of Oros' *Orthography*.

——— (1892–3), *Syriani in Hermogenem commentaria* (Leipzig). Standard edition.

——— (1895), "Nachtrag zum Lexicon Messanense de iota ascripto," *RhM* 50: 148–52. Addenda and corrigenda to 1892 edition.

——— (1906), *Scholia in Lucianum* (Leipzig). Standard edition, but not complete.

Raffaelli, Lucia M. (1984), "Repertorio dei papiri contenenti scholia minora in Homerum," in *Filologia e critica letteraria della grecità* (Pisa; Ricerche di filologia classica, 2): 139–77. List of papyri with discussion of distribution of material.

Ranke, Karl Ferdinand (1840), *Hesiodi quod fertur Scutum Herculis* (Quedlinburg and Leipzig). Latest edition of scholia to *Scutum*, pp. 19–65.

Rashed, Marwan (1995), "Alexandre d'Aphrodise et la 'magna quaestio': Rôle et indépendance des scholies dans la tradition byzantine du corpus aristotélicien," *Les études classiques*, 63: 295–351. Discusses some scholia to Aristotle.

——— (1997), "A 'New' Text of Alexander on the Soul's Motion," in Richard Sorabji (ed.), *Aristotle and After* (London; Bulletin of the Institute of Classical Studies suppl. 68) 181–95. On some scholia to Aristotle.

Rechenauer, Georg (1993), "Stachellose Drohnen bei Hesiod, *Erga* 304?," *QUCC*, NS 44: 27–48. Uses scholia to understand a *hapax*.

Rehm, Albert (1899), *Eratosthenis Catasterismorum fragmenta Vaticana* (Ansbach; Programm des königlichen humanistischen Gymnasiums Ansbach für das Schuljahr 1898/99). Text and discussion of some fragments not found in Olivieri (1897).

Reitzenstein, Richard (1888), "Die Ueberarbeitung des Lexicons des Hesychios," *RhM* 43: 443–60. Also discusses Cyrillus.

——— (1894), "Zu den Pausanias-Scholien," *Hermes*, 29: 231–9. Most important study.

——— (1897), *Geschichte der griechischen Etymologika: Ein Beitrag zur Geschichte der Philologie in Alexandria und Byzanz* (Leipzig; repr. Amsterdam 1964). Important work on ancient scholarship, particularly the etymologica, Oros, Eulogius, Choeroboscus, and Herodian.

Rengakos, Antonios (1993), *Der Homertext und die hellenistischen Dichter* (Stuttgart; *Hermes* Einzelschr. 64). Considers how the scholarship of Zenodotus, Aristophanes, and Aristarchus influenced Apollonius Rhodius, Callimachus, and other Hellenistic poets.

——— (1994), *Apollonios Rhodios und die antike Homererklärung* (Munich).

Reynolds, Leighton D., and Wilson, Nigel G. (1991), *Scribes and Scholars: A Guide to the Transmission of Greek and Latin Literature* (Oxford, 3rd edn.). Accurate and enjoyable introduction.

Richard, Marcel (1950), "'Ἀπὸ φωνῆς," *Byzantion*, 20: 191–222. Explores what the MS designation of a commentary as ἀπὸ φωνῆς means, concluding that through the 8th cent. it usually means "taken from the oral teaching of" but that from the 9th cent. it means simply "by."

Richardson, Nicholas J. (1980), "Literary Criticism in the Exegetical Scholia to the *Iliad*: A Sketch," *CQ*, NS 30: 265–87.

——— (1994), "Aristotle and Hellenistic Scholarship," in F. Montanari (1994): 7–28. Argues that the Hellenistic scholars took more from Aristotle than is generally thought.

Riddle, John M. (1984), "Byzantine Commentaries on Dioscorides," *Dumbarton Oaks Papers*, 38: 95–102. On scholia to Dioscorides.

Riemann, O. (1877), "Remarques sur les scholies de Démosthène et d'Eschine du manuscrit de Patmos," *BCH* 1: 182–94. Commentary on Patmos scholia on Demosthenes.

Rijksbaron, Albert (1986), "The Treatment of the Greek Middle Voice by the Ancient Grammarians," in Joly (1986): 427–44. Discusses the views of Dionysius, the scholia to his work, Apollonius Dyscolus, Choeroboscus, and the Latin grammarians.

Ritschl (*or* Ritschelius), Friedrich Wilhelm (1832), *Thomae Magistri sive Theoduli monachi Ecloga vocarum Atticarum* (Halle; repr. Hildesheim 1970 with title *Thomas Magister: Ecloga vocum Atticarum*). Standard edition.

Robert, Carl (1878), *Eratosthenis Catasterismorum reliquiae* (Berlin; repr. 1963). Superseded as text of *Catasterismi* epitome, but useful for comparison between that and other texts drawn from the same lost source.

Robins, Robert Henry (1986), "The *Technē Grammatikē* of Dionysius Thrax in its Historical Perspective: The Evolution of the Traditional European Word Class System," in P. Swiggers and W. van Hoecke (edd.), *Mot et parties du discours* (Louvain): 9–37. Illuminates the origins of the divisions of language (esp. into parts of speech), with special attention to the Τέχνη.

——— (1992), "Les grammairiens byzantins," in S. Auroux (ed.), *Histoire des idées linguistiques*, ii: *Le Développement de la grammaire occidentale* (Liège): 65–75. Useful general introduction and overview.

——— (1993), *The Byzantine Grammarians: Their Place in History* (Berlin). Helpful work with extensive discussion of (ps.-) Dionysius Thrax, Theodosius, epimerismi, Michael Syncellus, Gregory of Corinth, John Glykys, and Maximus Planudes. Factual information and Greek quotations are not reliable.

——— (1996), "The Initial Section of the *Tékhnē Grammatikē*," in Swiggers and Wouters (1996): 3–15. Explores the meaning of Dionysius' definition of grammar.

Romano, Francesco (1989), *Proclo: Lezioni sul "Cratilo" di Platone: Introduzione, traduzione e commento* (Catania). Reprints Pasquali's text (1908) with Italian trans. and notes.

Rome, Adolphe (1931–43), *Commentaires de Pappus et de Théon d'Alexandrie sur l'Almageste* (Vatican; Studi e testi, 54, 72, and 106). Standard editions of these commentaries on Ptolemy, with good, detailed introductions and notes.

Roselli, Amneris (1979), "Un frammento dell'epitome περὶ ζῴων di Aristofane di Bisanzio: P. Lit. Lond. 164," *ZPE* 33: 13–16.

—— (1996), "Nota su οὐκ ἄμουσος παιδία nel proemio del *Lexicon Platonicum* di Timeo Sofista," *SCO* 46: 213–7. Uses Timaeus' lexicon.

Rosén, Haiim B. (1962), *Eine Laut- und Formenlehre der Herodotischen Sprachform* (Heidelberg). Contains good explanation of ancient scholarship on Herodotus and edition of glossaries.

—— (1987–97), *Herodoti Historiae* (Leipzig). Prints scholia at bottom of relevant pages; also glossary entries and other ancient witnesses. Includes edition of Moschopulus' work on Ionic, and index to words discussed in scholia etc.

Rossum-Steenbeek, Monique van (1998), *Greek Readers' Digests? Studies on a Selection of Subliterary Papyri* (Leiden; *Mnemosyne* suppl. 175). Discussion of hypotheses, Mythographicus Homericus, etc., with re-editions of texts.

Ruhnken, David (1789), *Timaei sophistae lexicon vocum Platonicarum* (Leiden). Good text with extensive Latin commentary. Often (but by no means always) cited in the second edition (Leipzig 1828; repr. 1971) edited by G. A. Koch.

Rupprecht, Hans-Albert (1994), *Kleine Einführung in die Papyruskunde* (Darmstadt).

Russell, Donald A., and Konstan, David (2005), *Heraclitus: Homeric Problems* (Atlanta). Best edition, with introduction and trans.

Rusten, Jeffrey (1982), "Dicaearchus and the *Tales from Euripides*," *GRBS* 23: 357–67. Argues that the "Tales" were composed in the 1st or 2nd cent. AD and falsely attributed to Dicaearchus.

Rutherford, William G. (1881), *The New Phrynichus: Being a Revised Text of the Ecloga of the Grammarian Phrynichus* (London). Superseded as a text, but still useful for extensive discussion of how Phrynichus' pronouncements relate to actual classical usage.

—— (1896), *Scholia Aristophanica* (London). Text based on only one manuscript and now superseded, but still useful for its interpretive commentary (in English)—though the interpretations as well are superseded in places.

—— (1905), *A Chapter in the History of Annotation* (London; as 3rd vol. of Rutherford 1896); repr. New York 1987). Wide-ranging discussion of the Aristophanes scholia, with classification of scholia into different categories and extremely useful lists of passages exemplifying various classes. Now superseded in some respects.

Rzach, A. (1912), "Hesiodos," *RE* viii.i (xv): 1167–1240. Discusses scholia, cols. 1226–9.

Saffrey, Henri D. (1969), "Nouveaux oracles chaldaïques dans les scholies du *Paris. Gr.* 1853," *RPh* 43: 59–72. Discusses some important Aristotle scholia.

Sakellaridou-Sotiroudi, A. (1993), "Ὁ Ἡρόδοτος στις παρεκβολές του Ευσταθίου Θεσσαλονίκης στον Διονύσιο τον Περιηγητή," *Hellenica*, 43: 13–28. On Eustathius' use of Herodotus in his commentary on Dionysius Periegetes; proposes some new readings in the text of Eustathius. French summary, p. 261.

Sakkelion, Ioannes (1877), "Λέξεις μεθ' ἱστοριῶν—Lexicon Patmense," *BCH* 1: 10–16, 137–55. Publication (with introduction in Greek) of Patmos scholia to Demosthenes. Text (only) repr. in Latte and Erbse (1965: 140–65); corrections in Kontos (1877).

Salazar, Christine F. (1997), "Fragments of Lost Hippocratic Writings in Galen's Glossary," *CQ*, NS 47: 543–7.

Sandbach, Francis H. (1967), *Plutarchi Moralia*, vii (Leipzig). Includes fragments from the Aratus scholia and the commentary on Hesiod.

—— (1969), *Plutarch's Moralia*, xv: *Fragments* (Cambridge, Mass.). Loeb text of Plutarch fragments gives a translation of some of the Aratus and Hesiod scholia.

Santini, Carlo (1981), "Il salto delle costellazioni: Da Germanico ai glossatori," *Giornale italiano di filologia*, NS 12 [33]: 177–91. On Germanicus and the Aratus scholia.

Savorelli, Gabriella Messeri (1992), "Hermippus 3T: *De Aristotele* II," in *Corpus dei papiri filosofici greci e latini* (Florence) i.i.ii. 265–6. Repr. with discussion and bibliography of a portion of the papyrus of Didymus' commentary on Demosthenes.

Scaffai, Marco (1997), "Valerio Flacco e gli scolii: Sondaggi dai libri 3 e 4 degli Argonautica," *Prometheus*, 23/1: 40–58. On Valerius' use of the scholia to Apollonius.

Scattolin, Paolo (2003), "Su alcuni codici degli scoli all'*Elettra* di Sofocle," in G. Avezzù (ed.), *Il dramma sofocleo: Testo, lingua, interpretazione* (Stuttgart), 307–19. Edition and discussion of a few scholia (some old, some Byzantine) to Sophocles.

Schaefer, Arnold (1866), "Historisches aus den neuen Scholien zu Aeschines," *NJPP* 93 (= *JCP* 12): 26–9. Examples of the usefulness of the Aeschines scholia for understanding Greek history.

Schaefer (or Schäfer), Gottfried Heinrich (1811), *Gregorii Corinthii et aliorum grammaticorum libri de dialectis linguae graecae, quibus additur nunc primus editus Manuelis Moschopuli libellus de vocum passionibus* (Leipzig). Contains the standard edition of Gregory of Corinth's Περὶ διαλέκτων (pp. 1–624), as well as some short, anonymous works on dialects. Lots of notes and excellent indices.

—— (1813), *Apollonii Rhodii Argonautica*, ii (Leipzig). Edition of P scholia only; largely superseded by Wendel (1935) but contains some material omitted from that text. The work as a whole is a second edition, revised by Schaefer, of a 1780 edition by R. F. B. Brunck, but the scholia are not in the earlier edition.

Schäfke, Rudolf (1937), *Aristeides Quintilianus: Von der Musik* (Berlin). German trans. and commentary; difficult to read, and based on a now superseded Greek text.

Schamp, Jacques (1987), *Photios historien des lettres: La Bibliothèque et ses notices biographiques* (Paris).

—— (2000), *Les vies des dix orateurs attiques* (Fribourg). Compares part of Photius' *Bibliotheca* to Plutarch.

Schartau, Bjarne (1981), "Observations on the Commentary on Euripides' Phoenissae in the MSS Parma 154 and Modena, a. U.9.22," *ICS* 6: 221–41. Edition and discussion of some exegetical scholia in P and M. See Günther (1995) for background.

Scheer, Eduard (1908), *Lycophronis Alexandra* (Berlin; repr. 1958). Vol. ii is an edition of scholia with detailed discussion. Indices in Gualandri (1962, 1965).

Schenck, Horst (1974), *Die Quellen des Homerlexikons des Apollonios Sophistes* (Hamburg; Hamburger Philologische Studien, 34; repr. of 1961 Hamburg dissertation).

Schenkeveld, Dirk Marie (1982), "Studies in the History of Ancient Linguistics I: Σύνδεσμοι ὑποθετικοί and ὁ ἐάν ἐπιζευκτικός," *Mnemosyne*, 4th ser. 35: 248–68. Discusses the treatment of words for "if" in Apollonius Dyscolus and *P.Lit.Lond.* 182 (*c.*300 AD).

—— (1983), "Linguistic Theories in the Rhetorical Works of Dionysius of Halicarnassus," *Glotta*, 61: 67–94. Argues on the basis of Dionysius' mentions of (current, he claims) grammatical theories that the main development of ancient grammar occurred in the 1st cent. BC.

—— (1988), Review of Slater (1986), *Mnemosyne*, 4th ser. 41: 178–81. Some useful corrections.

—— (1990), "Studies in the History of Ancient Linguistics IV: Developments in the Study of Ancient Linguistics," *Mnemosyne*, 4th ser. 43: 289–306. Discussions of Callanan (1987) and Ax (1986).

—— (1994), "Scholarship and Grammar," in F. Montanari (1994): 263–301. Discusses a number of key ideas and their dates.

Schenkeveld, Dirk Marie (1999), Review article, *Mnemosyne*, 4th ser. 52: 598–610. Useful observations on Lallot (1997, 1998), Ildefonse (1997), Swiggers and Wouters (1998), and Petrilli (1997).

Schenkl, Henricus (1913), *Marci Antonini imperatoris in semet ipsum libri XII* (Leipzig, editio maior). Prints a selection of scholia, pp. 160–1.

Schironi, Francesca (2004), *I frammenti di Aristarco di Samotracia negli etimologici bizantini: Introduzione, edizione critica e commento* (Göttingen: Hypomnemata, 152). Complete edition of fragments of Aristarchus from the etymologica.

Schlunk, Robin R. (1974), *The Homeric Scholia and the Aeneid: A Study of the Influence of Ancient Homeric Literary Criticism on Vergil* (Ann Arbor).

—— (1993), *Porphyry: The Homeric Questions* (New York). Greek text (following Sodano 1970, but with many misprints) with English trans.

Schmidhauser, Andreas (forthcoming), edition and trans. of Apollonius Dyscolus' *Pronouns* (Diss. Geneva). Some material, including an unusually complete but error-prone bibliography, is currently available at http://andreas.schmidhauser.ch/apollonius.

Schmidt, Martin (1976), *Die Erklärungen zum Weltbild Homers und zur Kultur der Heroenzeit in den bT-scholien zur Ilias* (Munich; Zetemata, 62).

Schmidt, Moritz/Mauricius (1852), "Dionys der Thraker," *Philologus*, 7: 360–82. Edition of the fragments of Dionysius Thrax (other than the Τέχνη), superseded by Linke (1977).

—— (1853), "Dionys der Thraker," *Philologus*, 8: 231–53 and 510–20. Argument in favor of the authenticity of the Τέχνη that was definitive for a century; pp. 243–7 discuss the supplement Περὶ προσῳδιῶν.

—— (1854), *Didymi Chalcenteri grammatici Alexandrini fragmenta quae supersunt omnia* (Leipzig; repr. Amsterdam 1964). Standard edition of some of the fragments of Didymus, though when there is a more recent edition of the source of a fragment, that edition should also be consulted. Extensive discussion.

—— (1858–68), *Hesychii Alexandrini Lexicon* (Jena; repr. Amsterdam 1965). Best edition of Hesychius for those portions missing from Latte (1953–66); has a good apparatus but is not based on personal examination of the manuscript.

—— (1860), Ἐπιτομὴ τῆς Καθολικῆς προσῳδίας Ἡρωδιανοῦ (Jena; repr. Hildesheim 1983). The better edition of Arcadius' epitome of Herodian.

—— (1867), *Hesychii Alexandrini Lexicon, editio minor* (Jena, 2nd edn.). Edition to be avoided.

Schmit-Neuerburg, Tilman (1999), *Vergils Aeneis und die antike Homerexegese: Untersuchungen zum Einfluß ethischer und kritischer Homerrezeption auf imitatio und aemulatio Vergils* (Berlin).

Schmitter, Peter (1991) (ed.), *Sprachtheorien der abendländischen Antike* (Tübingen; Geschichte der Sprachtheorie, 2). Useful collection of articles on ancient grammatical thought.

Schneider, Jean (1994), "Les scholies de Lucien et la tradition parœmiographique," in A. Billault (ed.), *Lucien de Samosate* (Lyons), 191–204. Uses scholia and offers good summary of previous work on them.

Schneider, Otto (1856), *Nicandrea: Theriaca et Alexipharmaca* (Leipzig). Contains edition of *Theriaca* scholia by H. Keil and one of *Alexipharmaca* scholia by Bussemaker.

Schneider, Richard (1874), "Zu den Scholien des Dionysios Thrax," *RhM* 29: 183–6. Discussion of a point of interpretation of these scholia.

—— (1887), *Bodleiana* (Leipzig). Contains important corrections to some of the texts edited in Cramer (1835).

—— (1894), *Excerptum Περὶ διαλέκτων* (Leipzig; Beigabe zu dem Jahresbericht des königlichen Gymnasiums zu Duisburg). Only edition of this work of ps.-Theodosius.

—— (1895), *Excerpta Περὶ παθῶν* (Leipzig; Beigabe zu dem Jahresbericht des königlichen Gymnasiums zu Duisburg). Only edition of this work of Trypho.

Schönberger, Leander, and Steck, Max (1945), *Proklus Diadochus 410–485: Kommentar zum ersten Buch von Euklids "Elementen"* (Halle). German trans. with long introduction and detailed notes.

Schrader, Hermann (1880–2), *Porphyrii Quaestionum Homericarum ad Iliadem pertinentium reliquias* (Leipzig). Only complete edition, but problematic.

—— (1890), *Porphyrii Quaestionum Homericarum ad Odysseam pertinentium reliquias* (Leipzig). Only complete edition, but problematic.

Schröder, Bianca-Jeanette (1999), *Titel und Text* (Berlin). On the nature and history of book titles; primarily Latin but also relevant to Greek.

Schultz, Ferdinand (1865), *Aeschinis Orationes* (Leipzig). Edition of scholia, pp. 247–355; now superseded.

—— (1866), "Die Scholien zu Aeschines," *NJPP* 93 (= *JCP* 12): 289–315. Discusses sources and interpretation.

—— (1868), "Nachtrag zu den Aeschinesscholien," *NJPP* 97 (= *JCP* 14): 749–52. Corrections and supplements to F. Schultz (1865); now superseded.

Schultz, Hermann (1910), *Die handschriftliche Überlieferung der Hesiod-Scholien* (Berlin; Abhandlungen der königlichen Gesellschaft der Wissenschaften zu Göttingen, philologisch-historische Klasse, NF 12, Nr. 4). Fundamental work on textual history of these scholia, and edition of one commentary not found elsewhere.

—— (1912), "Harpokration (5)," in *RE* vii.ii (xiv): 2412–16. Useful information and bibliography, but somewhat dated.

—— (1913*a*), "Zur Nebenüberlieferung der Hesiodscholien," *Nachrichten von der königlichen Gesellschaft der Wissenschaften zu Göttingen,* philologisch-historische Klasse, 2: 252–63. Addenda to H. Schultz (1910).

—— (1913*b*), "Hesychios (9)," in *RE* viii.ii (xvi): 1317–22.

Schwartz, Eduard (1887–91), *Scholia in Euripidem* (Berlin). Standard text of the old scholia; omits Byzantine material.

Sedley, David (1996), "Three Platonist Interpretations of the *Theaetetus,"* in C. Gill and M. M. McCabe (edd.), *Form and Argument in Late Plato* (Oxford): 79–103. Includes discussion of an anonymous papyrus commentary.

Segonds, Alain P. (1985–6), *Proclus: Sur le premier Alcibiade de Platon* (Paris). Text with facing French trans., detailed introduction, notes, bibliography.

Sell, Hartmut (1968), *Das Etymologicum Symeonis (α-ἀίω)* (Meisenheim am Glan). Edition now superseded, but introduction still useful.

Severyns, Albert (1963), *Recherches sur la* Chrestomathie *de Proclos,* iv: *La* Vita Homeri *et les sommaires du cycle: texte et traduction* (Paris). Standard text; discussion also in vol. iii.

Sgarbi, Romano (1990), "Tecnica dei calchi nella versione armena della γραμματικὴ τέχνη attribuita a Dionisio Trace," *Memorie dell'Istituto lombardo, accademia di scienze e lettere, classe di lettere, scienze morali e storiche,* 39: 233–369. Examination of the terminology used in the Armenian translation of (ps.-) Dionysius' Τέχνη.

Sicking, C. M. J. (1970), "Kallimachos, Epigramm XXI Pf.," *Mnemosyne,* 4th ser. 23: 188–9. Uses Hesiod scholia to emend text of Callimachus.

Sider, David (2001), " 'As is the generation of leaves' in Homer, Simonides, Horace, and Stobaeus," in D. Boedeker and D. Sider (edd.), *The New Simonides: Contexts of Praise and Desire* (New York): 272–88. Lists the ways Stobaeus cites authors and works, and the kinds of manuscript corruption his system suffered.

Siebenborn, Elmar (1976), *Die Lehre von der Sprachrichtigkeit und ihren Kriterien: Studien zur antiken normativen Grammatik* (Amsterdam). A good study of the development of prescriptive grammar.

Skov, G. E. (1975), "The Priestess of Demeter and Kore and her Role in the Initiation of Women at the Festival of the Haloa at Eleusis," *Temenos*, 11: 136–47. Uses historical information from scholia to Lucian.

Slater, William J. (1976), "Aristophanes of Byzantium on the Pinakes of Callimachos," *Phoenix*, 30: 234–41. On Aristophanes' work on the *Pinakes*; argues that information on the grammarians must be treated with caution.

────── (1977), Review of Fischer (1974), *Gnomon*, 49: 258–62. Useful discussion, in English.

────── (1982), "Aristophanes of Byzantium and Problem-Solving in the Museum," *CQ*, NS 32: 336–49. Reappraisal of Aristophanes' work, suggesting that work in the Museum may have been less "serious" than normally thought. Counter-arguments in Blank and Dyck (1984).

────── (1986), *Aristophanis Byzantii Fragmenta* (Berlin; SGLG 6). Standard edition of the fragments of Aristophanes' Λέξεις, with notes and introduction in English and with a long bibliography. Not entirely complete. Useful corrections in Dyck (1989) and Schenkeveld (1988).

────── (1989a), "Problems in Interpreting Scholia on Greek Texts," in J. N. Grant (ed.), *Editing Greek and Latin Texts* (New York): 37–61. Useful set of warnings.

────── (1989b), Review of Callanan (1987), *Kratylos*, 34: 5–9. Useful discussion of specific points.

Sluiter, Ineke (1988), "On ἤ διασαφητικός and propositions containing μᾶλλον/ἧττον," *Mnemosyne*, 4th ser. 41: 46–66. More about logic than grammar, but contains useful information on terminology.

────── (1990), *Ancient Grammar in Context: Contributions to the Study of Ancient Linguistic Thought* (Amsterdam). Discusses the Stoics and Apollonius Dyscolus, with useful summary and discussion of much earlier work on Apollonius; particular focus on the idea of the interjection. Excellent bibliography.

────── (1997a), "The Greek Tradition," in W. van Bekkum, J. Houben, I. Sluiter, and K. Versteegh (edd.), *The Emergence of Semantics in Four Linguistic Traditions: Hebrew, Sanskrit, Greek, Arabic* (Amsterdam): 147–224. Good introduction to the development of Greek linguistic thought.

────── (1997b), "Parapleromatic Lucubrations," in A. Rijksbaron (ed.), *New Approaches to Greek Particles* (Amsterdam): 233–46. On the meaning of σύνδεσμος παραπληρωματικός.

────── (2000), "The Dialectics of Genre: Some Aspects of Secondary Literature and Genre in Antiquity," in M. Depew and D. Obbink (edd.), *Matrices of Genre* (Cambridge, Mass.): 183–203. On the ancient views of the genres of commentaries etc.

Smith, Andrew (1993), *Porphyrii philosophi fragmenta* (Stuttgart). Includes fragments of the Plato commentaries.

Smith, Ole Langwitz (1967), "Random Remarks on the Scholia to Aeschylus' Supplices," *C&M* 28: 75–85.

────── (1974), "A New Source of Triclinius' Commentary on Aeschylus' *Prometheus Vinctus*," *RhM*, NF 117: 176–80. Important supplements to Smyth (1921), from a newly discovered copy of T.

────── (1975), *Studies in the Scholia on Aeschylus*, i: *The Recensions of Demetrius Triclinius* (Leiden; Mnemosyne suppl. 37). Excellent discussion of Triclinius' work, with extensive bibliography; pp. 240–52 give text of proto-Triclinian scholia on *Septem* and *Persae*.

────── (1976a), *Scholia Graeca in Aeschylum quae exstant omnia: pars I: Scholia in Agamemnonem Choephoros Eumenides Supplices continens* (Leipzig; repr. with corrections 1993). Standard text of these scholia.

—————— (1976*b*), "On the Problem of a Thoman Recension of Aristophanes," *GRBS* 17: 75–80. Argues that Thomas only produced one edition of Aristophanes.

—————— (1977) *Scholia metrica anonyma in Euripidis Hecubam, Orestem, Phoenissas* (Copenhagen). Edition of Byzantine scholia in manuscripts P and M, which are argued to be proto-Triclinian. See Günther (1995) for background.

—————— (1979), "The Scholia on the Eumenides in the Early Triclinian Recension of Aeschylus," *Philologus*, 123: 328–36.

—————— (1980), "The A Commentary on Aeschylus: Author and Date," *GRBS* 21: 395–9. Argues that author is J. Tzetzes.

—————— (1981), "Classification of MSS of the Scholia on Aeschylus," *ICS* 6: 44–55. Shows that textual tradition is an open one.

—————— (1982*a*), *Scholia Graeca in Aeschylum quae exstant omnia: pars II fasc. 2: Scholia in Septem Adversus Thebas continens* (Leipzig). Standard edition of these scholia.

—————— (1982*b*), "The So-called 'Sch. Rec.' in Editions of the Scholia on Aeschylus," *Philologus*, 126: 138–40. Shows that readings so designated may really be the corrections of an early modern editor and not exist in any manuscript.

—————— (1982*c*), "Tricliniana," *C&M* 33: 239–62. Analysis of the different phases of Demetrius Triclinius' work on Aristophanes, Sophocles, Aeschylus, and Euripides; in English.

—————— (1992), "Tricliniana II," *C&M* 43: 187–229. On Triclinius' early work on Aeschylus, Sophocles, and Aristophanes, and on his final recension of Pindar; in English.

Smith, Wesley D. (1979), *The Hippocratic Tradition* (Ithaca). General introduction to scholarship on Hippocrates through the 2nd cent. AD.

Smyth, Herbert Weir (1921), "The Commentary on Aeschylus' *Prometheus* in the Codex Neapolitanus," *HSCP* 32: 1–98. Standard edition of T and useful (though dated) discussion.

Sodano, Angelo Raffaele (1964), *Porphyrii in Platonis Timaeum Commentariorum Fragmenta* (Naples). Edition of fragments (many in Latin), brief introduction, bibliography.

—————— (1970), *Porphyrii Quaestionum Homericarum liber I* (Naples). Standard edition with good introduction, but does not cover whole work.

Solmsen, Friedrich (1981), "The Academic and the Alexandrian Editions of Plato's Works," *ICS* 6: 102–11. Discusses early work on Plato.

Sorabji, Richard (1990) (ed.), *Aristotle Transformed: The Ancient Commentators and their Influence* (Ithaca). Good introduction to the ancient commentaries; bibliography.

Soubiran, Jean (1972), *Cicéron: Aratea, fragments poétiques* (Paris). Best edition of Cicero's translation of Aratus, which used the scholia; excellent introduction.

—————— (1981), *Aviénus: Les phénomènes d'Aratos* (Paris). Best edition of Avienus' translation of Aratus, which used the scholia and commentaries; excellent introduction.

Spanoudakis, Konstantinos (2000), "Hesychiana minima," *ZPE* 130: 31–41. Notes on entries related to Philitas; in English.

Spengel, Leonhard (1856), *Rhetores Graeci*, iii (Leipzig). Includes editions of Choeroboscus' Περὶ τρόπων ποιητικῶν, Trypho's Περὶ τρόπων, the Περὶ τρόπων misattributed to Gregory of Corinth, and the Περὶ σχημάτων misattributed to Herodian.

Spiro, Friedrich (1894), "Pausanias-Scholien," *Hermes*, 29: 143–9. Best edition.

—————— (1903), *Pausaniae Graeciae Descriptio* (Leipzig). Reprints scholia, without discussion, in vol. iii.

Spoerri, Walter (1980), "Die Edition der Aischylosscholien," *MH* 37: 1–24. Useful overview of the history of modern work on these scholia, with critiques of various editions; not always 100 percent accurate about contents of editions.

Spooner, Joseph (2002), *Nine Homeric Papyri from Oxyrhynchos* (Florence; Studi e testi di papirologia, NS 1). Edition of some papyri with marginal scholia to *Iliad* 2.

Stallbaum, Gottfried/J. G. (1825–6), *Eustathii archiepiscopi Thessalonicensis commentarii ad Homeri Odysseam* (Leipzig). Best edition of this commentary; index in Devarius (1828).

———— (1827–30), *Eustathii archiepiscopi Thessalonicensis commentarii ad Homeri Iliadem* (Leipzig). Superseded edition; index in Devarius (1828).

Stammerjohann, Harro (1996) (ed.), *Lexicon Grammaticorum: Who's Who in the History of World Linguistics* (Tübingen). Includes (among much later material) entries on many Greek grammarians and linguistically oriented philosophers. Tends to be more complete than the *OCD* but less thorough than *RE* or *NP*. Slightly peculiar inclusions and omissions. In English.

Stein, Heinrich M. (1871), *Herodoti Historiae*, ii (Berlin). Edition of scholia, pp. 431–40 and of glossaries, 441–82; the latter is repr. in Latte and Erbse (1965: 191–230). Largely superseded.

Steinicke, K. (1957), *Apollonii Sophistae Lexicon Homericum, litteras* α–δ (Diss. Göttingen). Re-edition of part of the lexicon.

Steinthal, Heymann (1890–1), *Geschichte der Sprachwissenschaft bei den Griechen und Römern* (Berlin; repr. Bonn 1961). Very important study, only partially superseded.

Stichel, Rudolf H. W. (1988), "Eine Athena des Phidias in Konstantinopel?," *Boreas*, 11: 155–64. Uses Byzantine scholia to Aelius Aristides.

Struck, Peter T. (2004), *Birth of the Symbol: Ancient Readers at the Limits of their Texts* (Princeton). Discusses some ancient scholarship of a literary-critical nature.

Studemund, Wilhelm (1867): "Der pseudo-Herodianische Tractat über die εἴδη des Hexameters," *NJPP* 95 (= *JCP* 13): 609–23. Edition of ps.-Herodian, *De metris* (pp. 618–19) with extensive discussion.

Sturz, Friedrich Wilhelm (1818), *Etymologicum Graecae linguae Gudianum* (Leipzig). Standard edition except for letters α–ζ, for which superseded. In appendix, on pp. 611–17, prints Werfer excerpts from Orion's etymologicum.

———— (1820), *Orionis Thebani Etymologicon* (Leipzig). Standard text of the largest epitome of Orion, followed by text of Koës excerpts.

Susemihl, Franz (1891–2), *Geschichte der griechischen Litteratur in der Alexandrinerzeit* (Leipzig). Old but still the most comprehensive study of the Alexandrians.

Sutton, Dana Ferrin (1980), "Plato Comicus Demoted: A Reconsideration," *ZPE* 38: 59–63. On a papyrus commentary on Aristophanes (*P.Oxy.* 2737).

Swiggers, Pierre (1997), *Histoire de la pensée linguistique: Analyse du langage et réflexion linguistique dans la culture occidentale, de l'Antiquité au XIXe siècle* (Paris). Conceptual history of linguistics; discussion of Greeks, largely pp. 9–68. More concerned with philosophy than with scholarship.

———— and Wouters, Alfons (1990) (edd.), *Le Langage dans l'antiquité* (Louvain). Collection of articles giving useful background on the wider context of linguistic thought across the ancient Mediterranean.

———— ———— (1994), "La *Technê grammatikê* de Denys le Thrace: Une perspective historiographique nouvelle," *Orbis*, 37: 521–49. Review article based on an earlier edition of Lallot (1998); useful observations and additions (especially concerning the papyri), and good bibliography.

———— ———— (1995a), "The Treatment of Relational Nouns in Ancient Grammar," *Orbis*, 38: 149–78. Discusses the meaning and origins of the terms πρός τι, ὡς πρός τι, and ἀπολελυμένος in the Τέχνη, looking carefully at the scholia and at philosophical antecedents. Good bibliography.

———— ———— (1995b), "*Techne* et *empeiria*: La Dynamique de la grammaire grecque dans l'antiquité à la lumière des papyrus grammaticaux," *Lalies*, 15: 83–100. Considers the grammatical papyri and their relationship to the Τέχνη of (ps.-) Dionysius Thrax, advocating a relatively early date for that work and emphasizing the fluidity of the tradition. Good bibliography (continued on errata sheet at front of volume).

———— ———— (1996) (edd.), *Ancient Grammar: Content and Context* (Louvain). Good collection of articles on ancient grammar.

———— ———— (1998), De *Tékhnē Grammatikḗ van Dionysius Thrax: De oudste spraakkunst in het Westen* (Louvain; Orbis linguarum, 2). Highly useful Dutch edition of the Τέχνη, containing an excellent introduction, repr. of the standard text, Dutch trans., German trans. (= Kürschner 1996), glossary, and extensive bibliography.

Taillardat, Jean (1967), *Suétone: Περὶ βλασφημιῶν, περὶ παιδιῶν (extraits byzantins)* (Paris). Standard text and good study.

Tannery, Paul (1893–5), *Diophanti Alexandrini opera omnia cum graecis commentariis* (Leipzig). Contains (ii. 73–7) edition of anonymous prolegomena to Nicomachus.

Tarán, Leonardo (1969), *Asclepius of Tralles: Commentary to Nicomachus' Introduction to Arithmetic* (Philadelphia; Transactions of the American Philosophical Society, 59.4). Critical text with good introduction (covering the relationships among the different Nicomachus commentaries) and notes.

———— (1976), Review of A. Carlini, *Studi sulla tradizione antica e medievale del Fedone*, *Gnomon*, 48: 760–8 (repr. in Tarán, *Collected Papers (1962–1999)* (Leiden 2001): 279–90). Argues that there was no Alexandrian edition of Plato.

———— (1978), *Anonymous Commentary on Aristotle's De Interpretatione* (Meisenheim am Glan; Beiträge zur klassischen Philologie, 95). Edition of a late commentary not in *CAG*; also of some scholia by Olympiodorus.

Tarrant, Harold (2000), *Plato's First Interpreters* (Ithaca). Useful study of Middle Platonism.

Taylor, Daniel J. (1987) (ed.), *The History of Linguistics in the Classical Period* (Amsterdam). Collection of essays on ancient grammatical thought, repr. from *HL* 13 (1986). Cf. Householder (1989).

Tessier, Andrea (1989), *Scholia metrica vetera in Pindari carmina* (Leipzig). Good edition, text-critical introduction, and bibliography.

Theodoridis, Christos (1972), "Drei übersehene Bruchstücke des Apollodoros von Athen," *Glotta*, 50: 29–34. Includes information about Didymus and Apollodorus.

———— (1976*a*), *Die Fragmente des Grammatikers Philoxenos* (Berlin; SGLG 2). Standard edition; excellent text and introduction. Asterisks mark fragments for which the authorship is deduced by Theodoridis rather than being stated in the ancient source.

———— (1976*b*), "Zwei neue Wörter für Aischylos und der P.Oxy. 1083, fr.1," *ZPE* 20: 47–53. Uses Pollux.

———— (1980), "Der Hymnograph Klemens terminus post quem für Choiroboskos," *BZ* 73: 341–5. Shows that Choeroboscus wrote no earlier than the end of the 8th cent. AD.

———— (1982–), *Photii Patriarchae Lexicon* (Berlin). Best edition, but not yet complete. Includes important discussion.

———— (1988), "Quellenkritische Bemerkungen zum Lexikon des Suidas," *Hermes*, 116: 468–75.

———— (1989), "Drei neue Fragmente des grammatikers Apion," *RhM* 132: 345–50. Important addendum to Neitzel (1977).

———— (1993), "Kritische Bemerkungen zum Lexikon des Suidas," *Hermes*, 121: 484–95.

———— (1996), "Ein unbeachtetes Zeugnis für Menanders Dyskolos v. 492–493," *RhM* 139: 375–6. Finds a fragment of Menander in scholia to Euripides.

Thierfelder, Andreas (1935), *Beiträge zur Kritik und Erklärung des Apollonius Dyscolus* (Leipzig; Abhandlung der sächsischen Akademie der Wissenschaften zu Leipzig, philologisch-historische Klasse, 43.2. Detailed commentary on numerous specific passages in *Pronouns*, *Adverbs*, and *Syntax*. Cf. Mette (1938); Sluiter (1990: 83, 118–21).

Thompson, Wesley E. (1983), "Harpocration on γεννῆται," *Hermes*, 111: 118–21. Uses Harpocration for historical information.

——— (1985), "Chabrias at Corinth," *GRBS* 26: 51–7. Uses historical information from the scholia to Aelius Aristides.

Thomson, George (1966), *The Oresteia of Aeschylus, edited with an introduction and commentary, in which is included the work of the late Walter Headlam* (Amsterdam, 2nd edn.). Vol. i pp. 63–4 is a brief introduction to the scholia; on pp. 211–77 is a text of the *Oresteia* scholia (M, with excerpts from T and F; numerous errors and very little app. crit.). Superseded.

——— (1967), "The Intrusive Gloss," *CQ*, ns 17: 232–43. Clear and engaging discussion of the different types of scholia in T.

Tihon, Anne (1973), "Les scolies des Tables Faciles de Ptolémée," *Bulletin de l'institut historique belge de Rome*, 43: 49–110. Edition with trans. and commentary.

——— (1976), "Notes sur l'astronomie grecque au Ve siècle de notre ère (Marinus de Naplouse—un commentaire au *Petit commentaire* de Théon)," *Janus*, 63: 167–84. Study of unpublished scholia to one of Theon's commentaries on Ptolemy, and other material on Marinus.

——— (1978), *Le "Petit commentaire" de Théon d'Alexandrie aux Tables faciles de Ptolémée* (Vatican; Studi e testi, 282). Edition and trans. of commentary, with study of textual history.

——— (1987), "Le livre V retrouvé du *Commentaire à l'Almageste* de Théon d'Alexandrie," *AC* 56: 201–18. Remains discovered in scholia to Ptolemy.

——— (1991), *Le "Grand commentaire" de Théon d'Alexandrie aux Tables faciles de Ptolémée, Livres II et III* (Vatican; Studi e testi, 340). Edition, trans., and commentary.

——— (1999), *Le "Grand commentaire" de Théon d'Alexandrie aux Tables faciles de Ptolémée, Livre IV* (Vatican; Studi e testi, 390). Edition, trans., and commentary.

Tittmann, Johann A. H. (1808), *Iohannis Zonarae Lexicon* (Leipzig; repr. Amsterdam 1967). Only edition.

Tolkiehn, Johannes (1915), "Der Grammatiker Diokles," *WKP* 32: 1143–6. Discusses the different references to "Diocles" in ancient writers and the identities of the referents.

Tosi, Renzo (1980–2), "Scoli-fantasma a Tucidide," *MCr* 15–17: 209–18.

——— (1988), *Studi sulla tradizione indiretta dei classici greci* (Bologna). On the way fragments of ancient literature are preserved in various types of ancient scholarship.

——— (1990–3), "Lexicographica Alexandrina," *MCr* 25–8: 297–304. Discusses Aristophanes of Byzantium, frs. 6, 7, and 27 (Slater), as well as some other lexicographical fragments of the early Alexandrians.

——— (1997), "Osservazioni sul rapporto fra Aristofane di Bisanzio e l'Antiatticista," in *Μοῦσα: Scritti in onore di Giuseppe Morelli* (Bologna): 171–7. On Aristophanes' lexicographical ideas and their preservation in the Antiatticista.

——— (1998), "Hesychios (1)," in *NP* v: 514–15.

——— (2001), "Suda," in *NP* xi: 1075–6.

Treadgold, Warren T. (1980), *The Nature of the Bibliotheca of Photius* (Washington).

Trojahn, Silke (2002), *Die auf Papyri erhaltenen Kommentare zur Alten Komödie: Ein Beitrag zur Geschichte der antiken Philologie* (Munich and Leipzig; Beiträge zur Altertumskunde, 175). Contains texts, translations, and excellent detailed study of papyrus commentaries to Aristophanes and Eupolis.

Turner, Eric G. (1962), "L'érudition alexandrine et les papyrus," *Chronique d'Égypte*, 37: 135–52.

——— (1980), *Greek Papyri: An Introduction* (Oxford, 2nd edn.).

Turyn, Alexander (1943), *The Manuscript Tradition of the Tragedies of Aeschylus* (New York). Crucial work on textual tradition, and superseded edition of T scholia to *Eumenides*, pp. 123–37.

———— (1944), "The Manuscripts of Sophocles," *Traditio*, 2: 1–41. Extensive discussion of scholia.

———— (1949), "The Sophocles Recension of Manuel Moschopulus," *TAPA* 80: 94–173. Much discussion of textual history of scholia, including good survey of editions.

———— (1952), *Studies in the Manuscript Tradition of the Tragedies of Sophocles* (Urbana). Discusses textual tradition of Byzantine scholia.

———— (1958), "On the Sophoclean Scholia in the Manuscript Paris 2712," *HSCP* 63: 161–70. On a group of Byzantine scholia.

Uhlig, Gustav (1902), Review of *GG* i.ii, *Deutsche Literaturzeitung*, 23: 1179–84. A few useful observations and some amusing general discussion of Apollonius Dyscolus and his difficulties.

Valckenaer, Lodewijk Caspar (1822), *Ammonius: De differentia adfinium vocabulorum* (Leipzig, 2nd edn.; 1st edn. 1739 has title *Ammonius: De adfinium vocabulorum differentia*). Superseded for Ammonius, but contains still-necessary edition of Περὶ πνευμάτων compilation.

Van der Valk, Marchinus (1955), "A Few Observations on the Atticistic Lexica," *Mnemosyne*, 4th ser. 8: 207–18.

———— (1963–4), *Researches on the Text and Scholia of the Iliad* (Leiden). Very important study.

———— (1971–87), *Eustathii archiepiscopi Thessalonicensis commentarii ad Homeri Iliadem pertinentes* (Leiden). By far the best edition of Eustathius; index in Keizer (1995).

———— (1984), "Manuscripts and Scholia: Some Textual Problems," *GRBS* 25: 39–49. Uses scholia on several authors.

Van Groningen, Bernhard A. (1963), "Ἔκδοσις," *Mnemosyne*, 4th ser. 16: 1–17. Argues that an ἔκδοσις was not an "edition" in our sense, because it was not intended for publication in our sense.

Van Heusde, Jan Adolf Karel (1864), *Aeschyli Agamemnon* (Hagae Comitis [i.e. The Hague]). Contains a superseded edition of M, F, and T scholia beneath text.

Van Looy, Herman (1991–2), "Les Fragments d'Euripide," *AC* 60: 295–311 and 61: 280–95. Bibliography including works on papyrus hypotheses.

Van Ophuijsen, Johannes M. (1987), *Hephaestion on Metre* (Leiden; *Mnemosyne* suppl. 100). Translation and commentary on *Encheiridion* and parallel passages from Aristides Quintilianus.

———— (1993a), "The Semantics of a Syntactician: Things meant by verbs according to Apollonius Dyscolus Περὶ συντάξεως'," in *ANRW* II 34.1: 731–70. Good discussion covering the meanings (in Apollonius) of πρᾶγμα, διάθεσις, ἐνέργεια, ἔννοια, (παρ)εμφαίνω, and related words.

———— (1993b), "On Poems: Two Hephaestionic Texts and One Chapter from Aristides Quintilianus on the Compostion of Verse," in *ANRW* II 34.1: 796–869. Reprints most (but not all) of Consbruch's text of the two fragments on poems and parallel passages from Aristides, with trans. and commentary.

Van Thiel, Helmut (1992), "Zenodot, Aristarch und Andere," *ZPE* 90: 1–32. Collection of papyri with text-critical scholia, pursuant to an argument about how the ideas of the Alexandrian editors were passed down.

———— (2000a), "Die D-scholien der Ilias in den Handschriften," *ZPE* 132: 1–62 (also on Web at http://www.uni-koeln.de/phil-fak/ifa/klassphil/vanthiel/index.html). Introduction to his edition; provides good, clear explanation of D scholia.

———— (2000b), *Scholia D in Iliadem* (available on Internet only, at http://www.uni-koeln.de/phil-fak/ifa/klassphil/vanthiel/index.html). Latest edition of D scholia.

Vári, Rudolphus (1909), "Parerga Oppianea," *Egyetemes Philologiai Közlöny*, 33: 17–32, 116–31. Edition of A scholia to Oppian's *Halieutica*, books 1–4 and lines 1–153 of book 5.

Velsen, Arthur von / Arthur de (1853), *Tryphonis Grammatici Alexandrini Fragmenta* (Berlin; repr. Amsterdam 1965). Standard edition of the fragments of Trypho; does not contain the extant treatises. See Pasquali (1910) for an additional fragment.

Ver Eecke, Paul (1948), *Proclus de Lycie: Les commentaires sur le premier livre des Éléments d'Euclide* (Bruges: Desclée de Brouwer). French trans.

—— (1960), *Les œuvres complètes d'Archimède, suivies des commentaires d'Eutocius d'Ascalon* (Paris). French trans.

Vinson, Steve (1996), "Πακτοῦν and πάκτωσις as Ship-Construction Terminology in Herodotus, Pollux and Documentary Papyri," *ZPE* 113: 197–204.

Viré, Ghislaine (1992), *Hygini de astronomia* (Stuttgart and Leipzig). Standard text of this work, which used material that was later turned into a commentary on Aratus.

Vitelli, Girolamo (1889), "Handschriftliches zu Herodian Περὶ ἀκυρολογίας," *BPW* 9: 907. Provides readings from a second MS of this work to supplement the text produced by Nauck (1867).

Von Fritz, Kurt (1936), "Timaios (8)," in *RE*, 2nd ser. vi.i (xi): 1226–8. Good discussion and bibliography.

Von Staden, Heinrich (1989), *Herophilus: The Art of Medicine in Early Alexandria* (Cambridge). Contains information on early commentaries and glossaries to Hippocrates.

—— (1992), "Lexicography in the Third Century BC: Bacchius of Tanagra, Erotian, and Hippocrates," in J. A. López Férez (ed.), *Tratados Hipocráticos* (Madrid), 549–69. On the early Hippocratic glossaries.

—— (2002), " 'A Woman does not Become Ambidextrous': Galen and the Culture of Scientific Commentary," in R. Gibson and Kraus (2002): 109–39. On Galen's work on Hippocrates.

Wachsmuth, Kurt/Curtius, and Hense, Otto (1884–1912), *Ioannis Stobaei Anthologium* (Berlin; repr. 1974; index 1923). Standard edition.

Wackernagel, Jacob (1876), *De pathologiae veterum initiis* (Diss. Basle). Repr. in *Kleine Schriften* (Göttingen 1955–79): iii. 1427–86. Important discussion of πάθος in a variety of grammarians.

—— (1893), *Beiträge zur Lehre vom griechischen Akzent* (Basle; repr. in *Kleine Schriften* (Göttingen 1955–79): ii. 1072–1107). Important discussion of the grammatical tradition for the Greek accent.

—— (1914a), "Akzentstudien II," *Nachrichten von der königlichen Gesellschaft der Wissenschaften zu Göttingen, phil.-hist. Kl.*, 1914: 20–51. Repr. in *Kleine Schriften* (Göttingen 1955–79): ii. 1122–53. On pp. 50–1 discusses the sources of Herodian's knowledge of Homeric accentuation.

—— (1914b), "Akzentstudien III," *Nachrichten von der königlichen Gesellschaft der Wissenschaften zu Göttingen, phil.-hist. Kl.*, 1914: 97–130. Repr. in *Kleine Schriften* (Göttingen 1955–79): ii. 1154–87. Discusses the sources of the grammarians' knowledge of Homeric accentuation.

Waitz, Theodor (1844), *Aristotelis Organon Graece*, i (Leipzig). Prints a small selection of commentary extracts to these works, pp. 30–77; superseded by *CAG*.

Walz, Christian (1832–6), *Rhetores Graeci* (Stuttgart; repr. Osnabrück 1968). Contains several works attributed to Gregory of Corinth, Herodian, Choeroboscus, etc.

Wartelle, André (1963), *Inventaire des manuscrits grecs d'Aristote et de ses commentateurs* (Paris). Useful introduction discusses scholia, pp. x–xi, but inventory itself is not very accurate; supplement in Argyropoulos and Caras (1980).

—— (1971), *Histoire du texte d'Eschyle dans l'antiquité* (Paris). Argues that old scholia to Aeschylus are based on a commentary of Didymus.

Wecklein, Nicolaus (1885), *Aeschyli Fabulae cum lectionibus et scholiis codicis Medicei et in Agamemnonem codicis Florentini ab Hieronymo Vitelli denuo collatis* (Berlin; also known as "Wecklein and Vitelli" and as "Vitelli and Wecklein"). Good edition of M scholia beneath text (also F scholia on *Agamemnon* separately after the text; for portions of *Agamemnon* missing from M, scholia beneath the text supplied from T and other sources), now often superseded.

Wellmann, Max (1906–14), *Pedanii Dioscuridis Anazarbei de materia medica libri quinque* (Berlin; repr. 1958). Prints scholia in apparatus.

——— (1931), *Hippokratesglossare* (Berlin; repr. Würzburg 1973). Study of lexica to Hippocrates (through Erotian only).

Wendel, Carl (1914), *Scholia in Theocritum vetera* (Leipzig; repr. 1966). Standard edition, excellent.

——— (1920), *Überlieferung und Entstehung der Theokrit-Scholien* (Berlin; Abhandlungen der königlichen Gesellschaft der Wissenschaften zu Göttingen, philologisch-historische Klasse, NF 17, Nr. 2). Indispensible study of Theocritus scholia, including their origins, the indirect tradition, and the Byzantine scholiasts.

——— (1932), *Die Überlieferung der Scholien zu Apollonios von Rhodes* (Berlin). Now largely superseded.

——— (1935), *Scholia in Apollonium Rhodium vetera* (Berlin; repr. 1958). Standard text of these scholia, but see H. Fränkel (1968) for corrections.

——— (1939*a*), "Orion (3)," in *RE* xviii.i (xxxv): 1083–7. Useful, clear study.

——— (1939*b*), "Tryphon (25)," in *RE*, 2nd ser. vii.i (xiii): 726–44. Detailed study, with extensive bibliography.

——— (1942), "Späne III," *Hermes*, 77: 216–18. Some use of scholia.

——— (1948*a*), "Tyrannion (2)," in *RE*, 2nd ser. vii.ii (xiv): 1811–19. Detailed, useful explanation of the life and writings of Tyrannio the Elder, with extensive bibliography.

——— (1948*b*), "Tyrannion (3)," in *RE*, 2nd ser. vii.ii (xiv): 1819–20. Short but useful piece on Diocles / Tyrannio the Younger.

West, Martin L. (1965*a*), "Alcmanica," *CQ*, NS 15: 188–202. Suggestions for interpretation and supplementation of ancient commentaries.

——— (1965*b*), "Tryphon *De Tropis*," *CQ*, NS 15: 230–48. Gives a new edition of the treatise on tropes attributed to Gregory of Corinth, and shows that this work cannot be by Gregory and may well be by Trypho.

——— (1973), *Textual Criticism and Editorial Technique* (Stuttgart). Useful explanation.

——— (1974), "The Medieval Manuscripts of the *Works and Days*," *CQ*, NS 24: 161–85. Explains use of etymologica as source for scholia.

——— (1978), *Hesiod: Works and Days* (Oxford). Excellent section on ancient scholarship.

——— (2001), *Studies in the Text and Transmission of the Iliad* (Munich). Includes much discussion of ancient scholarship.

——— (2003), *Homeric Hymns, Homeric Apocrypha, Lives of Homer* (Cambridge, Mass.). Latest edition of *Lives*, with trans.

West, Stephanie R. (1984), "Lycophron Italicised," *JHS* 104: 127–51. On date of poem; uses scholia.

Westerink, Leendert Gerrit (1956), *Olympiodorus: Commentary on the First Alcibiades of Plato* (Amsterdam). Best edition of text, with short introduction in English.

——— (1959), *Damascius: Lectures on the Philebus Wrongly Attributed to Olympiodorus* (Amsterdam; repr. with some updates 1982). Best edition, with facing English trans. and introduction.

——— (1962), *Anonymous Prolegomena to Platonic Philosophy* (Amsterdam). Text, facing English trans., and detailed introduction. Updated French version in Westerink, Trouillard, and Segonds (1990).

——— (1967), *Pseudo-Elias (Pseudo-David): Lectures on Porphyry's Isagoge* (Amsterdam). Edition of a commentary on a commentary to Aristotle.

Westerink, Leendert Gerrit (1970), *Olympiodori in Platonis Gorgiam Commentaria* (Leipzig). Best edition, includes short bibliography.

—— (1976), *The Greek Commentaries on Plato's Phaedo*, i: *Olympiodorus* (Amsterdam). Best edition, with facing English trans. and introduction.

—— (1977), *The Greek Commentaries on Plato's Phaedo*, ii: *Damascius* (Amsterdam). Best edition, with facing English trans. and introduction. Two commentaries probably represent the same set of lectures as given in two different years.

—— and Combès, Joseph (1997–2003), *Damascius: Commentaire du Parménide de Platon* (Paris). Best edition, with facing French trans., detailed introduction, and notes.

——, Trouillard, J.; and Segonds, A. Ph. (1990), *Prolégomènes à la philosophie de Platon* (Paris). Updated French trans. of Westerink (1962), with short commentary.

White, John Williams (1912), *The Verse of Greek Comedy* (London; repr. Hildesheim 1969). Contains a text (now superseded) of those parts of Heliodorus' metrical commentary on Aristophanes that survive in the scholia, with an excellent introduction.

—— (1914), *The Scholia on the Aves of Aristophanes* (Boston). The text given here is now superseded, but the introduction is still extremely useful, as is the index.

Whitehead, David (1994), "Site-Classification and Reliability in Stephanus of Byzantium," in D. Whitehead (ed.), *From Political Architecture to Stephanus Byzantius: Sources for the Ancient Greek Polis* (Stuttgart; *Historia* Einzelschr. 87): 99–124.

—— (1997), "Harpocrationiana," *Eikasmos*, 8: 157–64. Useful notes on specific points, in English.

—— (1998), "Harpocrationianis addenda," *Eikasmos*, 9: 209–12. Useful notes, in English.

Whittaker, John (1990), *Alcinoos: Enseignement des doctrines de Platon* (Paris). Best edition, with scholia, detailed introduction, facing French trans., and extensive indices.

Wieseler, Friedrich (1870), *Commentatio de difficilioribus quibusdam Pollucis aliorumque scriptorum veterum locis, qui ad ornatum scaenicu spectant* (Göttingen). Helpful in reading Pollux's sections on the stage.

Wifstrand, Albert (1932), "Två Apolloniospapyrer i Berlin," *Eranos*, 30: 1–6. Fragment of papyrus commentary on Apollonius.

Wilamowitz-Moellendorff, Ulrich von (1894), "Pausanias-Scholien," *Hermes*, 29: 240–8. Study of their usefulness.

—— (1889), *Einleitung in die griechische Tragödie* (= *Euripides Herakles*, i) (Berlin; repr. 1910 and Darmstadt 1974). Includes a discussion of ancient scholarship.

—— (1918), "Dichterfragmente aus der Papyrussammlung der Kgl. Museen," *Sitzungsberichte der Königlichen Preussischen Akademie der Wissenschaften zu Berlin*, 36: 728–51. Edition of papyrus commentary on Pindar, pp. 749–50.

Wilcken, Ulrich (1907), "Der Anonymus Argentinensis," *Hermes*, 42: 374–418. Text and discussion of papyrus fragment on Demosthenes.

Wilson, Nigel G. (1962), "The Triclinian Edition of Aristophanes," *CQ*, NS 12: 32–47. On the discovery of a manuscript of Triclinius' edition of Aristophanes (with scholia).

—— (1967), "A Chapter in the History of Scholia," *CQ*, NS 17: 244–56. On the change of hypomnemata into scholia.

—— (1971), "Two Notes on Byzantine Scholarship," *GRBS* 12: 557–60. On Photius and scholia to Dioscorides.

—— (1983a), *Scholars of Byzantium* (London; revised edn. 1996). Accurate, enjoyable introduction to the Byzantine scholars.

—— (1983b), "Scoliasti e commentatori," *SCO* 33: 83–112. Good general overview.

—— (1984), "The Relation of Text and Commentary in Greek Books," in C. Questa and R. Raffaelli (edd.), *Atti del convegno internazionale "Il libro e il testo"* (Urbino): 103–10. On the change of hypomnemata into scholia.

—————— (1994), *Photius: The Bibliotheca: A Selection* (London). Trans. with notes of select entries, with useful introduction.

Wilson, Penelope (1980), "Pindar and his Reputation in Antiquity," *Proceedings of the Cambridge Philological Society*, NS 26: 97–114. Uses scholia to explore Alexandrian view of Pindar and better understand *Odes*.

Winnington-Ingram, R. P. (1963), *Aristidis Quintiliani de musica libri tres* (Leipzig). Standard text.

Winter, Richard (1908), *De Luciani scholiis quaestiones selectae* (Diss. Leipzig). Important study.

Wirth, Peter (1980), *Eustathiana: Gesammelte Aufsätze zu Leben und Werk des Metropoliten Eustathios von Thessalonike* (Amsterdam).

Wolf, Hieronymus (1559), *Εἰς τετράβιβλον τοῦ Πτολεμαίου ἐξηγητὴς ἀνώνυμος: In Claudii Ptolemaei quadripartitum enarrator ignoti nominis, quem tamen Proclum fuisse quidem existimant* (Basle). Edition of anonymous commentary.

Woodhead, A. G. (1959), *The Study of Greek Inscriptions* (Cambridge).

Wouters, Alfons (1973), "A Compendium of Herodian's Περὶ κλίσεως ὀνομάτων (A Note on the New Grammatical Papyrus in Florence)," *ZPE* 11: 242–4. On the Herodian papyrus Florence P. inv. 3005.

—————— (1975), "Dionysius Thrax' Definition of the λόγος (sentence) and P. Yale I 25," *Orbis*, 24: 217–23. Argues for an emendation in the text of the Τέχνη based on a papyrus fragment of the 1st cent. AD; counterarguments in Lallot (1998: 122).

—————— (1979), *The Grammatical Papyri from Graeco-Roman Egypt: Contributions to the Study of the "Ars Grammatica" in Antiquity* (Brussels; Verhandelingen van de Koninklijke Academie voor Wetenschappen, Letteren en schone Kunsten van België, Klasse der Letteren, jaargang 41, nr. 92). Good edition of the grammatical papyri, with thorough discussion of each one, some translations, extensive indices, and detailed introduction with a discussion of the relationship between (ps.-) Dionysius' Τέχνη and these papyri. Cf. Holwerda (1984).

—————— (1991–3), "Dionysius Thrax on the *Correptio Attica*," *Orbis*, 36: 221–8. Discusses Dionysius' treatment of syllable length before mute + liquid, and the relationship between his theories and Hephaestion's.

—————— (1993), "The Grammatical Term ἀπολελυμένον in the School Book Brit. Mus. Add. MS. 37533 (=Pack² 2712)," *Chronique d'Égypte*, 68: 168–77.

—————— (1994), "The Ancient Greek (and Latin) Grammarians and the μετ' ὀλίγον μέλλων Tense," in De Clercq and Desmet (1994): 97–129. Argues that for the ancient grammarians the future perfect tense was less marginal than is normally thought. Good bibliography.

—————— (1997), "The Grammatical Papyrus *P.Berol. inv.* 9917," in *Akten des 21. Internationalen Papyrologenkongresses* (Stuttgart; APF Beiheft 3): ii.1021–33.

—————— (2000), "Les conjonctions dubitatives: La définition (originale) de la *Technè* retrouvée?," *Histoire Épistémologie Langage*, 22.2: 29–39. Discusses a grammatical papyrus that bears a strong relationship to a passage in [ps.-] Dionysius Thrax and thus sheds light on the evolution of that text.

Wyss, Bernhard (1936), *Antimachi Colophonii reliquiae* (Berlin). Text of long papyrus commentary (2nd cent. AD), pp. 76–89.

Zabrowski, Charles J. (1984), *The Older Scholia to Aeschylus's "Persae"* (Diss. Fordham). Text and Study of Φ scholia to *Persae*.

—————— (1987), "The Annotation *Sch. Rec.* in Dindorf's and Wecklein's Editions of the Medicean Scholia on Aeschylus' Persae," *C&M*, 38: 287–303. Follows O. L. Smith (1982*b*).

Zecchini, Giuseppe (1999) (ed.), *Il lessico Suda e la memoria del passato a Bisanzio* (Bari). Collection of essays.

Zetzel, James E. G. (1975), "On the History of Latin Scholia," *HSCP* 79: 335–54. Supports N. Wilson (1967).

Zhmud, Leonid (2002), "Eudemus' *History of Mathematics*," in I. Bodnár and W. W. Fortenbaugh (edd.), *Eudemus of Rhodes* (New Brunswick, NJ: 263–306. Uses Proclus' commentary to Euclid.

Ziegler, Konrat (1941), "Photios (13)," in *RE* xx.i (xxxix): 667–737. Important study.

Zuntz, Günther (1955), *The Political Plays of Euripides* (Manchester). Discusses hypotheses, pp. 129–52, with bibliography, p. 130 n. 3.

——— (1965), *An Inquiry into the Transmission of the Plays of Euripides* (Cambridge). Includes discussion of ancient scholarship.

——— (1975), *Die Aristophanes-Scholien der Papyri* (Berlin, 2nd edn.). Slightly updated version of articles published nearly 40 years earlier (*Byzantion*, 13 (1938): 631–90 and 14 (1939): 545–613); extremely influential in its time, but less so now. Concerned primarily with proving that the transfer of scholia to margins did not take place until the 9th or 10th cent. AD.

Index Locorum

Aeschines, scholia to
  on 1. 29: 207
  on 1. 39: 160, 184
  on 1. 59: 160, 185
  on 1. 64: 207
  on 1. 157: 207
  on 1. 182: 159, 184
  on 2. 10: 161, 185
  on 2. 157: 206
  on 3. 95: 160, 184
  on 3. 160: 160, 184
  on 3. 222: 207
Aeschylus, scholia to
  on *Ag.* 503a: 155, 182
  on *Ch.* 899: 204
  on *Ch.* 973: 155, 182
  on *Pers.* 34–5: 155, 182
  on *PV* 397b: 155, 182
  on *PV* 472b: 204
  on *PV* 561d: 155–6, 182
  on *Septem* 311a: 204
Ammonius
  26: 145, 176
  30: 144, 176
  140: 196
  144: 196
  180: 145, 176
  329: 196
  334: 145, 176
  386: 145, 176
  451: 196–7
  480: 196
Apollonius Dyscolus
  Adv. 119. 10: 116
  Adv. 177.5: 119
  Pron. 65. 20: 119
  Synt. 19. 4: 122
  Synt. 51. 1ff.: 217–18

Synt. 81. 5: 116
Synt. 156. 2: 116
Synt. 273. 9ff.: 173, 192–3
Synt. 389. 13ff.: 173–4,
    193
Synt. 392. 9–10: 122
Synt. 434. 1ff.: 174–5, 194
Synt. 455. 15–16: 122
Apollonius Rhodius, scholia to
  on 1. 436: 210
  on 1. 936–49q: 210–11
  on 1. 985: 164, 187
  on 1. 1081: 164, 187
  on 1. 1085–87b: 164–5, 187
  on 1. 1089a: 165, 187
  on 1. 1207b: 211
  on 2. 896: 210
  subscription: 164, 187
Apollonius Sophista
  4. 8–11: 146, 177
  4. 32–4: 118
  68. 11: 119
  106. 4–6: 146, 177
  106. 15–19: 197
  107. 3–4: 197
  107. 24–6: 117
  133. 14: 111–12
Aristophanes, scholia to
  on *Clouds* 540: 88 n. 21
  on *Pax* 123d: 206
  on *Pax* 728b: 157, 183
  on *Pax* 755a: 205–6
  on *Pax* 1244c: 157–9, 183–4

Choeroboscus
  GG iv.i. 305. 7: 113
  GG iv.i. 307. 5ff.: 167, 189
  GG iv.i. 333. 5ff.: 212–13

Index of Greek Words Discussed

Words discussed in Chapters 1–4 are systematically included, those found in the reader (Ch. 5) are selectively included, and those in the glossary (Ch. 6) are included only if also mentioned elsewhere.

General Index

More detailed discussions are italicized.

Lightning Source UK Ltd.
Milton Keynes UK
UKHW021412151119
353513UK00015B/266/P